MOON

ROME, FLORENCE & VENICE

ALEXEI J. COHEN

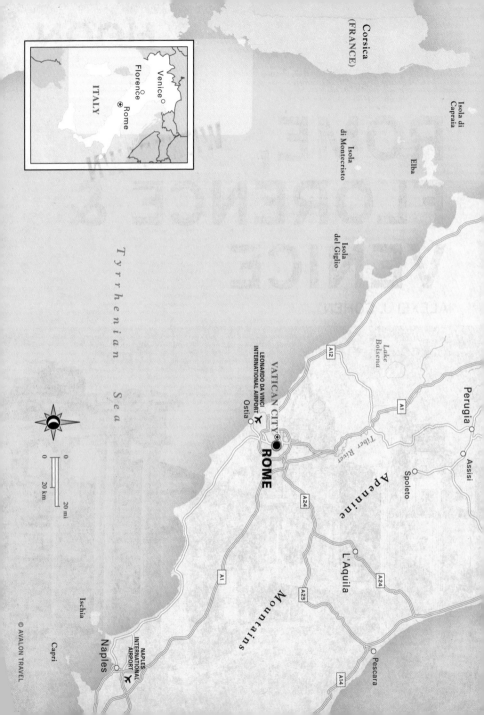

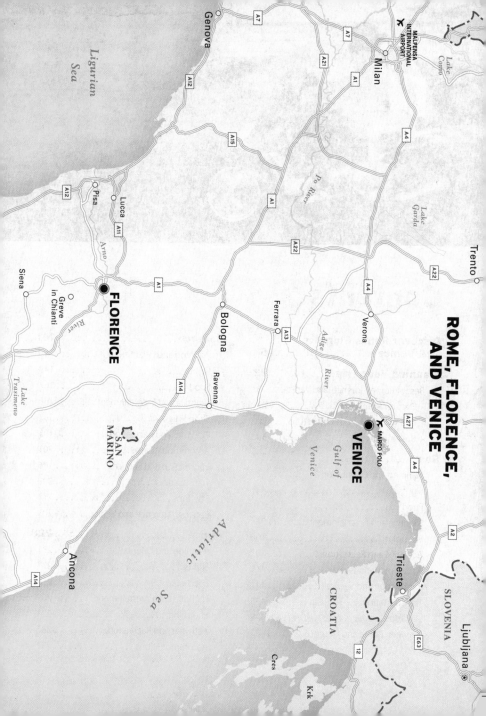

Contents

DISCOVER

Rome, Florence & Venice

These are no ordinary cities. They've witnessed remarkable events, given birth to revolutionary ideas, and formed the foundation on which modern culture and civilization rest. When it comes to beauty and influence, few places can compete.

There are no limits to what can be experienced in this Italian triumvirate. You may begin with a list of must-see museums, churches, monuments, and ruins, but you will discover much more. Follow in the footsteps of emperors, saints, and artistic geniuses by walking into the Vatican, crossing the Arno, and stepping into a gondola on the Grand Canal. It's easy to imagine the Roman Colosseum, Michelangelo's statue of *David,* and St. Mark's Basilica, but the true scale and grandeur of such sights must be seen to be believed.

Balancing the creativity of the past and the beauty of the present requires effort. To appreciate *la dolce vita* today, immerse yourself in each city and discover the characteristics and customs that make it unique. Notice the smell of freshly baked bread each morning; and silent squares after the masses have gone to sleep, surrendering the cobble-stoned streets to the

Clockwise from top left: gondola in Venice; Florence's Duomo; *cicchetti* in Venice; street market in Florence; Florence by night; view of St. Peter's Basilica in Rome..

adventurous. Learn to greet locals with a confident *buon giorno* and order espresso like an Italian. Sample new flavors in rustic trattorias, enter unexpected doorways, and ask locals which hillside provides the best view. With a little determination, you'll begin to distinguish a Romanesque church from a Renaissance *palazzo*, Florentine *aperitivi* from Venetian *cicchetti,* and good leather from bad.

Rome, Florence, and Venice offer all the delights and satisfaction of a sumptuous three-course meal. Savor every bite.

Clockwise from top left: lion statue at Piazza della Signoria in Florence; Basilica di Santa Maria della Salute in Venice; Venice vegetable market; Basilica di San Marco.

20 TOP
EXPERIENCES

1 **Colosseum:** Circle it, touch it, stand above it, go inside during the day—then return to see it by moonlight. Rome's ancient amphitheater exceeds all expectations (page 48).

2 **Roman Forum:** Ancient artifacts tell the story of the rise and fall of the Roman Empire (page 50).

3 **Pantheon:** Rome's largest temple has survived nearly 2,000 years and counting (page 55).

4 **St. Peter's Basilica:** The center of the Roman Catholic faith is also the largest church in the world (page 64).

5 **Vatican Museums:** You could easily get lost in the treasure trove of art and artifacts, but don't miss Michelangelo's **Sistine Chapel**—arguably the greatest work of art ever created (page 65).

6 **Borghese Gallery:** Masterworks by Bernini, Botticelli, and Caravaggio are displayed in a sumptuous villa (page 62).

7 **Cycling Villa Borghese:** Rome's central park is the best place to take refuge from the summer heat (page 108).

8 **Regional Italian Cuisine:** Each city offers its own specialties, from *cacio e pepe* pasta in Rome (page 78) to steak and *pappa al pomodoro* in Florence (page 170) and *fritto misto* in Venice (page 260).

9 **Michelangelo's *David*:** Amid the masterworks in the **Accademia,** *David* gets an entire room to himself (page 156).

10 **Florence's Duomo:** Rising above the city, the structure of Brunelleschi's iconic dome defies gravity (page 148).

11 **Uffizi Gallery:** Florentine artists added a realistic dimension to paintings that transformed art forever. See their masterworks up close here (page 154).

12 **Bargello National Museum:** One of the least crowded museums in Florence offers a look at a less famous *David* by Donatello, as well as ancient military hardware and the city's first police headquarters (page 152).

13 St. Mark's Basilica: Golden mosaics line the ceilings and walls of Venice's magnificent church (page 238).

14 Hiking to Basilica San Miniato al Monte: Climb to the highest point in Florence to get undisturbed views of the skyline (page 166).

15 **Gelato:** This thick, creamy ice cream is one of Italy's simplest, yet most satisfying pleasures (page 174).

16 **Italian Coffee:** Learn to appreciate coffee the Italian way. More than a daily fix, it's a ritual (page 177).

17 **Happy Hour, Italian-Style:** *Aperitivo* is the snacking and drinking tradition in Rome and Florence (page 182), while sampling seafood snacks called *cicchetti* is a quintessential Venetian experience (page 265).

18 Cruising Venice's Canals: The true romance of old Venice is on the water (page 254).

19 Doge's Palace: Wander through centuries of Venetian history and lore (page 239).

20 Venetian Glass: Tour the furnaces of Murano to learn the secrets of Venetian glassblowers (page 306).

Planning Your Trip

Where to Go

Rome

Italy's largest city is an heirloom of art, history, and culture. Its vast historic center contains some of the world's most famous sights. The **Roman Forum** and **Palatine Hill** are the focal points of antiquity, where ancient Romans once debated, worshipped, and played. Ruins including the **Colosseum** and **Pantheon** are remarkably intact, and thousands of archeological relics are now preserved inside **Museo Capitolino**. Meanwhile, across the Tiber River lies the **Vatican**. The world's smallest state packs a punch with the Vatican Museums and the **Sistine Chapel**, along with **Basilica San Pietro**, the massive structure that houses Michelangelo's *Pieta*.

Rome is more than its famous sights, animated by 3 million citizens proud of their modern metropolis and even prouder of their soccer teams. Stylish men and women rush past on mopeds without a second glance at the beauty around them. The city also has a more visible **nightlife scene** than Florence or Venice, with clubs and *aperitivo* **bars** hosting the Italian version of happy hour. Wandering the medieval alleys of **Trastevere** or kicking back with a *pizza al taglio* are good opportunities to allow the Eternal City's history to soak in.

Florence

Stepping off the train in Florence feels like entering a bygone era. Cars and mopeds move slowly along cobbled streets. Meticulous artisans practice age-old traditions to produce **leather**, paper, and perfume, vending their wares along the **Ponte Vecchio** and in **studio workshops** across the Arno.

The **birthplace of the Renaissance** has inspired a grand city, but on a human scale that never overwhelms. Visitors flock to Florence to circle the *David*, the world's most famous statue;

exploring Rome

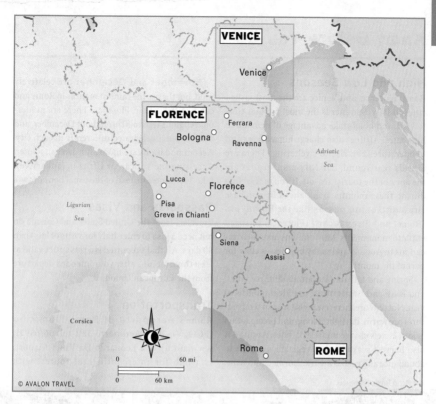

to glimpse Renaissance masterpieces inside the **Uffizi** museum; and to climb Brunelleschi's **Duomo,** an engineering masterpiece that rises majestically above the terra-cotta rooftops. Experiencing the city also means sampling delectable **Tuscan food** and uncorking bottles of locally produced **Chianti.** Outside the lively center, hillsides are dotted with sumptuous **villas** and **gardens.**

Venice

It's hard not to feel romantic in Venice. Founded after the fall of the Roman Empire, this island city's glorious past is still evident within mosaic-encrusted **Basilica di San Marco** and inside **Palazzo Ducale,** the home of the former rulers of the Mediterranean waterways. This is a city that always looked outward, eager to push the boundaries of trade and commerce.

Today, the **gondolas** that glide across the **Grand Canal** infuse the city with otherworldly charm. Flavors and smells inherited from the Orient enrich the local cuisine. Venetians toast with *prosecco,* snack on delectable finger food known as *cicchetti,* and keep **seafood** on every menu. Artisans still practice **glass-blowing** and **lacemaking,** keeping age-old traditions alive.

Know Before You Go

High and Low Seasons

Rome, Florence, and Venice are the most visited cities in Italy. Summer is the most popular time to visit, and hotels take advantage of demand to hike rates. Airlines also charge higher fares and temperatures can rise to sweltering. There are crowds year-round, but **July** and **August** are the apex of the tourist season. If you're traveling during these months, book ahead or purchase city **sightseeing passes** like the **RomaPass** (Rome) and **Firenzecard** (Florence) to speed entry to monuments. Most Italians take their vacations in August, and many businesses close for part of the month.

Spring and fall are pleasant in all three cities, and **May** and **September** are ideal months to visit. Not only are there fewer visitors, but temperatures are warm, daylight is long, and precipitation is low. Hotels charge midseason rates. Autumn is also harvest season, when vegetables appear in abundance and grapes are transformed into wine.

November and **December** are relatively mild, but they're the rainiest months in Rome and can be very cold in Florence. There are numerous religious festivals throughout December, and *Carnevale* is celebrated differently in each city. Accommodations are more affordable in winter. Accessing the Vatican or Uffizi in January can take 30 minutes instead of the usual hour or two.

Passports and Visas

Travelers from the United States and Canada do not need a visa to enter Italy for visits of less than 90 days. All that's required is a **passport** valid at least three months after your intended departure from the European Union.

Transportation

Rome's **Aeroporto di Roma-Fiumicino** (FCO, Via dell' Aeroporto 320, tel. 06/65951, www.adr.it), aka Leonardo Da Vinci Airport, is a hub for intercontinental routes, with

the Arno River, Florence

nonstop flights to dozens of North American cities. **Ciampino** (CIA, Via Appia Nuova 1651, tel. 06/65951, www.adr.it), Rome's second airport, is used by charter and low-cost airlines flying to Italian and European destinations. Venice's **Aeroporto di Venezia** (VCE, Via Galileo Galilei 30, tel. 041/260-6111, www.veniceairport.it) offers fewer direct flights to North America but many connecting flights from across Europe. Florence's **Aeroporto di Firenze-Peretola** (FLR, Via del Termine 11, tel. 055/30615, www.aeroporto.firenze.it) has no direct flights to the United States.

Traveling between Rome, Florence, and Venice by **train** is fast, easy, and convenient. Both the state-owned **Trenitalia** (www.trenitalia.com) and private **Italo** (www.italo.it) provide frequent daily departures between all three cities. The Trenitalia **Frecciarossa** (red arrow) service is slightly more expensive and operates more trains, making it popular with business travelers; tourists generally prefer Italo. **Travel time** between Rome and Florence is 90 minutes, Florence to Venice is 2 hours, and Venice to Rome 3.5 hours.

If you prefer to drive, guarantee yourself a **car rental** is to reserve one prior to departure. You'll need your passport and a driver's license if you plan on renting a car. An international license is not required, but it can avoid con... pulled over. It only costs $15 and i... any AAA office in the United Stat...

Within Italy, **buses** are a chea... with a half-dozen companies opera... Rome, Florence, and Venice, includin... ...nes (www.eurolines.com), **Flixbus** (www.flixbus.com), and **Megabus** (www.megabus.com).

What to Pack

Some **formal clothes** may be necessary for fine dining or clubbing. Plan to dress conservatively at **religious sites:** Knees and shoulders must be covered. Flip-flops are fine for the beach, but the Swiss Guard won't permit them inside the Vatican. Keep in mind that when entering religious buildings.

Most hotels provide **hairdryers,** but if you are staying in a bed-and-breakfast or camping you may want to pack a small one. It should be adaptable to Italy's 220 voltage. A **European plug converter** is useful for recharging MP3 players, digital cameras, and cellular phones. Adapters can be hard to find in Italy and airports are usually the best place to pick them up.

Binoculars are helpful for observing the ceiling of the Sistine Chapel, church facades, and wildlife.

ˍest of Rome, Florence, and Venice

Rome is a convenient starting point for a three-city tour of Italy. Most transatlantic flights land directly in the Italian capital and tickets are less expensive than to Florence or Venice, which often require connecting flights. The 327 miles that separate the cities are covered by high-speed trains, which are the quickest and easiest way of getting between destinations. A Rome-to-Florence-to-Venice itinerary also allows you to travel from the most populated to the least populated city and from oldest to newest, which can facilitate appreciation and understanding of each.

Seeing everything in these three cities is impossible, and visiting one museum after another will leave you exhausted and unable to absorb what you have seen. You're better offer taking it slow and balancing days with a mix of sights and everyday activities, like lingering in *piazze*, tasting gelato, and enjoying *aperitivo* (happy hour). Using local travel cards like **RomaPass**, **Firenzecard,** and **Venezia Unica** will help you get the most out of your journey without wasting time in lines.

ROME

DAY 1

Walking is the best cure for jet lag, so after you settle into your room, head out for lunch and a stroll. The *pizza al taglio* parlors in the center provide a good introduction to Roman pizza. Point to the variety you like and have it wrapped up for takeaway. Grab a seat on the stone bench at the base of **Palazzo Farnese** and observe the comings and goings in the busy square. At the first sign of a yawn enter a bar and order an **espresso.** Although most Romans drink at the counter, outdoor seating is common. Afterwards ride the number 23, 44, or 280 bus or 8 tram to Aventino and Testaccio. If it's close to *aperitivo* (happy hour) order a cocktail at **Porto Fluviale**

the Colosseum, Rome

Best for Romance

Rome, Florence, and Venice enchant eyes, ears, and palates. Romance waits around every corner and you don't have to be Casanova to take part.

DINE *AL FRESCO*

In Rome, outdoor tables are set up from April to October. Ditch crowds by choosing undisturbed streets and intimate alleys like **Via della Reginella,** where you can dine facing a fountain and forget about time.

WATCH THE SUNSET

In Florence, watching the **sun set over the Arno** is particularly moving. It's best seen from the **Ponte Santa Trinità** bridge just west of the Ponte Vecchio, where you can sit on the stone siding and watch the sun's final rays transform city surfaces (page 159).

SPLURGE ON A MICHELIN-STAR MEAL

At Florence's **La Bottega del Buon Caffè** (page 176), love costs less than you might expect. **Gusto** (page 83) in Rome and **Antiche Carampane** (page 264) in Venice may not have as many stars but are still seductive.

SIP *PROSECCO*

Aman, Venice's only seven-star resort, has a lounge, **Blue Bar** (page 273) that anyone can access. Come dressed for the décor—a casual suit and a light evening dress will do just fine. Sit in one of the plush armchairs overlooking the Grand Canal, order a flute of *prosecco*, and let the city do the rest.

gondola ride, Venice

TAKE A MOONLIT STROLL

After dark, **Venice** clears of crowds, and stillness descends on the canals. Walking hand-in-hand through starlit streets is as romantic as it sounds.

CRUISE BY GONDOLA

Nothing is more romantic than a gondola ride along **Venice's canals** (page 254). Just make sure to start your journey in one of the city's less crowded neighborhoods, where you can exchange sweet words in solitude.

and enjoy the buffet that can double as dinner. The longer you resist sleep the easier it will be to adapt to Italian time.

DAY 2

The **Colosseum** is a sight that cannot be missed. Walk to the ancient stadium, or ride Metro B to Circo Massimo and approach from the south.

Skip the lines with your preordered tickets or RomaPass and spend an hour exploring the interior with the audio guide. Then head next door to the **Roman Forum,** where you can wander through ruins and get a feel for ancient Rome. To see more artifacts, climb nearby Capitoline Hill and visit the **Museo Capitolino.** Michelangelo designed the square outside the museum and there's a great view of the city from the adjacent **Vittoriano** monument.

Walk down to the **Jewish Ghetto** for a taste of artichokes prepared in the Jewish style at **Nonna Betta** or the other kosher restaurants on Via del Portico D'Ottavia. Alternatively, ride the number 8 tram to the Piramide station and swap ancient for 19th-century history. Pay your respects to Keats in the **Protestant Cemetery** before heading to the covered **Testaccio Market.** Pick a stand and create an improvised picnic of a beef sandwich, cheese, and bread, all washed down with local wine served in plastic cups. On the way back, explore the residential streets of Aventino and the shaded **Giardini degli Aranci** (Orange Garden) with a view of the Vatican. Return at night to **Monte Testaccio** via the Metro B to Piramide for dancing and Roman nightlife, or dine *al fresco* at one of the informal kiosks along the Tiber and let your feet have the night off.

DAY 3

Zigzag along the pedestrian streets towards **Campo De' Fiori.** Browse the market for household souvenirs and order *pizza bianca* from **Il Forno** on the northwestern corner of the square. There's a flow of tourists on their way to **Piazza Navona,** but plenty of scenic side streets offer less crowded opportunities to reach the square. Choose one and admire the former athletic track with the help of a **gelato** from **Frigidarium.** Street musicians play near the fountains and there's a lot of art on display. Avoid cafes with waitstaff out front recruiting tourists, and order an espresso at **Antico Caffè della Pace.**

The **Pantheon** is less than ten minutes away and free to enter. After visiting it, browse the boutiques along **Via del Corso** as you head towards the newly refurbished **Spanish Steps,** which you can climb to reach **Villa Borghese.** Escape the summer heat by **cycling** in the city's biggest park or visiting the **Borghese Gallery** (advance reservations required). Afterward, walk down to **Piazza del Popolo** and follow Via Ripetta to the **Ara Pacis museum,** then have dinner at **Gusto.** End your day by visiting the **Trevi Fountain** after dark.

DAY 4

Walk or ride the Metro A to the Ottaviano station

The Pantheon, Rome

Vatican Museums, Rome

and follow the pilgrims to Vatican City. Remember to dress properly, and arrive early to the **Vatican Museums** where you can choose from several itineraries taking in the immense collection. Most visitors beeline to the **Sistine Chapel,** but there are less crowded parts of the museum. Once you've gotten your fill of art, take the guided bus tour of the gardens before entering **St. Peter's Basilica.** Light a candle and descend into the crypt to pay tribute to past popes, then make your way to the top of the cupola. The elevator only goes so far and you'll need stamina to climb the highest structure in the city. If you arrive on Sunday morning you can join the faithful in the square below and receive the pope's blessing.

The nearby streets of **Borgo Pio** and **Borgo Vittorio** have catered to pilgrims since the Middle Ages and are lined with eateries and souvenir shops. Follow one of these parallel streets to **Castel Sant'Angelo.** You can climb the castle and enjoy the view from the rooftop bar. Then walk or catch a bus to **Trastevere** and mingle with the crowds in **Piazza Trilussa.** Order *cacao pepe* pasta at **Da Giovanni** and explore the streets of this lively neighborhood packed with bars and clubs.

WITH MORE TIME

Ride the train from Piramide station to **Ostia Antica** and walk along the well-preserved streets of an ancient city. Explore the baths, theater, shops, and villas to understand how the Romans once lived. Afterward, have lunch in the small medieval enclave near the entrance to the archeological site or take the train back and get off at the Magliana station to explore **EUR.** There are dozens of eateries along Viale Europa and Viale America, along with Fascist-era architecture and a man-made lake where Japanese cherry blossoms bloom in spring.

Via Appia Antica is closer to the center and can be reached on the 118 bus from Circus Maximus in 15 minutes or on foot in a little over twice that time. Rent a bike from the park office and then saddle up and set off on a leisurely trot down the first road that led to Rome.

Rome, Florence, and Venice offer remarkable feats of engineering, from iconic monuments and palatial estates to improbable domes and humble homes. Most surprisingly, much of it was built quickly and is still standing.

ROME

- **Pantheon:** Two thousand years after being built, the Pantheon still features the largest unreinforced concrete dome in the world (page 55). It has inspired countless others—including Florence's Duomo.

- **St. Peter's:** It's not just the scale of this cathedral that's impressive; it's the fact so many different architects (including Michelangelo and Bernini), working in different centuries, were able to create so harmonious a structure (page 64).

- **Colosseum:** Setting the standard for stadium design, the Colosseum was equipped with features many modern arenas lack—such as retractable roofs and underground storage facilities. Incredibly, it took only eight years to build (page 48).

- **Trevi Fountain:** This baroque fountain was meant to impress. It does that, not just for its size but the dramatic quality of its statues and stage-like setting that can be viewed from every angle of the piazza (page 60).

- **MAXXI:** Rome isn't only about ancient architecture. New structures, like this one designed by starchitect Zaha Hadid, are becoming contemporary classics (page 63).

FLORENCE

- **Duomo:** Filippo Brunelleschi's ingenious dome design relied on a double shell and eight ribs bound together by horizontal rings (page 148).

- **Campanile:** None of the many bell towers in Italy are as graceful or elegant as this one, begun by Giotto (page 150).

- **Ponte Vecchio:** The oldest bridge in Florence is also the only one with a private corridor for getting the rich and powerful across unseen (page 159).

- **Palazzo Davanzati:** Not quite medieval, not

the dome of St. Peter's in Rome

quite Renaissance, this modest palace sits on the cusp of two eras and was equipped with early examples of indoor plumbing and dumbwaiters for moving goods between floors (page 152).

VENICE

- **Basilica di San Marco:** This one-of-a-kind church is an early example of architectural multiculturalism and a result of Venice's cultural ties to the Orient. Domes, mosaics, and exotic sculptures are the work of Middle Eastern craftsmen hired to decorate the elaborate exterior and stunning interior (page 238).

- **Ca' D'Oro:** Of all the Venetian Gothic palaces along the Grand Canal, this is the finest. The delicate exterior façade looks like it's made of fine linen rather than stone (page 253).

- **Rialto Bridge:** Mocked by many at the time it was built, this bridge today remains an innovative example of Venetian architecture (page 249).

- **Cottages of Burano:** Sometimes simplicity and understatement are the best solution. Each colorfully painted cottage in Burano has an individual charm some say helped fishermen find their way home (page 306).

FLORENCE
DAY 5

The journey from Rome to Florence on board Italo or Trenitalia trains takes less than two hours. Both operators run frequent departures from Termini station in the center of the city and Tiburtina slightly to the east. Depart midmorning so you can have lunch in Florence. There are taxis and buses waiting outside Santa Maria Novella station, but the historic center is small and flat enough to navigate on foot, with no two monuments more than 20 minutes apart. If you're driving, consider stopping in **Assisi**, burial site of St. Francis, or **Siena**. Florence's historic rival is famous for its shell-shaped piazza, annual horse race, and enormous unfinished cathedral.

Once you've deposited your bags, find a small *trattoria* like **Trattoria Sostanza** and discover the difference between Florentine and Roman gastronomy. Order *papa al pomodoro* or the steak from Chianina cattle raised along the Tuscan coast. The two covered markets in the center are also good places to learn about local culinary traditions. The 2nd floor of **Mercato Centrale** is a food emporium, while downstairs you can sample **tripe sandwiches**, a Florentine specialty.

Work off your meal by **hiking to Basilica San Miniato al Monte** via the less traveled footpath, which has a panoramic payoff. Just cross the Pont alle Grazie bridge and follow the signs through the old city gate before turning right and up the grassy path. On the way back walk along the medieval walls to **Forte Belvedere**, where free outdoor exhibitions are organized, and enter the **Pitti Palace** gardens from the side entrance. If there's time catch the sunset over **Ponte Vecchio** from nearby **Ponte Santa Trinità**. Otherwise order an *aperitivo* at **Volume** or any of the bars with outdoor seating lining **Piazza Santo Spirito.** During the summer, head to the riverside beach where DJs spin lounge music until late.

DAY 6

Start the day with an espresso at **Café Rivoire** and purchase a Duomo card for a tour of the cathedral. There are a lot of steps to climb up the **Duomo,** but the inside is nearly as impressive as the outside. (Note: It's not for the claustrophobic.)

night view of Palazzo Vecchio in Florence

Basilica di Santa Croce in Florence

Once you've reached the top, circle the terrace for a 360-degree view of the city. The card includes entry to the **Campanile** bell tower and newly renovated **Museo dell'Opera,** where you can learn how the Duomo was built. Just a few blocks away is the **Piazza della Signoria** in the center of the city and another steep climb to the top of **Palazzo Vecchio.**

Sample Florentine pizza at **Cucina Torcicoda** or a thick local steak at **Mario's** before visiting the **Museum of San Marco,** which contains colorful frescoed cells where monks lived. Nearby and a couple of blocks north is the **Accademia** that houses the statue of *David* and only lets in 300 visitors at a time. That explains the line, which will require patience if you haven't booked your tickets in advance.

Next pay homage to Michelangelo, who grew up in Florence and is buried inside **Basilica di Santa Croce.** Arrive a couple of hours before closing (5:30pm) if you want to get in. Then stop into nearby **Vivoli** for **gelato.** Try their *crema de' Medici* (cream-flavored gelato). At night, wineries offer cellars full of local **Tuscan vintages,** and the happy hour cocktail of choice is **Negroni**

served with cured meats and cheese. The **Soul Kitchen** and **Winter Garden by Caino** are both good options with happy hour appetizers that can easily substitute for a sit-down dinner.

DAY 7

Mornings are the only time to see the city's *Last Supper* frescoes, which were painted inside Florence's smaller churches like **Cenacolo di Ognissanti** and **Cenacolo di Sant'Apollonia** and are often overlooked by tourists. This is your opportunity to be alone with a masterpiece. Afterwards enjoy an enormous takeaway sandwich stuffed with Tuscan ham from **All'Antico Vinaio.**

Brace yourself for crowds and join the line at the **Uffizi,** home to works by Botticelli and other greats. After visiting the galleries, take a break in the museum bar overlooking Piazza della Signoria. The museum is considerably smaller than the Vatican Museums and you can see it all in a couple of hours. If the line is too long or you want to discover the city's most underrated museum, head to the **Bargello** nearby and prepare to be blown away by another *David* with far fewer admirers. For a caffeine pick-me-up stop into **Ditta Artigianale,** or pull up a lounge chair at **Amble** and start the evening with a cocktail. For dinner, the rustic **Angiolino** is a good choice for handmade pasta dishes, but if you want to sample Michelin-rated flavors and dine in a romantic interior reserve a table at **La Bottega del Buon Caffè** overlooking the Arno.

WITH MORE TIME

Fiesole is a half-day excursion just outside the city with stunning views overlooking Florence. You can get there on the number 7 bus from the train station in around 20 minutes. During the summer there's a musical festival and evening concerts are held in the ancient Roman amphitheater.

The hills around Florence are dotted with **medieval villas** where influential families retreated during hot Renaissance summers. There are finely furnished interiors and manicured gardens to explore with fountains, sculptures, and occasional views of the Duomo in the distance. Beyond these elegant homes is Tuscany and some of Italy's most iconic landscapes. Use **Enjoy** or **Car2Go,** Florence's car-sharing program, or rent a scooter from **Walkabout** or **Tuscany Vespa Tours** and motor down the SP 222 into Chianti country to sample the latest vintages from roadside vineyards.

If you prefer not to drive, board a regional train from SMN station to **Lucca.** An hour later you'll be inside one of Italy's best-preserved fortified towns and can cycle along the ramparts and climb medieval towers in the center. Soccer fans in town from September to June can walk or catch a bus to **Artemio Franchi** stadium. Home games are usually played on Sunday afternoons at 1pm and tickets are available at the gates. Make sure to wear purple.

VENICE
DAY 8

If you're driving from Florence to Venice, consider a stop for lunch in **Ferrara** or **Bologna,** two cities that are famous for food. The latter is also on the same high-speed train line that connects Rome, Florence, and Venice, which makes it a convenient stop. Journey time by train to Venice is around two hours with several stops. Venice is

St. Mark's Basilica in Venice

Rome, Florence, and Venice offer incredible views. Behold the city from magnificent cathedrals and bell towers one day, then hike to distant hillsides to take in sweeping landscapes the next. Some vantage points are major tourist attractions, while others are in remote areas where you can reflect on the city undisturbed.

ROME

Strangest View of the Vatican
Peek through **Buco di Roma,** a keyhole on Aventine Hill, for a head-scratching optical illusion.

Best Glimpse into the Past
The Forum can appear like an archeological disaster when you're in it, but head to the top of the **Vittoriano** monument to put ancient Rome in perspective.

Holiest Ascent
It doesn't get higher than **St. Peter's Basilica** (page 64), and there's no better view of the square below and the city stretching out in all directions.

Longest Climb
Gianicolo Hill (page 72) may not be the most accessible view, but once you arrive it's clear why it's the most popular. From here, it feels like you can touch the domes and towers in front of you.

Best Panorama
The pathways and terraces above the **Spanish Steps** (page 60) leading to **Villa Borghese** (page 108) provide an ongoing view of the city that shifts with every step.

Brews with a View
What **Castel Sant'Angelo** (page 68) lacks in height it makes up for in location. At the rooftop bar, views of the historic center are accompanied by cold beers.

FLORENCE

View *from* the Duomo
Climb the famous **Duomo** (page 148) for a view over Florence's rooftops.

Views *of* the Duomo
A view of Florence is better with the Duomo. Viewpoints on the hillsides of the Oltrarno, from **Piazzale Michelangelo** to **San Miniato al Monte** (page 166) provide the most complete views of the city.

view of the Duomo, in the historic center of Florence

Ponte Vecchio Vision
The best views of the pastel-colored houses flanking **Ponte Vecchio** are from **Ponte Santa Trinità** to the west and along the embankments lining the Arno (page 159).

Drinks with a View
Cocktails accompany views from the rooftop terraces of **Plaza Luchese** and **Empireo** (page 181).

Florence from Afar
Fiesole (page 212), a half-day excursion just outside the city, is famous for its stunning views overlooking Florence.

VENICE

Bird's-Eye View of Venice
The **Campanile di San Marco** (page 241) provides the most complete panorama of the city. Alternatively, across the lagoon on **Isola San Giorgio** (page 247) is a similar bell tower with a shorter line.

Drinks with a View
Sip cocktails at the **Skyline Rooftop Bar** (page 275), which sits atop the tallest building in Venice.

A Long View of Venice
No one regrets the trek to the *campanile* in **Torcello** (page 310) for a view of Burano and the wide-open lagoon with the mirage of Venice in the distance.

the end of the line, and Santa Lucia station drops passengers off on the city's doorstep. You can reach your accommodations on foot or via water taxi on the **Grand Canal**, which is more expensive but also more fun.

After you've settled in to your hotel, follow the yellow signs to **St. Mark's Square** and take the secret tour of the **Doge's Palace** to discover why they call it the **Bridge of Sighs**. Enter **St. Mark's Basilica** next door and listen to the audio guide explain the mosaics. Restaurants are expensive in Venice, but snacking at local bars is affordable and a chance to sample lagoon fish transformed into tapas-like appetizers called *cicchetti*. Try **All'Arco** across the **Rialto Bridge** and near the animated fish market. From there you can hitch a ride over the **Grand Canal** in a **gondola** and spend the evening in **Campo Santo Stefano** listening to Vivaldi.

DAY 9

Purchase a ferry pass and go island hopping on the 4.1 or 4.2 *vaporetto* from Fondamente Nuove. Get a window seat or stand on deck for the best views. Get off at the first stop on **Murano**. From here, you can visit **workshops** and watch a **glassblowing demonstration.** Some require a small fee while others are free.

Continue on the 12 *vaporetto* from the Faro station to **Burano**. It's a 45-minute ride past lagoon wildlife, and you can order fried calamari and cold beer at **Fritto Misto** near the main dock once you get there. Afterwards, circumnavigate the island on foot and put your camera to good use. Along the way are **colorful houses** and **galleries** where locals make and sell textiles and glassware.

Just north of Burano is the nearly uninhabited island of **Torcello**. There's only one path to follow unless you decide to cross the Ponte del Diavolo (Devil's Bridge) and follow the dirt trail to **Santa Maria Assunta** cathedral. On the way back stop at **Locanda Cipriani,** where Hemingway wrote and drank, before returning to Venice by *vaporetto* as the sun sets over the lagoon.

DAY 10

If it's a weekday morning, watch the fishmongers and greengrocers under the colorful **Rialto**

Rialto Bridge, Venice

market and **shop for masks** along the adjacent streets. **Atelier Pietro Longhi** is a good place for dressing up and getting into the Carnevale spirit. Head to any of the traditional *bacari* bars nearby and accompany every meal with *prosecco* from the Veneto region. If you don't want to wander unknowingly past Marco Polo's house or the oldest ghetto in Europe, spend a couple of hours with a certified guide who can provide an insider's perspective on the city. Take a break inside the first pastry shop you see and sample as many delicacies as your appetite can handle. There's a different sweet for every season, but *burranei* are baked all year long.

Hop a *vaporetto* to the **Galleria dell'Accademia** for a glimpse of Venetian Renaissance art. Alternatively, if you prefer contemporary canvases, keep going to the **Guggenheim Foundation** and **Punta della Dogana** at the very tip of Dorsoduro. Escape the narrow streets of the center and take a walk along the sun-drenched **Fondamenta Zaterre** promenade and stop for a gelato at **Da Nico.** Enjoy a cup or cone on the dock overlooking Giudecca and the southern lagoon. At night the squares near the university fill up. **Campo Santa Margherita** is the most animated in town, where you can listen to street musicians and join improvised parties spilling out into the square on weekends. If you haven't tried risotto with fish, make your way to **Osteria da Codroma.**

WITH MORE TIME

It's difficult to tire of Venice, but if you long for a different landscape spend a morning cruising up the **Brenta Canal** on a boat tour with **Il Burchiello** and then take the train back to Venice. Ride a *vaporetto* out to the **Lido** and lie on the beach or rent a bike near the main landing and cycle along this narrow strip of an island to the wild reserve where Goethe was inspired and Mussolini played golf.

Back in Venice, do your own sailing with a boat from **Brussa Is Boat.** A license isn't required but you will need to learn the rules of the lagoon. If that sounds too risky, try paddling through the city by kayak or riding a wakeboard.

If you happen to be in town during the **Venice Biennale** (May-November, odd-numbered years) art festival, visit the pavilions in the public gardens and installations set up around the city. All the gambling houses in the city have closed except one—you can still place bets at the **Venice Casino** and play familiar American table games or harder-to-master European games until 2am.

BACK TO ROME
DAY 11

It takes a little over 3.5 hours to get back to Rome by train. Leave Venice early enough to enjoy a final meal in the capital. Take the subway, tram, or bus to **Trastevere** for a tasty farewell, and if you haven't ordered *amatriciana* or *carciofi alla romana* this is the time to do so. Before heading off to the airport, climb the nearby **Gianicolo Hill** for one last look at the Eternal City and say your good-byes to Italy.

Rome

Highlights

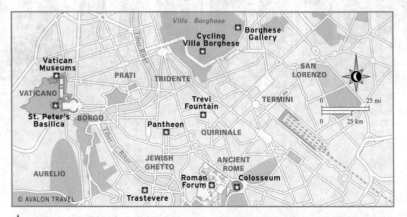

★ **Colosseum:** Circle it, touch it, stand above it, go inside during the day—then return to see it by moonlight. Rome's ancient amphitheater exceeds all expectations (page 48).

★ **Roman Forum:** Politics, commerce, and justice were all centered here from the rise of the Roman Republic to the fall of the Empire. A treasure trove of ancient Roman artifacts tell the tale (page 50).

★ **Pantheon:** Rome's largest temple has survived nearly 2,000 years and counting. Its immense portico columns still influence architects today (page 55).

★ **Trevi Fountain:** This baroque fountain is one of Rome's most popular photo-ops. Throw a coin into the water and guarantee yourself a return trip (page 60).

★ **Borghese Gallery:** Masterworks by Bernini, Botticelli, and Caravaggio are displayed in this sumptuous villa (page 62).

★ **St. Peter's Basilica:** Bernini, Michelangelo, and Raphael all contributed their talents to the design of this center of the Roman Catholic faith, the largest church in the world (page 64).

★ **Vatican Museums:** It would take days to see everything inside the Vatican Museums, but a visit to the **Sistine Chapel** is mandatory. Its 3,000 square feet of frescoes by Michelangelo are arguably the greatest work of art ever created (page 65).

★ **Trastevere:** Escape the crowds and get lost among the narrow streets, hidden squares, and spectacular views of this medieval enclave, a village within the city (page 70).

★ *Pizza al taglio:* Rome has an obsession with Italy's cheesy culinary masterpiece (page 82).

★ **Cycling Villa Borghese:** Rome's central park is the best place to take refuge from the summer heat. Rent a bike and cycle the shaded paths past gardens, museums, and panoramic terraces (page 108).

Rome isn't a single city; it's many cities built on top of one another over thousands of years. These layers blend together into a collage of art and architecture that makes it possible to travel from antiquity to the Middle Ages, from the Renaissance to the present, and back again within a single neighborhood. Every street, facade, fountain, and fresco has an invisible history and a unique splendor that dazzles the senses.

Even before you set foot in the city it's hard not to have an idea of what to expect. Monuments in Rome are global icons. The Colosseum, Spanish Steps, Trevi Fountain, Piazza Navona, and the Sistine Chapel are ingrained in the collective imagination and attract millions of travelers every year. Experiencing these wonders in person is what a visit to Rome is all about.

The past is fundamental, but it's not everything. Rome is alive with a contagious energy that pulsates through its streets, markets, and squares. You feel it the moment you take a breath of freshly baked *pizza bianca*, taste the bitter sweetness of Roman espresso, or catch a glimpse of rush hour traffic. The city's nearly three million residents seem oblivious to the magnificence all around them.

If you remain on the well-trodden tourist trail, you'll only catch a glimpse of Rome. Getting the wider picture requires wandering Trastevere's village-like streets and elegantly elbowing through crowded bars. It requires not only observing the grand monuments and masterpieces, but also meeting locals, who are nearly always willing to talk, especially when the conversation revolves around family, soccer, and food.

Old timers in Testaccio or Trastevere may claim that things aren't what they used to be—and they're probably right. But globalization has only put a small dent in Rome's age-old routines. Most shops still close at 1pm and reopen at 3pm, the pope still blesses pilgrims every Sunday morning, and daily fruit and vegetable markets still feed the masses. Artichokes appear in spring, peaches ripen in late summer, and grapes are pressed in autumn. There is an underlying rhythm to the city from *Carnevale* to Christmas, with

Previous: Colosseum; view of St. Peter's. **Above:** Trevi Fountain.

Rome

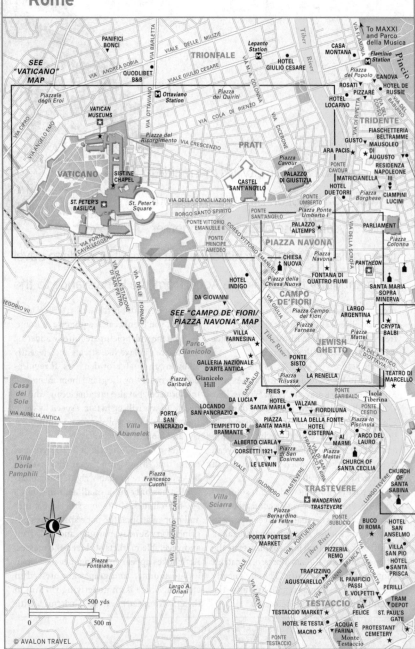

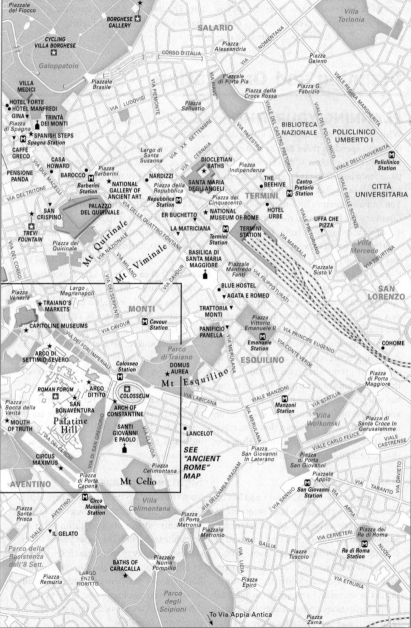

resilient traditions and perennial dishes that have whet appetites for generations.

What at first appears mysterious slowly begins to make sense. If you cross the tourist divide and enter the everyday reality of the city, you will absorb the local body language and pick up a few melodic phrases in Italian. At the very least, you will learn how to order pizza by the slice and defend your place in line. The learning curve is steep but gratifying for stomach, mind, and spirit.

Planning and Orientation

PLANNING YOUR TIME

While you can hit the highlights in two days, it's worth spending three days or more to really experience Rome. With this much time you should be able to explore most of the historic center as well as several major museums. You can also venture into the outskirts and discover what lies beyond the center.

Before arriving, spend some time planning an itinerary based on your interests and not just what you're expected to see. Tourism is a year-round reality in Rome that peaks in August and during the Christmas and Easter holidays. In summer, lines to popular sites can stretch for hours, making sightseeing passes and advance bookings a good idea. The Vatican Museums alone require at least a half-day to appreciate. Getting up early can help avoid tour groups that generally don't leave their hotels until midmorning, and staying up late will give you a chance to admire fountains and squares undisturbed. Most of all, don't be afraid to go with the Roman flow and enjoy everything without the agonizing feeling you should be doing something else.

Daily Reminders

Most museums close on Mondays, and box offices stop selling tickets an hour before entry. The Vatican closes on Sundays, except the last Sunday of every month, and churches restrict visiting hours during masses. Some monuments like the Baths of Caracalla and many parks have different closing times according to the season and amount of daylight. All public institutions close on December 25 and January 1, and some smaller museums also take national holidays off. Roman monuments and museums are free on the first Sunday of every month. The majority offer informative audio guides that are essential to understanding the art and history on display.

Advance Bookings and Time-Saving Tips

Most monuments and museums, including the **Vatican, Colosseum,** and **Borghese Gallery,** offer convenient online prebooking services that can save you the frustration of waiting in line. There's a small fee and reservations should be made a couple of weeks in advance. The Colosseum, Roman Forum, and Palatine Hill share a single ticket; if you haven't prebooked, get it at the San Gregorio ticket office instead of the Colosseum, which is usually very crowded. Many museums now require visitors to check large bags and backpacks, which can lead to further waiting. If you don't want to stare at the back of someone's head for another 20 minutes, travel light and avoid the Vatican and Borghese cloakrooms.

Sightseeing Passes

RomaPass (tel. 06/0608, www.romapass.it) is the city's visitor card that includes a map, museum entry, discounts, and unlimited travel on public transport. The 3-day pass (€34) includes free entry to two museums, while the 48-hour option (€28) is good for one museum. Both will save you money and time, especially if you plan on moving around Rome by bus or subway. The Vatican is a separate state and not covered by RomaPass.

The **Omnia Card** (tel. 06/6989-6375, Mon.-Sat. 9am-6pm, www.omniakit.org) is the most comprehensive card available and comes in a 24-hour (€50) or 72-hour (€108) format. It provides entry to the Vatican Museums, an audio guide to St. Peter's, an 18-stop bus tour of Christian sights, plus all the benefits of the RomaPass. If you do everything it offers you can save 15 percent; if you don't you may be better off with single entries. The card also permits direct access to all sights, which can be priceless. It's available at Fiumicino airport (Terminals 1 and 2), Termini station (Via Giolitti 34, track 24), the Vatican (Piazza Pio XII 9), or online.

The **Archaeologia Card** (tel. 06/3996-7700, €23) is dedicated to archeological sites such as the Colosseum and Foro Romano and seven other ancient Roman destinations and museums. It doesn't include public transportation, but it does allow access to a special archeology bus line and is valid for seven days from first use.

The **National Museum of Rome ticket** includes four sights (Palazzo Massimo, Palazzo Altemps, Crypta Balbi, and Baths of Diocletian). It costs €8 and is valid for three days.

Exploring the City

Walking is the best way to experience Rome. Public transportation is mostly efficient, and a single-or three-day **ATAC** (Rome's transportation authority) pass can get you around the city quickly. The two-line metro is limited, but there are myriad bus and tram lines that link different neighborhoods and are a fun way to explore the city once your feet tire.

ORIENTATION

Rome is the biggest city in Italy. On a map, it looks relatively compact, but once you hit the ground the vastness of the historic center quickly becomes evident. There are no sharp divisions between neighborhoods other than the Tiber River; there is no east side or west side, no left bank or right bank with distinct characteristics. It takes time to really know

Rome and even locals get lost in their city. Don't feel bad—just check for *piazza* names, which can usually be quickly found on a map, and don't be too proud to ask directions.

Ancient Rome and Monti

The remnants of ancient Rome can be spotted throughout the city, but are especially concentrated and impressive around the **Roman Forum** and **Colosseum.** For thousands of years, this was the commercial, political, religious, and entertainment hub of the city. It's the only part of Rome that hasn't been covered over by medieval or modern constructions. The area sunk into ruin after the decline of the empire and it wasn't until the 17th century that artists and archeologists began to discover and preserve the foundations visible today. Many of the sculptures, personal belongings, and artifacts they unearthed are preserved inside **Museo Capitolino** on **Capitoline Hill.** The area's ancient monuments attract thousands of visitors every day—along with tour operators, souvenir vendors, imitation gladiators, horse-and-buggy drivers, street artists, and beggars.

Monti competes with Trastevere and Testaccio for the title of most Roman neighborhood. **Via Urbana** is one the area's characteristic thoroughfares. The cobblestoned street, which locals petitioned to have pedestrianized, follows a gentle incline and is dotted with boutiques, workshops, eateries, barbers, and jewelry stores. There are no major museums or monuments in Monti, which makes it relatively tourist-free and a good place to rub shoulders with locals.

Public transit lines: Metro B Circo Massimo, Colosseo; Tram 3; Buses 40, 70, 75, 80, 85, 175, C3.

Campo De' Fiori/ Piazza Navona

Campo De' Fiori and **Piazza Navona** are Rome's most characteristic areas and make up the historic core of the city. These neighborhoods flanking the Tiber are home to the finest **Renaissance and baroque buildings**

Rome in Two Days

Rome is a big city with more World Heritage Sites than anywhere else in the world. Seeing it all would take a lifetime. You can get a memorable introduction in 48 hours, though it may leave your senses reeling. Wear comfortable shoes for this whirlwind introduction to Rome.

DAY 1

- Check in to your hotel and relieve yourself of any unnecessary luggage.

- Head to the **Colosseum** and bypass the lines with a **RomaPass.**

- Cross the street and explore the ruins of the **Forum** and **Palatine Hill.**

- If it's raining or cold enter the **Capitoline Museums** to see Roman relics.

- Climb the stairs of the **Vittoriano** monument and get a panoramic look at the city.

- Leave ancient Rome behind and descend into the **Jewish Ghetto.**

- Try a kosher hamburger at **Fonzie's** or keep going to **Campo de'Fiori.**

- Browse the market stalls and enter **Il Forno** to sample *pizza bianca.*

- If you don't have sunglasses, buy a pair and check out the street artists in **Piazza Navona.**

- Avoid the cafes lining the square and sit outside at **Antico Caffè della Pace** to people watch.

- Walk through the enormous bronze doors of the **Pantheon** and follow Via dei Pastini to the **Trevi Fountain.**

- Deposit a coin and grab a gelato topped with *panna* whipped cream from **San Crispino.**

- Navigate your way to the **Spanish Steps** and climb up to **Villa Borghese** to watch the sun set over the city.

DAY 2

- Make your way to Vatican City and leave Rome—and Italy—behind.

- Admire the immensity of **St. Peter's Basilica** and climb to the cupola for a great view.

- Enter the **Vatican Museums** and follow the guided itinerary to the **Sistine Chapel.**

- Join the tour of the **Vatican gardens,** but don't ruin your appetite at the museum café.

and a maze of streets that are ripe for exploration. Both are vibrant and filled with **animated squares** where locals get their freshly baked pizza and kosher treats. Rome's highest concentration of **eateries** is in these two neighborhoods, though they can veer toward touristy. During the day, Campo De' Fiori fills up with flowers and market stalls. At night partygoers congregate around the lively square enjoying *al fresco* happy hours.

The area is divided by Corso Vittorio Emanuele II, which runs from the Tiber River to Piazza Venezia. Campo De' Fiori and the **Jewish Ghetto** are south and Piazza Navona and **Pantheon** are north.

Public transit lines: Tram 8; Buses 23, 40, 62, 70, 80, 81, 116, 119, 280, C3.

Tridente

The Tridente neighborhood is the result of 17th-and 18th-century urban planning. Great artists were commissioned to leave

view of Rome from the dome of St. Peter's Basilica

- Have lunch in **Borgo Pio** or a traditional plate of pasta at **Pastasciutta** nearby.

- Walk it off along the Tiber River or ride the bus to **Trastevere.**

- Stroll through the medieval streets and enter **Santa Maria di Trastevere** to view its mosaics.

- Climb to the top of the **Gianicolo Hill** and have a look at everywhere you've been.

- Order *aperitivo* at café in a square below or cross the Ponte Sisto bridge and try the wine at **Roscioli.**

- Start searching for a *trattoria* with tables outside or sit indoors at **Filetti di Baccala** for Italian fish-and-chips.

- Enjoy getting lost after dark until **Jerry Thomas Speakeasy** opens, and then have them mix you the house cocktail.

- Go to bed—or don't, and wait until the first bakeries open and start serving the first *cornetti* of the day.

their mark on this corner of Rome. Under popes and leaders like Napoleon, **Piazza del Popolo,** the **Spanish Steps,** and the **Trevi Fountain,** were constructed along with imposing homes and elaborate churches. Today, this neighborhood is Rome's most glamourous **shopping district,** with the action centered on Via Condòtti and Via del Corso. From the top of the Spanish Steps it's possible get a wonderful view of the city and reach **Villa Borghese**.

Public transit lines: Metro A Barberini, Spagna, Flaminio; Tram 8; Buses 62, 70, 80, 116, 119, 175, 224, 280, C3.

Vaticano

Within the walls of the Vatican (the smallest state in the world) lie the former **papal residences,** now converted into museums. Whether you are a believer or not, it's hard not to be impressed by the grandeur of **St. Peter's Basilica,** the view from its cupola, or the works on display within the museums—not to mention the **Sistine Chapel.**

The Vatican is easily reached by bus, tram, or subway, but the only way to appreciate its monumental size is on foot. Via Della Conciliazione was built to provide a grand entrance to the square and is packed with visitors throughout the day. If you want to see Pope Francis in person, Sunday morning is the time to come.

Public transit lines: Metro A Ottaviano, Lepanto; Tram 2; Buses 23, 32, 34, 40, 49, 62, 70, 81, 115, 280.

Trastevere

Trastevere means "across the Tiber." This neighborhood's proximity to the river attracted sailors and fishermen including many Syrian and Jewish immigrants. Later, wealthy Romans built their villas here, the remains of which can be found underneath **Villa Farnesina.** During the Middle Ages the population increased and the neighborhood grew haphazardly. Much of Trastevere's **medieval character** remains; there are still plenty of labyrinthine passages to explore. Residents here have always been slightly secluded from the rest of the city, and the neighborhood offers a vibrant and characteristic slice of Roman life. Trastevere has a high concentration of *trattoria*-style restaurants and cocktail bars that makes parking in the area on weekends nearly impossible.

Unless your hotel is in Trastevere, you'll probably have to cross a bridge to get to the neighborhood. The most scenic and convenient options are **Ponte Sisto** if approaching from Piazza Navona, or Ponte Cestio from the Forum.

Public transit lines: Tram 8; Buses 23, 115, 125, 280, H.

Aventino and Testaccio

Testaccio and Aventino lack major tourist attractions—but that's arguably what makes them worth exploring. These primarily **residential areas** have maintained their

Roman identity and provide an authentic feeling of daily life in the city.

Testaccio is a working-class neighborhood with a grid-like street pattern that was laid in the 1930s under the orders of Mussolini. Tucked between a bend in the Tiber, the Aurelian wall, and Via Marmorata, it's populated with spirited residents who are proud of their neighborhood and their soccer team. On weekday mornings the streets are alive with locals going about their business. Especially animated are the small parks and covered market where residents shop and socialize. Most businesses are concentrated around these areas. After dark, the **nightclubs** and restaurants at the base of Mount Testaccio attract a young crowd.

Aventino lies on one of Rome's famed seven hills a short distance from Testaccio. Unlike its gritty neighbor, Aventino is well heeled and predominately **residential.** Streets are lined with trees and elegant apartment buildings are interspersed with large 19th-century villas. Most of the points of interest are concentrated along **Via di Santa Sabina.** Here you can get the famous keyhole view of the Vatican through the **Buco di Roma,** visit a Franciscan church or Dominican basilica, and look out over the city from the intimate **Giardini degli Aranci** (Orange Gardens). What you won't find is many shops or restaurants, so come before or after lunch or bring a picnic.

Public transit lines: Metro B Piramide; Tram 3; Buses 23, 75, 118, 175, 280, 715, 716.

Termini

Termini train station is Rome's **transportation nerve center,** the place from where high-speed trains leave, the city's two subway lines (Line A and B) intersect, and dozens of buses depart. The streets around the station are full of **hotels** and **fast-food joints** catering to commuters and travelers. It's been cleaned up in recent years and much of the seediness is gone, but there's not much to see in the immediate area besides the **Museo Nazionale Romano, Baths of**

Diocletian, and daily rush hour, which is often hectic.

HISTORY

Rome has been changing the course of history for 2,770 years. It was the first city with a population over a million; the first to have running water; and the first to organize prostitution and build apartment buildings. It spread the Latin alphabet and a language whose traces are evident in the words you're reading. Romans transformed the calendar and the perception of time, built roads that changed the concept of distance, established laws that regulated behavior, and designed stadiums that standardized entertainment.

Rome didn't start out as an eternal city nor was it built in a day. It started out as a quiet place near a river with a few hills to which no roads led. It was an attractive spot for Iron Age settlers searching for food and safety. The first buildings were not the marble and travertine ruins of the Forum but timber huts on Palatine Hill. Time passed, numbers grew, tribes merged, and before anyone knew it clash of clans had evolved into age of empires.

The early civilized centuries were influenced by the Etruscans, who ruled the town until 509 BC when they were expelled and a republic was founded. The next 500 years saw the steady growth of the city. One by one the peoples of the Italian peninsula were conquered or absorbed before attention was turned overseas. It was during this period that Rome's first roads were built, Hannibal was defeated, and Spartacus's revolt nearly changed the course of history.

Caesar's assassination in 44 BC marked the beginning of a new age, and it took 17 years of civil war before his adopted son Augustus eliminated the competition and declared himself emperor of Rome. The empire increased the city's size in territory and splendor. The brick of the Republican age was replaced with marble and the city took on new dimensions. Subsequent emperors used architecture to influence public opinion and ensure a legacy that has survived to this day.

Invading Goths and Vandals put an end to 1,200 years of Roman hegemony in the 5th century AD. The centuries that followed marked a drastic decline in population and prestige. Even the papacy could do little to save the city from feuding families and frequent invasions. Rome gently withered until the 16th century when Renaissance ideals snapped the city out of its medieval stupor. Popes and aristocrats began to value the city's past as well as its present and hired artists and architects to build the churches and palaces that fill the city today. It was the beginning of a rebirth that continued through the unification of Italy, a brief flirtation with fascism, and the modern age.

Sights

Rome is the most visited city in Italy and one of the most popular destinations in the world. Each neighborhood in the historic center contains countless churches, monuments, and museums. Some, like the Colosseum, are crowded; others are nearly empty. Many, such as Circus Maximus, are free, but others charge an entry fee or require reservations. Lines outside major sights can be long during the summer but are avoidable by prebooking or using the RomaPass.

There's something for everyone in Rome. If you fancy antiquity and dream of gladiators your first stop should be Ancient Rome and Ostia Antica; anyone with a love of painting or sculpture could stop into the Vatican Museums or Villa Borghese. There's modern at the MAXXI and baroque throughout the city. Piazza Navona and Fontana di Trevi are mandatory stops, but the lesser-known squares and fountains in between can be equally appealing.

What's New?

Visitors who imagine Rome as a static city are mistaken. The city is very much alive, and change is constant. Here's what's new in the Eternal City:

Spruced-up monuments. Many monuments have been or are currently undergoing restoration. Scaffolding was recently removed from the Piramide di Cestio (Pyramid), and the structure has never been whiter or more accessible to visitors, who can now discover the interior. Work continues on the Colosseum and Spanish Steps, with the latter scheduled to reopen in early 2017.

Walkable streets. Ex-mayor Ignazio Marino made mobility a priority and quite a few pedestrian projects were launched under his brief mandate. Traffic around the Colosseum was completely rerouted and the Via dei Fori Imperiali that connects the monument with Piazza Venezia restricted to buses and taxis only. Routes along the Tiber were also improved and precedence given to joggers and cyclists along the riverside path.

Better public transit. The new Tiburtina train station with high-speed connections to Florence and Venice opened, the Linea B subway line was extended four stops, and several new bridges now cross the Tiber River. The biggest urban project and the one that directly affects visitors is the construction of a third subway line (Line C), which has disfigured parts of the city including the area around the Colosseum. Construction is made difficult by the occasional discovery of Roman ruins and the completion date is unknown.

More culture. Several important institutions have opened or reopened in the last couple of years, including the MAXXI 21st-century art and architecture museum designed by Zahad Hadid and the MACRO art museum. The riverside has also been revived and outdoor films are now projected on Tiburtina Island.

New eats and libations. New bars and restaurants include the Eataly emporium, modern-day speakeasies like Jerry Thomas and Race Club, and beer bars lined with taps such as Queen Makeda Grand Pub and Argot. Burger joints have gone kosher and healthy street food continues to trend. The Testaccio food market reopened and temporary food and drink kiosks are set up along the river from June to September.

ANCIENT ROME

What to visit first in Ancient Rome is a tough question. If you want to be chronologically correct, you'll start with the Forum—but the monumental size and reputation of the Colosseum is hard to resist, which is why many visitors make it their first stop. The sites share a single ticket. Save time by buying yours at the San Gregorio ticket office instead of the Colosseum.

The center of ancient Rome can be approached from different directions. The traditional route along **Via dei Fori Imperiali** leads directly to the Colosseum. This road was recently pedestrianized (except for buses and taxis), but ongoing work on a new subway line may leave eyes sore. For an instant impression, take the subway to the **Colosseo station.** Get out and be wowed. **Via di San Gregorio** from Circo

Massimo is less crowded and provides a subtler entrance.

TOP EXPERIENCE

★ Colosseum
(COLOSSEO)

The **Colosseo** (Piazza del Colosseo, tel. 06/774-0091, daily 8:30am-7:15pm summer and 8:30am-4:30pm winter, €12 combined with Palatino and Forum, audio guides €6, Metro B: Colosseo) was ancient Rome's largest amphitheater, where citizens came to be entertained. It's nearly as impressive today as it must have been in AD 80 when it was inaugurated, with a crowd of 50,000 gathered to witness. Remarkably it only took eight years to build and survived pillaging by generations of architects and builders. Restoration began in the 19th century when pioneering

Ancient Rome

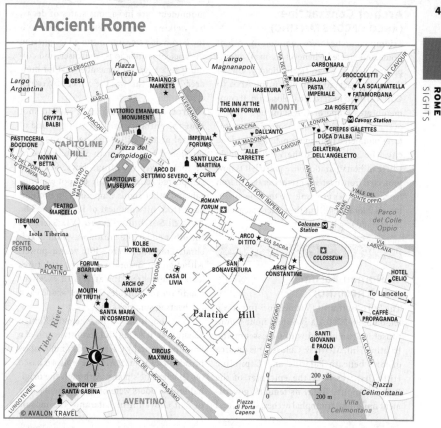

© AVALON TRAVEL

archeologists and the Vatican recognized the building's historical significance and safeguarded the area.

Today, the Colosseum still towers over visitors and looks like many of the modern sporting stadiums it inspired. The monument consists of three levels of stone archways that have been stripped of their original marble facing but remain impressive. Archaeologists added a platform at ground level to partially cover the passageways and storerooms underneath the arena where wild animals and gladiators waited to entertain the masses. From here, you can climb to the second tier, which can be entirely circumnavigated and provides the best views of the monument. Other parts of the sight can only be accessed by special tours.

The Colosseum teems with visitors (along with those hoping to make a euro off the masses). It costs €5 to pose with one of the modern-day gladiators circling the area and slightly more for an unofficial guided tour. Lines to visit the interior, which was a cow pasture in the Middle Ages and once housed a barbershop, are long, and there is only one entrance. **RomaPass** provides quicker access as well as transport and discounts for other museums. English-language tours of the Colosseum (€5) depart daily every 30-45 minutes between 9:45am and 5:15pm. Tours of the underground and third tier are €9 with frequent departures from the ticket office. It's worth making early-morning and evening visits when crowds thin and the stadium's travertine surface takes on yellowish tones.

Arch of Constantine
(ARCO DI CONSTANTINO)

Triumphal arches were common in ancient Rome and erected whenever a consul or emperor obtained a significant victory. One of the best-preserved examples is the **Arco di Constantino** next to the Colosseum. It commemorates Emperor Constantine's victory over a rival in 312 BC and incorporates sculptures plundered from monuments around the city. The arch spanned the Via Triumphale where military parades once passed; it is now protected from overeager sightseers by an iron fence. The arch's proximity to the Colosseum makes it look small, but the closer you get the more imposing it becomes.

TOP EXPERIENCE

★ Roman Forum
(FORO ROMANO)

The **Foro Romano** (Via dei Fori Imperiali, tel. 06/3996-7700, daily 9am-1 hour before sunset, €12 combined with Colosseum and Palatine Hill, Metro B: Colosseo) is an area of land beneath Palatine and Capitoline Hills that was once the epicenter of the Roman Empire. Today its temples, government buildings, triumphal arches, shops, and monuments are in various states of decay, but walking along the **Via Sacra** path into the Forum is a step into history. Deciphering the ancient foundations, staircases, and columns isn't easy, but remember that for hundreds of years this was the center of Western civilization.

Arco di Tito (Via Sacra), easy to spot near the entrance of the Forum, is one of several arches still standing. It was commissioned by the Roman Senate to honor victories over rebellious Jews. Scan the sculptured relief carefully to spot a menorah and other spoils Emperor Tito brought back from his conquest of Jerusalem. The **Arco di Settimio Severo** (Via Sacra) at the other end of the Forum was built to celebrate Emperor Severo's 10th year in power. Although the decorative bronze sculptures have disappeared, the arch is in excellent condition and provides welcome shade from the beating summer sun.

Next door is the **Curia,** where the Roman Senate met. It's a faithful reconstruction of a building begun by Caesar and completed by his adopted son in 29 AD. The replica is based on Diocleziano's plans. Although the original bronze doors were moved to the Basilica of San Giovanni in Laterano, the mosaic

Colosseum

flooring, which illustrates daily Roman life, is authentic. It's a good place to understand what the Forum was like in its heyday.

Several entrances lead into the Forum; the least crowded is on Via di San Gregorio beneath the aqueduct.

Palatine Hill
(PALATINO)

Palatino (daily 9am-1 hour before sunset, €12 combo ticket with Colosseum and Roman Forum, Metro B: Colosseo or Circo Massimo), one of Rome's seven hills, is far less crowded than the Forum below. It is dominated by the remains of palaces, once inhabited by Rome's ancient elite, and is covered with wildflowers in spring. Some cats also call it home. From the top, there are wonderful views of the Forum on one side and the Circus Maximus on the other.

One of the most interesting villas on Palatine Hill is **Casa di Livia** near the site where Augustus, Rome's first emperor, lived with his family. The home is one of the hill's best-preserved dwellings. Time has raised the ground level above the house, and a short flight of steps leads to the rooms. The original mosaic paving and religious frescoes provide insight into Roman decorating standards.

You'll see many of the same colors and patterns used here throughout the city.

Nearby is a small **stadium** Emperor Domiziano built inside his estate. Though its exact use is unknown, it may have served as a garden, riding track, or outdoor gym. Thinking that it might make a good place for footraces, an Ostrogoth king added a circular enclosure at the southern end in the 6th century. There's enough room for an impromptu 50-yard dash, but the baths next to the track have been out of order for centuries.

You can reach Palatine Hill from the Roman Forum or Via San Gregorio, the entrance beneath the arches of the aqueduct that once provided running water to residents.

Imperial Forums

Caesar wasn't satisfied with just one forum. What today is known as the Roman Forum had become cramped and overcrowded in his day and he decided to expand. First, he had Cicero purchase nearby land for a small fortune. Then, on the battlefield of Pharsalus in 48 BC, he vowed to build a temple in honor of Venus. What was initially intended as a simple structure soon laid the pattern for the Imperial Forums, which lie on the northern side of Via dei Fori Imperiali. Although they

Roman Forum

can be viewed from several angles, they may not be entered.

The **Forum of Augustus** (Foro Augusto) is adjacent to Caesar's and was built to mark the defeat of his stepfather's assassins Brutus and Cassius. The centerpiece is a temple dedicated to Mars the Avenger, of which a short flight of stairs and four Corinthian columns are still visible. Nearby is the high wall Caesar built to protect his forum from the densely packed neighborhoods nearby and the ever-present menace of fire. The area is rarely open to the public, but can be observed from the street or a small footbridge that runs behind the site.

After successful military campaigns in Dacia, Trajan used his vast booty to build a forum next to the others. **Trajan's Forum** was the last and greatest, designed by a Syrian architect who dispersed 30 million cubic feet of soil to make way for a vast semicircular market, the largest basilica ever built in ancient Rome, and Greek and Latin libraries. It became the center of political and administrative action where laws were passed and wars declared.

At the end of the complex, **Trajan's Column** tells the story of the emperor's two campaigns in Dacia (modern-day Romania). The column is wrapped with sculpted reliefs that show Roman troops in action defeating local chieftains. It also includes over 60 portraits of the emperor so no one could forget his success. The statue of Trajan at the top, however, was removed by Pope Sixtus V and replaced with one of St. Peter. The column also marks the height of the hillside, which was removed to make way for the market and has survived nearly intact except for the emperor's gold funeral urn. Small slits on the outside allow light to reach the spiral staircase on the inside that isn't open to the public.

Piazza Venezia

Piazza Venezia (Metro B: Colosseo) is one of the busiest squares in the city and difficult to cross at rush hour when cars from five different streets fight for the right of way. Watching the traffic cop on the raised pedestal in the center tame unruly drivers is a treat. On the southern side of the chaos is the massive **Vittoriano** (www.ilvittoriano.com, daily 9:30am-5:30pm, free, Metro B: Colosseo) monument also known as the Altar of the Republic. It is where Italy's unknown soldiers are honored. If you're wondering what the Forum looked like in its heyday, this building completed in 1925 is a decent rendering of classical ancient style. It overshadows everything in the square below and is not particularly loved by locals who refer to it as "the wedding cake." A steep set of stairs lead to the altar where an honor guard is permanently stationed, and there are three terraces with increasingly great views of the city. Inside is the **Complesso del Vittoriano** (Via di San Pietro in Carcere, tel. 06/871-5111, Mon.-Thurs. 9:30am-7:30pm, Fri.-Sat. 9:30am-10pm, and Sun. 9:30am-8:30pm, €13) exhibition space where international art shows are temporarily staged, as well as the **Museo del Risorgimento** (Via dei Fori Imperiali, tel. 06/679-3598, daily 9:30am-6:30pm, closed first Tues. of every month, €5) dedicated to Italy's mid-19th-century struggle for unification.

Piazza del Campidoglio

Capitoline Hill, the smallest of Rome's seven hills, was the most revered. It's here that the Temple of Juno once stood and where Roman coins were minted. **Piazza del Campidoglio** (Metro B: Colosseo or Tram 8) lies at the top and is a sharp contrast from the ruins below. Michelangelo designed the marble paving of this elegant square as well as the well-proportioned facades of the Renaissance buildings (Palazzo Nuovo, Conservatorio, and Senatorio) that now house city hall and the **Musei Capitolini.**

The stairs to the right of Palazzo Nuovo (the one with a clock tower) lead to the **Vittoriano** monument and a great view of the forums. You can enter by way of the monumental steps from Piazza Venezia or via the back way from Piazza Campidoglio. There's a bar at the top with a scenic terrace that makes a good stop.

Capitoline Museums
(MUSEI CAPITOLINI)

Musei Capitolino (Piazza del Campidoglio 1, tel. 06/3996-7800, daily 9:30am-7:30pm, www.museicapitolini.org, €14 or RomaPass, audio guide €6, Metro B: Colosseo or Tram 8) comprise one of the oldest museums in the world. It got its start in 1471 when Pope Sisto IV donated a collection of ancient statues to the city. Subsequent popes contributed relics that were periodically dug up in the area and a pinacoteca art gallery was added in the 18th century.

The museums are located in Piazza del Campidoglio inside Palazzo Nuovo and Palazzo dei Conservatori. The ticket office is in the latter along with the original bronze equestrian statue of Marcus Aurelius (the one in the square is a copy). There's a mix of ancient and Renaissance art including Bernini's marble version of Medusa (room 10) and a bronze statue of Rome's legendary twin founders, Romulus and Remus (room 9). Upstairs in the painting gallery are works by Caravaggio, an outdoor terrace with panoramic views, and a café.

Palazzo dei Conservatori is connected to Palazzo Nuovo by way of an underground corridor; the perpendicular passageway near the end leads to the oldest part of the complex overlooking the forums. This side of the museum is smaller and contains mostly ancient sculpture including *The Dying Gaul* (room 53) and the Hall of Emperors featuring busts of ancient Roman VIPs.

Circus Maximus
(CIRCO MASSIMO)

Circo Massimo (daily 24/7, free, Metro B: Circo Massimo) is where ancient Romans cheered their favorite charioteers, and where present-day locals jog or walk their dogs. Most of the stone structure has been stripped away over the centuries, but the original shape of the immense oval racetrack is still clear. Although there are few relics here, there is plenty of atmosphere.

The Circus Maximus accommodated up to 250,000 spectators, including the emperor, who watched races from the comfort of Palatine Hill. Chariots were released from 12 gates at the northern end of the track. Drivers attempted to complete 7 laps; races lasted around 10 minutes. Not everyone finished in one piece, which may be why horse racing was

inside the Capitolene Museums

so popular in ancient Rome. Gambling was another reason, and successful charioteers became wealthy and famous.

Today the area is a pleasant refuge from traffic and a good place to exercise or rest. You can walk along the long stretches of track or the raised *spina,* which divided the course and was decorated with obelisks and other spoils of conquest.

Baths of Caracalla
(TERME DI CARACALLA)

Hygiene was important to ancient Romans, who visited public baths daily. Hundreds of these were built throughout the city and could be used free of charge. **Terme di Caracalla** (Via delle Terme di Caracalla, tel. 06/3996-7700, Apr.-Sept. Tues.-Sun. 9am-7:15pm, Mon. 9am-2pm, Oct.-Feb. Tues.-Sun. 9am-4:30pm, Mon. 9am-2pm, Feb.-Mar. Tues.-Sun. 9am-5pm, Mon. 8:30am-2pm, €6 or RomaPass, Metro B: Circo Massimo) were some of the largest, and are among the best-preserved examples of an imperial spa. These baths could accommodate up to 1,600 bathers at one time. Facilities included pools of different temperature for keeping clean and socializing. Slaves kept the water warm, while servants attended to the wealthier patrons. Changing rooms, libraries, and a courtyard for exercising are still visible. Guided tours can be arranged on weekend mornings, and are a good idea. Otherwise, the lack of signage leaves a lot to the imagination.

Forum Boarium

Before the Roman Forum became the center of the ancient world, business was conducted in the **Forum Boarium** (Piazza della Bocca della Verita) close to the Tiber. This forum was adjacent to Rome's first port, which explains the presence of the **Temples of Hercules** and **Portunus.** Portunus was the god of rivers and ports and Hercules was the protector of trade and livestock. The temple celebrating the former is circular in shape and was commissioned around 120 BC by a wealthy merchant who belonged to the oil guild. Both temples show the influence of Greek civilization on early Roman architecture and were recently restored. Neither is open to the public.

Arch of Janus
(ARCO DI GIANO)

The **Arco di Giano** (Via del Velabro, Metro B: Circo Massimo), a rare four-faced arch, lies across a busy street from the temples and was erected in the 4th century. Although the statues of the gods that once adorned the 12 niches on either side have disappeared along with the marble covering, the monument is still imposing. It now lies slightly off the beaten path, but once marked a busy crossroads where herders brought their cattle to market and merchants took cover whenever it rained. During the Middle Ages it was converted into a fortress and the structure on top that once decorated the arch was dismantled.

Santa Maria in Cosmedin

Santa Maria in Cosmedin (Piazza della Bocca della Verita 18, daily 9am-1pm and 2:30pm-6pm, free, Metro B: Circo Massimo) is famous for the ancient drain cover that hangs in the portico and supposedly distinguishes between fact and fiction. There's usually a long line of people waiting to put their hand into the **"mouth of truth"** during the summer, and many forget to enter the church. That's too bad, considering the quality of the mosaics in this simply designed 6th-century building. The ceiling is flat rather than arched (making it cheaper to build) and prayer seems more important than any embellishments. There's a small souvenir shop in the lobby.

Basilica di Santa Maria Maggiore

There are four basilicas in Rome. St. Peter's attracts the most attention but **Basilica di Santa Maria Maggiore** (Piazza di Santa Maria Maggiore 42, tel. 06/698-6800, daily 7am-7pm, free, Metro B: Cavour) is just as breathtaking, and the one locals consider the most beautiful. The front façade doesn't look much like a church and if it wasn't for the medieval bell tower you might mistake it for something else. It was built on top of an older church beginning in AD 423 under the orders of Pope Sisto III and progressively aggrandized over the centuries. That included adding magnificent marble flooring, placing mosaics along the walls, and installing a finely carved ceiling. It is of particular importance to pilgrims who come to behold the ancient relics dating from Jesus's nativity stored in the crypt and church museum. Bernini, who created several of the statues decorating the chapels, is buried inside. A large crowd gathers in the inclined square behind the church on August 5 every year to celebrate the Madonna and watch artificial snowfall in the middle of summer. Security has been tightened in light of recent events and metal detectors are now used to check all visitors entering the basilica.

CAMPO DE' FIORI/ PIAZZA NAVONA

To visit this neighborhood, you can stick to the well-indicated routes that tourists use out of convenience or you can begin a visit from the **Isola Tiberina** or **Ponte Sisto** bridges. The former takes you through the Jewish Ghetto and then continues on Via dei Giubbonari towards Campo De' Fiori, while

the latter is a more direct route to the major squares. If time isn't a luxury, walk along less frequented, largely pedestrian streets such as **Via Giulia, Via del Pellegrino, Via del Governo Vecchio,** and **Via di Panico.**

★ Pantheon

The **Pantheon** (Piazza della Rotonda, tel. 06/6830-0230, daily 9am-6:30pm, free, Buses 40, 70, 80, 130) is the best-preserved ancient Roman building in the world. This former temple's first incarnation dates from 27 BC when it was dedicated to Jupiter, Mars, and Venus. Three gods meant pulling out all the stops, and Emperor Hadrian completely rebuilt the structure less than 100 years later. The 16 monolithic columns his architects used in the portico entrance are 12 meters high. The darkest one was recently traced to a forced labor camp that the Romans operated in Egypt.

After the empire fell the building was consecrated as a church in AD 663 and survived centuries of ravaging. It was used as a fortress and poultry market, and bell towers were added and removed, but no misuse or abuse managed to cause permanent damage.

the dome of the Pantheon

Campo De' Fiori/Piazza Navona

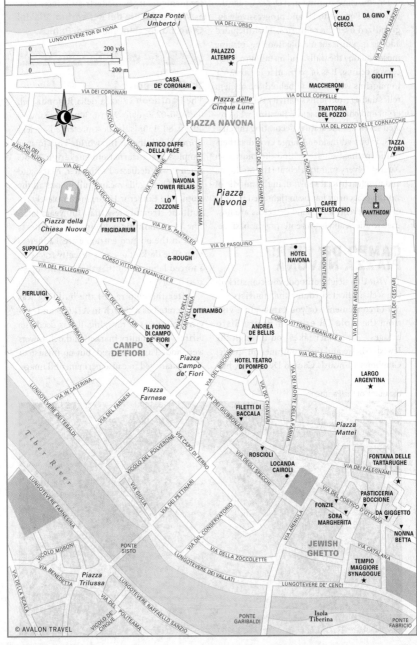

Piazza Ponte Umberto I

VIA DELL'ORSO

CIAO CHECCA

DA GINO

VIA DI CAMPO MARZIO

LUNGOTEVERE TOR DI NONA

0   200 yds

0   200 m

PALAZZO ALTEMPS ★

CASA DE' CORONARI

VIA DEI CORONARI

Piazza delle Cinque Lune

MACCHERONI

VIA DELLE COPPELLE

GIOLITTI

TRATTORIA DEL POZZO

PIAZZA NAVONA

VIA DEL POZZO DELLE CORNACCHIE

VICOLO DELLE VACCHE

VIA DEI BANCHII NUOVI

ANTICO CAFFE DELLA PACE

VIA DEL GOVERNO VECCHIO

VIA DI PARIONE

NAVONA TOWER RELAIS

LO ZOZZONE

VIA DI SANTA MARIA DELL'ANIMA

Piazza Navona

CORSO DEL RINASCIMENTO

VIA DELLA SCROFA

TAZZA D'ORO

CAFFE SANT'EUSTACHIO

PANTHEON ★

Piazza della Chiesa Nuova

BAFFETTO
FRIGIDARIUM

VIA DI S. PANTALEO

SUPPLIZIO

VIA DI PASQUINO

VIA DEL PELLEGRINO

CORSO VITTORIO EMANUELE II

G-ROUGH

HOTEL NAVONA

VIA MONTERONE

VIA DI TORRE ARGENTINA

VIA DEI CESTARI

PIERLUIGI

VIA GIULIA

VIA DI MONSERRATO

VIA DEI CAPPELLARI

PIAZZA DELLA CANCELLERIA

DITIRAMBO

ANDREA DE BELLIS

CORSO VITTORIO EMANUELE II

CAMPO DE' FIORI

IL FORNO DI CAMPO DE' FIORI

Piazza Campo de' Fiori

VIA DEL SUDARIO

HOTEL TEATRO DI POMPEO

LARGO ARGENTINA ★

VIA IN CATERINA

VIA DEL FARNESI

Piazza Farnese

VIA DEL BISCIONE

VIA DEI GIUBBONARI

VIA DI CHIAVARI

VIA DEL MONTE DELLA FARINA

LUNGOTEVERE DEI TEBALDI

FILETTI DI BACCALA

Piazza Mattei

Tiber River

VICOLO DEL POLVERONE

VIA CAPO DI FERRO

VIA DEGLI SPECCHI

ROSCIOLI

LOCANDA CAIROLI

FONTANA DELLE TARTARUGHE

VIA DEI FALEGNAMI

LUNGOTEVERE FARNESINA

VIA GIULIA

VIA DEI PETTINARI

VIA DEL CONSERVATORIO

VIA DEL PORTICO D'OTTAVIA

PASTICCERIA BOCCIONE

FONZIE

SORA MARGHERITA

DA GIGGETTO

NONNA BETTA

VICOLO MORONI

VIA BENEDETTA

Piazza Trilussa

PONTE SISTO

VIA DELLA ZOCCOLETTE

VIA DELLA SCALA

VIA DEL POLITEAMA

VICOLO DE' CINQUE

LUNGOTEVERE DEI VALLATI

LUNGOTEVERE RAFFAELLO SANZIO

JEWISH GHETTO

VIA CATALANA

TEMPIO MAGGIORE SYNAGOGUE ★

LUNGOTEVERE DE' CENCI

PONTE GARIBALDI

Isola Tiberina

PONTE FABRICIO

© AVALON TRAVEL

Piazza Navona

Back then, it could hold up to 30,000 spectators who came to watch athletic competitions rather than horse racing. Piazza Navona can be entered from six streets and is entirely free of automotive threats, allowing fountains, churches, musicians, street artists, and pigeons to be leisurely observed. Bernini's **Fontana di Quattro Fiumi** in the center is the most intricate of the waterworks and was installed in 1651. Four mythical figures representing the Nile, Ganges, Danube, and Rio de la Plata support a Roman obelisk that once stood in Circo di Massenzio on the Via Appia Antica.

The church in front of the fountain is **Sant'Agnese in Agone** (Piazza Navona, tel. 06/6819-2134, Tues.-Sun. 9am-12:30pm and 3:30pm-7pm, free). According to legend, Agnese was stripped naked in an attempt to make her renounce her faith. The hair she miraculously grew to cover herself is depicted in a marble relief near the altar. Boromini completed a restructuring of the church in 1657, giving it a unique concave appearance topped with twin bell towers. The underground chambers can be reached through a passage on the right wall and lead to the foundations of the stadium, a mosaic floor from the same period, and medieval frescoes.

The 6-meter-thick walls, one of the keys to the building's longevity, continue to support the largest dome built in antiquity. It weighs over 5,000 tons and became a model for churches, mosques, museums, and universities throughout the world. Anyone who has attended the University of Virginia or visited Monticello will spot the similarities. Even today, the dome is one of the largest in the world and supersedes both St. Peter's and the Duomo in Florence.

The only light enters through an oculus 9 meters in diameter embedded in the coffered vault high above. Most of the colored marble is original, as is Hadrian's inscription on the frieze outside. It's no wonder Italy's two first kings are buried here and Renaissance artist Raphael requested to be entombed inside.

Piazza Navona

Piazza Navona (Buses C3, 40, 81, 87) is not a typical square—in fact, it's not square at all. The piazza inherited its oblong shape when it was an ancient Roman stadium.

Palazzo Altemps

Palazzo Altemps (Piazza Sant'Apollinare 4, tel. 06/3996-7700, Tues.-Sun. 9am-7:45pm, €8 or Archaeologia card, audio guide €6, Buses C3, 40, 81, 87) is home of the Museo Nazionale Romano and houses Egyptian, Greek, and ancient Roman sculptures within a magnificent Renaissance palace. The most noteworthy statue in the collection is *Galata Suicida* (Galatian Suicide), commissioned by Caesar in the 1st century BC to commemorate his conquest of Gaul. It was later unearthed alongside the *Dying Gaul,* on display in the Capitoline Museums. The museum provides a unique opportunity to see how sculpture evolved through the centuries. Free one-hour tours are conducted in Italian every Sunday at noon.

Campo De' Fiori

Activity goes on at all hours in **Campo De'
Fiori** (Buses 23, 40, 62, 280). During the day,
the square fills with stalls selling flowers, vegetables, and knickknacks that attract locals
and visitors in search of souvenirs. At night,
the cafes, bars, and eateries that line the *piazza* are bursting with business. In summer,
crowds spill outdoors and occupy the square
until the late hours. The hooded statue in the
center is a tribute to philosopher Giordano
Bruno, who was burned at the stake here for
being a little too ahead of his time.

Piazza Farnese

Piazza Farnese is a large residential square
dominated on one side by an enormous
Palazzo Farnese (Buses 23, 40, 62, 280).
The palace was built by the Farnese family
and considered one of the finest in Rome.
If you're wondering where the missing half
of the Colosseum ended up, the answer is
standing in front of you: stones from the
Colosseum was repurposed to build the palazzo. The two large fountains in the *piazza*, on
the other hand, were swiped from the Baths
of Caracalla.

Michelangelo was asked to design the facades of the *palazzo* after the original architect died. He's responsible for the cornice,
central balcony, and the third floor of the
courtyard. The building has belonged to the
French government since 1635 and now serves
as an embassy. Guided visits in Italian or
French are free and can be arranged through
the **French Consulate** (Via Giulia 251, tel.
06/686-011). The lavish residence is highlighted by an enormous reception hall where
the Farnese family once entertained hundreds
of guests, and a lovely walled garden where the
French ambassador still does.

Largo Argentina
(AREA SACRA DELL'ARGENTINA)

Largo Argentina is a large rectangular sunken
area where four temples known simply as A,
B, C, and D were discovered in the 1920s. All
that remains today are foundations, stairs,
and a dozen columns that look like part of
a marble jigsaw puzzle. Near temples C and
D are the remains of Pompeii's Curia where
the Senate convened and Caesar was stabbed
to death. Today, Largo Argentina is undergoing restoration and is closed to visitors, but
the area has become a home for stray cats and
the **Roman Cat Sanctuary** (Corner of Via
Florida and Via Torre Argentina, tel. 06/6880-
5611, www.romancats.com, daily noon-6pm)
welcomes volunteers to help care for felines
at their underground refuge. An information
panel at street level provides details about the
relics still standing and illustrates how the
temples once looked.

Crypta Balbi

Crypta Balbi (Via delle Botteghe Oscure 31,
Tues.-Sun 9am-7:45pm, tel. 06/3996-7700, €8
or Archaeologia card, Tram 8) is located on
a street named after the Middle Ages craftsmen who patiently transformed blocks of
marble into lime for construction. The museum displays artifacts illustrating how the
city reinvented itself over the ages. It's small
and often overlooked by tourists, but the well-
organized and informative itinerary helps
visitors discover different layers of the city's
past. Afterwards you should be able to recognize different eras and distinguish between
antiquity and Middle Ages. The museum is
part of a group of four sites that also includes
Palazzo Massimo, Altemps, and the Baths of
Diocletian. A single ticket allows entry to all
four museums over a three-day period.

Jewish Ghetto

Jews have inhabited Rome for over two thousand years and have occupied the area opposite Isola Tiberina for nearly half that time.
As religious hatred ebbed and flowed, so did
their fortunes. One century they were limited
to selling fabrics, clothing, and second-hand
iron; the next, they found themselves cramped
behind the high walls of the **Jewish Ghetto**
(Buses 23, 63, 280, 780 or Tram 8), under the
watchful eyes of the Swiss Guard. The neighborhood is slightly dilapidated in an appealing

way and the inhabitants are renowned for being more Roman than the Romans. The best time to visit is on Sunday after Sabbath when the pedestrian square is bustling with activity and the shops are open.

Via Del Portico di Ottavia is the heart of the Ghetto. It's also the place to sample Kosher Roman cuisine. The street was recently recobbled, and new benches installed that are usually occupied by old-timers watching children playing.

Tempio Maggiore Synagogue, or Great Synagogue (Lungotevere Cenci, tel. 06/6840-0661, www.museoebraico.roma.it, Sun.-Thurs. 10am-7pm and Fri. 10am-4pm summer, Sun.-Thurs. 9am-5pm and Fri. 9am-2pm rest of the year, €11), is a product of Greek and Assyrian design, and one of the largest synagogues in Italy. Its museum displays ancient manuscripts and recounts the history of Roman Jews. There's also a 30-minute video and a 3-D reconstruction of the Ghetto as it appeared in the late 19th century. Entry includes a guided tour in English, held on the hour. Police have been stationed outside since a terrorist attack in 1982.

Via della Reginella became part of the neighborhood in 1823, when Pope Leo XIII allowed the Ghetto to expand. The air is medieval and the courtyards all around provide a clue as to what the area once felt like. Farther ahead is **Piazza Mattei.** Have a seat at the bar on the corner of this intimate square and enjoy the graceful, recently restored fountain, **Fontana delle Tartarughe,** in its center.

Isola Tiberina

Whoever said the more things change the more they stay the same was probably thinking of Rome, and the Isola Tiberina in particular. This small island of volcanic rock played a crucial role in putting Rome on the map. It's here that Aesculapius, the god of medicine, was worshipped, where ancient Romans waited to be healed outside his temple, and where a hospital has been operating since 1548. The island itself was altered to resemble a ship in the 1st century AD, and the **Ponte Fabricio** bridge that links the island to the Jewish Ghetto is the oldest in the city. It's a popular crossing point into Trastevere and is often lined with street vendors and musicians entertaining the passing crowds. During the summer locals often sun themselves on the embankment below, an open-air cinema is set up, and food and drink kiosks line the riverside.

relaxing on the Spanish Steps, Piazza di Spagna

TRIDENTE

Looking down on the Tridente, it's clear how this part of the city got its name: The neighborhood is made up of three streets that radiate out from **Piazza del Popolo**. Via del Corso, the longest, lies in the center and leads to the Vittoriano monument. It's lined with international chain stores and is partly pedestrianized. Each of the side streets is narrower and less trafficked. Via Babuina was the traditional home of antiques dealers that have gradually been replaced by luxury boutiques. It runs into **Piazza di Spagna** and runs parallel to picturesque Via Margutta, where Federico Fellini once lived. Via di Ripetta, the third prong, is the least explored and contains historic shops and more practical ones where students from the nearby art school go for lunch. It leads to the **Ara Pacis** and ends near the Pantheon.

Piazza del Popolo

Rome is a dense city, which may be why the wide-open space of **Piazza del Popolo** (Metro A: Flaminio Piazza del Popolo) is so refreshing. Here in this circular, cobblestone square commissioned by Napoleon, there's room to breathe and admire the twin Santa Maria churches that mark the beginning of the Tridente. All three of Tridente's streets intersect here, and the square is a major thoroughfare for pedestrians on their way to work or the next monument. In the middle of the *piazza* is a giant Egyptian obelisk flanked by enormous lions. Concerts are organized during the summer, and crowds gather here for national holidays or spontaneous soccer celebrations.

Piazza di Spagna

Piazza di Spagna (Metro A: Spagna) is one of the most elegant and refined squares in the city. The luxury shops nearby add to its character, as do the ingenious fountain, remarkable steps, and church that overlooks everything. The area was the headquarters of the Spanish embassy to the Vatican. In the center of the square is the **Fontana della Barcaccia**, believed to be the work of Gian Lorenzo Bernini, who overcame the lack of water pressure by sculpting a half-sunken boat that collects the water. It's a working fountain, so you can drink directly from the spout. The stone bees and suns decorating the fountain are identical to those on the coat of arms of Pope Urban VIII and are a reminder of who financed the project.

Spanish Steps

Directly in front of Fontana della Barcaccia in Piazza di Spagna are the **Spanish Steps** (Metro A: Spagna). This majestic outdoor staircase was actually built by the French, who wanted to connect their church with the square below in the 17th century. Wrangling between popes and French monarchs delayed the project until a design was found that satisfied both parties. The result is a stunning combination of terraces, curves, and balustrades where everyone wants to sit. Continuous sitting, however, has damaged the stairs over the years and they were partially closed for a restoration expected to be completed in 2017.

The view gets better the higher you climb, reaching perfection from the platform in front of **Trinita dei Monti** (Piazza della Trinita dei Monti, daily 7am-7pm). The panorama can easily distract visitors from this 15th-century church, which was also recently restored, and whose interior includes paintings by Daniele da Volterra, a pupil of Michelangelo. Volterra was chosen to cover up his master's *Last Judgment* nudes deemed too racy by the pope. The muscled bodies in his *Deposition* show signs of his teacher's influence.

★ Trevi Fountain
(FONTANA DI TREVI)

Fontana di Trevi (Piazza di Trevi, 24/7, free, Metro A: Barberini Fontana Trevi) is the largest fountain in Rome and probably the most famous fountain in the world. Like many in the city it's linked to an ancient aqueduct that's been supplying water from miles away since Augustus was emperor. Over the years different basins were erected here but it wasn't until 1732 that things got fancy. That's when Pope Clement XII decided to forgo modesty and create a triumphal fountain. The resulting baroque masterpiece took Niccolò Salvi 30 years to complete and completely dominates the small square in which it was built.

The fountain rises up against the side of an elegant *palazzo* and is framed by four imposing columns representing the major known rivers of the time. The central niche is occupied by Oceanus, god of the sea, who stands in a shell-shaped chariot guiding two horses (one agitated and one less so). On his right is a statue representing health and on his left is abundance. The water emerges from the center, and flows over jagged rocks into an immense pool around which hundreds of visitors gather.

It's a spectacular scene that sounds and looks even better at night when the fountain is illuminated. Avoid visiting at noon (especially in August), when the small *piazza* is crammed with visitors and merchants selling selfie sticks. Legend has it that tossing a coin into the water with your back turned ensures a return trip to Rome. The origin of the habit is unknown, but wishing wells were an ancient tradition that modern tourists have happily adopted. Every day over €3,000 worth of coins lands in the fountain and the funds are collected twice a month and donated to charity.

Villa Medici

Villa Medici (Viale della Trinita dei Monti 1, tel. 06/676-1311, www.villamedici.it, Tues.-Sun. ticket office 9:30am-6pm, guided tours 10am-6pm, €12, half-off with RomaPass, Metro A: Spagna), one of the best-preserved villas in Rome, provides an idea of how Italian nobles once lived. The Medici family acquired the immense *palazzo* in the 16th century and added the austere façade that was fashionable at the time. Lightheartedness was reserved for the rear of the building, which is much more ornate and overlooks a park complete with hedged pathways, secret gardens, and fountains. In 1804 Napoleon moved the French Academy into the villa and helped inspire such talents as Berlioz and Debussy.

Tickets include entry to contemporary art exhibits and guided tours of the villa. There are several different itineraries that last 90 minutes and reveal the history, art, and architecture of the remarkable dwelling. The **historic visit** is offered from Tuesday to Sunday and covers everything from the symbolism of the façade to the private chambers

Trevi Fountain

of the cardinal who once called the villa home. English-language sessions start at noon in the inner courtyard. On weekends there are tours for children and garden enthusiasts but these are only available in Italian. A pleasant cafeteria with wonderful views of Rome serves light snacks on the second floor. Security has been beefed up since the Paris terrorist attacks of 2015 and a couple of soldiers are stationed at the entrance.

TOP EXPERIENCE

★ Borghese Gallery
(GALLERIA BORGHESE)

Galleria Borghese (Piazzale del Museo Borghese 5, tel. 06/841-3979 or 06/841-6542, Tues.-Sun. 9am-7pm, www.galleriaborghese. beniculturali.it, €11 or RomaPass, audio guide €5, Metro A: Spagna or Buses 53, 910) is one of Rome's finest art galleries. It is located inside the villa of the same name, begun in the 17th century, that once belonged to the influential Borghese family whose members included popes and cardinals. They were passionate about art and amassed a unique collection of sculpture and painting that was purchased by the Italian state in 1902.

The two-story villa is elaborately decorated with frescoes, stucco, and marble detailing that recount the family's glorious past. The ground floor is devoted to sculpture, and paintings line the walls upstairs. There are two extraordinary depictions of David: a marble statue by Gian Lorenzo Bernini portraying the hero a moment before striking Goliath, and a vivid canvas by Caravaggio of David holding the giant's severed head. Both artists are well represented in the gallery.

Getting into the gallery isn't straightforward and requires advance booking. Visits are limited to two hours with designated slots at 9am, 11am, 1pm, 3pm, and 5pm; these can be reserved online (www.galleriaborghese.it) up to four months in advance. **Guided tours** (€5.50) are available in English at 9:10am and 11:10am and can be reserved with the tickets. RomaPass holders must also reserve (tel. 06/32810) in advance and pick up tickets 30 minutes prior to entry.

Ara Pacis

This monumental stone altar was commissioned by the Roman Senate in 13 BC to celebrate Emperor Augustus and mark a new era of peace after years of civil war. Part temple, part archway, it's adorned with figures recounting the city's legendary past

Borghese Gallery

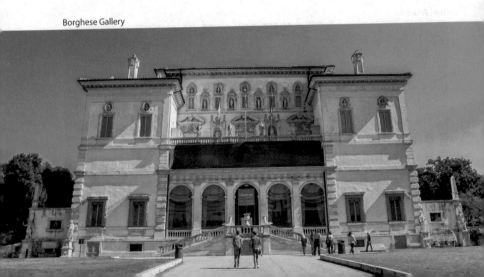

and present and was an ancient example of the propaganda and self-promotion at which the Romans were experts. There are finely carved images of the imperial family including Caesar, Tiberius, and Augustus and his wife, Livia, along with a frieze depicting how the Roman state functioned. The glass-roofed **Ara Pacis Museum** (Via di Ripetta, daily 9:30am-7:30pm, www.arapacis.it, €10.50 or €13 with entry to exhibition, Buses 70, 81, 87, 280) was designed by Richard Meier to house the altar and an exhibition space located on the lower level. Initially criticized by purists, the building has become popular with visitors who can walk through the altar while listening to a multilingual audio guide (€6) that vividly deciphers the monument's limestone reliefs.

The **Mausoleo di Augusto** (Piazza Augusto Imperatore, tel. 06/0608) across from the Ara Pacis is one of several impressive and monumental tombs ancient Romans of wealth and distinction built for themselves. Like many others, this one is circular and was once topped with poplar trees. Later generations of Romans transformed it into a fortress, palace, and prison. Guided tours are periodically available while the monument undergoes renovation.

National Gallery of Ancient Art
(GALLERIA NAZIONALE DI ARTE ANTICA)

The **Galleria Nazionale di Arte Antica** (Via delle Quattro Fontane 13, tel. 06/481-4591, Tues.-Sun. 8:30am-7pm, €7, audio guide €3, Metro A: Barberini) in Palazzo Barberini is one of the best places to understand the evolution of Italian painting from the 12th century all the way to neoclassicism. The vast gallery is the permanent home of over 1,500 works of art of which Caravaggio, Raphael, and Bernini are the stars. The premises were partially restored in 2009 and are nearly deserted compared to other museums of equal stature. Paintings are carefully labeled with Italian and English explanations, and it's hard

not to get a neckache admiring the frescoed ceilings.

MAXXI

MAXXI (Via Guido Reni 4A, tel. 06/32180, www.fondazionemaxxi.it, Tues.-Sun. 11am-7pm, Sat. 11am-10pm, €10 and RomaPass, Tram 2) is the Italian abbreviation for National Museum of XXI Century Arts. The museum is Rome's attempt to document and display contemporary creativity. The Zaha Hadid-designed building is split into temporary exhibitions and a permanent collection of art, architecture, design, photography, and fashion. Many of the names are still as yet unknowns, but there's plenty of off-the-wall drawings, models, photographs, and video to contemplate inside this immaculate museum. It's the perfect balance to antiquity and a pleasant place to spend a couple of hours admiring the present instead of the past.

MAXXI is located slightly outside the Tridente but can be easily reached on tram number 2 or buses 53, 168, or 280. Gallery 4 of the permanent collection is free from Tuesday to Friday and entry is complimentary on your birthday as long as you can prove it.

VATICANO

The modern Vatican city-state dates from the Lateran Treaty of 1929 when its present boundaries were officially recognized. Although the population does not exceed 1,000, its religious and cultural importance is inestimable.

St. Peter's Square
(PIAZZA SAN PIETRO)

Walking through the crowds at **St. Peter's Square** (Castel Sant'Angelo Buses 34, 40, 280, 870) may feel like a marathon, but it actually takes about five minutes to cross the square. *Square* is actually the wrong word for what Bernini began building in 1656—it is more of an ellipse superimposed on a trapezoid. The *piazza* was designed for outdoor masses and can accommodate over 80,000 pilgrims. Bernini intended the space to symbolically

Vaticano

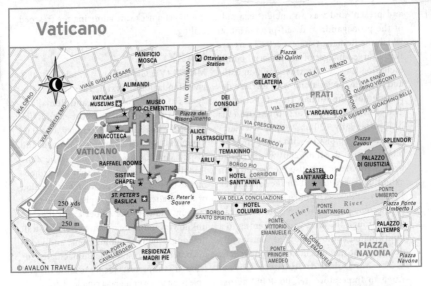

embrace the world, and that's what it looks like from the cupola above St. Peter's. The semicircular colonnades are made up of four rows of columns and topped with statues of 140 saints. Stand on either of the marble discs near the fountains and the columns disappear behind one another. Pope Sixtus V had the granite obelisk in the center erected, the only visible reminder of the ancient Roman racetrack that once occupied the site. Every Sunday morning at 11am from September to June thousands of worshippers gather in the square to hear Pope Francis deliver his weekly message in a half-dozen languages. It gets quiet at night and worth a second visit when the dome is lit up and tourists have retreated to their hotels.

TOP EXPERIENCE

★ St. Peter's Basilica
(BASILICA SAN PIETRO)
Basilica San Pietro (Piazza San Pietro, tel. 06/6988-3731, daily 7am-7pm, free, Metro A: Ottaviano) was built on the site of a Roman racetrack and the spot where St. Peter is believed to have been buried in AD 64. Early Christian pilgrims began visiting the site

almost immediately after Peter's death, which made it the obvious place for freshly converted Emperor Constantine to build the first incarnation of the basilica in AD 324. That building was expanded and remained standing until 1503, when restoration proved impossible and Pope Julius II opted for demolition. Bramante was chosen to design a new basilica, and the next century and a half saw the church slowly take the its current shape. Michelangelo engineered the cupola, Carlo Maderno constructed the façade, and Bernini designed the *piazza*. The result is remarkably uniform considering how many different hands worked on the building.

The gargantuan interior leaves no doubt that this is the largest church in the world and is as impressive as the outside. Measuring 187 meters from entrance to apse and 136 meters to the top of the cupola, the basilica contains 11 chapels and 45 altars. Popes didn't cut corners when it came to interior design, and only the finest materials were used. Immediately on the right behind bulletproof glass is Michelangelo's *Pieta*. Completed when he was just 25, the sculpture is his only signed work. It depicts Jesus shortly after his crucifixion in the arms of his mother. In the center is Bernini's **Baldacchino** that covers the Papal Altar, where only popes are permitted to celebrate mass. The sculpted bronze canopy is supported by four twisting columns directly under the dome. Nearby is the entrance to the grottoes where relics of the original basilica, including fragments of Giotto's mosaic, can be seen. This is where popes are buried. The original Christian necropolis is also open to visitors and provides insight into the origins of modern religion.

One of the greatest challenges in building St. Peter's was completing the **cupola,** which needed to express the grandeur of the pope's ambition while withstanding the laws of gravity. By the time of his commission Michelangelo already enjoyed an indisputable reputation and was a master of both expression and form. He was also a native of Florence, where an impressive dome had already been built. When the pope called he accepted the commission. The solution, which he never saw realized, consists of two domes, one fitted inside the other. The best way to appreciate this engineering marvel that occupied 600 skilled workers for years is by climbing to the top. An elevator can take you partway up, but you'll have to use your legs to reach the summit and one of the best views of the

city. All of Rome is visible from the top, and St. Peter's Square below reveals its true shape.

★ Vatican Museums
(MUSEI VATICANI)

The **Musei Vaticani** (Viale Vaticano, tel. 06/6988-4676, www.museivaticani.va, Mon.-Sat. 9am-6pm with last entry at 4pm, €16, free on the last Sun. of every month 9am-12:30pm, Metro A: Ottaviano) are a group of museums, and visiting all of them in one a day is nearly impossible. The most popular destinations are the Raphael rooms and the Sistine Chapel, which takes nearly 20 minutes to reach from the entrance without a single sideways glance or tourist jam. Visitors wearing sleeveless shirts, miniskirts, or flip-flops will be refused entry. Food and drink is also not permitted, and large bags and selfie sticks must be checked at the entrance. To avoid lines, buy your ticket beforehand from the Vatican Museums website and travel as light as possible so you don't have to spend time waiting in line at the cloakroom. Video recording and photography is prohibited inside the chapel, but you can take pictures in the rest of the museum as long as you don't use a flash.

St. Peter's Basilica at Vatican City

There's a lot to see inside the Vatican and not all of it is easy to understand. Fortunately, various color-coded itineraries that vary in length from 90 minutes to five hours can be followed. A range of official tours of the museum and gardens are also available as well as an audio guide (€5) for children and adults. These can be booked online up to three months in advance and last one to three hours. The tour of the gardens (Mon.-Sat. 8:15am-12:45pm, €36) is on board an open bus and lasts 40 minutes. There's also an interesting 90-minute tour (€10) of the 1st-century necropolis and remains of the original basilica belowground. Private tour operators may also approach you near the entrance, and if you haven't already reserved they can be a good option. Just make sure the price includes museum entry and that the visit includes what you want to see.

SISTINE CHAPEL

The **Cappella Sistina** (Viale Vaticano, tel. 06/6988-4676, Mon.-Fri. 8:45am-3:20pm, Sat. and last Sun. of the month 8:45am-12:20pm), where cardinals gather to elect new popes, attracts 15,000 visitors a day. The chapel is narrow and long with a ceiling that's 20 meters (65 feet) from the ground. Skipping it would be like leaving the Louvre without seeing the *Mona Lisa*. When it comes to frescoes nothing is bigger, more closely associated with a single artist, or more impressive.

The chapel was painted by Michelangelo, and consists of over three hundred figures. A special theological committee determined what scenes to depict and decided episodes from the book of Genesis would make up the central spine of the vault. These include the *Creation of Adam* and *Temptation* in the center of the ceiling. Michelangelo worked alone on special scaffolding that allowed him to paint every corner of the 3,000-square-foot ceiling, which took four years to complete.

The ceiling was an immediate hit and resulted in Michelangelo being appointed the Vatican's chief architect, sculptor, and painter. Pope Paul III later commissioned him to paint the two walls on either end of the chapel. Only *The Last Judgment* was completed. It covers the entire altar wall and depicts humanity lining up to be condemned or saved by an athletic-looking Jesus flanked by his mother and saints. Down below are the flames of hell and desperate sinners escorted to their fate by grotesque demons, while angels point to the pages of the Bible and trumpet the word of God. It's powerful and took the master even longer to

one of the rooms in the Vatican Museum

complete than the ceiling frescoes. Some of the nudity was later covered up but the work remains breathtaking by any standard.

The chapel is a ten-minute walk from the museum entrance. It's best to arrive early or take the **guided tour** (€32) if you want to get a good look before it becomes shoulder-to-shoulder tourists. Video recording and photography is prohibited.

RAPHAEL ROOMS

While Michelangelo was busy painting a ceiling, Pope Julius II put Raphael to work on his personal apartments, known today as the Raphael Rooms. It took the artist 12 years (working on and off) to paint large sections of the four interconnected rooms, and he died before completing the project. What he left behind rivals the Sistine Chapel in brilliance if not size.

The largest room is **Sala di Constantino,** which was used for formal receptions and completed by students of Raphael after he died. The main theme on the walls and ceiling is the life and times of Constantine, Rome's first Christian emperor. **Stanza di Eliodoro** was reserved for private audiences with the pope and the second room Raphael painted himself. The pictures have a political undertone and illustrate key episodes of the Old Testament and God's relation to the Catholic Church.

Stanza Segnatura, the first room Raphael painted, contains the most stunning works. *La Disputa* portrays saints, doctors, and laborers debating the meaning of the Bible while Christ offers himself as a sacrifice for sin. *The School of Athens* depicts a meeting of philosophers and includes Plato and Aristotle at the center of the fresco as well as a self-portrait of the artist at the extreme right of the picture. The last room is **Stanza dell'Incendio di Borgo,** which was used as a meeting and dining room. Raphael had his students do most of the work here, and the paintings symbolize the aspirations of Pope Leon X. They tell the stories of his papal

predecessors and illustrate the coronation of Charles the Great.

MUSEO PIO-CLEMENTINO

Museo Pio-Clementino is opposite the Sistine Chapel and Raphael Rooms, and far less crowded. It's a museum unto itself with eight large rooms containing the classical Roman sculpture that formed the nucleus of the Vatican's initial collection. The most famous piece is the *Laocoon* located in the courtyard. The 1st-century AD work was unearthed in Nero's villa near the Colosseum and depicts a Trojan priest punished for warning his fellow citizens about the large wooden horse gifted by the Greeks. The rooms of the museum are filled with mosaics and portraits of emperors who have surprisingly contemporary faces. The museum also contains Rome's first spiral staircase.

PINACOTECA

The Pinacoteca houses 460 paintings, tapestries, and statues arranged chronologically from the 12th to the 19th century in 18 elegant rooms. The picture gallery is a recent addition to the Vatican Museums and was opened in 1932. The collection includes works by some of the all-time greats such as Giotto, Beato Angelico, Perugino, Raphael, and Tiziano. Many of the paintings in the first nine rooms were created on wood and are highly religious in nature, after which canvas and perspective begin to dominate.

Room 8 is entirely dedicated to Raphael and is where his vibrantly colored *Transfiguration* hangs. This was his last work and meant to be sent to France but Cardinal Giulio de' Medici changed his mind after the artist's death. Like many paintings in the museum it was confiscated and moved to Paris during Napoleon's reign over the peninsula, but it was later returned. In the small room next door is Leonardo da Vinci's unfinished *St. Jerome,* which has puzzled art historians for decades. The second-to-last room contains the clay models Bernini made before casting the larger bronze versions that now decorate St. Peter's Square.

Castel Sant'Angelo

Castel Sant'Angelo (Lungotevere Castello 50, tel. 06/681-9111, www.castelsantan-gelo.com, Tues.-Sun. 9am-7:30pm, €10.50 or RomaPass) didn't start out as the castle, prison, or the papal escape pad it would later become, but as a mausoleum for Emperor Hadrian. Respect for the dead did not out-live the fall of the empire, and the castle has been repeatedly modified over the centuries. In 1277, walls were enlarged, and the **Vatican Corridor,** which allowed popes to quickly and safely reach the castle in times of unrest, was added.

The monument gets its name from the Archangel Michael, who allegedly appeared in AD 590 and whose statue now adorns the tower on top. There are many rooms to ex-plore over five floors, including the prison cell where Florentine sculpture Benvenuto Cellini was locked up and more comfortable apart-ments where popes slept and fortunes were kept. The terrace provides a 360-degree view of the city and there's a nice rooftop bar serv-ing soft drinks and beer. Lines to enter are usually short and there are three highlighted itineraries to follow.

Hadrian built the bridge known as **Ponte Sant'Angelo** to connect his mausoleum with the city. Pope Clement VII added statues of Peter and Paul, and Bernini lined the parapets with musically inclined angels. Today, itiner-ant salesmen hawk their wares here to passing tourists on their way to or from the Vatican.

TRASTEVERE
Ponte Sisto

Ponte Sisto is one of the oldest bridges in Rome and connects Trastevere with the rest of the city. It was name after Pope Sixtus IV, who opened the bridge in 1474 and financed the endeavor with taxes paid by prostitutes. The Renaissance comprised the boom years for the oldest profession, who numbered 6,800 in a city of barely 50,000. Flooding destroyed

previous bridges on this site and the remains of the Pons Auerelio were incorporated into the medieval version. The round hole in the center serves as a flood alert—if water reaches that level it's time to head for the hills. On most evenings someone is playing an instru-ment, asking for change, or selling fake Gucci bags on the bridge.

Piazza Trilussa

Piazza Trilussa lies across the street from the Ponte Sisto bridge and is named after the Roman poet Carlo Alberto Salustri (1871-1950), who wrote under the pseudonym Trilussa. There's a sculpture of him on one side of the small square and an elaborate foun-tain on the other reached by a short flight of steps. The square is the main entrance to the neighborhood and a popular meeting place. It starts filling up with locals most afternoons and remains lively until well after midnight.

Villa Farnesina

When banker Agostino Chigi decided to build himself a villa in 1506, his goal was to set a new standard in palace design. **Villa Farnesina** (Via della Lungara 230, tel. 06/6802-7538, www.villafarnesina.it, Mon.-Sat. 9am-2pm, €6, garden €2, audio guide €2, Buses 23, 125, 280) did just that. The building's deceptively simple plan of a central block with two projecting wings is enhanced through the paintings and imagination of its architect Baldassarre Peruzzi, who also worked on St. Peter's. His *Salone delle Prospettive* on the sec-ond floor creates the illusion of looking out on 16th-century Rome and alters depending on the viewer's perspective. Raphael had a hand in the decoration of **Loggia of Psyche** on the ground floor, which has a distinctly botanic theme and depicts over 200 different plants including some recently discovered varieties from the Americas. Flash photography and video are not permitted.

Only a part of the original gardens re-mains, and it was carefully replanted ac-cording to original designs. There are many ornamental species and a small collection of

Mission Michelangelo: Rome

Michelangelo's *Pietà* in St. Peter's Basilica

Sculpture, painting, and architecture: Michelangelo Buonarroti could do it all. He was recognized as a genius nearly from the moment he picked up a chisel, and he spent his long life executing high-profile commissions for cardinals, popes, and princes. Yet for someone with such a monumental reputation, he wasn't especially prolific; rather, he combined frenetic periods of nonstop creativity with long bouts of idleness. What he did produce has captivated viewers for half a millennium and inspired generation after generation of artists. The majority of his works are in Rome and Florence, which makes a Michelangelo pilgrimage possible.

The **Sistine Chapel** contains the mother of all ceilings, a project that took Michelangelo four years to complete. It covers 8,600 square feet and recounts man's ascent to heaven. Two decades after the frescoes were finished, Pope Clement VII recalled the artist to paint *The Last Judgment* in the same chapel. It's a rare opportunity to compare Michelangelo's creative evolution and witness how changing politics had an influence on his brushstroke.

One of Michelangelo's earliest sculptures, the *Pietà,* is now safely behind glass after it vandalized in 1972. But the figure of the lifeless Christ in the arms of Mary still makes a strong impression. Although commissioned as a funeral monument, it was later moved to St. Peter's and was the only work signed by the artist.

Michelangelo wasn't just paid to decorate the Vatican; he also had a hand in its expansion. He was appointed chief architect in 1564 and spent most of his time planning **the dome**. Although he died before its completion, the designs he left behind served as the blueprint for what was eventually built.

To see a building that Michelangelo did complete, cross the Tiber and head to **Palazzo Farnese.** The building's third floor and its elaborate cornices are all his doing, along with a renovation of the inner courtyard. It can be seen upon request from the French embassy, which is now housed inside.

★ Wandering Trastevere

Scenic Trastevere is known for its bohemian medieval charm and uneven cobblestoned streets where maps can be set aside and every direction has its merits. Here you can be forgiven for backtracking and going around in circles. That's part of the fun of this maze-like neighborhood that doesn't go out of its way to satisfy tourists. Wandering off from the main thoroughfare you'll discover narrow alleys, dead ends, vine-covered facades, and graffiti of all kinds. The colors of the houses are a delightful patchwork of worn-out red, yellow, and orange, and the plants and flowers stationed next to doorways provides the greenery.

a typical, picturesque street in Trastevere

Trastevere is divided in two by Viale Trastevere. The half opposite Isola Tiberina is smaller and less visited than the other side where most sights are located. The pedestrianized **Via Lungaretta** links both and provides a good introduction to the area, which can also be entered by crossing the **Ponte Sisto** bridge. Both eventually lead to **Piazza Santa Maria** in the center of the neighborhood, around which many restaurants and bars are clustered. From here there are many possible directions to follow. If you arrive in the morning you can shop for vegetables or watch locals getting their groceries at the **Piazza San Cosimato market** south of Piazza Santa Maria. If you walk uphill you'll eventually reach the Gianicolo terrace overlooking the city and can visit Tempietto di Bramante along the way, or come back at night and congregate with locals in **Piazza Trilussa**, wondering where to wander next.

ancient relics. Garden tours (€4) in English are available every Saturday at 10am while special musical performances are organized on the second Saturday of each month.

Piazza Santa Maria in Trastevere

Piazza Santa Maria, which fronts the church of the same name, is the heart of Trastevere, and the fountain in the middle is one of the oldest in the city. It was remodeled in the 17th century by Carlo Fontana, who also designed the fountains in St. Peter's Square. The steps around the fountain are usually occupied by street musicians and children. There are several outdoor cafes lining the square from where the church and street life can be observed in comfort.

According to legend, **Chiesa Santa Maria in Trastevere** (Piazza Santa Maria in Trastevere, daily 7:30am-1pm and 4pm-7pm, free, Buses 23, 125, 280 or Tram 8) dates back to a dispute early Christians had with tavern keepers in the area. One party wanted a place to worship and the other a place to drink. The matter reached the attention of Emperor Alexander Severus, who sided with the fledgling religious order, preferring faith over revelry. This church was built, rebuilt, and remodeled many times since the 3rd century, and its present form dates from Pope Innocent II in 1140. It's notable for the external mosaics, added in the 13th and 14th centuries, that represent the Virgin Mary and Child. The mosaics continue inside with a series illustrating the life of the Virgin Mary.

Church of Santa Cecilia
(CHIESA SANTA CECILIA)

The **Chiesa Santa Cecilia** (Piazza di Santa Cecilia, tel. 06/589-9289, daily 9am-1pm and 2pm-7pm, €2, Buses 23, 125, 280 or Tram 8) was commissioned by Pope Pascal I in 821 in honor of a martyred saint who resisted her torturers through song and was eventually beheaded. The church includes a convent, bell tower, cloister, and the immense *Last Judgment* fresco by Pietro Cavallini located in the choir of the nuns. The fresco is one of the finest examples of medieval painting in existence and the church is rarely crowded. Guided tours are available on the last Saturday of the month from September to June. Dr. Neda Parmegiani (331/409-3253) takes visitors under the church to see ancient Roman dwellings, the 5th-century baptistery, and the crypt where remains of the saint are preserved. Tickets are €5 for a tour that lasts over an hour and should be reserved.

Galleria Nazionale d'Arte Antica

Before housing the **Galleria Nazionale d'Arte Antica** (Via della Lungara 10, tel. 06/6880-2323, Tues.-Sun. 8:30am-7:30pm, €5, Buses 23, 125, 280), Palazzo Corsini was the residence of cardinals and noblemen, including Cardinal Neri Corsini, for whom it is named. Over the course of its long history the building has hosted Michelangelo, Erasmus, and Queen Christina of Sweden. Today, the gallery is filled with a first-rate collection of 17th-and 18th-century Italian art as well as a smattering of Rubenses and Van Dykes. The elaborate frescoed interiors are almost as interesting as the paintings hanging on the walls.

Tempietto di Bramante

The **Tempietto di Bramante** (Piazza San Pietro in Montorio, tel. 06/581-2806, Tues.-Sun. 10am-6pm, free, Bus 115, 125) was designed by Bramante between 1502 and 1507 and commemorates the site where St. Peter was martyred. The circular temple set a new standard for proportions and became a model for countless other buildings in the 16th century. Gian Lorenzo Bernini built the entrance of the crypt more than one hundred years later. Inside stands a statue of the saint dating from the same period. The temple is entered through the adjacent Spanish Academy and hosts frequent art exhibitions and events.

Chiesa Santa Maria in Trastevere

Exploring Roman Piazze

Piazze (the plural of *piazza*, or square) are one of Italy's great contributions to urban architecture. You'll find them all over Rome's historic center in all sizes, shapes, and styles, from the circular Piazza del Popolo to the ornate Campidoglio. A good place to start or finish a tour is the cozy **Piazza Mattei** near the Jewish Ghetto, with its recently renovated fountain featuring turtles and nymphs. If you're thirsty, the bar facing the fountain is a pleasant place to have a drink while admiring the square.

It's a short walk down Via della Reginella to **Via del Portico d'Ottavia.** Although not technically a square, the wide street has been pedestrianized and serves as a gathering place for the Jewish community. Locals congregate at the benches along the way, and you can spend a moment observing the hustle and bustle of the neighborhood. When you've gotten your fill of Roman chutzpah, head towards the synagogue and cross the Ponte Fabricio bridge to Isola Tiberina. **Piazza di San Bartolomeo all'Isola** is open on two sides and contains a statue of its namesake saint in the center. Search for the French cannonball that landed inside the church of the same name. If you have a pang for coffee or gelato, take a break at the café on the corner.

Continue over the Ponte Cesto to the other side of the Tiber, cross the street, and go down the steps until you reach Via della Lungaretta. This long, narrow street is a gateway to the Trastevere neighborhood. Walk straight until you reach **Piazza di Santa Maria in Trastevere,** where you'll find a church and a fountain that is curiously not in the center of the square. Images of apostles decorate the church exterior, and there are several cafes and restaurants from where you can admire the scene.

Backtrack slightly and walk down Via Del Moro. If you want to sample local fare, take a left on Via della Pelliccia and hope there's a free table at **Da Augusto** serving *cacio e pepe* and other local favorites in the **Piazza De Renzi.** Otherwise, continue walking until you reach **Piazza Trilussa.** This square gets very crowded on summer evenings and is a meeting place for young Romans.

Cross the Ponte Sisto back over the Tiber and turn left onto Via Giulia. When you reach the fountain topped with a fleur-de-lis turn right. **Piazza Farnese** is a grand square with twin fountains recycled from ancient Roman baths. The stone bench that runs the entire length of the impressive Palazzo Farnese is a convenient spot from which to observe the square. Locals read their papers at the bar on the far corner, but for the most part the *piazza* is a place of transition rather than a destination.

Most of the action takes place day and night a few meters away down Via Dei Baullari in **Piazza Campo De Fiori,** the "field of the flowers," so named because it was initially just that. Today, there's a lively market in the morning and all sorts of revelry in the bars and restaurants at night. The Forno on the corner is the place to sample Roman white pizza.

Piazza Navona is only five minutes away, but if you prefer to avoid the tourists, explore any of the dozens of lesser-known squares nearby.

Gianicolo Hill
(COLLE DEL GIANICOLO)

Trastevere is mostly flat, but the farther you walk from the river, the steeper it gets. **Gianicolo Hill** (Giancolo Hill Buses 115, 870) flanks the western edge of the neighborhood and is a popular weekend gathering spot for local couples and families. At the top is a long terrace with one of the best views of the city, from where you can spot the Pantheon, Vittoriano monument, and much of the historic center. Nearby is a small café and amusement area for kids. A cannon is fired every day just below the terrace to mark noon. Pope Pio IX started the tradition in 1846 so that Roman church bells were synchronized and would ring at the correct time. The long way to Gianicolo Hill is up the winding Via Garibaldi; the shortcut is Via Porta di San Pancrazio.

Piramide di Cestio

models from which it was inspired, the structure was incorporated into the defensive walls of the city. Latin inscriptions indicate that the structure was built in 333 days. Tours are organized every 2nd and 4th Saturday of each month and can be arranged by calling tel. 06/3996-7700.

St. Paul's Gate
(PORTA SAN PAOLO)

The Aurelian walls, which flank both Testaccio and Aventino, were built during the late empire when foreign invasions became a real possibility. Much of the fortifications are still standing and in good condition, especially near the Pyramid where St. Paul's Gate stands. This was and remains one of the strategic entrances to the city, consisting of two imposing towers with living quarters where soldiers were permanently stationed. The ancient gateway now contains the small and rarely visited **Museum of the Ostian Way** (Porta San Paolo, Tues.-Sat. 9am-1:30pm, free, Metro B: Piramide). Walking along the narrow corridors provides a feel for Roman military architecture and a detailed model shows how the area looked in ancient times.

Monte Testaccio

Monte Testaccio (Via Nicola Zabaglia 24, tel. 06/0608, €4; Metro B: Piramide or Tram 3) is an antique dumping ground. This artificial hill stands 50 meters high and consists of discarded *amphorae* (clay vases), which were used to carry oil from Spain and other Roman provinces to the warehouses lining the Tiber. Jars were smashed after being emptied, and then were piled up here. The area is now a popular nighttime retreat for young Romans who gather in the bars and restaurants that surround the hill. Visits to the hill must be reserved in advance and take you on a steep climb to the top, where there's a decent view and you could pocket yourself an ancient souvenir.

MACRO

MACRO (Piazza O. Giusiniani 4, tel.

AVENTINO AND TESTACCIO
Protestant Cemetery

The **Protestant Cemetery** (Via Caio Cestio 6, tel. 06/574-1900, Mon.-Sat. 9am-5pm, Sun. 9am-1pm, free, Metro B: Piramide or Tram 3) is a romantic escape from the city. Located on a quiet side street, it's an oasis of tranquility, filled with cats and tombs. A small visitors center provides maps of the tombs, along with other information. On Monday and Wednesday mornings a kind American woman volunteers and will gladly answer questions or point you towards **Keats's tomb.** This is the best place to observe the newly polished Pyramid and Aurelian walls away from traffic and underneath the shade.

The **Piramide di Cestio** (Piazzale Ostiense) is the largest and most impressive tomb in the cemetery. Although the name Caius Cestio may have faded from history, this pyramid (which functions as a monumental tomb) remains. Like the Egyptian

06/6710-70400, www.museomacro.org, Tues.-Sun. 2pm-8pm, €6, Metro B: Piramide or Tram 3) is a branch of Rome's contemporary art museum located in the former meatpacking district. It occupies one building close to the entrance of the complex and puts on regular exhibits, some of which are located outdoors. The afternoon hours make it a good post-lunch or predinner destination.

Testaccio Market
(MERCATO DI TESTACCIO)

The new **Mercato di Testaccio** (Mon.-Sat. 6am-2pm, Metro B: Piramide or Tram 3) is located across the street from the MACRO. The large covered space is clean and airy, with over 100 stalls selling fruit, bread, cheese, wine, housewares, clothes, and more. There's a pleasant bar with outdoor seating near the main entrance and another in the center of the complex near the remains of the Roman road uncovered during construction. Arrive with an appetite and browse the stalls until you find what you need for an impromptu picnic. **Box 15** is run by Sergio and Giuliano, who prepare traditional beef sandwiches for €3. Sandra Dominici serves local red and white wine at **Box 7** by the glass (€0.50) or bottle (€2.50).

Buco di Roma

Most of the sites and curiosities of Aventino can be found along Via di Santa Sabina. One of the most popular is the **Buco di Roma** (Piazza dei Cavalieri di Malta) or Hole of Rome. At first glance, it appears to be an ordinary keyhole in a big door, but wait your turn to look through and you'll get a surprising close-up view of St. Peter's Basilica. Lines are usually short, and the optical illusion never disappoints.

Church of Santa Sabina
(CHIESA SANTA SABINA)

The **Chiesa Santa Sabina** (Piazza Pietro d'Illaria 1, daily 8:15am-12:30pm and 3:30pm-6pm, Metro B: Circo Massimo or Bus 715) dates from the 5th century and is one of the best-preserved early Christian churches in Rome. The outside gives little hint of the enormous space within, which is pleasantly cool on hot summer days. The flat roof covers two rows of giant columns probably recycled from the Roman Temple of Juno on the same site. The only ornate part of the basilica is the small chapel on the far side, which has colorful frescoes that were added during the Middle Ages.

Entry is through the side door. The main

the Diocletian Baths

entrance that links the church with the adjacent monastery is rarely opened, as it contains some of the oldest wooden carvings (AD 430-432) in existence. One of the 18 surviving panels features an early depiction of Christ's crucifixion. Mass is held on Sundays at 8am, 10:30am, and 11:30am (sung).

TERMINI
National Museum of Rome
(MUSEO NAZIONALE ROMANO)

The Palazzo Massimo branch of the **Museo Nazionale Romano** (Largo di Villa Peretti, tel. 06/3996-7700, daily 9am-7:30pm, €8 or Archaeologia card, audio guide €5, Metro A or B: Termini) contains the most important collection of classical art in the world. The four-story building near Termini station contains sculptures, frescoes, mosaics, jewelry, and coins that document the transformation of Roman art and culture from the foundation of the republic to the fall of the empire. It's the place to understand how ancient Romans saw themselves and how they portrayed their everyday lives. The second floor is particularly rich in paintings that were unearthed in the city and the interior decorations of several villas have been perfectly reconstructed.

The museum is a little on the shabby side and generally overlooked by tourists who prefer to head straight to the Colosseum. That's an advantage for amateur historians with a fondness for learning about antiquity who can admire the exhibits in peace.

Diocletian Baths
(TERME DI DIOCLEZIANO)

The **Terme di Diocleziano** (Viale Enrico de Nicola 79, tel. 06/477-881, daily 9am-7:30pm, €8 or Archaeologia card, Metro A or B: Termini) are also part of the National Museum of Rome and diagonally across the street from Palazzo Massimo. They originally covered 32 acres and could accommodate up to 3,000 bathers (twice as many as the Baths of Caracalla). The complex was transformed during 16th century when Pope Pio IV commissioned Michelangelo to build the Basilica di Santa Maria degli Angeli e dei Martiri. Like many ancient buildings the baths were stripped of useful materials and partially transformed into a church. This one honors Christian martyrs and looks Roman on the outside and Renaissance on the inside.

The visit winds through the remaining structures of the baths, an epigraph museum devoted to communication in the ancient world, and a collection of prehistoric relics discovered in the Lazio region. A 3-D film makes it easy to understand how the baths once looked and functioned.

Food

Romans take food seriously and are attached to their culinary traditions. The city's fortunate location provides kitchens with a great variety of fresh ingredients from land and sea. These are transformed into dishes that have been prepared for generations and that make eating in Rome special.

There are thousands of restaurants in Rome, from simple pizza shops to historic *trattorie* that have been serving local specialties for decades. The dining scene, however, isn't stuck in the past. New establishments open every week. The best put a gastronomic twist on old favorites and an emphasis on quality. That doesn't mean you can't have a bad meal in Rome—you can, especially if you stick to main streets where tourists gather. Eating well requires curious nosing about before committing to a place.

Breakfast is not the most important meal for Romans. Locals start the day with an *espresso* and may have a *cornetto* pastry. *Cornetto* are the Roman version of the croissant, served in the morning at bars and

Best Food and Drink

★ **Gusto:** This cozy *trattoria,* pizzeria, restaurant, and bookstore is greater than the sum of its parts (page 83).

★ **Er Buchetto:** This miniscule neighborhood institution has been serving famous roasted-pork sandwiches since 1890 (page 91).

★ **Splendor:** Don't miss a chance to sample wood-fired Neapolitan pizza—a taste of southern Italy in Rome (page 87).

★ **Il Gelato:** Locals' favorite gelato is scooped at this outpost of an ice cream empire (page 91).

★ **Race Club:** Sip late-night cocktails next to hip Romans at this underground speakeasy (page 92).

★ **Roscioli:** This modern *trattoria* carries more than 2,800 bottles of wine and hosts wine-tasting dinners (page 80).

★ **Antico Caffè della Pace:** You can tell by the old-fashioned coffee machine that the espresso will be good (page 83).

bakeries around the city. They come in many varieties including plain, whole wheat, chocolate, jelly, or cream, and go well with *cappuccino.* The best are prepared when ordered and served warm. A *cornetto* costs €1 and can be ordered by pointing at the one you like. Romans eat them standing at the counter and don't tend to linger over breakfast—the meal usually over in less than five minutes and is just a minor precursor for the main gastronomic events, which are lunch and dinner.

ANCIENT ROME AND MONTI

It's best not to visit the Roman Forum on an empty stomach, but besides the cafe at the top of the Vittoriano monument and the expensive snack bars lining Via dei Foro Romani, choices in the immediate vicinity are limited. Avoid the restaurant at the entrance to the Colosseum subway station. The view may be good, but the pasta is likely to have been frozen minutes before arriving at your table. For more authentic flavors explore the neighborhood immediately behind the Colosseum

in the direction of **Villa Celimontana** or the streets of **Monti.**

Roman

When you've been serving food for over a hundred years in a working-class neighborhood and haven't had to change your signage in fifty, the pasta can't be bad. That's the case with **La Carbonara** (Via Panisperna 214, tel. 06/482-5176, www.lacarbonara.it, Mon.-Sat. 12:30pm-2:30pm and 7pm-11pm, €10-12). The restaurant's namesake is the first dish diners should try. The Rossi family are a friendly bunch, and the typical Roman dishes Simone and Nando bring out from the kitchen are memorable. The small restaurant focuses on flavors rather than décor, which is bland and only notable for the walls covered in autographs by past patrons. Bring a pen if you want to add your two cents.

Broccoletti (Via Urbana 104, tel. 06/9027-1389, daily 12:30pm-3pm and 7:30pm-11:30pm, €13-16) serves classic Roman fare with a dash of fantasy. The decor is simple yet cozy and diners are seated fairly close together, but the real star here is the food. Ingredients are fresh and the enthusiastic chef isn't afraid to change a recipe for the sake of flavor.

Rome is full of restaurants serving regional Italian food. **Trattoria Monti** (Via San Vito 13a, tel. 06/446-6573, Tues.-Sun. 1pm-2:45pm and 8pm-10:45pm, closed Sun. dinner, €12) offers a taste of the Le Marche region. The Camerucci clan has successfully imported Adriatic flavors to Rome, and one taste of the *tortello di rosso d'uovo* (stuffed rabbit with roast potatoes baked in truffle oil) is almost as good as being there. The small, single-room trattoria is tucked in between Santa Maria Maggiore and Piazza Vittorio. Reservations are recommended on weekends.

Italian

A couple that cooks together stays together, which explains the longevity of **Agata e Romeo** (Via Carlo Alberto 45, tel. 06/446-6115, Mon.-Fri. noon-3pm and 7pm-11pm, €16-20). The couple in question has been serving *fusilli con radicchio e speck* and *risotto zizzania* to locals for over 30 years. The interior of this family restaurant has been updated since then but does not distract from the food, which is fresh and comes in large portions. A tasting menu is available with fine cheeses and wines from the cellar.

Pizza

There's nothing fancy about **Alle Carrette** (Via della Madonna dei Monti 95, tel. 06/679-2770, Thurs.-Tues. noon-4pm and 7pm-11:30pm, Wed. dinner only, €8-10), just good pizza served fast and accompanied by fried starters. It's a popular weekend spot and on summer nights the best seats are outside at the small wooden tables where most diners are speaking Italian and enjoying cold pints of beer. The hand-scribbled check is a pleasant surprise given the location so close to the Imperial Forums.

International

Maharajah (Via dei Serpenti 124, tel.

06/474-7144, daily 12:30pm-2:30pm and 7pm-11:30pm, €12-14) may be a welcome sight to diners tired of Italian cuisine. All the Indian favorites like *rogan josh* and *chicken tikka* are on the menu, as are a variety of North Indian specialties and prix fixe options. Furnishings are in line with the cuisine and the service is far politer than that received from the average Italian waitperson.

Sushi has made inroads in Rome, and **Hasekura** (Via dei Serpenti 27, tel. 06/483-648, Mon.-Sat. lunch and dinner, €12-18) was one of the first restaurants to introduce sashimi and tempura to Italian palates. There's table or counter service from which you can watch chef Kimiji Ito demonstrate his knife skills. The lunchtime menu is light on stomachs and wallets.

Crepes Galettes (Via Leonina 21a, 389/668-3360, daily noon-11pm, €5) was opened by a young Frenchman. Inside the narrow and informal *creperie* are a couple of stools facing one wall, with an open kitchen on the other wall. The kitchen serves both sweet and savory crepes, including the *completa*, filled with egg, cheese, and ham.

Bakeries

Rosetta, a traditional Roman bun that resembles a rose, is the star ingredient of ★ **Zia Rosetta** (Via Urbana 54, tel. 06/3105 2516, Tues.-Fri. 11:30am-3:30pm and 6pm-9pm, weekends 9am-9pm, €2-6). This little sandwich bar 10 minutes from the Colosseum offers more than 30 creative fillings served inside miniature or standard-size buns. They also make fresh salads and mix fruit and vegetable shakes in interesting combinations in their cramped but elegant shop.

In Rome, bread is nearly a religion, and few places take it more seriously than **Panificio Panella** (Largo Leopardi 2, tel. 06/487-2344, Mon.-Sat. 8:30am-11pm, Sun. 8:30am-4pm, €5). This is where to try traditional local loaves like the rose-shaped bun known as *rosetta* as well as cakes, tarts, and Italian-style doughnuts. The bar also turns out some of the creamiest cappuccino in town using an

Roman Cuisine

Traditional Roman fare is about getting the most flavor from the humblest ingredients. Roman cooking is a tale of inventiveness and thrift. Nothing is wasted. A good example of that is *Fiori di zucchini*, in which the zucchini flowers are deliciously prepared rather than thrown away once the vegetable has been cooked. Food here is also seasonal: Some dishes can be enjoyed year-round while others appear only during certain holidays or seasons. *Pizza al taglio* (page 82) is a good and thoroughly Roman choice for a quick meal.

APPETIZERS (ANTIPASTI)

Most menus offer a plate of mixed fried starters, which is a good introduction to the genre and will help you identify your favorites.

- *Fiori di zucchini:* Zucchini flowers stuffed with anchovies and mozzarella, battered, and fried. *Fiori di zucchini* are generally served in *pizzeria* or *trattoria* along with *suppli* and potato croquettes.

- *Suppli:* A ball of rice mixed with meat sauce, stuffed with mozzarella, covered with breadcrumbs, and deep fried.

- *Bruschetta aglio e olio:* A thick slice of bread rubbed with garlic and seasoned with oil and salt or diced tomatoes.

FIRST COURSES (PRIMI)

Every town and region in Italy has developed its own particular pasta shapes and sauces. In Rome, these pasta dishes are particularly famous; each began as a working-class meal made from humble ingredients.

- *Cacio e Pepe:* Pasta seasoned with a mix of sharp *cacio* goat cheese and pepper.

- *Amatriciana:* Pasta with *guancia di maiale* (fried bacon) and tomato sauce.

- *Pasta alla Carbonara:* Spaghetti with egg, bacon, and *Parmigiano* or *pecorino* cheese, which gives it a tangy flavor.

- *Pasta e Ceci:* A soup-like dish traditionally served on Fridays consisting of short *cannolicchi* pasta combined with beans.

---

antique coffee machine. On weekdays after 6pm they prepare an extensive all-you-can-eat buffet for €15 that includes the cocktail of your choice.

Sardinian fare is hard to find in Rome, which is why **Dall'Antò** (Via della Madonna dei Monti 16, tel. 06/678-0712, Tues.-Sat. noon-11pm and Sun. noon-3pm, €6) is a such a novelty. This humble establishment specializing in several types of traditional breads and desserts uses a small wood-burning oven, chestnut flour, and other surprising ingredients to keep the past alive. It may also be

the only place in the world to sample *neccio*, a crepe-like dish filled with ricotta or ham, and learn baking secrets from the passionate owner.

Gelato

★ **Fatamorgana** (Piazza degli Zingari 5, tel. 06/4890-6955, daily 1pm-11pm, €1 per scoop) doesn't just serve the usual ice-cream flavors. This little gelato lab 10 minutes from the Colosseum experiments with unlikely combinations like grapefruit and ginger, rum and coffee, or basil and nuts. Although

SECOND COURSES (SECONDI)

- *Trippa alla Romana:* Tripe stewed with onions and tomatoes.
- *Saltimboca alla Romana:* Veal cutlet covered with a slice of *prosciutto* ham and sage leaf, cooked in butter and wine.
- *Abbacchio alla Romana:* Oven-roasted lamb usually served with potatoes. The dish is available year-round but is most popular during Christmas and Easter.

SIDES (CONTORNI)

The artichoke holds a special place in Roman cuisine. It is served nearly year-round, except during the summer.

- *Carciofi alla Romana:* Artichokes stewed with olive oil and parsley.
- *Carciofi alla Giudea:* Artichokes prepared in the Jewish style: deep fried until the leaves are golden and crispy. Sample this dish in Rome's Jewish neighborhood.
- *Broccoletti:* A leafy variety of broccoli boiled and sautéed with garlic and oil.

SANDWICHES

- *Tramezzini:* Triangular sandwiches made of crustless white bread and filled with cold cuts, shrimp, tuna, egg salad, artichokes, or vegetables. They are inexpensive and make a perfect snack. Most bars in the capital have a selection of *tramezzini* sandwiches on display from midmorning to late afternoon.
- *Panini:* Sandwiches made with pizza *bianca* or rolls and containing prosciutto, ham, and mozzarella; grilled zucchini and mozzarella; or some other appetizing combination. Freshness is essential, so if you doubt it, walk away.
- *Porchetta:* Several slices of roasted pork in a Roman *rosetta* (little rose) bun. The pork in question is usually on display and cut while you wait.

combinations may initially seem outlandish, they'll make a lot of sense to taste buds. The friendly clerks behind the counter are happy to provide samples and the little square outside is a wonderful spot to enjoy a cone or two.

Down the street and around the corner is another *gelateria* vying to be the neighborhood's best. **Gelateria dell'Angeletto** (Via dell'Angeletto 15, tel. 06/487-4760, daily midnight-noon, €2.50-5) has a fine pedigree, with an owner who learned the craft working at one of the city's historic ice-cream shops. Now that he's on his own there's more room

for creativity, and he experiments with gluten-free and vegan flavors. Portions are generous and can spoil an appetite.

Coffee

★ **Caffè Propaganda** (Via Claudia 15, tel. 06/9453-4255, Tues.-Sun. noon-2am) is a short walk uphill from the Colosseum in a direction few tourists head. The bistro-style interior is covered in white ceramic tiles and gritty antique furnishings that make it a nice place to sit and relax. Coffee can be ordered at the bar or at one of the tables lining the front window. Homemade desserts are available, and if you want to drink something stronger try the award-winning *El Especialista* cocktail.

Snacks and Street Food

The quickest way to eat a delicious plate of pasta is to enter ★ **Pasta Imperiale** (Via del Boschetto 112, tel. 324/072-3203, daily noon-5pm and 6:30pm-11:30pm, €5-7). Just choose the sauce (tomato basil, pesto, mushroom parsley, ragu, etc.) and the type of pasta (fettuccine, farfalle, tortellini, ravioli, etc.) you like and it'll be on a paper plate ready to devour in a couple of minutes. Everything is handmade in the little kitchen behind the counter and can be eaten on the stools in the cramped dining area or outside wherever you find something to lean on. Extra-large portions are €2 extra.

CAMPO DE' FIORI/ PIAZZA NAVONA

Rome's highest concentration of eateries is in these two neighborhoods. Restaurants around Campo De' Fiori are loud and boisterous, and it's been a while since an Italian stepped into those lining Piazza Navona. Authenticity is often proportional to the width of the street. If you want to taste the Jewish contribution to Roman cooking, head to the Ghetto, where you can decide if you prefer artichokes *alla Romana* (stewed) or *alla Guidea* (deep-fried).

Roman

Sora Margherita (Piazza Delle Cinque Scole 30, tel. 06/687-4216, Mon.-Fri. 12:30pm-3pm, Fri. 8pm-11:30pm, closed Mon. in winter, €8) has been written up before and they have the reviews mounted on the walls to prove it. Lucia, Mario, and Ivan haven't let the attention go to their heads. This popular hole-in-the-wall restaurant in the Ghetto features down-home decor along with handwritten menu that changes daily. Thursday is dedicated to *gnocchi,* Friday is for *baccala,* and *pasta e fagioli* is prepared daily.

It would be hard to find a more historic restaurant than **Da Giggetto** (Via del Portico di Ottavia 21, tel. 06/686-1105, Tues.-Sun. noon-3pm and 7:30pm-11pm, €15), where Lidia and her husband have been welcoming customers for the last 50 years. Inside is a maze of spacious rooms where uniformed waitstaff whisk fried zucchini flowers, fish soup, and *carciofi alla giudia* from kitchen to table.

London may have fish-and-chips, but Rome has **Filetti di Baccala** (Largo dei Librari 88, tel. 06/686-4018, daily noon-10pm, €10). Here the fried cod is served with *puntarelle* (a traditional Roman green) and the atmosphere is so simple they only accept cash. A very drinkable house wine is available by the full, half, or quarter carafe.

Italian

★ **Roscioli** (Via dei Giubbonari 34, tel. 06/686-4045, deli Mon.-Sat. 7am-7:30pm, restaurant 12:30pm-4pm and 7pm-midnight, €12) started out as a deli counter selling the finest cheeses and hams from France, Spain, and Italy. A good thing got better when they opened a restaurant in the back and began serving wine. The starters are a good introduction to local cured meats and are best enjoyed with the house wine. Unfortunately, there aren't enough tables to meet demand and you may have to settle for a spot at the small counter—though you'll still be able to enjoy the gastronomic sights and smells.

Touristic isn't always bad, especially when classic dishes are served in a spacious and elegant setting. That's the hallmark of **Pierluigi** (Piazza de' Ricci 144, tel. 06/686-1302, daily 12:30pm-3:30pm, 7pm-midnight, €16-20). You can try artichokes prepared in both the Roman and Jewish styles, lots of fresh fish, and nearly any kind of wine you like. It comes at a price though. The outdoor tables overlooking the small square are perfect for lingering.

Most restaurants stopped making their own bread a long time ago. That's not the case at **Ditirambo** (Piazza della Cancelleria 74, tel. 06/687-1626, daily 1pm-3pm and

7:30pm-11:30pm, closed Mon. lunch, €15), where fresh loaves appear nightly and form a natural partnership with the wide selection of pasta dishes.

Pizza

★ **Il Forno di Campo De' Fiori** (Campo De' Fiori 22, tel. 06/6880-6662, Mon.-Sat. 7:30am-2:30pm and 5pm-10pm, €5) is a local institution on the northeastern corner of the square. Everything is baked on-site, and you can watch pizza being prepared and pulled from the ovens before going in to make your selection. The most popular are the white, red, and zucchini but several other tempting varieties are also served. It gets chaotic at lunch, so arrive early if you want to avoid the crowds. The pastry counter in the back features breads, cakes, and cookies including a delicious apple tart. Everything is sold by weight and can be ordered using gestures. To pay, bring your receipt to the cashier at the entrance.

At **Baffetto** (Via del Governo Vecchio 114, tel. 06/686-1617, daily noon-3:30pm and 6:30pm-1am, €8), expect eager crowds waiting to enjoy thin-crust pizza served by waitstaff with attitude. Arrive early or late after a visit to Piazza Navona, and make sure to sample the fried appetizers.

Pizza purists may scoff at the thought of electric ovens, but that's what **Lo Zozzone** (Via del Teatro Pace 32, tel. 06/6880-8575, daily lunch and dinner, €10) uses to produce great white pizza they then transform into sandwiches. The *pizzaoli* working the dough are all veterans. The takeaway option is perfect for a picnic on the benches of Piazza Navona, or you can grab one of the small tables on the street outside.

Kosher

Roman kosher is a unique combination of Italian and Jewish culinary traditions. The dishes that emerged in the Ghetto can now be found across the city but ordering them here provides added authenticity. Note that many businesses in the Ghetto observe the Sabbath and close on Friday evenings.

There are a handful of small historic restaurants along Via del Portico D'Ottavia. Like most, **Nonna Betta** (Via del Portico D'Ottavia 16, tel. 06/6880-6263, Wed.-Mon. 11am-11pm, €15) hasn't changed menu or décor in decades. Waiters have the character that comes with a lifetime of experience, and the long, narrow dining room is lined with paintings of yesteryear. Any item with *alla giudia* at the end means it's prepared in the Jewish style. Artichokes, pasta, meat, and desserts have all been given the kosher treatment, with delicious results.

Fonzie (Via di Santa Maria del Pianto 13, tel. 06/6889-2029, Sun.-Thurs. 10:30am-11pm, Fri. 10:30am-4pm, Sat. 5:30pm-midnight, €6.5-8) is a popular burger joint near the western entrance to the Ghetto. The faux-1950s interior has a counter at the entrance where 20 burgers and all the usual sides are grilled and served up fast. All the beef is certified kosher from Italian cattle, and the vegetables are organic. Seating is on stools along the walls but many customers opt for takeaway and enjoy their chili burgers on the nearby benches. Sabbath is observed here, so don't arrive Friday night expecting to eat.

For Jewish pastries head to **Pasticceria Boccione** (Via del Portico D'Ottavia 1, tel. 06/687-8637, Sun.-Thurs. 7am-7pm, Fri. 7am-3pm, €4) and hope that that they haven't sold out of the chocolate or honey *mostaccioli* cookies. The pastries in the window are not the good-looking dainty kind available from most shops but the hefty imperfect variety that are no less delicious. Lines can be long in the morning when locals come for the freshly baked *pizza ebraica* (sweet Jewish pizza).

Snacks and Street Food

Fried rice balls, or *suppli,* are a mainstay in Rome, but few restaurants are based around them. Fortunately that hasn't stopped **Supplizio** (Via dei Banchi Vecchi 143, tel. 06/8987-1920, Mon.-Sat. 12:30pm-3:30pm and 6:30pm-10:30pm, Thurs. noon-9:30pm, €5) from specializing in this wonderful finger food. It's perfect for takeaway if there isn't

★ *Pizza al Taglio*

pizza al taglio

Roman pizza is thin, prepared in long trays, and served by the kilo at hundreds of *pizzerie al taglio* (takeaway pizza shops) around the city. Varieties range from *bianca* (plain white toppingless pizza) and *margherita* (tomato and mozzarella) to potato and sausage or four-cheese and some creative alternatives. The best thing to do is enter a pizzeria and check out what they have behind the counter. If you like the selection order a few different cuts and indicate with your hands how much you want and if you intend to eat in (*per mangiare qui*) or take it to go (*per portare via*). Most restaurants also serve the familiar round pizzas baked in wood-burning ovens. Menus are divided into red and white pizzas and nearly always include a selection of fried appetizers. Good places to try *pizza al taglio* include:

· **Il Forno di Campo De' Fiori** (page 81)

· **Pizzarium** (page 87)

· **Alice** (page 87)

· **Ai Marmi** (page 89)

· **Il Panifico Passi** (page 90)

room on the wooden stools or leather couches inside.

Bakeries

Gourmet pastry shops are rare in Rome, and none are as enticing as the small laboratory **Andrea De Bellis** (Piazza del Paradiso 56, tel. 06/6880-5072, €4-5), located near Campo de Fiori. Inside the bakery a colorful array of pastries tempts the eyes and can be enjoyed

sitting down with a cup of coffee or tea. *Sablé al cioccolato, millefoglie,* plum cake, and croissants are all stalwarts and are wonderful any time of day.

Gelato

Frigidarium (Via del Governo Vecchio 112, daily noon-2am, €2-4.50) is a standing-room-only *gelaterie* with two refrigerated cases filled with ice cream that's prepared from scratch every morning. Pistachio and chocolate lovers should taste the *Mozart* flavor with *panna* (whipped cream). You can choose from various sizes and enjoy your gelato from a cone (*cono*) or cup (*coppa*). If you can't make up your mind the friendly owner or his assistant can suggest the best pairings.

Limited selection isn't always a bad thing, and what **Ciampini Lucini** (Piazza San Lorenzo in Lucina 29, tel. 06/687-3620, €3) lacks in quantity it makes up for in quality. As long as the *zabaglione* (hazelnut chocolate) is available, there's really no reason to taste anything else. You can order a scoop at the dedicated bar section or outside on a terrace where it comes served in a metal bowl by the uniformed waitstaff.

Coffee

★ **Antico Caffè della Pace** (Via della Pace 5, tel. 06/686-1216, Tues.-Sun. 8:30am-2am, Mon. 4pm-2am, €3) is a Roman institution frequented by local artists and personalities as well as visitors who fall for the beauty of its ivy-clad exterior and wood-paneled interior. You can tell by the old-fashioned coffee machine behind the narrow counter that the espresso will be good, but if you prefer tea or a glass of wine the bar staff are happy to oblige.

Strong, aromatic coffee is standard fare at **Tazza d'Oro** (Via Degli Orfani 84, tel. 06/678-9792, Mon.-Sat. 7am-8pm), where the house blend may be purchased and *granita al caffè* (iced coffee) is served in summer.

The interior at **Caffè Sant'Eustachio** (Piazza Sant'Eustachio 82, tel. 06/6880-2048, daily 8:30am-1am) hasn't changed since 1938—and neither has the café's unique blend of locally prepared beans. The uniformed baristas take pride in serving the presweetened *Gran Caffè* and *Monachella* house coffees with chocolate and whipped cream. At lunch, the café is crowded and wonderfully chaotic.

TRIDENTE

Tridente isn't an obvious dining destination. Most of the stores around Piazza di Spagna are dedicated to retail shopping, and restaurants are rare along Via del Corso or Condotti. Those present are often expensive and not always worth the price. There are exceptions, and south of Via Corso and away from the major shopping district culinary options and quality improve significantly. The neighborhood is also known for historic tearooms and bars where poets and aristocrats once drank (and elegantly dressed ladies and groups of crumpet-craving tourists still do).

Roman

★ **Da Gino** (Vicolo Rosini 4, tel. 06/687-3434, lunch and dinner, closed Sun. and August, €12-14) stands out. Don't be surprised if your server forgets to bring a menu at this *osteria,* where the limited selection is a good sign. *Pasta e ceci* is usually served on Tuesdays, and with any luck the *pollo con peperoni* will have been prepared that morning. Da Gino can be a little difficult to find and is not very glamorous inside, but it is authentic and satisfying to the stomach.

The name says it all at **Maccheroni** (Piazza delle Coppelle 44, tel. 06/6830-7895, daily 1pm-3pm and 7:30pm-11:30pm, €11). Expect pasta in all its Roman incarnations including *amatriciana, carbonara,* and *cacio e pepe,* all prepared within a glass-enclosed kitchen. The restaurant is popular with couples, who are seated at a dozen tableclothed tables inside the well-lit interior or along the pedestrian-only cobblestone street outside. Service is fast and friendly.

Italian

★ **Gusto** (Piazza Augusto Imperatore 9, tel. 06/322-6273, daily noon-midnight, €10) is greater than the sum of its parts, which include a *trattoria,* pizzeria, restaurant, and bookstore. The buffet brunch is the perfect break between the Ara Pacis and Piazza di Spagna. The wine bar regularly features live jazz and the cheese corner is well stocked with Italian and French hard and soft varieties served with honey and fruit.

What **Matricianella** (Via del Leone 4, tel.

Best Brunches

Food fads come and go, but brunch has endured in Rome and been embraced by eager locals and curious visitors. Restaurants have added their own twists to the meal. Here, it's not so much about bacon and eggs, but long buffet tables stocked with enticing all-you-can-eat vegetarian and meat dishes. Some brunches are accompanied by live music, others provide play areas for children, and a few offer great views of the city while you eat. If you can't arrive early, make reservations to avoid a line.

BRUNCH BUFFETS

If you wake up hungry on Saturday or Sunday, **CamilloB** (Vatican, Piazza Cavour 21/A, Sat.-Sun. noon-3:30pm, tel. 06/683-2077, €18) can help. This bistro a block from Castel Sant'Angelo serves a changing menu of sweet and savory dishes for both gluttons and the health conscious. The buffet includes quiches, omelets, curry chicken, pizza, and many other freshly prepared delicacies competing for space on your plate. Leave room for the desserts, and compare their cheesecake with the one back home. Children are kept occupied in a dedicated fun zone overseen by a qualified "brunchsitter." In between refills you can try your hand at table soccer or Ping-Pong.

Margutta Ristorarte (Tridente, Via Margutta 118, tel. 06/3265-0577, Sat.-Sun. 12:30pm-3:30pm, €25) is a vegetarian institution that has thrived in a city of carnivores. The classy interior and strictly biological buffet may even make you reconsider your diet. The buffet has over 30 vegetarian and vegan plates along with four themed menus. Bread, water, juice, fruit salad, and coffee are included in the price, and a pianist in the corner provides the atmosphere.

Queen Makeda Grand Pub (Aventino, Via di San Saba 11, tel. 06/575-9608, Sat.-Sun. 12:30pm-3:30pm, €19) is a couple of blocks from the Circus Maximus in a leafy residential neighborhood. The industrial interior and bamboo garden give it a Brooklyn-meets-Japan look, while the long row of taps dispensing craft beers answers any questions about the name. The buffet strays from traditional Italian into spicy international flavors and a roasted meat table where chicken, pork, and lamb are carved. Toddlers have a place to play, and several tables are equipped with self-service taps.

If you don't get to **Gusto** (Piazza Augusto Imperatore 9, tel. 06/322-6273, daily noon-midnight, €10) early you'll be left salivating in line. The problem isn't the lack of tables inside or underneath the monumental portico facing the mausoleum where Rome's first emperor is buried. It's just a popular place. Here, price is determined by weight. Brunchers are given large metal plates and unleashed on a fairly standard but well-executed buffet of Italian classics. The first 500 grams is €15 and every 100g after that is an additional €2.50. Plates are weighed after each filling.

06/683-2100, Mon.-Sat. 12:30pm-3pm and 7:30pm-11pm, €12) lacks in space it makes up for in wine. It stocks more than 700 bottles, which makes choosing one of the roasted lamb dishes simple. There are tables outside on a shaded terrace or inside underneath wood-beamed ceilings and walls covered with framed reviews from the past.

Fiaschetteria Beltramme (Via della Croce 39, tel. 06/6979-7200, daily 12:15pm-3pm and 7:30pm-10:45pm, €10-15) mixes the best of Lazio with a dash of Tuscany. The *tagliolini* and *penne* dishes are worth the risk of a sauce stain, and meat dishes are cooked

in almost every way imaginable. Italians outnumber tourist here and owners Silvia and Arturo keep everyone smiling. As with many restaurants in Italy, you'll be charged a couple euros for bread.

Watching chef Stefano Galbiati operate in his open kitchen at **Trattoria del Pozzo** (Via del Pozzo delle Cornacchie 25, tel. 06/6830-1427, Mon.-Fri. 6pm-11pm, €15) puts a stomach at ease. The chef's ingredients vary depending on the season, but the results are always delicious. Emerging Sicilian vineyards dominate the wine list. This modern Piedmontese eatery is a hit with locals.

the brunch buffet at Gusto

OTHER BRUNCH VENUES

La Veranda (Vatican, Via Borgo Santo Spirito 73, tel. 06/687-2973, Tues.-Sun. 12:30pm-3:15pm and 7:30pm-11:15pm) offers a baby (€15), light (€18), veg (€24), or big (€27) fixed brunch menu served in a medieval *palazzo* with vaulted ceilings and original frescoes. This is brunch with historic charm, plenty of space between linen-covered tables, and a soothing courtyard view.

Coromandel (Piazza Navona, Via di Monte Giordano 60, tel. 06/6880-2461, Sat.-Sun. 8:30am-3pm, €8-12) takes what is probably a more familiar approach to brunch. There is no buffet; instead there is a special brunch menu filled with American classics given an Italian treatment. You can order freshly squeezed juices, pancakes with banana and almonds, eggs Benedict, bagels, cheeseburgers, or one of the two daily specials. The bohemian furnishings and wood-beamed interior make for an ideal place to linger over coffee and plan the day.

Pizza

PizzaRe (Via di Ripetta 13, tel. 06/321-1468, daily noon-midnight, €6-10) serves some of the best Neapolitan pies in town. The large dining room is perpetually full of people eyeing the wood-burning oven with anticipation. Fried starters are excellent, and if you have any room left try one of the traditional desserts like *cassata napoletana* or *torta caprese*. Reservations are essential on weekends.

Snacks and Street Food

★ **Ciao Checca** (Piazza di Firenze 25/26, tel. 06/6830-0368, Mon.-Tues. 8:30am-3:30pm, Wed.-Fri. 8:30am-10:30pm, weekends 9am-10:30pm, €6.50-8.50) serves contemporary slow food made from organic ingredients. You'll feel healthier the moment you walk into to the brightly lit eatery lined with green and white stools where health-conscious office workers and visiting vegans get their calories. The menu consists of pasta salads, soups, fruit smoothies, and vegetable shakes. It's the place to go if you're missing durum wheat and gluten-free burgers.

Healthy can be chic, and **Ginger** (Via Borgognona 43, tel. 06/6994-0836, daily 10am-midnight, €10-13) is the proof. There's something about the overwhelming whiteness, the skylights, and the plants inside this modern organic food emporium that make quinoa and steamed vegetables tempting. Grab a stool at the immaculate bar for a soy milk shake and gourmet *panino* or sit down at the marble-topped tables and try one of the main courses. Service can be a tad slow during the lunch hour rush, but there's plenty to look at while you wait.

Searching for picnic ingredients in a market or Roman deli is a sure way to build an appetite, but if you'd rather someone else do the preparing **Gina** (Via di S. Sebastianello, 7A, tel. 06/678-0251) can simplify matters. Their ready-made baskets include pasta and rice salads, sandwiches, bread, cheese, and desserts that can be enjoyed on the grounds of nearby Villa Borghese.

Roasted chestnuts are available on the streets of the Tridente from late autumn to early spring. It's an age-old tradition carried on by new faces who operate mobile roasting carts and serve warm unshelled chestnuts in paper cones (€5). There are several vendors stationed along Via del Condotti and another facing the Spanish Steps.

Gelato

If you're serious about gelato, sooner or later you'll find yourself standing outside ★ **San Crispino** (Via della Panetteria 42, tel. 06/679-3924, daily noon-12:30am, €3). The owners only serve the flavors they like, so expect lots of hazelnut, cinnamon, honey, and ginger. The ice cream is hidden from view in metal vats but each flavor is labeled in Italian and English. There's some seating inside but most customers enjoy their cups outside.

Giolitti (Via Uffici del Vicario 40, tel. 06/699-1243, daily 7:30am-1:30am, €3) pioneered gelato and has been making it the same way since the early 20th century. Much of the day, there's a lione of people waiting to get inside, where bow tie-wearing staff scoop legendary gelato. Coffee and pastries are also available.

Coffee

Caffè Greco (Via dei Condotti 86, tel. 06/679-1700, daily 9am-8pm) was around long before the designer boutiques that now surround it. This is where grand tour stalwarts like Goethe and Stendhal drank their coffee, and portraits of many famous sippers can be seen in the room farthest from the entrance. It's a great place to write postcards and get your literary kicks while sipping tea from porcelain cups.

There are two historic cafes overlooking Piazza del Popolo where celebrities and intellectuals once gathered and paparazzi still occasionally stake out. Today, **Canova** (Piazza del Popolo 16-17, daily 7:30am-1am) and **Rosati** (Piazza del Popolo 5a, daily 7:30am-11:30am) attract tourists who sit on the outdoor terraces and watch the constant stream of pedestrians leaving and entering the square. The drinks are expensive, but you can people watch for free from a bench nearby.

VATICANO

Borgo Pio, a long narrow street parallel to Via della Conciliazione, is a good place to find sustenance after a visit to the Vatican. **Borgo Vittorio** is another good place to quench an appetite.

Roman

L'Arcangelo (Via G.G. Belli 59, tel. 06/321-0992, Mon.-Fri. 1pm-2:30pm and 8pm-11pm, Sat. 8pm-11pm, €14-16) is a gourmet *trattoria* with a limited but high-quality menu of dishes combining the city's culinary past and present. Marble-topped tables are arranged around a medium-sized dining room with dark wood paneling and family photos.

Arlu (Borgo Pio 135, tel. 06/686-8936, lunch only, €14) serves Roman specialties within a refined setting. The family that runs the restaurant serves their fresh bread and pasta with a smile. The house wine goes well with everything on the menu, including the *saltimbocca alla Romana.*

The latest restaurant trend in Rome is express pasta bars. The pasta and sauces at **Pastasciutta** (Via delle Grazie 5, tel.

333/650-3758, daily 10:30am-6:30pm, €4.50-6) are made fresh daily. You can watch dishes being prepared in the miniature kitchen. It only takes a couple of minutes before *cacio e pepe* or *pappardelle al ragu* are served to you on a plastic plate. There are only six options and very little space to eat inside, but the prices are unbeatable and the pasta is good.

Pizza

Not all pizza is alike in Italy, and the closer you get to Naples the better it becomes.

★ **Splendor** (Via Vittoria Colonna 32c, tel. 06/683-3710, daily noon-2am, €12-20) has successfully transplanted those Neapolitan flavors to Rome and serves a memorable margherita topped with fresh tomatoes and mozzarella. The oven is wood burning and the extensive menu includes fried mixed plates and many southern Italian specialties. It's an elegant eatery with several different seating options on two floors where a young crowd gathers after work. Service is efficient. Prices are a little higher than average, but nothing scandalous.

Alice (Via delle Grazie 7/9, 06/687-5746, Mon.-Fri. 7:30am-8pm, Sat. 7:30am-4pm, Sun. 10am-4pm, €5) is perfect for a quick slice of takeaway pizza on the way to or from St. Peter's. From noon onwards the counter is filled with trays of pizza topped with vegetables, sausage, and other appealing ingredients. There's not much space inside, so tourists gather on the steps out front.

Pizzarium (Via della Meloria 43, tel. 06/3974-5416, Mon.-Sat. 10am-10pm, Sun. noon-4pm and 6pm-10pm, €8) is a *pizza al taglio* shop behind the Vatican where legendary baker Bonci and his crew of dough fanatics are busy manning the ovens most of the day. Toppings are generous and creative, and you're likely to find figs, goat cheese, and plenty of vegetables in between. It's a simple neighborhood joint without any seating and plenty of regulars congregating outside. Price is by weight and the pizza is thick, so expect to pay more than average for a pizza that's far better than average.

Fusion

Temakinho (Borgo Angelico 30, 06/9291-9949, daily 12:30pm-3:30pm and 7pm-12:30am, €12-15) combines Japanese sushi culture with Brazilian fish and meat traditions. It's an unlikely restaurant spread out among four brightly decorated floors. Caipirinha is the house drink, but there are plenty of South American beers and refreshing fruit smoothies, too, all of which can be sipped from the panoramic rooftop terrace.

Snacks and Street Food

Panino Divino (Via dei Gracchi 11a, tel. 06/3973-7803, Mon.-Sat. 10am-9pm, €5-6.50) is an informal sandwich shop with cold cuts hanging from the ceiling and bottles of wine lining the walls. The menu includes over 25 *panini* as well cured meat and cheese plates (€9.50) served on wooden cutting boards. Sandwiches are prepared while you wait by the jovial owners, who like to chat while they work. There a half-dozen stools inside and a barrel outside that's been converted into a table. Prices are very reasonable.

If you're tired of Roman takeaway, try **Bacio di Puglia** (Via del Mascherino, 59, 06/6830-7697, daily 9am-9pm, €8-12) for a taste of southern Italian comfort food. It's a favorite with Vatican workers who come for the *calzone* and fried *panzerotti,* but you can also get a first and a second course like orecchiette pasta with turnips or potatoes and mussels that can be wrapped up or eaten at handful of tables. Most of the ingredients come directly from Puglia including the wine, which can be ordered by the carafe.

Grattachecca is an Italian ice once sold by itinerant vendors who hauled large blocks of ice around looking for customers needing refreshment. Those days are gone but **Tempio della Grattachecca** (Lungotevere in Augusta/Corner Ponte Cavour) has somehow survived, and the metal kiosk opposite the Ara Pacis is one of the last places selling the concoction. Rafaello and his mother crush the ice and mix it with fruit syrup (cherry, melon, strawberry, peach, etc.) they prepare themselves. The treat is served in a large glass with a spoon and a straw and can be eaten at the counter or one of the tables nearby. The only downside is the traffic.

Bakeries

Gabriele Bonci, a local culinary guru, recently turned his attention to bread and opened **Panificio Bonci** (Via Trionfale 36, tel. 06/3973-4457, €5). In a year he bakes more than 1,200 different loaves, none of which use industrial flour or additives. Country bread, whole grain, brown, salt-free, seasonal, brioche, focaccia and many other bread varieties line the shelves of this neighborhood bakery. The oven also turns out broccoli and sausage rolls and loads of sweets. Everything is priced by the kilo and it's possible to ask for half a loaf or even a single cookie.

The smell inside **Panificio Mosca** (Via Candia 16, tel. 06/3974-2134, €4), located near the Vatican walls, has been seducing residents since 1916. Locals come for the handmade pastries in the morning and trays of freshly baked white and red pizza at lunch. Although it's crowded and chaotic at noon, lines move fast, and the ladies behind the counter are in a joyful flutter.

Pasticceria Colapicchioni (Via Tacito, 76, tel. 06/321-5405, €5) has been baking bread, biscuits, pastries, pizza, and focaccia since 1934 and even created their own unique cake. It's called Pangill'Oro and is a variation of an ancient Roman dessert made from dried fruit, honey, nuts, and grapes that's been trademarked by the shop's owner. One side of the bakery is dedicated to oven-fresh ingredients while the other is filled with regional specialties.

Gelato

Their hazelnut is good, but it's the chocolate flavors that have kept **Mo's Gelateria** (Via Cola di Rienzo 174, tel. 06/687-4357) on the map. Fruit is delivered fresh weekly and everything is made without preservatives by a friendly staff.

TRASTEVERE

There is no shortage of restaurants in Trastevere, and the vast number of choices can be confusing. Most serve classic Roman fare, and it's hard to go wrong at any of them. Nevertheless, refrain from stopping at the first *trattoria* you pass, and don't be rushed into sitting down by an overzealous waitperson. Side streets are a good place to search for authenticity.

During the summer many bars and restaurants set up shop on the banks of the Tiber. It's a fun place to enjoy a light meal or cocktail, although hygiene can be questionable.

Roman

Italians have a way of putting people at ease, and it doesn't take long for **Da Giovanni** (Via della Lungara 41a, tel. 06/686-1514, Mon.-Sat. 12pm-3pm and 7pm-10:30pm, €8-10) to feel like a second home. The menu reads like all the rest of the Roman trattorias in the neighborhood, but tastes slightly better—especially when the check arrives. The small dining room is charmingly untrendy and full of 1950s nostalgia. The *carciofi alla romana* (Roman-style artichokes) and *tonarelli cacao e pepe* pasta are must-tries.

The menu at **Da Lucia** (Vicolo del Mattonato 2, tel. 06/580-3601, Tues.-Sun. 12:30pm-3pm and 7:30pm-11pm, €12-15) may seem limited—but it's better to perfect a few great dishes than master none. Specials include *gnocchi al pomodoro* on Thursdays and helpings of *coniglio alla cacciatora* (roasted rabbit) all week long. The *trattoria* has been satisfying locals since 1938 and is located on one of Trastevere's most photogenic streets.

Corsetti 1921 (Piazza San Cosimato 27, tel. 06/581-6311, daily noon-3:30pm and 7:15pm-midnight, €15-20) doesn't change. It's been run by the same family for three generations and still serves *bucatini all'amatriciana.* What they have renovated is the décor, which is tastefully modern with careful attention to table settings, lighting, and flower arrangements. There's also a downstairs lounge bar with a piano set underneath stone arched ceilings, where well-dressed patrons retreat to before and after dinner.

Italian

Pianostrada Laboratorio di Cucina (Vicolo del Cedro 26, tel. 06/8957-2296, Tues.-Thurs. 11:30am-3:30pm and 5:30pm-1am, Fri.-Sun. 11am-midnight, €8-10) isn't interested in serving the usual. The staff like to experiment. Fortunately, they know what they're doing, and the daily menu can include everything from apple pie to fishburgers. It's all prepared in an open kitchen behind a long metal counter that's usually crowded.

Pizza

Regulars call ★ **Ai Marmi** (Viale Trastevere 53-57, tel. 06/580-0919, Thurs.-Tues. noon-2:30am, €6-8) "the morgue" in reference to the white marble tables. The pizza is blue-chip Roman with a thin crust that doesn't disappoint. Starters include *suppli* (mozzarella-filled rice balls), fried olives, and cold cut platters. A large blackboard lists the options. Waiters move about the space frenetically, and getting their attention can be a challenge.

Seafood

How a former rugby player swapped scrum for kitchen is uncertain, but the move produced one of the best fish restaurants in Rome. Fans of **Alberto Ciarla** (Piazza San Cosimo 1, tel. 06/588-4377, 12pm-3pm and 7pm-10:30pm, €18-22) swear by the shrimp salad and spaghetti with bass.

Snacks and Street Food

If you're craving french fries and you want them fast, head to **Fries** (Vicolo del Cinque 22, Mon.-Thurs. 5pm-2am, Fri.-Sat. noon-4am, Sun. noon-2am, €5). This standing-room-only potato shack is about one thing and one thing only. Their hand-cut Italian spuds are fried in cholesterol-free peanut oil and served with a selection of 20 homemade sauces that range from classic to exotic. Everything comes in paper cones that locals line up for until dawn.

Bakeries

All it takes to make a mouth water is stone-ground wheat from an antique mill outside Rome and a hazelnut-burning oven. That's the way things are done at **La Renella** (Via del Moro 15, tel. 06/581-7265) and have been for 130 years. They also serve pizza, which students and travelers eat at the long wooden counter running down one side of this bakery where English isn't always spoken.

Don't worry about language at **Valzani** (Via del Moro 37, tel. 06/580-3792, Tues.-Sun. 10am-8am). Just point to the torrone or chocolate sweets you desire and they'll understand. This pastry shop has made no attempt to keep up with the times and has stuck with making traditional Roman desserts that come in single portions (€1.50). Many are temptingly on display in the window, which takes on festive colors during the Christmas and Easter seasons.

Giuseppe Solfrizzi learned the art of pastry in France under Alain Ducasse and returned to Italy to open **Le Levain** (Via Luigi Santini 22, tel. 06/6456-2880, Tues.-Sun. 8am-8:30pm, €4-6). Now Romans enjoy his knowledge of baguettes, croissants, pain au chocolat, and other mouth-watering creations. He's usually busy baking away in the lab or restocking the counter with chocolate treats.

Gelato

Fresh, seasonal ingredients and an obsession with quality are what makes **Fiordiluna** (Via della Lungaretta 96, 06/6456-1314, daily 11:30am-12:30am, €2.50-5) so good. You won't find strawberry ice cream in winter or additives at any time, but you will discover dozens of chocolate varieties and flavors made with mule's milk. They take the purist approach all the way and only serve their thick, creamy gelato in cups.

Tiberino (Piazza Fatebenefratelli 18, tel. 06/687-7662, Mon.-Tues. 7:30am-6pm, Wed.-Fri. 7:30am-11pm, Sat. 10am-11:30am, Sun. 10am-8pm, €3-5) is a reliable gelato stop on the island separating the Jewish Ghetto from Trastevere. You can also have a coffee or a sit-down meal, but the ice cream is the most portable option and can be licked on the sunny cobblestone square outside.

AVENTINO AND TESTACCIO

Roman

Agustarella (Via G. Branca 98, tel. 06/574-6585, Mon.-Sat. noon-11pm, €12) is a classic Roman *osteria* in a quintessentially Roman neighborhood. They prepare simple dishes known as *cucina povera*, or poor food. Recipes originated from necessity and use nearly all parts of an animal. Those with adventurous palates will give the *trippa alla romana* (tripe) a try, while the *rigatoni alla pajata* is the safe bet for pasta lovers.

At **Perilli** (Via Marmorata 39, tel. 06/574-2415, Thurs.-Tues. 12:30pm-3pm and 7:30pm-11pm, €10-14), the owner won't answer many questions and the welcome may not be especially warm, but people who know their *gnocchi* from their *rigatoni* swear by this place (and its immense portions). Large murals on the walls offer something to contemplate as you eat.

Historic digs don't translate into appetizing food—except when trattorias like **Da Felice** (Via Mastro Giorgio 29, tel. 06/574-6800, daily 12:30pm-3pm and 7:30pm-11:15pm, €14) are concerned. It's a little less rustic and a little more elegant than other options in the area and perfect for romantic evenings. There are two dining rooms, both of which have black-and-white-checkered paving, brick walls, and carefully set tables. Expect to eat well and leave satisfied.

Porto Fluviale (Via del Porto Fluviale 22, tel. 06/574-3199, daily 10:30am-2am, €8-12) is on the border of Testaccio within walking distance of the Piramide in an up-and-coming part of town. The restaurant is divided into several sections and vaguely resembles a diner, albeit with a darker tone. The food comes in full or miniature portions that allows you to taste a little of a lot. Happy hour is well attended and the mustached barman mixes excellent cocktails.

Pizza

★ **Il Panifico Passi** (Via Mastro Giorgio 87, Mon.-Sun. 9am-1pm and 4pm-8pm) has been baking bread in the same wood-burning oven since 1931. The *pizza bianca* (white pizza) is tempting and filling. It's cut according to your hunger, so just indicate how much you want to the patient woman behind the counter. They also bake interesting breads and prepare lasagna fresh daily. Even if you're not hungry it's worth stopping in to see an Italian bakery in action.

Pizzeria Remo (Piazza Santa Maria Liberatrice 44, tel. 06/574-6270, Mon.-Sat. 7pm-1am, €10), on a corner across from a park, serves Roman thin-crust pizza. It's a popular place that has lines on weekends, when you're better off arriving early or late. Waiters seem to have a lot of fun navigating the crowded tables, bantering with clients and speaking in heavy Roman slang about soccer. The appetizers are delicious, and the mixed plate with fried zucchini flowers is particularly recommended.

Acqua e Farina (Piazza Orazio Giustiniani 2, tel. 06/574-1382, daily noon-12:30am, €7-10) is another place to look for Testaccio's best pizza. Their mini option offers a chance to taste different pizzas in a single sitting. Starters include *crostini di patate* with sliced potatoes, mushrooms, mozzarella, and *tartufo* (truffle). A line generally forms on weekends, but watching the people gathered in the *piazza* opposite helps pass the time. Once you get a table don't expect a lot of elbow room or a quiet evening. It's loud and you'll need to speak up if you want to get the waitperson's attention.

Snacks and Street Food

Most street food vendors serve fast-food classics, but **Trapazzino** (Via Giovanni Branca 88, tel. 06/4341-9624, Tues.-Sun. noon-1am, €5) has created a new classic and sells it inside a small takeaway eatery. The item everyone comes for is a cross between pizza, calzone, and stew. It doesn't take much courage to try, and once you've sampled one it's hard not to want more. Fillings include chicken cacciatora, meatballs, mozzarella, and vegetables.

Tram Depot (Corner of Via Marmorata and Via Manlio Gelsomini opposite the fire station, tel. 06/575-4406, daily 7:30am-2am, €5) is a reliable destination for light sandwiches, salads, and fruit shakes. There's outdoor seating and the tram is open day and night. Food and drinks are ordered at the counter and can be enjoyed sitting in the shade. They mix excellent cocktails and attract a loyal happy hour crowd.

Gelato

Claudio Torce is the maestro of a small gelato empire and runs eight shops around the city.
★ **Il Gelato** (Viale Aventino 59, daily 11am-10pm, €2.50-4.50) in Aventino is one of the smallest, which isn't a problem. Here you can focus on a select number of classic chocolate and cream flavors. Pistachio and *nocciola* are found in nearly every ice cream shop in Rome, but the nuts taste better here. The colorful and friendly staff are happy to give you a sample before you commit to a flavor. Just ask *posso provare?* (can I try?).

TERMINI

The area surrounding Rome's train station isn't very attractive and caters mostly to tourists and travelers who don't have the time or energy to find a nicer area to eat. There are dozens of fast-food joints inside the station and along the streets south of Termini. If you continue in this direction you'll enter one of the most culturally diverse neighborhoods in the city, home to low-priced Chinese, Korean, and Indian restaurants. North of the station, towards the university district, is less commercial and more residential with a higher number of local eateries that don't survive on commuters. The general rule of thumb is that the farther you get from Termini the better the food gets.

★ **Er Buchetto** (Via del Viminale 2f, tel. 329/965-2175, Mon.-Fri. 9:30am-3pm and 5pm-9pm, Sat. 9am-2:30pm, €5) is a Roman-style tavern famous for porchetta (roast pork) sandwiches. The name means "little hole" and that's not an exaggeration: There are three tables at most and they're not even normal-size tables, but that's the fun of this neighborhood institution that's been feeding locals since 1890. If you do get to sit on one of the stools, order the white wine from the tap; otherwise have your sandwich wrapped and head to the nearest park.

La Matriciana (Via del Viminale 44, tel. 06/488-1775, daily noon-2:30pm and 7pm-11pm, Sat. lunch only, €14-16) is a large brasserie-style restaurant with a 1930s interior and uniformed waitstaff in continual movement. The menu doesn't stray from the Roman classics, and if you haven't yet tasted tripe this could be the place to take a gastronomic leap of faith. There's a tempting appetizer cart filled with grilled vegetables and a sommelier ready to make suggestions from the extensive wine list.

Uffa Che Pizza (Via dei Taurini 39, tel. 06/4436-2444, Mon.-Sat. noon-3pm and 6pm-11:30pm, €7-9) is on a tree-lined residential street north of the station near the university. It's a simple, clean, one-room pizzeria with reasonable prices, air-conditioning, and quick service. Toppings don't get very creative but that doesn't seem to bother the tables of locals and students who fill the pizzeria at lunch and dinner.

Nightlife and Entertainment

Evenings in Rome start in neighborhood squares and continue inside theaters, clubs, and discos. Romans aren't heavy drinkers, but they are extremely sociable and enjoy conversing until late. *Aperitivo* is usually how they begin an evening. It's the rough equivalent of happy hour except it can last a couple of hours and usually includes food. It starts on weekdays around 6pm in bars and cafes around the city. Drink and buffet offers are usually posted outside and rarely exceed €10. Some places fill counters with cold pasta, frittata omelets, couscous, cheese, cold cuts, and bread while others simply provide olives and potato chips. Wine is the most commonly ordered drink, but beer and cocktails always available.

There are many ways to have a good time after *aperitivo*. The city is sprinkled with theaters and concert halls where symphony, opera, and ballet are performed. Talented musicians play to intimate clubs and wine bars entertain the palate. There are also month-long festivals dedicated to the arts, and outdoor performances in Piazza del Popolo and the Baths of Caracalla are frequent. Pick up Rome's quarterly event calendar at any TIP office, or swing by a newsstand to buy a copy of *La Repubblica*, the entertainment supplement that's published on Thursdays and includes an English section.

The city has a few known nightlife districts. **Piazza Trilussa** is a popular outdoor meeting area where locals plan what to do next. **Campo De' Fiori** is lined with bars filled with foreign travelers and exchange students. **Monte Testaccio** is a reliable late-night destination for all orientations where the hillside is ringed with clubs spinning lounge or deep house. Throughout the summer, dozens of temporary bars and restaurants are set up along the Tiber, while some establishments close from June until August and relocate to the beaches in Ostia.

BARS AND PUBS

Mentioning Rome doesn't conjure up images of beer, but maybe it should. Peroni and Nastro Azzurro are the name-brand lagers but there's plenty of lesser-known craft beer worth sampling and plenty of places to drink it in. Some resemble Irish pubs and attract foreigners fond of familiarity, but a growing interest in brewing has inspired new locales where a beer can be properly savored. *Aperitivo* or happy hour at these establishments starts at 6pm and lasts a couple hours. Drinks come with finger food or a buffet that can often substitute dinner.

Ancient Rome

Looks are deceiving at the ★ **Race Club** (Via Labicana 52, tel. 06/9604-4048, www.theraceclubroma.org, daily 6pm-2am, cash only, €3 entry). This modern-day speakeasy could be mistaken for a garage, but once you've gotten past the motorcycles, paid the €3 membership fee, and walked downstairs, it's clear you've come to the right place. This underground lounge down the road from the Colosseum is a popular late-night haunt where you can order original cocktails and hard-to-find craft beers, then relax on cozy armchairs and listen to DJs or live performers entertain the fashion-conscious crowd.

Campo De' Fiori/ Piazza Navona

Anyone craving a Guinness can satisfy their thirst at the **Abbey Theatre** (Via del Governo Vecchio 51, tel. 06/686-1341, daily noon-2am). This cozy wood-paneled pub is fully equipped with Irish stouts and ales as well as some good bourbons. Flat-screen TVs make it an ideal place to watch *calcio* (soccer) or rugby.

Choosing a beer at **Open** (Via Degli Specchi 6, tel. 06/683-8989, daily noon-2am) isn't easy. The counter is lined with taps, and the wall behind the friendly bar staff is covered with bottled beers that prove Peroni and Nastro Azzuri aren't the only beers brewed in Italy. Whatever you choose, it can be enjoyed with thick burgers served all day long in the busy front room or cozier rear dining area.

The trio who opened **Argot** (Via dei Cappellari 93, tel. 339/269-7421, Tues.-Sun. 11pm-4am) aren't interested in sleek design or fashionable interiors. Their mantra is retro comfort and they succeeded in creating a quirky underground space where you can order unique cocktails, relax on vintage furniture, and listen to live music on weekends. The bar is popular with locals and visitors tired of the mundane bars around nearby Campo De' Fiori.

Circus (Via della Vetrina 15, tel. 06/9761-9258, daily 10am-2am) is a sprawling neighborhood bar with an informal interior that attracts a young crowd who surf the free Wi-Fi, browse the international papers scattered on the table in back, or just drink. The daily happy hour (6:30pm-9pm) is hard to beat, and €5 gets you the wine, beer, or cocktail of your choice along with a cutting board of cured cheeses and hams. Brunch (Sun. 11:30am-4:30pm, €15) is also good and includes familiar dishes like cupcakes, pancakes, and smoothies prepared Italian style.

Jerry Thomas Speakeasy (Vicolo Cellini 30, tel. 370/114-628, www.thejerrythomasproject.it, Tues.-Sat. 10pm-4am, no entry fee) makes some of the best cocktails in Rome. If you know the difference between single malt and blended whiskey, this is where to drink. Getting into this low-lit, cash-only joint with portraits of Al Capone on the wall and bearded barmen isn't so simple. You'll need to make a reservation the day before between 2pm and 6pm, memorize a password, and join the club (it's free). Yes, it's worth the effort.

Tridente

The crisp, cold beer on tap at **Antica Birreria Peroni** (Via S. Marcello 19, tel. 06/679-5310,

Mon.-Sat. noon-midnight) is perfect for washing down Tirolese dishes like sausage and sauerkraut. Drinkers are merry, and the proximity of the dark wooden tables increases the opportunity to socialize. It can get loud, however, so if you're searching for something intimate this is not the place.

Pint glasses filled to the rim, raucous bartenders, and loud pop music have made **Trinity College** (Via del Collegio Romano 6, tel. 06/678-6472, daily noon-3am) popular with locals and visitors alike. It's packed on the weekends when crowds overflow into the narrow streets and the small dance floor requires precision movements.

Freni e Frizioni (Via del Politeama 4/6, tel. 06/4549-7499, daily 6:30am-2am) in Trastevere is a popular bar with a large outdoor terrace where locals love to gather in the early evening. Getting a drink on a Friday night can be a challenge, but the crowd is festive and there's a good chance you'll have made some new friends by the time the night is over.

WINE BARS

The vineyards on the hillsides around Rome aren't as famous as their Tuscan cousins, but the volcanic soil provides distinctive flavor, and some craft wineries are beginning to distinguish themselves. Menus offer local, regional, and international vintages. Most *enoteche* (wine bars) in Rome also offer smoked meats and cheeses, and food only adds to the pleasure of a tasting.

Ancient Rome

La Barrique (Via del Boschetto 41b, tel. 06/4782-5953, Mon.-Sat. 12:30pm-3:30pm and 5:30pm-1am, closed Sat. lunch, €6-8) is a bare-bones wine bar with few distractions on the walls or the tables. The wine list changes frequently and unlike many places doesn't overwhelm with endless choices. It's divided into bubbly, white, red, and dessert wines that can be ordered by the glass, carafe, or bottle. Most of the selection is not aged and includes both single-grape and blended wines from very small Italian vineyards. Light snacks and a handful of dishes are also available.

Campo De' Fiori/ Piazza Navona

Do not go to ★ **Roscioli** (Via dei Giubbonari 21, tel. 06/687-5287, Mon.-Sat. 7am-7:30pm, €6-9) if it takes you a while to select wine. This deli/modern *trattoria* carries more than 2,800 bottles for takeaway and a fraction of that for immediate consumption. Getting a table at the counter, along the wine-covered wall, or in the back isn't always easy, but it's worth the wait. If you like to drink without the bustle, attend one of their wine-tasting dinners (www.winetastingrome.com, Tues.-Sat., €65) that includes 8 wines, 12 food pairings, pasta, and dessert. It lasts three mouthwatering hours and is hosted by a team of sommeliers.

Cul de Sac (Piazza di Pasquino 73, tel. 06/6880-1094, daily noon-midnight, €5-10) means "dead end" in French, and that's what this place feels like. It's one long corridor lined with bottles and wooden booths where tables are already set with wine glasses. That's a good sign, as is the little kitchen area at the front where cheese and cured meat plates are prepared. The wine list could take an entire evening to read but if you want to cut to the chase order the Barbera d'Asti Montalberra 2012.

Enoteca Corsi (Via del Gesu 88, tel. 06/679-0821, Mon.-Sat. noon-3:30pm and 5pm-8pm, €4-7) is an old-style wine bar with old-style prices. Nostalgia attracts a steady crowd who come for the daily menu of Roman specialties handwritten in chalk. They occasionally run out of some dishes if you arrive late for lunch, but they never run out of wine. Over three hundred bottles cover the back room from ceiling to floor, with just enough space for a lucky few to sit and admire labels from every region in Italy.

A glass of red at **Vineria** (Campo De' Fiori 15, tel. 06/6880-3268, Mon.-Sat. 9pm-1am, €4-10) is a must for many Romans. The choice of bottles is wide, and the recent renovation

hasn't affected the charm of the place. Tables overlooking the *piazza* are hard to come by. If you can snag one, savor it.

Casa Bleve (Via del Teatro 49, tel. 06/686-5970, www.casableve.it, Tues.-Sat. 12:30am-3pm and 7pm-11pm, €6-10) is more expensive than the average wine bar and not the kind of place in which you wear sandals and shorts. Wine is stored in a temperature-controlled cellar and the list is notable for its Lazio whites and Tuscan reds. You can sample those and other bottles from around the world at the bar or in the historic main dining room where a selection of appetizers and pasta dishes are served.

Tridente

Enoteca (Via della Croce 76b, tel. 06/679-0896, noon-1am) was around long before the area near the Spanish Steps was flooded with clothing boutiques. In fact, it's the perfect place to escape fashion and taste something timeless. The wood-beamed interior is larger than most wine bars, and you can sit at the long counter, in the elegant back room, or outside along the quiet side street. There are plenty of by-the-glass wine options and a menu that includes pizza.

Palatium (Via Frattina 94, tel. 06/6920-2132, Mon.-Sat 11am-11pm, €7-10) is the place to sample local dishes with local wines. Its central location and spacious, well-heeled interior make it popular with the after-work crowd.

LIVE MUSIC
Campo De' Fiori/ Piazza Navona

Piano bar enthusiasts won't want to miss a night at kitschy **Jonathan's Angels** (Via della Fossa 16, tel. 06/689-3426, daily, 4pm-3am). All tables will be taken unless you arrive early.

Tridente

Quirinetta (Tridente, Via Marco Minghetti 5, tel. 06/6992-5616, www.quirinetta.com) isn't quite underground, but it gets pretty close. With live shows most nights of the week, it's a regular stop for indie Italian and European bands with names like Amycanbe, Zibba, and O.R.K. The venue is small, and it's easy to get close to the stage or just enjoy the music from the bar. They also host a regular Sunday vintage market.

Vaticano

Alexanderplatz (Via Ostia 9, tel. 06/3972-1867, daily 8pm-1am) is the club of reference for Roman jazz musicians and one of the oldest in the city. Established players appear nightly in solo and combo arrangements. The club itself is dark and gritty, with photographs and autographs of past greats on the walls. Concerts start at 10pm and a cover is often charged. A select menu is also available.

The Place (Via Alberico II 27, tel. 06/6830-7137, Tues.-Sun. 8pm-3am) vibrates with funk, Latin, and R&B. The reputation for good music is deserved, and visitors should definitely seize the opportunity to enjoy live acts while dining on creative Mediterranean cuisine. The Place is one of larger clubs in the city, with a stage that can fit a small orchestra and audiences that watch from two long rows of tables.

Trastevere

For over twenty years, **Big Mama** (Vicolo S. Francesco a Ripa 18, tel. 06/581-2551, Tues.-Sun. 9pm-1:30am) has been an authentic home for top jazz and blues musicians searching for a groove in Trastevere. The small club is the most likely place to find a jam session in Rome.

Aventino and Testaccio

Casa del Jazz (Viale di Porta Ardeatina 55, tel. 06/704-731, www.casajazz.it) was converted from a mobster's villa to a permanent home for jazz. It now regularly hosts local and international musicians in a 100-seat hall and the outdoor stage on summer evenings. There's a bookshop and bar where a jazz trio accompanies the Sunday all-you-can-eat brunch (€25), held in the restaurant's tranquil garden.

The chances of hearing some variation of rock or jazz are about equal at **Villaggio Globale** (Lungotevere Testaccio 1, tel. 06/5730-0329). This alternative cultural space presents frequent live events within a former slaughterhouse. Show up early if you want to stand near the stage.

Further Afield

Don't let Northeastern Rome's distance from the center put you off. The neighborhood is on the rise and clubs and restaurants are now replacing the factories and warehouses that once operated in the area. **Lanificio 159** (Via di Pietralata 159, tel. 06/4178-0081, www.lanificio.com, daily 9am-4am) is one of the most interesting. This multifaceted cultural center with eating, learning, exhibition, and performing spaces is located in a converted wool mill. The music area on the ground floor is largely dedicated to electronic and experimental sounds and is a popular destination for Roman clubbers. The restaurant and bar are open daily for lunch and dinner, and the weekend brunch makes the journey worthwhile.

CLUBS

If you're searching for a party in Rome, you'll find it. The city's clubs present a range of scenes. Monday nights are generally slow, Thursdays are up-tempo, and weekends always pull in a crowd. Whatever your style is, you're likely to hear it. You can also discover a new genre spun by one of the Italian or international DJs who liven up the city's nocturnal hours. During the summer many clubs relocate to the beaches of Ostia where the dancing is done in the sand. Many bars also have a house DJ and straddle the bar-disco divide. The slightly secluded hillside around Monte Testaccio is where a lot of the capital's clubbing is concentrated, and lines start forming from 11pm. Dress codes are casual by Italian standards, which are higher than most other countries.

Campo De' Fiori/ Piazza Navona

La Maison (Vicolo dei Granari 4, tel. 06/683-3312, Tues.-Sun. 11pm-4am) is home to glamour, made clear by the vintage theater interior adorned with velvet and crystal. Sunday nights with DJ Flavia Lazzarini and artistic direction by Marco Longo make finding this place worthwhile. Playlists vary from commercial to reggae with a heavy dose of experimental thrown into the mix.

Tridente

Don't miss an evening mixing with beautiful people beneath the vaulted ceilings of the **Micca Club** (Via degli Avignonesi 73, 393/323-6244, www.miccaclub.com). A small stage hosts regular musical events and burlesque shows. Weekends reverberate with lounge and chill-out music spun by guest DJs.

Gilda (Via Mario de Fiori 97, tel. 06/678-4838, daily noon-3am) is an old-school disco where neckties outnumber nose rings. The crowd is mature, and paparazzi are on the prowl for players, politicians, and showgirls.

Eat, drink, and dance on a two-story boat moored on the Tiber at **Baja** (Lungotevere A. da Brescia, tel. 06/94368869, daily 5pm-midnight), a floating party with an underground feel. Happy hour is from 7pm to 9pm, and the restaurant serves food until late.

Aventino and Testaccio

Night owls will feel at home within **Akab's** (Via Monte Testaccio 69, tel. 06/5725-0585, Thurs.-Sat. 11:30pm-5am,) two floors of minimalist décor in Testaccio. The dancing is done to upbeat sounds with a heavy synth flavor (Saturday) as well as hip-hop (Thursday) and reggae. Live performances are frequent. **Caffè Latino** (Via Monte Testaccio 96, tel. 06/578-2411, Tues.-Sun. 10:30pm-3am), also in Testaccio, is a laid-back music café where DJ sets alternate between rock, soul, and jazz. Sunday is dedicated to Latin America.

Hip-hop and house are the bread and butter of **Alpheus** (Via del Commercio 36, tel. 06/574-7826, 10pm-4am Tues.-Sun.).

Partygoers alternate between four dance floors, while the garden is reserved for fresh air and conversation. Live rock is also frequently played.

For house and techno head to **Goa** (Via Libetta 13, tel. 06/574-8277, daily 8pm-4am). Thursday night Ultra Beat hosted by one of the six resident DJs is a sure bet for a good time, as is the late-afternoon party on Sundays.

Termini

Rimini mixed with Ibiza equals tribal house harmony at **Alien** (Via Velletri 13, tel. 06/841-2212, Tues.-Sun. 11pm-4am). The large space is filled with a youthful crowd spread across several dance floors.

PERFORMING ARTS

Culture is king in Rome, and there is no shortage of high-quality music, dance, and theater experiences available each week. Many standout venues exist. The city attracts international artists of the finest caliber performing in front of audiences who know when to applaud.

Music and Dance

Modern architecture and music harmonize at the **Parco della Musica** (Viale De Coubertin 30, tel. 06/802-411, www.auditorium.com). Rome's main music venue showcases the world's best classical, jazz, and contemporary performers on three world-class stages. The three Renzo Piano-designed halls resemble metallic whales beached in the north of Rome. The auditorium regularly hosts classical, contemporary, and experimental performances of all types. Acoustic connoisseurs will appreciate the modular wooden ceilings, which are adjusted according to the genre of music performed. The outdoor amphitheater holds summertime concerts and the restaurant/bar and café complement any evening.

The Orchestra Sinfonica di Rome performs regularly at the **Auditorium della Conciliazione** (Via della Conciliazione 4, tel. 06/684-391). Guest conductors and international soloists often join them in an eclectic symphonic program.

Teatro dell'Opera (Via Firenze 62, tel. 06/481-601, €10-100) may not be as famous as La Fenice in Venice, but the lavish interior and persistently good productions will thrill both eyes and ears. The season runs from November to January and generally includes the classics performed the way their creators intended them to be. During the summer the stage moves to the baths of Caracalla, giving performances an entirely different dimension. A resident ballet company also performs within the opera house.

Teatro Olimpico (Piazza Gentile da Fabriano, tel. 06/320-1752) presents modern dance, ballet, and orchestral music. The theater is the permanent home of the Filarmonica, who give one performance per week during the musical season.

Teatro del Vascello (Via G. Carini 72, tel. 06/588-1021) is committed to contemporary dance. Companies like Momix and Merce Cunningham have performed here in the past. Lesser-known names are given the chance to experiment, and the RomaEuropa festival uses the theater as one of its venues. Outdoor performances occur during the summer.

Classic productions are staged at **Teatro Argentina** (Largo Argentina 56, tel. 06/6840-00311), which inherited an opera house interior and is one of the few permanent theater companies in the city. Famous Italian actors often make their debuts here. The **Eliseo** (Via Nazionale 183, tel. 06/474-3431) and the **Piccolo Eliseo,** its sister theater next door, are as close as Rome gets to Broadway. Musicals and farce are regularly posted on the marquee outside.

Shakespeare liked Italy so much he set many of his plays here. So it's no surprise to find a reconstruction of the **Globe Theater** (Largo Aqua Felix, tel. 06/0808) in Villa Borghese. It regularly presents the Bard's work in both English and Italian. Open-air comic performances are held from July to September at the **Anfiteatro Quercia del Tasso** (Passeggiata del Gianicolo, tel. 06/575-0827)

and at the nearby Neapolitan puppet booth, which fascinates kids.

Cinema

Movies cost around €8 in Rome and are often discounted on Wednesdays. Some theaters show films in their original language, but most are dubbed—providing you an opportunity to see *Star Wars* in Italian.

Time Elevator (Via dei S.S. Apostoli 20, Piazza Venezia, tel. 06/6992-1823, daily 10:30am-7:30pm) projects films in 5-D. Besides the usual three dimensions there are moving seats and multisensory effects. Films include one on the foundation and growth of Rome, which puts the city into instant historical perspective.

Movies are projected in *v.o.* (original version) at the **Alcazar** (Via Merry del Val 14, tel. 06/588-0099), **Pasquino** (Vicolo del Piede 19, tel. 06/580-3622), and **Greenwich** (Via G. Bodoni, 59, tel. 06/574-5825). All three are independently owned and operated, which means the popcorn tastes better and isn't overpriced.

The **Nuovo Sacher** (Largo Ascianghi 1, tel. 06/581-8116) was the idea of an Italian director fed up with the films shown in most chain cinemas. Its single screen is dedicated to art rather than happy endings. They also project films outside in the summer.

Art Galleries

Living up to Michelangelo's legacy isn't easy, but Rome's contemporary artists are constantly finding new ways of expressing themselves. The art scene has experienced a revival in recent years, and new galleries have opened to meet the demand of a growing number of collectors. To find out exactly what's going on in the Roman art world pick up a copy of **Art/Guide,** which publishes a monthly list of events, exhibitions, and gallery locations. It's available at all tourist information points.

Il Gabbiano (Via delle Frezze 51, tel. 06/322-7049, Mon.-Sun. 10am-1pm and 4:30pm-7:30pm) shows many veteran artists and tends to concentrate on painting done on non-canvas materials like cardboard or wood.

Experimental video, photography, and some less traditional means of expression are on exhibit at **LaPortaBlu Gallery** (Arco degli Acetari 40, tel. 06/687-4822, Tues.-Sun. 5pm-8pm). Nearby **Magazzino d'Arte Moderno** (Via dei Prefetti 17, tel. 06/687-5951, www. magazzinoartemoderna.com, Tues.-Sun. 11am-3pm and 4pm-8pm) continually pushes the envelope with one-artist shows that leave an impression.

Altri Lavori in Corso (Vicolo del Governo Vecchio 7, tel. 06/686-1719, www.altrilavori-incorso.com, daily 5pm-8pm) spotlights international artists working in Rome. Appointments for private visits can be made. **AAM** (Via dei Banchi Vecchi 61, 1st Fl., tel. 06/6830-7537, daily 4pm-8pm) mixes architecture and art-inspired work from the likes of Roberto Caracciolo and Alan Fletcher. Established artists like Tracey Emin entrust their creative juices to **Lorcan O'Neill** (Via Orti d'Alibert 1e, tel. 06/6889-2980, daily noon-8pm).

If you prefer street art and murals in particular, the Ostiense neighborhood has become a hub for artists with an urban edge. There are giant murals covering walls along Via del Gazometro and many of the intersecting streets nearby.

FESTIVALS AND EVENTS

Rome has a rich calendar of cultural, sporting, and religious events that can make a trip even more memorable. Some, like the marathon or summer opera series, require registration or tickets; others like the Easter festivities and anniversary of Rome celebrations are free to attend.

Spring

Pilgrims flock to the city's basilicas during **Easter,** following the Procession of the Cross at 9pm to the Colosseum on Good Friday and attending the pope's Sunday morning mass outside St. Peter's.

For two weeks starting in mid-May, Via dei Coronari rolls out the red carpet, candles are lit, and banners fly. It's time for the **Antiques Fair,** when the dealers who occupy nearly every shop on the street bring out their best merchandise and prospective buyers put on their poker faces.

Rome celebrates its birthday every year on April 21. Concerts and cultural events are organized in the Circus Maximus to honor

A historical reenactment celebrates the anniversary of the city's foundation on April 21.

the legendary **anniversary of the city's foundation** in AD 753. The highlight is the historic reenactments charting ancient Rome's rise to greatness and the defeat of its enemies. Hundreds of costumed enthusiasts play the part of battle-ready centurions and their barbarian foes. Spectators surround the mock battlefield and afterward you can get up close to the warriors, who prefer to remain in character.

Summer

Summer brings entertainment and art to unexpected places around Rome. An outdoor cinema projects films nightly on the Isola Tiberina, world-renowned authors recite their works in the Forum, and concerts are held in the Circus Maximus. Bars and restaurants are also installed along the Tiber River and remain open until late.

Throughout the summer, Terme di Caracalla becomes the backdrop for the **Rome Opera Summer Series** (www.operaroma.it) from late June until the middle of August. Classics like *Aida* and *Madame Butterfly* are performed within the ancient baths. Tickets range from €20 to €90 and can be purchased online or at the Teatro di Roma box office in Piazza Beniamino Gigli 7.

According to legend, it snowed heavily in Rome on the August 5 in AD 352. Since then, with little interruption, the **Festa della Madonna delle Neve** (tel. 06/6988-6800) has been held at Santa Maria Maggiore. Crowds gather throughout the day and white petals are thrown from the dome of the cathedral during an outdoor evening liturgy.

The **Jazz Festival** (tel. 06/0608) in the Villa Celimontana gardens presents two months of nightly concerts in one of Rome's most beautiful parks, moments from the Colosseum. Prices rarely exceed €15 and the intimate outdoor amphitheater is bordered by an assortment of bars and restaurants.

Ferragosto is the midsummer Italian holiday originally created to honor Emperor Augustus in 8 BC. It takes place on August 15 every year and many Romans leave the city and head for the beach or countryside. Many restaurants and bars close for a week or two at this time and traffic is greatly reduced.

Fall

In mid-November, cinema stars walk down the red carpet during the **Festival Internazionale del Film di Roma** (www.romacinemafest.it). The festival is held in the Auditorium della Musica and has proved quite popular since its debut in 2006. If you are interested in catching a world premiere, book ahead because tickets (€10-20) sell out quickly.

Throughout November and December, the **RomaEuropa Festival** (www.romaeuropa.net) presents avant-garde music and dance in venues around the city. Artists come from all over the world and provide a snapshot of the latest cultural innovations. Tickets cost €15-37 and performances are exuberant and full of innovative ideas.

Winter

Romans get into the Christmas spirit in early December and traditionally put up their trees on the 8th, the day of the feast of the Immaculate Conception. Markets sell sweets and traditional decorations throughout the month in Piazza Navona and sellers of roasted chestnuts can be found on many street corners.

Italian children look forward to the arrival of **La Befana,** a witch-like figure who rides a broomstick and brings candy to the good and coal to the bad on January 6. The carousel (€2) in Piazza Navona operates throughout December and January, and gives parents a chance to treat children before schools reconvene.

Confetti-strewn streets are a signal that **Carnevale** is near. The other more edible indication are the *frappe* (thin strips of fried or baked dough covered in sugar), which appear in bars and bakeries from late January until *Martedi Grasso* (Mardi Gras) and pair perfectly with cappuccino. Each of the city's neighborhoods organizes events that take place in larger squares like Piazza Navona and

Piazza del Popolo. The **Bioparco di Roma** (www.bioparco.it) prepares a children's carnival on the Saturday before Mardi Gras with an animal parade and face painting.

The number of joggers increases after New Year's Eve, but that doesn't necessarily have to do with resolutions. Many are preparing for the **Rome Marathon** (www.maratonadiroma.it), which takes place at the end of March or early April. Over 20,000 runners participate and the start and finish line is next to the Colosseum. If you don't feel like running the entire 42 kilometers you can register for the 5-kilometer fun run.

Rugby fans can catch the **Six Nations** tournament at the Stadio Olimpico. There are two or three matches every year, taking place on Sunday afternoons in February and March. The Italian national team faces off against England, France, Wales, Scotland, and Ireland. Win or lose there's a great ambience between fans before, during, and after the match, and unlike soccer games where opposing supporters are divided the seating at rugby is mixed.

Shopping

While Florence has leather and Venice has glass, Rome doesn't really have a standout shopping specialty. Still, there are many opportunities to be enticed by high and low fashion, shoes, accessories, antiques, art, home goods, and oddities. If you're searching for something unique, you'll find it, as skilled hands are at work across the city. A handmade shirt, earrings, or panoramic watercolors make nice souvenirs of the city.

Shops are scattered around the historic center but there are some streets with a high concentration of international chains, boutiques, and specialty stores that attract large numbers of shoppers. The pedestrianized **Via del Corso** is the main shopping drag with a succession of international chain stores. Higher-end brands cluster along **Via Condotti** and the surrounding streets near Piazza di Spagna. Antiques can be found along **Via dei Coronari** in the Navona area, while handicraft workshops and small galleries are scattered around **Campo De' Fiori.** Each neighborhood has its own markets, and the city's biggest flea market, **Porta Portese,** is held every Sunday in Testaccio.

ANCIENT ROME AND MONTI

The shops that once lined Trajan's Forum went out of business a long time ago. Today, the sales continue behind those ruins in Monti, which competes with Trastevere and Testaccio for the title of most Roman neighborhood. There is something a little edgier here though and the boutiques aren't run of the mill. You'll find young designers and old-timers carrying on ancient crafts inside narrow storefronts.

Via Urbana is one of the Monti neighborhood's characteristic thoroughfares. Here, artisans and merchants go about their business with no concern for the Colosseum. It lies parallel to the souvenir shops and tourist traps of **Via Cavour,** but feels miles away. The cobblestoned street, which locals petitioned to have pedestrianized, follows a gentle incline and is dotted with boutiques, workshops, eateries, barbers, and jewelry stores. It isn't very long but may lead to backtracking and can easily absorb an hour or two.

Arts and Crafts

Silver and gold are the ingredients in nearly every object within **Longobardi** (Via dei Fienili 43, tel. 06/678-1104, Mon. 3:30pm-7:30pm, Tues.-Sat. 9:30am-7:30pm). Most of the handcrafted tableware, frames, and jewelry are produced in Italy. The shop gets its name from the owner, who is always willing to discuss his favorite topic: the history of Rome. Tourists can be reluctant to enter the elegant shop but there's no pushiness to buy inside and you can browse as long as you like.

Inside **Silice** (Via Urbana 27, tel. 06/474-5552, Mon.-Sat. 10am-7pm) Anna Preziosi cuts glass and carefully puts it into place. She doesn't use a blowing technique; instead, she works with plate sheets that she melts in an oven at the back of her studio workshop. Lamps and decorative pieces are displayed in the front room and temptingly priced. She'll be happy to explain her process and show you around.

Books

Don't judge **IBS** (Via Nazionale 254, tel. 06/488-5405, Mon.-Sat. 9am-8pm and Sun. 10am-1:30pm) by the entrance. The nondescript front doors lead to a palatial hall filled with every category of book imaginable. Used books are in the basement, travel and fiction on the ground floor, and design and architecture are next to the bar on the second. There are a few shelves of the latest best sellers in English if you need something to read on the way to Venice.

Clothing and Accessories

Handbags, handbags, and more handbags are what you'll find displayed at **Alexia** (Via Nazionale 76, tel. 06/488-4890). Fendissime, Coccinelle, and Moschino are just a few of the brands competing for the attention of prospective buyers across two floors. Like many of the shops along Via Nazionale this one attracts tourists, and the friendly sales team have had a lot of opportunities to practice their English.

Vintage may have gone out of fashion in some cities but it's still available at **King Size Vintage** (Via del Boschetto 94, tel. 06/481-7045, daily 11am-8:30pm). This small and well-organized one-room shop sells men's and women's secondhand shirts, dresses, shoes, and accessories dating from the 1940s to the 1990s. They have a good selection of leather jackets as well as sneakers from yesteryear. It's located near the center of Monti and many good browsing opportunities.

M.A.S. (Via dello Statuto 11, tel. 06/4938-3011, daily 9am-12:35pm and 3:45pm-7:45pm) is a discount store where it's possible to spend next to nothing for a new wardrobe. Granted, the quality is low, but the two immense floors of men's, women's, and children's clothing are crammed with everything from underwear to overcoats that will leave bargain hunters breathless. Everyone once in a while they have a going-out-of-business sale but always somehow manage to hang in there.

Shoes

If you like the idea of a shoe that breathes, then **Geox** (Via Nazionale 232, tel. 06/481-4518, daily 10am-8pm) is just the thing. This ever-expanding franchise produces patented casual and elegant models renowned for comfort and durability. There's something for both men and women, and they design a new line of fashionable footwear every season. U.S. sizes are indicated and they've recently branched out into accessories and jackets. Prices range from €80 to €120.

Markets

The **Monti Urban Market** (Grand Hotel Palatino, Via Leonina 46, Sept.-June Sat.-Sun. 10am-8pm) is held in a hotel. It's not kitsch, just comfortable and friendly with lots of interesting stands. Merchants are part of an extended family that encourages new talents like **Annabella Cuomo,** who paints engaging illustrations on T-shirts, and the **COSMOOS** collective, who create one-of-a-kind jewelry out of natural stones and noble metals. There are scores of tables to scan and clothes racks to consider.

CAMPO DE' FIORI/ PIAZZA NAVONA

These virtually chain-free neighborhoods are full of original clothing and jewelry boutiques. **Via dei Giubbonari** is lined with shops from Piazza dei Fiori to Via Arenula. Anyone interested in antiques can get their fill along **Via dei Coronari.** If you prefer your art fresh from the easel, the artists in **Piazza**

Navona paint oil and watercolors canvases fit to be framed. **Via del Governo Vecchio** is a long, gently winding street dotted with hip shops that don't attract the crowds of Via del Corso. It's a perfect stroll on a hot afternoon.

Antiques

The number of antiques stores are especially high around Campo De' Fiori, and Via dei Coronari is the center of the trade. Don't expect bargains, and don't hesitate to negotiate if the price seems exorbitant. For a break from the baroque furnishings that dominate many shops try **Antiquariato Valligiano** (Via Giulia 193, tel. 06/686-9505, daily 10:30am-2pm and 4:30pm-7:30pm). It's a sure place to find objects descended from 19th-century farmhouses.

If you're after limited-edition books, prints, and paintings from past centuries, then **Antiquaria Sant'Angelo** (Via del Banco di S. Spirito, tel. 06/686-5944, Mon.-Fri. 10am-1pm and 4pm-8pm) is bound to oblige. This well-furnished store opposite Ponte Sant'Angelo even has a selection of antique frames.

Arts and Crafts

Art is good for the eyes and a small painting or photograph is a good souvenir start. There are dozens of **street painters** in Piazza Navona and at the top of the Spanish Steps filling canvases with images of Rome. Some artists sell reproductions, while others paint lovely streetscapes themselves. Prices aren't exorbitant and usually worth the effort.

The contents of **Laboratorio Marani** (Via di Monte Giordano 27, tel. 06/6830-7866) are all covered with a light coat of white powder. That's the price to pay for working with plaster and creating antique sculpture imitations that are hard to distinguish from the originals. The workshop is continually creating new objects, and it's worth taking a moment to observe how they do it.

The best souvenirs aren't for sale, they're self-made. That could mean filling a glass vial with water from the Fontana di Trevi, creating a collage from receipts and ticket stubs, or making charcoal rubbings from ancient inscriptions. It could also mean making random recordings while traveling around the city or just keeping a diary. If you need pen and paper or any art materials **Poggi** (Piazza Navona, Via del Gesù 74-75, tel. 06/679-3674, Mon.-Sat. 9am-2pm and 3pm-7:30pm) has been supplying writers and painters since 1825. The shop is crammed

outdoor market of Campo de' Fiori

with art supplies and everything else you need to assist inspiration.

Books

How places like **Il Museo del Louvre** (Via della Reginella 28, tel. 06/6880-7725, Mon.-Fri. 10am-8pm) stay in business is a delightful mystery. This combination gallery and secondhand bookstore specializes in Italian literature and no doubt has a loyal following of readers. A signed edition of Neruda is kept under glass and costs €1,200. Next door is a collection of 20,000 photographs organized by subject and crammed with anonymous shots of everyday Rome from the 1960s to the present day as well as works by celebrated photographers.

Feltrinelli (Largo di Torre Argentina 5a, Mon.-Fri. 9am-9pm, Sat. 9am-10pm, Sun. 10am-9pm) is the Italian version of Barnes & Noble with better coffee and fewer sofas. They also carry music, and if you've never listened to an Italian singer before the staff can fix that. Find CDs for under €6, including music from the legendary Mina, singer-songwriters like the late Lucio Dalla, aging rockers of the Vasco Rossi and Luciano Ligabue variety, sophisticated songs by Manika Ayan, and Jovanotti's Italian pop. There are several branches around the city but this is the largest.

Clothing and Accessories

Strategic Business Unit (Via di Pantaleo 68, tel. 06/6880-2547, Mon.-Sat. 10am-7:30pm) doesn't sound like it would create comfortable men's clothing, but the originators of this Roman label obviously have a sense of irony as well as a talent for designing sportswear in a variety of fabrics.

There are three boutiques at one at **Civico 93** (Via del Governo Vecchio 72-93, tel. 06/687-6572). Each carries its own style of women's clothhiung, starting at casual and moving to elegant. Clothes are on the minimal side and the brands are primarily Italian names including Mezzo, Diva, and Rossodisera.

Sirni (Via della Stelletta 33, tel. 06/6880-5248, Mon.-Sat. 10am-7:30pm) sells pizzazz you can carry. Their bags are all created from high-quality leather that's transformed into every size and shape imaginable. If you don't find what you're looking for on the shelves it can be ordered and sent to your home.

Getting a handmade shirt may sound extravagant, but it is made accessible at men's shops like **Camiceria Bracci** (Via dei Funari 18 and Via delle Coppelle 73, tel. 06/6476-0440, Mon.-Sat. 10am-7:30pm, €50). The made-to-measure products provide another level of comfort and confidence. It will take a little longer than buying off the rack and requires you to learn about collar types, thread thickness, and cotton quality, but once you do it's hard to go back. Clerks are patient with newcomers and they'll file your details so you can reorder whenever you like.

Laura Tonatto (Piazza di Pietra 41, tel. 06/6979-7625, Tues.-Sat. 10:30am-7:30pm, Sun. 3pm-7:30pm, Mon. 3:30pm-7:30pm) will satisfy the nose. Her perfume shop is a mix of ancient and modern where knowledgeable staff guides clients through shelves of niche scents and historic brands for body and home. Her Rome-inspired perfumes *Magnolia Romana* by Eau d'Italie and *Roma* by Laura Biagiotti are sold in distinctive bottles and available for men and women in most beauty stores.

Shoes

A peek into **Alex Shoes** (Via del Governo Vecchio, tel. 06/6813-9447, Mon.-Sat. 10:30am-8pm and Sun. 11:30pm-7:30pm) will raise spirits. This tiny shop carries women's and men's casual and dress shoes that go with everything. Prices aren't out of reach and the salespeople are happy to serve.

Mauro Leon (Via del Biscione 8, tel. 06/6880-4918, Tues.-Sat. 10:30am-7:30pm, Sun.-Mon. 2:30pm-7:30pm) is an Italian brand with an extensive collection of men's and mostly women's shoes. The shop is tiny and many models are in the back room. If you see something appealing in the window just point to it and ask for your size.

If you forgot your favorite shoes or the ones you did pack are no match for the cobblestones of Rome, **Totem** (Via della Maddalena 45, tel. 06/6978-1701) can help. There are flats and high heels of all styles and descriptions. The shop offers proof that style and comfort can coexist.

Housewares

Lela (Via dei Pettinari 37, tel. 06/8777-5792, Mon.-Sat. 10:30am-7:30pm) sells Nordic and Italian household goods in an inviting one-room shop near the Ponte Sisto bridge. The friendly owner and charming selection make this a fun place to browse and a perfect place to find small gifts. Wooden items are on display along with glass carafes, colorful tin mugs, and honey-scented candles at reasonable prices.

Leather

Leather isn't as closely associated with Rome as it is with Florence, but you can still find places like **Mancini** (Via della Palombella 28, tel. 06/686-1485, daily 10:30am-7:30pm) where they've been making leather bags, wallets, and belts since 1918. There's a wide range of traditional luggage and briefcases that come in many colors. Prices reflect the handmade quality of the products, and a small handbag can easily cost €200.

Toys

Three shops in the vicinity of Piazza Navona will please both parents and kids, though it's a challenge to leave each one empty handed. **Al Sogno** (Piazza Navona 53, tel. 06/686-4198, daily 10am-8pm) is just off the famous square. Inside, it's hard to decide what mask, puppet, car, sword, or medieval pistol to grab first. Many items are wrapped and the most realistic toy soldiers are safely behind glass, but the salespeople are relaxed and touching is allowed.

Berte (Piazza Navona 107, tel. 06/687-5011, daily 9:30am-9pm) is a classic toy store with

wooden dollhouses and all the accessories to inspire young imaginations. There are lots of huggable teddy bears, expressive dolls, and wooden construction kits. They also carry original costumes in the run-up to Halloween and *Carnivale*.

If your offspring aren't into traditional toys, just walk out of Piazza Navona and zigzag over to **Città del Sole** (Via della Scrofa 65, tel. 06/6880-3805, Mon.-Sat. 10am-7:30pm, Sun. 11am-7:30pm). This ecofriendly toy chain fosters creative play. Plenty of wood and educational items are in stock and ready to try along with art supplies, musical instruments, board games, outdoor activities, books, and a fun assortment of safe gadgets for children under three.

Markets

Activity goes on at all hours in Campo De' Fiori. During the day, the square fills with stalls selling flowers, vegetables, and knick-knacks that attract locals and visitors in search of souvenirs.

Herbs aren't generally the first item on a shopping list, but that may change after a visit to **Antica Erboristeria Romana** (Via Torre Argentina 15, tel. 06/687-9493, daily 9:30am-7:30pm). This emporium of dried plants has been selling spices since 1752. Noses will be grateful for a sniff.

TRIDENTE

Tridente is the most glamorous place to shop in Rome. It's primarily about women's clothing, though men are catered to as well. The neighborhood epicenter of high fashion is **Via Condotti,** while other shopping is concentrated along **Via del Corso.** The parallel pedestrian streets are filled with boutiques and megastores from Armani to Zara.

Antiques

It's getting harder and harder to spot an antiques shop along Via Babuina, but **Turchi** (Via Margutta 91a, tel. 06/323-5047, Mon.-Fri. 10am-7pm and Sat. 10am-1pm) is one of the remaining pillars of the trade. The father-and-son institution is all about ancient statues that can be thousands of years old and cost many times that. Most items aren't allowed out of the country and museum curators from around the world covet those that are. Large groups are dissuaded from entering the dimly lit shop but serious visitors are always welcome.

Everything at **Apolloni** (Via del Babuino 133, tel. 06/3600-2216, Mon.-Sat 9:30am-1pm and 3:30pm-7:30pm) was made in Italy hundreds of years ago. Furniture, paintings, and silver are in impeccable condition and mostly date from the 18th century.

Arts and Crafts

Silvio is a remnant of a lost age. Most days you'll find him inside **Il Marmaro** (Via Margutta 53b, tel. 320-7660, Mon.-Sat. 9am-7:30pm) engraving stone or stirring his soup on an open fire. He's been doing both for decades. The little marble plaques displayed in the basket by the window are a unique souvenir. They come with short epithets (€15) or can be personalized with the words of your choosing (€20) in under an hour.

Clothing and Accessories

It takes talent and hard work for a name to become synonymous with style. Just ask Ennio Capasa, who has transformed **CoSTUME NATIONAL** (Via del Babuino 106, tel. 06/6920-0686) into a premier avant-garde label. Celebrity clients swear by the his-and-hers lines that include hard-to-resist accessories.

Zeis House (Piazza del Popolo 21, tel. 06/324-0908, Mon.-Fri. 9am-8pm and Sat. 10am-7pm) puts sneakers on the pedestal they deserve. Trendy brands like Merrell, Dutch, and Bikkembergs all compete for your feet's attention.

If *Breakfast at Tiffany's* had been filmed in Rome it would have been called *Breakfast at Bulgari's* (Via dei Condotti 10, tel. 06/679-3876, Tues.-Sat. 10:30am-7pm). This jewelry institution founded by a Greek immigrant has been adorning women since 1884 with timeless designs. Don't be intimidated—pretend you're Hepburn or Peppard and have a look.

There comes a time when you have to declare your soccer loyalty and reveal your team colors. If you make the popular choice you'll support AS Roma, but before you buy a cheap acrylic jersey hanging from an outdoor souvenir kiosk check out the authentic uniforms, scarves, and gadgets available at the **AS Roma Store** (Piazza Colonna, tel. 06/679-3591, daily 10am-7:30pm). Prices are higher for official merchandise but you're more likely to find proper sizes and the latest home and away kits.

Nau (Via del Corso 100, tel. 06/6992-4828, daily 10am-7:30pm) makes it possible to get a stylish pair of prescription eyeglasses or sunglasses for under €100. There are scores of models to try inside this colorful chain store where frames are made from recycled plastic and all the designs are Italian.

Housewares

The scent of pastries and sweet Roman air can't be bottled, but some smells can be reproduced—and coffee is number one among these. It's brewed differently in Rome and the steam coming out of a **moka** filled with distinct Arabica blend will rekindle images of street-side terraces and busy neighborhood bars. You'll find all sorts and sizes of coffeemakers at **Bialetti** (Largo Chigi 4, tel. 06/8927-6836, daily 10am-8:30pm) that can be easily used at home.

Malls and Department Stores

Galleria Alberto Sordo (Via del Corso 79, tel. 06/6919-0769, Mon.-Sat. 8:30am-9pm, Sun. 9:30am-9pm), an indoor gallery with glass ceilings and wonderful mosaics, was inaugurated in 1922 and is as elegant as ever. Inside, there's a toy shop, bookstore, Zara, and department store. Two bars supply light snacks and **Illy** is the one for coffee. **Imaginarium** (Galleria Alberto Sordi, daily 10am-8pm) is a stimulating stop for kids and the place to find quality games, building kits, and instruments.

Shoes

Aldo (Via del Corso 162, tel. 06/6992-4803, daily 10am-9pm) is a haven for shoe-happy shoppers and often crowded. Quality varies, but for a reasonable price women get a pair of flats or pumps that won't fall apart after the first pothole.

Not all Italian shoes have heels. **Superga** (Via Della Vite 86, tel. 06/678-7654, Tues.-Sat. 10:30am-7:30pm, Sun.-Mon. 2:30pm-7:30pm) makes casual street sneakers for men and women that regularly come into and out of fashion. Whatever the fad, they are comfortable for walking and very colorful, like an Italian Converse without the branding.

If you're not ready for the stiletto edge of fashion, stay away from **Michele di Loco** (Via del Leone 7, tel. 06/4547-9103, Tues.-Sat. 10am-7:30pm, Sun. 11am-7:30pm. Mon. 3:30pm-7:30pm). The selection is small and occasionally outrageous, but the craftsmanship is undeniable and so are the prices.

Markets

If you're searching for magazine covers of Sophia Loren or old Piranesi prints of 17th-century Rome, **Mercato delle Stampe** (Largo delle Fontanella di Borghese, Mon.-Sat. 7am-1pm) is your jackpot. Everything here looks as though it would be the perfect addition to that blank wall back home.

Kitsch, curiosities, and the occasional gem are reason enough to visit **Il Mercatino del Borghetto** (Piazza della Marina 32, Sun. 10am-7pm). This flea market housed in a former bus depot is more about quantity than quality, but there are bargains to be had.

A **vintage market** (Via Marco Minghetti 5, tel. 06/6992-5616, 11am-8pm) is held indoors in a small theater on the third Sunday of every month. It's a big rummage sale of a market with some interesting stalls featuring young designers, couture classics, and used vinyl, books, and art.

VATICANO

Shopping is a religion to some, so it's no surprise to find stores in the shadow of St. Peter's.

Via Cola di Renzo houses the majority of these, including a branch of the Coin department store. The lack of parks means the best place to take a break from spending is inside one of the historic cafes that line this busy street.

Arts and Crafts

Italia Garipoli (Borgo Vittorio 91, tel. 06/6880-2196) makes it clear that clear embroidery is an art form. Intricate patterns on napkins, tablecloths, and handkerchiefs make you wonder how they did it. (The answer is decades of practice and a steady hand.)

Small, very small, and even smaller mosaics are created at **Savelli** (Via Paolo VI 27, tel. 06/6830-7017, Mon.-Sat. 9:30am-6:30pm, Sun. 9:30am-2pm). Find out how these little gems are made by having a look in the studio, where an assortment of religious objects are also under construction.

Books

There are two kinds of Roman readers: Those that prefer buying their books at Feltrinelli, and those that only shop at **Mondadori** (Piazza Cola di Rienzo 81, tel. 06/322-0188, daily 9am-10pm). Find out what kind you are at this large megastore with an extensive English section.

Clothing and Accessories

Before you buy a bag anywhere else check **Maxim** (Via Ottaviano 17, tel. 06/3972-3718). Popular labels like Coccinelle, Nannini, and Biasia are all here and they're priced a lot less expensive than some of the other stores in the area.

Shoes

Guja (Via del Cola di Rienzo 36, tel. 06/4555-5371, Mon.-Sat. 10am-7:30pm, Sun. 11am-7:30pm) is a small chain shop that stocks lots of brands. The heels come in all heights and are perfect for romantic escapades. Leather quality is generally good, and prices not excessive. There's a second location near Corso in Via Gambero 9.

Department Stores

Coin (Via Cola di Rienzo 173, tel. 06/3600-4298, daily 10am-8pm) has several stores around the city, but the newly refurbished, upscale location near the Vatican is the sleekest and most appealing. It's a complete shopping experience spread out on three luminous floors with designer men's, women's, and children's clothing, kitchenware, tech gadgets, and an ample selection of gastronomic goods that can be eaten on the spot or wrapped up to go.

TRASTEVERE
Antiques

The cousins who run **Le Cugine** (Via dei Vascellari 19, tel. 06/589-4844, Tues.-Sun. 10am-8pm) have put together an eclectic range of odds and ends. Sabrina Alfonsini happily shows visitors around the birdcages, tableware, and furniture. Most objects come from Roman homes.

Pandora (Piazza Santa Maria in Trastevere 6, tel. 06/581-7145, daily 10am-midnight) sells Murano glass, small antique furnishings, and fashion accessories.

Arts and Crafts

Bottega Artigiana (Via Santa Dorotea 21, tel. 06/588-2079, Mon.-Sat. 9:30am-1:30pm and 3:30pm-7:30pm) displays all the ceramics Domenico and Lavinia Sarti produce in their Anzio studio. The small shop contains terra-cotta vases and urns, some of which might fit in a suitcase. There's also an interesting selection of light fixtures and wall hangings. Nearby, **La Galleria** (Via della Pelliccia 30, tel. 06/581-6614) offers a wide selection of handmade products from around Italy. This large space tends towards the rustic whether it be textile, ceramic, or sculpture.

Time is the theme at **Polvere di Tempo** (Via del Moro 59, tel. 06/588-0704, Mon.-Sat. 10am-8pm). Sundials, hourglasses, and vintage-style clocks put minutes and hours into a new perspective. It's also a break from the overload of clothing boutiques in the area.

Handmade paper feels different at **Officina della Carta** (Via Benedetta 26b, tel. 06/589-5557, Mon.-Sat. 10:30am-7:30pm), where the owners transform authentic fibers into miniature diaries and leather-bound photo albums perfect for storing Roman memories.

Books

Cinephiles will feel at home at **Libreria del Cinema** (Via dei Fienaroli 31d, tel. 06/581-7724, Sun.-Fri. 10am-9pm, Sat. 11am-11pm) where books, magazines, and DVDs dedicated to the seventh art are the main attraction. Italian producers, writers, and actors regularly meet at the comfortable bar.

The Corner Bookshop (Via del Moro 45, tel. 06/583-6942, daily 10am-1:30pm and 3:30pm-8pm) is a no-frills haven of English-language literature where it can easily take a couple of hours to choose a novel.

Clothing and Accessories

Livia Risi's (Via Dei Vascellari 37, 334/676-0920, Mon.-Sat. 10:30am-8pm) bohemian boutique down a back street of Trastevere is hard to pass without a double take. The niece of director Dino Risi is a young designer whose avant-garde clothes straddle past and present. One of her many versatile creations is the TransformHer cape, which can be worn as a skirt or shawl. Dresses and accessories are one of a kind and priced that way.

Markets

Porta Portese (Via Ippolito Nievo, daily 5am-2pm) has the flavor of a souk where you can find anyone and anything. In recent years, made-in-China goods have replaced antiques, and the crowds seem more interested in knockoffs than authentic wares. Still, the market is an experience. The stretch near Piazza Ippolito Nievo is the best chance to spot a Roman coin, illustrated text, or vintage Leica.

Piazza San Cosimato Market (Piazza San Cosimato, Mon.-Sat. 6am-1:30pm) is primarily dedicated to food and is the place to go for fruit, vegetables, cheese, meat, and fish. It's also a great place to observe a Roman market in action.

AVENTINO AND TESTACCIO

Markets

SPECIALTY FOOD

Technically **Eataly** (Piazzale XII 1492, tel. 06/9027-9201, www.eataly.it, daily 10am-midnight) is beyond Aventino and Testaccio, but it's close enough to make a trip worthwhile especially if you love food. This emporium with branches in several Italian cities as well as New York and Tokyo is a mecca of Italian gastronomy. The Roman branch is located in a former train station and is filled with markets, shops, books, wine, gelato, bars, and a dozen restaurants. Whatever your taste you will find it here served fresh.

Window shopping at **E. Volpetti** (Via Marmorata 47, tel. 06/574-2352, Mon.-Sat. 8am-2pm and 5pm-8pm) will affect your taste buds. This gourmet emporium covers nearly every food group from thick-crusted breads and cured meats to freshly made pasta and dessert. Immaculately dressed attendants serve a steady stream of regulars, but you don't need to feel obliged to buy—the smell alone is worth the visit.

The biggest flea market in the city, **Porta Portese** (Sun. 6am-2pm) attracts thousands of Romans and tourists every Sunday morning. It's located just outside the old Aurelian walls along Via Portuense. While it isn't particularly scenic, it is animated, with stalls selling clothing, bags, kitchenware, electronics and a wide range of knicknacks. Haggling is customary and can save you a couple of euros. The best deals can be had when the market opens and closes.

Activities and Recreation

There's more to do in Rome than view the Sistine Chapel or throw a coin into the Trevi Fountain. Rome is an active city, and the prevalence of clear blue skies and fine weather means life is lived outdoors.

Sport in Italy is synonymous with *calcio* (soccer) and Romans are especially mad for the game. Anywhere there's grass there's likely to be people kicking a ball around. Tennis is also popular and is played on clay courts. Cycling is another common (if dangerous) pastime, and what the city lacks in bicycle lanes it makes up for in beautiful parks and manicured gardens.

PARKS AND GARDENS

★ Villa Borghese

Private gardens of the rich and famous have been bequeathed to the city over the centuries, leaving Romans with wonderful places to spend their lunch breaks or take a Sunday-afternoon stroll. The largest and most accessible of these is **Villa Borghese** (Piazzale Flaminio, tel. 06/0608, www. sovraintendenzaroma.it, open daily from dawn to dusk), covered with immense umbrella pines that provide plenty of shade and make natural goalposts for children who play on the grassy lawns in between the trees. It features museums, a zoo, playgrounds, cafes, and a small lake. The different areas are well indicated and connected by a series of paved alleys shared by walkers, bikers and in-line skaters.

Cycling is a good way to explore the park and take refuge from the intense summer heat. Pedal the shaded paths past its gardens, museums, and panoramic terraces. Bicycles, quadricycles, go-karts and Segways can be rented from five locations and are a great way to explore the tree-lined alleys that crisscross Villa Borghese. Most of the paths are paved and inclines are gentle. An hour on a bike

costs €8 and a passport or ID must be left as collateral.

The park is home to **Galleria Borghese** (Piazzale del Museo Borghese 5, tel. 06/841-3979 or 06/841-6542, Tues.-Sun. 9am-7pm, www.galleriaborghese.beniculturali.it, €11 or RomaPass, audio guide €5) one of the world's finest art collections (see also page 62). Reservations are required for Galleria Borghese, but you can show up unannounced at the **Museo Carlo Bilotti** (Viale Fiorello La Guardia, tel. 06/0608, www.museocarlobilotti.it, June-Sept. Tues.-Sun. 1pm-7pm, Oct.-May Tues.-Sun. 10am-4pm, €6.50), also located within the park. The former greenhouse has been transformed into an exposition space and contemporary gallery featuring 17 paintings by Giorgio de Chirico, which make up the core of the small permanent collection.

Children can enjoy pony (€5) and carousel rides or visit the **Bioparco** (Villa Borghese, Piazzale del Giardino Zoologico 1, tel. 06/360-8211, daily 9:30am-6pm, €8.50) nature reserve. The park is also home to the world's smallest **cinema for kids** (Viale della Pineta 15, tel. 06/855-3485, Wed.-Sat. afternoon, €5), which shows cartoons in Italian.

Giardini degli Aranci

Rome specializes in romantic spots like the **Giardini degli Aranci** (Via di Santa Sabina, daily 7am-dusk) next to Santa Sabina where couples regularly practice their kissing. It's called the Orange Garden because of the numerous orange trees growing on either side of the gravel walkway that no one ever seems to pick. The terrace at the far end of the garden provides a view of Trastevere and St. Peter's. If you need more green the **Roman Rose Garden** (Via di Valle Murcia 6, April 21-June 24, daily 8am-7pm) just down the street features 1,100 varieties and a view of the Circus Maximus. The garden is only open in late spring/early summer when the roses are in bloom.

Villa Doria Pamphilj

Villa Doria Pamphilj (Via di San Pancrazio, daily dawn to dusk), located above Trastevere, is populated by dog owners and their pets. The park is full of pickup soccer games on weekends. The villa and fountains in the center were financed by Pope Innocent X and have been inspiring joggers to run that extra kilometer since the park was opened to the public.

the boat pond in Villa Borghese

Rome with Kids

Rome is enjoyable at any age and will appeal to toddlers, kids, teenagers, and parents. It's hard not to be amused by cobblestones, gladiators, ice cream, fountains, bicycles, horses, toy stores, parks, and tech museums. These activities and events will keep all members of the family smiling.

- Many Roman museums have special activities and workshops for children. The **Vatican** has created a **Family Tour** (www.museivaticani.va tel., 06/6988-1351) for 5-12-year-olds. It includes an audio guide and map that explores 32 stops from the Pinacoteca to the Sistine Chapel. The kit is available in English for €5 and can be rented from the Antena International office near the entrance to the museum.

- Roman parks are full of fun activities, and **Villa Borghese** is the safest bet for keeping children amused. There are **playgrounds** near the entrance at Via Veneto where **bikes** are available to rent and toddlers can go for **pony rides.** The park also has a **zoo, boat pond,** and miniature **carousel.**

- Once they've visited the Colosseum, boys and girls may want to be put to the gladiatorial test. The only way to do that is at the **Scuola Gladitori Roma** (Via Appia Antica 18, tel. 06/5160-7951, www.scuolagladiatoriroma.it, daily 9am-5pm) where they'll learn about the everyday life of these ancient heroes and practice wielding a sword in a small outdoor arena. The instructors are part history teachers, part sparring partners who passionately re-create ancient Rome.

- Older children may enjoy the challenge of climbing to the top of the **Gianicolo Hill, cupola of St. Peter's,** or the **Vittoriano** monument. All three come with satisfying views.

- Kids can take part in fun, quick traditions, such as sticking a hand inside the **Mouth of Truth,** tossing a coin into the **Trevi Fountain,** and looking through the **Buco di Roma** in Aventino. They can also watch the **changing of the guards** every hour at the **Presidential Palace** (Piazza del Quirinale). The ritual lasts about 10 minutes and is more elaborate on Sundays at 4pm when the mounted Corazzieri regiment takes part in the pageantry. Even using a simple fountain and collecting different denomination euro coins can be fun and form the basis of a treasure hunt-like adventure.

- **Explora** (Tridente, Via Flaminia 80, tel. 06/361-3776, www.mdbr.it, Tues.-Sun. 10am, noon, 3pm, and 5pm, closed Aug. 13-19, €8), Rome's children museum, is located in a former tram depot and is filled with hands-on activities about nature and science. Most kids are attracted to the water and fire engine exhibits, and tots can tumble in total safety in the upstairs play zone. On weekends reservations are required to ensure a place in one of the designated time slots, but the museum is less crowded during the week and throughout the summer.

- **Zoomarine** (Torvaianica, tel. 06/91534, www.zoomarine.it, weekends Apr., May, Sept., daily Jun.-Aug. 10am-7pm, €28), on the outskirts of the city, is a combination water park and animal preserve with hourly shows that may not be on par with SeaWorld but still delight young audiences. Dolphins, penguins, and parrots all have their dedicated areas in a park that's easy to navigate, but crowded, in summer. Shuttle buses depart from the **Visitor Center** (Termini Station, Via Marsala) from 9:30am and round-trip tickets cost €10.

- At **Via Appia Antica,** Rome's ancient road, **bikes** can be rented at the visitors center and **horses** are available to mount from the nearby stable. No previous riding experience is necessary and the stable also provides picnic lunches. **Ostia Antica** is another good half-day excursion that will stimulate young imaginations and help them understand what a **Roman town** was like.

- **CamilloB** (Vatican, Piazza Cavour 21/A, brunch Sat.-Sun. noon-3:30pm, tel. 06/683-2077, €18), a block from Castel Sant'Angelo, serves brunch on Saturdays and Sundays. In addition to the wide variety of items available, there is a dedicated fun zone for kids, overseen by a qualified "brunchsitter." Try your hand at table soccer or Ping-Pong between bites.

Villa Celimontana

Villa Celimontana (Piazza della Navicella, daily 7am-dusk) is a small hillside park a ten-minute walk from the Colosseum. It fills up with families on weekends and children enjoying the slightly dilapidated playground where pony rides are usually available. During the summer a monthlong jazz festival (www.villacelimontanajazz.com) is organized on the grounds and the gravel paths are lit by candlelight to guide the way.

CYCLING

There's little chance of confusing Rome with Amsterdam when it comes to cycling. Rome isn't an ideal training ground for first-time riders, as there are thousands of mopeds with impatient riders roaring through the streets. Pedal with caution! Bike lanes are rare, but one of the few routes that does exist is a 15-kilometer path that runs along the Tiber from Castel Giubileo to Ponte Risorgimento near the center. You can also avoid traffic by remaining in Rome's parks. Viale Gioacchino Rossini is a safe street for getting from the meticulous paths of Villa Borghese to the wilder off-road track at Villa Ada, which is more suited for mountain rather than city bikes. Bike maps are available from all tourist info points. Bikes can be transported on the first car of the Rome-Lido di Ostia railway on weekends. The final stop is a good place for a leisurely ride along Ostia's boardwalk.

Hourly and daily rentals are available from **Collalti** (Via dei Pellegrino 82, tel. 06/6880-1084, €15 per day) near Campo De' Fiori and **Eco Move Rent** (Via Varese 48, tel. 06/4470-4518, €11 per day) close to Termini. **Bike 95** (Via Marsala, tel. 347/625-3458, www.bikerentalrome.com, Wed.-Mon. 10am-7pm) is near Termini station and rentals are €8 for four hours or €12 per day. Helmets, locks, and child seats are included. **Bici & Baci** (Via del Viminale 5 and Via Cavour, tel. 06/9453-9240, www.bicibaci.com, daily 8am-7pm) provides bikes and scooters to adventurous travelers. Prices for scooters range from €19 per day to €80 depending on the number of riders and cylinders of the engine. Helmets, locks, and child seats are included. **Biciebike** (tel. 339/715-5964, €15 plus cost of rental) provides half-day tours of the city every Sunday. Riders meet outside the Colosseum metro station at 9:30am.

If you prefer a more relaxing ride with reduced traffic you can rent bikes in **Villa Borghese** (Viale di Villa Medici, 9am-10pm) or from the **Park Information Office** (Via Appia Antica 58, tel. 06/513-5316, daily 9:30am-5pm, €3 per hour, €15 per day) on Via Appia Antica. The latter offers several itineraries along the ancient road that stretches many kilometers outside the city and through the surrounding park, which contains many ancient remains.

HORSEBACK RIDING

There are more stables in Rome than any other Italian city. Most are located on the outskirts but a few are near the historic center and can be reached by public transportation or taxi. **Riding Ancient Rome** (Via dei Cercenii 15, tel. 392/788-5168, www.ridingancientrome.it, daily 7am-8pm, €40 per hour) is one of the most accessible and provides scenic itineraries along an ancient Roman road and parkland. Horses are mellow, and riders of all experience levels can set off on 1-to 3-hour tours accompanied by expert guides. Home-cooked lunches and dinners are served in the clubhouse and ready-made picnics are available.

Roma River Ranch (Lungotevere degli Inventori 69, tel. 328/698-3077, www.romariveranch.it, Mon.-Sat. 9am-1pm and 3pm-7pm, Sun. 9am-1pm, €50) is a small stable on the banks of the Tiber with horses and ponies that can be taken out for a trot along the river and away from the chaos of the city. Riding gear is provided and first-timers of all ages can take lessons from licensed instructors.

Many parks around Rome have pony-riding areas where children can handle the reins for a few minutes. The most convenient location is Villa Borghese near the Casa del Cinema entrance where a pony grazes throughout the summer. Rides cost €5 and parents are encouraged to accompany young-sters along the way.

TENNIS

Rome is a clay court town with no shortage of tennis clubs, some of which do not require membership. Anyone looking for a game can find it at **Circolo della Stampa** (Piazza Mancini 19, tel. 06/323-2452), where an hour of singles is €10 and doubles €12. The night supplement is €2 and you can choose from one of six clay or synthetic surfaces. **Oasis di Pace** (Via degli Eugenii 2, tel. 06/718-4550) runs a similar service near Via Appia Antica. Courts here should be booked in advance.

GOLF

Rome has six golf courses of varying dimen-sions, many of which are in the countryside and lined with pine trees. All you need to play is a reservation. **Circolo del Golf Fioranello** (Via della Falcognana 61, tel. 06/7138-0800, fax 06/713-8212, €20) features an 18-hole, par-72 course, clubhouse, restaurant/bar, driv-ing range, and outdoor swimming pool. It's a 35-minute taxi ride from the center, which should not exceed €40.

SPECTATOR SPORTS
Soccer

Rome's two soccer teams play in the **Stadio Olimpico** (Viale Gladiatore 2, tel. 06/36-851). There's a game nearly every weekend. The season runs from late August to late May and most matches are held on Sunday afternoons. **Rome** (yellow and red), the more popular and successful of the teams, was recently bought by a wealthy American businessman. Their hardcore supporters live in Testaccio and Garbatella. **Lazio** (sky blue and white) won the Italian Serie A championship in 2000 and has languished in mid-table ever since. Tickets for *le curve* (the seats behind the goal), where the most faithful fans sit, are €15, while more comfortable seating in the stands costs €25 and up. Games don't generally sell out. Tickets can be purchased at the gates or the **AS Roma Store** in Piazza Colonna.

Rugby

Italian rugby has come a long way in recent years. Although clubs remain amateurish, the national team is now respectable and doesn't lose by the margins it once did. They even manage to beat Scotland or France now and again. The **Six Nations** (tel. 0862/404-206, €25-90) tournament runs from January to March and allows the opportunity to watch England, Wales, or Ireland compete at the Olympic Stadium. Unlike soccer, rival fans don't require a restraining order and post-game celebrations go on for hours at pubs around the center.

TOURS

The majority of tourists see Rome's ancient monuments without understanding why they were built and what they were used for. A large number of companies and individu-als offer guided tours that they promise will help you understand the city. These best of these are insightful, entertaining, and make you want to learn more. The worst (usually touted around the Colosseum, Vatican, and other popular sites) are monotonous and crowded. Of course, one of the biggest ben-efits of a guided tour is skipping lines and having access to areas that may be off-limits to the general public. Do a little research be-forehand to make sure your guide is qualified. (Unfortunately, not all recruits are up to the task of revealing the Renaissance or the ex-plaining the difference between the Roman Republic and Empire.) Costs vary widely and may or may not include entry to the individ-ual sights.

Walking

Walks of Italy (tel. 1-888/683-8670 in U.S. or 069-480-4888 in Italy, www.walksofitaly. com, €39-95 pp) can help you gain a better appreciation for what this unique civilization achieved, and maybe transform how you view the city. One of their most popular tours is the VIP Colosseum option, which leads small groups into the intricate guts of the arena where gladiators and animals waited to enter the fray above. There's little waiting, and participants enjoy access to areas few tourists get to see. The visit lasts three hours and also includes the Forum and Palatine Hill. All participants are equipped with headsets and led by experienced guides.

Besides the many companies operating in the city, there are hundreds of registered freelance guides—many of whom are passionate lifelong residents—who provide a more intimate take on the city. **Annalisa Cingolani** (tel. 328/645-8588, www.visitareroma.net, €145/3-hour tour for 1-6 people) is one of these and has been leading tours since 2005. All her tours are for single parties only and allow greater personalization than the larger agencies can offer. She will customize tours around your interests, whether that's Caravaggio, sculpture, or fountains. The only downside is that participants are expected to get their own tickets, and entry fees are not included.

If you decide to hire a guide once you arrive in Rome and prefer not to join a large group, head to **Guide Center** (Via dei Fori Imperiali, tel. tel. 06/0608-7707, www.guides.roma.it, daily 10am-4pm, €150/tour for 1-5 people). This organization is operated by the city and matches visitors with certified guides. These are primarily intended for families or groups. Seven fixed itineraries include hidden, ancient, and contemporary Rome. Tours last three hours and can be booked directly from the tourist office near the Colosseum. Entry fees are not included.

Not all tours focus on ancient sights. Rome has a surplus of graffiti. A lot of it is the nondescript scribbled kind, but there has been a recent effort by street artists to leave a creative mark on the cityscape with murals that cover entire buildings in the capital's grittier neighborhoods. The best way to see what's being sprayed on walls today is to join a **Rovescio tour** (tel. 389/992-1126, www.rovescio.org, €12/person). This group of urban art enthusiasts leads walking and cycling tours through the most graphically interesting neighborhoods to see the work of international street artists like Axel Void, StenLex, and Ozmo. Walks last two hours and depart from locations in Ostiense, Garbatella, and Testaccio.

Segway

Segways are a common sight in the historic center. They combine a fun and convenient mode of transportation with a bit of history and allow travelers to see more in less time. **Rolling Rome** (Via del Cardello 31, tel. 320/807-6437, www.rollingrome.com, €79) has a modern fleet of two-wheeled vehicles that set out on prearranged itineraries around the city. Riders must be over 16, less than 250 pounds, and have a decent sense of balance. Tours start with a 30-minute orientation and practice session. After that it's mostly smiles and occasional stops where guides briefly explain sights and answer questions. These tours are popular with families and a sure way to keep older teenagers and adults entertained for hours. If you prefer the freedom to roam wherever you want, they also rent Segways and electric bikes in Villa Borghese. It's €15 per hour or €60 for the day.

Pedicab

Near the exit of the Colosseum subway station, rickshaw bikes are lined up and drivers await their next fare. These three-wheeled vehicles seat two comfortably and are well adapted to the newly pedestrianized areas around the Colosseum. Prices vary from €50 per hour to €10 per monument and should be negotiated prior to departure. If you prefer to do your own pedaling, four-wheeled bikes are available nearby. **Ecotour** (tel. 389/589-0587) operates a one-or two-hour tour through the historic center. Drivers point out monuments and stop for photo ops along the way.

Tram

Reserve a seat on **TramJazz** (Anna Maria, tel. 338/114-7867, www.tramjazz.com, €65 pp) and spend an evening listening to music and enjoying regional food aboard a vintage tram. Departure is at 9pm from Piazza Porta Maggiore, and the tram returns three hours later after crisscrossing the city. Reservations are required and the musical program is available online.

Ape

There are a lot of ways of touring Rome, and one of the most nostalgic is aboard a three-wheeled *ape* (pronounced *ah-pay*). It's a cross between a scooter and a micro-van that was popular in the 1950s and remains ideal for navigating the narrow streets of the center. It now comes in a convertible electric version that **Ape Rome Tour** (Via Lorenzo il Magnifico 150, tel. 06/8767-2327, €150) uses to give passengers a fun view of the city. You can take one of their Highlights, Night, or James Bond Tours that last two hours and seat three. Pickup can be arranged in advance or you can hire one of the guides parked in Piazza Venezia or near the Pantheon.

Horse and Buggy

Before Rome became infested with cars the horse and buggy ruled the streets. Today they've been relegated to tourist attractions and await clients near Piazza di Spagna and the Colosseum. Prices are negotiated with the driver and tours vary depending on interest. A 50-minute visit of ancient sights costs around €100 and can be split between up to four passengers.

CLASSES
Cooking

Cooking Classes in Rome (Via dei Fienaroli 5, www.cookingclassesinrome.com, €65 pp, reservations required), located in Trastevere, could be the best part of your journey. Once you've discovered how to make pasta and prepare homemade tomato sauce, dinner will never be the same. Chef Andrea Consoli teaches the basics of Mediterranean cooking in a professionally equipped kitchen and leads participants through the preparation of a classic four-course meal. As everyone rolls up their sleeves, fellow aspiring cooks quickly become friends. The five-hour course starts at 10am and ends with a meal. Recipes are emailed to participants in case any of the steps or ingredients are forgotten along the way.

Wine-Tasting

There are plenty of opportunities to sample wine in Rome, but learning about what you're drinking from an experienced sommelier educates the palate and makes reading wine menus easier. **Vino Roma** (Via In Selci 84/G, tel. 328/487-4497, www.vinoroma.com, €50 pp) isn't a wine tour around the city. They have their own storefront location where participants learn about local vintages and what to order where. Their introductory course to Italian wines features six bottles from different regions that small groups choose from the well-stocked cellar and uncork at a long tasting table.

Language

There are a number of language schools offer intensive Italian courses that can get you from zero to the fundamentals in under a week. **Torre di Babele** (Via Cosenza 7, tel. 06/4425-2578, www.torredibabele.com, €240) offers one-week courses in small classes that meet several times a day and begin with a placement test to determine level. The benefits are immediate. If you'd like to dive deeper into Italian culture, the school also offers workshops related to food, architecture, and art.

Scuola Leonardo da Vinci (Piazza dell'Orologio 7, tel. 06/6889-2513, €270) provides intensive one-week courses for groups and individuals. They also have an office in Florence, so travelers can begin learning the basics in Rome and continue developing language skills at the next stop on the journey. Like most language schools, they also offer a range of single-day cultural activities.

Accommodations

Happily, hotels in Rome have gone through a renaissance in recent years, and many of the faded carpets and soft mattresses have been replaced with modern furnishings. Design hotels have helped shake things up, along with bed-and-breakfasts that were virtually unknown a decade ago.

Rates change throughout the year, but high season is nearly year-round. Prices must be displayed in every room by law and do dip slightly from November to March, with many hotels offering discounts for multiple-night stays. Around €120 usually gets you a decent double with private bath, air-conditioning, and Wi-Fi, although you'll need to spend more for facilities like a sauna or rooftop terrace with a view. Most 3-star or higher hotels come equipped with satellite television. Channels include CNN, BBC, and pay-per view films in English.

CHOOSING WHERE TO STAY

Ancient Rome and **Monti** are convenient to the city's major monuments. Choose from small hotels and B&Bs. Several streets and squares are lined with inviting bars and restaurants but for the most part the neighborhood is tranquil.

Campo De' Fiori/Piazza Navona in walking distance from most sights. Accommodations tend to be expensive side, but there are reasonably priced apartment rentals. Nightlife around the main squares remains boisterous until late during the summer months.

Rome's most exclusive hotels are located in **Tridente.** It costs an arm and a leg for four- or five-star treatment at establishments concentrated around Via Veneto and Piazza di Spagna. Many offer luxurious rooftop gardens and fine dining. Renowned shopping draws crowds throughout the day, but there's noticeable depopulation at night.

Trastevere is one of the most vibrant neighborhoods in the city and a good place to stay if you for nightlife. Hotel rooms are small and early birds are likely to have their dreams interrupted by the festivities. Some quieter streets offer romantic escapes from the revelry.

There are many mid-priced accommodations near the **Vaticano,** convenient for pilgrims visiting the Vatican Museums and St. Peter's, as well as secular shopping and along 19th and 20th century streets to the north.

Testaccio and **Aventino** are mostly residential, with few hotels. Both make good refuges for travelers who value peace and quite and don't mind walking or using public transportation to reach the main attractions. That said Monte Testaccio is a popular party zone with many bars and discos where young Romans gather all year long.

The streets around **Termini** are packed with accommodations of all types, catering to business travelers, tourists, and backpackers. Some of the best-priced hostels in the city are near the train station and subway, but the scenery is unattractive.

ANCIENT ROME AND MONTI
Under €100

★ **La Scalinatella** (Via Urbana 48, tel. 06/488-0547, www.lascalinatellaroma.com, €80-160 d) is a charming B&B in the Monti neighborhood, which is near all the antiquities and is full of restaurants, bars, and boutiques. The three large rooms have original furnishings, modern en suite bathrooms, Wi-Fi, and safes. The vaulted reception area is equally comfortable. Hosts Elisabetta and Annamaria provide a warm welcome plus all the guidance you could hope for.

Blue Hostel (Via Carlo Alberto 13, tel. 340/925-8503, www.bluehostel.it, €75 d) has nothing to do with bunk beds or dormitories.

Best Accommodations

★ **The Inn at the Rome Forum:** Climb down for a glimpse of ancient underground ruins; climb up for afternoon drinks served on a panoramic split-level terrace (page 116).

★ **Casa de' Coronari:** This sleek, industrial-chic boutique hotel is close to all of the sights and sounds of Campo de' Fiori (page 117).

★ **G-Rough:** Get the rock-star treatment at this neo-rustic hotel (page 118).

★ **Hotel de Russie:** Take a vacation from your vacation with the spa facilities at this luxury hotel (page 119).

★ **QuodLibet B&B:** Its authentic, warm welcome will make you feel at home in Rome (page 1.).

★ **Hotel Santa Maria:** Get a taste of Trastevere village life in this former 17th-century cloister (page 120).

★ **The Beehive:** This hostel/hotel is easy—easygoing, easy on the eyes, and easy on the wallet (page 121).

Instead it's intimate and cozy, and just far enough from the train station to make it a decent location that's close to Monti and all the sights of ancient Rome. Rooms are small but the curtains, lamps, exposed beams, and parquet floors make it feel like it could be home. If you need more space, they have a bright suite with an eat-in kitchen and foldout bed. Prices aren't hostel prices but they start at €49 depending on the season and rarely exceed €150.

The **Kolbe Hotel Rome** (Via di San Teodoro 44, tel. 06/679-8866, €90 s/d) is a comfortable, down-to-earth hotel located moments from the Forum, Capitoline Hill, and Circus Maximus. Rooms in the back look out on a garden and are all equipped with TV and Wi-Fi. The hotel restaurant serves lunch and dinner in a simple yet welcoming dining room. Guests are primarily young northern Europeans who have come to explore antiquity.

€100-200

★ The Inn at the Rome Forum (Via degli Ibernesi 30, tel. 06/6919-0970, www. theinnattheromanforum.com, €150-400 d) is a luxury retreat hidden down a forgotten street. The 14 superior, deluxe, and executive rooms are plush with mildly extravagant carpets, bed frames, and curtains. An attentive concierge manages all requests with a smile and invites guests to visit the ancient underground ruins below the inn. Upstairs afternoon drinks are served on a panoramic split-level terrace where couples gaze upon rooftops, towers, and domes.

An ideal location and Danilo at the front desk make the **Duca d'Alba** (Via Leoni 14, tel. 06/484-471, www.hotelducadalba.com, €130-180 d) a convenient choice. A continental breakfast is included, and the shops of Via Nazionale are just around the corner. Antiquity is only minutes away, and the vibrant Monti neighborhood will liven up your nights. Danilo can help quench any curiosity about the city or provide directions to your next destination. The 27 rooms are small but comfortable. Each contains an electronic safe.

€200-300

The Lancelot (Via Capo d'Africa 47, tel.

06/7045-0615, www.lancelothoco.com, €200 d) is a bit of Britain in Rome. The rooms of this small hotel could be set in an Agatha Christie novel with their plush couches, gilded mirrors, and antique desks. Rooms are bright and cheerful, and some have balconies. Breakfast is served on large round tables that make meeting fellow travelers easy. Many guests are return visitors, and the majority are English speakers. The garden is a pleasant place to plan the next sojourn and the hotel restaurant (€25 fixed price) is conveniently right at your doorstep. Airport transfers and car or scooter rental can be arranged upon request.

Over €300

Situated in a restored 19th-century *palazzo* two blocks from the Colosseum, **Hotel Celio** (Via dei Santi Quattro 35c, tel. 06/7049-5333, www.hotelcelio.com, €280-300 d) makes an immediate impression. The lounge is elegant and the staff is unusually attentive in a city where customer service is often neglected. Michelangelo and Caesar are the most charming rooms, with high ceilings and comfortable beds. End a grueling day of sightseeing with a swim in the hotel pool.

CAMPO DE' FIORI/ PIAZZA NAVONA
Under €100

A location next to one of the Rome's last medieval towers and barely 40 yards from Piazza Navona makes **Navona Tower Relais** (Via di Tor Millina 19, tel. 06/6880-9777, www. navonatowerrelais.com, €80 d) hard to resist. It's somewhere between a hotel and a B&B in terms of services, but the five recently refurbished rooms are well sized, clean, and comfortable. It's nothing fancy, but the owners are friendly and happy to look after bags before or after check-in.

€100-200

★ **Casa de' Coronari** (Via dei Coronari 234, tel. 06/6880-3907, www.casadecoronari.com, €180-220 d) is a small boutique residence on one of Rome's first linear streets close to all the neighborhood sights and nightlife. The industrial chic lounge on the ground floor leads to six minimalist rooms with original wood-beamed ceilings and terra-cotta floors. The modern furniture in white and grayish tones is sleek and stylish. In-room breakfast is provided, and bikes are free to use for guests. Vacancy is limited during the summer, when multiday bookings are required.

Tastefully decorated rooms and 15th-century charm await at **Hotel Navona** (Via dei Sediari 8, tel. 06/6821-1392, www.hotelnavona.com, €120-155 s/d). Gilt-framed paintings of the city hang above the beds and heavy green curtains keep the sunlight out of the 20 rooms. They also have several large apartments with frescoed ceilings and fully equipped kitchens where guests can spend a weekend or more just minutes from Rome's most famous square. Breakfast is served on a long table in the communal dining room that encourages conversation among travelers.

At **Hotel Teatro di Pompeo** (Largo del Pallaro 8, tel. 06/6830-0170, €170 d), guests can enjoy a continental breakfast under the original vaults of a Roman theater. The 12 rooms are spacious and clean, and half face a courtyard. You'll have to stick your neck out the window to see the sky, but these rooms are quiet and conducive to late risers. Rooms in front face a small square and have tiled flooring and dark wood ceilings. A bar near the entrance is open throughout the day and free Internet access is available throughout the hotel. Piazza Navona, the Spanish Steps, and Fontana di Trevi are all within walking distance.

€200-300

It doesn't get much more central than **Hotel Due Torre** (Vicolo del Leonatta 23, tel. 06/687-6983, www.hotelduetorreroma.com, €150-230 s/d). Parquet floors and antiques give the hotel a distinctive and refined feeling. It's like staying in a museum or 1970s time capsule. All 22 rooms and four apartments have air-conditioning, mini-bars, and paintings that depict how the neighborhood once looked. English-language newspapers are stacked in the lobby, which is a comfortable staging point before heading out into the thick of the city.

Falling in love is easy at **Locanda Cairoli** (Piazza Benedetto Cairoli 2, tel. 06/6880-9278, www.hotelcairoliroma.com, €180-240 s/d). This small hotel mixes period furnishings with modern art and photographs of Ernest Hemingway. The hominess is reinforced by the Greek-and English-speaking owner who can organize shopping and cultural tours of the city. Breakfast is included. Rooms include satellite TV.

Over €300

Italian hotels may have a reputation for cramped rooms and low water pressure, but those days are over if you have the money to spend. The ten rooms at ★ **G-Rough** (Piazza Navona, Piazza di Pasquino 69, tel. 06/6880-1085, www.g-rough.it, €350-500 d) are spacious and suited for rock stars. The 17th-century *palazzo* moments from Piazza Navona have been given the stripped-down, neo-rustic treatment. Surfaces have a rough, incomplete look that contrasts with designer 1920s-1940s furniture and contemporary art. Originality permeates the hotel and the ground-floor **bar** (7am-midnight) is a convenient destination for nightcaps and gaiety.

Hotel Indigo (Via Giulia 62, tel. 06/686-611, www.hotelindigorome.com, €300 d) is an unpretentious five-star boutique hotel behind Piazza Farnese that's close to all the major sights. The 64 rooms range from standards to two-bedroom suites. All are equipped with air-conditioning, docking stations, and satellite TV. There's a wonderful view from the rooftop terrace, and a spa facilities help guests relax after a day pounding the cobblestones. If you don't feel like exploring the vibrant neighborhoods nearby, the restaurant and bar provide a mix of local and international flavors.

TRIDENTE
Under €100

Sober rooms at sober prices could be the slogan for **Pensione Panda** (Via della Croce 35, tel. 06/678-0179, www.hotelpanda.it, €88-93 d). So what if the decoration is dull? The beds are comfortable, and guests come for Piazza di Spagna, which is only moments away. Rooms are spread out on two floors of a 19th-century palazzo that has preserved some of its original frescoes. A couple of the rooms have balconies overlooking a central courtyard and are quieter than those facing the street. Air-conditioning costs extra and may be worth the euros if you're traveling in August.

€100-200

★ Barocco (Via della Purificazione 4, Barberini, tel. 06/487-2001, www.hotel-barocco.com, €150-210 s/d) is the essence of elegance. Some of the 41 rooms have balconies overlooking Roman rooftops. Interiors are on the flowery side, with primary colors favored throughout and lots of marble in the large bathrooms. Digital safes, air-conditioning, and satellite TV are standard and sound-proofed windows guarantee traffic won't interfere with your dreams.

Anyone with an aversion to big hotels will appreciate the intimacy of **Casa Howard** (Via Capo delle Case 18, tel. 06/6992-4555, www.casahoward.com, €150 d). Each of the five rooms is neatly decorated, some with antiques the owner has brought from her Tuscan farmhouse. The Verde Room is especially beautiful. There is a high standard of service, with perks like massages available upon request.

€200-300

No two rooms are the same at **Hotel Locarno** (Via della Penna 22, tel. 06/361-0841, www.hotellocarno.com, €210-240 d), where a view of the Tiber is only as far as the roof terrace. You may never want to leave the enchanting garden on the ground floor with its miniature fountain and overflowing vegetation. All 60 rooms have high ceilings and rustic fittings. Room 201 is especially comfortable, as are the two deluxe rooms on the 6th floor. Bicycles are provided for free.

One vine-covered entrance on a quiet street just moments from Piazza di Spagna leads to two hotels: **Hotel Manfredi** (Via Margutta 61, tel. 06/320-7676, www.hotelmanfredi.it, €170-240 s/d) and **Hotel Forte** (tel. 06/320-7625, www.hotelforte.com, €160-230 s/d). Both offer comfortable, chic accommodations that aren't overdone and make no attempt to be trendy. Each provides large beds in silent curtained rooms and professional three-star service. Breakfast can be eaten in your room or in either of the pleasant breakfast rooms.

It's hard to leave **Casa Montana** (Piazzale Flaminio 9, tel. 06/3260-0421, www.casamontani.com, €200-300 d). The five deluxe rooms and suites of this contemporary guesthouse on the edge of Piazza del Popolo are all warm and inviting. The furniture is elegant but cozy, the bathrooms small but stunning. The in-room breakfast encourages lingering. Room service can satisfy most desires from 7am to 8pm, and when you do decide to leave, Piazza di Spagna and the rest of the city are only a short walk away.

Over €300

★ **Hotel de Russie** (Via del Babuino 9, tel. 06/328-881, www.roccofortehotels.com, €450-500 classic double) feels like a miniature Club Med, with enough luxury to make guests forget they're in Rome. There are several levels of rooms with city and garden views decorated in contemporary fashion, which may be a refreshing change from rustic. Downstairs you can dine at the fusion-inspired restaurant or relax with a perfectly mixed cocktail in the lively bar. Guests are free to use the extensive spa facilities and state-of-the-art gym. Mercedes-Benz smart bikes and walking tours can be reserved from the very attentive front desk.

There aren't many places to live like an emperor, but there is one in Rome. The emperor at **Residenza Napoleone III** (Piazza di Spagna, Via Fontanella Borghese 56, 347-7337098, www.residenzanapoleone.com, €730 and €1400) was the nephew of Napoleon who resided in this opulent residence in 1830. The grand suite has been restored to the highest aristocratic standards with antique oil paintings, tapestries, and gold-leafed furnishings that fill a mammoth bedroom, two sitting rooms, a powder room, and the bath. History here comes at a price and you'll need to be a modern-day emperor to afford it.

VATICANO
Under €100

A B&B isn't just a bed and a breakfast. What makes it a special way of experiencing Rome are the hosts. The best provide the right balance of hospitality and privacy, are eager to share their knowledge of the city and make you feel like an honorary citizen. Not only can Gianluca do that but he also has a great apartment. ★ **QuodLibet B&B** (Via Barletta 29, tel. 347/122-2642, €70-100 d) is located in a grand 19th-century *palazzo* 10 minutes from St. Peter's and near a convenient Metro stop. You'll get all the advice you need and a rich breakfast served in an immaculate kitchen or one of three colorful bedrooms with private bath, air-conditioning, and Wi-Fi.

Travelers looking to make friends from all over the world should book a room at the **Alimandi** (Via Tunisi 8, tel. 06/3972-3948, €80-100 s/d). The low cost attracts a youthful crowd that can survive without luxury. Rooms are clean, and conversations can go on for hours on the spacious rooftop terrace.

€100-200

A night at **Residenza Madri Pie** (Via Alcide de Gasperi 4, tel. 06/631-967, www.residenzamadripie.it, €77-123 s/d) is a good way to prepare for the Vatican, which is just 150 meters away. Many of the 73 rooms have views of St. Peter's; and all of them have pictures of saints hanging over the beds. The residence is favored by student travelers and pilgrims, who congregate in the small chapel throughout the day. There's also a lovely garden out back that's cool in the summer and makes up for the lack of air-conditioning.

A new addition to the area's four-star hotel scene, the **Dei Consoli** (Via Varrone 2d, tel.

06/6889-2972, www.hoteldeiconsoli.com, €125-200 s/d) distinguishes itself with professionalism, modern furnishings, and the fact that they welcome pets. The 26 rooms are divided into superior, deluxe, and junior suites where whirlpools help weary guest recuperate. Everyone else can count on power showers and lots of Spanish porcelain in the bathrooms.

After facing the crowds of the Piazza San Pietro, the tranquility of **Hotel Sant'Anna** (Borgo Pio 133-4, tel. 06/6880-1602, www.santannahotel, €160-200 s/d) is a godsend. All it takes is a few moments in the garden of this small hotel for serenity to return. If that doesn't work, the minibar in each room should do the trick. Vatican colors of yellow and white predominate. Breakfast is included and rooms on the third floor have a terrace.

€200-300

Hotel Giulio Caesar (Via degli Scipioni 287, tel. 06/321-0751, www.hotelgiuliocaesar.com, €170-210 d) is as majestic as the name suggests. The lounge and entrance are decorated with antiques and tapestries. A hearty breakfast is served in the garden, and there's free parking. The fireplace is lit in winter and the high-backed leather chairs in the lounge are perfect for reflecting on the day's events.

Before **Hotel Columbus** (Via della Conciliazione 33, tel. 06/686-5435, www.hotelcolumbus.net, €210-250 d) became a hotel it was the home of medieval princes and cardinals. The 15th-century pedigree still shows: Most rooms have vaulted ceilings, wood beams, and decoration fit for an aristocrat. (Internet access and modern concessions to comfort have been made, too.) The restaurant in the veranda looks out on a romantic courtyard.

TRASTEVERE
Under €100

The noise of boisterous Trastevere seems far away once you settle into **Locando San Pancrazio** (Via di Porta San Pancrazio 32a, tel. 06/9727-3171, www.hotelsanpancrazio.

com, €85-130 d). Maybe it's the dead-end street on the edge of the neighborhood; maybe it's the seven cozy bedrooms overlooking a park. Whatever it is, staying here feels like a romantic retreat from the city below. Three-star comfort gets you air-conditioning, a minibar, and good water pressure in a pleasantly decorated room. Breakfast can be ordered in or taken on a lovely terrace.

Arco del Lauro (Via Arco De Tolomei 29/27, tel. 06/9784-0350, www.arcodellauro.it, €85-145 d) is a B&B near a medieval arch a short walk from Tiberina Island. Though simple and small by most standards, rooms are cheery and comfortable. A continental or international breakfast is served at a nearby bar. Reception is friendly, but only open mornings.

€100-200

★ **Villa della Fonte** (Via della Fonte d'Olio 8, tel. 06/580-3797, www.villafonte.com, €110-160 s/d) is a five-room hotel run by a friendly mother-daughter team. What the villa lacks in size it makes up for in charm. Rooms are bright and include a minibar and satellite TV. Mattresses were recently replaced and are quite firm. Parking is available nearby for a small fee and chocolate croissants from a neighborhood bakery are served in your room or on the sun-filled patio. The balconies are perfect for watching the Trastevere street scene down below.

Hotel Cisterna (Via della Cisterna 7-9, tel. 06/581-7212, www.cisternahoit, €130 d) gets its name from the fountain in the nearby courtyard. There are 20 rooms, and those on the upper floors have pitched ceilings and wood beams. There is no lack of bars and restaurants near the hotel, but the side-street location keeps the hustle and bustle of Trastevere at a safe distance. Don't expect posh here, but it's clean and friendly. Breakfast (included in the price) is served until 10am.

€200-300

★ **Hotel Santa Maria** (Vicolo del Piede 2, tel. 06/589-4626, www.hotelsantamaria.info, €180-220 s/d) is quaint with a capital Q. A stay here is like entering a small village miles from Rome, a feeling that has to do with the building's 17th-century cloister past. All the bricks, beams, tiles, and cobblestones have been restored. A buffet breakfast is included and may be eaten in the orange tree-filled courtyard or in the high-ceilinged dining room. The half-dozen rooms come in double, triple, and quadruple options that all look out on a lovely portico where guests like to spend the afternoons sipping wine from the hotel bar.

TESTACCIO AND AVENTINO
Under €100

Hotel Re Testa (Via Beniamino Franklin 4, www.hotelretesta.com, €85 d) is located above the market across from the Testaccio nightlife scene. Rooms are modern and well equipped with free Wi-Fi, air-conditioning, hairdryer, flat-screen TV, and concierge service. There are a variety of different-sized rooms, with the smallest a 29-square-meter double bed option costing €85 with breakfast included.

€100-200

If you can handle 1980s decor in a Fascist-era building—and you manage to reserve a room facing the courtyard away from the traffic on Via Marmorata—**Hotel Santa Prisca** (Largo M. Gelsomini 25, tel. 06/574-1917, www.hotel-santapriscaroma.com, €100-150 s/d) may grow on you. The medium-size hotel is managed by nuns who care less about innovation than providing a good night's sleep at reasonable prices. That explains the linoleum flooring and antiquated decor. Breakfast is included, and the lunch and dinner prix fixe options are a bargain. Both Testaccio and Aventino are nearby, and the Colosseum is only 15 minutes by foot.

Surrounded by an attractive garden on a quiet residential street in Aventino, **Villa San Pio** (Via Santa Melania 19, tel. 06/578-3214, www.aventinohotels.com, €130-200 s/d) provides elegant rooms with baroque flair. Much of the furniture is antique. Bathrooms are all done up in black-and-white marble and

equipped with hair dryers and hydromassage bathtubs.

€200-300

★ **Hotel S. Anselmo** (Piazza S. Anselmo 2, tel. 06/570-057, www.hotelvillasanpio.com, €220-270 d) is as memorable as Rome. Each of the 34 rooms in this four-star hotel has its own personality. The *Camera con Vista* (room with a view) boasts a bucolic panorama while the *Renaissance* room could save you a trip to Florence. Downstairs, old and new blend seamlessly into a timeless style. The breakfast buffet includes smoked salmon, fresh fruit, and homemade cakes. It's served in the pleasant dining room or in the garden where a giant palm shades guests. Uniformed staff provide impeccable service, and Ari at the bar specializes in exotic cocktails.

TERMINI
Under €100

★ **The Beehive** (Via Marghera 8, tel. 06/4470-4553, www.the-beehive.com) is a recently remodeled accommodation two blocks north of Termini station that's part hostel and part hotel. It's owned by an American couple who came to Rome and stayed. All the rooms have been redone in bright colors and are friendly on the eye and the pocketbook. You can choose from a mix-gender dorm (€25) or private rooms with (€80) and without (€70) bath. There are three neat common areas where guests hang out and breakfast (not included) is served and where you can order eggs, French toast, or Korean rice porridge. The couple also manage the eight-room **Hotel Urbee** (www.hotelurbee.com, €70) with the same easygoing philosophy.

If you've done the B&B thing but aren't quite ready for couch surfing, **Cohome** (Via di Porta Labicana 56, 328/790-6089, www.cohome.it, €80 d) may be the perfect compromise. This bohemian accommodation near Termini station in the edgy, graffiti-covered San Lorenzo neighborhood is all about meeting people from all over the world. The three friendly residents provide four private rooms and a shared living and dining space where guests dine together and a guitar is often being played. There's a strong emphasis on ecology and bikes can be rented for the day.

€100-200

Hotels like the **Nardizzi** (Via Firenze 38, tel. 06/4890-3916, www.hotelnardizzi.it, €105-145 d) only exist in Italy. This family-run operation obviously takes hospitality seriously. A few minutes on the terrace is all it takes to feel as Roman as the owners. Rooms are spacious and the service goes beyond the two stars listed at the entrance.

Information and Services

TOURIST INFORMATION
Tourist Information Centers

The **Rome Tourist Office** (Via Parigi 11, tel. 06/0608, www.turismoroma.it, Mon.-Sat. 9am-7pm) operates a dozen **Tourist Information Points** (TIP) around the historic center, at both airports, and in Termini train station. Each is open daily from 9am to 7pm and operated by multilingual staff. It's where to pick up a RomaPass, the city's quarterly event guide, and a detailed map (€1.50).

TIP locations include: Stazione Termini (Piazza dei Cinquecento), Colosseum (Piazza Tempio della Pace), Piazza Navona (Piazza delle Cinque Lune), Trastevere (Piazza Sonnino), Fontana di Trevi (Via Minghetti), Vatican (Via della Conciliazione 4) and Leonardo da Vinci Airport (Terminal B). The city's **tourist information number** (tel. 06/0608) operates daily 9am-9pm. The call center provides information in English about events, accommodations, restaurants, and transportation. Tickets to museums, exhibitions, and shows can also be purchased and picked up on-site. Tickets to many sights and guided tours can be reserved from **Coop Culture** (www.coopculture.it).

The **Visitor Center** (Via dei Fori Imperiali, tel. 06/679-7702, Tues.-Sun. 9:30am-6:30pm) in Ancient Rome is a useful stop if you intend to purchase a RomaPass or are searching for event information. Next-day tours can be arranged and the adjacent courtyard is a good place to sit and plan the next stage of a journey. There's also a snack bar and restrooms.

If you just need directions, the **vigili urbana** (urban vigils) in white-and-blue uniforms and on duty near most of the city's attractions can help.

Business Hours

Shops generally open between 8am and 9am, close at 1pm for the *pausa pranzo* (lunch break), and reopen at 3pm or 4pm. Department stores and boutiques in the center have continual hours, but the farther you get from Piazza di Spagna the more likely you are to find shutters drawn in the early afternoon. Many small shops and restaurants remain closed on Sundays or one weekday and generally shut down for a week or two in mid-August and over important holidays. Few eateries provide continual service: Most kitchens operate noon-2:30pm and 7:30pm-10pm. Many establishments have winter and summer hours that are extended as days get hotter.

HEALTH AND SAFETY
Emergency Numbers

Dialing **118** in Italy is like calling 911 in the United States. Call that number if you break something while frolicking in the Fontana di Trevi. An ambulance with a unique siren will be on the scene within minutes.

Police

There are a lot of uniforms on the streets of Rome. The white ones issue parking tickets, the blue ones chase criminals, and the ones carrying machine guns deter terrorists. The *vigili urbani* (white, tel. 06/888-7620) are the most common in the city and can direct you

Roman Economics

Although most Italians are honest, tourists can be easy targets for unscrupulous business owners who charge one price for locals and another for anyone holding a map. Note that taxis, bars, and shops must clearly display their prices. Markets can be murkier but all food is generally sold by weight. Clothes and other objects should be labeled. If they aren't, inquire about price and ask for a discount if you feel it's too high. A receipt (*ricevuto*) should accompany all transactions (except those conducted by nomadic salespeople). It's always a good idea to ask for the receipt if it isn't provided.

Prices fluctuate slightly depending on neighborhood and location, but the average costs listed below should give you an idea of what to expect:

FOOD AND DRINKS

- espresso: €1

- cappuccino: €1.20

- *cornetto* (breakfast pastry): €1

- *tramezzino* (light sandwich): €2

- other sandwiches: €3-4.50

- fresh-squeezed juice: €2.50-3.50

- small bottle of water: €1

- large bottle of water: €2

- small beer: €2-3

- large beer: €3-5

- bottle of house wine: €7-10

- first course: €8-11

- second course: €11-15

TRANSPORTATION COSTS

- bus/metro fare: €1.50

- unleaded/diesel fuel: €1.30/1.50 per liter

- street parking: €1 per hour

SOUVENIRS

- postcard: €0.50

- stamp to North America: €2.20

to the Colosseum. The *polizia* (blue, 113) will listen to you recount how your iPad was stolen. The *carabiniere* (blue with red stripes, 112) shouldn't be disturbed unless you suspect terrorist activity.

Hospitals and Pharmacies

There are dozens of hospitals in the city center. The **Rome American Hospital** (Via Emilio Longoni 69, tel. 06/225-51) has no shortage of English-speaking doctors. **Policlinico Umberto I** (Viale del Policlinico 155, tel. 06/446-2341) is one of the largest facilities.

You'll find well-equipped **pharmacies** on Via Cola di Rienzo 213/215, (tel. 06/324-4476), Piazza Risorgimento 44 (tel. 06/397-38166), Piazza Barberini 49 (tel. 06/487-1195), Via Nazionale 228 (tel. 06/488-0754), and Viale Trastevere 229/229a (tel. 06/588-2273).

Foreign Consulates

If you misplace your passport, lose a friend, or need to declare a birth abroad, your consulate can help. The **United States consulate** (Via Veneto 119a/121, tel. 06/467-41) is located near the center, while the **Canadian consulate** (Via Zara, tel. 06/445-981) is located in the northwest of the city.

Lost and Found

Lost and found at **Leonardo da Vinci Airport** (tel. 06/6595-5253) is located inside Terminal 3. If your luggage doesn't arrive within a couple of hours you're better off leaving your details, telephone number, and address where you'll be staying. It's also worth checking with your airline in the arrivals halls outside.

If you've forgotten something on a bus call 06/581-6040 Monday to Friday between 7am and 6pm to see if it's been found. Lost items may also end up at the **Central Lost and Found Office** (Garbatella, Circonvallazione Ostiense 191, tel. 06/6769-3214, weekdays 8:30am-1pm, Thurs. 8:30am-5pm). Each line of the subway has its own lost-and-found office: Metro A (tel. 06/487-4309, daily 9:30am-12:30pm) and Metro B (tel. 06/575-4295,

daily 9am-6pm). Passports and other documents remain for 15 days before being transferred to police, and consulates are notified if items belong to foreigners. All offices provide information over the phone and there's a €9 recovery fee at the main office. The people who work in these offices are not especially sympathetic. However, a lot of stuff is recovered and being nice to them will facilitate the search.

COMMUNICATIONS
Wi-Fi

Rome has gone wireless, and anyone with a Wi-Fi-equipped device can access the Internet throughout Villa Borghese and many other locations throughout the city. The plan is to provide total coverage in the near future. Most of Rome's historic center is covered and the area around Piazza Navona is one continuous hot spot. Registration is quick and a confirmation call is required.

Internet cafes are still common in Rome. The cost for one hour of surfing is about €3. The most popular Internet point is the **EasyInternet** (Via sei Marrucini). You can also log on at **Internet Point** (Via Gaeta 25, tel. 06/4782-38662) and **TreviNet Place** (Via in Arcione 103, tel. 06/6992-2320).

Newspapers

Italian newsstands are crammed with newspapers and magazines on everything from knitting to military aviation. *La Repubblica* and *Corriere della Sera* are the two most popular papers, and both print local editions. Journalists in Italy don't seem to be familiar with objectivity, and most newspapers have some political agenda. For example, *L'Unità* represents the Communist Party, while *La Padania* serves the interest of the right-wing Lega Nord party. Italians really care about sports, and the best-selling broadsheets are the *Corriere dello Sport* and the pink *Gazzetta dello Sport*. Several Roman papers have an events listing that comes out midweek with a small English section. When in doubt, ask the newspaper attendant.

Transportation

GETTING THERE
Air
Rome has two international airports, Leonardo da Vinci and Ciampino.

LEONARDO DA VINCI
Leonardo Da Vinci Airport (FCO, tel. 06/65951, www.adr.it), also known as **Fiumicino**, is located near the sea 26 kilometers from the city center. It's the main intercontinental entry point, with three terminals and scheduled nonstop flights to and from dozens of North American and European cities. **Alitalia** is the Italian national carrier and provides service to many of these, although it is not necessarily the cheapest option. Alitalia is based in T3 while U.S. airlines are housed in the newly built T5 terminal. A tourist office is located in the arrivals hall along with currency exchange, bars, newsstands, and transportation services.

Trenitalia (www.trenitalia.com) operates two train shuttle services between Fiumicino and Termini station. **Leonardo Express** (€14) is a direct link that departs every 15-30 minutes from the airport between 6:23am and 11:23pm and from tracks 23 and 24 inside Termini station between 5:35am and 10:35pm. The trip takes 32 minutes and the service is guaranteed even during strikes. **FL1** (€11) service leaves every 15 minutes on weekdays and 30 minutes on weekends but makes a few extra stops along the way including Trastevere and Ostiense, which is convenient for anyone staying in Aventino or Testaccio. The journey takes 47 minutes. Tickets for both are available from the Trenitalia website, automatic ticket machines at the airport and train station, and many *tabacchi* shops and newsstands in the center.

SIT (www.sitbusshuttle.com, daily 8:30am-11:50pm, €6) and **Terravision** (www.terravision.eu, daily 5:35am-11pm, €4) buses provide service to Fiumicino. Journey time is around one hour with multiple departures per hour from outside the arrivals hall to Termini station.

Travelers in groups of three or four may find it convenient to take a **taxi**. Taxis are parked outside and drivers wait inside for travelers to clear customs, which is usually only a formality. Rides into the city center are fixed at €48 from Fiumicino. Bags are included in the fare.

CIAMPINO
Ciampino (CIA, tel. 06/65951, www.adr.it) is a smaller, one-terminal airport used by low-cost airlines flying to domestic and European destinations. **SIT** (www.sitbusshuttle.com) and **Terravision** (www.terravision.eu) buses outside the arrivals hall shuttle passengers to and from Termini station in the center. Both companies charge €4 for a one-way trip that takes 40 minutes.

Travelers in groups may want to consider a **taxi**. Rides into the city center are fixed at €30 from Ciampino. Bags are included in the fare.

Train
Trenitalia (www.trenitalia.com) operates the Italian rail network and runs local, intercity, and high-speed services. All types generally have a first-and second-class option and arrive at **Termini station** (www.romatermini. com, Metro A or B: Termini), which is the hub of the rail network and is located ten minutes east of the city center. The station itself contains many shops and eateries. The large number of travelers attracts some less-than-savory characters and only train spotters should linger; a barrier was recently added near the tracks to keep pickpockets away from passengers and tickets are necessary in order to access the platforms. The A and B lines of the subway intersect downstairs at the station and the main bus terminal is out front in Piazza dei Cinquecento.

There are several other train stations around the city including the ultramodern **Tiburtina station** (Metro B: Tiburtina) 2km east of Termini, where high-speed trains also stop; and **Porta San Paolo station** (Metro B: Piramide) in Testaccio, where commuter trains connect the city with Ostia Antica and the sea.

From Florence: High-speed trains arrive in 1.5 hours from Florence's Santa Maria Novella station. One-way standard fares start from €19. There are approximately 50 departures per day with either **Italo** or **Trenitalia.**

From Venice: Trains arrive in under 4 hours from Venice's Santa Lucia station. One-way standard fares start from €29. There are approximately 50 departures throughout the day. Trains departing from Venice also stop in Florence.

Car

Drivers arriving from the north on the A1 highway should exit at Rome Nord; those coming from the south should exit at Rome Est. Both lead to the Grande Raccordo Anulare (GRA), or ring road, from where the center can be easily reached via the Aurelia, Flaminia, or Colombo. The GRA also leads to both of the city's airports.

From Florence: There are several ways to reach Rome, and the fastest is also the simplest. Just get on the A1 highway on the western outskirts of Florence and follow it all the way to the Roma Nord/Aeroporti exit, which leads to the GRA ring road. The 280 kilometers (174 miles) can be covered in around 3 hours and there's an €18 toll at the exit.

From Venice: The journey from Venice is slightly less straightforward and requires merging onto several highways. Cross the bridge connecting Venice to the mainland and follow signs for the A57 towards Bologna. On the outskirts of Padova exit onto the A13 and continue following signs for the A1 Firenze near Bologna. There are a couple merges to make and then it's all A1 until Rome. The 530km (330-mile) journey takes around six hours and a costs €38 in a single final toll.

Bus

Eurolines (www.eurolines.com), **Flixibus** (www.flixbus.com), **Baltour** (www.baltour. it), and **Megabus** (www.megabus.com) operate daily service between Venice, Florence, and Rome. In Rome, passengers are dropped off in either Tiburtina or Termini stations. Most companies offer special discounts for travelers under 26 years old, and there are multiple-week passes that provide the freedom to board buses whenever you like.

From Florence: Most buses depart from or near Santa Maria Novella station and may make a couple of stops before getting onto the highway. The journey takes four hours (280km) and prices start at around €14 for a one-way ticket.

From Venice: Buses leave from the Tronchetto terminal west of the train station, which can be reached via the People Mover monorail from Piazzale Roma. Times for the 530km (330-mile) journey vary depending on the company but generally take between eight and eleven hours. Fares start at €17 and rise to €45.

GETTING AROUND

Rome's concentration of interesting sights makes walking the most convenient and rewarding form of transportation. Many streets in the center are now pedestrian-only. Although pedestrians do have the right of way at crosswalks, play it safe and pay special attention to moped and motorcycle drivers who often follow their own rules of the road.

The ferry that once carried visitors up and down the Tiber is no longer active, and bike sharing has suffered a similar fate. Luckily, **ATAC Rome** (www.atac.roma.it) offers a variety of transit options including subway, tram, bus, and train service to destinations throughout the city. Rush hour is best avoided and peaks 7am-9am and 5pm-7pm. For safety reasons, it's best to avoid Termini station after dark.

Transit Passes

There are a variety of travel passes available

from **ATAC** (www.atac.roma.it, tel. 800/431-784). A single **BIT ticket** (€1.50) allows unlimited transfer between subway, bus, and tram for 75 minutes after the ticket is first used. A full-day **BIG pass** costs €6. A three-day **BTI pass** is €16.50 and the **7-day CIS** version is €24. Tickets can be purchased at automated machines within subway stations as well as at most *tabacchi* (tobacco shops). All tickets and passes must be validated upon initial use of the transport network.

Metro

Rome's subway system is made up of two lines, **Metro A** and **Metro B,** which intersect at Termini train station. Daily service begins at 5:30am and the last train departs at 11:30pm (12:30am on Sat.). This two-line subway system doesn't cover all of the historic center, but you can easily reach the Colosseum, Vatican, Spanish Steps, and many other sights underground. Connecting commuter and shuttle trains travel to Ostia Antica and Fiumicino airport.

Most subway stations on the Metro B line are equipped with elevators, which isn't always the case with Metro A. However, **bus 590** follows the same route as this line and is wheelchair accessible.

Bus and Tram

Six trams and hundreds of bus lines operate throughout Rome day and night. Getting on and off city buses and trams provides the freedom to follow your instinct and discover the city in unexpected ways. Just remember to avoid the morning and evening rush hours (7am-9am and 5pm-7pm).

Many public buses travel through the city center, and riding these is both less expensive and more authentic than an organized bus tour. **Bus 40** from Termini to the Vatican, **23** from Piramide to the Vatican, and mini electric buses **116** and **119** through the historic center are all good options. **Tram 3** from Piramide to Villa Borghese is a long, pleasant ride passing the Circus Maximus, Colosseum,

and many 19th-century neighborhoods that are often overlooked by tourists.

The square outside Termini station is the starting point for over a dozen bus lines that connect all parts of the city. From here you can catch **Bus H** to Trastevere, which isn't served by the metro, **Bus 40** to Piazza Navona and the Vatican or **Bus 170** to Testaccio. The H and 40 bus lines, as well as Tram 8, terminate at **Largo Argentina,** which is a convenient stop for visiting the Vatican.

Bicycle

Exploring Rome on two wheels is risky and many drivers haven't gotten used to the idea of sharing the road. If you do rent a bike, wear a helmet and ride in parks, along pedestrianized streets, or along the few bike paths that do exist. Weekends are the best time to cycle because traffic is lighter and many locals get on their bikes. A route map for cyclists can be picked up at any TIP info kiosk and bicycles are available from rental shops around the city.

If you prefer a more relaxing ride with no cars, rent a bike in **Villa Borghese** or from the Park Information Office on **Via Appia Antica.** The latter offers several itineraries along the scenic ancient road that stretches many kilometers outside the city.

Taxi

Cabs can be useful, especially at night, and may be reserved by phone or picked up at taxi stands located within the larger squares (Piramide, Venezia, Popolo, and Trilussi). **Radio Taxi** (tel. 06/3570) and **Pronto Taxi** (tel. 06/6645) are two 24-hour options. Taxis are not generally hailed NYC or London style but that shouldn't stop you from trying. Payment can be made by credit card, and tipping is optional.

Fares are calculated by an initial rate of €3 on weekdays (€4.50 on weekends and €6.50 from 10pm to 6am) plus a combination of distance (€1.10 per kilometer) and time (45 cents per minute). Journeys to Leonardo da Vinci airport and the center are fixed at €48.

Ciampino airport is €30. To contest a fare make sure to get the receipt, which specifies the route, taxi number, and amount paid.

Car

Driving is the most challenging transportation option and more suited for leaving rather than entering the city. Cars offer little gratification unless you have hired a patient driver as well. Finding parking is time-consuming and expensive, and large sections of the historic center compose a limited traffic zone (ZTL) that requires a residential permit to enter. The ZTL is active on weekdays 6:30am-6pm and on Saturdays 2pm-6pm. Most hotels can provide a pass if you're arriving by car and cars rented within the ZTL are exempt.

Still, anyone determined to experience life in the Italian fast lane can do it easily and quickly. Rome has two car-sharing services that have become popular with residents and can be used by visitors as well. The blue-and-white Smart cars of Car2Go (www.car2go.com, €0.29 per minute/€14.90 per hour) are parked throughout the center. These are two-passenger vehicles, so if you need more space choose the red Fiat 500s of Enjoy (enjoy.eni.com, €0.25 per minute, €60 per day). Both services require online registration and possession of a passport, driver's license, and credit card. There are hundreds of cars parked around the city that can enter the historic center and be left anywhere without the need to pay for parking. Having a car at your disposal without the hassles of traditional renting is liberating and can help you discover the outskirts of Rome. It's also great for short journeys, and the same system operates in Florence.

For longer trips outside the city or between cities, traditional rental agencies can be found inside Termini (Platform 1, Via Marsala 29) or at either airport. Avis (tel. 06/481-4373), Europcar (tel. 06/488-2854), Maggiore (tel. 06/488-0049), and Sixt (tel. 06/3211-0194) have the largest fleets in Italy.

Day Trips

Rome is a big city. Its historic center is the most visited area, but that's just the beginning. Beyond the Aurelian walls lie ancient roads, a Roman town that rivals Pompeii, and Fascist-era suburbs. None of these are very far or difficult to reach, and each makes for interesting half-day excursion that will provide a different perspective on Rome. All are served by public transportation, and it only takes 30 minutes to get to Ostia Antica.

VIA APPIA ANTICA

Via Appia Antica is a magnificent thoroughfare, now part of a park, that served as the ancient gateway to Rome. This road lined with pine trees once connected Rome with the port of Brindisi, 570 kilometers to the southeast. It's a good place to better your understanding of the city's history. Once you arrive you'll be immersed in Roman countryside and surrounded by remnants of villas, tombs, and racetracks.

Walking from the Circus Maximus, it takes 20 minutes or more to reach the best parts of the ancient road. Several stretches along the way are not equipped with sidewalks. A visit can last anywhere from an hour to a half day depending on how much of this picturesque road you decide to explore. Although most of the ruins are clustered near the beginning, the farther you go the more scenic the landscape becomes. Stop at the park office (Via Appia Antica 42, tel. 06/512-6314, www.parcoappiaantica.it, daily 9:30am-5pm) pick up a guide or map of the area. Bike rentals (€3 per hour or €15 per day) are also available.

If you choose no tto walk, hop on the Archeobus / Bus 118, which departs Termini every 40 minutes, for a condensed overview of the sight. Tours of the park on horseback can be organized at **Riding Ancient Rome** (Via dei Cercenii 15, 392/788-5168, daily 7am-8pm, www.ridingancientrome.it, €40 per hour).

Sights

The first eye-openers on the road are two ancient residences once populated by wealthy Romans. **Torre Selce** can only be seen from the outside but **Villa dei Quintili** (tel. 06/3996-7700, Tues.-Sun. 9am-6:30pm, winter 9am-4pm, €6 combo ticket) was recently opened to the public. It was built by a consul and was the home of emperor Commodus during the second century AD. Guided tours are available upon reservation. Aqueducts can be seen in the distance and several of the Roman thirst quenchers are still in use today.

Further down the road is the **Circo di Massenzio** (€2). Private sponsorship of stadiums is another Roman innovation and this one is in better condition than its larger cousin the Circus Maximus. Here, ten thousand Romans regularly came to cheer their favorite charioteers.

Cecilia Metella (Via Appia Antica 161, daily 9am-4:30pm, €6 combined ticket) is the first of several monumental tombs. Like the others it has been transformed over the ages according to the whims of its owners. It's now a museum where visitors can examine the interior of an ancient grave.

Food

A bottle of wine, a loaf of bread, cold cuts, cheese, and clementines are all you need for a good picnic along the grassy banks of Appia Antica. If you prefer something less improvised, there are several restaurants lining the road. **Antica Hosteria L'Archeologia** (Via Appia Antica 139, daily 12:30pm-3pm and 8pm-11pm, €14) near the Catacombs of San Sebastiano is one of the oldest and a good way to start or finish a day on the ancient road. **Trattoria Da Priscilla** (Via Appia Antica 68, Tues.-Sun. 12:30pm-2:30pm and 7:30pm-10:30pm, €10) is a rustic option serving traditional Roman dishes in humble surroundings.

They only accept cash and the bathroom is outside next to the park office.

EUR

EUR is a suburb 10 kilometers south of the historic city that Benito Mussolini began in the 1930s. The acronym stands for the Universal Exposition of Rome, which was planned for 1942. The world had other priorities at the time and Il Duce's dream neighborhood wasn't completed until the 1960s. Buildings are monumental and clad in white marble that has aged well. In the center there's an artificial lake and an arena built for the 1960 Olympics where concerts are held today.

Sights

Palazzo della Civilta del Lavoro (Piazza G. Agnelli) is the symbol of the area and one of the first buildings completed. You'll understand why Romans call it the *Colosseum Quadrato* (square Colosseum) very quickly. Coincidentally, the six vertical and nine horizontal arches correspond with the number of letters in Benito Mussolini's first and last name. From the front steps there's an architecturally uniform view towards **Palazzo dei Congressi** (Piazza John Kennedy 1, tel. 06/5451-3705), which hosts trade fairs and events. It's also where Rome Marathon participants pick up their bib numbers. **Museo della Civilta Romana** (Piazza G. Agnelli 10, tel. 06/592-6135, Tues.-Sun. 9am-2pm, €8.50) is a must for die-hard fans of antiquity and contains both a scale model of Imperial Rome and a replica of Trajan's Column.

The artificial lake is a pleasant break for anyone with time to spare. In spring the cherry blossoms around the lake bloom and you can rent a pedal boat or sailboat (€10) from the little dock near the waterfall. Small children will enjoy the two playgrounds or feeding the ducks and turtles who call the lake home. There's a weekly Sunday market during the summer that sells street food, antiques, clothing and knickknacks in front of Palazzo della Civilta del Lavoro. Several blocks away,

Viale Europa is a mix of boutiques and chain stores primarily geared towards women.

Food

There are a variety of eateries on Viale America, which runs parallel to Viale Europa and faces the lake. You can choose from Chinese, Japanese, kebab, or modern Italian. **Il Bistrot** (Vialeamerica 3, tel. 06/8892-0800, daily 6:30am-10pm, €5) is a good option for a sandwich or buffet washed down with a local craft beer. It gets crowded at lunch so you may just want to grab takeaway and eat on a park bench.

Getting There

EUR is 20 minutes from Termini on the Metro B line towards Laurentina. The neighborhood has three stops. EUR Magliana is the first and most convenient for visiting Palazzo della Civilta del Lavoro, while EUR Fermi and EUR Palasport are near the lake and shops. The Roma-Ostia train leaves from Piramide every 15 minutes and stops at EUR Magliana. Most 700 bus lines terminate in EUR day and night. The 714 runs express from Termini and provides a different view of the city. Once in EUR all the sights are within walking distance although there is a taxi stand on Viale Europa.

OSTIA ANTICA

The ancient city of Ostia Antica provides an instant sense of how the Romans lived. The ruins here are more extensive than those in the city center, and it's easy to imagine oneself on the way to the forum.

The town was founded as a fort at the mouth of the Tiber to protect Rome from invaders. When threats faded, it evolved into a major port where Egyptian grain and other materials from across the empire were stored. Today, Ostia Antica contains warehouses, apartment buildings, shops, ands temples. At its peak, the population numbered nearly 100,000 and might have continued growing if the river here hadn't silted up and a second port been built. The consequence was a slow decline and gradual burial that has yet to be fully excavated.

Sights

The entrance to **Ostia Antica** (Viale dei Romagnoli 717, tel. 06/5635-0215, www. ostiaantica.beniculturali.it, winter Tues.-Sun. 8:30am-5pm, summer Tues.-Sun. 9am-7:15pm, €8) is on the Decumanus, the Roman main street that ran from east to west. Immediately on the left are dozens of stone **sarcophagi,** and behind these are small

the lake in EUR

family burial chambers where the remains of cremated relatives were placed and frequently visited. (Death was kept outside the city walls and cemeteries ran along the major roads.) Farther along on the right is the first of several **baths,** a major component of every Roman city. From the top of the steps you can get a good view of the various rooms and the mosaics depicting Neptune. Citizens came here once a day to wash, relax, exercise, or socialize.

Even if actors weren't particularly respected in Roman times, theater was popular and Greek-style plays were regularly performed. Ostia's **amphitheater** is a short distance from the baths. Its surprisingly good condition is a result of restoration during the 1930s. The theater has a semicircular shape, and the three large masks on the stage once formed part of the backdrop. From the last row of the amphitheater **Piazzale delle Corporazioni** is visible directly in front. This large complex once held the offices of importers and the various guilds responsible for keeping ships afloat. The mosaics in front of each doorway were similar to modern-day neon and indicated the origin and business of the traders inside.

The **forum** is located where the Decumanus intersected with the Cardo to form the heart of the city. This is where citizens gathered on religious or civic occasions and where business was conducted. The temple in the center was built by Hadrian in the 2nd century AD. Adjacent to the forum are the largest baths that include a public latrine, which could still function in an emergency. The apartments nearby include the **House of Diana,** which was lined with shops and a bar where antique happy hours were once served.

Ostia Antica is quite extensive. Most visitors turn back after reaching the forum, although much remains to be explored farther south. If you have time, get off the main road and get face to face with history. Most of the time the site is fairly empty except for school groups and adventurous visitors. The **museum** (daily 10:30am-4pm) near the middle contains the artifacts discovered over the years and offers further insight into daily Roman life. A snack bar and gift shop handle any food and postcard needs.

Food

It's easy to work up an appetite exploring the past, and **Il Monumento** (Piazza Umberto

Ostia Antica

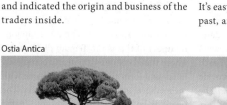

18, tel. 06/565-0021, Tues.-Sun. 12:30pm-3:30pm and 8pm-11pm, €13-16) has the solution. The *spaghetti monumento* is the house dish for a reason and is served with fresh seafood sauce. Outdoor dining is available in the carefully tended garden. The restaurant is located near a small castle in the pleasant village-like *borgo* opposite Ostia Antica.

Getting There
The train from Piramide station departs every 15 minutes and takes less than 30 minutes to reach Ostia Antica station. From there, it's a 5-minute walk to the entrance of the ancient city. If you don't feel like heading straight back after your visit, ride the train to the last stop and have a walk along the Mediterranean.

Between Rome and Florence

ASSISI
As one of the most important artistic and religious centers in Italy, Assisi attracts a crowd. Over six million pilgrims visit the town every year, with many of them there to see the home and burial site of St. Francis. To find peace from the rush of busy thoroughfare Corso Mazzini, climb the steep streets behind Piazza del Comune towards the castle looming above the town.

Sights
BASILICA DI SAN FRANCESCO
Basilica di San Francesco (Piazza Superiore, tel. 075/819-9001, www.sanfrancescoassisi.org, Basilica Inferiore daily 6am-6:50pm, free; Basilica Superiore daily 8:30am-6:50pm, free, audio guide available) consists of two churches built on top of each other. Two booths outside the basilica provide free audio guides to the entire complex. The lower church was begun in 1228 several years after St. Francis's death. It has a more intimate feel and was intended to accommodate the growing number of pilgrims who venerated Francis. The upper church dates from 1230 and has a grander style. The crypt that houses the saint's body was dug in 1818 and is below the lower church.

Both churches attracted the finest artists of the time, and nearly every centimeter of the interior is frescoed. The lower church contains biblically themed frescoes by Lorenzetti and Martini, but the most impressive works are those by Giotto, who nearly singlehandedly invented a new perspective. His paintings gave depth to landscapes and figures that had previously appeared flat. He painted a series of 28 frescoes inside the upper church over five years starting in 1290. The panels illustrate the life of St. Francis, with the most dramatic panel showing the saint renouncing his father's wealth and stripping himself before God. Giotto's cycle starts on the far right side of the church near the choir. The first painting depicts the future saint in his youth; a man spreads a cloth over the ground where he will step, foretelling his destiny of purity.

PIAZZA DEL COMUNE
Piazza del Comune is located on the spot of the old Roman Forum. The most obvious reminder of this is the Tempio di Minerva, whose fluted columns are nearly completely intact and form an interesting contrast with the medieval Palazzo del Popolo nearby. The inside is lavishly decorated in gold-leafed sculptures.

BASILICA DI SANTA CHIARA
Basilica di Santa Chiara (Piazza Santa Chiara, tel. 075/812-282, daily 6:30am-noon and 2pm-7pm, free) was constructed from pink stone dug from the nearby mountains. Its 12th-and 14th-century frescoes are particularly well preserved and depict the saint who founded the Clarissa order of nuns. In the chapel on the right along the single nave is the cross on which St. Francis vowed to reform the church.

Food

Every time the bell rings at the **Trattoria Pallotta** (Vicolo della Volta Pinta, tel. 075/815-5273, www.pallottaassisi.it, Wed.-Mon. noon-2:30pm and 7pm-10pm, €8-12) something good comes out of the kitchen. There are three tasting menus for those who can't decide, and the choices include many vegetarian options. Visitors are greeted with a smile as soon as they enter and are given a choice of tables in one of two rustic rooms. The family also runs a small hotel nearby.

A medieval atmosphere in the center of Assisi is only half the attraction of **Buca di San Francesco** (Via E. Brizi 1, tel. 075/812-204, Tues.-Sun. noon-3pm and 7pm-10:30pm, €10-14). The other half is the food, which excels from the appetizers to the desserts. *Fantasia di bruschette* is a good way to start and will arrive on your table within minutes. Trust Giovanni Betti to make the right wine selection to accompany your food.

What started out as a hobby among four friends has become **La Piazzetta dell'Erba** (Via San Gabriele dell'Addolorato 15b, tel. 075/815-352, Tues.-Sun. 12:30pm-2:30pm and 7pm-10:30pm, €12-15). Their interpretation of Umbrian classics includes a salad of pecorino, pear, nuts, and honey. Meals are served inside amid modern décor or outside on a quiet pedestrian street.

Getting There and Around

Assisi is 183km (114 miles) from Rome and is less than two hours from the capital by car. The fastest route is north on the A1 highway to the Orte exit, after which drivers should follow the E45 and SS3. **Sulga** (www.sulga.it, tel. 075/500-9641, €18.50) buses connect Rome and Assisi and depart twice daily Monday-Saturday (7am and 10:30am) and once on Sunday (8:15am) from Tiburtina station and Fiumicino airport Terminal 3. There are several stops along the way and the journey takes three hours.

Most trains from Termini in Rome require a transfer in Foligno, and it can take anywhere from 90 minutes to 3 hours to reach Assisi

depending on the service. The nearest train station to Assisi is six kilometers outside of town in Santa Maria degli Angeli. Travelers can complete the journey by bus or taxi. The journey costs €10. **APM buses** (tel. 800/512-141, www.apmperugia.it) connect Perugia and surrounding towns with Assisi. All journeys start and terminate in Piazza Matteotti. A minibus service operates within the town and connects the principal monuments and *piazze*. It runs every 30 minutes and tickets may be purchased at newsstands or *tabacchi*. Taxi stands are located in Piazza Unità d'Italia and Piazza del Comune, or cabs may be ordered 24 hours a day from **Radio Taxi Assisi** (tel. 075/813-100, www.radiotaxiassisi.it).

SIENA

Siena offers a refreshing break between the endless monuments of Rome and the extraordinary art of Florence. It feels more like a small town than a city and can easily be navigated in an hour or two on foot. Most of the streets lead to the shell shaped piazza del campo in the historic center. The other essential stop in Siena is the Duomo which was built in Roman-Gothic style and is one of the great churches of Italy.

Siena first rose to prominence under the Lombards in the 6th century A.D. It experienced a population influx during the Middle Ages when wealthy families began building their houses along the Via Francigena on the highest part of town. Prosperity brought about conflict with Florence and the numerous battles that ensued are immortalized in Dante's *Divine Comedy*. Beating the Florentines was one thing, but surviving the plague of 1348 was another. The Black Death brought construction to a halt and began a long period of instability, which ended with Siena's submission to its larger neighbor.

Siena is divided into 17 contrade or neighborhoods. They are located within the medieval walls of the city and each has its own colors, coat of arms and motto. Numbers have special relevance in Siena. The nine sections of the Piazza del Campo represent the Council

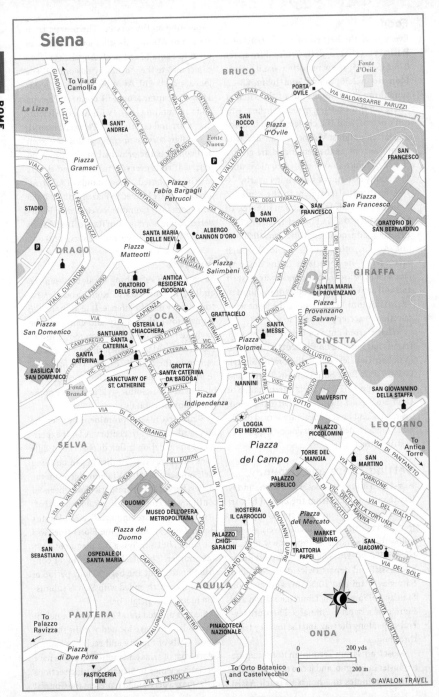

Siena

of Nine, which ruled the city in the 13th and 14th centuries. There are 17 *contrade* (parishes) that inspire loyalty from birth and from which contestants are selected during the two annual *palios* (horse races). Then there are the Terzi, the three districts the town has been divided into since its founding. Terzo di Città is where the Duomo and Siena's oldest buildings stand. The central Capitana dell'Onde borders Piazza del Campo and stretches south of the square.

Sights
PIAZZA DEL CAMPO
Wherever you enter Siena, you are inevitably drawn to **Piazza del Campo.** The main square has inherited its famous seashell shape from the whims and jerks of medieval urbanization. Fonte Gaie fountain at the northern end is a beautiful replacement for the 15th-century original sculpted by Jacopo della Quercia and now kept safe in Santa Maria della Scala. It's also the location of Siena's famous horse race, the Palio delle Contrade.

    Palazzo Pubblico (Piazza del Campo, tel. 05/7729-2226, 10am-6pm, €7) is at the bottom of the sloping piazza and was constructed in a Gothic style at the end of the 12th century. The elegant structure has a gentle concave facade and on the side **Torre del Mangia** (Mangia Tower) rises 88 meters into the sky, providing a great views of the Tuscan countryside in the distance. All that separates you from a view reminiscent of the frescoes in the rooms below is 300 steps.

DUOMO
The Duomo is hard to miss. It's the largest building in town, an immense marble ship moored in the center of everything. Built in Roman-Gothic style, it is one of the great churches of Italy and might even have been the biggest church in the world had the plague not brought construction to a halt. The alternating white-and-black marble is its most striking feature, and the large number of columns on the inside creates many unexpected perspectives. The pavement built in the 15th century is unique and made of 56 immense squares featuring mythological and biblical figures. The pulpit carved by Nicola Pisano illustrates the life of Christ in a highly dramatic fashion. Inside the Duomo are the library and **Museo dell'Opera Metropolitana** (tel. 05/7728-3048, www.operaduomo.siena. it, 9am-7:30pm, €6), featuring remains of the unfinished section of the church, paintings, and sculpture that once resided in the church.

Piazza del Campo in Siena

OSPEDALE DI SANTA MARIA

Ospedale di Santa Maria (Piazza Duomo 2, tel. 05/7722-4828, daily 10:30am-6:30pm, €6) was the first hospital in the city. It was where pilgrims would get their blisters looked at and anyone with a serious disease might find a little relief. It was operational until a few years ago and now houses a museum. Inside, Sala del Pellegrinaio is a monumental vaulted corridor, built in the 14th century as a passageway for the many pilgrims on their way to or from Rome. The ceilings and walls are covered with frescos predating the Renaissance style that would later make Florence famous. Exhibitions are frequent and cover a wide variety of interests.

PINACOTECA NAZIONALE

Since the 1920s, Palazzo Buonsignori has housed the **Pinacoteca Nazionale** (Via San Pietro 29, tel. 05/7728-6143, Tues.-Sat. 9am-7pm, Mon. and Sun. 8:30am-1pm, €6) and a premier collection of Sienese artwork. Most of the paintings date from the 13th-17th centuries, and the collection presents a clear picture of how art developed in the city over the years. There is an unrivaled quantity of gold-painted canvases, many of which were donated by local churches and convents. Works by Ambrogio and Pietro Lorenzetti, Sassetta, and Beccafumi are all on display. The sculpture room in the second-story loggia has an excellent view of the city.

TERZO DI CAMOLLIA

The Terzo di Camollia district is on the northern edge of the city; although it was rebuilt in recent centuries, many of its medieval monuments have been preserved. **Via di Camollia** runs through the center of the neighborhood and is the home of churches San Pietro and Santa Maria, completed in 1484. At the end of the road is Porta Camollia, one of the original medieval entrances to the city. Anyone who understands Latin will be able to read the inscription welcoming visitors to Siena.

BASILICA DI SAN DOMENICO

Catherine Benincasa is the patron saint of Italy and Europe. She lived in the area and had her visions inside **Basilica di San Domenico.** There are several portraits of her within this Gothic church overlooking the Fontebranda Valley. Halfway along the nave on the right side is a chapel dedicated to the saint with a sculpture and frescoes by Sodoma recalling her short life.

Siena's Duomo

TERZO DI SAN MARTINO

East of Piazza del Campo is **Terzo di San Martino** neighborhood. Via di Città is the main thoroughfare and is flanked by the city's finest palazzi. **Palazzo Piccolomini** is distinguished by immense blocks of ashlar Rossellino used to bring a little Florentine style to Siena. Almost directly opposite is the slightly curved **Palazzo Chigi-Saracini** that now houses a music academy. Farther down on the right is **Loggia dei Mercanti,** which marked a transition between Gothic and Renaissance architecture when it was added in the 16th century. The street also passes **Piazza Salimbeni,** enclosed on three sides by three buildings in three different styles. It's a good test for anyone who gets Gothic, Renaissance, and baroque confused.

ORTO BOTANICO

Biagio Bartalini liked plants so much he founded the **Orto Botanico** (Via P. A. Mattioli 4, tel. 05/7729-8871, Mon.-Fri. 8am-12:30pm and 2:30pm-5:30pm, Sat. 8am-noon, free) in 1784. The 2.5-acre botanical garden situated in a small valley near Porta Tufi is divided into three sections. The first contains the most local Tuscan species you'll see in one spot. They include herbs, aromatics, and medicinal varieties that were used by Ospedale di Santa Maria in the 18th century. Aquatic plants, fruit trees, and cacti grow in the other areas and a tepidarium protects vulnerable leaves. The garden is a favorite destination of birds that serenade visitors with song. Serious horticulturists can reserve a tour of the grounds.

Food

Mass tourism may have lowered the standards of some Siena restaurants, but **Castelvecchio** (Via Castelvecchio 65, tel. 05/774-9586, Mon.-Sat. noon-3:30pm and 7pm-11pm, €7-12) is not one of them. Simone Romi is attentive to the quality of food he serves and the service he provides both locals and visitors. The menu changes daily and the prix fixe (€25) is a good option if you want to get a wide sampling of Tuscan flavors. It comes with an antipasto, three different pastas, two seconds, and dessert.

"Historic" may be a strange way to describe a restaurant, but it's the only way to summarize the traditional food and lively atmosphere of **Trattoria Papei** (Piazza Mercato 6, tel. 05/7728-0894, €10-14). The selection of grilled meats will satisfy carnivores and the informality of the waitstaff provides excellent entertainment while waiting for the next carafe of house wine to arrive.

Thanks to the outdoor tables added in the summer the wait at **Osteria la Chiacchera** (Costa di Sant'Antonio 4, tel. 05/7728-0631, daily 12:30pm-3:30pm and 7pm-11pm, €8-9) is considerably reduced. In all other seasons it's wise to make a reservation and ensure you get a taste of traditional dishes served in this minuscule restaurant.

Cravings for cheese and cured meats can strike at any moment in Siena. When they do, **Grattacielo** (Via dei Pontani 8, tel. 05/7728-9326, €10) has a cutting board ready. The restaurant also prepares one locally inspired dish each night. But perhaps the best thing about this place is the feeling you get walking in the streets afterwards realizing how little you paid for such good food.

Getting to **Grotta di Santa Caterina da Bagoga** (Via della Galluzza 26, tel. 05/57728-2208, Tues.-Sat. noon-3pm and 7-11:30pm, Sun. noon-3pm, €8-11) is half the fun. The labyrinth of streets leading to the restaurant are some of the most suggestive in the city. The owner is a former *palio* rider and the tables outside provide a unique environment to have lunch or dinner. The cooking is strictly Sienese and offers a wide choice of seasonal dishes. Wine is mainly from the Rufina and local hillsides.

Hosteria il Carroccio (Via di Casato di Sotto 32, tel. 05/774-1165, Thurs.-Tues. noon-3:30pm and 7pm-11pm, €7.50-10) remains one of the most affordable options around Piazza del Campo. Service may be a little hurried but it's always efficient. Waitstaff dispense with menus in the evening and you may have to ask them to repeat themselves a few times. Antipasto includes *salumi* and there is generally some variation of wild boar pasta. Surprisingly good salads are also served. The dozen or so tables on the inside are set within a small room carved out of rock. Nearby on the same street **Cantina in Piazza** sells nearly all of the wines produced in the DOCG (appellation) areas of the province.

Antica Trattoria Botteganova (Via Chiantigiani 29, tel. 05/7728-4230, Mon.-Sat. 12:30pm-2:30pm and 7:30pm-10:30pm, €10-14) is considered one of the best restaurants in Siena. It's outside the city walls on the SS408 in the direction of Montevarchi, but gourmets won't mind the detour. An elegant, rustic interior and refined table settings complement the elaborate fish and meat dishes chef Michele prepares. The three tasting menus (€37-45) are an introduction to creative Sienese cuisine and should be approached on an empty stomach. Reservations are almost always required on weekends.

Nannini (Via Banchi di Sopra 22, tel. 05/7723-6009) is the most famous bar in Siena and earned its reputation one espresso at a time. The sweets are especially memorable and gelato fans may add it to their top-10 list.

Since 1943, **Pasticceria Bini** (Via Stalloreggi 91, tel. 05/7728-0207) has baked all of the town's high-octane specialties, from *panforte margherita* to *cannoli alla mandorla*. The selection is best in the morning but midafternoon is a quiet time when you can browse the sweets in relative calm.

Festivals and Events

Lots of saints are celebrated in Siena but it's **Festa di San Giuseppe** on March 19 that's the most spirited. Via Dupre in citry center is lined with stalls displaying of arts and crafts and selling toys and sweets. Around Piazza del Campo and the church of San Giuseppe the intoxicating smell of *frittelle* (fried rice) is hard to resist and outdoor stands remain open until late.

Twice a year Siena turns back the clock and transforms the Piazza del Campo into a racetrack where thousands cram to watch the **Palio delle Contrade.** For locals the main event is on July 2, while the second race on August 16 is nicknamed the "*palio* of the tourists." Both days begin with a parade around the outer perimeter of the piazza, which is covered in sand to prevent horses from slipping. It's best to arrive several hours before the midafternoon start. The best places to stand are on the outer edges to the left or right of the fountain from where nearly the entire course can be observed. The race consists of three laps and an anything-goes approach with the winner carried back to his *contrade* for a victory dinner where the horse is the guest of honor.

Shopping

Via di Città is the main shopping street in Siena and contains clothing, book, food, and craft shops. Most days it's filled with tourists hunting for souvenirs. Don't let that stop you from taking a look and stopping by some of the more interesting addresses.

Antiques aren't hard to find in Siena. What is hard to find is a selection as vast as that at **Antichità Monna Agnese** (Via di Città 60, tel. 05/7728-2288). The store is a favorite with collectors who appreciate Italian country furnishings and can date objects down to the decade. Novices who can't distinguish between centuries may still find the collection of antique jewelry interesting. Agnese usually participates in the craft and antiques market held on the third Sunday of each month in Piazza Mercato.

Bruna Fontana spends so much time chatting with clients it's hard to believe she ever has time to finish any of the needlework that fills her small shop. **Siena Ricama** (Via di Città 61, tel. 05/7728-8339, Mon.-Sat. 9am-1pm and 3pm-6pm) is the place to go for embroidery. You'll find everything from handmade lampshades to handkerchiefs that can be personalized. The designs Bruna creates have a medieval quality and are nearly as interesting as the frescos nearby.

The ceramics of **Ceramiche Artistiche**

Santa Caterina (tel. 05/7728-3098, Mon.-Fri. 9am-11am and 4:30pm-6:30pm) are produced in Via P.A. Mattioli 12 and displayed in several shops on Via di Città 74-76. Marcello Neri and his wife have been behind the pottery wheel for decades and trained at the most important studios in Tuscany. The Sienese style is recognizable by its exclusive use of black and white, with designs inspired by the Duomo. Utilitarian and more fanciful objects line the shelves. It's best to ask before touching anything.

Stained glass may not be high on your souvenir list but the artists at **Vetrate Artistiche Toscane** (Via della Galluzza 5, tel. 05/774-8033, Mon.-Sat. 9am-1pm and 3pm-6pm) may change your mind. Their secular and religious creations come in every size and shape and make a nice addition to nearly any wall. The store doubles as a workshop where craftsmen can often be observed. They also run glassblowing apprentice workshops during the summer.

The goods sold at **Antica Drogheria Manganelli** (Via di Città 73, tel. 05/7728-0002) should be tasted. It's pasta is all handmade by small producers in the area and some of the vinegar is 80 years old.

Accommodations

San Francesco (Vicolo degli Orbachi 2, tel. 05/774-6533, www.bb-sanfrancesco.com, €75-100 s/d) is in the *contrada* Bruco, a working-class neighborhood where support for the local *palio* rider is always high. The 16 rooms at the bed-and-breakfast are immaculate and equipped with the essentials. There's something homey about the simplicity and the Tuscan greeting that guests receive from owner Massimo Giuliani. He is the best person to ask for shopping, dining, or sightseeing advice. A 30 percent advance deposit may be required depending on the season; check with Massimo.

Dante mentions **Albergo Cannon d'Oro** (Via Montanini 28, tel. 05/774-4321, www.cannondoro.com, €80-99 s/d) in his "Purgatory" poem and it may have something

to do with the old set of stairs guests must climb to reach their rooms. If stairs aren't a problem (there are several rooms on the ground floor), this medium-sized hotel at the intersection of a vibrant neighborhood near Piazza Salimbeni is an excellent option. Breakfast is included and the friendly staff can provide assistance 24 hours a day.

The Cicogna family has restored a medieval *palazzo* and turned it into an ideally located bed-and-breakfast minutes from the Piazza del Campo and Duomo. Each of the five rooms of **Antica Residenza Cicogna** (Via dei Termini 67, tel. 05/7728-5613, www.anticaresidenzacicogna.it, €83-100 s/d) is decorated in a unique style and benefits from high frescoed ceilings. Breakfast is the occasion to taste local biscuits and breads such as *cavallucci, copate,* and *panforte.* Fresh fruit and yogurt are also served.

Antica Torre (Via di Fieravecchia 7, tel. 05/7722-2255, www.anticatorresiena.it, €90-120 s/d) has preserved the marble paving and cast-iron beds that might have greeted medieval travelers. There are two rooms per floor at this small hotel 10 minutes from Piazza del Campo. The two on the top floor provide rooftop views and a glimpse of the Tuscan countryside in the distance. Breakfast is an additional €7.

Palazzo Ravizza (Pian dei Mantellini 34, tel. 05/7728-0462, €120-180 s/d) is a vintage *palazzo* with 30 rooms that haven't lost their Renaissance charm. The hotel dates from the 1920s and has been run by the same family in a peaceful *contrade* within walking distance of everything. Modern comforts have been added without sacrificing the building's character and the shaded garden provides a welcome refuge in summertime. Parking is available and the restaurant is more than adequate.

The parishioners who run **Santuario Santa Caterina** (Via Camporeggio 37, tel. 05/774-4177, €65 d) understand the relation between cleanliness and godliness. Rooms may be stark but they couldn't be any cleaner, and if you don't mind the 11:30pm curfew this may be the best place to contemplate Siena. Many of the 31 rooms in the sanctuary have views of the Duomo and San Domenico. It goes without saying that there's no TV and the front desk can be slightly irritable.

Information and Services

The Siena **APT office** (tel. tel. 05/7728-0551, www.terresiena.it, daily 9am-7pm) is located on Piazza del Campo and is extremely well organized. If you've come without a plan, they have countless ideas for spending time in the city and province. Museum tickets are on sale and there are various combination offers.

Getting There

FROM ROME

Trains from Rome leave every hour for Siena between 5:32am and 11:07pm. Most departures are at 10 minutes past the hour. The two-hour trip costs €5.70 for a second-class seat. All trains require a transfer at Grosseto or Chiusi.

There are several ways to reach Siena from Rome by car. The fastest is the A1 highway, which covers the 230 km (140 miles) in 2.5 hours. The A12 coastal highway is slightly more scenic but adds an additional hour to the journey. Tolls cost less on this route and drivers will need to exit onto the E78 near the town of Grosseto to reach Siena. The slowest and most picturesque alternative is the SR2, a one-lane state road that can be crowded at times and passes through many small towns and villages.

FROM FLORENCE

Florence and Siena are linked the 78-km (50 mile) stretch of Raccordo Autostradale Firenze-Siena highway. It's a Journey time is under an hour. When arriving from the south, use the A1 exit at Chiusi for a scenic drive along the N146 or take the following exit at Valdichiana to reach Siena more quickly.

Regular **SITA** and **Train** (Piazza Gramsci, tel. 05/7720-4246, www.trainspa.it) buses leave from Florence's Piazza Santa Maria Novella. The journey takes 1.5 hours and makes a dozen stops along the way. A one-way ticket to Siena costs €6.50 and may be purchased at the SITA office in the piazza.

Getting Around

The historic center of Siena has been pedestrian-friendly since the 1960s and there is no better way of exploring the narrow streets and alleys than on foot. Public buses run through the modern parts of town and there is extra-urban service to many of the surrounding communities leaving from Piazza Gramsci. A car is useful for reaching destinations further afield and can be rented from **Hertz** (Via Sardegna 37, tel. 05/774-5085, daily 9am-7pm).

Florence

Highlights

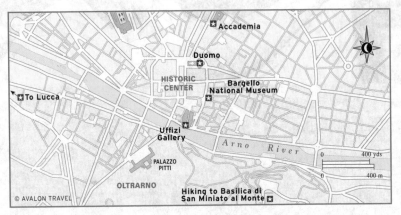

★ **Duomo:** Rising above the city is a monumental reminder of Brunelleschi's creative genius. Take a look inside the dome to see how its unique structure defies gravity (page 148).

★ **Bargello National Museum:** One of the least crowded museums in Florence offers a look at Donatello's *David,* ancient military hardware, and the city's first police headquarters (page 152).

★ **Uffizi Gallery:** Florentine artists added a realistic dimension to paintings that transformed art forever. Get a close-up view at the Uffizi (page 154).

★ **Accademia:** Michelangelo's masterworks are the stars here. The *David* sculpture gets an entire room to itself and is surrounded by adoring fans (page 156).

★ **Hiking to Basilica San Miniato al**

Monte: This church marks the highest point in Florence, providing undisturbed views of the skyline. Take the back route up the hillside and avoid the crowds (page 166).

★ **Gelato:** There are 136 *gelaterie* (gelato shops) in Florence. Sample as many as possible (page 174).

★ **Italian Coffee:** The Florentine contribution to coffee-making made caffeine history (page 177).

★ **Aperitivo Bars:** Enjoying an *aperitivo* alongside a *Negroni* cocktail is the perfect transition from afternoon to evening (page 181).

★ **Lucca:** Florence is only a fraction of Tuscany. This charming, immaculately preserved walled city is less than an hour away by train (page 216).

Firenze, as locals call their city, has a justified marble chip on its shoulder. After all, this was the cradle of the Renaissance, where civilization was given an injection of creativity after centuries of artistic stagnation.

Visiting Florence means walking the same streets that were graced by the presence of great artists and thinkers, including Dante Alighieri, Leonardo da Vinci, Machiavelli, and Galileo Galilei. Today, the Ponte Vecchio still stands, and the Uffizi remains the place to go for art. On the other side of town, Michelangelo's *David* waits to be examined, and Brunelleschi's majestic dome is never far from view.

Museums and basilicas aren't the only attractions. Florence gradually seduces with its clean, well-ordered streets and pleasant yellow facades. Beauty is everywhere in this city. Many old towers and lavish homes as well as large portions of the defensive walls can still be seen today. There are secluded monasteries and chapels to explore, where a little curiosity leads to unexpected discoveries. The city hasn't lost its creative touch, either (although the Renaissance will always be a hard act to follow). Artisans pound away on the backstreets of the Oltrarno neighborhood, and the wallets sold along Via de' Tornabuoni are hard to resist.

Discovering Florence also means getting to know its inhabitants. Florentines may be more reserved than their Roman cousins, but they are always ready to talk about their city and remain as devoted to it as the Medici family, Florence's famed patrons of the arts. Their pride is visible in workshops, markets, and squares where young and old congregate daily. It can be heard on summer nights when music echoes down the streets on both sides of the Arno, and tasted at the *trattorie* faithfully serving traditional *pappa al pomodoro* and *ribollita*. Experiencing this side of Florence is a lot easier than getting into the Uffizi—and equally satisfying.

Previous: Piazzale Michelangelo; Ponte Vecchio. **Above:** Piazza della Signoria.

Florence

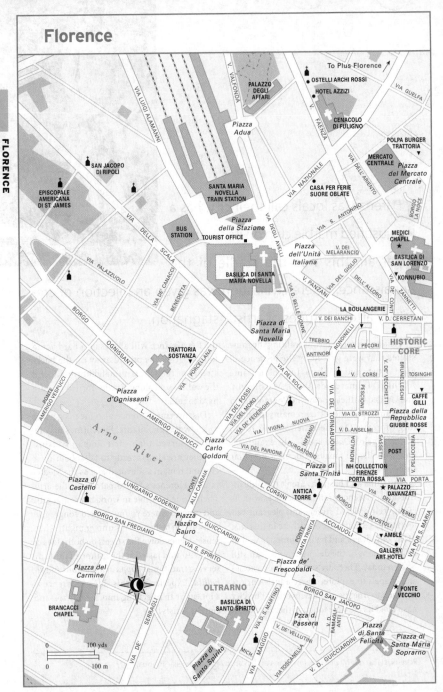

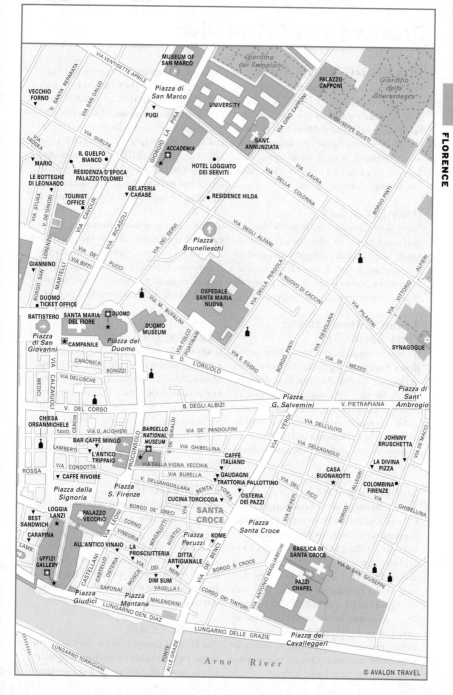

Planning and Orientation

PLANNING YOUR TIME

Florence may be ten times smaller than Rome, but that doesn't mean it deserves less attention. Three days will allow you to visit a number of major sights and still have time to climb the hills overlooking the city, explore landscaped gardens, observe a half-dozen *Last Suppers,* take a bus out to Fiesole, and ride a bike through Parco delle Cascine.

Daily Reminders

Many sights (monasteries in particular) are only open mornings while others close for lunch or on Mondays. Sights also tend to have seasonal hours, closing a few hours earlier from November to March. Check opening times ahead of time to avoid disappointment.

Advance Bookings and Time-Saving Tips

It's easy to spend more time waiting in line than actually visiting the iconic monuments in Florence. It's therefore vital to make reservations for the sights you intend to visit, or purchase a Firenzecard, which offers quicker entry. Advance reservations for many sights, including the **Accademia** and **Uffizi,** can be made on the city's official website www.firenzeturismo.it.

Sightseeing Passes

The **Firenzecard** (www.firenzecard.it) costs €72 and is valid for 72 hours after its first use. It provides free entry to all major museums in the city, including the Duomo sights, and speedier access to the most popular sights such as the Uffizi and cathedral dome. Just look for the Firenzecard sign and have your card ready to be scanned. It also provides Wi-Fi access and free bus and tram transport over a three-day period. Even if you're only staying two days, or are unsure it's worth the investment, remember the card will save you from spending many hours in line.

Piazza del Duomo is the religious heart of Florence and contains six of the city's most popular sights: the Cattedrale di Santa Maria del Fiore, Cupola di Brunelleschi, Campanile di Giotto, Battistero, Cripta, and Museo dell'Opera. All six attractions can be accessed with **Il Grande Museo del Duomo card** (€15) available online or from the **ticket office** (Piazza San Giovanni 7, tel. 055/230-2885, www.museumflorence.com, daily 8:15am-6:30pm) opposite the northern entrance of the baptistery. If you purchase the Duomo card at the ticket office you may want to pick it up the day before to save time. Once you've entered the first monument you have 24 hours to visit the others and aren't allowed into the same monument twice.

Exploring the City

If arriving by rail, don't bother hunting for a tourist information office inside **Santa Maria Novella** station. It's across the street in Piazza Stazione 4 but it's usually crowded. If you don't want to begin your stay by waiting in line, visit the other office in Via Cavour 1. The Historic Center of Florence is compact and flat, making walking the best way of getting around the city.

ORIENTATION

Florence is relatively small, and the majestic Duomo, visible from nearly every angle in the city, makes getting lost difficult. The Arno River also creates a distinct divide. There are a handful of bridges that connect the two sides of the city, but **Ponte Vecchio** is by far the most popular. The bridge is crowded with visitors en route to Palazzo Pitti.

Historic Center

The Historic Center (*Centro Storico*), north of the river, is made up of three neighborhoods (Santa Maria Novella, San Giovanni,

Florence in One Day

It's possible to hit the majority of Florence's top museums and monuments on foot. The only time you may want to consider hopping a bus or hailing a taxi is on the climb to San Miniato al Monte, which is the steepest part of this itinerary.

- Start the morning at **Galleria dell'Accademia** before the crowds arrive to admire Michelangelo's larger-than-life *David*.

- From the Accademia, it's a short stroll to the **Duomo**. The line to the top can be over an hour long during the summer. Visit the inside of the church for free, then get an equally good view of the city a few blocks south at **Palazzo Vecchio**, where things are generally quieter. The inside of the city's most illustrious building also provides a vivid idea of how the Renaissance elite once lived.

- Visit the **Mercato Centrale**, Florence's biggest and most animated neighborhood market. Hundreds of Florentines arrive every day to purchase fresh produce and meet with friends. Grab lunch at the 2nd-floor food court.

- Getting into the **Uffizi** is always tough, even with reservations. If it's frescoes or sculpture you're after, the **Museo Nazionale del Bargello** is a valid alternative. There are far fewer visitors here and you can admire sculptures by Michelangelo and Donatello nearly alone.

- Visit **Basilica di Santa Croce** where Michelangelo is buried and pilgrims have come for centuries. Afterwards, stop for an espresso break or find a *gelateria* and take your cone for a walk without consulting a map. The best discoveries are serendipitous, and Florence's side streets are a destination unto themselves.

- Cross the **Ponte Vecchio** and climb up to **San Miniato al Monte** along the uncrowded side street to discover Florence's bucolic side. From here you can backtrack and follow the medieval walls towards **Forte Belvedere** and the **Boboli** or **Bardini** gardens, which are the loveliest in the city.

- Disappear into the side streets of the Oltrarno neighborhood for dinner. Sample local specialties like *pappa al pomodoro* or *bistecca al fiorentina* accompanied by a carafe of house wine. Choose a *trattoria* with outdoor tables like **Osteria Antica Mescita** and observe Florentine street life while you eat.

and Santa Croce). This is where the Romans founded the city, influential families like the Medici built imposing *palazzi*, and many Florentines still live and work today. Most of the major sights, including the **Duomo**, **Uffizi**, and **Palazzo della Signoria**, are located here. **Piazza della Repubblica** is the geographical center and lies above where the Roman Forum once stood. The center becomes less organized towards Santa Croce, where streets show the medieval tendency of mazelike randomness.

Oltrarno

Oltrarno translates to "beyond the Arno," and includes the Santo Spirito and San Niccolò neighborhoods. This area developed later, and it's a noticeably quieter part of the city that many tourists skip. The main attractions are **Palazzo Pitti** and the views from **Piazzale Michelangelo**. The village-like atmosphere is ideal for seeking refuge from the crowds. Wander past medieval walls, along deserted streets overlooking olive groves, and through elaborate shaded gardens that remain pleasantly cool during the summer. Squares such as **Piazza Santo Spirito** are lined with bars and restaurants that fill up with locals on summer nights and remain open late. The hillside beyond the medieval walls provides some of the best views of Florence.

HISTORY

Florence's history is a long one, and it involves the usual suspects. There were once Etruscans here, preceded by Iron Age tribes. The settlement along the Arno was one of the only ones in the region on flat terrain. It proved a natural funnel for traffic coming down from Bologna and Venice. The sea was also close, and the Mediterranean opened up markets for wool merchants and other trades that brought wealth to the town. With wealth came leisure and with leisure came art. The town's craftsmen became the best in the world, and fine jewelers still line the Ponte Vecchio. It was only a small jump from creating beautiful ornaments to creating beautiful sculptures, frescoes, and eventually entire buildings.

The greatest geniuses of Italy—Giotto, Dante, Machiavelli, Brunelleschi, Michelangelo, Donatello, Raphael, and so on—resided in or had some connection with Florence. With minds like these and a wealthy political class, the result was explosive. They didn't call it the Renaissance then; to them, revitalizing the Western world was simply business as usual.

Sights

Florence's three most popular sights (the **Galleria dell'Accademia, Duomo,** and **Uffizi**) are nearly always inundated with visitors. To avoid long lines, make advance reservations, or consider a Firenzecard. And remember that Florence offers much more than its most famous sights, and many other wonderful options are surprisingly empty. Make it a point to seek these out if you have the time and energy.

Museum staff have passed rigorous state exams and are passionate and knowledgeable about where they work. Don't hesitate to ask questions even if you don't speak Italian. You can also learn a lot from the audio and app guides available at many sights. These are inexpensive, easy to use, and very informative especially if you didn't attend (or don't remember) catechism and are unversed in the Old and New Testaments.

HISTORIC CENTER

Piazza del Duomo is the religious heart of Florence and contains six of Florence's most popular sights: the Cattedrale di Santa Maria del Fiore, Cupola di Brunelleschi, Campanile di Giotto, Battistero, Cripta, and Museo dell'Opera. Visiting requires patience and stamina. Those determined to do it all may want to start with the **Battistero,** which opens earliest and is the oldest of the bunch. You can then continue to the top of the dome before going inside the **Cattedrale** (also called the **Duomo**) and exploring the **Cripta.** The bell tower is open the latest. You can end a visit there or at the **Museo dell'Opera,** which was completely renovated in 2015 and is vital to understanding how Brunelleschi constructed the cupola. It also contains many works of art that have been removed from the other buildings for safekeeping. The **Cupola** and **Campanile** involve climbing hundreds of steps. You may want to choose one or the other, as the views from the top are fairly similar.

TOP EXPERIENCE

★ Duomo
(SANTA MARIA DEL FIORE)

Florence was undergoing significant change at the end of the 13th century. The churches of Santa Maria Novella and Santa Croce were completed, an outer ring wall surrounding the city was erected, and the newly built Palazzo Vecchio towered over the city. The ancient cathedral in Piazza del Duomo, however, was decrepit in comparison, and leading citizens decided to build a bigger and better cathedral to express Florence's new ambitions.

Work began on **Santa Maria del Fiore** (Piazza del Duomo, Mon.-Sat. 10am-5pm, Sun. 1:30pm-4:45pm, free), or Duomo for short, in 1296 and took nearly six hundred years to complete. Today, many consider Santa Maria del Fiore the finest church in Italy. The cupola, or dome, may look like a simple matter of bricks, but it presented a huge dilemma, as the traditional methods of construction would not work for a dome this size. In 1417, self-taught architect Filippo Brunelleschi won a competition to design the dome. His ingenious design, which relied on a double shell and eight ribs bound together by horizontal rings—without scaffolding—led to the completion of the dome in a mere 16 years and transformed architecture forever. This magnificent dome can be seen from nearly everywhere in the city and far beyond. The cathedral itself is spectacular at night, when floodlights illuminate the decorative carvings and sculptures that aren't always visible during the day.

Inside, the Duomo appears even bigger, and can easily hold 3,000 worshippers. The nave is 45 meters (148 feet) high and over a football field and half long. The interior is austere, reflecting the Renaissance preference for geometrical harmony over decoration.

The dome reveals itself as you approach the altar. Standing underneath, you can feel its immensity. The 3,600 square meters of frescoes illustrating the *Universal Judgment* seem to lead towards the heavens.

The **Cripta** (Mon.-Sat. 10am-5pm, €15 or Firenzecard) is down a set of marble stairs on the south side of the Santa Maria del Fiore. This crypt is the oldest part of the church, with some walls dating back to the city's Roman origins. Mosaic floors are still intact and embedded with the Latin names of the individuals who financed construction. There are also many gravestones, including the tomb of Brunelleschi. The vast, well-lit complex is an incredible sight and one of Florence's unique spots.

One-hour **tours** (€30) of the Duomo and rooftop terrace are available daily except Sundays from 10:30am to 11:30am. Vespers and Gregorian chants are sung on Sundays at 10:30am and 5:15pm. Around the corner is a dusty **workshop** (Via dello Studio 3) dedicated to maintaining the hundreds of carvings and sculptures inside and outside the church. You can have a glimpse of the modern stonemasons carrying on ancient traditions or take a 90-minute **tour** (www.museumflorence.com, Mon., Wed., Fri. noon-1:30pm, €30) to

Santa Maria del Fiore

learn how medieval tools are still used to keep the past in perfect condition. Both tours are conducted in English, must be booked online, and include entry to the dome, bell tower, and museum.

CLIMBING THE DUOMO

Climbing the Duomo (€15 or Firenzecard) is one of the most popular activities in Florence. It's 463 steps to the top. The journey begins in the southwestern pier. One-third of the way up, you arrive at an internal balcony where the massive scale of the dome is palpable. From here, a narrow staircase winds between the inner and outer shells that make up the dome. This method of construction is considered a great engineering innovation. Watch your step. It's narrow with many obstacles to trip over or hit your head. After a final set of steep steps, you emerge onto the circular platform to take in one of the most spectacular views of Florence. There are several mounted binoculars for examining the city and surrounding countryside, so if you haven't brought your own make sure to have a couple euro coins ready.

A limited number of visitors are allowed up at a time, and the line to climb the Duomo stretches for hundreds of yards along the northern side of the church. Firenzecard holders are given priority in a separate, far shorter line. If you're out of shape, have a fear of heights, or are claustrophobic you may want to reconsider the climb.

Campanile

The **Campanile** (Piazza del Duomo, daily 8:15am-6:50pm, €15 or Firenzecard) is one of the unique features of the Florentine skyline and arguably the most beautiful bell tower in Italy. Getting to the top is slightly easier than ascending the dome, and there's always a line of tourists ready to climb up the 414 steps. From the top, the Campanile offers a great view of the Duomo and the rest of the city.

The tower measures 279 feet (85 meters) in height and is only 50 feet (15 meters) wide. It's often called Giotto's Tower in reference

the Campanile

to the artist who began work on it in 1337. Unfortunately, he died three years later, and it was up to Andrea Pisano and Francesco Talenti to complete the job. They fitted the tower with its polychrome marble similar to the Duomo and added scores of sculptures illustrating the Old Testament and the *Redemption of Man*. Many pieces have been moved to the Museo dell'Opera to avoid being damaged by the elements. Completed in 1359, the Campanile remains one of the finest examples of Gothic architecture in the city.

Baptistery
(BATTISTERO)

The green-and-white marble **Battistero** (Piazza del Duomo, Mon.-Fri. 8:15am-10:15am and 11:15am-6:30pm, Sat. 8:15am-6:30pm, Sun. 8:15am-1:30pm, €15 or Firenzecard) was built around the 6th or 7th century. This is where citizens were baptized, and it was one of the most important buildings in Florence. Making it look good was a

detailed view of the magnificent *Gates of Paradise,* created by Lorenzo Ghiberti

their absence, a replica—a great work in its own right—was created and has remained at the Battistero. The original set is now on display inside **Museo dell'Opera del Duomo.** If you're interested in understanding the significance behind each panel of the *Gates of Paradise* download the **app** (€2.99) from the baptistery website.

Inside the baptistery, golden mosaics cover the dome above, depicting Jesus along with angels and saints recounting the *Last Judgment.* You'll also find the only pope buried in Florence, John XXIII. Donatello and Michelozzo built the tomb and the Latin epitaph ruffled a few feathers back in Rome. A dress code is enforced at the Baptistery.

Duomo Museum
(MUSEO DELL'OPERA)

The **Museo dell'Opera** (Via della Canonica 1, Mon.-Sat. 9am-7:30pm, Sun. 9am-1:45pm, €15 or Firenzecard), located directly behind the Duomo, is essential for understanding how the Duomo was built. Throughout construction of the adjacent monuments it was used as a repository and workplace. It's where Brunelleschi confronted the day-to-day challenges of building the dome and it still contains the large wooden model he used as a basis for construction. It's also where Michelangelo sculpted *David.*

Once the cathedral was completed the building was transformed into a museum focused entirely on preservation and the safekeeping of over 750 works of art. It reopened in 2015 and now covers 6,000 square meters over three floors. Exhibits include many of the original relics and artwork from the baptistery, cathedral, crypt, and bell tower. The *Gates of Paradise,* the famed doors Ghiberti created for the Battistero, have a befitting place behind an immense glass case. The doors consist of 10 large panels that portray scenes from the Old Testament.

Though visitors often skip this museum, to do so would be a mistake. It also contains one of the best gift shops in the city.

matter of civic as well as religious pride. The original wooden doors were eventually replaced with bronze doors that have been a major attraction ever since.

Andrea Pisano cast the first of the three sets of doors, which now face south, in 1336, and recount the life of John the Baptist. Lorenzo Ghiberti won the competition to design the next set of doors, and spent 21 years working on them. The project would cost millions in today's currency. His doors are located on the north entrance of the baptistery and tell the life of Christ in 28 panels read from left to right starting at the bottom.

The city liked the result so much they commissioned Ghiberti to create a third set. This one took him 27 years to complete and became known as the *Porta del Paradiso,* or *Gates of Paradise,* a dazzling achievement that marked the beginning of the Renaissance. The *Gates of Paradise* were severely damaged during a flood in 1966 and underwent restoration that was completed in 2012. During

Orsanmichele Church
(CHIESA ORSANMICHELE)

Chiesa Orsanmichele (Via dell'Arte della Lana, tel. 055/23885, church daily 10am-5pm, free) is a massive three-story church *palazzo* that looks more like a wealthy merchant's house than a place of worship. It began as a grain warehouse and the ground floor was later transformed into a church after sightings of the Virgin Mary. The site was destroyed and rebuilt several times, and in 1336 the city decided to erect a building that would serve both religious and civic functions. The ground floor became a place to worship the Virgin Mary, while the upper floors were set aside for grain storage.

The government encouraged the guilds to decorate the exterior of the building, which occupied a place of special prominence between the Duomo and Palazzo Vecchio. Fourteen niches were created along the north and south sides. Over decades, these were filled with sculptures that led to an artistic evolution that fueled the Renaissance. No two niches are the same, and competition between the guilds meant that the most talented artists in the city were commissioned to contribute.

Donatello created two of the finest statues. The Guild of Armor and Sword Makers hired him to represent San Giorgio, while the linen workers requested a portrait of San Marco. The resulting sculptures mark a rediscovery of classical forms of beauty. The statues have been replaced with copies that still have a powerful presence, while Donatello's San Giorgio now resides in the Museo Bargello.

The church on the ground floor is devoted to the Virgin Mary and dominated by Andrea Orcagna's tabernacle. He spent 10 years perfecting his marble bas-relief of *The Death of the Virgin* and *Assumption*. On the opposite wall is Bernardo Daddi's *Virgin and Child,* in which baby Jesus tenderly touches his mother's cheek while angels look on. The **museum** (Mon. 10am-5pm) is accessed from here. Inside, you can view many of the original sculptures that appeared in the niches around the outside of the church.

Palazzo Davanzati

To get an idea of how wealthy medieval Florentines lived, visit **Palazzo Davanzati** (Via di Porta Rossa 13, tel. 055/238-8610, Mon.-Sun. 8:15am-1:50pm, €2 or Firenzecard). The Davanzati were a family of lace merchants who ran their business on the first floor (where a small gift shop and ticket desk are now located) and lived on the upper floors. The difference between medieval and Renaissance-era *palazzi* is evident from the greater height of the building and its cramped courtyard and wooden staircase, which is humble by Medici standards. They did, however, have an internal well, good plumbing, and en suite bathrooms that can be seen as you tour the well-preserved living quarters refurbished with period antiques. The 3rd and 4th floors where the second banquet hall, kitchen, and medieval graffiti are located are accessible by tour only at 10am, 11am, and noon for a maximum of 25 visitors.

TOP EXPERIENCE

★ Bargello National Museum
(MUSEO NAZIONALE DEL BARGELLO)

While some of Florence's museums and monuments are besieged by tourists, the **Bargello** (Via del Proconsolo 4, tel. 055/238-8606, daily 8:15am-5pm, €4 or Firenzecard) is often deserted. This is where you'll find Donatello's *David,* which preceded Michelangelo's version. Although it's overshadowed by the latter, Donatello's *David* marks an important moment in the early Renaissance. Donatello accompanied Brunelleschi to Rome and played an essential role in the rediscovery of classical art. His sculpture was the first cast in bronze since the fall of ancient Rome and inspired an entire generation of artists.

The building itself is a holdover from the Middle Ages and was the first public office in the city. It was the headquarters of the chief of police (known as the *Bargello*) and used as a prison for centuries. Torture and executions that were torn down by the Guelphs in the mid-13th century to make sure their enemies never recovered. The resulting square became the administrative center of the city and is home to **Palazzo Vecchio, Loggia Lanzi,** and many fine statues and monuments. It's where Florentines gathered to defend the city, prisoners were executed, and where public celebrations are still held today.

In the center of the *piazza* is the round plaque marking the spot where Savonarola was hanged and burned at the stake. Nearby, there's a bronze statue of Cosimo I on horseback and a marble Neptune that exalts the seafaring glories of the city. The *piazza* is one of the great urban spaces in Florence. It fills up with visitors during the day and is used to stage concerts on summer nights.

Chiasso dei Baroncelli, adjacent to Loggia Lanzi, is closer to an alley than a street and the perfect escape from the crowds in the square. If you walk to the end, turn right and continue through the intersection along Borgo Santi Apostoli; you'll arrive at **Piazza Santa Trinità,** where street musicians perform throughout the day and night.

Donatello's bronze statue of *David* at the Bargello

were conducted in the courtyard as punishment for offenses that would be classified as misdemeanors today. The death penalty was abolished and the gallows destroyed in 1786, making Tuscany one of the first states to ban capital punishment.

The immense rooms overlooking the courtyard are nearly as interesting as the art within the museum. On the ground floor are a number of marble and bronze sculptures and several works by Michelangelo. The great hall one flight up contains Donatello's *David* and the bronze door panels Ghiberti and Brunelleschi submitted for the Baptistery competition. A little further on is the chapel with faded frescoes where prisoners were given their last rites. On the upper floor is a fine collection of antique armor and weapons including swords, crossbows, lances, and early firearms.

Piazza della Signoria
Piazza della Signoria's asymmetrical shape has a lot to do with the buildings and towers

Loggia Lanzi
The triple-arched **Loggia Lanzi** is the imposing structure next to Palazzo Vecchio on the southern side of Piazza della Signoria. A *loggia* is an open-air building popular in the Renaissance that generally functioned as a market or meeting place. This one was completed in 1382 and was used to shelter government officials during ceremonies. When the Republic fell in 1530 artists were allowed to use the covered space as a workshop. Today it's a public gallery with statues from different periods; the only two placed in the *loggia* during the Renaissance were Giambologna's *Rape of the Sabine Woman* and Cellini's *Persues*. The latter portrays the Greek hero holding Medusa's head and was an attempt to outdo Michelangelo's *David* standing nearby. It may not have succeeded, but the 12-foot bronze statue remains impressive. The number of visitors allowed to enter the *loggia* is limited,

but turnaround time is quick, and sculptures are clearly visible from the *piazza*.

Palazzo Vecchio

The Duomo may get more attention, but the decision to build the cathedral and countless others that shaped the city were made at **Palazzo Vecchio** (Piazza della Signoria, tel. 055/276-8325, museum Fri.-Wed. 9am-11pm, Thurs. 9am-2pm, tower Fri.-Wed. 9am-9pm, Thurs. 9am-2pm, €10 for single sights, €14-18 combined tickets or Firenzecard). This palazzo served as a political and administrative hub where magistrates lived and nobles, dignitaries, and citizens gathered. The exterior looks impregnable, which is exactly what Arnolfo di Cambio intended when he began construction in 1298. Walls are made of rough-cut stone and rise high above the square. The 308-foot (94-meter) tower is even more impressive.

Palazzo Vecchio can be entered from the gateway next to the statue of David. The ticket office is located off the internal courtyard designed by Michelozzo and decorated with a graceful fountain. Even if you don't intend to visit the *palazzo* it's worth a peek inside the courtyard and at the Roman remains underground, both of which are free. Take the stairs inside the ticket office and follow the walkway overlooking the massive brickworks. The courtyard is the best example of Roman architecture in the city and it provides an idea of what lies below street level.

The lower floors include residential quarters and reception halls that were the home of Cosimo I and other members of the Medici family when they rose to power. The grandest of these is the **Salone dei Cinquecento,** which has a high frescoed ceiling and two walls covered with gigantic paintings illustrating Florence's military successes. Michelangelo and Leonardo da Vinci were originally commissioned to undertake this project but neither ever completed the task. Had they done so the *salone* would be one of the unique artistic sights in Italy. Nonetheless it remains impressive,

especially when viewed from the balcony on the third floor.

The route to the **tower** starts at the staircase near the front entrance. The number of visitors within the tower is limited, so you may encounter a short wait after a few flights. On the way up, you'll pass a small prison cell known ironically as the *alberghetto,* or little hotel, where Savonarola and other illustrious prisoners were detained. Farther along, you can circumnavigate two terraces that offer the best panoramas from the tower. These are where soldiers once kept watch over the city. At the very top views are obstructed by high ramparts except for a ledge where visitors take turns photographing the Duomo. Lookouts once observed the countryside from here and rang the bells that hung in the wooden structure above if they spotted enemies approaching. A friendly attendant is always present and happy to answer questions. The tower is closed whenever it rains and is off-limits to children under six.

There are evening **tours** (€4) of the tower during the summer and **tablet guides** (€5) to the *palazzo*.

★ Uffizi Gallery
(GALLERIA DEGLI UFFIZI)

When Francesco I added a second story in 1584 to what was once a set of office buildings, **Galleria degli Uffizi** (Piazzale degli Uffizi 6, tel. 055/238-8651, www.polomuseale.firenze.it, Tues.-Sun. 8:15am-6:30pm, €12.50 or Firenzecard) became the world's first modern art gallery. This grand 16th-century building stretches from Palazzo Vecchio to the Arno. Inside are many of the world's finest works of art, from 13th-century religious frescoes to Renaissance masterpieces by the likes of Giotto, Beato Angelico, Botticelli, Mantegna, Leonardo, Raphael, Michelangelo, and Caravaggio. It's a match for any museum in the world and its relatively small dimensions make it possible to visit in a morning or afternoon. There's also an extensive collection of umbrellas, large bags, and food. On the top floor is a cafeteria where you can have an espresso or light snack and walk onto the spacious terrace. There's a great view of the *piazza* and Palazzo della Signoria from here.

Basilica di Santa Croce

Basilica di Santa Croce (Piazza Basilica di Santa Croce 16, tel. 055/246-6105, Mon.-Sat. 9:30am-5:30pm, Sun. 2pm-5pm, €6 or Firenzecard) lies on the eastern edge of the Historic Center in a working-class district (also called Santa Croce) that once housed tanning and leather workshops. The Franciscan monastery was enlarged in the late 13th century and the façade was completed many centuries later in 1863.

The basilica is designed in a Latin cross plan with three naves, a number of side chapels, and a vast wooden ceiling. The style is predominately Gothic with frescoes by Renaissance artists who set the early standards of Western art. None of these is more influential than Giotto, who decorated two chapels. His use of space and the positioning of figures influenced generations of Florentine artists and significantly impacted the Renaissance painting that would follow.

Santa Croce is the final resting place of Michelangelo, Machiavelli, and Galileo Galilei, all of whom are buried inside. Dante would be lying next to them had he not been banished from Florence; the city later made amends by installing a statue of the poet on the steps outside. Funerary monuments dedicated to the city's all-time greats are located along the walls. A passage, opposite the basilica entrance, leads to the peaceful 14th-century cloister and **Pazzi Chapel** designed by Brunelleschi. The architect died before work was completed and the façade has remained unfinished.

The basilica is the city's most visited church after the Duomo and lines form early. A tour app is available for download, but you're better off asking the friendly volunteers who wait inside the church and organize free impromptu guided tours.

Uffizi Gallery at night

Dutch masters including Dürer, Rembrandt, and Rubens.

You can pick up a plan of the museum and an **audio guide** (€6 single/€10 double), which is essential for understanding the paintings to come, at the information desk. The gallery itself begins on the 3rd floor, where 35 rooms are organized around both wings of the building. Tourists huddle in front of the pearls of the collection, such as Botticelli's *Birth of Venus,* on display in room 10. The floor below contains a permanent collection as well as a number of temporary exhibition spaces. The Dutch painters are housed in rooms 53 to 55, while works by Caravaggio hang in room 90.

Outside, painters and street vendors fill the long rectangular courtyard, while hundreds of visitors line up underneath the portico entrance. The shorter line is for reserved tickets (which can be picked up at the office on the opposite side) and Firenzecard holders. The longer one is for everyone else. If you take photos inside, turn your flash off. Selfie sticks are prohibited in the museum, as are

Worshippers can enter Monday through Saturday from 7:30am until 6:45pm from a separate entrance and are not required to wait in line or purchase tickets. Just inform attendants of your intentions and remain within the designated prayer areas on the left side of the nave. Mass is celebrated Monday through Saturday at 6pm and on Sunday at 11am, noon, and 6pm.

Casa Buonarotti

Michelangelo's last name was Buonarotti but he didn't live in **Casa Buonarotti** (Via Ghibellina 70, tel. 055/241-752, Wed.-Mon. 10am-4pm, €6.50 or Firenzecard), which was built by his nephew and transformed into a museum after the extinction of the family line. Today it houses Michelangelo's first serious attempts at sculpture, created when he was barely out of his teens. *Battaglia dei Centauri* and *Madonna della Scala* may not compete with his later work, but they do show clear signs of potential. In those early years Michelangelo used a bas-relief technique that requires chiseling away at a marble background and is best viewed from the front. Some of the artist's architectural models and drawings are also on display.

★ Accademia
(GALLERIA DELL'ACCADEMIA)

If you're looking for *David*, you'll find him inside the **Galleria dell'Accademia** (Via Ricasoli 58-60, tel. 055/238-8609, Tues.-Sun. 8:15am-6:50pm, €8 or Firenzecard). Michelangelo sculpted the masterpiece from an enormous piece of secondhand marble that had frustrated lesser artists. David was a popular subject and, like Donatello's version, this one is naked. Michelangelo, however, chose to capture the tense moments prior to the struggle with Goliath. The face is not relaxed but reveals the kind of apprehension you'd expect before facing a giant. The statue gets an entire room to itself and is easily visible regardless of the number of visitors. Remember to walk around the statue and observe what many consider *David's* finest asset.

The museum would be worth visiting even if it didn't contain Michelangelo's masterpiece, though the unique collection of medieval paintings, half-completed sculptures, Florentine art from the 12th to 15th centuries, and some surprises is often overlooked. Other works by Michelangelo include four unfinished sculptures that were ordered for the

lining up outside Galleria dell'Accademia

Mission Michelangelo: Florence

Florence produced many geniuses during the late middle ages and Renaissance but none acquired as much fame in life and after as Michelangelo. He left an unmistakable mark on the city that can still be seen today. Although some of his greatest works require standing in line for hours, others are far more accessible and can be visited in a morning or afternoon.

Casa Buonarotti houses Michelangelo's first serious attempts at sculpture, created when he was barely out of his teens. Some of the artist's architectural models and drawings are also on display.

Michelangelo found refuge in **Basilica di Santo Spirito** after the death of his benefactor Lorenzo the Magnificent. The young artist was allowed to dissect cadavers in the church hospital, a task that played an instrumental part in his growth as an artist. He paid the monks back for their hospitality by sculpting a wooden crucifix in 1493 that still hangs in the basilica. It's a realistic and human portrayal of Christ that hints of the sculptures to come.

After the Medici were exiled in 1494 Michelangelo journeyed to Rome where he carved the *Pieta di San Pietro* and *Bacco*. These sculptures are the first signs of a mature artist at the height of his talents. They were eventually returned to Florence and now reside in the **Museo Bargello.** The museum also contains other works from the same period, and comparing one with the other reveals a subtle evolution in style.

Upon returning to Florence in 1501 Michelangelo created some of his most famous masterpieces including the statue of David. The **Galleria del Accademia** also contains his sensual uncompleted statues, in which rough chisel marks can still be seen and the figures appear trapped in stone. Getting into the gallery is a challenge, as it is at the **Uffizi** where Michelangelo's first painting, *Tondo Doni*, is on display in room 35. It's a colorful portrayal of the Holy Family and the only one of his paintings in Florence.

Two members of the Medici family served as pope between 1515 and 1534, and during that time they commissioned Michelangelo to design and decorate the **Cappelle Medici** (Piazza di Madonna degli Aldobrandini 6, tel. 055/238-8602, daily 8:15am-6pm, €6) chapel. It's perhaps his most complete work, in which he demonstrated talent both as an architect and as a sculptor. He created two tombs on which muscular statues lounge and a symmetrical interior that was different from how chapels were designed to look at the time.

Michelangelo's final sculpture was created in Rome and later moved to Florence, where it now resides inside **Museo del Opera del Duomo.** The life-size figures are noteworthy for the expression of grief on their faces and the self-portrait of the artist in the center. Michelangelo intended it for his tomb but didn't complete it in time and the city commissioned another artist to decorate his final resting place inside **Basilica di Santa Croce.**

tomb of Pope Julius II but remained embedded in stone. The effect is eerie and inspired future generations of sculptors to adopt this *nonfinite* technique. The music room contains more than 50 antique instruments including a Stradivari violin and the oldest upright piano in the world.

The line for unreserved ticket holders to get into the Galleria dell'Accademia often stretches around the corner, and the wait can be over an hour during the summer. The reserved ticket and Firenzecard line is slightly shorter, but still requires patience. Only 600 are allowed inside at any one time. A good strategy for avoiding crowds is to arrive early.

Museum of San Marco
(MUSEO DI SAN MARCO)

The Dominican monastery that houses **Museo di San Marco** (Piazza San Marco 3, tel. 055/238-8608, Mon.-Fri. 8:15am-1:50pm, Sat.-Sun. 8:15am-4:50pm, €4 or Firenzecard) is a hidden gem just moments from the Galleria dell'Accademia but with only a fraction of the visitors. Inside you'll find frescoes by Beato Angelico, the city's first public library, and one and a half depictions of the Last Supper. This is also where the fanatical monk Girolamo Savonarola preached and resided. The completed *Cenacolo,* as the Last Supper is called in Italian, is by Ghiberti and notable for the vivid colors and the disciples' detailed expressions.

Upstairs, you'll find the 44 cells where monks lived. Each contains a fresco of Jesus in various states of crucifixion. San Domenico is also present and recognizable by the star above his head, while the order's first martyr (San Pietro di Verona) is usually depicted as bleeding. Beato Angelico oversaw the painting of the frescoes and worked on those closest to the entrance himself. Ginevra and other attendants on duty are happy to answer questions and share their insight with visitors. The library is on the same floor and is where the monks studied. The delicately colonnaded space was built during the Renaissance and contains hand-decorated manuscripts, some of which are now on display.

Downstairs, the fresco cycle along the cloister recounts the youth, conversion, and religious life of San Marco and begins diagonally from the entrance. It illustrates how Florence looked and how locals dressed and acted during the 11th century. Beato Angelico painted the spaces above the doorways, all of which hint at the rooms beyond. The "Half Supper" is located in the refectory where monks ate. It isn't the highest quality but remains interesting for its realistic portrayal of the monks who inhabited the monastery. The monk standing on the far left dressed entirely in white financed the work. Anyone who joined the brotherhood was required to give up their worldly wealth and applied any riches they had to the beautification and improvement of the monastery.

Medici Chapel
(CAPPELLE MEDICI)

Cappelle Medici (Piazza di Madonna degli Aldobrandini 6, tel. 055/238-8602, daily 8:15am-6pm, closed 2nd and 4th Sunday, €6, audio guide available) is the final resting place of the members of the Medici dynasty. The chapel inside San Basilica di San Lorenzo was the family's parish church and a short walk from their residence on Via Cavour. The complex consists of an Old and New Sacristy built by Brunelleschi and Michelangelo. The latter is notable for its scale and the muscular statues lounging on the monumental tombs. The main octagonal chapel is covered in precious marble and rises to a towering 59 meters (194 feet). The family members are not actually resting inside the stone tombs; their remains are instead within the walls of the crypt at the entrance of the museum. Restoration of the chapel's interior and exterior are ongoing, and scaffolding is not an uncommon sight.

Basilica di Santa Maria Novella

Basilica di Santa Maria Novella (Piazza Santa Maria Novella, tel. 055/219-257, www.chiesasantamarianovella.it, Mon.-Thurs. 9am-5:30pm, Fri. 11am-5:30pm, Sat. 9am-5pm, Sun. noon-5pm, €5 or Firenzecard) lies opposite the train station and is often ignored by travelers. The basilica is called *novella* (new) because was built over a smaller church by Dominican monks, who completed the structure in 1360. The recently remodeled *piazza* out front provides the best view of the green-and-white marble façade begun in the Middle Ages and completed in the Renaissance.

The basilica consists of a monumental church, a half-dozen chapels, and several cloisters. There's rarely a line to enter, and impressive artwork throughout. The most striking artifact is the large wooden crucifix by Giotto hanging above the altar, a small fresco by Botticelli near the entrance, and *The Trinity* by Masaccio that's one of the earliest examples of perspective in painting.

The **Chiostro Verde** (Green Cloister) is down a short flight of steps on the left side of the church. It's named after the green pigment used in the frescoes lining the walls that vividly illustrate stories of sinners and saints. Farther down is the **refectory** where monks ate meals and restored artworks. Hanging on the wall is a painting of the Last Supper, and below are glass cases containing religious garments.

Mass is held daily in the **Capella della Pura** chapel at 7:30am and 7pm in July and August and 7:30am and 6pm the rest of the year. Sunday mass is at 10:30am and 7am during the former and 10:30am, noon, and 6pm during the latter. Services (in Italian) last 45 minutes.

OLTRARNO
Ponte Vecchio

There are many bridges in Florence but Ponte Vecchio is the one everyone wants to cross. It's the oldest in the city and has spanned the Arno since 1342. What makes it special are the workshops built on both sides of the bridge by butchers who once plied their trade here and discarded waste in the gaps at the center (where tourists now line up to take pictures of the river). Above the eastern side of the bridge runs the corridor that connects the Uffizi and Palazzo Pitti. It was completed in less than five months and used by Cosimo I de Medici to avoid the chaos down below. A few years later in 1593 the butchers were ordered to leave and replaced with jewelers who didn't smell as bad.

During World War II, Ponte Vecchio was the only bridge in Florence that was not destroyed by the retreating German army.

For most of the day and night, Ponte Vecchio is filled with pedestrians half-admiring the storefronts and in no hurry to get to the other side. The bridge is best viewed from the streets running along the Arno and the neighboring bridges, which attract less attention. People gather on **Ponte Santa Trinità,** 150 yards downriver, to watch the setting sun transform the pastel-colored shops of the Ponte Vecchio. **Ponte Alle Grazie** on the opposite side is farther away and provides a better view in the morning. Both bridges lead to lesser-known parts of Oltrarno.

Basilica di Santo Spirito

Basilica di Santo Spirito (Piazza Santo Spirito 30, Mon.-Tues. and Thurs.-Fri. 9:30am-12:30pm and 4pm-5:30pm, Sat.-Sun. 11:30am-12:30pm and 4pm-5:30pm, free) is one of only two basilicas in Oltrarno. From the outside it looks a little like the Alamo, with a plain façade facing a modest tree-lined *piazza* that hosts a daily market in the morning and gets lively at night. It was founded by Augustan monks in 1250, but a devastating fire led to the hiring of Brunelleschi to work on the reconstruction.

Basilica di Santa Maria Novella

Searching for Last Suppers

Over the centuries, artists have illustrated hundreds of episodes from the Bible—and one of the favorite images is the *Cenacolo* or *Last Supper*. Monasteries and convents frequently commissioned Middle Ages and Renaissance artists to paint this iconic scene. The basic scene is nearly always the same: Jesus sits in the center of a long table, with followers seated on either side. John is to the left and often hunched over in near sleep. Each figure sports a halo, except Judah, who is usually seated across the table from the other figures and portrayed with a dark beard. Everything else including the background, expressions, and the food itself were up to the artist, many of whom specialized in painting this single scene.

Florence counts over 50 versions of the Last Supper, and tracking a few down is a rewarding venture that costs next to nothing. Searching for *Last Suppers* requires a little planning, as many of the monasteries where they're located are only open mornings on certain days. The ones listed below are all within walking distance of one another and can be covered in a couple of hours:

Cenacolo di Ognissanti (Borgo Ognissanti 42, tel. 055/294-883, Mon., Tues., and Sat. 9am-noon, free) stands near the Arno facing an elegant *piazza*. The *Last Supper*, completed by Domenico Ghirlandaio in 1488, covers the far wall in the refectory where monks gathered for meals. Ghirlandaio was an expert in the genre and completed several others around the city with the help of his brother and assistants. This one is notable for the detailed expressions and use of perspective. The artist sketched a rough draft that hangs on the side wall. Comparing the two makes for some interesting speculation about John. Botticelli is buried in the adjacent church.

Head north towards the train station to reach the **Cenacolo di Fuligno** (Via Faenza 42, tel. 055/286-982, Mon., Thurs., and Sat. 9am-midday, free). Pietro Perugino worked three years on the *fresco* and completed the work in 1496. It was covered over and only rediscovered a century ago during a restoration project. The apostles in this portrayal are hungry and all those to the left of Jesus are busy enjoying their food. The landscape above them is visible through the columns of an imaginary *palazzo* that adds depth to the scene.

Walk up Via Nazionale and take a left on Via Ventisette Aprile to reach **Cenacolo di Sant'Apollonia** (Via XXVII Aprile 1, tel. 055/238-8607, daily 8:15am-1:50pm, free). This was once the biggest convent in the city, but there's a good chance you'll be the only one observing the painting Andrea del Castagno completed in 1450. He imagined the scene taking place inside a finely decorated room with a long table and many geometric patterns. Judah is notable for his dark features and there's less interaction and more contemplation among the diners. Castagno painted each apostle's name (in Latin) near his feet.

Down the street inside **Museo di San Marco** (Piazza San Marco 3, tel. 055/238-8608, Mon.-

---

Rebuilding and expanding the church was so costly that the monks were forced to give up one of their daily meals until work was completed. The famed architect died a few years after construction started, but many of his plans were carried out, including the cupola and strict geometric proportions that give the interior an impressive harmony. Daily mass is held at 5:30pm.

A small **museum** (Piazza Santo Spirito 29, tel. 055/287-043, Mon.-Sun. only 10am-4pm, €4) to the left of the basilica was once part of the medieval convent and now contains a collection of religious artifacts and the remains of Andrea Orcagna's enormous *Last Supper* fresco. The apostles have disappeared but Jesus remains high above on a crucifix surrounded by angels. The room itself is full of Gothic fittings and is a stark contrast to the Renaissance concepts employed inside the church.

Brancacci Chapel
(CAPPELLA BRANCACCI)

Santa Maria del Carmine was founded by a group of Pisan monks in 1268. The inside

Last Supper on display at Museo di San Marco

Fri. 8:15am-1:15pm, Sat.-Sun. 8:15am-4:50pm, €4) is another *Cenacolo* designed by Ghirlandaio and completed with the help of his brother in 1480. The background, tablecloth, and perspective are very similar to his earlier work; however, the colors are more vivid here and the artist took the liberty of adding a cat. Today the painting shares a room with a small bookshop.

Seeing several *Last Suppers* in a single day requires getting up early, but if closing is still an hour off and you have the energy walk east towards the city's second train station and **Cenacolo di Andrea del Sarto** (Via di S. Salvi 16, Tues.-Sun. 8:15am-1:50pm, free). This one is the most recent of the bunch—it was completed in 1527—and is quite animated, with apostles on their feet in heated discussion. They haven't earned their halos yet and John is wide awake while Judah on the far right of the fresco doesn't look so villainous. One of the figures above the main scene is said to be a self-portrait of the artist.

Afterwards you can walk back to the center along the Arno or search for your own supper in a neighborhood *trattoria*.

was nearly completely destroyed by a fire in 1771, but the **Cappella Brancacci** (Piazza del Carmine 14, tel. 055/238-2195, Mon. and Wed.-Fri. 10am-5pm, Sat.-Sun. 1pm-5pm, €6 or Firenzecard) survived. This chapel was commissioned by Felici Brancacci, a wealthy merchant and politician, and recounts the life of St. Peter. The frescoes were the result of three successive artists including Masaccio and Filippo Lippi, who completed the chapel in 1480. The new interior is one of the few examples of Roman baroque in the city.

The most striking of the frescoes depict Adam and Eve before and after giving in to temptation, represented by a snake with a female head. Their body language and complexions are completely transformed. A keen observer might also notice the belly buttons on the first couple. Some speculate it was an oversight by the artist, as both Adam and Eve were created by God and would not have needed an umbilical cord.

Only 30 people are allowed in the chapel at a time, but lines are short, even in summer. The chapel is just beyond the bookshop on the far side of the cloister. If you're not well

Oltrarno

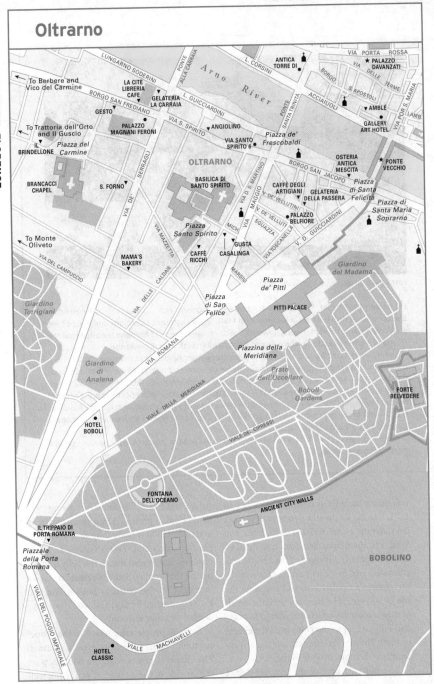

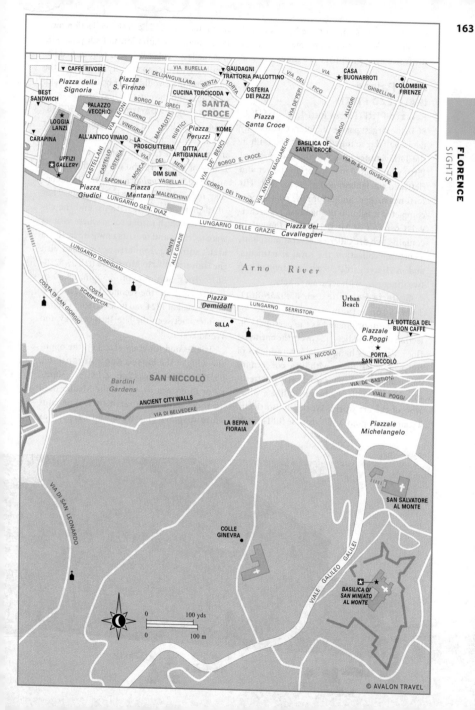

▼ CAFFE RIVOIRE

Piazza della Signoria

Piazza S. Firenze

V. DELLANGUILLARA

VIA BURELLA

▼ GAUDAGNI
▼ TRATTORIA PALLOTTINO

VIA DEL

VIA

★ CASA BUONARROTI

● COLOMBINA FIRENZE

BEST SANDWICH

CUCINA TORCICODA ▼

BORGO DE' GRECI

SANTA CROCE

OSTERIA DEI PAZZI

VIA DE PEPI

VIA DEL FICO

GHIBELLINA

PALAZZO VECCHIO

★ LOGGIA LANZI

CORNO

VINEGRIA

★ CARAPINA

ALL'ANTICO VINAIO ▼

LA PROSCIUTTERIA ▼

✚ UFFIZI GALLERY ★

CASTELLANI

CASTELLO

SAPONAI

Piazza Giudici

Piazza Peruzzi

KOME ▼

Piazza Santa Croce

DITTA ARTIGIANALE

DIM SUM

VAGELLA I

Piazza Mentana

MALENCHINI

VIA DEI NERI

BORGO S. CROCE

BORGO ALLEGRI

BASILICA OF SANTA CROCE ✚

VIA DI SAN GIUSEPPE

CORSO DEI TINTORI

VIA ANTONIO MAGLIABECHI

LUNGARNO GEN. DIAZ

LUNGARNO DELLE GRAZIE

Piazza dei Cavalleggeri

LUNGARNO TORRIGIANI

PONTE ALLE GRAZIE

A r n o   R i v e r

COSTA DI SAN GIORGIO

COSTA SCARPUCCIA

Piazza Demidoff

LUNGARNO SERRISTORI

Urban Beach

LA BOTTEGA DEL BUON CAFFÈ ▼

SILLA ●

Piazzale G. Poggi

★ PORTA SAN NICCOLÒ

VIA DI SAN NICCOLÒ

SAN NICCOLÒ

Bardini Gardens

VIA DE BASTIONI

VIALE POGGI

ANCIENT CITY WALLS

VIA DI BELVEDERE

LA BEPPA ▼ FIORAIA

Piazzale Michelangelo

VIA DI SAN LEONARDO

SAN SALVATORE AL MONTE ✚

COLLE GINEVRA ●

VIALE GALILEO GALILEI

✚ **BASILICA DI SAN MINIATO AL MONTE**

0   100 yds
0   100 m

© AVALON TRAVEL

versed in the Bible pick up the **tablet** (€3) at the shop. It's easy to use and makes sense of the fresco cycle one image at a time.

Pitti Palace
(PALAZZO PITTI)

Palazzo Pitti (Piazza Pitti 1, tel. 055/294-883), the largest palace in Florence, can easily take a half day to fully explore. It was built in the 14th century for a wealthy banker (Luca Pitti) who wanted to show off his power and flattened a neighborhood to get his wish. His fortunes turned, and before the *palazzo* was completed it fell into the hands of his archrival, Cosimo I de Medici. Today, the palace contains two art galleries, several museums, a costume collection, the royal apartments, and an 11-acre garden. Sights are divided into two itineraries with separate tickets.

Galleria Palatina (tel. 05/5238-8611, Tues.-Sun. 8:15am-6:50pm, €8.50 or Firenzecard) originated as the personal collection of the Medici and covers the entire 1st floor. Paintings hang as the last residents of the *palazzo* left them, with little concern for chronology. The haphazard display is refreshing, and the gallery labels read like a who's who of the art world. Works by Botticelli, Tiziano, Perugino, and Veronese fill 11 finely decorated salons. The entire collection owes its existence to Anna Maria Ludovica, who was the last Medici heir and bequeathed her family's treasures to the city in 1737 on the condition they would never be divided, sold, or taken from the city.

The Royal Apartments (tel. 05/5238-8614, Tues.-Sun. 8:15am-6:50pm, €8.50 or Firenzecard, audio guide €6) provide further insight into the family's taste for luxury. The Dukes of Lorraine, who were later residents and lived in the *palazzo* until the 19th century, ordered the neoclassical redesign. They liked their decor ostentatious, and the climax is the plush throne room where visitors were received and tourists now gather. If you aren't suffering from artistic overload visit the **Galleria d'Arte Moderna** (tel. 05/5238-8616, Tues.-Sun. 8:15am-6:50pm, €8.50 or Firenzecard) on the second floor. This gallery opened in 1924 and is dedicated to Italian painters between the late 18th century and World War I.

The second itinerary starts on the opposite wing at the **Museo degli Argenti** (tel. 05/5238-8709, Tues.-Sun. 8:15am-6:30pm, €7 or Firenzecard), which the Medici used as their summer apartments. The museum displays glassware and carpets, as

Palazzo Pitti

well as fine jewelry cherished by the family. This option also includes the **Galleria dei Costume** (Tues.-Sun. 8:15am-6:30pm, €7 or Firenzecard), which is worth visiting if you have an interest in 19th-century womens wear and ancient fashions. The real reason to get this ticket is for the **Giardini Boboli** (Tues.-Sun. Nov.-Feb. 8:15am-4:30pm, Mar.-May and Sept.-Oct. 8:15am-6:30pm, June-Aug. 8:15am-7:30pm, €7 or Firenzecard) gardens that come into full bloom in late spring and provide a tranquil escape from the city. There are four entrances to the gardens, which are free on the first Sunday of every month.

Forte Belvedere

Forte Belvedere (Via di San Leonardo 1, tel. 055/27681, Wed.-Mon. 10am-7pm, free) lies on the hill above the Boboli Gardens and provides one of the best views of the city. This fortress is a little harder to reach than Piazzale Michelangelo, whose convenient parking makes it a mandatory stop for busloads of camera-happy tourists, but offers a closer perspective of the city. If you aren't planning on visiting Lucca or any of the other fortified towns in Tuscany, Belvedere's star-shaped ramparts are also an excellent primer in military architecture. The fortress was built

at the end of the 16th century and served as insurance for the Medici, who were wary of attacks from outside the city and rebellions from within. It was also a reliable place to stash their treasure. Today you can walk around the upper and lower terraces, which often host summer art exhibitions.

The fort has two entrances. It can be reached directly from the northeastern exit of the Boboli Gardens or through the main entrance near the medieval walls, which also flank the nearby Giardino Bardini.

Piazzale Michelangelo

Piazzale Michelangelo is Florence's most famous observation point and a mandatory stop for many tourists. It was built during the city's brief stint as capital of Italy and sits on a hillside from where most of Florence is visible. You can arrive by car or bus (line 12) but most people climb up from the San Niccolò neighborhood. If you choose to walk you can take the pedestrian walkway past the rose garden or the winding monumental steps that begin from Piazza Giuseppe Poggi. In the center of the square stands a bronze copy of Michelangelo's *David*. There are several other copies of his work nearby. The elegant neoclassical *loggia* across the street was meant to

Basilica San Miniato al Monte

house a Michelangelo museum, but the project was never completed and it has since become a restaurant and cafe serving local specialties.

The 1870s was a period of urban restructuring in Florence. Along with the *piazza*, tree-lined avenues leading to the square were created. Two of these, Viale Galileo and Michelangelo, wind through the countryside and offer further glimpses of the city.

TOP EXPERIENCE

★ Basilica San Miniato al Monte

The hilltop church of **Basilica San Miniato al Monte** (Via delle Porte Sante 34, tel. 055/234-2731, daily 9am-1pm and 3:30pm-8pm, free) is one of the oldest Romanesque churches in the city and was dedicated to the first Christian martyr of Florence. It's rarely crowded and the cool interior provides relief on hot summer days. There are three levels connected by marble steps; each is decorated in the green-and-white marble common to the region. The walls are covered with ancient frescoes of saints. An audio booth near the entrance sheds light on the origins of the building.

From the wide gravel terrace in front of the church you can admire the entire city. Unlike at Piazzale Michelangelo, the view is unspoiled by tour groups and street vendors hawking selfie sticks. Look upon the Duomo and rooftops of the city while sampling sweets prepared by the Benedictine monks in the adjacent **monastic shop** (daily 10am-12:15pm and 4pm-6pm) or explore the **cemetery,** where the author of *Pinocchio* is buried.

Getting to San Miniato is a small endeavor. Although the church can be reached by bus 12 or 13, the most gratifying approach is **hiking** up along Via San Niccolò and through the old medieval gate. Take the second right onto Via dell'Erta Canina and continue a short way to the path on the left that leads uphill. It's also called Erta Canina, but you'll know you're in the right place if there's grass growing in between the rough paving stones and no one's in sight.

As you climb, you'll pass olive groves and cottages that appear more suited to a village than the city spreading out below. At the end of the narrow road you can turn left onto Viale Galileo or cross the avenue and continue up the improvised steps through a glade of pines until you come to the fortifications hastily constructed by Michelangelo during a siege of the city. The dirt path eventually disappears; follow the walls in either direction and you'll eventually reach the basilica.

Porta San Niccolò

If you're climbing back down from San Miniato, it's hard to miss **Porta San Niccolò** (Via dei Bastioni, tel. 055/276-8224, daily 4pm-8pm, €6 or Firenzecard), a tower that overlooks the Arno and once guarded the city. It's the only surviving tower to maintain its original height and is open to the public between July and September. Tours are conducted in Italian and English and depart on the hour. The 30-minute visit includes an explanation of Renaissance fortifications and a walk up the 160 steps to the terrace where you can get a riverside view of the city.

Food

It's hard to have a bad meal in Florence. Food here is a tale of traditional rural recipes prepared generation after generation. Ingredients are simple and in harmony with the seasons. The city offers a variety of unique dishes, many of which hail from a humble era when ingredients were whatever was available. For the most part that meant grains, legumes, vegetables, and meat. Florentines use all of these. The city is also famous for T-bone steaks and soups.

Long before the word *restaurant* was invented Italians were heading to *trattorie* for good food at next-to-nothing prices. Some of the oldest date back hundreds of years and are often run by different generations of the same family in historically working-class neighborhoods. They're not fancy and barely romantic, but they are full of charm and where *pappa al pomodoro* and *bistecca alla fiorentina* taste the best.

HISTORIC CENTER

There are hundreds of eateries in the *centro storico* in all categories and price ranges. The best and most authentic are nearly never located on a major squares or thoroughfares that rely solely on the tourist trade. Good restaurants look as though they've been around for decades. Many have wonderful rustic interiors and good-natured staff who usually have time to share a word or a joke.

Tuscan

If you can't decide between pizza, pasta, or a T-bone steak, the food emporium on the 2nd floor of the recently restored ★ **Mercato Centrale** (Piazza del Mercato Centrale, tel. 055/239-9798, daily 10am-midnight, €12-14) is the solution. It contains over 20 quality eateries that can satisfy multiple cravings. It's a popular lunch and dinner spot where diners bring whatever they like back to the central eating areas or sit and watch dishes being prepared at the counters. Beer and wine have their own dedicated sections and local soccer fans gather to watch games on Sundays.

★ **Trattoria Sostanza** (Via Porcellana 25r, Mon-Sat. noon-2pm and 7:30pm-10pm, €8-10) is on an anonymous street you'd probably avoid unless you were hungry. It has the character that comes from decades of preparing the same dishes a dozen times a day. No attempt is made at reinventing traditional recipes and no one seems to care. The daily handwritten menu includes pasta, soup, *Trippa alla Fiorentina, bistecca alla fiorentina* , and side orders of beans.

The word has been out about **Mario** (Via Rosina 2r, tel. 055/218-550, Mon.-Sat. 12:30pm-3:30pm, €10-12, cash only) since 1957, and this compact *trattoria* is nearly always busy with young and old seated close together eating whatever the daily menu has on offer. It's always delicious and the long, tiled dining room is nearly always full. Chefs prepare a steady stream of *ribollita* and roast chicken for eager customers drinking carafes of house wine. It's a good place to try *bistecca alla fiorentina* that's perfectly tender and always served rare. Reservations aren't accepted, but they'll take your name and seat you when a space opens up. Seating is often communal, which means there's a high probability of meeting people.

Baldini (Via il Prato 96r, tel. 055/287-663, Mon.-Fri. noon-2:30pm and 7:30pm-10pm, €14-16) may seem like a long way to walk for a meal but it's actually still within the old city walls and only minutes from the train station. It's hard to get more traditional than this. The fundamental ingredients are bread, olive oil, grilled meat, and wine. In addition, you'll find Tuscan classics like *tagliatelle* with wild boar, *ribollita,* and tripe. The desserts are homemade daily and fish is only served on Fridays.

Osteria Dei Pazzi (Via dei Lavatoi 1/3r,

Best Food and Drink

★ **Trattoria Sostanza:** This modest eatery serves Florentine classics in 1950s-era surroundings (page 167).

★ **Cucina Torcicoda:** It's restaurant, *osteria, pizzeria*—and wholly original (page 169).

★ **Mercato Centrale:** Browse the ingredients at this lively market—the center of Florentine food scene since 1872—before settling in at its 2nd-floor food court (page 167).

★ **All'Antico Vinaio:** Tourists and locals line up for mammoth sandwiches stuffed with local cold cuts. Don't worry; the line moves fast (page 171)!

★ **Osteria Antica Mescita:** Enjoy down-to-earth dishes at affordable prices en route to enjoy the views from the hillside of San Miniato (page 176).

★ **La Bottega del Buon Caffè:** This Michelin-rated restaurant facing the Arno makes dishes that are close to art—at an accessible price (page 176).

★ **Vecchio Forno:** Good-smelling Tuscan bread and pastries are baked in the oven out back at this cute corner bakery (page 172).

★ **Carapina:** Simone Bonini helped revolutionize gelato in Florence, taking a gourmet approach and experimenting with salty flavors, and brought a gourmet approach (page 173).

★ **Gelateria della Passera:** Enjoy the creamiest gelato in the city on the lovely little square facing this tiny shop (page 180).

tel. 055/234-4880, Tues.-Sun. 12:30pm-2:30pm and 7:30pm-10:30pm, €7-10) is an unassuming restaurant around the corner from Piazza Santa Croce. The sign above the entrance is vintage 1960s and little on the inside has changed since then. The food is typical Tuscan and Italians occupy most of the tables under ceiling fans that keep the large dining room cool.

Trattoria Pallottino (Via Isola delle Stinche 1r, Tues.-Sun. noon-2:30pm and 7pm-10:30pm, €8-10) has been serving local Tuscan dishes since 1911. It's a good place to try *pappa al pomodoro* and *ribollita*. The narrow dining room is paved with cobblestones and lined with wooden tables and chairs that have been used by generations of diners. There's outdoor seating along the pedestrian street near Santa Croce. Daily specials are written on a blackboard near the entrance.

Italian

Like many historic restaurants founded after World War II, **Giannino in San Lorenzo** (Via Borgo San Lorenzo 33-37r, tel. 055/239-9799, daily 11:30am-11:30pm, €12-20, pizza €7-9) has managed to survive thanks to a new generation of restaurateurs eager to keep old traditions alive. In this case Riccardo Bartoloni and his son are behind the renaissance. They serve great steaks, tripe in all its incarnations, and excellent pizza. There's something for everyone inside this venerable establishment where quality still matters.

Konnubio (Via dei Conti 8R, tel. 055/238-1189, daily 7:30am-11:30pm, €14-16) is proof that Florentine dining isn't only about traditional dishes served within rustic interiors. This cosmopolitan restaurant around the corner from Basilica San Lorenzo could easily be located in New York or Paris. The restaurant's four attractive rooms are decorated in contemporary style with wood and metallic furniture that is beyond cool. Tuscan, international, and vegan dishes are served nonstop from breakfast to dinner. Plate appearance matters as much as the ingredients selected.

Johnny Bruschetta (Via dei Macci 77r, tel. 055/247-8326, Mon.-Fri. 11am-3pm and 6pm-midnight, Sat.-Sun. 6pm-midnight, €7-11) is a fun place for beer and *bruschetta* near Mercato di San Ambrogio. They prepare 17 varieties of *bruschetta* that can be sampled on 30-inch (2 types), 50-inch (3) and 80-inch (4) long cutting boards. It's a lot like a tapas bar, and tables fill up with friends sharing this fun finger food. They also serve cured meats and cheeses, a vegetarian option, and craft beer from the taps. The area is animated at night and a good place to start or spend an evening.

Pizza

Pizza isn't native to Florence. It was introduced by Neapolitan expats and is thicker than the Roman version. Few restaurants are entirely devoted to pizza but it does appear on many menus.

In recent years ★ **Cucina Torcicoda** (Via Torta 5/r, tel. 055/265-4329, daily noon-3pm and 7:30pm-midnight, €8-10) has distinguished itself with its versatility: it's a restaurant, *osteria,* and *pizzeria* all in one. San Marzano tomatoes, Campania *mozzarella,* and Tuscan oil find their way into the daily pizza special and great *calzone.* All the ingredients from the menu can be purchased the little gourmet shop in the back.

Caffè Italiano (Via dell'Isola delle Stinche 11/13r, tel. 055/289-368, daily 7am-midnight, €8-10) has a wood-burning oven and are obsessed with using the best ingredients in traditional ways. That's probably why they only serve three types of pizza: *Margherita, Napoli,* and *Marinara.* The lack of variety hasn't stopped Vincenzo D'Anetra from building a loyal following that can make finding a table inside this delightful brick and wood-paneled *osteria* difficult.

The atmosphere at **Cucineria la Mattonaia** (Via della Mattonaia 19r, tel. 055/386-0564, daily 7:30pm-11:30pm, €9-12) is more refined than you'd expect for a *pizzeria,* but then again they also serve an extensive selection of meat and fish dishes. The pizza comes in over 20 varieties that includes the classics as well as some originals topped with cheese and vegetables.

Pizza enthusiasts who aren't interested in décor should visit **La Divina Pizza** (Via Borgo Allegri 50r, tel. 055/234-7498, Mon.-Sat. 10:30am-11:30pm, €6-8). It's a *pizza al taglio* shop run by an enthusiastic father-and-son team. They pull out mouthwatering tins of pizza and *focaccia* throughout the day that are served by the cut to a steady stream of clients. Choose three or four kinds and eat them inside on a little wooden tray or ask for takeaway (*per portare via*) and enjoy your pizza in Piazza Santa Croce or along the river.

International

The influx of Japanese and Chinese tourists as well as a steady stream of North African and East Asian immigrants has led to a diversification of dining options in Florence over the past few decades. Today it's easy to find sushi and noodles in the center and kebab shops and Indian takeaway along the streets north of Mercato Centrale where newcomers to the city tend to gather.

Dim Sum (Via dei Neri 37, tel. 055/284-331, Tues.-Sun. noon-3pm and 7pm-11pm, €14-16) is a small, modern restaurant with a bright interior and an open kitchen where chefs prepare southern Chinese specialties. Diners are greeted with a cup of tea (which is continually refilled) and a menu that includes steamed appetizers, dumplings, pot stickers, and vegetarian, noodle, and rice dishes. It fills up fast on weekends. Reservations can be useful.

There are quite a few sushi restaurants in Florence, and **Kome** (Via dei Benci 41r, Mon.-Sat. noon-3pm and 7pm-midnight, lunch special €14.90) is one of the liveliest. Choose between the *kaitan* belt (€25-40) on

Florentine Cuisine

In a country known for food, Tuscany is recognized by Italians as one of the best regions in which to eat. Meals don't have to be formal, and simple dishes are very often the best. Besides traditional *trattorie* where you can sample local cuisine the city has a long tradition of street food. Here are some tips for tasting Florence's most authentic dishes:

AT THE *TRATTORIA*

Nearly every Florentine *trattoria* has *ribollita* and *pappa al pomodoro* stews on their menu. Both are vegetarian friendly and highly filling. Fortunately, you can order a half portion *(mezza porzione)* of either and sample both.

- *Antipasti:* Appetizers, which are a delicious way to begin any meal. Choices include **crostini** along with local cold cuts and cheeses, often served in wine bars on wooden platters and accompanied by honey and olives. Central Italy is a great producer of **prosciutto** and other hams. The local variety is slightly spicy.

- *Crostini:* A lighter version of *bruschetta* that consists of grilled unsalted bread topped with oil, chopped tomatoes, or *fegato* (ground chicken liver similar to paté).

the ground floor where experienced chefs keep the sushi, sashimi, and tempura plates coming, or head to the grill-it-yourself tables for Japanese barbecue (€40-60 for 2). It's a lot of fun, but if all you're after is a shot of *sake* the downstairs lounge has a regular Wednesday happy hour that includes an extensive tasting menu.

Florence has experienced a recent boom in gourmet burger joints and **Polpa Burger** **Trattoria** (Piazza del Mercato Centrale 22r, tel. 055/286-770, daily 12:30pm-3pm and 8pm-midnight, €12) has put an Italian spin on the American classic. The key is quality local beef, lamb, and turkey that's selected and ground daily. Toppings include fresh vegetables, gorgonzola cheese, and grilled mushrooms. Crispy french fries are the default side dish and come in two different cuts. The €11 lunch special is hard to resist.

- *Ribollita:* An authentic vegetarian stew, often made in winter when the black cabbage in the recipe is in season, though it can be found throughout the year with substitute vegetables.

- *Pappa al pomodoro:* A vegetarian, tomato-based stew that's perfect in summer. It's reminiscent of gazpacho although the bread used gives it a thicker texture.

- *bistecca alla fiorentina :* A thick T-bone steak that is the most popular main course in Florence. It's cut from *Chianina* beef, a local cattle breed raised along the Tuscan coast and prized for its flavor. It's priced by the kilo. Don't bother asking for medium or well done: *Fiorentina* steaks are grilled for three minutes on either side and served alone on a plate close to rare. *Contorni* (sides) are ordered separately and generally consist of green beans (*fagioli*), broccoli, and zucchini. Roasted potatoes (*patate arrosto*) are also usually on offer.

- *Vino:* Wine! Tuscany is home to some of the finest vineyards in Italy. **Chianti** and **Barolo** are world renowned. If you're not an expert, the *vino della casa* (house wine) of any decent restaurant is always drinkable. Order it by the glass, quarter, half or full carafe. Cold *vino bianco* (white wine) is popular in summer while *vino rosso* (red wine) usually accompanies meat and cheese dishes.

STREET EATS

The favorite fast-food ingredient in Florence is tripe (*trippa*), made from the inside of a cow's four stomachs (not intestines). This traditional ingredient is a holdover from a hundred years ago, when people didn't throw away just anything. Tripe in fact has great gastronomic possibilities and has generated a variety of dishes. Locals can point the way towards the best of the remaining stands that serve tripe. Favorites depend on tenderness of the meat, concentration of spices, and personality of the vendors.

- *Lampredotto:* Tripe simmered for hours with tomatoes, onions, and parsley. It's eaten as a stew accompanied by a green herb sauce or in a sandwich. Find it at mobile kiosks around the city and inside Mercato Centrale.

- *Trippa alla Fiorentina:* Tripe sautéed with vegetables, tomatoes, and Parmesan, then simmered until the liquid slowly evaporates. It's on many menus and a good introduction to tripe.

- *Schiacciata:* The Florentine version of *focaccia,* served at bakeries to make sandwiches or enjoyed straight up. It's a speedy and delicious snack that's thick and doughy, and often topped with grilled vegetables or stuffed with local cold cuts.

Sandwiches

Tourists and locals line up outside ★ **All'Antico Vinaio** (Via dei Neri 74r, tel. 055/238-2723, Tues.-Sat. noon-4pm and 7pm-11pm, Sun. noon-11pm, €5) waiting to get their hands on the hefty sandwiches prepared behind the counter inside this tiny eatery. Although you can custom-select ingredients, the most popular *panini* are listed on a wooden board near the entrance. The *Favolosa,* stuffed with ham, goat cheese, and eggplant, is a good choice. Plastic cups of red or white wine are €2. Satisfied customers chew on the stools and steps outside.

If you don't want to wait and are looking for a little more than a sandwich, walk down the street to **La Prosciutteria** (Via de'Neri 54r, tel. 055/265-4472, daily 10:30am-11pm, €8-10). They specialize in Chianti wine and locally produced cold cuts and cheeses served on long wooden cutting boards. It's a fun place where groups of friends meet to share a meal in relaxed company that spills out onto the sidewalk.

The most reliable destination for thick sandwiches and generous platters of cold cuts and cheeses served with wine is **Via dei Neri**. It's one of the most mouthwatering streets in the city, with plenty of Florentine fast-food options to choose from.

Sandwichic (Via San Gallo 3r, tel. 055/281-157, daily 11am-8:30pm, €4.50) is housed inside a former haberdashery. *Panini* have replaced textiles and sewing machines, but thread and buttons are still on display. The three street chefs aren't trying to revolutionize the sandwich—they're just obsessed with using the best bread and local hams to make them. Wine is self-served for €1 a cup. Daily specials are written on the blackboard or fresh ingredients can be chosen to create an original sandwich.

The best thing about **Best Sandwich** (Via Vaccereccia 13, tel. 055/265-5847, daily 9am-11pm, €3-6) is that you can find a dozen kinds of Italian sandwiches all made with the regional products that make them unique. There's *mozzarella di bufala* from Campania, *porchetto* from Lazio, *'nduja* sausage from Calabria, and much more. The glass case facing the street is filled with tempting options that can be eaten at one of the stools inside the small shop or in Piazza della Signoria down the block.

Street Food

The areas around Mercato Centrale and Mercato San Ambrogio are havens for street food. Several long-standing *trippaio* or **mobile tripe stands** still operate throughout the city. **I Trippaio di Firenze** (Via Gioberti 103, 335/821-6880, €6) is recognizable by the metal stools surrounding a little van where Marco Bologesi has been preparing tripe sandwiches for over 20 years. It's usually surrounded by locals reading their newspapers and waiting for Marco to put the finishing touches on their order. **L'Antico Trippaio** (Via dei Cimatori 16) is a similar setup with the addition of photos identifying each of the sandwiches on offer. Hours may vary, but you can generally expect to find both operating from 11am until 9pm.

Tripe isn't the only ingredient available on Florentine streets. There's also a little blue mini-truck, equipped with a grill and deep fryer, parked in squares around the city and dishing out seafood. **Pescapane** (Via Arnolfo 27, €6) serves fish burgers, fish kebabs, and classic Italian-style fish-and-chips. The *mozzarella in carozza di mare* is full of mystery ingredients that go wonderfully well together. Water, beer, and wine are also available from this street-food eatery.

Alimentari are small deli-like shops most visitors never enter. They carry food and drink supplies as well as freshly prepared sandwiches, pasta salads, and occasionally pizza. **Gaudagni** (Via Isola delle Stinche, tel. 055/239-8642) is a neighborhood stalwart around the corner from Santa Croce run by husband and wife Stefano and Stefania. They've seen the neighborhood change dramatically in the last 30 years and greet local customers like old friends. It's the perfect place to improvise a picnic or enjoy a cold beer outside in the little square. Drinks are reasonably priced and can be drunk openly—though Stefania does suggest moderation.

Bakeries

Florentine bread lacks salt. According to legend this was due to a Pisan blockade and the inability to import the mineral for several years. The taste for unsalted loaves stuck and dozens of *forni* (bakeries) in the center are busy baking it every morning. ★ **Vecchio Forno** (Via Guelfa 32, tel. 055/265-4069, daily 7am-3pm, €3) is a small shop on a corner where locals come for typical *pan di ramerino* sweet bread made with raisins and rosemary. Glass cases display tempting sandwiches, cakes, and tarts, and the shelves are filled with an assortment of Tuscan breads. You can take it to go or sit at one of the half-dozen stools and listen to local chatter. The bar on the opposite corner is where the owners go whenever they want an *espresso*.

If you haven't tried *schiacciatta all'olio* (Tuscan focaccia), grab a number and get in line at **Pugi** (Piazza San Marco 9b, tel. 055/280-981, Mon.-Sat. 7:45am-8pm, €5). The *schiacciata* comes dabbed with olive oil and topped with zucchini, sliced potatoes, or red peppers or stuffed with *prosciutto* ham. When it's your turn just point and gesture to the friendly uniformed ladies behind the counter. They also have great desserts and seasonal specialties at Carnevale, Easter, and Christmas. There are several other locations around the city in case you develop a habit.

People obsessed with bread won't mind the long walk to **Garbo** (Via Dino del Garbo 2, tel. 055/437-8740, Mon.-Sat. 7am-8pm, Sun. 7.30am-1:30pm, €3-5), a neighborhood bakery run by Carlo Scorpio and his wife, Silvia. They can spend hours talking about flour and yeast. Everything here is made by hand using local ingredients and a grindstone Carlo claims is the secret to making great bread. You'll notice the difference from the smell wafting from the ovens and the perfectly stacked loaves behind the counter. Every day is dedicated to a different flavor: If you arrive on a Saturday you can sample the *paillasse* and dried fruit buns. They also create pastries and serve a light lunch menu that can be eaten there or taken away.

Gelato

Gelato prices start at around €2 for two scoops in a cup or cone. Each additional scoop is 50 cents. Whipped cream is free but you may have to ask for *panna* in case it's forgotten.

Simone Bonini helped revolutionize gelato in Florence, and his ★ **Carapina** (Via Lambertesca 18r and Piazza Oberdan 2/r, tel. 055/676-930, daily noon-10:30pm) was one of the first gelato shops to use old-fashioned refrigerated containers (called *carapina*) where the product remains hidden inside cold metal vats. He's experimented with salty flavors and brought a gourmet approach to gelato. The *crema al Vin Santo* and *stracciatella* flavors

are unbeatable. A second shop is east of the Historic Center.

Vivoli (Via dell'Isola delle Stinche 7r, tel. 055/ 292-334, Tues.-Sat. 7:30am-midnight, Sun. 9am-9pm) has maintained its quality since the 1930s. This is the old-school approach, with classic cream and fruit flavors and little concern about innovating or improving their English skills. Hazelnut, coffee, pear, and lemon are among the dozens of flavors available in a cone or cup at prices that may keep you coming back for more.

Le Botteghe di Leonardo (Via de' Ginori 21r, tel. 055/933-7083) makes a great dark chocolate flavor, but if you ask Francesco what he suggests combining it with he won't give you a straight answer. Fortunately, he'll let you sample any flavor that catches your interest on the menu board. The gelato is kept in metal containers and out of sight. Once you've made a decision you can enjoy it on the chairs facing a *fresco*. This *gelateria* is part of a cooperative and there are several others around the city.

Gelateria Carabè (Via Ricasoli 60r, tel. 055/289-476, Mon.-Fri. 3pm-midnight and Sat.-Sun. 10am-midnight) takes the Sicilian approach to gelato, which explains the *granite* and *cannoli* that are also available. Watch the gelato being made while you wait and enjoy it on one of benches inside or out. Every flavor is based on fresh ingredients, including almonds, hazelnuts, and pistachios imported from Sicily. There's even an olive oil and several gluten-free flavors. (Gelato is often gluten-free, but some shops use flour as a thickener, and flavors like tiramisu may contain wheat.)

Fans of chocolate should try **Gelateria De' Medici** (Via dello Statuto, 5/r, Tues.-Sun. 9:30am-1am), where cacao is combined with fruit, alcohol, and spices to create a vast and tempting assortment. *Crema de'Medici*, cream flavor, is the house specialty and sorbets are served inside frozen fruit.

Without *gelateria* written on the sign it would be easy to pass **Dario Ceccarelli's** (Via Capo di Mondo 40, tel. 055/660-561) small shop without a second thought. If you

★ Gelato

Gelato has been produced in Florence ever since the Medici developed a taste for the treat. Today there are over 136 *gelaterie* in the city and every Florentine has a favorite. The best have been around for generations, preparing their gelato and *sorbetto* on-site or close by using all-natural ingredients.

Gelato is just milk, sugar, and natural fruit and cacao flavors, but when those ingredients are fresh and combined with care something special happens. Understanding the difference between good and great gelato takes practice. A few basic guidelines for finding the best:

- **Avoid unnatural colors and showy displays.** If the color looks too bright or the gelato is displayed in gravity-defying mounds, artificial flavoring and preservatives may be to blame.

- **Start with the classics.** Start with the classics like chocolate, cream, and a wild card. Read labels next to each flavor carefully and remember the names of the ones you like.

- **Taste test.** Gelato clerks readily provide small samples on miniature plastic spoons.

- **Mind the line.** Unless you exert some authority inside a crowded *gelateria,* you may never place an order.

- **Go cone-less.** *Gelateria* always offer a choice between cup or cone. Purists advocate the former on grounds of taste.

- **Get the scoop(s).** Gelato is ordered in several different sizes that usually translate into two, three, and four scoops. Each scoop can be a different flavor. There's only one size of cone, while cups get progressively larger.

- **Enjoy *al fresco.*** Gelato is street food and best enjoyed while moving. It has an undeniable effect on the view, and walking through the streets of Florence with a gelato has a way of making even good days better.

did you'd be missing one of the best old-fashioned gelato joints in Florence. Dario uses the same machines he did a half century ago and you can taste the quality. The *Crema Antica* is made from a secret recipe and classics like *nocciola*, *noci*, *torrone*, and *stracciatella* are all served in this shop a short distance from the Historic Center.

Coffee

Florence's historic cafes are elegant institutions that have been in business for decades. They continue to serve regulars and curious visitors inside little-changed interiors where artists and literati of previous eras spent their days in animated discussion.

The key to great coffee is the bean. At ★ **Ditta Artigianale** (Via dei Neri 32r, tel.

055/274-1541, Mon.-Thurs. 8am-10pm, Fri. 8am-midnight, Sat. 9:30am-midnight, Sun. 9:30am-10am, €2-3) they choose theirs carefully and control every step in the blending process. The result is one of the best espressos in the city. You can also sip on tea, have a light lunch, or enjoy a predinner cocktail inside this hip coffee hangout adorned with repurposed and vintage furnishings.

Nothing matches at ★ **Amblé** (Piazzetta dei Del Bene 7a, tel. 055/268-528, daily 10am-10pm, €3-5), but that's part of the charm of this coffee and fruit bar moments from the Ponte Vecchio. The other part is the feeling of stumbling upon a place that can only be found by accident. Friends and couples relax outside on brightly colored deck chairs, benches, and stools all partially shaded by an ancient wall.

Which flavor of gelato will you choose?

Below are some of the best options for gelato in Florence:

- **Carapina** (page 173)
- **Le Botteghe di Leonardo** (page 173)
- **Vivoli** (page 173)

The only place an aspiring 20th-century Florentine writer or painter would consider entering was ★ **Giubbe Rosse** (Piazza della Repubblica 13/14r, tel. 055/212-280, daily 10am-1am, €2-5). Named after the red jackets still worn by the waitstaff, this tearoom was founded by two German brothers in 1896. It became famous a decade later as the principal hangout of Futurist artists. It's a mandatory stop for bibliophiles and traces of the café's literary past are still evident. On the other side of the *piazza* lies **Caffè Gilli** (Piazza della Repubblica 39r, tel. 055/213-896, daily 7am-midnight, €2-5) with its elegant chandeliers and closely spaced round tables. The location and Liberty-style décor have changed little since the 1920s.

Caffè Rivoire (Piazza della Signoria 5, tel. 055/214-412, Tues.-Sun. 7:30am-midnight, €2-5) is diagonally opposite Palazzo Vecchio and has been in business since 1872. Initially they only served chocolate, but coffee, tea, and pastries were soon added to the menu and attracted the cultural elite of the time. The shop still draws people who want to step into the past and enjoy a good view of the square. The only thing that has changed are the topics of conversation and the prices—which are double or triple that of an average bar.

La Boulangerie (Via de'Rondinelli 24r, tel. 055/281-658, €5) is a good place to take a break from sightseeing or shopping. It's an instant respite from the busy street outside and serves coffee, fresh-squeezed orange juice, pastries, and a variety of tempting baguette sandwiches. Take a seat at the long wooden counter or grab a stool near the front and observe the world walking by.

Bar Caffè Mingo (Piazza San Martino) is stuck in time on a little square that has nothing very special about it except its refusal to change. Sit outside on the metal chairs away from the sun and watch the pedestrians pass. It doesn't feel like the center of Florence, but it's around the corner from everything and is a good caffeine refuge.

OLTRARNO

There are fewer restaurants across the Arno. Most are small, rustic places serving traditional Tuscan food at affordable prices. There are some notable exceptions where Michelin-starred chefs create culinary masterpieces and al fresco dining includes views of olive trees and medieval walls. **Borgo San Frediano** near the river is particularly rich in gastronomic options and is lined with dozens of inviting eateries. Neighborhood squares like **Piazza Santo Spirito** are also reliable destinations for those in search of authentic flavors. Here coffee, pasta, cocktails, and gelato can all be had within a short radius. Snack bars and restaurants near the Ponte Vecchio and Palazzo Pitti often cater exclusively to tourists and are best avoided.

Tuscan

A number of restaurants and bars line the street leading towards Piazzale Michelangelo and San Miniato. ★ **Osteria Antica Mescita** (Via Borgo S. Jacopo 16r, daily noon-12:30am, €7-12) is one of the simplest. The outdoor tables are an excellent place to seek Tuscan nourishment before or after walking up to see the view. The menu consists of a half-dozen firsts and seconds, none of which exceeds €8 or has been translated into English (which is usually a good sign). If you're hungry you can have a two-course meal for a very reasonable €12 that includes water. The house wine is more than satisfactory and served by the glass or carafe.

Casalinga (Via Michelozzi 9r, tel. 055/218-624, Mon.-Sat. 12:30pm-3pm and

7:30pm-10:30pm, €13-15) has been serving lunch and dinner in the Oltrarno neighborhood since 1963. Nello and Oliviero have retired now, but their three children maintain the tradition inside this simple *trattoria* where waitstaff in red aprons dash from table to table delivering traditional favorites. The menu is quite dense and there are many possibilities for creating a memorable meal. One option is the mixed *crostini* plate, followed by minestrone soup and *bollito misto*. Ask the server about the daily special and leave room for the *torta della nonna*. If you can't arrive around opening time, make a reservation.

Il Guscio (Via dell'Orto 49a, tel. 055/224-421, Mon.-Fri. noon-2pm and 7:45pm-11pm, Sat. dinner only, €12-15) is a friendly, informal restaurant where first courses arrive before you can begin nibbling on the bread and seconds include *bistecca alla fiorentina* and seared tuna. Portions are enviable and prices honest. The wine cellar includes over 400 Tuscan bottles and you can order Chianti by the glass or carafe.

If décor isn't essential and all you're after is Florentine classics, **Il Brindellone** (Piazza Piattellina 10-11r, tel. 055/217-879, Tues.-Sun. 12:30pm-1:45pm and 7:30pm-9:45pm, €7-9) is a good choice for lunch or dinner. This *trattoria* is popular with locals and there's jovial banter between the owner and regulars who come for the beef. They also prepare a very tasty *ribollita* and *pappa al pomodoro* that can easily feed two. Don't worry about reservations or dressing up.

Italian

There are five Michelin-rated restaurants in Florence, but the elegant ★ **La Bottega del Buon Caffè** (Lungarno Benvenuto Cellini 69r, tel. 055/553-5677, Tues.-Sat. 12:30pm-3pm and 7:30pm-10:30pm, Sun. lunch only, €26-41) is the only one facing the Arno. Here, a team of young chefs diligently prepares dishes that look like they belong in a modern art museum. What each plate lacks in quantity it makes up for in flavor and creativity. The kitchen garden supplies vegetables; other

★ Italian Coffee

Un café per favore...

Coffee wouldn't be the same without Florence. Not only were the Medici the first to import beans to Italy in the early 18th century, but two local brothers pioneered the modern coffee machine in the 1930s. Their patented horizontal boiler simplified coffee making and made the drink accessible to all.

Today, coffee is a daily ritual for thousands of Florentines who crowd into bars for their morning fix and often end their lunches with a cup. Most of them drink at the counter and there's hardly ever a wait. It's one of the cheapest pleasures in the city and rarely exceeds a euro, unless you sit down at a table or find yourself in front of Piazza della Signoria where the views increase the cost. Before placing an order consider the following options:

- **Caffè:** Espresso served black. This is the most popular way of drinking coffee in Italy. (Espresso has become so popular that when you order a *caffè* you automatically receive an espresso.) The espresso is served in a ceramic cup, unless *al vetro* is requested—in which case it will be poured into a shot glass.

- **Caffè Corto:** An espresso served short (*corto*), making it slightly stronger.

- **Caffè Lungo:** An espresso served long (*lungo*), making it slightly weaker.

- **Caffè Macchiato:** Espresso with a dash of steamed milk. (*Macchiato* means stained; the milk "stains" the *espresso*).

- **Latte Macchiato:** The opposite of *caffè macchiato*—a glass of milk stained with a little coffee.

- **Cappuccino:** One of Italy's greatest exports. In Florence it's almost always ordered in the morning and often accompanied by a pastry. A cappuccino is served in a larger cup and is creamier than a caffè macchiato.

- **Marocchino:** A cross between a caffè *macchiato* and miniature *cappuccino* topped with cacao and served in a glass or ceramic cup.

- **Caffè Freddo:** Italians don't stop drinking coffee in summer, but they often order iced *espresso* when temperatures rise. It's served black, with milk or topped with whipped cream.

- **Shakerato:** An espresso blended with crushed iced and served in a glass. It occasionally comes presweetened and presented in a martini glass.

- **Spremuta d'Arancia:** Not coffee, but fresh-squeezed orange juice. Most bars have sophisticated juicers and oranges are in season nearly all year long.

Below are some of the best coffee shops in Florence:

- **Amblé** (page 174)

- **Ditta Artigianale** (page 174)

- **Giubbe Rosse** (page 175)

ingredients, like venison, lamb, and pigeon, are all locally sourced. The interior is simple but refined, with vaulted brick ceilings and comfortable chairs, and waitstaff anticipate every need. There's a memorable four-course tasting menu at lunch. Reservations are recommended.

Owner-chef Arturo Caminatti spends his mornings selecting ingredients from local meat and vegetable suppliers and the rest of the time in his kitchen at **Trattoria dell'Orto** (Via dell'Orto 35r, tel. 055/244-148, Wed.-Mon. noon-3pm and 7:30pm-11:30pm, €8-12). The result is mouthwatering plates of *crostini,* cold cuts, and chargrilled steaks that look as good as they taste. The bottles lining the movie set-like interior aren't only for show, and there's more in the vaulted cellar down below. The garden is a lovely place to eat during the summer.

Angiolino (Via di Santo Spirito 36r, tel. 055/239-8976, daily 11:30am-11:30pm, €10-14) is a historic *trattoria* run by three jubilant brothers where Florentine families come for long Sunday lunches. Their menu includes handmade pasta, grilled meats, and specialty sandwiches like lobster roll and roast beef club. Wine can be ordered by the bottle or glass and the dark wood interior is perfect for escaping the heat outside.

Gesto (Borgo San Frediano 27r, 393/954-0021, daily 6pm-2am, €3-5 per plate) is an eco-friendly eatery where menus are written on tables and orders are taken using small chalk-boards that double as trays. Martina Luccatelli and her all-female staff have created a welcoming space that's artsy and comfortable. The food is tapas-style with some vegetarian twists that surprise the senses. Portions are small and the fish, meat, vegetable, and sweet plates are suited for a light dinner rather than a heavy feast.

Make the second right just beyond the medieval gates and you'll stumble onto **La Beppa Fioraia** (Via dell'Erta Canina, tel. 055/234-7681, www.labeppafioraia.it, daily 12:30pm-2:30pm and 7:30pm-midnight, €8-11). This large restaurant with indoor and outdoor seating is popular with locals for the convenient parking and bohemian atmosphere. It's perfect for families. The large lawn facing an olive grove allows children to play while parents relax in the shade. The menu includes a variety of *tagliere* tasting platters with different combinations of cheese, cold cuts, honeys, and fruits. Vegetarians are catered to and fresh bread is served with every meal by an enthusiastic staff.

Pizza

Florence doesn't have the same pizza-making tradition as Rome, but there are still plenty of places where it can be found. Most common is the thin, soft-crust Neapolitan variety. You'll also find *pizza al taglio* shops offering freshly baked trays of pizza with various toppings. These are sold by the cut *(taglio)* and you can choose whatever dimensions you like.

outdoor dining at La Beppa Fioraia

Gusta

generations of stomachs. The family also prepares southern Italian specialties, fried *antipasti,* and homemade desserts. The rustic interior is decorated like a small shrine to Naples. Getting there is a pleasant walk through the old city gates and down Borgo S. Frediano where tempting stops await.

Street Food

You can get tripe on this side of the river, and missing out on **Il Trippaio di Porta Romana** (Piazzale Porta Romana, 335/285-245, €5) is the gastronomic version of missing the Duomo. Mario and Manola Albergucci set up their mobile kiosk just outside the medieval walls and have been serving tripe sandwiches there for decades. He's a former butcher and prepares *lampredotto* with passion while she dishes out sides of beans, artichokes, and whatever else is in season. Eat at one of the portable counters underneath the trees. When you're done, take a stroll through the Boboli Gardens or up Viale Machiavelli to enjoy the view.

Bakeries

S. Forno (Via Santa Monaca 3r, tel. 055/239-8580, www.ilsantobevitore.com, daily 7:30am-7:30pm, €4) is more than a bakery. At breakfast they offer a tempting assortment of breads, muffins, scones, and tarts. At lunch soups, salads, and freshly made sandwiches are accompanied by fruit juice, wine, or beer. Pull up a stool and eat underneath the barrel vaulting or head to Piazza Santo Spirito to enjoy an *al fresco* picnic. If you have a canine friend inquire about their homemade dog biscuits.

Homesick? Make a beeline for **Mama's Bakery** (Via della Chiesa 34r, tel. 055/219-214, Mon.-Fri. 8am-5pm, Sun.-Sat. 9am-3pm, €5), where Matt Reinecke and his wife, Christina, prepare bagels, American-inspired cookies, cupcakes, pies, and brownies that can cure any gastronomic nostalgia. Matt can also inspire anyone contemplating a full-time move to Italy. The California native launched the bakery in 2008 and has rarely

★ **Berbere** (Piazza de'Nerli 1, tel. 055/238-2946, Mon.-Thurs. 7pm-midnight, Fri.-Sun. 12:30pm-2:30pm and 7pm-midnight, €7-11) has a modern, post-industrial interior with exposed brick, wood tables, and high vaulted ceilings. The pizza is thick and well suited to anyone with a passion for crust and vegetables. There is a good selection of regionally produced craft beer and the *piazza* outside becomes a popular hangout during the summer.

Gusta (Via Maggio 46r, daily 11:30am-3:30pm and 7pm-11:30pm, €5-8) is one of the most popular pizzerias in the neighborhood, with a mix of university students, locals, and visitors vying for tables inside or out of this small and unpretentious establishment. Service is fast but friendly. Arrive early to avoid the rush or ask for takeaway and eat on the steps of Santo Spirito just a minute away.

Vico del Carmine (Via Pisana 40r, Tues.-Sun. 12:30pm-2:30pm and 7:30pm-midnight, €6-9) is a traditional Neapolitan *pizzeria* with a wood-fired oven that has satisfied several been out of the kitchen since. Mama's is popular with expats and locals who have developed a taste for American flavors made with Italian ingredients.

Gelato

★ **Gelateria della Passera** (Via Toscanella 15r, tel. 055/291-882, daily noon-midnight) is a tiny shop facing a lovely little square. Flavors are made on the premises with fresh natural ingredients. A short line is always possible, as there's little space inside and some important decisions to make. Enjoy the flavors on one of the nearby benches where grandparents like to gather.

People come to **Gelateria La Carraia** (Piazza Nazario Sauro 25r, tel. 055/280-695, daily 11am-midnight) for the chocolate and come back for all the other flavors. The cones here are nearly as tasty as the gelato and come in different colors, shapes, and varieties. This inviting parlor is located on a corner facing the two Arno bridges west of the Ponte Vecchio.

Over in Piazza Tasso children play and locals pass the time on their cell phones. The only *gelateria* on the square is **La Sorbettiera** (Piazza Torquato Tasso 11, Mon.-Sat. 12:30pm-11:30pm, Sun. 11am-1pm and 3pm-11:30pm), from which people have been getting gelato since 1934. There's less variety but what they do have is top notch. A little counter faces the street and clients order from outside.

Enjoy the gelato on a stool facing a neat line of parked mopeds or in the park.

Coffee

There are coffee bars in most squares and a choice of three or four in Piazza Santo Spirito that all come with views of the church; the outdoor tables at **Caffè Ricchi** (daily 7am-11pm) are especially pleasant for sipping coffee or cocktails. Over in the triangular *piazzetta* where Via dello Sprone meets Via Toscanella **Caffè degli Artigiani** (daily noon-midnight) serves coffee out of an intimate little bar that barely seats one. Fortunately, the *espresso* is good and there's outdoor seating around the corner. By early evening orders for beer and wine outnumber those for coffee.

La Cité Libreria Café (Borgo San Frediano 20r, tel. 055/210387, Mon.-Sat. 9am-2pm and Sun. 3pm-2am, €2.5-5) is Florence's bohemian version of Starbucks. The relaxed space close to the Arno is a cultural lounge that mixes good coffee with literature, music, and theater. Rest here for as long as you like browsing the books, using the free Wi-Fi, and discussing politics with staff.

There are also several bars in Piazza Pitti facing the palace. Street traffic and the continual flow of tourists along the sidewalk make these less inviting regardless of the view. For a more relaxed and authentic afternoon coffee stick to the lesser-known streets and squares of the neighborhood.

Nightlife and Entertainment

In Florence, nightlife doesn't start at night. It begins in the lazy part of the afternoon when people stop thinking about work, and officially commences once an *aperitivo* is ordered. That leads to dinner and the opportunity to dine *al fresco* in another spot. Florence is a small and dynamic city, and you're bound to stumble upon music, dancing, or a lively, crowded square. Market workers dismantling their stalls along with the shutting of doors

and the opening of others are all clues to the onset of nightlife. Most of the city's nightlife options are located near the Historic Center, with a few in the Oltrarno.

If you opt out in favor of a good night's rest, you wouldn't be alone. Most Florentines turn in early, and the city doesn't have a reputation for nightlife like Rome does. Still, there are enough young professionals, artists, *bon vivants,* university students, and curious travelers to provide a pleasant, relaxed energy at night.

Much of the time that energy isn't organized—it's just dozens of people watching the Ponte Vecchio at sunset or hanging out in a square. Any search for nightlife should include both sides of the Arno. **Piazza Santo Spirito** is a good destination whatever the time, and the bars and restaurants along **Borgo San Friediano** in Oltrarno are bustling from dinner until midnight. Other likely sources of nightlife are villas and parks where stages with live music pop up during the summer. It can also be generated by a single bar or kiosk where people crowd onto sidewalks and steps, transforming a street into an outdoor lounge.

★ APERITIVO BARS
Historic Center

The ★ **Winter Garden by Caino** (Piazza Ognissanti 1, daily 11am-1am) recently earned its first Michelin star and deserves it on the decoration alone; come to this hotel along the Arno for drinks and its great hall will provide an eyeful of architecture and elegance. The meticulous bar and buffet are well stocked and cozy living room-like niches await. A Bloody Mary prepared with the addition of *Grappa di Brunello* is the house cocktail.

Many hotel bars have great views, and **Plaza Luchese** (Lungarno della Zecca Vecchia 38, tel. 055/26236, 9am-midnight) is no exception—but the **Empireo** bar inside this hotel also boasts a spectacular riverside terrace and swimming pool. From Monday to Thursday the *aperitivo* includes a meticulously prepared buffet with live music for a modest €14. On weekends there's an *a la carte* menu.

Soul Kitchen (Via dei Benci 34, tel. 055/263-9772, daily 5pm-3am, €8-10) is located on a lively street near Piazza Santa Croce. There's an extensive hot and cold buffet set on two long tables that can easily substitute dinner. Leather couches and brick walls provide the atmosphere, and the piano at the back is often played. If you can't

decide on a cocktail let the bartenders surprise you.

Oltrarno

★ **Negroni** (Via dei Renai 17r, tel. 055/243-647, daily 8am-2am, €7-10) is named after the city's favorite cocktail and the namesake is the obvious drink to order. The bar's been the backdrop for several films and was in the vanguard of the *aperitivo* movement. Crowds spill out onto the small terrace and surrounding sidewalks during the summer, and getting the bartender's attention can be difficult. Ask for finger snacks (*stuzzichini per favore*) if they aren't served.

Don't bother asking them to turn down the music at **Volume** (Piazza Santo Spirito 5r, tel. 055/238-1460, daily 9:30am-1:30am, €5-8). They like things loud at this workshop-turned-bar where carpentry tools are still on display and none of the armchairs match Bands often perform inside, though conversation is possible on the outdoor patio overlooking the square.

Viale Machiavelli is an elegant tree-lined avenue that begins in Piazzale di Porta Romana and snakes its way up the Oltrarno hillside. There are many villas along the way but **Villa Cora** (Viale Machiavelli 18, tel. 055/228-790, Thurs.-Sat, 7pm-10pm, €20) is where both Napoleon III's wife and conductor Claude Debussy chose to reside. There are several bars and restaurants inside this refined five-star hotel including a champagne bar, a bistro, and a poolside lounge. Fridays and Saturdays are devoted to enjoying cocktails, tapas, and live jazz.

Pasticceria Giorgio (Via Duccio di Boninsegna 36, tel. 055/247-9738, Tues.-Sat. 7am-8:30pm, Sun. 7am-1:30pm, €10-14) doesn't care about fancy. This pastry shop and bar is more concerned with the food. It puts on one of the finest buffet spreads in the city on its long bar where locals jostle to fill their plates and sip their drinks. If you manage to get a table the waitstaff will come by with new delicacies that are hazardous to diets. Although not in the center it's a good excuse

Aperitivo Hour

aperitivo hour in Piazza Santo Spirito

Florentines are social, so they love to sit down for an *aperitivo* (pre-dinner drink) with friends. The city even has its own cocktail invented nearly a century ago by Count Camillo Negroni. The drink, called a Negroni, consists of Campari, Vermouth, and gin. Today, cocktails are served with complimentary light snacks from 5pm onwards at bars throughout Florence. There's an abundance of venues to choose from, but these are some of the best:

- **Winter Garden by Caino** (page 181)
- **Volume** (page 181)
- **Negroni** (page 181)
- **Coquinarius** (page 183)
- **Le Volpe e L'Uva** (page 183)

to visit a real neighborhood and walk off the calories you're sure to gain.

WINE BARS

Tuscany produces good wine, and you'll taste proof of that at restaurants and bars around the city. But if you take wine seriously, visit an *enoteca*. These shops are entirely dedicated to grapes and stocked with thousands of bottles waiting to be uncorked. The varieties most commonly grown on the hillsides overlooking Florence are Sangiovese,

Canaiolo, and Trebbiano. These are pressed to create Chianti, which is the world's favorite wine and tastes good with everything. If your palate craves something more sophisticated you're ready for Brunello.

If you can't decide that's not a problem. *Enoteche* are run by people who love wine and love sharing their knowledge of wine. Wine rarely goes without food in Italy and *enoteche* are great for understanding how each vintage tastes when paired with meats, cheeses, and other staples of the Tuscan larder.

Historic Center

You'll find a mix of loyal regulars and satisfied visitors underneath the arched ceilings of ★ **Coquinarius** (Via delle Oche 11r, tel. 055/230-2153, €10-15). Every wine has a tale and you're likely to hear it by the end of the night. This jovial *enoteca* with bare wood tables and chairs is just around the corner from the Duomo. It's full of character and serves deliciously simple dishes. Come even if you aren't hungry to enjoy a glass and read a book within a timeless setting.

As you read this, Brunello, Chianti, and Montalcino are aging in the cellar below **Divina Enoteca** (Via Panicale 19, tel. 055/292-723, Tues.-Sun. 10:30am-8:30pm, €10-14) opposite the San Lorenzo market. What started as a deli serving fried cod has become a reliable address for sampling classic Tuscan vintages. To accompany a glass, choose from a *bruschetta*, *panini*, or mixed plates of cured meat served with bread. It's all eaten on a marble table where strangers frequently become friends.

They know wine at **Enoteca Fiorentina** (Via Pietrapiana 11-13r, tel. 055/388-0177, Thurs.-Tues. noon-11:30pm, €6-10) and are continually learning more about a subject that never ceases to surprise. They take pleasure in the infinite possibilities and have a preference for biological vineyards in Tuscany. Jonathal (that's his real name) can advise you on single or mixed varietals and accompany them with an original appetizer.

Oltrarno

Minutes from the Ponte Vecchio, ★ **Le Volpe e L'Uva** (Piazza dei Rossi 1, tel. 055/239-8132, Mon.-Sat. 11am-9pm, €10) has been serving some of the city's hardest-to-find Italian and French wines for more than 20 years. They do it unpretentiously and with a passion that is contagious. The *stuzzichini* (appetizers) are simple but satisfying. Cheese plates served with honey and mustard and *crostone* topped with Asiago are set tantalizingly on a circular counter where wine is the favorite topic of conversation. Reservations are useful for getting a table outside.

The San Niccolò section of Oltrarno has a wonderful bohemian feel that remains unspoiled by tourism. It's a great place to drink wine and the fact that **Fuori Porti** (Via del Monte alle Croci 10r, tel. 055/234-2483, daily 12:30pm-12:30am, €12) has wine glasses set on the tables is a good sign. In summer, you can sit on the large terrace and choose from over 500 labels the owners have personally selected from the region's smaller wineries. The *crostini* and *carpaccio* make wonderful appetizers and there's plenty on the menu if you suddenly gain an appetite.

DISCOS

If you consider nightlife to mean clubbing, you may be disappointed by Florence's options. Although discos exist, the good ones where you can dance until dawn are few. Still, Florence has a high concentration of foreign exchange students, and it's possible to listen to contagious electronic music and dance among locals and visitors. Many clubs are registered as private associations and operate a membership system in which first-time visitors must register before entering. It's a fairly straightforward process that requires filling out a short form with your name, details, and signature. There's usually a small fee (€5-10), which entitles you to a membership card and complimentary drink. Clubs that don't use this system charge a slightly higher cover that rarely exceeds €20 and is often waived for female revelers.

Historic Center

Blue Velvet (Via Castello d'Altafronte 16r, tel. 055/215-521, Thurs.-Sat. 11:30pm-late) is a small disco lounge on a narrow side street close to the river. The front room is filled with people sitting on velvet sofas and mingling in the blue-lit interior. Dancing is through the back where DJs, accompanied by live performers on Thursdays, keep bodies moving until late.

For a dose of glamour in stylish

underground surroundings head to **Full Up** (Via della Vigna Vecchia 23-25r, tel. 055/293-006, Thurs.-Sat. 11pm-3am). The door policy is lenient but there's usually a small entrance fee. It's popular with locals and visitors who regularly flock to the dance floors and lounge areas inside.

Most discos in the center are small and rather intimate. If you want big and brash try **Yab** (Via dè Sassetti 5r, tel. 055/215-160, Mon., Wed-Sat. 7pm-4am). Here you'll find cube dancers, international DJs, and a main dance floor populated by a mixed crowd most nights of the week. There's a hip-hop evening on Mondays, Wednesdays are for students, and from Thursday to Saturday you can dine and dance. Yab operates a pay-as-you-leave scheme in which you are given a drink card as you enter. It has one prepaid drink that can be used at any of the bars and is stamped each time afterwards. You pay when you leave and are charged €50 if you lose the card.

Further Afield

A location outside the center near the airport hasn't stopped **Tenax** (Via Pratese 46, tel. 055/30-8160, www.tenax.org, Fri. 10:30pm-4am and Sat. 10:30pm-5am) from becoming one of Florence's most popular nighttime destinations. It's a €6 taxi ride from the train station or you can use public transportation. Once you arrive you'll find several bars, lounges, a big stage, balconies, a VIP area, and lots of people. The club is ideal for live shows and international acts regularly turn up. Nobody's Perfect is the chill-out night on Saturdays when resident and guest DJs take turns spinning the latest vinyl.

THE ARTS
Concerts

Music isn't hidden away in Florence. It's played outside throughout the day by the violinist seated along a quiet street and the singer dressed in jeans belting out *arias* in Piazza Santa Trinita. Street musicians are common and a variety of instruments from accordions to flutes serenade pedestrians. Melodies reverberate off the stone walls in summer, and finding music only requires following your ears. Larger, organized concerts are also held in the larger squares like Piazza della Signoria where orchestras perform from the Loggia Lanzi. Summer events are also staged in parks and historic villas around the city. There are musical festivals from May to September and many bars regularly feature live music nights or DJ sets. Florence is also an occasional stop for international acts, and megaconcerts are held in the soccer stadium.

Squares, villas, and churches have concerts scheduled throughout the summer. The city's

a concert in Piazza della Signoria

youth orchestra performs several times a week in Piazza della Signoria. They usually start in the late afternoon and impromptu audiences sit wherever they can. **Villa Bardini** (Costa San Giorgio 2, tel. 055/2006-6206, €7) offers more intimacy and hosts talented musicians from the city's conservatory who play the classics. Reservations are required and entry includes an *aperitivo*. The grand baroque interior of **Santo Stefano al Ponte** (Via Por. Santa Maria, €12) near Ponte Vecchio becomes a regular backdrop for opera and soloist performances. On the other side of the river in Oltrarno **St. Marks** (Via Maggio 16, tel. 055/294-764, €15-35) organizes regular choral, lyrical, and orchestral events.

Many shows are free but if there's something specific you want to hear and tickets are necessary it's best to purchase them in advance to ensure decent seats. Otherwise you can wait until you arrive and decide spontaneously. In that case visit **Boxoffice Toscana** (Via delle Vecchie Carceri 1, tel. 055/210-804, Mon.-Fri. 10am-7pm, Sun. 10am-2pm) inside the refurbished prison on the eastern edge of the Historic Center. They provide tickets to all genres of musical events all year long.

Theater and Opera

Teatro Verdi (Via Ghibellina 97, tel. 055/212-320, www.teatroverdionline.it, box office Mon.-Sat. 10am-1pm and 4pm-7pm, €15 and up) is one of the longest-operating theaters in the city. It has a classic red velvet interior and six tiers of seating that soar above the stage. It seats over a thousand and is home to the Tuscan regional orchestra, which performs a varied repertoire from October until May. Throughout the year the theater also hosts concerts, musicals, ballet, and plays.

Teatro della Pergola (Via della Pergola 12-32, tel. 055/22641, www.teatrodellapergola. com, box office Mon.-Sat. 9:30am-6:30pm, €20 and up) is the oldest theater in Florence and the first to introduce box seats, which were owned by wealthy families. Some say the divisions in the three upper tiers were built to prevent bickering between rival clans.

Only one is still privately owned and they all provide great views of the ornate chandeliered ceiling and gilded wooden interior, which looks like a wedding cake. Plays are the mainstay of the theater and some of the finest Italian actors regularly appear on the illustrious stage. If you can't make a show, come for drink at **Caffè Italiano Guido Guidi** (tel. 055/362-059, Tues.-Sun. 10am-late) inside the grand entrance hall or enjoy the buffet *aperitivo* on performance nights from 7pm to 9pm.

The **Opera di Firenze** (Via Fratelli Rosselli 2, tel. 055/277-9309, www.operadifirenze.it) provides a stark architectural contrast to the rest of the city. Inaugurated in 2011, it's one of the only contemporary buildings in Florence. The modern interior is split into several levels. Classics like *Madame Butterfly* and *The Barber of Seville* are seasonal mainstays. Ticket prices range from €10 for the upper gallery to €80 for front-row seats. The opera house is located west of the center near Parco delle Cascine and can be reached via tram or on foot in less than 20 minutes from the train station.

Perhaps the most original theater in Florence is **Teatro del Sale** (Via de'Macci 111r, tel. 055/200-1492, www.teatrodelsale. com), located in a 14th-century convent. It is a dinner theater operated in association with the Cibreo restaurant and serving dazzling dishes created by Fabio Picchi. The curtain rises in the early evening and performances range from classical, jazz, and blues to poetry readings and one-act plays. To enter this versatile locale, you'll need to become a member; it's a formality practiced by many clubs in the city and in this case only costs €5. Reservations are a good idea.

FESTIVALS AND EVENTS

Florence has a rich and varied cultural calendar, but the most dramatic annual events are those related to religious holidays and feast days. Many involve re-creations with hundreds of participants in historical costume. It might appear like play acting for the sake of tourists, but these celebrations have ancient origins and are ingrained into Florentine consciousness. Although religious fervor has declined, thousands of locals still are still passionate about these unique events and participate with pride.

Spring

TASTE is a three-day gastronomic event held in early March in the newly renovated Stazione Leopolda (Viale Fratelli Rosselli 5, tel. 055/212-622, www.stazione-leopolda.com) arts center. There are over a hundred stands providing free samples of specialty items from all over Italy. Besides eating a lot of delicious ham and cheese it's an opportunity to speak directly with producers and understand how things are made. You can also purchase a glass near the entrance in order to sample the many wines. Complete your tour with a stop in the gourmet gift shop.

Easter isn't a formality in Florence; it's an important event. Even if you aren't a fan of organized religion you can taste the treats and watch festivities like the Scoppo del Carro (Blowing Up of the Cart) on Easter morning. The tradition dates back to the Crusades when a local knight brought back three stones from Christ's tomb. The rocks were later used to light sparks symbolizing the renewal of life and bring fire to the hearths of all the city's families. It was a big deal then and still fills Piazza del Duomo with thousands of onlookers. Festivities start with a historical parade at 10am that weaves through the city and arrives at the Duomo at 11am, where the archbishop lights an enormous cart piled high with fireworks. It's a good idea to cover your ears.

Music takes center stage in May during Maggio Musicale (Teatro Comunale, Via Solferino 15, tel. 055/213-535, www.maggio-fiorentino.com). The festival was created as a means of exploring creative movements of the past and proposes a new theme every year, such as Romanticism or the works of Rossini. The world's finest conductors, soloists, and singers perform contemporary interpretations. Tickets range €15-120. The Teatro

Comunale (www.operadifirenze.it), which hosts the event, also presents ballet and opera.

Summer

The Feast of San Giovanni (June 24) celebrates one of the city's most loved individuals. Giovanni Battista was known for his teachings as well as his courageous and determined spirit. He was made patron saint of Florence in the 11th century, and June 24 has been his day ever since. Events are held throughout the day. At 8am, you can attend mass in the Baptistery or watch the long parade that sets off a half hour later from Via Folco Portinari. Participants in Renaissance-era dress move slowly through city streets until arriving in Piazza del Duomo. Honors are bestowed upon the deserving at Palazzo Vecchio in the afternoon and the Calcio Storico sporting event final is held at 5pm in Piazza Croce. The day ends with fireworks over the Arno (best viewed from the bridges and the Oltrarno hillside) at 10pm.

It may feel like most Florentines leave the city during the summer, but there are still enough left to celebrate the popular saint and protector San Lorenzo on August 10. At 10am a parade of people in Renaissance regalia heads from Palazzo di Parte Guelfa near Ponte Vecchio to Palazzo Vecchio; there the city banner is collected and brought to Basilica di San Lorenzo. Festivities continue from 9:30pm onwards in Piazza San Lorenzo with a traditional feast of *pasta al pomodoro* and free watermelon. There's music and dancing, too.

Fall

Festa della Rificolona (Sept. 7) is a popular feast connected to harvest season, when farmers would make the journey to Florence to sell their goods and celebrate the birth of Mary. They carried lanterns held aloft on long sticks that remain an integral part of the celebration. Find them in Piazza Santissima Annunziata behind Galleria dell'Accademia alongside a traditional folk and food market. At night floating lanterns are lit in the San

Niccolò neighborhood and drift slowly down the Arno.

Every guild has its day, and for winemakers it's the last Saturday of September. Since the 13th century this has been the time to bring new wine into town to be honored and blessed. The wine in question was Valdisieve, and today the **Carro Matto** (Crazy Cart) re-creates the winemakers' ingenious way of transporting 2,800 flasks in a single carriage. The event begins with an afternoon procession from Piazza del Duomo through the surrounding streets. It's a colorful parade of heralds, flag wavers, and trumpeters performing traditional pageantry. Later the cart is drawn to Piazza della Signoria where festivities continue and the wine flows freely.

Winter

La Cavalcata dei Re Magi is held on Epiphany (Jan 6th) and is celebrated with an elaborate parade. It begins at 2:15pm and is led by the wise men, who walk from Palazzo Pitti over Ponte Vecchio and through Piazza della Signoria to Piazza del Duomo. The most spectacular part is the 500 participants representing all walks of Renaissance society. There are soldiers, monks, farmers, aristocrats, and maidens bearing flags, playing drums, pulling

carts, and doing everything the way it was done in 1417 when the tradition started.

You can tell **Carnevale** season has begun when calorie-intensive desserts begin appearing in pastry shop windows. Festivities last from late January until *martedi grasso* (Mardi Gras or Fat Tuesday). It was the traditional day of excess when peasants filled up on the foods they would give up for Lent (meat, eggs, and milk) and occurs 47 days before Easter. The favorite temptation is *Schiacciata Fiorentina,* a two-level sponge cake with a cream filling topped with powdered sugar and a pinch of cacao. But eating isn't the only festivity: The masked fun begins on the Thursday prior to Mardi Gras. The highlight is the parade on the following Tuesday when floats leave Piazza Ognisanti and weave their way around the city until they reach Piazza della Signoria. There's always an international element with participants from Brazil, China, Mexico, and the United States. At the end a prize is awarded to the best costumes and a local children's choir performs. There are many other events around the city and younger travelers can wear their disguises to the **Carnevale dei Bambini** (Sat.-Sun. 2pm-6pm) in Piazza Ognissanti.

Shopping

Shopping in Florence ranges from international boutiques housed in Renaissance-era buildings to simple street markets. The city offers plenty of fashion products. After all, this is where Guccio Gucci was born, and where stylists from Ferragamo to Cavalli got their starts. The Historic Center is lined with luxury brands and smaller shops that attract the fashion conscious. For everyone else, there are outdoor leather markets lined with scores of stalls where bags and wallets come in countless variations. Clothes, antiques, leather, stationery, and ceramics can all be found in the city at prices that are lower than

in Rome or Venice. Even if prices are marked, asking for a discount is common practice in Italy and often leads to savings.

Although many traditional shops have closed or moved outside the city, handmade still means something in Florence. It can involve preserving papermaking traditions or skillfully operating vintage printing machines. A walk along the smaller streets leads to workshops where craftspeople hammer wood, sand shelves, paint shutters, weld metal, and perform other skills that have been repeated for generations. For curious travelers, these shops are a great opportunity to learn.

HISTORIC CENTER

Most of the city's commercial activity takes place in the Historic Center, so it's a good place to begin a shopping spree. Besides the megastores, the largest street and covered **markets** are located here and provide a lively experience that may require some bargaining. When negotiating, remember that if the asking price seems too high it probably is. There's also a good chance you may be approached on the street. Itinerant salespeople are less aggressive than in Rome; however, they usually offer the same selfie sticks, trinkets, and other gadgets of dubious quality. Unless you absolutely need a glow-in-the-dark rubber bracelet, save your money for something that's made in Florence.

Leather

A good place to start searching for leather is the **San Lorenzo street market** that runs along Via dell'Ariento adjacent to the central market. It is open from early morning to early evening 365 days a year. The street is lined with small stands selling every type of leather product. Behind these are narrow shop fronts with even more leather to be examined.

Maurizio arrived in Florence in 1970 from Iran to become an architect, but found himself in the leather trade. He opened **BiBi** (Via dell'Ariento 12r, tel. 055/230-2400, daily 9am-7pm) several decades ago and has been a fixture of the San Lorenzo street market ever since. Outside his stall is lined with handbags, wallets, book covers, and key chains of every type. Inside of the narrow store next door you'll find jackets, belts, and larger accessories that cover the walls.

There are many shops beyond the market that transform leather into stylish designer goods. If you're after shoes, Via dei Cerretani and Via Pellicceria near the Duomo are good streets to start the hunt. **Botegga Fiorentina** (Borgo dei Greci 5, tel. 055/295-411, Mon.-Fri. 10am-7pm) near Piazza Santa Croce is a good destination for bags, and there are several other stores nearby offering original styles. Everything is meticulously handmade at the **Bisonte** (Via del Parione 31-33r, tel. 055/215-722), where new collections are presented every year and exported all over the world.

Many leather bottegas were once located in the streets around Santa Croce, and the area remains a good place to shop for bags. You can even visit the **leather school** (Via S. Giuseppe 5r, tel. 055/244-533, www.

San Lorenzo street market

Made in Florence

LEATHER

Leather has a long history in Florence, where the transformation of hide into articles of clothing, bags, and other items goes back centuries. Most leather is still made near Florence but production has moved to large industrial sites outside the city. That doesn't mean leather is cheap. Both the raw material and the skilled labor are costly.

Today there are countless shops selling goods and not all quality is the same. There are a couple things every leather shopper should consider:

- **Label:** If the label is sewn on, it's a good sign. If it's glued on or the stitching is faulty, walk away.

- **Location:** Outdoor stalls and markets meet the demands of millions of tourists looking for low-priced souvenirs, but the best leather products aren't found on the street. If you're serious about leather you need to shop indoors, where the finest handcrafted items are displayed.

- **Price:** A nice wallet should be around €20, a handbag €50, and a medium-sized carrying bag €100. Prices vary, and browsing is the best way to find a compromise between quality and cost. Whatever sounds too cheap probably is. The saying around here is that it's better to pay more once than less many times. It's a convincing argument.

MARBLED PAPER

Paper production has a long history in Florence, though the marble variety for which the city is famous didn't originate here. Turks had been using the technique long before the Florentines, who did have the good sense to begin creating their own. The skill was widely diffused throughout Europe; however, today only Florence continues to produce significant quantities.

The process is fairly simple. First, colors are added to a rectangular glass basin containing a little water. Next, they're delicately brushed into the characteristic marble pattern. Finally, finally a sheet of stock paper is placed on top. The paper absorbs the color, and is removed and hung to dry. At that point it's only a matter of ten minutes before the piece is finished.

Papiro has a near monopoly on marbled paper and there are a handful of shops around the city where you can purchase stationery and see how it's made. The branch at Via de' Tavolini 13r periodically demonstrates the process and allows customers to make their own colorful sheets. **Giuliano Giannini e Figlio** on the other side of the Arno has no intention of becoming a chain store—and that's a good thing for anyone who stops in and learns from the father-and-son team who are keeping the art of stationery making alive.

scuoladelcuoio.com) to discover exactly how leather goods are made.

Perfume

Perfume isn't often associated with Florence, but it should be. During the Renaissance, the art of making perfume prospered in Florence. The city might still be associated with perfume if Caterina de Medici hadn't embarked to Paris with her personal perfumer, who shared his savoir faire with an eager audience of noblemen and women. They enthusiastically adopted the habit of dousing themselves in scent and helped make France the center of production.

They haven't forgotten how to make perfume in Florence, and a visit to **Aqua Flor** (Borgo Santa Croce 6, tel. 055/234-3471, daily 10am-7pm) will dazzle the nose. Inside this elegant shop you can sniff hundreds of essences and choose one of the unique blends contained in beautiful bottles on which your initials can be engraved. If you're really serious, spend an afternoon with the house perfumer who will analyze the PH level of your skin and help create a personalized scent. It's expensive and the session must be reserved in advance but there's nothing like *eau de you*. Ready-to-wear scents start from €50 and a one-of-a-kind perfume costs €500.

On the opposite side of town **Officina Profumo** (Via della Scala 16, Mon.-Sat. 8:30am-1pm and 2:30pm-7pm) is Florence's oldest pharmacy, dating back to when pharmacies sold mixed herbs and medicine was in its infancy. Locals don't understand what the fuss is about but the cavernous rooms attract a healthy number of visitors who come to sniff the neatly arranged essences, perfumes, and soaps. Many of the aromatic scents are created using centuries-old formulas. Helpful multilingual assistants can guide you through the assortment of cosmetic and holistic products.

Stationery

Florence's primary sustainer of the art of paper production is **Il Papiro** (Via de'Tavolini 13r, tel. 055/213-823, Mon.-Sat. 8am-8pm), which operates six shops in the Historic Center and one over the river in Oltrarno. These are like small temples devoted to stationery and the art of writing. If you still enjoy using a pen and sending letters or postcards this is a mandatory stop. Three of the shops provide demonstrations of how marbled paper is made. These occur spontaneously when stores aren't busy and shop assistants have the 15-20 minutes it takes to make a sheet of marbled paper. You can search for a colorful book cover, notepad, or card while you wait for your piece of craftsmanship to finish. Although a purchase isn't necessary, it is appreciated and is hard to resist in any case. Prices range, but there's stationery for every budget.

Giuliano Giannini e Figlio (Piazza Pitti 37r, tel. 055/212-621, Mon.-Sat. 10am-7pm and Sun. 11am-6:30pm) is one of the oldest shops in Florence and has been selling stationery since 1856. There's a pleasant smell of paper and ink inside this unlikely shop near Palazzo Pitti. The inside is lined with shelves full of temptations for office or home, and workshops are organized by the fifth generation

of the same family. Basic demonstrations last 30-40 minutes, but if you want to learn how to bind a book you should count on a couple of hours. Reservations are required and prices vary depending on the number of participants.

Recycling is the key word at **La Tartaruga** (Borgo Albizi 60r, tel. 055/234-0845, Mon.-Sat. 9am-1pm and 3pm-7pm), where paper is transformed into everything imaginable. There are practical objects such as calendars and stationery as well as imaginative paper toys.

Books

Bibliophiles and librarians will appreciate the amount of shelf space in the city. Anyone looking for secondhand editions and out-of-date manuscripts should browse the bookshops on **Via dei Servi** (Bartolini at 24-28r and Cornici Campani at 22r) or around the **Biblioteca Nazionale** (Piazza S. Ambrogio 2, Mon.-Fri. 8:15am-7pm and Sat. 8:15am-1:30pm). The smell of old books is strong at **Alberto Cozzi** (Via del Parione 35r, tel. 055/294-968, Tues.-Sat. 9am-1pm and 2:30pm-7pm). Paper is all locally made and artisans spend their days rebinding and restoring worn-out editions.

Fashion and Clothing

The area around **Piazza della Republic** is the fashion heart of Florence. Gucci, Prada, and many other designer labels are all located here. Luxury is concentrated around **Via de' Tornabuoni** and **Via della Vigna Nuova** and many flagship stores are housed within *pallazi* that would make any museum envious. The big names can be slightly intimidating, but entering does not necessarily lead to buying—and walking through the elegant interiors is a pleasure in itself. There are also many appealing lesser-known boutiques that are usually a great deal less expensive. If you happen to arrive in July or January, you'll also be in time to enjoy the sale season when merchandise is significantly discounted.

Salvatore **Ferragamo** began making shoes

in Hollywood before returning to Florence and setting up shop in **Palazzo Spini Feroni** (Piazza di Santa Trinita 5, daily 10am-7:30pm). It's one of the largest buildings in the city and the ground floor is still used to display the fashion house's latest creations. The architecture is as interesting as the shoes, but if you have a fetish **Museo Ferragamo** (tel. 055/356-2846, daily 10am-7:30pm, €6, free first Sunday of every month) contains hundreds of pairs from many different eras. An audio guide is available and guided tours are offered on the first Saturday of every month at 10am and 11am upon reservation (tel. 055/356-2466).

On a side street off Via de' Tornabuoni, somewhat less glamorous shops like **Desii Vintage** (Via de'Conti 17-21r, tel. 055/230-2817, Mon.-Sat. 10:30am-7:30pm) wait to be discovered. Desii is an original vision of menswear that combines old and new, hip and classic into one wearable look. It's difficult to resist buying at least one shirt or sweater and making the rest of your wardrobe jealous.

Gerard Loft (Via dei Pecori, 34-40r, tel. 055/282-491, Mon. 2:30pm-7:30pm, Tues.-Sat. 10am-7:30pm) sells cool. The shop stocks men's, women's, and children's brands that are a couple of seasons ahead of fashion. Labels include Munich Vintage 55, Swear, N.D.C., and limited-edition lines. The store feels like a gallery where the clothes are the art.

Antiques

Tuscany has always been a good source of antiques, and there's been a thriving trade in relics, artwork, furniture, and bric-a-brac since the Renaissance. Dozens of stores can be found along **Via dei Fossi** and **Via del Moro**. These vary from galleries with a limited number of fine pieces to small shops cluttered with collectibles.

Barbara Gallorini Antichita (Piazza degli Ottaviani 9r, tel. 055/230-2608, daily 10am-7pm) is crowded with interesting items. The owner believes that anything can become a collectible, and it shows in her shop, which is filled with jewelry, candelabra, frames, books,

and sculptures from many different eras. Although prices are marked, don't hesitate to ask for a discount *(un sconto)* when wavering to purchase or not.

Antichita' Le Colonne (Via del Moro 38, tel. 055/283-690, Mon.-Fri. 10am-7pm, Sat. 9am-6pm) is a large shop filled with furniture and curiosities. Merchandise is randomly displayed between stone columns and not always easy to reach. The owners can date items and explain the use of some devices that haven't been operated for centuries.

Ceramics

In Italy, pottery is a little like pasta—every region produces its own particular style. Historically, the town of Montelupo a short distance down the Arno supplied ceramics to Florence and became famous for its colorful style depicting floral and abstract patterns. Today, decorative and everyday pottery is still produced and sold.

Armando Poggi (Via dei Calzaiuoli 103, tel. 055/211-719, Mon.-Sat. 10am-7:30pm, Sun. 11am-7pm) has been selling ceramics since the 1930s. The store has an array of elegant objects as well as platters, trays, vases, and pitchers for everyday purposes. They're used to dealing with international customers and ship everywhere in the world.

The pottery inside **Il Sole Nel Borgo** (Borgo la Croce 50, tel. 055/246-6495, Mon.-Sat. 10am-1:30pm and 4pm-7:30pm) is less traditional in design and has a vibrant country feel that can brighten a meal. Colorful jugs, plates, and platters are hand painted by the two sisters running this shop, which doubles as a bistro where you can try drinking from the ceramics before you buy.

Souvenirs

La Botegga del Chianti (Borgo SS Apostoli 41r, tel. 055/283-410, Mon.-Fri. 8am-7pm, Sat. 9am-7pm, Sun. noon-6pm) hasn't changed much since it opened in 1934. You'll find the same wooden spoons, olive oil, copper tins, and ceramics they've always sold. It may be a little dusty and crammed with an eclectic mix of Tuscan products, but you're bound to find an interesting gift.

Markets

★ **Mercato Centrale** (Piazza del Mercato Centrale/Via dell'Ariento, tel. 055/239-9798, Mon.-Fri. 7am-2pm and Sat. 7am-5pm, closed Sat. summer) is the largest covered food market in Florence and attracts as many local shoppers as curious visitors. Florentines huddle around the fruit, vegetable, meat, and fish stands while tourists take pictures and browse the cheese and wine shops. There are dozens of stalls selling dried as well as fresh foods, making it a good place to purchase ingredients for a picnic. Mornings are busy with green grocers entertaining clients and sharing gossip. At one end of the ground floor are a number of stalls selling specialty dishes that can be eaten at the tables and counters that fill up at lunchtime. Head to **Narbone**, part of the market since it opened in 1872, where Stefano has been preparing beef and tripe sandwiches over half his life. Salt and pepper are the traditional condiments, and if there's room at the marble tables you can sit and watch the stream of visitors who come to this historic eatery. The food court on the second floor of the market is open daily 10am to midnight.

The **San Lorenzo Street Market** (Piazza San Lorenzo and Via dell'Ariento) is a busy open-air market on the pedestrian streets immediately surrounding Mercato Centrale. There are hundreds of regulated stalls selling T-shirts, jewelry, notebooks, and most of all, leather. It's a browser's paradise and the multicultural vendors aren't too pushy. Many operate stand-alone stores behind their stalls where you can find higher-quality products. Prices are pretty standardized throughout the market and relatively cheap, but haggling is not uncommon and feigning disinterest can save you money. It's open 365 days a year from early morning to late afternoon.

Mercato di Sant'Ambrogio (Piazza L. Ghiberti) is a smaller, livelier food market a few minutes north of Piazza Santa Croce. It hasn't been sanitized for tourists and locals make up the majority of shoppers. Outside (Mon.-Sat. 8am-2pm) it's a bazaar with a little of everything on display including seasonal fruit and vegetables. Inside (Mon., Tues., Thurs. 7:30am-2pm, Wed. and Fri. 7:30am-7pm, Sat. 7:30am-5pm) is entirely dedicated to gastronomy, with stalls covering all food groups. If you're not looking for ingredients but just want to sit down and eat, **Trattoria da Rocca** is the neighborhood institution.

La Botegga del Chianti

Arrive as close to noon as possible because booths fill up fast. The menu is as simple as the décor but soup and pasta dishes are substantial and priced to sell.

Loggia del Mercato Nuovo (Intersection of Via Calimala and Via Porta Rossa) is one of the prettiest covered markets in the city and has been used for different commercial activities since it was completed in 1551. Where silk and straw hats were once sold leather is now the trade of choice and a dozen or so kiosks set up shop every day from 9am until 7:30pm. Visit the *loggia* after the market has closed and see the *pietra dello scandalo*, a circular stone embedded in the center of the market where debtors were chained and beaten during the Renaissance. Also within the market is the bronze boar whose shiny nose locals and tourists rub for good luck.

The **Mercato delle Pulci** flea market (Piazza dei Ciompi, daily 9am-7:30pm) is small and dilapidated in a good way. In summer it isn't very crowded and many of the rickety-looking shops are closed. Those that are open contain an odd mix of objects including 19th-century postcards and undated doorknobs. The market has been operating since 1967 near the old covered fish market but has been temporarily moved to Largo Pietro Annigoni near Mercato di Sant'Ambrogio while asbestos is removed from the site.

Department Stores

There are a couple of department stores in the center. The two biggest are convenient for finding a wide selection of clothing for men, women, and children. **Coin** (Via dè Calzaiuoli 56r, tel. 055/280-531, daily 10am-8pm) is a mid-range chain between the Duomo and Palazzo Vecchio selling international brands in modern semi-anonymous surroundings. They also carry shoes, household goods, and children's toys. The upscale alternative is **La Rinascente** (Mon.-Sat. 9am-9pm, Sun. 10:30am-8:30pm) in Piazza della Repubblica. Even if you're not interested in shopping you can take the elevator up to the rooftop terrace bar and get a great view of the Duomo.

OLTRARNO

In Oltrarno shopping takes on more intimate dimensions. Few if any fashion labels are located here and the area is home to smaller shops and studios devoted to objects of art, antiques, craft, and one-of-a-kind items.

Leather

Production of leather goods in Florence has decreased dramatically over the last few decades and the workshops that were once common are getting harder to find. Those that do remain operate on a very small scale and produce everything on site. At **Ali Firenze Laboratorio** (Via Toscanella 9r, tel. 055/217-025), Alicia and Ivana cut and sew leather into handbags, key chains, and other accessories. Prices are reasonable and you can watch them at work inside their one-room studio.

Jewelry

Jewelry means one thing in Florence: **Ponte Vecchio.** The bridge is lined with dozens of stores selling rings, necklaces, bracelets, pendants, and earrings of all sorts. The downside of shopping here is that the bridge is jammed with visitors most of the day, and browsing can become a claustrophobic endeavor. Avoid the crowds by arriving early or late and enter the boutiques in order to examine gold, silver, diamonds, and gems undisturbed. If you don't like the look of merchandise at one shop, simply say *grazie* and pop into the next.

T. Ristori (Ponte Vecchio 1-3r, tel. 055/215-507, Mon.-Sat. 9:30am-7:30pm) is an elegant and tasteful place to start shopping on Ponte Vecchio and carries well-known jewelry brands as well as their own handcrafted line. This is also a good opportunity to see the inside of a *bottega* and catch a glimpse of the Arno without being crushed by the people outside. The red staircase in the corner of the shop was built for Francesco I de' Medici and is the only direct access from the corridor above to the bridge.

Antiques

There are a number of antique stores in Oltrarno. **Via Maggio** is the main thoroughfare for serious antique hunters.

Maurizio of **Maurizio & Salici** (Via Santo Spirito 32r, 328/716-7049, Mon.-Sat. 9am-7pm) sells items you don't need but would like to own anyway. Don't call it shabby chic, or he'll remind you everything is antique down to the 1920s office plaques and late-19th-century gilded mirrors. Generally speaking, nothing here is more than two hundred years old. It all looks good on a coffee table, shelf, or mantle. Prices are not listed and there's some room for negotiation, but like every good dealer, Maurizio knows the value of everything he sells.

The Malenotti family has operated **Piumaccio d'Oro** (Borgo San Frediano 65r, tel. 055/239-8952, Mon.-Sat. 8:30am-1pm and 2:30pm-7:30pm) for more than 70 years. That's a lifetime of antique restoration and creation. The techniques practiced in the small workshop and displayed in the store result in one-of-a-kind tables, chests, chairs, and smaller objects found nowhere else.

Markets

There are fewer markets on this side of the river. Those that do exist don't thrive off tourists, but instead attract locals who buy their fruits and vegetables and browse racks of cheap clothing, shoes, and household gadgets. The busiest is in **Piazza Santo Spirito** and is held Monday through Saturday from 8am until 2pm. It has a handful of stands hawking cheap womens wear, shoes of every kind, undergarments, and vegetables. The **Arti e Mestieri D'Oltrarno** arts and crafts market also takes place 7am-7pm in the square on the second Sunday of every month except July and August.

OUTLETS

There are two outlets near Florence where serious shoppers can find discounted brand-name clothing. Both are outdoors and provide shuttle bus service from SMN train station. **Barberino Designer Outlet** (Barberino di Mugello, tel. 055/842-161, daily 10am-9pm) is 30 minutes away and has a Renaissance theme that feels like being on a film set. The experience is about as pleasant as shopping can be, and there's a large shaded playground that keeps young children busy. Black double-decker buses leave from Piazza della Stazione 44 daily at 9:30am, 11:30am, 2pm, and 4pm. Round-trip tickets are €15 and may be purchased on the bus.

The Mall (Leccio Reggello, tel. 055/865-7775, daily 10am-7pm) is a small luxury outlet popular with Asian and North American visitors searching for Armani, Fendi, Gucci, and other premium brands. Savings can be significant depending on what you're after. The Gucci Café is a nice place to stop for lunch and enjoy views of the Tuscan countryside from the rooftop terrace. Buses from Via Santa Caterina da Siena 17 near the station depart hourly between 8:50am and 6pm. It's a half-hour journey and a round-trip ticket is €10.

Activities and Recreation

PARKS AND GARDENS

It's easy to overdose on art in Florence. Fortunately, there are gardens like **Giardini di Boboli** (daily 8:15am-7:30pm in summer and until 5:30pm in winter, €7 or Firenzecard) where you can relax and give your eyes a rest. The garden was created for the Medici and blends an initial perfectly manicured section with a wilder natural park opened to the public in 1766. Even here art isn't entirely absent, and there are grottoes, fountains, and statues lining many of the alleys. Boboli Gtardens are off-limits to cyclists and pickup soccer games. Visitors must keep off the grass, remain on the footpaths, and refrain from climbing trees. You can, however, bring food and drink into the garden and eat on the benches as long as you clean up after yourself.

Giardino Bardini (Costa San Giorgio 2, tel. 055/263-855, Tues.-Sun. 10am-7pm, €8) is a fraction of the size of the Boboli Gardens and only a short distance away near Forte Belvedere. The advantage of this park is not only its manageable dimensions (divided into three distinctive areas), but the wonderful gravel terrace overlooking the city. The villa at the entrance of the property was built in 1641 and was opened to the public in 1965. It contains two small museums and an exhibition space.

Giardino delle Rose (Viale Giuseppe Poggi 2, tel. 055/234-2426, daily 9am-sunset, free) is located off the stairs leading up to Piazzale Michelangelo and is a fragrant stop in late spring and early summer when more than a hundred varieties of roses are in bloom. Interspersed among the plants are metal sculptures, small fountains, and wooden benches with wonderful views.

Parco delle Cascine is Florence's largest park. It's located just west of the Historic Center along the Arno and can be easily reached by foot, tram, or bike. The latter is the best option for exploring the long paths that run through the park and lead past meadows, woods, and sporting complexes. On summer weekends it can be quite animated. It's a park where few tourists tread and locals come to cycle, run, or just stroll along the banks of the Arno. There's a pedestrian bridge over the

Giardini di Boboli

Arno you can cross to explore the residential neighborhood of low-rise apartment blocks immersed in green, or ride along the dirt path overlooking the river. In summer, the former racetrack and amphitheater within the park are used for concerts and exhibitions.

CYCLING

Cycling is a safe and convenient way to explore Florence. Most of the city is flat and traffic is respectful of cyclists. There are bike racks in nearly every *piazza* and dedicated bike lanes along both sides of the river and many streets. Rental prices for an hour or an entire day are reasonable and some bike shops also offer tours. If you're serious about cycling and aren't just out for a leisurely ride around the Historic Center, you can head for the hills surrounding the city and discover the Tuscan countryside on two wheels.

The long paths in **Parco delle Cascine** are excellent for exploring by bicycle. **Viale Galileo** and **Michelangelo** near Piazzale Michelangelo both wind through the countryside and have **bike lanes** that fill up with local cyclists on weekends.

Florence By Bike (Via S. Zanobi 54r, tel. 055/488-992, www.florencebybike.it, Mon.-Fri. 9am-1pm and 3:30pm-7:30pm, Sat. 9am-7pm, Sun. 9am-5pm) is close to the train station and provides city, mountain, touring, and road bikes that can be rented for an hour, half day, full day, or multiple days. Prices depend on the model and a half day with a good Dutch-style city bike is €9 while a mountain bike is double that. All sizes are available and accessories like baskets and child seats are an additional €3. Helmets and locks are included in the rental price. Florence by Bike also offers tours in and around Florence.

Mille e Una Bici (tel. 055/933-1356, www.bicifirenze.it) is a local initiative to encourage two-wheeled transportation in the city. Bikes can be rented from Stazione SMN weekdays and Saturdays 7:30am-7pm and Sundays 9am-7pm. One hour costs €1.50 while a full day is €8. A similar service is operated from Piazza Ghiberti.

Travelers who prefer to discover Tuscany on their own can rent a bike and board any regional train with a bike symbol. There are special bike compartments for 5-15 vehicles that must be loaded and unloaded by the cyclists themselves. Tickets for transporting bikes are €3.50 one-way and valid 24 hours.

MOPEDS

If you've never ridden a moped, Florence is a good place to start and is significantly safer than Rome. Drivers don't go very fast and there are fewer cars overall. Mopeds are perfect if you have a little experience and want to get outside the city. The best direction is south along the SR222 state road that winds its way through Chianti and plenty of picturesque countryside. **Alinari** (Via San Zanobi 38r, tel. 055/280500, www.alinarirental.com) rents classic Dutch bikes and Honda SH 125 mopeds for €55 per day. Credit card and ID are required.

BEACHES AND SWIMMING

Florence is only 55 miles (90km) from the sea and many residents spend their weekends and holidays on the Tuscan coast—but if you can't make it to the beach, the beach can make it to you. Every summer the city organizes a riverside beach along the sandy southern bank of the Arno River east of Ponte alla Grazie bridge. **Spiaggia sul Arno** (Piazza Poggi, www.easylivingfirenze.it, May-Sept. daily 10am-1:30am) attracts families and hipsters looking to relax. During the day you can sip drinks at the kiosk bar, rent lounge chairs, or practice beach yoga; after the sun goes down on weekends musicians and DJs alternate rhythms.

Costoli (Viale Paoli 9, tel. 055/623-6027, Mon. 2pm-6pm, Tues.-Sat. 10am-6pm, €8) is equipped with an Olympic-size pool and two smaller pools. ID and swimming cap are required at this complex surrounded by greenery near the soccer stadium. **Le Pavoniere** (Viale Catena 2, tel. 055/362-233, daily 10am-6pm, €8) is located within Parco delle Cascine and is easy to reach from the center. The large pool has various depths, while a smaller one is intended for young children. Lawn chairs can be hired and there's a bar and restaurant if you want to spend a leisurely afternoon near the water.

SPAS AND SAUNAS

Asmana (Viale Allende 10, tel. 055/892-723, Thurs.-Sun. 10am-11pm, €29 full day) is an elegant spa northwest of the city that provides relaxing aquatic activities all year long. There are a number of heated saline pools, three saunas, and a large hammam. It's equipped with plenty of areas to rest or receive head-to-toe treatments that last from 20 to 80 minutes. Drinks can be enjoyed in the water from a poolside bar, and nouveau Tuscan cuisine is served at the restaurant. Caps, slippers, robes, and shower kit are extra.

WATER PARKS

Hidron (Via di Gramignano, tel. 055/892-500, www.hidron.it, Mon.-Fri. 10am-9pm, Sat.-Sun. 9am-7:30pm, €15) is closer to a water playground than a spa and is popular with families more interested in playing than relaxing. The outdoor slide, waterfall, geyser, and vortex keep kids happy, and there's a designated area for newborns to discover water. Adults can keep fit with aqua gym or try a Turkish bath. The center is also open in winter and children under 12 get in free on Sundays. To get there take bus 30 towards Campi Bisenzio and get off at the stop in front of the Esselunga store.

SKIING

The slopes of **Abetone** (057/360-001, www.abetone.org) are 50 miles (85km) from Florence and have been a popular winter destination since **Hotel Ristorante Excelsior** (Via Brennero 313, 057/360-010, €110 d) and **Albergo Regina** (Via Uccelliera 5, 057/360-007, www.albergoregina.com, €100 d) opened in the early 1900s. There are four valleys full of trails that keep downhill racers and cross-country enthusiasts occupied. Snowboarders can enjoy the new snow park equipped with a half pipe, moguls, and three-meter jumps. The season officially opens on December 8 and artificial snow machines guarantee coverage whether nature cooperates or not. Renting equipment is convenient and accommodations plentiful if you decide to stay the night. **Copit** (tel. 055/21463, www.copitspa.it) operates daily bus service from Largo Alinari near Stazione SMN.

SPECTATOR SPORTS
Calcio Storico

According to popular belief the English invented soccer, but Florentines know that *Calcio Storico,* an early form of the game, originated here in the 16th century—which may explain why Italy has won four World Cups. It's a bruising game that combines elements of soccer and rugby and in which head butting, punching, and elbows are allowed. A competition is held every year between teams representing the four historic neighborhoods of the city and takes place in Piazza Santa Croce during the second and third weeks of June. Matches last 50 minutes and enthusiastic crowds fill the bleachers around the square. The final is played on June 24, the feast day of Florence's patron saint, and the winning team wins bragging rights and a free dinner. Tickets (www.boxol.it) are priced €21-52 and go on sale in May.

Soccer

Fiorentina is the local soccer *(calcio)* team. They regularly finish in the top half of the Italian Serie A championship, although they haven't won a title in over four decades. They play at the **Artemio Franchi** (Viale Manfredo Fanti 4, tel. 055/503-011) stadium, which opened in 1931 and was remodeled to host matches during the 1990 World Cup. Capacity is 47,000 but games are rarely sold out unless one of the league's top teams is in town. Matches are usually played on Sunday afternoons. Tickets can be purchased directly at the stadium or the team shop on the 2nd floor of the **Mercato Centrale** (Mon.-Fri.

10am-2pm and 3:30pm-7:30pm). Seating is relatively close to the action, and unlike in Rome there's no running track around the field. The side tribunes provide the best views, while the curves offer more atmosphere and are where you're likely to hear fans singing support for their squad. The stadium is a couple kilometers northeast of the center and can be easily reached from Stazione Santa Maria Novella or Piazza San Marco via buses 7, 17 or 20.

TOURS

There are over 2,000 registered guides in Florence and dozens of agencies offering tours of the city and Tuscany region. These range from walking and cycling tours to Segway and Vespa outings. All tours recommended here are led by English speakers.

Walking

Elisa Acciai (tel. 055/527-0455, elisaacciai@libero.it) always dreamed of being a tour guide in her native city, and she's been doing it professionally for more than a decade. Her interest began on school trips when monotone guides put her classmates to sleep with a dull monologue of names and dates. She decided to take the opposite approach and brings her city to life with facts and insights that will transform your perspective on Florence. You can customize tours based on your interests (monuments, neighborhoods, markets, etc.) or let her surprise you. Tours are €50 per hour for groups of up to six and conducted in English.

Cycling

Florence By Bike (Via S. Zanobi 54r, tel. 055/488-992, www.florencebybike.it) offers guided tours of various lengths inside and outside of Florence. The four-hour tour (€39 including rental) along the Arno and through Parco delle Cascine leaves weekdays at 3:30pm and 9am on weekends. If you want to pedal even farther they organize 40-60 mile (60-100km) trips to Chianti, Siena, and other Tuscan destinations.

I Bike Tuscany (Via Belgio 4, 335/812-0769, www.ibiketuscany.com, €145) specializes in single-day and multiday rides outside the city. Destinations include Siena, Chianti, and San Gimignano. Groups leave every morning and follow scenic routes through the Tuscan countryside past olive groves, vineyards, and villages where riders stop for lunch and gelato. Experienced local guides conduct tours in English that include 27-speed hybrid bikes, transfers to starting points, tastings, helmets, and water.

Vespa

The Vespa is Italy's most famous scooter brand and a synonym for mobility. It's easy to ride even if you have little or no motoring experience and is a delightful way of exploring the countryside around Florence. All agencies require a valid drivers license and include insurance in the prices.

Walkabout (Via Vinegia 23r, tel. 055/264-5746, www.walkaboutflorence.com) uses restored vintage Vespas to take small groups on four-hour tours outside the city. There are several stops along the way to admire the views and explore narrow roads past castles and villas. Lunch is eaten *al fresco* and includes *prosciutto*, cheese, and Chianti. Tours depart at 9am and 2:30pm all year long and cost €110 for a single rider and €170 for two. Helmets with two-way radios are provided by the English-speaking guides.

For longer tours that go a little deeper into the region try **Tuscany Vespa Tours** (Via Ghibellina 34r, tel. 055/386-0253, www.tuscany-vespatours.com, Mar.-Oct.). These depart at 10am and head south into Chianti for seven-hour visits of the area. Along the way there's a stop at a 12th-century castle with a wine cellar and olive oil-producing facilities. Once you've climbed the tower and enjoyed the view, it's back on the moped along winding country roads to a family-run *trattoria* where a traditional lunch is served. Total distance is 21 miles (35km) completed at a very leisurely pace. Drivers pay €120 and passengers €90.

Bus

Several companies offer bus tours. **Florence City Sightseeing** (tel. 055/290-451, www.firenze.city-sightseeing.it) operates red double-decker buses with open tops along three different routes. Ride them all for one (€20), two (€25), or three (€30) days. The starting point is Santa Maria Novella train station and a complete circuit lasts one or two hours with numerous stops where passengers are free to get on and off whenever they like. Tickets can be purchased online or onboard and include audio commentary. They also provide group walking tours of the Uffizi and other monuments.

Horse-and-Buggy

Horse-and-buggy teams line the *piazza* around the Duomo waiting to pick up fares for a trot around the city. It can be a lovely way to discover Florence; just avoid the five o'clock rush hour, and negotiate the price prior to departure. A 30-minute ride usually costs around €80 and a buggy can seat up to four adults.

Wine

Wine tours can seem expensive but the best provide a memorable day of discovery that's hard to replicate on your own. **Grape Tours** (Via De' Bardi 23r, 331/358-3823, www.tuscan-wine-tours.com, €150 pp and up) organize half-and full-day visits to local wineries that include a light lunch and vineyard visits. At each stop you'll meet vineyard owners and learn about what makes their vintage different. The quality of the soil, the amount of rain, and the type of containers used for storage all influence taste. You'll get to sample a number of bottles at each stop, and with the help of passionate guides you'll begin to distinguish the flavors of Chianti and other Tuscan wines.

   Italy and Wine (Corso dei Tintori 13, tel. 331/874-9912, Mon.-Fri. 9am-6pm, www.italyandwine.net) offers dozens of one-day private and group tours of the region. A typical day out includes a tasting at two wineries and a light lunch at an authentic *trattoria* along

the way. Participants are picked up at their hotel and accompanied by a sommelier who can help all levels of drinkers distinguish between grape varieties and understand the subtleties of wine production. The big advantage Vittorio and his team have are the relationships they've developed with vineyards over the years. Participants get more than a generic tour and tasting; they get an intimate, behind-the-scenes look at what it means to live and breathe wine every day. There are a number of itineraries to choose from and shared tours start from €135 per person; the cost of private tours varies according to the number of participants, which never exceeds eight.

CLASSES
Cooking

Mama Florence (Viale Petrarca 12, tel. 055/220-101, www.mamaflorence.it, €100 and up) is a cooking school geared towards visitors who already know how to handle a knife. Classes are run by an all-star lineup of mostly female chefs, including Beatrice Segoni from the Convivium restaurant, who balance theory with practice inside a state-of-the-art kitchen. Once you've finished cooking you get to enjoy your effort with a good bottle of wine and the company of other gastronomic enthusiasts. Classes cover the classics like making homemade pasta and pizza and last around four hours, including time spent eating your creations.

   Cucina Lorenzo de'Medici (Piazza del Mercato Centrale, tel. 334/304-0551, www.cucinaldm.com) is located on the 2nd floor of Mercato Centrale and has been spreading Italian culture for the last 40 years. The cooking school is equipped with 16 single workstations and all the utensils needed to complete any recipe as well as tablets for following chefs who are filmed as they cook. Lessons start from €90 while lunch or dinner with a chef is €38 and up. Classes last three hours and are based around menus of meat, fish, pasta, and desserts. All ingredients are top quality and positive feedback is provided from beginning to end.

Family-Friendly Florence

Florence has little traffic and plenty of churches, gardens, streets, parks, and gelato shops to explore.

- The city offers a **family tour kit** (www.familytour.it) for ages 6-13 that includes materials for discovering the city. It's free and there are two itineraries that depart from **Museo di Palazzo Vecchio** (Piazza della Signoria, summer daily 9am-8pm, winter daily 9am-3pm) and **Istituto degli Innocenti** (Piazza SS Annunziata, Mon.-Sat. 9am-4:30pm). These treasure hunt-like activities are a journey for the hands, eyes, and imagination that bring the city to life.

- Toddlers can chase pigeons in the city's *piazze* or explore elaborate gardens like **Giardini Boboli** where they can race Mom or Dad to the next fountain.

- Younger children can ride the old-fashioned **merry-go-round** (€2) in Piazza della Repubblica or board a **horse and buggy.**

- Older kids and teens may enjoy getting on **bikes** and pedaling around the city or to **Parco delle Cascine** where local families cool off in the Olympic-size pool.

- For budding scientists there's the **Museo di Storia Naturale** (Via Romana 17, tel. 055/275-6444, summer Tues.-Sun. 10:30am-5:30pm, winter Tues.-Sun. 9:30am-4:30pm, €6), which is rarely crowded and home to an extensive and surprisingly detailed anatomy collection.

- **Markets** are enjoyable for all ages and a good place to put allowance money to use. And there's nothing like **gelato** to bring a family together.

- Temper tantrum? Head to the nearest **newsstand.** Most kiosks have several racks filled with small toys, collectibles, playing cards, and gadgets that offer instant distraction.

- Consider allowing **older teenagers** to spend a couple hours on their own. Florence is one of the safest cities in Italy and exploring it alone is an experience they'll never forget.

The low-cost way to wear an apron and get your hands into dough is with **Cucina Riciclona** (Caffeteria delle Oblata, Via dell'Oriuolo 26, www.cucinariciclona.it, €50). The recipes proposed are fairly simple and half the fun is getting to know other participants who may or may not speak your language. There's a "less is more" philosophy going on here that favors simplicity and creativity. During classes participants work at their own station and will have something to show for their effort by the end. Courses are generally held from 7:30pm to 10:30pm for 3-5 participants and cover topics like pasta with unusual sauces, pizza with alternative flours, special-occasion desserts, and dining on leftovers.

Art

Why buy a painting from an artist in front of the Uffizi when you can create your own work of art? At **Studio D'Arte Toscanella** (Via Toscanella 33r, 340/737-1239, www.studiotoscanella.com, €30 per hour) you can do just that. Lukas provides all the materials you need inside his small street-side studio where both beginners and veteran painters are welcome. Just let the city inspire you and put your impressions of Florence on the canvas. You can work for an hour or return to your easel for as many days as you like.

Accommodations

Florence has a range of accommodation options including hostels, *pensiones*, residences, B&Bs, apartments, hotels, and monasteries. There are many low-star hotels and residences clustered near Stazione Santa Maria Novella where tour groups tend to stay. That isn't always bad, especially on short visits, but the city is small enough to make getting to and from most accommodations easy. If arriving by car, check the availability of hotel parking and ask for the necessary permits in order to enter the ZTL (limited traffic zone).

The proximately of the Tuscan countryside makes *agriturismo* (farmhouse accommodation) feasible. This is especially pleasant during the summer on extended stays when you can spend the morning visiting the city and hot afternoons relaxing by a pool. *Residenza d'epoca* (period residences) are another interesting option. This category of accommodation is based on meticulous attention to historical detail as well as comfort.

There are generally two seasonal rates in Florence: high season extends throughout late spring, summer, and on major holidays and low season comprises the rest of the year. Overall, hotel prices are lower than in Rome or Venice, and this is the place to spend a little extra in order to get a lot more. All accommodation types charge a daily city tax that's not included in the list price; it varies from €1.50 to €5.50 based on the category of accommodation.

HISTORIC CENTER

Most hotels are located in the Historic Center but very few have over a hundred rooms. Residences and lower-end hotels are concentrated around Stazione Santa Maria Novella, especially on Via Nazionale. Large buildings are often shared between several establishments of which the plaques can be seen out front. Higher-end hotels are located close to major monuments and along the Arno where prices grow incrementally. Many of these are located within historic *palazzo* where only the furnishings have changed and guests can get an idea of how the Florentine elite once lived.

Under €100

The hippest hostel in town is ★ **Plus Florence** (Via Santa Caterina d'Alessandra 15, tel. 055/628-6347, www.plushostels.com, €60 d, €16-20 shared), which attracts a young and international crowd who often forget about sightseeing and remain frolicking by the pool or panoramic terrace and drinking sex-inspired cocktails (€6). Private and shared, mixed, and female-only rooms are clean and minimal in design. An all-you-can-eat breakfast is served in the restaurant lounge, which transforms into a disco at night.

Ostelli Archi Rossi (Via Faenza 94r, tel. 055/290-804, www.hostelarchirossi.com, €90 d, €28 for bed in shared room) is a laid-back hostel around the corner from the train station that's popular with students, families, and solo travelers. There are simple private rooms with en suite baths as well as dorm-style rooms with bunk beds and lockers that sleep up to nine. Guests eat downstairs at the convivial shared tables where a cafeteria-style breakfast (7am-9:30pm) with eggs and bacon is served. Dinner and bar are service also available along with €8 walking tours that leave the hostel at 10am.

Once you enter the thick wooden doors of **Casa Per Ferie Suore Oblate** (Via Nazionale 6, tel. 055/239-8202, www.oblate-spiritosantofirenze.it, €58 d, summer only) the noise of the city disappears. This accommodation run by Catholic nuns houses university students during the academic year and visitors during the summer. Rooms are simple, large, and clean. Doubles consist of two single beds and a private bathroom. Several of the nuns speak fluent English. An

Best Accommodations

★ **Plus Florence:** The hippest hostel in town attracts a young, international crowd who enjoy cocktails by the pool or panoramic terrace (page 201).

★ **Il Guelfo Bianco:** Soak in the genuine Tuscan hospitality a the best three-star option in Florence (page 202).

★ **Hotel Loggiato Dei Serviti:** Travel back in time at this former monastery, located on one of Florence's most beautiful squares (page 203).

★ **Antica Torre:** Live like a Medici at this medieval tower house with rooftop terraces and stunning views (page 203).

★ **Monte Oliveto:** Enjoy a warm welcome at this B&B tucked away in a charming neighborhood that most tourists never see (page 205).

★ **Via Santo Spirito 6:** Choose from ten rooms named after illustrious women at this lovingly restored 18th-century *palazzo* minutes from the Ponte Vecchio (page 204).

★ **Torre di Bellosguardo:** This *Agriturismo* is a virtual Eden on the outskirts of Florence (page 205).

11pm curfew is enforced, but that will seem reasonable after a day walking the streets of Florence.

Colombina Firenze (Via dell'Agnolo 23, tel. 05/8340-3228, www.colombinafirenze. com, €80 d) is a cozy little apartment in the center of Florence. The simply furnished two-room retreat is a quiet place to wake up and start the day like a local. It comes with a kitchenette, wood-beamed ceilings, air-conditioning, and free Wi-Fi. There is a two-night minimum stay in summer.

Bed & Breakfast Rovezzano (Via Aretina 507, tel. 05/569-0023, www.rovezzano.com, €65-80 s/d) is located in a residential area a 10-minute stroll from the center. There's free parking and a swimming pool. Rooms are rustic, with thick shutters that block light. Breakfast is served in a large common living room where fellow travelers gather in the evening.

Johanna II (Via Cinque Giornate 12, tel. 055/473-377, www.johanna.it, €85-100 s/d) is located on a quiet street in a small villa with a garden. Rooms are bright and inviting. An extensive breakfast buffet encourages late risers to start the day early. Parking is free. The owners of the residence operate three similar accommodations in the neighborhood.

Casa Schlatter (Viale dei Mille 14, tel. 347/118-0215, www.casaschlatter-Florence. com, €85-105 d) was the home of a 19th-century Swiss painter. His ancestors have transformed the house into an elegant B&B. There are three rooms with large en suite bathrooms and modern fittings. Alessandra, the great-granddaughter of the artist, is an excellent host and serves breakfast in the small garden or the bright communal area where guests can relax.

€100-200

Why ★ **Il Guelfo Bianco** (Via Cavour 29, tel. 055/288-330, www.ilguelfobianco.it, €180-225 d) only has three stars is a mystery. The colorful hotel moments from Galleria dell'Accademia provides instant hominess and effortless charm that more luxurious accommodations struggle to match. All the rooms, from singles to suites, have been tastefully restored to their Renaissance best with the addition of antique furnishings, modern art, minibars, and air-conditioning. A sweet and savory breakfast is served inside a bright breakfast room or outside in the private courtyard where staff are on the lookout for cups to refill with coffee. The front desk is on duty 24 hours a day and can make reservations at local museums or the adjacent hotel restaurant (daily 12pm-10pm).

Many hotels near the train station survive on location rather than quality, but **Hotel Azzizi** (Via Faenza 56, tel. 055/213-806, www.hotelazzi.com, €130-150 d) benefits from both. This friendly three-star establishment offers a handful of bright, recently renovated rooms with modern bathrooms on the edge of the Historic Center. They all come with air-conditioning, Wi-Fi, and an abundant buffet breakfast served in the comfortable common area where guests can relax on the sunny balcony.

Hotel Liana (Via Vittorio Alfieri 18, tel. 055/245-303, www.hotelliana.com, €150-170 s/d) is a short walk from the Duomo in an elegant residential neighborhood near the botanical gardens. The 18th-century *palazzo* once housed the English consulate and has maintained an old-world atmosphere uncorrupted by bad taste. Each of the 24 rooms contains refined furnishings.

On the eastern edge of the Historic Center close to a number of parks, **Alfieri9** (Via Vittorio Alfieri 9, tel. 055/263-8121, www.alfieri9.it, €160-180 d) provides 18th-century character and guesthouse comfort. Rooms come in three categories (classic, superior, and junior suite) and all are uniquely decorated with personalized details that make it feel like home. Breakfast is served around a large table filled with Italian flavors and as much coffee as you need.

€200-300

★ **Hotel Loggiato Dei Serviti** (Piazza della Santissima Annunziata 3, tel. 055/289-592, www.loggiatodeiservitihotel.it, €180-220 d) is the quickest way to travel back in time. Located inside a former monastery, this

historic residence is in one of the most beautiful squares of the city and underneath an ancient portico that monks once called home. The inside has changed very little and there's an antique atmosphere that history buffs and anyone fascinated by the past will love. About the only concession to modernity is the Wi-Fi access and the armchairs scattered around cozy sitting rooms.

A night at ★ **Antica Torre** (Via de' Tornabuoni 1, tel. 055/265-8161, www.tornabuoni1.com, €350-450 d) provides a feel for how the Medici once lived. This medieval tower house in the center of Florence was restored with comfort and authenticity in mind. All rooms and suites have original antique furnishings and are equipped with a minibar, air-conditioning, and Wi-Fi. The best reason to stay here, however, are the stunning views from two rooftop terraces where breakfast is served and guests spend summer evenings sipping Chianti.

A stay at **Residence Hilda** (Via dei Servi 40, tel. 055/288-021, €230 d) gives you an idea of what it's like to live in Florence. The suites are all decorated in light tones with simple modern furniture. Each is equipped with a small kitchen and there's a food delivery service if you don't feel like choosing your own tomatoes. Robiglio downstairs is the perfect coffee bar to start the day. From here, all major sights are within walking distance.

Although part of a chain, the **NH Collection Firenze Porta Rossa** (Via Porta Rossa 19, tel. 055/271-0911, www.nh-hotels.it, €175-250 s/d) has plenty of character and all the quality you'd expect from a four-star hotel. Rooms range from standard to presidential and mix modern furnishings with original vaulted ceilings and 13th-century detailing. The multilingual personnel are friendly and an extensive buffet breakfast is served in an elegant dining hall.

If after a day of gazing upon the past you crave something trendy and modern, **Gallery Art Hotel** (Vicolo dell'Oro 5, tel. 055/27263, www.lungarnocollection.com, €250 d) doesn't disappoint. From the sculptures of spoons attached to the facade to the dark and cozy hotel bar, nothing is farther from the Renaissance than this luxury hotel around the corner from the Ponte Vecchio. Fashion designer Ferragamo designed the well-proportioned interiors and offset the whiteness of the walls with elegant brown furnishings. Rooms on the upper floors have private terraces with spectacular views. The Fusion restaurant downstairs provides a delicious alternative to traditional Tuscan flavors.

Staying at **Residenza d'Epoca Palazzo Tolomei** (Via de' Ginori 19, tel. 055/292-887, www.palazzotolomei.it, €200-300 d) is a little like staying inside a museum and would satisfy members of the Medici family: Rooms are spacious; ceilings high and frescoed; floors covered in terra-cotta, marble, and wood; and mirrors gilded. Waking up here is the perfect beginning to a day in Florence. An Italian breakfast can be enjoyed in your room or at a nearby bar.

Gallery Art Hotel

OLTRARNO

There are considerably fewer accommodations on this quiet side of the river, but waking up here provides an opportunity to observe the everyday habits of residents as they go about their morning routines. Several luxury hotels cluster around the Ponte Vecchio but for the most part accommodations consist of comfortable B&Bs, residences, and low-star hotels.

Under €100

Recently refurbished **Hotel Boboli** (Via Romana 63, tel. 055/229-8645, www.hotel-boboli.com, €65-85 s/d) is one of the best two-star establishments in the city. The bar downstairs is open 8am-midnight. Breakfast is an Italian-style buffet with pastries, cakes, and juice. Rooms are compact, and lack televisions. Air-conditioning is optional. The staff is friendly and available to advise guests 24 hours a day.

Antique furniture, wrought-iron beds, and parquet flooring are the hallmarks of **Hotel David** (Viale Michelangelo 1, tel.

055/681-1695 www.davidhotel.it, €88-95 s/d). All rooms are soundproof and equipped with both shower and bath.

Residence Michelangiolo (Viale Michelangiolo 21, tel. 055/681-1748, www.residencemichelangiolo.it, €90-120 d) is in a quiet neighborhood along the Arno a short walk from the center. The attractive three-story villa is surrounded by a garden with outdoor seating and free parking. Rooms are bright and spacious with compact kitchenettes and real king-size beds that aren't just two twins pushed together. Reception staff are attentive and can reserve museum tickets or restaurants should the need arise.

€100-200

Caterina studied restoration and is extremely knowledgeable about her city's artistic past. She renovated her family home herself and transformed the 18th-century *palazzo* into ★ **Via Santo Spirito 6** (tel. 055/288-082, www.viasantospirito6.it, €140 d) a historic residence with ten lovely rooms named after illustrious women. All are elegantly furnished and conveniently equipped with kitchenettes, Wi-Fi, and air-conditioning. It's a tranquil place where guests relax in the courtyard garden or the 2nd-floor lounge equipped with sofas and a fireplace. The residence is on a wonderful street minutes from the Ponte Vecchio, Palazzo Pitti, and the unexplored sights of Oltrarno.

★ **Monte Oliveto** (Via Domenico Burchiello 67, tel. 055/231-3484, www.beb-monteoliveto.it, €140 d) is a slightly off-the-beaten-track B&B near neighborhood restaurants and shops most tourists never see. Donatella provides a warm welcome along with a generous homemade breakfast that can be served in her private garden or the comfortable common area. The four guest rooms are bright and airy with views of the hillside or the quiet street out front.

Colle Ginevra (Via dell'Erta Canina, tel. 055/245-197, €100 d) could probably do with a makeover, but the husband-and-wife hosts are so friendly and the views so good it really doesn't matter. This B&B on the hillside overlooking Florence is one of the most secluded in the city. It feels like a rural oasis. It's just a 15-minute walk uphill from the center (easy unless you're carrying lots of luggage). The large and peaceful garden looks out onto olive groves as well as the Duomo. Breakfast is waiting whatever time you get up. Consider taking a taxi if you're traveling with heavy luggage.

It's easy to forget you're in a city once you enter **Hotel Classic** (Viale Machiavelli 25, tel. 055/229-351, www.classichotel.it, €133-166 s/d). Nature is all around this delightful villa. A continental breakfast is served in the vaulted dining room, garden, or in your room. Parking is available and the Ponte Vecchio is just 12 minutes away on foot.

The **Silla** (Via De' Renai 5, tel. 055/234-2888, www.hotelsilla.it, €180-220 d) isn't the most modern hotel in Florence but it is one of the friendliest. Everyone from the front desk to the kitchen staff go out of their way to help guests. If you need an electrical adaptor, want to make restaurant reservations, or have any

dietary concerns they'll resolve the matter quickly. Rooms are pleasantly decorated and those in the front have a view of the Arno. The streets nearby are filled with good restaurants and the center is only a short walk away.

€200-300

The team at **Palazzo Belfiore** (Via de' Velluti 8, tel. 055/264-415, www.palazzobelfiore.it, €190-230 d) like sharing their city with travelers. They do that by welcoming guests to their 14th-century residence with real gusto and making loads of suggestions. Saying they care is an understatement, and if you don't already have a friend in Florence it will feel like you do the moment you arrive. The eight cozy apartments have terra-cotta floors, wood beams, plush sofas, and antique furnishings that can be used rather than admired. They all come with small cooking corners and good Wi-Fi connections.

Palazzo Magnani Feroni (Borgo San Frediano 5, tel. 055/239-9544, www.florencepalace.com, €280 d) takes spacious to new heights. Each of the suites has 20-foot-high ceilings and enough room for a good pillow fight. Bathrooms are decked out in precious marble and there are no hustlers in the billiard room downstairs. A rooftop terrace and bar provides postcard-perfect views.

AGRITURISMI NEAR FLORENCE

Agriturismi are working farms that also provide accommodations and encourage guests to take part in rural activities. There are hundreds throughout Tuscany that produce everything from artichokes to wine and provide urbanites with an opportunity to relax and understand how the food chain functions.

You don't have to travel far from Florence to leave the crowds behind and immerse yourself in green fields, olive groves or vineyards. ★ **Torre di Bellosguardo** (Via Roti Michelozzi 2, tel. 055/229-8145, www.torrebellosguardo.com, €300 d) is barely ten minutes from the center by car yet a world away. This grand historic residence surrounded by lush gardens seems trapped in time and occupies a quintessential corner of Tuscany. The inside of the palatial estate is fit for a Medici and every antique-clad room hints of other eras and the city's fabulous past. On the grounds is a bountiful vegetable patch that supplies the kitchen, and owner Ana Franchetti can show guests how to transform seasonal ingredients into traditional local dishes. There are donkeys, ducks, and rabbits that are an instant hit with children who can fill their days exploring the garden paths and diving into the pool overlooking the city.

Casale Giuncarelli (Via di Baccano 4, www.casalegiuncarelli.com, €140 d, 3-night minimum stay) is on a hillside about a 10-minute walk from Fiesole overlooking Florence. The rustic farmhouse contains five self-catering flats of different sizes, all with private entrances and access to a nice garden with barbecue area and pool. Furnishings keep in style with the house and are perfect for travelers who don't feel the need to sightsee in the city all day. Car is the most convenient way of reaching the bumpy dirt road leading to the property, which can be a little hard to find; you can also take a taxi. Daniela provides a warm welcome and the location is great for anyone with the time to discover Florence and the countryside.

There's no possibility of running out of wine at **Fattoria Montignana** (Via Montignana 4, San Casciano Val di Pesa, tel. 055/807-0135, €140 d, 2-night minimum stay). This family-owned winery 20 minutes south of Florence has been producing Chianti Classico for generations, and the vines are right outside the door. During a stay you can visit their cellars and sample as much of the latest vintages as you like. Accommodation is in one of 11 authentically restored apartments that accommodate from two to six guests. Outside there's a pool and plenty of countryside to explore on foot or by bike.

Information and Services

TOURIST INFORMATION
Tourist Information Centers
There are three official tourist offices in the center, one in Parco delle Cascine, and another at the airport. The office opposite the train station (Piazza Stazione 4, tel. 055/212-245, Mon.-Sat. 9am-7pm and Sun. 9am-2pm) is the busiest and is best avoided. You'll find a friendly multilingual staff at the office on Via Camillo Cavour 1r (tel. 055/290-832, Mon.-Fri. 9am-6pm). Another one is located on Piazza San Giovanni (tel. 055/288-496, Mon.-Sat. 9am-7pm and Sun. 9am-2pm) near the Duomo. All the office provides useful maps, event calendars, and the Firenzecard.

HEALTH AND SAFETY
Emergency Numbers
For medical emergencies, call **118** and an ambulance will be sent.

Police
Florence is a safe city and there's less chance of being targeted by pickpockets than in Rome. There are a number of state and municipal police stations in the center. The most centrally located is the **Polizia Municipale Zona Centrale** (Via delle Terme 2, tel. 055/261-6057). This is where to go to report a theft or criminal activity.

Hospitals and Pharmacies
Ospedale Santa Maria Nuova (Piazza Santa Maria Nuova, tel. 055/693-8832) is a hospital located in the Historic Center just east of the Duomo. If you can't walk, call a taxi or take bus 1, 7, 11, 17, or 23. If you're staying in a hotel, notify the front desk; many accommodations are prepared to handle any medical issues that may arise. For general health questions call 05/527-581. **Hospital Pediatrico Meyer** (Viale Pieraccini 24, tel. 055/56621) is

a couple of miles north of Florence and one of the most modern children's hospitals in Italy.

There are dozens of pharmacies on both sides of the river. Locals can usually direct you to the nearest one. **Farmacia Comunale** (Piazza della Stazione 1, tel. 055/216-761) inside the main train station is open 24 hours a day. You can also call 800/420-707 to find the nearest open pharmacy.

Public Restrooms

There are a half dozen public toilets in the Historic Center and a couple in Oltrarno. They cost €1 to use but you can also walk into any bar and use the restrooms for free. Bars will also provide a glass of tap water to anyone in need of hydration in a hurry.

Foreign Consulates

The **U.S. Consulate** (Lungarno A. Vespucci 38, tel. 055/266-951) is open weekdays 9am-12:30pm and can assist travelers in a jam. Canadians in trouble should head to the **Canadian Consulate in Rome** (Via Zara 30, 06/854-441, Mon.-Fri. 8:30am-noon and 2pm-4pm) or the **Canadian Consulate in Milan** (Via Vittor Pisani 19, 02/67581).

Lost and Found

If you lose something in Florence, you have a good chance of recovering it. Head to the **Ufficio Oggetti Smarriti** (Via Veracini 5, tel. 055/334-802, Mon., Wed., Fri. 9am-12:30pm and Tues., Thurs. 2:30pm-4pm) 20 minutes northwest of SMN station. They receive thousands of objects every year and it's worth checking with them before giving up all hope. It's better to go in personk, as they may have difficulty understanding your English over the phone.

COMMUNICATIONS
Wi-Fi

The city of Florence has created more than 450 free indoor and outdoor Wi-Fi hotspots (info-wifi@comune.fi.it). Most of the center is now covered, along with public libraries and the tram line. However, there is a 2-hour/300 megabyte limit and the network can be difficult to access without a European smartphone account. Ensure coverage for 72 hours by purchasing the Firenzecard or visit any of the many bars and restaurants that offer free Wi-Fi. Most accommodations provide unlimited-access Internet, as do high-speed trains to and from the city.

Internet cafes are nearly a thing of the past but the **Internettrain** (Via Guelfa 54-56r, www.internettrain.it) still operates a few shops where you can check email, rent cell phones, and buy phone cards. They don't serve coffee and these days are more geared towards immigrants than tourists.

Newspapers

Newspaper stands are getting harder to find in Florence but still operate in the larger squares like Piazza Santo Spirito and Piazza Pitti. They sell a variety of local, national, and international papers as well as **Firenze Spettacolo** (€2), a monthly event guide to the city with a dedicated English section. The influx of foreign visitors means that many European dailies are available at the **Feltrinelli** (Piazza della Stazione, daily 7am-10pm) bookstore inside the train station.

Transportation

GETTING THERE
Air
Aeroporto di Firenze-Peretola, also known as **Amerigo Vespucci Airport** (FLR, Via del Termine 11, tel. 05/530-615, www.aeroporto.firenze.it), is located a couple miles west of Florence. There are daily flights to and from major European and Italian cities including Rome's Fiumicino Airport but no connections to Venice. Most **Alitalia** (www.alitalia.com) flights land in Pisa. Total travel time from Rome can exceed five hours and leave passengers severely winded. Taking a plane for such a short journey doesn't make much sense and is far less convenient than other options.

Amerigo Vespucci Airport is the smallest of the three destination airports, with no direct flights to the United States. A new runway and renovated arrivals hall are projected to open in 2017 along with a direct rail link to the city center with the aim of developing intercontinental routes. The airport suffers from a high percentage of cancellations due to fog and wind, and even minor inclement conditions cause delays.

Ataf/SITA (800/424-500, www.ataf.net) operates **Volainbus** (€6) shuttle buses that depart every 30 minutes from outside the arrivals terminal 6am-11:30pm and drop visitors off at Santa Maria Novella train station. A taxi ride to or from the center takes 15 minutes and costs €15-20.

Tuscany's busiest airport is **Aeroporto di Pisa-San Giusto** (Piazzale D'Ascanio 1, 050/849-111, www.pisa-airport.com), an hour from Florence by bus, train, or car. **Terravision** (www.terravision.eu, €4.99) buses depart from outside the arrivals terminal and drop passengers off at Stazione Santa Maria Novella in Florence daily between 8:48am and 12:20am. The slightly longer, more expensive option is to ride the **PisaMover** (daily 6am-12am, €1.30) bus that

departs every 10 minutes from the airport to Pisa Centrale train station, and from there board a regional train (€8) to Florence SMN station. Combined tickets (€9.30) are available from the Information Office inside the arrivals hall. Delta operates scheduled flights to Pisa five times per week from New York City (JFK).

Train
The easiest, most convenient way of getting to Florence is high-speed train to **Stazione Santa Maria Novella,** near the city center. Rail tickets can be purchased online through **Italo** (www.italo.it) or **TrenItalia** (www.trenitalia.it) or directly from train stations in Rome and Venice. Both operators provide frequent daily service and multiple levels of comfort that makes rail a great option.

From Rome: Trains are direct, and arrive in less than two hours from Termini and Tiburtina stations. One-way standard fares start from €10 with over 50 daily departures between 6am and 10:30pm. All passengers have access to Wi-Fi and outlets for charging electronic devices.

From Venice: The journey from Venezia Santa Lucia station takes just over two hours. One-way standard fares start from €18 with dozens of departures throughout the day.

Car
Florence is roughly halfway between Rome and Venice. Driving is a viable option, although the cost of tolls and fuel as well as the challenge of finding parking in the city center can offset any benefits.

If you prefer taking a car but don't want to drive there are a number of sharing services available. The most popular is **BlaBlaCar** (www.blablacar.it), which costs around €15 per passenger. There are plenty of daily offers for the Rome-Florence route by drivers who are rated and insured. It's a memorable way to cut costs and get to know a stranger at the same time.

From Rome: The journey north from Rome along the **A1** highway is direct and the 230 kilometers (143 miles) can be covered in less than three hours. You'll need to get onto the **Grande Raccordo Annulare** ring road and take exit 10 towards Florence. There's a toll (€17.80) that's paid at the end of the trip and several rest stops along the way. The speed limit on Italian highways is 120kmp and there are a half-dozen speed traps that are indicated in advance. The single-lane **Cassia state road** (SS2) is the scenic alternative. It won't get you to Florence quickly but it does cross some remarkable Tuscan countryside. Once you've left Lazio and entered Tuscany, there are opportunities for panoramic lunch stops and interesting detours in Viterbo, Siena, or smaller hill towns along the way.

From Venice: Florence is 260 kilometers (162 miles) from Venice and the distance can be driven in under three hours. It's not as direct as the trip from Rome: You'll have to take the **A57, A13,** and **A1** highways. Fortunately, signage is clear and Firenze (Florence) is well indicated. During the final 20 miles of the route, which cross the Apennine Mountains, drivers should be wary of tunnels, curves, and speed traps.

Bus

Bus is the cheapest and slowest way of getting to Florence. It's only an option if you enjoy cramped seating, dodgy toilets, and the din of strangers speaking on cell phones, and it doesn't provide significant savings. A number of companies operate the Rome-Florence and Venice-Florence routes, and depart from the train stations in those cities.

From Rome: Tickets start from €7 and the trip takes over three hours. There are a half-dozen companies that operate the route and nearly all depart from Tiburtina station. **Flixbus** (02/9475-9208 www.flixbus.it, daily 7am-10pm) is a low-cost operator with a modern fleet of buses. There are six daily departures (€11) on weekdays between 8:15am and 11pm and slightly fewer on weekends. Onboard amenities include Wi-Fi, restrooms, plugs, and snacks. **Eurolines** (0861/199-1900, www.eurolines.it) provides a similar service with 2-3 daily departures and single tickets start from €25. They also offer an **ItalyPass** that allows unlimited travel on all routes for a week or more. The 7-day pass in high season is €125; a 15-day pass is €135. It's not a bad option if you prefer to improvise, but it's still a bus.

From Venice: Eurolines provides daily service from the Tronchetto bus terminal in Venice to Santa Maria Novella station in Florence. Journey time is close to five hours and one-way tickets are €24.

GETTING AROUND

Addresses in Italy consist of street names followed by numbers. The system in Florence, however, is slightly different and distinguishes between residential and commercial properties. Black numbers are used for houses and red ones for shops and businesses. Most restaurants, therefore, will have an "r" (*rosso* means red) and may sometimes be out of chronological order. Via Garibaldi 50r, for instance, is not necessarily next to Via Garibaldi 48 and can be several doors or blocks away. If you can't find the address you're looking for, don't assume they've gone out of business. Just keep searching for the right letter.

Much of the center is pedestrianized and distances between monuments are short, and if your accommodation is located in the Historic Center or Oltrarno you won't need public transportation unless you want to visit Fiesole or Parco delle Cascine. That said, getting on a bus or tram from the train station and riding it to the end of the line is always fun. Florence has many lovely residential suburbs where tourists rarely tread and you can get a different perspective on the city.

Bus and Tram

Florence ATAF (www.ataf.net) operates a transit network that consists primarily of buses. The **C1, C2, C3,** and **D** buses crisscross

Cycling from Rome to Florence

Cycling may seem like an extreme option, but it's probably the most memorable way of getting to Florence. It requires time, a good bike, and traveling light. Intermediate and advanced riders can cover the 300km (186 miles) from Rome in three days along the **Via Cassia.** The road is sparsely trafficked and although there are many hills the climbs and descents are manageable. Along the way you'll pedal past vineyards, lakes, Roman amphitheaters, and tiny hill towns. Rome to Bolsena, Bolsena to Siena, and Siena to Florence are convenient stages, but there are many possible itineraries for travelers on two wheels.

Anyone considering this mode of transportation would probably prefer to bring their own trusted bike from home, but there are several long-term bicycle rental companies in Rome. **Top Bike Rental** (Via Labicana 49, tel. 06/488-2893, www.topbikerental.com, daily 10am-7pm) has one of the largest selections of sturdy mountain, trekking, and electric bikes. You'll need a good carbon frame and needle bearing forks to offset the ruts along the way. Cannondales, Haibikes, and KTMs don't come cheap, and a three-day rental ranges €49-120 depending on the model. Subsequent days are cheaper and cost €12-35. Rentals include helmets and locks, but you need to contact the shop in advance if you want to attach a luggage rack.

You can continue pedaling from Florence to Venice but that requires crossing steep, rugged terrain. It's more convenient to bypass the Apennine Mountains on board the regional trains that permit bikes and then get off in Bologna. The rest of the journey is flat and can be covered in a couple of days.

the Historic Center and can be boarded at **Stazione Santa Maria Novella** (Piazza della Stazione, tel. 055/89-2021, daily 4:15am-1:30am), which is practically in the center of the city and is a major transportation hub. Scenic lines include the **Bus 7** between Stazione Santa Maria Novella, San Domenico, and Fiesole, and **Bus 12** or **13** from Stazione Santa Maria Novella to Piazzale Michelangelo. One tram line terminates at the station and connects the Historic Center with the southwestern outskirts of the city. It's fun to ride and provides an entirely different view of the Florence. Work is underway on two other lines scheduled to open in 2017 and 2018.

The second train station is **Stazione Campo di Marte** (Via Mannelli, daily 6:20am-9pm) northeast of Basilica di Santa Croce. It is accessible on the 12, 13, and 33 bus lines.

A single ticket (€1.20) is valid 90 minutes on buses or trams. Tickets can be purchased at the **Ataf Point** (www.ataf.net, Mon.-Sat. 6:45am-8pm), located at windows 8 and 9 inside Santa Maria Novella, and at many newsstands or tobacco shops around the city. They can also be purchased on board with a 50-cent surcharge. Tickets are also available in discounted **Carta Agile** blocks of 10, 21, or 35. Daily (€5), 3-day (€12), and 7-day (€18) travel cards are also available along with a **Daily Family** (€6) card valid 24 hours for up to 4 members of a family.

Bicycle

Bikes are everywhere in Florence, and most of the Historic Center is flat and easy to pedal around. Most rental agencies offer one-hour or five-hour periods on standard city bikes. If you want a more challenging ride you can rent a mountain bike and head over the river to the hillsides above Oltrarno or make an entire day of it and climb up to Fiesole. There are bike paths stretching along both sides of the Arno but the center is often a free-for-all. Locals ride fast and the sound of bells warning distracted tourists to get out of the way is frequent.

Florence by Bike (Via S. Zanobi 54r, tel. 055/488-992, www.florencebybike.it, Mon.-Fri. 9am-1pm and 3:30pm-7:30pm, Sat. 9am-7am and Sun. 9am-5pm) and **Tuscany Cycle**

(Via Ghibellina, 133r, tel. 328/071-4849, www. tuscanycycle.com, daily 9am-7pm) are near the train station and carry a range of bikes for different rider needs. The former rents single-gear city bikes with hand brakes and rat trap pedals for €3 per hour or €14 for an entire day; the price includes a helmet and lock. Reservations are wise during the summer. Both shops also run cycling tours of the city and the surrounding countryside.

Taxi

Taxis aren't that useful in a city this small, but they are available from stands in Piazza Santa Maria Novella and most other large squares. They can also be summoned by calling **Taxi Firenze** (4390 or 4242) and are useful at night or if you want to reach Fiesole quickly without taking a bus. On weekdays fares start at €3.30 and increase €0.85 per kilometer. Weekends start from €5.30 and at night the initial charge is €6.60. There's also a €1 supplement for bags and for a fourth passenger. A ride from the train station to Palazzo Pitti costs €13.77. To calculate the fare of a specific journey, visit www.taxifarefinder.com.

Car

If entering Florence by car, keep in mind the city operates a **ZTL** (Limited Traffic Zone) in the Historic Center and beyond that's active weekdays 7:30am-8pm and Saturdays 7:30am-4pm (hours may change during the summer). The zone is clearly indicated and a map of the boundary is available from **SAS** (tel. 055/40401, www.serviziallastrada.it). The best thing to do if your hotel is located within the zone is contact them and obtain a waiver or park at one of the lots on the edge of the ZTL. Vehicles rented in Florence are not subject to ZTL restrictions.

Street parking is hard to find in Florence, and you can avoid the headache of searching for a spot by using one of the lots **Firenze Parcheggi** (www.firenzeparcheggi.it) manages around the city. Rates range €1-3 per day or €15-20 per day unless you park in their underground Stazione SMN or Mercato Centrale garages where rates are inflated. There are a number of private garages on both sides of the Arno and hotels can usually provide better deals.

Most rental companies have multiple locations and there are many on Via Borgo Ognissanti minutes from the train station. **Sixt** (Via Borgo Ognissanti 96, tel. 055/277-6374, www.sixt.com, Mon.-Sat. 9am-1pm) rents compact and larger models with both manual and automatic transmissions. **Avis** (Borgo Ognissanti 128, 05/213-629, www.avisautonoleggio.it, Mon.-Fri. 8am-6pm, Sat. 8am-4:30pm, Sun. 8am-1pm) and **Europcar** (Via Borgognissanti 53/55, tel. 055/290-438, www.europcar.it, Mon.-Fri. 8am-7pm, Sat. 8am-4pm, Sun. 8:30am-12:30pm) have multiple locations near the center.

Car2Go (www.car2go.com) and **Enjoy** (enjoy.eni.com) car sharing offer hundreds of two-and four-passenger vehicles around Florence. They're permitted to enter the ZTL, exempt from street-parking fees, and can be used for however long or little you like. Costs are reasonable and based on a formula of time and mileage (15 minutes is €3.75 and an entire day costs €50). Registration is simple and completed online. All you need is a passport, drivers license, international diving permit (available from AAA for €15), and credit card. It's a good alternative to traditional renting and a convenient way to set off on day trips with zero hassle. Enjoy also operates a scooter sharing service.

Day Trips

Tuscany is one of the most scenic regions in Italy, and the countryside around Florence is dotted with hill towns, castles, wineries, and villas waiting to be explored. This is the place to take a day trip. Unlike Rome or Venice, getting out of Florence is quick and easy by rail or road.

FIESOLE

If you've been to the top of the Duomo or climbed the slopes of Oltrarno you've probably already spotted Fiesole in the hillside northeast of Florence. It's a sleepy little town just outside the city, founded in the 7th century BC by Etruscans. Florentines spend summer evenings here, and visitors come to escape the city for a few hours and enjoy the views.

Sights

The **Duomo** (daily 7:30am-6pm, free) stands in the center of town in the space once occupied by the Roman Forum. It was completed in 1208 and contains frescoes by Cosimo Rosselli and a triptych above the altar by Bicci di Lorenzo. The bell tower looks more defensive than spiritual and is nearly 160 feet (50 meters) tall.

Behind the Duomo is an ancient **Archeological Area** (Via Fiorentina 6, tel. 055/596-1293, www.museidifiesole.it, summer daily 9am-7pm, winter Wed.-Mon. 10am-6pm, €7, €10-12 combo ticket, or Firenze Card) that's in better condition than the Roman remains in Florence. There's a well-preserved outdoor **amphitheater** with seating for 3,000 and thermal baths dating from Emperor Adriano's reign. Close examination sheds light on how the Romans heated their saunas and an informative multimedia guide is included with the entry fee. **Etruscan ruins** are also visible in the shape of a massive stone wall and the foundations of a temple excavated in the 19th century.

Relics from successive digs are on display at the **Archeological Museum** (Via Portigiani 1, tel. 055/596-1293, same hours as archeological area, €10-12 combo ticket or Firenze Card). Guided tours of the museum and archeological site are available for €5. There's also a small book and souvenir shop inside.

Museo Bandini (Via Dupre 1, tel. 055/59118, www.museidifiesole.it, summer Fri.-Sun. 9am-7pm, winter Fri.-Sun. 10am-3pm, €5, €12 combo ticket or Firenze Card), the little museum across from the Roman ruins, contains a small collection of 12th-century religious icons and Della Robia ceramics. There's a small, unkept garden and nice views.

A combo ticket (€10) is available for the Archeological Area and the Archeological Museum. A second combo ticket option (€12) covers those sights along with Museo Bandini.

Food

There are many bars and restaurants in the main square and along Via Antonio Gramsci. Most of these have outdoor seating and some include views of Florence. **Perseus** (Piazza Mino da Fiesole 9r, tel. 055/9143, daily 12:30pm-2:30pm and 7:30pm-10:30pm, €8-12) is famous for homemade cooking without any pretensions. Start with a plate of their mixed Tuscan *antipasto* and continue with a homemade pasta dish. Choose from ravioli, *pici* (thick, spaghetti-length pasta), or *tagliolini* (long, ribbonlike pasta). Brightly colored tables and chairs are set outside from early spring to late autumn. The *gelateria* next door is a reliable place for dessert.

For an excellent meal with a view try **La Reggia degli Etruschi** (Via San Francesco 18, tel. 055/59385, €12-14) on the outskirts of town near the Franciscan convent, which is still active and welcomes visitors.

Entertainment and Events

Anyone who decides to extend an afternoon

in Fiesole into an evening affair can settle down at **Blu Bar** (Piazza Mino da Fiesole 39b).

Estate Fiesolana (www.estatefiesolana. it) is a music, dance, and theater festival held annually throughout June and July. Events are staged in an ancient Roman amphitheater and performers from around the world demonstrate their takes on classical, jazz, pop, rock, and many other genres. The **box office** (Via Portigiani 3, tel. 055/596-1293, daily 10am-6:30pm) is near the Archeological Area and performances usually take place in the evening.

Getting There

Fiesole is 15 minutes from Florence by car or taxi along the panoramic Via San Domenico that snakes its way up to town. The trip is slightly longer by bus from Stazione SMN on the **number 7 bus**. Make sure to validate your ticket on board as checks are frequent and unvalidated tickets result in a fine of €50. It's a pleasant ride that ends in Piazza Mino da Fiesole.

City Sightseeing (tel. 055/265-6764, www.city-sightseeing.com) tour buses on Line B also regularly make the journey. Get a map and event information from the **tourist office** (Via Portigiani 3) just north of the main square near the Roman ruins. The area around town is quite steep and anyone contemplating cycling there should bring plenty of water. Otherwise you can rent a mountain bike in Fiesole from **Fiesolebike** (Piazza Mino, www.fiesolebike.it, by appointment only) and join one of their countryside tours or bike downhill back to Florence and return your rental at their office in Via G. Orsini 4a.

MEDIEVAL VILLAS

The hills to the north and south of Florence are dotted with medieval villas where the town's elite once retreated during the warm summer months. A visit offers great views of the city as well as walks through some of Italy's most delightful gardens.

La Petraia Villa

La Petraia Villa (Castello, Via della Petraia 40, tel. 055/452-691, summer daily 8:15am-7:30pm, winter daily 8:15am-6:30pm, closed second and third Mon., free) was constructed in the 13th and 14th centuries and changed hands several times before becoming property of the Medici. Additions to the house and garden were frequent and Ferdinando I hired Bernardo Buontalenti to rebuild it from scratch.

The Italian-style garden that surrounds the villa on three sides was laid out to complement the building. It contains a variety of geometric designs around a central fountain. There's also a long rectangular pool on the second terrace where fish were once stocked. The views of the city are magnificent. Free tours of the villa are organized hourly from 8:30am until closing. La Petraia is about 20 minutes from Florence by car. Head northeast towards Sesto Fiorentino and follow the signs for the villa. Or take bus 2 or 28 from SMN train station in Florence.

Villa Gamberaia

Villa Gamberaia (Via del Rossellino 72, tel. 055/697-205, www.villagamberaia.com, Mon.-Sat. 9am-7pm, Sun. 9am-6pm, €15 garden, €10 villa) is just outside the small village of Settignano and has attracted sculptors and painters for centuries. The building was greatly damaged during World War II and painstakingly restored. Today, it's an expensive luxury hotel, but the gardens are open to all visitors and the elegant interior can be toured Tuesday-Saturday 9am-noon by reservation only.

Anyone who has ever planted a bush or seeded a lawn will appreciate the gardens divided into a succession of unique environments. The most interesting part is on the south side of the building, where two local gardeners divided the area into four rectangular pools of water, bordered by box hedges and arch-shaped cypress trees. Nearby there's a long lawn adorned with statues and a gate that leads to a smaller garden bordered by hydrangeas. The grotto at the end was built out of sandstone and contains terra-cotta statues. The view from the shaded terrace is worth a long pause.

The villa is 3 miles (6km) from the center and can be easily reached with the number 6 bus from SMN train station or Piazza San Marco. Get off at the end of the line in Settignano and walk the rest of the way.

GREVE IN CHIANTI

Greve is the first sizable town on the road from Florence to Siena and is considered the gateway to Chianti. It's an ancient market town notable for its architecture and gastronomy. The arcades that run along the sides of **Piazza Matteotti** are filled with traditional shops and restaurants. The statue in the middle is Giovanni da Verrazzano, who was born nearby in Castello di Verrazzano and made several journeys to the New World.

If the trademark rolling hills of Chianti don't excite you the wine surely will. The wineries, which are located a short distance from town, are the real reason to visit the area. Each has its own personality and produces a different variety of Chianti Classico. The first mention of grapes in the region dates from the 12th century and an export business

began soon after that. By the 18th century cultivation was firmly established and early European visitors were taking note.

Sights

Santa Croce (Piazza Santa Croce, free) lies at the pinnacle of the *piazza* on the site where a medieval chapel once stood. It's not as old as it looks: It was completed in 1835 by Luigi de Cambray-Digny in a neo-Renaissance style. Inside the works of art include a triptych of the Madonna and Child by Bicci di Lorenzo.

Entertainment and Events

The market spirit has not faded in Greve, and the *piazza* regularly fills up with farmers and merchants selling locally produced goods. On the last Sunday of each month **Il Pagliaio** (Piazza Matteotti) is the occasion to sample handmade olive oils and cheeses. Producers are happy to explain the process involved to curious visitors discovering new flavors. Between May and September on the third Thursday of each month late-night snacks are served in the square. **Stelle e Mercanti** (Piazza Matteotti) is a nocturnal market that starts at 6pm and runs until 11pm.

Cantina Aperta (Open Cantina) is the best time for a wine lover to be in Tuscany.

Greve in Chianti

It's when wineries open up their doors and let anyone who wants a drink sample the wines on offer. Not every vineyard in the region takes part in the event but there's a high level of participation in Greve. The event is scheduled every year on the last Sunday in May.

Food and Nightlife

Underneath the porticos is a small restaurant where Mirna serves her husband's dishes. **Mangiando** (Piazza Matteotti 80, tel. 055/854-6372, Tues.-Sun, 12:30pm-3pm and 7:30pm-11pm, €7-10) doesn't stray very far from tradition and the *crostini* are a classic Tuscan appetizer. There are a half-dozen pastas, but if you've had your fill of carbohydrates the steaks are an excellent alternative. Chianti is the prevalent wine.

If you prefer making your own *panini*, **Antica Macelleria Falorni** (Piazza Matteotti 71, tel. 055/853-029, Mon.-Sat. 8am-1pm and 3:30pm-7:30pm, Sun. 10am-1pm and 3:30pm-7pm) can slice up some *prosciutto crudo, capocollo,* or *soppressata.* For wine, visit **Le Cantine di Greve** (Piazza delle Cantine 6, tel. 055/854-6404, daily 10am-7pm). This well-stocked *enoteca* carries 1,200 types of wines, 150 of which can be sampled. There's also a small museum inside.

Wineries

You can learn a lot about wine in Florence, but there's something raw and earthy about drinking it at the source. There are two ways to do that: Either you join a wine tour and follow a preordained path or you set out on your own. The latter is the adventurous option and only requires reaching Chianti. Almost as soon as you leave the city limits you'll see signs pointing to wineries. Dozens are clustered around the SR222 and it's impossible not to stumble on great wine.

Most vineyards around Greve in Chianti have their own shops where tours and tastings are organized. Vineyard tours often need to be reserved but tastings are spontaneous and nearly always available. They usually involve several different vintages and may include light snacks or lunch. Whenever something strikes your palate, buy a bottle or have a case shipped directly home. The fun thing about visiting several vineyards in a single day is discovering how much difference a few kilometers make on what's poured into your glass.

Villa Calcinaia (Via Citille 84, tel. 055/054-0137, www.villacalcinaia.it, shop hours Mon.-Fri. 9am-6pm) is located on an elegant estate a couple of kilometers north of town. They produce red, white, and rosè from a number of different grape varieties. Visits can be booked with Vincenzo, who will show you around the vineyard and explain the production process. Tours last one hour and start on weekdays at 11am and 2:30pm. Afterwards you'll sample four recent vintages with cheese and cured meats (€18). Lunch and dinner can also be organized for a minimum of six people and accommodation is available in case you want to extend your stay.

On a hilltop five minutes away lies **Castello di Verrazzano** (Via Citille 32a, tel. 055/854-243, www.verrazzano.com), where grapes and olives have been grown since 1150. The estate belonged to the Verrazzano family and is the birthplace of the famous explorer. There's a lot of history here and plenty of great stories waiting to be told. Guided visits reveal the vineyards, gardens, and cellars where wine ages in oak casks. The **Wine Tour Classico** (Mon.-Fri. 10am and 3pm, €18) lasts 90 minutes and includes three glasses of Chianti Classico and a sampling of the family's olive oil, goat cheese, and balsamic vinegar. If you plan on being hungry, book the **Wine and Food Experience** (€58) and have a lunch you'll never forget.

Information and Services

The **tourist office** (Viale Giovanni da Verrazzano 59, tel. 055/854-6287, Mar.-Oct. Mon.-Sat. 9am-1pm and 2:30pm-6:30pm) can help find last-minute accommodations and provides a list of monthly events. **Chianti Slow Travel** (Piazza Ferrante Mori 1, tel. 055/854-6299) is a source for gastronomic itineraries and events in the area.

Getting There and Around

Greve is 18 miles (30km) south of Florence on the SS222. SITA buses from Stazione SMN are available daily and take 45 minutes to reach the town. There's a taxi stand in the central *piazza* where scooter and car rentals are also available.

You can pay someone to take you on a wine tour or you can set off on your own vineyard journey to discover grapes firsthand. A car is necessary; you can rent one or use either of the car sharing options available in Florence. Once you've decided who the designated driver will be, head south along the SR222 that starts on the outskirts of Florence.

★ LUCCA

Few Italian towns are as thoroughly well preserved as Lucca, where winding alleys, bell towers, and squares have changed little over the centuries. The street pattern is a remnant of ancient Roman engineering, and they built their designs atop Ligurian and Etruscan foundations. A thriving silk trade and shrewd banking led to steady growth during the late Middle Ages and Renaissance. There were periods of friction and war with larger cities including Pisa and Florence, but Lucca's independence was never extinguished due in large part to the massive walls surrounding the town. Accessible by direct train from Florence, Lucca is an easy day trip to organize and a great opportunity to see the Tuscan countryside.

Sights

The **ramparts** of Lucca are the symbol of the city and probably have had a lot to do with preserving the beauty inside. They're actually the fourth set of walls; they were transformed into a park during the 20th century before being rediscovered as one of the great attractions of the town. A walk around the four-kilometer, tree-lined perimeter provides wonderful views of Lucca and the surrounding countryside. The walls include 10 heart-shaped bulwarks that stick out from the wall and were built to resist attacks. The ramparts can be reached from any of the six gates or by way of numerous streets within the town.

San Michele in Foro (Piazza San Michele, 058/358-3150, Mon.-Sat. 7:40am-noon and 3pm-5:30pm, free) may not be as large as the churches in Florence, but size doesn't matter when the details are this good. Each column in the triple-tiered facade is different and the inlaid marble fits to perfection. Religious iconography is absent from the exterior except

panoramic view of Lucca

Lucca

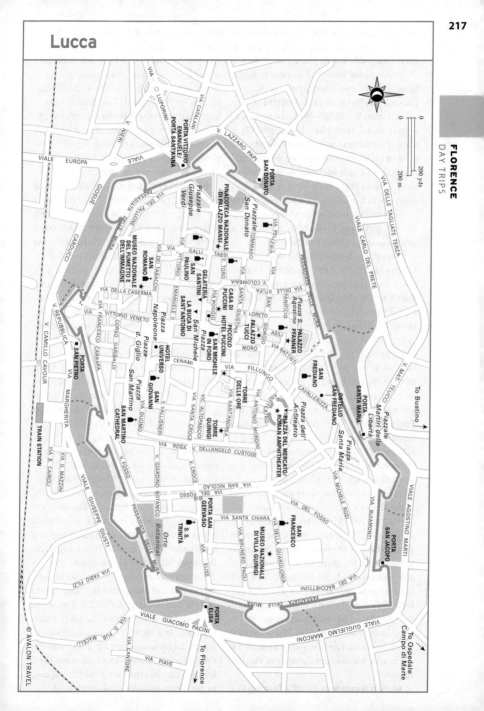

VIA CATALANI
V. NIERI
V. LUPORINI
VIALE EUROPA
VIALE
PASSAGGIATA DELLE MURA
CARDUCCI
V. CAMILLO CAVOUR
V. REPUBBLICA
TRAIN STATION
VIA GIUSEPPE GIUSTI
VIA FABIO FILZI
@ AVALON TRAVEL

PORTA VITTORIO EMANUELE/ PORTA SANT'ANNA
Piazzale Giuseppe Verdi
V. LAZZARO PAPI
PORTA SAN DONATO
VIALE CARLO DEL PRETE
VIA DELLE TAGLIATE TERZA
VIA FELTRIA
Piazzale San Donato
V. COLOMBAIA
PINACOTECA NAZIONALE DI PALAZZO MANSI
TASSI
SAN ROMANO
MUSEO NAZIONALE DEL FUMETTO E DELL'IMMAGINE
VIA DEI TABACCHI
VIA DELLA CASERMA
VIA VITTORIO VENETO
GELATERIA SANTINI
SAN PAULINO
GALLI
LA BUCA DI SANT'ANTONIO
Piazza Napoleone
Piazza d. Giglio
HOTEL UNIVERSO
San Martino
SAN GIOVANNI
SAN MARTINO CATHEDRAL
CASA DI PUCCINI
V. POGGIO
PICCOLO HOTEL PUCCINI
SAN MICHELE IN FORO
Piazza CENAMI
VIA S. GIUSTINA
V. LORETO
PALAZZO TUCCI
MORO
V. BATTISTI
Piazza S. Agostino
PALAZZO PFANNER
PANIFICIO
ASILI
SAN FREDIANO
Piazzale Martiri della Libertà
PORTA SANTA MARIA
OSTELLO SANTA MARIA
Piazza Santa Maria
FILLUNGO
TORRE DELLE ORE
TORRE GUINIGI
CAVALLERIZZA
Piazza dell' Anfiteatro
PIAZZA DEL MERCATO/ ROMAN AMPHITHEATER
VIA ANTONIO MORDINI
VIA DEL TEATRO
VIA SANT'ANDREA
VIA BUIAMONTI
VIALE AGOSTINO MARTI
PORTA SAN JACOPO
VIA MICHELE ROSI
VIA FOSSO
VIA DEL FOSSO
SAN FRANCESCO
MUSEO NAZIONALE DI VILLA GUINIGI
VIA DELLA QUARQUONIA
PORTA ELISA
PORTA SAN GERVASIO
VIA SANTA CHIARA
VIA BRUNERO PAOLI
s.s. TRINITA
Orto Botanical
VIA DEL BACCHETTONI
VIALE GIACOMO PACINI
VIALE GUGLIELMO MARCONI
PASSAGGIATA DELLE MURA
VIA CANTORE
VIA PIAVE

To Buatino
To Florence
To Ospedale
Campo di Marte

0   200 yds
0   200 m

for the winged figure of St. Michael above the pediment. The inside is unusually bare, which makes it a good place to pause and think.

Catty-corner from the cathedral is the house where the great opera conductor Puccini was born. **Casa di Puccini** (Corte San Lorenzo 9, 058/358-4028, www.puccinimuseum.org, Wed.-Mon. 10am-7pm, €7) is where the maestro was born in 1858 and spent most of his youth. The museum was recently restored, and each of the rooms returned to their 19th-century best. Even if you don't enjoy opera the house provides insight into Victorian-era tastes and standards of living. A small **gift shop** (daily 9:30am-6:30pm) is located nearby in Piazza Cittadella 5.

Several of the towers that once dotted Lucca's skyline are still standing. Legend has it that the devil was once spotted on **Torre delle Ore** (daily 9:30am-7:30pm, closed Nov.-Feb., €3.50 or €5 combo ticket) along Via Fillungo, the main thoroughfare of the city. It's the city's highest tower and so named for the clock that was installed in 1754. If you climb the 207 wooden steps to the top, you'll pass the clock mechanics that require daily winding. You can get an equally great view of town from **Torre Guingi** (Via S. Andrea, winter daily 9:30am-4:30pm, summer daily 9:30am-6:30pm, €3.50 or €5 combo ticket). The tower was built in the 14th century and distinguishes itself by the holm oaks growing on top. On clear days there are good views of the Historic Center and the Apuan Alps.

Piazza del Mercato has a strange shape to it. The reason lies in the **Roman amphitheater** that once stood here. In the Middle Ages the stone from the amphitheater was used to build houses, but in 1830 the Bourbons cleared the central area to preserve the original elliptical form. Remains of the two rows of 54 ancient arches can still be seen. Even though it's called Market Square, the stalls once set up here were transferred to the nearby Mercato del Carmine in the 19th century.

Museo Nazionale di Villa Guinigi (Via della Quarquonia, 058/355-570, www.lucca-museinazionali.it, Tues.-Sat. 8:30am-7:30pm, €4 or €6.50 combo with Pinacoteca) displays cultural artifacts and paintings across three floors of an elegant villa. The archeological section on the ground floor contains many fragments from the past and examples of ancient funerary monuments. The shield once worn by a medieval Lombard warrior is impressive, as are paintings by Fra Bartolomo and his Renaissance contemporaries.

Pinacoteca Nazionale di Palazzo Mansi (Via Gallitassi 43, 058/358-3461, Tues.-Sat. 8:30am-7:30pm, €4 or €6.50 combo with Villa Guinigi) was the home of a 16th-century nobleman and has since been transformed into a museum. The luxurious interior includes a hall of mirrors and hall lined with intricate tapestries. The museum has a varied collection donated by Leopold II in 1847. Venetian, Lombard, Roman, and Flemish artists are all present. Tuscan paintings include work by Bronzino, Andrea del Sarto, and Pontormo's *Portrait of a Young Man*.

For a complete change of scenery without having to leave the Historic Center you can chose between the 18th-century formal gardens and baroque statues of **Palazzo Pfanner** (Via degli Asili 33, 058/395-4029, www.palazzopfanner.it, Apr.-Nov. daily 10am-6pm, €3 garden, €6 garden and residence) and the **Orto Botanico** (Via del Giardino Botanico, 058/395-0596, www.lemuradilucca.it, Nov.-Mar. upon reservation only, Apr.-Oct. daily 10am-6pm, €4). The latter was built along the walls and contains hundreds of rare species. Both are quiet places to take a stroll under shaded trees and flowering plants that reach full bloom in late spring.

For serious comic-strip junkies **Museo Nazionale del Fumetto e dell'Immagine** (Piazza San Romano 4, 058/356-326, www.museoitalianodelfumetto.it, Tues.-Fri. 10am-6pm, €4) is a must. The museum demonstrates the techniques used by Italy's premier illustrators, and hands-on exhibits will thrill Disneyphiles whether you speak the language or not. Entry includes a free comic book.

Food

Lunchtime service at **Buatino** (Borgo Giannotti 508, 058/334-3207, Mon.-Sat. noon-3pm and 7:30pm-10:30pm, €10-14) can be hectic—everyone's eager to get their forks into the specials. Dinner is more relaxed and the atmosphere often includes live music. The *tagliatelle al piccione* (pasta with pigeon) makes a good first course and seconds include *bollito misto in salsa verde* (mixed meat stew with green sauce). The wine menu lists over 150 bottles from Tuscany and other Italian regions.

What started out as an inn where weary travelers could rest their horses and feed themselves hasn't changed much. Although the horses are gone the hearty soups at **La Buca di Sant'Antonio** (Via della Cervia 3, 058/35-5881, Tues.-Sat. 12:30pm-3pm and 7:30pm-10pm, Sun. lunch only, €14-16) is pretty much the same. Puccini and Pound were known to dine here, and the candles and white tablecloths make it popular with couples.

Agli Orti di Via Elisa (Via Elisa 17, 058/349-1241, Thurs.-Tues. 1pm-3pm and 7pm-11pm, €7-11) is operated with gusto by an enthusiastic team of chefs. The two large dining rooms offer traditional gastronomy and oven-baked pizzas within an elegant interior. **Gelateria Santini** (Piazza Cittadella 1, 058/355-295, summer daily 9am-midnight, winter Tues.-Sun. 9am-9pm, closed Nov., €2.50-4) has been open since 1916 and they've learned a lot about gelato in that time. Besides a dozen homemade flavors they prepare delicious *zuccotti* and *semifreddi* desserts.

Entertainment and Events

Sagra Musicale Lucchese is a series of concerts held throughout May and June and performed within the town's churches. Recent editions were dedicated entirely to the organ. Newly restored ancient instruments often take center stage. The repertoire varies between forgotten classics and new compositions sung by local choirs. Tickets rarely exceed €15 and concerts start at 9pm.

Luminara di Santa Croce (Sept. 13) honors the cross that was supposedly brought back from Palestine by a monk and now rests in the Duomo. The nighttime procession is illuminated by thousands of torches that add a surreal effect to the celebration.

Shopping

Lucca's shopping district is concentrated along **Via Fullungo.** The town's many **markets** provide pleasant atmospheres and original gifts. **Mercato dell'Antiquariato** is the second-largest antiques and ethnic market in all of Italy, and it fills half a dozen squares in the center with hundreds of stalls. Treasure hunters will find furniture and collectibles of every style, period, and type. The popular event is held on the third weekend of every month and closes much of the center to traffic.

A weekly **food and clothing market** is held on Wednesdays and Saturdays from 8am to 1pm in Piazza Varanini. There's a daily fruit and vegetable market in Piazza Santa Maria and the town's only **covered market** is open Monday to Saturday in Piazza Carmine. **Mercato rionale di Corte del Biancone** (Mon.-Tues. 9am-1:30pm and 2:30pm-7:30pm) carries secondhand books, stamps, comics, prints, and postcards.

Sports and Recreation

There are two parks close to Lucca that can be easily reached after a visit to the town center. **Parco del Nottolini** starts 50 meters from the train station and extends three kilometers towards the Pisani Mountains. Walk or bike along the 12-meter-high aqueduct completed in 1851 by local architect Lorenzo Nottolini. The 400 arches carry water from a source in **San Quirico di Guamo,** and if you make it all the way to this small village you can fill up a bottle from the large public fountain.

Northwest of town along the Serchio River is the **Parco Fluviale.** There are several itineraries to choose from, including one by horse through forested paths that periodically reveal great views of Lucca and the valley beyond. A two-hour tour (€40) includes detailed explanations of the surrounding country-side. Contact Susanna or Marcella at **Club Ippico Lucchese** (Via della Scogliera 877, tel. 058/346-7054 or 349/074-5600) to reserve a saddle.

Cycling is a great way to explore the city, circle the ramparts, and move out into the countryside. Bikes can be rented at the tourist office in Piazzale Verdi, at **Cicli Bizzarri** (Piazza S. Maria 32, daily 9am-7pm), or at **Crono** (Corso Garibaldi 93, tel. 058/349-0591, www.chronobikes.com), where personalized cycling tours can also be arranged. Olympia hybrids rent for €20 a day while ultralight Pinarello bikes for racing enthusiasts are €40. Tandems, quads, and rickshaws are also available for slower rides.

Guided walks dedicated to showing visitors around Lucca are organized by the tourist office and reveal lesser-known aspects of the town. Tours begin at 10am on Saturdays in Piazza San Donate. Reservations (accoglienza@consorzioitinera.com) should be made a week in advance. Two-hour walks cost €3.50.

Accommodations

Lucca is the perfect day trip from Florence, but if you decide to spend the night there are plenty of inexpensive accommodations.

Ostello San Frediano (Via della Cavallerizza 12, tel. 058/346-9957, www.ostellolucca.it, €28 pp or €68 d) challenges many of the stereotypes surrounding hostels. First, it's not a large dormitory for backpackers; and second, it's not located far from the city center. Instead rooms are of many different sizes and the location between Piazza San Frediano and Piazza Antifiteatro is enviable. What remains true, however, is affordability. A buffet breakfast is included in the price and the €20 all-inclusive lunch and dinner served in the large dining room is one of the best deals in Lucca. Guests do need to register for a AIG hostel card, but that can be done on-site at the front desk.

It doesn't get more central than **Piccolo Hotel Puccini** (Via di Poggio 9, tel. 058/355-421, www.hotelpuccini.com, €70-100 s/d). All of the town's monuments are around one corner or the other of this comfortable hotel. Breakfast is an extra €3.50 that will seem wisely spent.

Hotel Universo (Piazza del Giglio 1, 058/349-3678, www.universolucca.com, €130-200 s/d), offer rooms with views of the Duomo, Piazza Napoleone, or Piazza del Giglio. Room 15 is where Chet Baker stayed during his numerous visits to town and is one of the least refined. The standard of service is high and the newly refurbished restaurant offers haute cuisine in a quiet setting.

The entrance is the first clue **Palazzo Tucci** (Via C. Battisti 13, 058/349-6078, www.palazzotucci.com, €170-230 d) is not an average bed-and-breakfast. This historic residence provides an idea of how 19th-century nobles once lived. The high frescoed ceilings and six spacious rooms decorated in period furnishings are authentic down to the bedposts. Satellite TV, Wi-Fi, and air-conditioning are the only concessions to modernity.

Information and Services

Lucca goes a long way to welcome visitors. There are three main tourist offices in the center as well as several smaller information kiosks around the city. **Centro di Accoglienza Turistica** (Piazzale Verdi, tel. 058/358-3150, www.luccaturismo.it, daily 9am-7pm) near Porta San Donato provides the most services. You can deposit bags, find a hotel, rent a bike or audio guide, and purchase tickets to museums. Detailed maps and updated event listings are available and restrooms are nearby. The offices in Piazza Napoleone (daily 10am-6pm) close to the train station and Piazza Santa Maria (daily 9am-5pm) provide slightly slimmed-down service.

All offices can advise you on **ticket options.** Besides single entrance to monuments and museums you can opt for several combination tickets. There's a €5 ticket for visiting the towers and botanical gardens and a €6.50 ticket that includes entry to both national museums.

services depart from Stazione Santa Maria Novella and arrive in **Stazione Ferroviaria di Lucca** (Piazza Ricasoli, 05/834-7013) just outside the city walls and within walking distance of Lucca's Historic Center. The last train back to Florence is at 10:30pm and arrives at 11:50pm. Tickets can be purchased from automated machines in SMN or the ticket office. Most trains aren't crowded and there is plenty of scenic countryside to enjoy along the way.

There's a taxi stand near the station in Lucca as well as in Piazza Santa Maria, Piazzale Verdi, and Piazza Napoleone. To order a cab, call **Radio Taxi** (05/8333-3434) or **Taxi Lucca** (05/8395-5200). Lucca is located off the A11 highway that links the A1 near Florence with the A12 near Pisa. Drivers can choose from 10 parking lots within the walls or park outside in Viale Europa.

LEANING TOWER OF PISA

Italy is full of leaning towers but the **Torre Pendente di Pisa** or Leaning Tower of Pisa (Piazza dei Miracoli, www.opapisa.it, daily 9am-8pm, €18) is the most famous. It's only 5 degrees off-kilter but that's enough to make it look like a disaster waiting to happen. Construction of the bell tower began in 1173 and took nearly two centuries to complete. Unstable soil caused it to start leaning before it was finished, and the remarkable building has puzzled architects and attracted tourists ever since. Fortunately, recent interventions have stabilized the 58-meter high monument and allowed it to reopen to the public.

Today visitors can climb the 251 steps to the top via an inner staircase that leads to a circular terrace with good views of the city and seven bells that ring out before mass and at noon. Children under six and people with heart conditions aren't allowed to enter. Walking up a leaning tower feels strange and can cause wooziness but the view at the top and the knowledge that this is one of the man-made wonders of the world makes it worthwhile. Don't expect to just show up and enter the Leaning Tower:

Torre Pendente di Pisa

Ospedale Campo di Marte (Via dell'Ospedale, tel. 058/39701 or 800/869-143) is just outside the walls near Porta San Jacopi. Consultations can be made over the phone and there are several pharmacies in the center for resolving minor mishaps. If you can't find the right words just mime the injury or ailment. **Farmacia Comunale** (Piazza Curtatone, 058/349-1398) is open 24 hours and located in front of the train station. Most *tabacchi* carry stamps, but a stop at the **post office** can also be an interesting cultural experience. The main office is on Via Vallisneri 2 and there are smaller branches near Piazza Carmine and outside the walls near Piazza del Risorgimento. Make sure to grab a ticket or you'll lose your place in line.

Getting There and Around

The easiest way to reach Lucca from Florence is by train. There are many hourly departures. The direct line takes 70 minutes and costs €7.30. The second route requires a transfer in Pisa and takes nearly two hours. Both

Reserve a ticket in advance online at www. opapisa.it. You will be assigned 30-minute time slot to climb the tower. Don't be late or you'll miss your turn.

The Leaning Tower is only one of the monuments in Pisa's Piazza dei Miracoli, and the **Duomo** (daily 10am-8pm), **Baptistery** (daily 8am-8pm), and **Sinopie Museum** (daily 8am-8pm, €5 for 1, €7 for 2 or €8 to enter all 3) would receive more attention if it wasn't for their unbalanced neighbor. Mornings are the best time to visit. The walkways around all three buildings are a circus most of the day, cluttered with tour groups and street merchants tempting tourists with selfie sticks and cheap souvenirs. If you get hungry do not consider any of the restaurants near the tower or you'll risk eating something average. The center of Pisa is full of good eateries and you can explore the center in a couple of hours before heading back to Florence.

Getting There

You can take the A11 highway or Strada Grande Communicazion Firenze-Pisa to reach Pisa. It's a 90-minute drive on either one and both have tolls. Otherwise, board a train from Santa Maria Novella to Pisa Centrale station (€8.40). The journey lasts one hour and it's a 15-minute walk from the station north across the Arno River and up Via Santa Maria to the Leaning Tower.

Between Florence and Venice

BOLOGNA

Bologna, directly between Florence and Venice on the A1 highway, is home to the world's oldest university, founded in 1088. The city is relaxed about its scholarly reputation, and there's a pleasant and collegial atmosphere throughout the city's historic center. It's a great place to meet students from all over Europe at the many bars and cafes along Via Zamboni and its offshoots, where famous regional ingredients are served.

Bologna is surrounded by fertile lands and has a strong gastronomic reputation. It's particularly famous for *tortellini* (ring-shaped pasta filled with meat or cheese) and *mortadella*, cured ham that tastes remotely like bologna (but much, much better).

Sights

Bologna's central **Piazza Maggiore** gets away with looking majestic yet lively and lived-in at the same time. The centerpiece is **San Petronio Basilica** (daily 7:45am-2pm and 3pm-6pm, free), which is flanked by the Notaries' Palace, City Hall, and the Governor's Palace, all of them elegant without being ostentatious. You can see it all here: Large-screen movies every night of the week during the summer, businesspeople bustling to work, and students crooning Italy's beloved resistance song, *Bella Ciao,* on the church steps in the wee hours of the morning. The basilica is the world's fifth-largest church and a stunning example of Gothic architecture. Work on it was started in 1390, initially with the intention of making it larger than St. Peter's in Rome (that ambition was blocked by the Vatican). The immense, austere, and unfinished facade is well guarded by volunteers who make sure you turn off your mobile phone before entering. The simple but magnificent interior bodes well for symphonic concerts at Christmas and other major Roman Catholic holidays.

Rain or shine, Bologna feels like a medieval and slightly dark town, owing to its 654 **arcades**—roughly 24 miles long—that were constructed during the Middle Ages. The arcades have spawned a life of their own, particularly throughout the historic center and university area, with students and everyone else can be seen engaged in lively conversation or contemplative pause under the stately protection of the arcades.

Le Due Torri (twin towers) are fraternal, rather than identical, towers in the center of the city. The **Garisenda Tower** leans more and is about half as tall as the **Asinelli Tower.** They're named for the families believed to be responsible for their construction in 1109-1119. Visitors can climb to the top of the Asinelli Tower (97.2 meters/498 steps) for the best view of the city. It's open every day 9am-7pm (until 5pm during the winter) and costs €3.

Food

With its colder climes, Bologna does not follow the Mediterranean diet, and winter is the best time to get a taste of why the city is known for its food. The entire country has embraced Bologna's staple dish, tortellini with broth, as a Christmas Eve dinner tradition. The ring-shaped pasta comes stuffed with meat, ricotta cheese, or pumpkin.

Try tortellini with broth in the elegant **Cesarina** (Via Santo Stefano 19/b, tel. 051/232-037, Tues.-Sun. 12:30pm-2:30pm and 7:30pm-10:30pm, €10-15), a legendary restaurant in a 14th-century palazzo beneath the arcades in the city center. Also worth sampling are the lasagna, ravioli, and gnocchi, followed by oven-roasted rabbit or goat seasoned with truffles and herbs. In winter they serve *zampone*, pork sausage stuffed inside *zampa* (pig's foot). Italians all over the country eat it with lentils on New Year's Eve for good luck.

If you like meat, **Da Bertino** (Via Lame 55, tel. 051/522-230, Mon.-Sat. 12:30pm-2:30pm and 7pm-10:30pm, €10-12) is the place to eat. Brave travelers should try the *bollito,* boiled parts of animals most people have never tasted—such as beef tongue and veal brisket. More traditional dishes such as roast lamb and pork can sate carnivorous appetites, while cold meats like mortadella and prosciutto serve as tasty appetizers. Fresh pasta is also made daily.

Known as the temple of *tagliatelle* pasta, **Antica Trattoria della Gigina** (Via Stendhal 1/b, tel. 051/322-300, daily 12:30pm-3pm and 7:30pm-11pm, €8-14) has developed a solid reputation over 50 years for some of the best handmade pasta in the city: lasagna, *tortelli,* and tortellini served with classic Bolognese meat sauce (which the rest of world calls *ragù*) or butter and sage. Try the *zuppa inglese* to finish it off. It's close to the town racetrack just outside of the city center.

Getting There and Around

Bologna is easy to reach by car from Florence.

Piazza Maggiore in Bologna

The drive takes less than 90 minutes along the A1 highway. It's only slightly longer from Venice by way of the A57 and A13. Getting to Bologna does not require a detour for those traveling between Florence and Venice. Bologna is also on the same high-speed train line that connects Rome, Florence, and Venice, so it makes a convenient stop if you're curious about *tortellini*. **Bologna Centrale** station is a 15-minute walk from the center on Via dell'Independenza and bags can be deposited (€6) inside 7am-9pm. **Guglielmo Marconi International Airport** (tel. 051/647-9615, www.bologna-airport.it) is located seven kilometers northwest of the city and serves domestic and European destinations.

Although Bologna is small enough to traverse on foot, buses operate in the historic center and stop at Piazza Nettuno and Piazza Maggiore. Tickets are available at newspaper stands and *tabacchi* shops. Single tickets costs €1.30 and are good for one hour; for €5 you can get a 24-hour pass. Validate your ticket as soon as you get on board to avoid being fined.

RAVENNA

Ravenna is an often-overlooked small city that hosts relatively few tourists. That means there's little wait to view the town's main attraction, a collection of early Christian and Byzantine mosaics. Ravenna is also the final resting place of the great Florentine poet Dante Alighieri, who nearly singlehandedly codified the Italian language. His tomb is in the center of town, as are many ancient churches that can be visited in a couple of hours.

Sights

The **Mosaic Ticket** (€11.50) allows entry to several of the town's mosaic-related sights. Buy it at the first sight you visit.

Basilica di San Vitale (Via San Vitale, tel. 05/4454-1688, www.ravennamosaici.it, daily 9am-7pm, covered by €11.50 Mosaic Ticket) is one of Ravenna's eight UNESCO World Heritage Sites. The octagonal church, begun in AD 527, has the largest and best-preserved Byzantine mosaics outside of Constantinople. Ceilings and walls are covered with golden portraits of Emperor Justinian, Empress Theodora, and images of the Old Testament. Tickets allow entry to a half-dozen sites nearby.

The city's oldest mosaics are housed in the **Mausoleo di Galla Placidia** (Via San Vitale, daily 9am-7pm, covered by €11.50 Mosaic Ticket), built by Emperor Teodorico for his

Basilica di San Vitale in Ravenna

daughter Galla Placidia. The mausoleum contains many powerful images, particularly *The Good Shepherd,* which utilizes rare blue and yellow tiles rarely seen anywhere else.

You can feel the silence of reverence as you approach **Dante Alighieri's tomb** (Via Alighieri Dante 9, free), in part because of a city ordinance and in part because Italians have great respect for their premier poet. Ravenna was the last place he lived, and where he wrote the final verses of *Il Paradiso,* part of his masterpiece trilogy *The Divine Comedy,* before his death in 1321. A votive lamp filled with oil from Florence hangs above his tombstone. The temple where the literary giant's tomb rests is open daily 10am-8pm. However, dusk or thereafter provides a particularly moving atmosphere.

The austere-looking **Chiesa di San Francesco** (daily 7:30am-noon and 3pm-7pm), near Dante's tomb, is where the poet's funeral was believed to have taken place. Hold your breath before you visit the stunning 10th-century mosaics beneath the flooded crypt.

Food

Ca' De Ven (Via Corrado Ricci 24, tel. 054/430-163, Tues.-Sun. 11am-3pm and 6:30pm-11pm, €8-12) is a cavernous winery and restaurant in the center of town that serves traditional meat-and-potato-style dishes. Even the basic *pasta e fagioli* (pasta with beans) is done exceptionally well, not to mention the *cappelletti* and *tortelloni.* The house red wine is excellent and *ravioli con marmalade* makes for a sumptuous dessert.

The family-run **Antica Trattoria al Gallo** (Via Maggiore 87, tel. 054/421-3775, Wed.-Sat. 12:30pm-3pm and 7:30pm-11pm, Sun. 12:30pm-3pm, €7-11) has been cooking pasta right for nearly a century. The largely vegetarian menu owes nothing to trends; they simply use Italy's best products, and never stray from seasonal ingredients.

Perhaps the world's best *brioche* (Italianstyle croissant) can be found in a cozy bar located just before the entrance to the historic center and appropriately called **Caffè del Arco** (Via Cesarea 5, tel. 345/955-3905, daily 6am-7:30pm) as it lies directly in front of a small triumphal arch.C hoose between cream, ricotta cheese, marmalade, or chocolate versions. Even the *tramezzino* (triangular whitebread sandwich) stuffed with ham or tuna is delectable.

Getting There and Around

Ravenna is 188 km (117 miles) from Florence on the Adriatic coast. By car, head north on the A1 until you reach Bologna and then take the E45 and A14 highways to the city, which is clearly indicated. The town is 144 km (90miles) from Venice. To get there, drive south from Venice on the scenic SS309, a one-lane state road that skirts the coast. The journey by train from either Florence or Venice takes a little under three hours and requires a transfer in Bologna. One-way tickets cost around €30.

FERRARA

Ferrara is roughly halfway between Florence and Venice and easily reached by car or train. It's a beautiful small city that makes a nice extended lunch stop.

Great minds worked hard to make Ferrara spectacular. There was a sharp increase in building activity during the Renaissance and the city paved the way for modern urban planning. The center is easily visited on foot or bike and was added to UNESCO's heritage protection list in 1995. A couple of hours are all you need to relish the architecture and explore the streets that are ideal for pedestrians and cyclists.

Sights

Palazzo del Diamante (Corso Ercole I d'Este 21, tel. 053/224-4949, daily 9am-7pm) was named for its stunning facade made from white diamond-shaped stones. It was the residence of the Estes family, who were the local equivalent of the Medici in Florence, and is used for exhibitions and to house the city's art gallery. **Pinacoteca Nazionale** (Corso

Ercole I d'Este 21, tel. 053/220-5844, Tues.-Wed. and Fri.-Sat. 9am-2pm, Thurs. 9am-7pm, Sun. 9am-1pm, €4) is located on the 2nd floor and displays a permanent collection of regional masters.

In the center of town **Castello Estense** (Viale Cavour, tel. 053/229-9233, Tues.-Sun. 9:30am-5:30pm, €8) is the epitome of a castle and even has a shallow moat. It was built to defend the Estes family against tax rebellions at the end of the 14th century. It's said that inside the invincible walls is where one of the Estes nobles discovered that his wife and son were lovers. Visit the underground prison where he tortured them before having them beheaded. Today the government occupies most of the *castello* but a few rooms replete with original frescoes are open to the public along with a café and bookshop.

Ferrara's **Duomo** (Piazza della Cattedrale, tel. 053/220-7449, Mon.-Sat. 7:30am-noon and 3pm-6:30pm, Sun. and holidays 7:30am-12:30pm and 3:30pm-7:30pm) combines beauty and substance. Its three-tiered marble facade attracts and holds the gaze. Inside, Sebastiano Filippi's fresco of *The Last Judgment* inspired Michelangelo's version in the Sistine Chapel. Along the church's right-hand side are 15th-century artisans' shops known as the *Loggia dei Merciai* that re-create Ferrara during the Renaissance.

The Estes family went to **Palazzo Schifanoia** (Via Scandiana 23, tel. 053/224-4949, Mon.-Sat. 9:30am-6pm, €3) to escape boredom, and that's literally what the name of the palace means in Italian. Celebrations, banquets, and festivities were all held here, and the interior is fit for a pope or a king. Today, the main attractions are the frescoes portraying the Greek gods at play.

Gallerie d'Arte Moderna e Contemporanea (Corso Porta Mare 9, tel. 053/224-4949) is three museums in one, all housed within Palazzo Massari. **Museo Giovanni Boldini** (tel. 053/224-4949, Tues.-Sun. 9am-1pm and 3pm-6pm, €5) displays the work of 19th-century painter Giovanni Boldini, who was born in Ferrara and emigrated to Paris. His portrayal of women is reminiscent of Edgar Degas, who was a close friend. Two of Degas's portraits are in the museum. There's also a collection of 18th-century paintings and a modern and contemporary art museum featuring local 20th-century painter Filippo De Pisi.

Food

The best reason to visit Ferrara is the food. The Emilia Romagna region has a strong gastronomic reputation, with local dishes to savor. At **Al Brindisi** (Via Adelardi 11, tel. 053/220-9142, Tues.-Sun. 9am-1am, €9-11) they claim to have fed Renaissance greats Titian and Benvenuto Cellini. The restaurant opened in 1435 and has had plenty of time to hone the marriage of good regional cooking and fine wine. The menu changes with the seasons but usually includes the town's famous *tagliatelle* and *cappellacci* pasta dishes.

Quel Fantastico Giovedì (Via Castelnuovo 9, tel. 053/276-0570, Fri.-Tues. noon-2:30pm and 7pm-10:30pm, closed Aug., €11-14) is a favorite with locals who come for eclectic dishes that include duck liver. If you're not feeling adventurous they also prepare less intimidating handmade pasta. Meals are often accompanied by live jazz and improvised singing. Service is friendly and the atmosphere relaxed.

La Ripa (Via Ripagrande 21a, tel. 053/276-5310, Wed.-Mon. 12:30pm-3pm and 7pm-11pm, €8-10) serves traditional *Ferrarese* cuisine in a characteristically elegant 15th-century *palazzo*. The pasta filled with pumpkin and *scaloppa alla estense* (veal steak) are traditional local recipes. Try the pineapple mousse for dessert.

If you develop an appetite during a visit to the Certosa Monastery, **La Provvidenza** (Corso Ercole d'Este 92-94, tel. 053/220-5187, Tues.-Sun. noon-3pm and 7pm-10:30pm, €8-10) is just around the corner. Try the fresh pasta with porcini mushrooms and truffles or stuffed ravioli.

Information and Services

The **tourist office** (Largo Castello 1, tel. 053/229-9303, www.ferrarainfo.com, daily 9am-6pm) is located inside Castello Estense and provides free maps and sight information. The friendly multilingual staff can direct you to **Todisco Bike** (Corso Biagio Rossetti 31, tel. 346/139-4287, Mon. 3pm-7pm, Tues.-Sat. 8:30am-1pm and 3pm-7pm) or one of the other rental shops if you get an urge to join locals pedaling about town.

Getting There

Ferrara is a two-hour drive from Florence in the direction of Venice. Take the A1 and then follow the A13 after Bologna. There are two exits for Ferrara; the second gets you to the center slightly quicker. Paid parking is available on Viale Cavour and the side streets near Piazza Castello.

Ferrera is 114km (70 miles) from Venice, which can be reached in a little over an hour by rejoining the A13 highway or SS16 state road in double that time.

The train service to Ferrara is high speed or regional and may require a transfer in Rovigo. Tickets start from €17 and there are hourly daily departures from Florence and Venice.

Venice

This improbable city—famously built on islets in a flood-prone lagoon—is known as La Serenissima (Her Most Serene) to Italians. It's arguably the world's most romantic city—a beautiful dream with a thread of melancholy that makes it seem more real.

Historically, Venice's role as a seafaring town and trade center brought openness unequaled elsewhere in Italy. Its trade with Asia opened it to new ideas, goods, and lifestyles that came in and out of the port. The heady aroma of exotic spices and perfumes mingled with the sea air and added a sensual component unrivaled by other Italian cities. That East-meets-West atmosphere is still evident in many ways, from textile design to grand architectural expressions. It's even in the spices still used in Venetian dishes.

Hospitality is nothing new to Venice, where Renaissance doges entertained visiting ambassadors and dignitaries met with foreign merchants. Today, visitors may sometimes have the sense that the 20th century never fully arrived, let alone the 21st. Buildings may be decaying, but Venice has lost little of its golden-age flair, and there are thousands of artisans, shopkeepers, fishermen, and chefs preserving the Venetian way of life. Gondolas glide along the canals and glass is still blown in Burano, and the absence of cars and the extraordinary presence of boats make Venice even more magical. *Vaporetto* ferries are a necessary part of the daily commute, while on land, the best—and only—way to explore the maze of streets and squares is on foot.

It's no wonder millions of tourists want to see Venice for themselves. The best approach is to get lost in Venice. Put away your map and resist the urge to know where you are. Whichever byway, bridge, or canal you follow, it's impossible to stray from the enchanting labyrinth that is Venice. When you're tired, do as the locals do and step inside a *bacaro* bar for a glass of *prosecco* and delectable Venetian finger food known as *cicchetti*.

Let the city lead you in unexpected directions. At the end of your sttay, you may be left wondering if Venice exists in reality, or just in your imagination.

Previous: Isola San Giorgio; Piazza San Marco and Doge's Palace. **Above:** Grand Canal and Basilica Santa Maria della Salute.

Look for ★ to find recommended
sights, activities, dining, and lodging.

Highlights

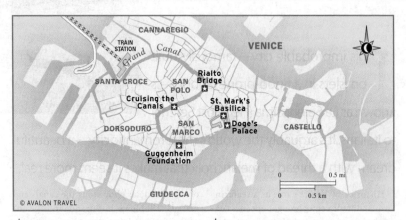

★ **St. Mark's Basilica:** Thousands of golden mosaics line the ceilings and walls of this magnificent church—you may wonder if you've walked into another world (page 238).

★ **Doge's Palace:** No building in Venice has more history than this one. Step inside to understand what made Venice great over the centuries—and what happened to anyone who broke the rules (page 239).

★ **Guggenheim Foundation:** Leave historic Venice behind to fast forward a few centuries at this unique collection of 20th-century masterpieces (page 245).

★ **Rialto Bridge:** This bridge is the center of Venetian life, with markets, food stalls, and commerce of all types (page 249).

★ **Cruising the Canals:** Experience all the romance of old Venice on its canals. With a single-day pass, you can circumnavigate the city (page 254).

★ *Cicchetti:* Enter an age-old *bacaro* bar to sample a tempting array of Venetian appetizers, all accompanied by sparkling *prosecco* (page 265).

★ **Shopping for Masks:** Papier-mâché and plastic masks are both souvenirs of Venice's famed *Carnevale* and iconic symbols of the city (page 281).

★ **Glassblowing:** Tour the furnaces of Murano to learn the secrets of authentic Venetian glass (page 306).

Planning and Orientation

PLANNING YOUR TIME

While many visitors spend as little as one day in Venice, it really shouldn't be rushed. Each *sestiere* (neighborhood) has its own character, and aimlessly exploring these is the most enjoyable activity of all. Three or four days will allow you to discover the secrets of the Doge's Palace and to stroll through remote parts of the city where tour groups rarely tread. It will also provide sufficient time to explore the lagoon islands of Burano and Murano and follow any path you choose without having to check your watch.

Plans are very often affected by weather in Venice. Although the city is hot during the summer it rains considerably more than Rome or Florence, and flooding is a possibility throughout the year. The busiest flood seasons are autumn and spring. Most flooding doesn't last more than a day and not all parts of the city are affected equally. San Marco is usually the first place to flood, as it's built at sea level. The city has learned to deal with the inconvenience and developed a warning system for residents and visitors. If you hear a siren followed by a series of high pitched tones you should get your boots on. The higher and longer the tone, the higher the water. The flooding may be a regular nuisance for residents but is a memorable adventure for everyone else.

Daily Reminders

Some sights in Venice, such as the Doge's Palace, are open daily. Others, including the Guggenheim Foundation and Galleria dell'Accademia, are closed or close early on Mondays. Museums also shut on January 1, May 1, and December 25. Hours are usually extended from March to October and reduced during the winter months. Outdoor markets operate in the morning and are closed on weekends. The Burano market is open on Monday, Wednesday, and Saturday mornings.

Advance Bookings and Time-Saving Tips

Mornings are best for visiting major monuments, and the lines to the bell tower and Basilica di San Marco are still reasonably short at 9am before they open to the public. Other than the monuments lining Piazza San Marco and the pedestrian jam over Rialto Bridge, museums and monuments aren't overcrowded. If you aren't planning on entering more than a couple of sights, you can rely on single-entry tickets rather than a sightseeing pass.

Sightseeing Passes

Sightseeing passes can be useful depending on how much you intend to see. If you plan on visiting three or more sights, you would be better off with a pass that allows you to skip the lines and enter directly. Passes can be purchased at tourist information points and most ticket offices.

The **Venezia Unica Pass** (price varies, www.veneziaunica.it) is the most comprehensive. This multifunctional card provides entry to museums, ferry transportation, Wi-Fi, and other services that can be customized according to interest. It's useful for visitors on short or long stays and covers most major museums, churches, and monuments. The Venezia Unica Pass is available from the main tourist office in Piazzale Roma, automated machines near the train station, authorized shops around the city, and online.

The **Museum Pass** (€24, www. en.turismovenezia.it) allows entry to Venice's 11 civic museums, including the Doge's Palace, Museo Correr, and the Glass Museum in Murano. Available at tourist offices and all participating museums.

Saint Mark's Square Pass (€19, www. palazzoducale.visitmuve.it) provides access to the Doge's Palace and three museums around Piazza San Marco. Whether you visit one or

Venice

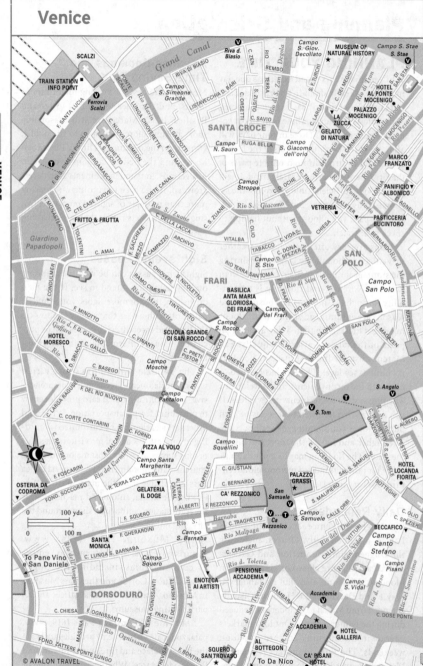

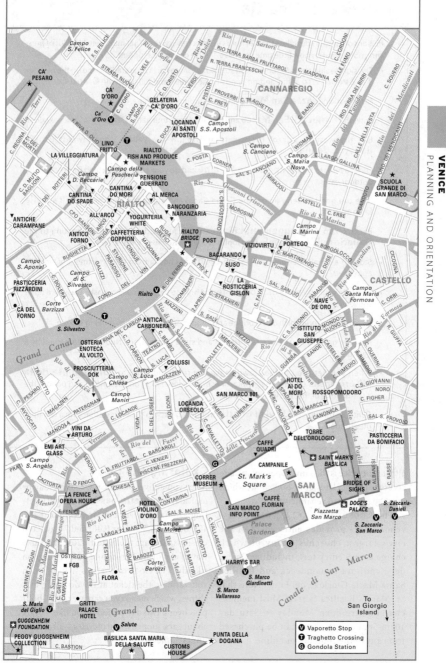

Legend:
- **V** Vaporetto Stop
- **T** Traghetto Crossing
- **G** Gondola Station

Venice in One Day

Millions of visitors spend less than 24 hours in Venice every year. That may seem like a lot of pressure, but no matter how little time you have, Venice doesn't disappoint.

- The sightseeing starts as soon as you step out of Santa Lucia train station. Hop on the number **1** or **2** *vaporetto* at the landing opposite the station and sail down the **Grand Canal.**

- Disembark in **Piazza San Marco** and walk around the square.

- Enter the **Basilica di San Marco** and take the secret tour at the **Doge's Palace** next door.

- Exit the western side of the square and follow the yellow signs towards **Ponte dell'Accademia.**

- Order a *prosecco* in **Campo Santo Stefano** and do your people-watching from one of the outdoor cafes.

- Ride the gondola ferry across the Grand Canal and enjoy the view from **Punta della Dogana.**

- Backtrack to the **Guggenheim Foundation** for modern art or keep walking to the **Galleria dell'Accademia** for a look at Venetian Renaissance paintings.

- Stop for a canal-side snack at **Al Bottegon** and choose from the assortment of *cicchetti* appetizers.

- Navigate your way to the **Rialto Bridge** and browse the stalls selling masks, glass, and other souvenirs.

- Hunt for a *trattoria* north of the bridge and choose one where Italian is being spoken.

- Ride the gondola ferry to **Cannaregio** and stroll along Strada Nuova accompanied by a gelato.

- When you get tired of the crowds, take any right and head to **Fondamenta della Misericordia.** Order a beer, spritz, or espresso depending on your mood and ponder the city from one of the bars lining the canal.

- Continue through the **Jewish Ghetto** and zigzag back to the train station with a few minutes to spare.

all four the price is the same. Does not include access to the clock tower or *campanile*, which must be purchased separately.

The **Chorus Card** (€12, www.chorus-venezia.org) provides entry to 18 of the city's largest churches (many of which charge a €3-5 entry fee), including Chiesa del Renditore in Giudecca and Basilica Santa Maria Glorioso dei Frari. Note that St. Mark's Basilica is free. Most member churches are open Monday to Saturday 10am-5pm and the card can be purchased from any of the churches or online.

Exploring the City

After you arrive, purchasing a single-day or multiday *vaporetto* **pass** can simplify getting around. These come in 24-hour (€20), 48-hour (€30), 72-hour (€40) and 7-day (€60) versions, and are the fastest, most enjoyable way of exploring Venice and outlying lagoon islands. The clock only starts ticking when you validate the ticket at the dockside machines, which means you can use the 24-hour pass over a two day period if you like. Forget about cars, mopeds, and bicycles—all are off-limits in the city.

Venice is divided into six *sestiere* (neighborhoods). All but one of these borders the Grand Canal, which snakes through the city like a backwards *S*. Venice is smaller but far denser than Florence and Rome. With no visible landmarks to facilitate navigation, getting a sense of direction isn't easy. Plus, there are countless dead ends and the constant disorienting effect of canals. Few streets run straight for very long other than **Strada Nuova** and the wide *fondamente* embankments overlooking the lagoon. The Grand Canal and its bridges can facilitate navigation a little, and the famous Rialto Bridge lies right in the center of Venice.

San Marco

Most of the city's sights are concentrated in San Marco. This is where you'll find the symbols of the city like the **Basilica di San Marco** and **Palazzo Ducale,** all located in the magnificent **Piazza San Marco,** which draws thousands of tourists every day. There are also five-star hotels, luxury boutiques, and **historic cafes** where exorbitantly priced coffee comes with spectacular views. The neighborhood is easily reached on foot along clearly indicated routes from the Rialto or Accademia Bridges, or from the sea, which is how 18th-century travelers arrived (and purists still do).

Dorsoduro

Dorsoduro lies on the western side of the Grand Canal. It's a residential *sestiere* with few shops and a large student community that gathers in **Campo Santa Margherita** on weekends. Some of the best museums and galleries are located here. The views from the eastern tip of the neighborhood are superb, and the visitors gathered to watch the boats motoring into the Grand Canal are serenaded by talented street musicians. The **Fondamenta Zattere** promenade runs along the entire southern edge of Dorsoduro and leads to the quiet streets and canals where gondoliers bring their boats for repairs and where stumbling across reasonably priced *trattorie* and outdoor cafes is easy.

San Polo and Santa Croce

Santa Croce lies opposite the Santa Lucia station and can be easily reached by way of the Ponte degli Scalzi or Costituzione Bridges to the immediate left and right of the train station. It's the smallest of the six *sestiere* and remains underexplored by visitors. Stray from the main thoroughfare to discover quiet back streets, empty churches, and impressive palaces facing the Grand Canal. **Ca' Pesaro** is one of the finest of these and now houses the city's museum of modern art.

San Polo to the south is the commercial hub of Venice; it was one of the first areas settled thanks to its slightly elevated position. Shakespeare mentioned it in *The Merchant of Venice,* and there are still lively **markets** where Venetians come for fish, vegetables, and fruit and tourists shop for glass and lace. The *sestiere* was named after the church of San Polo in the *campo* of the same name. The closer you get to the **Rialto** the busier things get. Crossing the city's most famous bridge can be frustratingly slow in summer, while the district's main sights—**Santa Maria Gloriosa Dei Frari** and **Scuola Grande di San Rocco**—are practically deserted. It's also possible to find refuge inside the neighborhood's many *bacari* bars.

Cannaregio and Castello

Cannaregio and Castello are the two largest *sestieri* in Venice. They're mostly residential and largely untouched by mass tourism. **Cannaregio,** where **Santa Lucia train station** is located, is a good neighborhood to begin exploring if you're not in a hurry. The gateway to the area is **Rio Terra Lista di Spagna,** which is lined with shops selling souvenirs and leads to **Strada Nuova.** That street is usually packed with visitors on their way to the Rialto. Other than this busy thoroughfare, most of the neighborhood is quiet. Not far away, boats depart the **Fondamente Nuove** *vaporetto* station for the islands of Murano and Burano. The bars and restaurants lining **Fondamenta della Misericordia** are animated with a mix of locals and visitors from early evening until late at night.

Streets become narrower the closer you get to **Castello** and regularly intersect with tiny squares where locals congregate. Castello is one of the least-visited *sestieri* in the city—except during the **Venice Biennale,** when art lovers converge at the southern tip of the neighborhood. It's also where Venetian galleons were built in the **Arsenale** shipyards and period vessels can be seen inside the **Museo Storico Navale.** There are several lovely squares and some of the finest **workshops** where masks are patiently made by hand. At the southern edge of Castello is the wide **Riva degli Schiavone** embankment lined with boats, souvenir stands, and outdoor cafes with great views of the lagoon and **Sant' Elena.** This tranquil islet is one of the greenest parts of the city, with tree-lined paths where locals still outnumber visitors.

Giudecca

Although Giudecca is technically considered part of Dorsoduro, it has a different atmosphere than the rest of the city. This is the only area in Venice that can't be reached on foot. Few tourists visit, and most of the narrow island south of Dorsoduro is residential. The northern edge is flanked by a long quayside *fondamenta* overlooking the Giudecca Canal. There aren't many blockbuster attractions other than the **Chiesa del Redentore.** In recent decades this traditionally blue-collar neighborhood of laborers and fishermen has gradually been gentrified. Abandoned factories have been converted into luxury lofts and **five-star hotels.** Of the five water stations along the northern embankment, **Palanca** is the most central and a good place to disembark and explore the mix of modern and 19th-century architecture. At the eastern end of the neighborhood is the island of **San Giorgio,** which has a bell tower where you can survey San Marco and the lagoon.

HISTORY

Venice is the result of coincidence. It just so happened that the Roman Empire was in decline, Germanic tribes were entering the Italian peninsula, and local people needed a place to hide. In Tuscany they built walls and in Venice the sea became the wall. The small fishing villages on the mainland were no longer safe and the best refuge from Vandals were the maze of small islets scattered around the Venetian Lagoon.

Many of these islands were settled, but Venice is the one that eventually emerged thanks to its position and geography. The land was gradually urbanized over the centuries and trade with Adriatic port cities and exotic Eastern empires began to flourish. The city was organized into a semi-democratic republic ruled by doges, who were king-like figures with great power and privilege; they were guided by a council of advisers and supported by influential Venetian families. There were 120 doges in all and many of their portraits appear within the Doge's Palace from where they reigned.

After the body of St. Mark was smuggled to the city in an attempt to gain prestige and religious clout, pilgrims from across Europe began flooding into Venice. Visitors have been welcomed ever since, and along with trade were fundamental in the city's rise. Goods, language, and ideas from Asia Minor left a unique cultural impression that still permeates the city today. New palaces were built, basilicas consecrated, canals dug, and sailing ships launched. At its height Venice had a population of 160,000 and controlled large stretches of the Mediterranean from Crete to Lebanon. Vast wealth was accumulated and invested in art and architecture.

A thousand years of independence came to an end in 1797 when Napoleon captured the city, and the Venetian Republic—already past its heyday and slowly degenerating—went out with a whimper. But a city like Venice could never decline for long, and it was only a matter of time before it was rediscovered and glorified by 19th-century intellectuals, writers, and musicians. Soon the entire world knew about Venice and has been trying to get there ever since.

Rules of Venice

A unique city requires unique rules. Some of the following are simple courtesy for the city and other visitors, while others are the law and can result in a fine if broken:

- **Walk on the right, and avoid blocking other pedestrians.** This is especially pertinent when stopping to look at shop windows or examine restaurant menus on crowded streets.

- **Make way for the two-wheeled trolleys.** These are often used to transport merchandise and luggage around the city.

- **Do not sit on steps leading to bridges.** Doing so creates unnecessary and annoying obstruction.

- **Keep shoulders and knees covered when entering churches.** In fact, this is a good rule to follow throughout the city. Also keep in mind that flip-flops are better for the Lido than the stones of Venice.

- **Do not drag luggage over bridges.** Lift suitcases and trolleys to avoid damaging steps.

- **Remove backpacks while on board *vaporetto*.** Carry them in your hands. This is less a matter of pickpocket (rare in Venice) prevention than to maximize space and avoid disturbing other passengers.

- **Never discard waste in streets or canals.** This includes cigarette butts, unwanted food, and everything else. There aren't many trash cans in Venice but you can walk into a bar and use their bin in a pinch.

- **Do not feed the pigeons in Piazza San Marco.** It's forbidden. Offers of birdseed should be politely declined.

- **No swimming in canals.** They are for maritime navigation only.

Sights

Each neighborhood in Venice has a distinct character that's a result of both the city's history and its present-day inhabitants. Take time to explore the streets—and especially the squares—where life tends to congregate. These squares can be large and vibrant or small and intimate settings where Venetians come to shop, socialize, and stretch their legs. You're as likely to see extraordinary things here as anywhere else, and the journey to so-called sights can be as gratifying as the sights themselves.

SAN MARCO

San Marco is located where your right thumb would be if you put your hands together and made a map of Venice. Home of the famous Piazza San Marco, it's the most visited *sestiere* in Venice and the first place visitors have come for centuries.

St. Mark's Square
(PIAZZA SAN MARCO)

Piazza San Marco, the largest square in Venice, is the heart of the city, where citizens and pilgrims have gathered for centuries. The sprawling open space is bordered on one end by the **Basilica di San Marco** and **Palazzo Ducale,** where leaders of the city resided and reigned. The remaining three sides are enclosed by **Museo Correr** and the colonnaded palaces that housed the Procurators of St.

Marks who were responsible for looking after the basilica. A little off center are the *campanile* **bell tower** and **Torre dell'Orologio** clock tower, where Venetians came when they wanted to know the time and visitors come for great views of the city.

Today, the *piazza* is animated with competing quartets playing on outdoor stages at elegant cafes, tour groups waiting to enter Palazzo Ducale, fearless pigeons, and itinerant salesmen hawking umbrellas or sunglasses, depending on the season. They may also offer birdseed that you should decline, as pigeons damage buildings and feeding them is prohibited. All the sights (except the bell and clock towers) can be accessed with a combination ticket (€19), and some like the Basilica and **Bibliotheca Marciana** are partially free.

The *piazza* can be entered from a number of directions. Each has its particular charm. You can take the direct route from the Rialto through the clock tower archway or approach from the Ponte dell'Accademia bridge along the winding streets behind Museo Correr. The most dramatic approach, however, is by boat, which was the most common way of reaching the *piazza* before the train station was built.

★ St. Mark's Basilica
(BASILICA DI SAN MARCO)

Basilica di San Marco (Piazza San Marco 328, tel. 041/270-8311, www.basilicasanmarco.it, Mon.-Sat. 9:45am-5pm and Sun. 2pm-4pm, free), founded in 832, was built to house the remains of St. Mark, which were looted from Egypt in a pork-laden basket (meant to deter Muslim customs officials) after two Venetian merchants decided that Mark should be the patron saint of their city. The basilica was influenced by Greek, Byzantine, and Islamic art and architecture. The five domes are reminiscent of a mosque, and the layout is a Greek-cross floor plan. The mosaics above the doorways recount the saint's arrival to the city, and a team of four bronze horses plundered from Constantinople stands triumphantly above the central portal.

Inside, golden mosaics embellish over 40,000 square feet of the cavernous interior. The uneven floor is also decorated in exotic patterns, and it's very clear how much it has shifted over the centuries. Biblical tales like the *Descent of the Holy Ghost* are beautifully illustrated on the dome interiors. Just behind the altar is the Pala d'Oro, or Golden Ball,

Piazza San Marco

which was created by the city's goldsmiths and is adorned with hundreds of precious gems. The chapel is connected to the church and although a velvet rope separates it from the rest of the basilica you can get a good look at the interior in relative peace. Over the centuries the basilica was decorated with columns, marble, sculptures, gold, the other spoils of war brought back by the city's merchants ships after the sack of Constantinople and other military successes.

Also inside the Basilica is the **Museo di San Marco** (Basilica di San Marco, tel. 041/270-8311, 9:45am-4:45pm, €5), dedicated to mosaics, textiles and ancient relics such as the original quadriga statue of four bronze horses. A detour here provides access to the 2nd-story balcony overlooking Piazza San Marco. This is where doges and dignitaries stood on special occasions and visitors now gather to get a great view of the square below. The basilica's Treasury (€3) and Pala d'Oro (€2), a stunning gold and gem encrusted altarpiece begun in the 10th century by Byzantine jewelers can also be seen.

There's no better time to visit the basilica than during **Sunday mass** (6:45pm), when the lights are switched on and the thousands of mosaics are fully illuminated. Mass isn't for tourists, so if you aren't religious, be prepared to sit through a 45-minute sermon conducted in Latin and Italian. Mass is held every morning, but only the Sunday evening service comes with spotlights.

When visiting the basilica, remember to dress appropriately (no bare shoulders or knees), keep quiet, and refrain from taking photographs. **Tours** (tel. 041/241-3817, Apr.-Oct. Mon.-Sat. 11am) highlighting the religious significance of the basilica start in the atrium and should be reserved in advance. If the line at the main entrance is long you can also enter the church through the prayer door on the side of the church in Campo Leoni. The façade and other parts of the basilica are often undergoing restoration and may be partially covered or closed.

TOP EXPERIENCE

★ Doge's Palace
(PALAZZO DUCALE)

To understand Venice, you must visit **Palazzo Ducale** (San Marco 1, tel. 041/271-5911, www.palazzoducale.visitmuve.it, Apr.-Oct. 8:30am-7pm, Nov.-Mar. 8:30am-5:30pm, €19, €20 with tour or Museum Pass, audio guide €5). This imposing palace on the southeastern corner

mosaics inside Basilica di San Marco

of Piazza San Marco is where the doge resided and the Venetian senate met to make the decisions that made the city a leading power for centuries. It's a White House and Capitol Hill rolled into one building. This is where dignitaries were received, powerful men slept, and prisoners were kept.

The palace is an immense U-shaped complex with a stunning façade and sumptuous interior. The exterior is wrapped in a columned arcade that supports an intricate *loggia*. The upper stories are covered in smooth brick decorated in a diamond pattern. Doges once greeted citizens gathered below from the ornate balconies. Inside, there's a vast courtyard, grand reception rooms, a chapel, luxurious sleeping quarters, prison cells, and a museum. This is where you'll find several of the world's largest oil paintings by the likes of Tintoretto, Titian, and Veronese.

The fixed itinerary leads visitors through grand chambers where the city counselors gathered and an extensive armory is stocked with swords and early firearms used by the doge's guards and auxiliary troops. Sala dei Consigli, the next stop, is one of the biggest rooms in Europe. Here, new doges were elected, and up to 2,000 counselors met the doge every Sunday to express their grievances.

Paintings depicting Venice's greatest triumphs and the portraits of 76 doges cover the ceiling and walls. The hall is lined with wooden benches and no matter how crowded the palace gets there's always room to sit and admire the scope of it all.

Sala dei Consigli is exited through a small doorway that leads to the cramped Palazzo dei Prigioni prisons. The narrow stone passageway leads across the **Bridge of Sighs**, where prisoners were once led to the gallows and through a long series of cells and chambers that make it pretty clear how the Republic deterred citizens from breaking the law. This is where Casanova was briefly detained and less fortunate prisoners met their end. Visitors must recross the bridge back into the main building. The itinerary ends in a bookshop and café near the courtyard.

The Doge's Palace is the most visited monument in Venice. Lines form early, but if you arrive at 9am the efficient ticket office is nearly empty. **Secret itineraries** (daily, 9:55am, 10:45am, and 11:35am) or **hidden treasures** (daily, 11:45am) tours are available. These 75-minute guided walks through the lesser-known parts of the *palazzo* are conducted in English. They only cost a euro more than a regular ticket and afterwards

Doge's Palace

What's a Doge?

Doge is a title that derives from the Latin *dux*, or commander (duke in English). It was used in Venice from AD 697 until the fall of the Republic in 1797. During those thousand years, the position evolved from primitive military leader to something close to a king and eventually a mere figurehead.

Becoming a doge was nearly as complicated as becoming a pope. The elaborate and complicated rules of the election system were intended to dissuade any overeager aristocrats from taking shortcuts to power. Each *doge* was, however, required to pay for his furnishings and expenses, which meant only the richest Venetians could aspire to the position. In the city's 15th-century heyday the doge's primary responsibility was representing Venice during public ceremonies and proceeding over diplomatic relations with other states. He could recommend foreign policy but his advice was not always taken and he wasn't allowed to meet with ambassadors without the presence of his counselors.

Eventually the election of doges became the responsibility of a council of aristocrats, and the freedom of doges was severely limited. They could not marry foreign princesses, abdicate, write or receive letters without the presence of a witness, conduct business, own land outside the palace, or leave the city without a special license. Towards the end of the Republic the position was limited to presiding over the government without having real control, and by then a doge was simply a fancy magistrate whose gondola was no nicer than those of other nobles. The biggest benefit was residing in the most prestigious palace in town. The only power that was never stripped from him was commander in chief of the navy in times of war.

Doges can be seen in many paintings inside Palazzo Ducale and are often portrayed wearing scarlet robes with a fur collar and an oddly shaped hat. Power was eventually siphoned away from the *doge* by an emerging merchant class who distrusted too much power in one place. The sculpture of a *doge* bowing in submission to a lion above the palace entrance closest to the basilica is the expression of that distrust and a constant reminder of who was serving whom.

you're free to visit the rest of the building. Reservations are required; although they can be made online, calling can be the simplest option. Visitors may be checked with metal detectors. All backpacks and large bags must be left at the cloakroom on the right side of the courtyard.

Campanile di San Marco

The **Campanile di San Marco** (Piazza San Marco, daily Jul.-Sept. 9am-9pm, Mar., Apr., Oct. 9am-7pm, Nov.-Feb. 9:30am-3:45pm, €8), or bell tower, is nearly 100 meters high and would be the oldest in the city if it hadn't collapsed in 1902. It was entirely rebuilt to 12th-century specs. Only one of the original bells survived the crash. Each bell had a specific purpose, from announcing the start and end of the working day to calling senators to the doge's place and foretelling an execution. In 1609, Galileo demonstrated his first telescope

here. The lightning conductor fitted on the roof a century and half later was the first of its kind.

Lines form early to ride the elevator to the top of the bell tower. From the terrace there's an unobstructed view of the city and lagoon. On clear days, the Alps are visible to the north. The elevator has a capacity of 16 passengers, and the terrace accommodates 20-25 visitors at a time. There are coin-operated binoculars at the top and there is no time limit for coming down. Tickets are available inside the bell tower, which may be closed in the event of high winds or adverse weather.

Torre dell'Orologio

In the 15th century, knowing the time meant looking at the sun or listening to church bells. The **Torre dell'Orologio** (Piazza San Marco, tel. 848/082-000 or tel. 041/4273-0892 from abroad, www.torreorologio.visitmuve.

it, €12, €7 with Museum Pass) clock tower in the northeastern corner of Piazza San Marco changed all that with Renaissance high-tech ingenuity.

The blue façade of the enormous astronomical clock contains rotating panels that tell the hour (like many old clocks in Venice, there is no minute hand), day, lunar phase, and zodiac sign. That was essential information for sailors, senators, and merchants, all of whom came to rely on the clock and checked it regularly. Visitors gather hourly in front of the clock to see the bronze sculptures on the top of the tower strike a large bell. The statue on the left strikes two minutes before the hour to represent the time that has past, while the statue on the right hammers two minutes after the hour to foretell the time to come.

You can observe the clock tower for free from the square or reserve a tour of the inside and discover what keeps it ticking. Reservations can be made in advance or on the same day at the Correr Museum, where the 50-minute visits begin. English-speaking **tours** are held Monday to Wednesday at 10am and 11am and Thursday to Sunday at 2pm and 3pm. Tour groups do not exceed 12 visitors.

Campanile di San Marco

Correr Museum
(MUSEO CORRER)

Museo Correr (Piazza San Marco 52, tel. 041/240-521, www.correr.visitmuve.it, daily Apr.-Oct. 10am-7pm, Nov.-Mar. 10am-5pm, €18 or Museum Pass) is a behemoth of a museum on the western edge of Piazza San Marco. The 17th-century palace contains over 70 rooms. Most people head straight to the rooms filled with Venetian Gothic art, but you could also see where an Austrian princess resided, admire 19th-century sculpture, or learn some Venetian history.

The **Quadreria** picture gallery located on the 2nd floor is filled with religious effigies, portraits of aristocrats, and scenes documenting everyday Venetians like the *Two Ladies of Venice* in room 15. The **neoclassical rooms** on the same floor display the marble sculptures of Antonio Canova, a skilled artist-diplomat who managed to bring back much of the art shipped off to France by Napoleon.

Before Museo Correr became a museum it was a royal residence and hosted Empress Sissi of Austria during her mid-18th-century visit to Venice. The **Imperial Apartments** are a miniature Versailles and include a throne room, dining area, audience hall, study, bedroom, and boudoir complete with period furnishings. The **Civilita di Venezia** rooms downstairs provide insight into how the city once operated and are organized by themes including the doge, the military, maritime trade, and daily life. Most rooms contain explanation panels in English. **Tours** (€100/1-4 people) are available.

The museum cafeteria is one of the least expensive places to have a coffee or light snack in Piazza San Marco. The views are great and the drink-sandwich combo only costs €10. The **Bibliotheca Marciano** (Piazzetta San Marco 7, Mon.-Fri. 8am-7pm and Fri. 8pm-1:30pm, free) can be entered through the museum.

The library contains a monumental reading room decorated by Tiziano, Tintoretto, and Veronese. **Tours** (tel. 041/240-7238, mazzariol@marciana.venezia.sbn.it, free with museum ticket) in Italian last 50 minutes and can be arranged in advance with Mariachaira.

La Fenice Opera House
(TEATRO LA FENICE)

Opera is an Italian invention, and the theaters where Rossini, Verdi, and other composers premiered their works are legendary. **Teatro La Fenice** (Campo San Fantin, tel. 041/786-672, www.festfenice.com, daily 9:30am-6pm) is among the most prestigious in the world and has staged thousands of hours of melodies since it was opened in 1792. It has seen more than its own share of drama and twice burned down only to be rebuilt, most recently in 1996. The simple neoclassical exterior gives little hint of the opulent five-tiered seating inside. Unless you attend a performance the only way to visit the theater is with a self-guided **audio tour** (€10) that lasts 45 minutes and includes a visit to a permanent exhibition dedicated to Maria Callas. Music lovers can go backstage, see contemporary sets, sit in the royal box, and learn about singers like Callas who performed here.

Campo Santo Stefano

The largest *campo* in San Marco is a vibrant intersection where visitors pause on their way to and from Piazza San Marco and local children run free. It was once used for bullfights, masked balls, and processions during *Carnevale* and is lined with modest *palazzo* and outdoor cafes. The statue in the center honors Niccolò Tommaseo, one of the city's hometown writers, and the steps at the base are usually occupied with people-watchers. The Gothic church of Santo Stefano has a simple brick façade and a ceiling shaped like a ship's keel. There's a small **museum** (tel. 041/522-2362, Mon.-Sat. 10am-5pm, €3 or Chorus Card) in the adjacent cloister with a *Last Supper* by Tintoretto. On the other side of the *campo* is the Chiesa di San Vidale, where classical concerts are held every evening. The repertoire nearly always includes Vivaldi.

Palazzo Grassi

Palazzo Grassi (San Marco, Campo San Samuele 3231, tel. 041/200-1057, www.palazzograssi.it, Wed.-Mon. 10am-7pm, €15 single, €20 combo with Punta della Dogana) was the last palace built before the fall of the Republic. It's owned by French businessman and art collector Francois Pinault Grassi,

Campo Santo Stefano

Lingering in *Campi*

Venice would be a dark and dreary place without its *campi*. These oddly shaped squares provide light and space for locals to commune, children to play, and pigeons to gather. They come in all sizes and are recognizable by the wellheads, flagpoles, and red benches that characterize them. Tourists walk quickly through, but these aren't just stone paving between destinations—they are destinations in themselves, where you can observe daily life, fill up a bottle of water, and enjoy a spritz at an outdoor café.

There are dozens of *campi* in each neighborhood and they are difficult not to stumble upon. Some are large and busy at all hours like **Campo Santo Stefano** (Dorsoduro), which is lined with eateries and popular with students from the nearby university; others are semi-deserted and lacking in commerce such as **Campo S. Agnese** (Dorsoduro), where the biggest attraction is the shade from the trees and the entertainment by the street musicians playing violins and accordions.

On the other side of the Grand Canal **Campo Santo Stefano** (San Marco) is a mix of the two types. It is flanked on either end by churches and sees a constant stream of visitors on their way to and from Piazza San Marco. At its outdoor tables you can enjoy a drink in the sun and try to spot the Venetians among the tourists. (Hint: They're the ones walking a little faster and seem to know where they're going. They also don't have an expression of exhaustion or amazement on their faces and tend to be better dressed.)

Some *campi* overlook canals like **Santa Maria Formosa** and **Campo San Lorenzo** (Castello), where gondoliers wait patiently for fares and lines form outside small ice-cream shops. They are natural places to enjoy gelato and browse vegetable stalls in search of exotic fruit. **Campo San Polo** (San Polo) is one of the biggest and is nearly empty most of the year—except during the Venice Film Festival when a screen is set up and spectators watch the latest international releases outdoors followed by a pint at the pizzeria on the corner.

There is a *campo* for everyone whether you like yours boisterous or desolate, and whichever you choose you'll be able to admire the immense beauty of the city from these unique urban settings and have a proper moment to take it all in.

who also owns Punta della Dogana. Palazzo Grassi is generally used for retrospectives of established artists, and also has a fabulous interior that competes with the art for visitors' attention. There are free **guided tours** in Italian every Saturday at 3pm; group tours are available the rest of the week by reservation (tel. 041/2719031, visite@palazzograssi.it, €80, €150 for Palazzo Grassi and Punta della Dogana).

DORSODURO
Accademia
(GALLERIA DELL'ACCADEMIA)
Gallerie dell'Accademia (Campo della Carità 1050, tel. 041/522-2247, www.gallerie-accademia.org, Mon. 8:15am-2pm, Tues.-Sun. 8:15am-7:15pm, €15) is Venice's answer to the Vatican museums and Uffizi in Florence,

although it's only a fraction of the size and much less crowded. The collection of paintings and sculptures is housed in a deconsecrated church and former confraternity that first opened to the public in 1817.

The collection spans the 13th to the 18th centuries. Paintings are arranged chronologically. There is no better place in the world to find Venetian masters like Mantegna, Titian, Tintoretto, Veronese, and Tieplo. Even the lesser-known works demonstrate brilliance and the Venetian love of vibrant colors and light. One of the most interesting pieces is Veronese's *Last Supper* that includes dogs, midgets, and drunkards. It was deemed too racy for the time and nearly got the artist locked up. He eventually passed the censors by changing the title of the work to *Feast in the House of Levi* (room 10).

Bags must be checked (€0.50) and fire regulations limit the number of visitors allowed into the museum at any one time. That causes a 30- or 45-minute wait in summer that can be reduced by reserving tickets in advance at the official museum website www.gallerieaccademia.org for a small fee. The **audio guide** (€6) helps reveal the story behind every canvas. Note that the various buildings have been undergoing renovation since 2005, which means less than half of the artwork is on display and many paintings have been temporarily moved.

★ Guggenheim Foundation

America's savviest art patron, Peggy Guggenheim, moved to Venice in 1949 and assembled a vast collection of modern art in Palazzo Venier. The **Guggenheim Foundation** (Fondamenta Venier 704 or 701, tel. 041/240-5411, www.guggenheim-venice.it, daily 10am-6pm, €15) is her legacy and a lasting gift to art lovers. It's located along the Grand Canal in a modest 18th-century *palazzo* where she lived and encouraged artists to push artistic boundaries until her death in 1979. The all-star cast of painters includes Chagall, Dali, Duchamp, and Miro, and other big names of 20th-century art.

The museum is entered through two stone archways that can be easily missed and lead to a peaceful sculpture garden that encourages lingering. The villa is smaller than you might expect and filled with eager visitors getting close-up views of Pollocks and Picassos. A photograph in each room shows how things looked in Peggy's time. Most of the furniture is gone but the artwork remains. If you have any questions about the art or the heiress, you can ask the multilingual interns stationed around the foundation. You can also enjoy the view of the canal from the terrace at the front of the building.

Visitors can opt for the **audio guide** (€7) or free 10-minute **talks** (daily 11am and 5pm) that focus on a different painting each day. There are also 30-minute **talks** (daily 10am and 4pm) in Italian and English about the life and times of Peggy Guggenheim. The café is bright but slightly overpriced and the foundation gift shop is down the street on Fondamenta Venier.

Basilica Santa Maria Della Salute

Basilica Santa Maria della Salute (Campo della Salute 1, daily 9am-noon and 3pm-5:30pm, free) dominates the entrance to the

the Guggenheim Foundation

Grand Canal and has dazzled visitors with its white baroque façade since it was erected in the 17th century. The basilica was commissioned by the Venetian senate in gratitude for the ending of the plague and consists of an octagonal plan topped by an enormous dome that can be seen from around the lagoon. The monumental steps are a wonderful place to sit and watch boats traveling up and down the canal.

Inside are works by Titian and Tintoretto as well as a small **gallery** (daily 3pm-5:30pm, small fee) in the sacristy to the left of the altar. There are frequent free concerts, usually on Saturday afternoons, when the massive organ is played. Venetians are still thankful to the Virgin Mary for ending the plague and every year on November 21 they show their respect. A pontoon bridge is built from San Marco and locals come to receive votive candles and gondoliers to have their oars blessed.

Punta della Dogana

Old and new are a surprisingly good fit in Venice, and there are several galleries where cutting-edge exhibitions are regularly organized. One of the individuals behind this renaissance is French businessman and enthusiastic art collector Francois Pinault, who somehow convinced the city to lease **Punta della Dogana** (Campo della Salute 2, tel. 041/271-9031, Wed.-Mon. 10am-7pm, €15 single or €20 combo with Palazzo Grassi) to his foundation. The former warehouse on the triangular tip of Dorsoduro was restored by the Japanese architect Tadao Ando and now hosts regular international art exhibitions and retrospectives. The 5,000-square-meter exhibition space is always filled with visually challenging installations that hit more than they miss. There are free **guided tours** in Italian every Saturday at 4:30pm; group tours are available the rest of the week by reservation (tel. 041/2719031, www.palazzograssi. it, €80, €150 for Palazzo Grassi and Punta della Dogana). Even if you don't like art, you should come for the spectacular **view** of

Basilica Santa Maria Della Salute

the lagoon from the easternmost tip of the neighborhood and long canal-side promenade facing Giudecca.

Squero San Trovaso

Although the number of gondoliers is in continual decline, new boats are still needed and old ones require repair, fresh paint, and regular maintenance. **Squero San Trovaso** (Fondamenta Bonlini 1097, tel. 041/522-9146, free to watch), one of only four gondola shipyards still active, can do all those things.

The best view of the small alpine-like huts and teams of workers hammering, sawing, and painting away is from Fondamenta Nani, which links the Grand Canal with the Giudecca Canal. There are usually several gondolas in dry dock being cared for by a team of workers. It can take up to a year to complete a new gondola, and each artisan has his own specialty handed down from generation to generation. Although there are occasional tours they prefer if you watch from afar unless you're interested in buying.

Campo Santa Margherita

Campo Santa Margherita is a relief from history. There are no major monuments, no earth-shattering churches, and no reason not to relax in this square. It's simply a popular university hangout lined with pretty houses, neighborhood shops, and regulars eating at affordable *trattoria*. Most mornings there's an animated fish and vegetable market, and there's always plenty of space on the red benches that dot the large rectangular square. The oddly positioned building at the southern end of the square is the confraternity where the tanners of the city once met.

San Giorgio Island
(ISOLA SAN GIORGIO)

The island of **San Giorgio** lies in front of Piazza San Marco and can only be reached by *vaporetto*. Travelers who make the extra effort can visit the **Chiesa di San Giorgio Maggiore** (Isola di San Giorgio Maggiore, daily 7am-6pm, free) and adjacent Benedictine monastery where Cosimo de Medici stayed while banished from Florence. The church was built by Palladio and houses several paintings by Tintoretto, but the main attraction is the view from the bell tower. The *campanile* inside the church complex is slightly smaller than its San Marco counterpart but lines to enter are shorter. There's a fee and the viewing platform is reached by an elevator that takes a little of the fun out of getting to the top.

The church and bell tower can be combined with a look at the permanent collection of the **Cini Foundation** (tel. 041/271-0217, www.cini.it, Apr.-Sept. daily 10am-5pm, Oct.-Mar. daily 10am-4pm, €5), which includes paintings, sculpture, and furniture. The foundation is located in a former monastery and has played an instrumental part in redeveloping the island and supporting local culture. The gallery and exhibition spaces can be visited daily, but if you want to see the cloisters, garden, *Last Supper*, library, and labyrinth you need to sign up for the **tours** organized by **Civita Tre Venezia** (tel. 041/220-1215 or 347/338-6426, www.civitatrevenezie.it, €10). These are held on Saturdays and Sundays at 11am, 1pm, 3pm, and 5pm.

The island can be reached via the number 2 *vaporetto* from the San Marco, Zattere, or Zitelle stops in a matter of minutes.

SAN POLO AND SANTA CROCE
Ca' Pesaro

Ca' Pesaro (Santa Croce, Fondamenta de Ca'

Isola San Giorgio

Pesaro 2076, tel. 041/721-127, www.capesaro. visitmuve.it) isn't just a pretty facade along the Grand Canal. It's also home to two remarkable museums in one stunning 17th-century *palazzo*. The first two floors are occupied by the **Galleria Internazionale d'Arte Moderna** (Tues.-Sun. 10am-6pm, €10 or Museum Pass) with works by Chagall, Kandinsky, Klee, Matisse, and Moore. This is also where many pieces from early editions of the Venice Biennale ended up. Highlights include *Giudetta II* by Klimt and a version of *The Thinker* by Rodin. Guided **tours** (education@fmcvenezia.it, €100/1-4 people) of the collection explore the artistic trends and innovations of the 20th century and last two hours.

Upstairs, the **Museo d'Arte Orientale** (tel. 041/524-1173, Tues.-Sun. 10am-6pm, €10 or Museum Pass) displays more than 30,000 artworks and artifacts Prince Enrico di Borbone gathered during his grand tour of Asia. It's the largest collection of Edo-era objects outside of Japan and a drastic departure from the Venetian landscape. There are kimonos, lacquer furnishings, porcelain, paintings, shadow puppets, weaponry, and many personal items. The dark wood-paneled rooms also contain jade-and-gold-painted shells from China. A short video in Italian and English explains the origins of the collection.

A single ticket provides entry to both museums. There's a small cafeteria, a cloakroom, and a bookshop near the main entrance.

Museum of Natural History
(MUSEO DI STORIA NATURALE)

Venice's natural history museum, **Museo di Storia Naturale** (Santa Croce, Salita Fontego 1730 1730, tel. 041/520-9070, www.museiciviciveneziani.it, Jun.-Oct. Tues.-Sun. 10am-6pm, Nov.-May Tues.-Fri. 9am-5pm and Sat.-Sun. 10am-6pm, €8 or Museum Pass), isn't just for kids interested in dinosaurs (although there are plenty of those)—it's the only place in Venice to learn about lagoon fauna and biodiversity. Many exhibits are interactive and several rooms contain pre-Roman artifacts dating from the Iron Age.

The Museo di Storia Naturale is housed in the former **Fondaco dei Turchi,** a warehouse used by Turkish merchants. (Foreign merchants operating in Venice all had their own designated warehouses.) This allowed city officials to keep an eye on their movements and confiscate money and weapons upon arrival. No Christian women or children were allowed to enter the area, which was originally equipped with a bathhouse and Turkish eateries. The Fondaco was used for trade until 1838 and eventually transformed into Museo di Storia Naturale after an extensive restoration one hundred years later.

Palazzo Mocenigo

The ornately decorated rooms of **Palazzo Mocenigo** (Santa Croce, Salizzada di San Stae 1992, tel. 041/721-798, www.mocenigo.visitmuve.it, Apr.-Oct., Tues.-Sun. 10am-4:30pm, Nov.-Mar., Tues.-Sun. 10am-3:30pm, €8 or Museum Pass) make it easy to imagine the lives of 18th-century aristocrats. The first floor is dedicated to perfume. In the 18th century, Venice was continually importing new scents from the Orient and transforming them into perfumes for the city's well-to-do. Visitors have an opportunity to smell the most popular scents of the day and visit a laboratory where this ancient craft was conducted. Upstairs is filled with fashionable Venetian clothing from yesteryear. The collection includes lavish ball gowns, hats, and shoes. The walls and ceilings of the former residence are covered in frescoes, textiles, and Murano chandeliers.

The museum conducts olfactory **workshops** (two hours, includes tour of museum) during which participants learn the basic concepts and classifications of perfume making and create their own personal scent. Workshops must be reserved at least four days in advance and are usually held weekdays from 10am to noon. The cost ranges €80-100 depending on the number of participants, which never exceeds 12. Participants must be over 18 years of age.

The Mocenigo family who once inhabited

the Palazzo included a number of doges and financed the **San Stae** church down the street from their residence. The grand classical façade is anything but modest and opens out on the Grand Canal where visitors wait on the watery steps for the next *vaporetto* to arrive.

★ Rialto Bridge

There are four bridges spanning the Grand Canal, but the Rialto is the grandest, and the one everyone wants to cross. It's divided into three lanes, the outermost of which provides good views of the canal. Like the Ponte Vecchio in Florence it's flanked with shops and has become a magnet for commercial activity. It's crowded at the best of times and can be difficult to cross let alone enjoy. Early mornings and late evenings are about the only time you can appreciate the harmonious stonework and twin archways in the middle without being bumped. The Rialto can also be viewed from the embankments on both sides of the canal, although the bridge is now partially covered in scaffolding and undergoing restoration that's scheduled to finish in 2017.

There's been a succession of bridges on the same spot since the 13th century and each increased in size as the city grew in power and wealth. The current version of the Rialto was the result of a competition held in 1524 to replace a wooden bridge. Although Palladio and Michelangelo were among the participants, a little-known local architect named Antonio de Ponte (*ponte* happens to mean bridge in Italian) got the job. He completed the project in less than three years using stone and a single 48-meter arch to span the canal. Critics at the time predicted the audacious design would end in collapse but so far the Rialto has passed the test of time.

Rialto Fish and Produce Markets

There are fish and vegetable markets in squares around the city where everyday Venetian life goes on as it always has, but the Rialto markets are the original center of the action. The area even has its own *vaporetto* stop. If you disembark at *Rialto Mercato* you'll discover a **fish market** (Tues.-Sat. 7:30am-1:30pm) where you can smell the authenticity. Early mornings are the best time to stroll underneath the shaded colonnades watching chefs, housewives, and old-timers carry on with gesticulating fishmongers. There are more kinds of fish and crustaceans

Rialto Bridge

than at any supermarket, and having a look is the perfect preview for lunch or dinner. Next door are the green stalls of the **fruit and vegetable market** (daily, 7am-5pm) that remain open until midafternoon and provide the latest harvest from the region and the rest of Italy.

Basilica di Santa Maria Gloriosa dei Frari

The Basilica di San Marco may be Venice's most famous church, but **Basilica di Santa Maria Gloriosa dei Frari** (San Polo, Campo dei Frari 3072, Mon.-Sat. 9am-5:30pm, Sun. 1pm-5:30pm, €3 or Chorus Pass, audio guide available) is the biggest—and that's not the only thing it has going for it. Inside the plain brick façade favored by Franciscan monks are works by Venetian masters including Vivarini, Bellini, and Titian, who died of the plague and is buried here along with several doges. A monument dedicated to him is near the entrance on the right while the enormous *Annunciation* he painted hangs over the altar. It's not just paintings that stand out—it's the overall craftsmanship visible in the choir stalls, tombs, murals, and wooden sculptures. The 15th-century choir in the center of the church is a masterpiece of carpentry, with 50 carved panels illustrating everyday life in Venice.

Scuola Grande di San Rocco

Scuola Grande di San Rocco (San Polo, Campo di San Rocco 3052, tel. 041/523-4864, www.scuolagrandesanrocco.org, daily 9:30am-5:30pm, €10) was the last confraternity founded in Venice and is the best preserved. The interior somehow avoided looting during Napoleon's sojourn in the city in 1797 and is filled with more than 50 paintings by Tintoretto. He won the competition to decorate the building by submitting a completed painting rather than the sketch the judges were expecting. Tintoretto later became a member of the brotherhood and spent the next 23 years painting the inside of the building.

Elaborate wall and ceiling paintings are located in the rectangular Sala Terrena on the ground floor where religious ceremonies were held, and upstairs in the Sala dell'Albergo where members gathered. Tintoretto began work on the Sala Capitolare next door in 1575 for a very reasonable 1,000 ducats per year, which was a little like getting a Ferrari for

Basilica di Santa Maria Gloriosa dei Frari

the price of a Fiat. Most of the paintings are religious in nature. Ceilings recount stories from the New Testament, including the *Fall of Man* and the *Sacrifice of Isaac,* while walls are dedicated to New Testament themes like the *Last Supper*. The Sala dell'Albergo contains Tintoretto's competition-winning entry *St. Roch in Glory* and a stunning *Crucifixion*. A written guide to the paintings is available in English at the entrance.

The Tintoretto tour can continue at the **Chiesa di San Rocco** (daily 9:30am-5:30pm, Sun. mass 11am, free) opposite the Scuola Grande. The church contains several paintings that predate his work in the confraternity and recount the life of St. Roch assisting victims of the plague. The church and school were both named after the saint and the brotherhood was active in plague relief.

Campo San Polo

Campo San Polo became the largest square in the *sestiere* when a canal was filled in and paved over. The parallel lines of white stone on the curved end of the square indicate exactly where the waterway once ran. Venetians have used the square for horse racing, bullfights, and masked *Carnevale* parties for centuries. Today it's a playground for children and a peaceful retreat for residents who sit on the red benches in the shade of a half-dozen trees. A newsstand at one near the flagpole gets used on special occasions. From July to September the *campo* is transformed into an **open-air cinema** (€5-8, or 6 films for €24) and throughout the Venice Film Festival films are projected after their Lido previews.

Chiesa di San Polo (Salita San Polo, Mon.-Sat. 10am-5pm, €3 or Chorus Pass), located in Campo San Polo, is even older than the square and was founded by Doge Pietro Gradonico in AD 737 with significant modifications in the 14th and 15th centuries. The church doesn't face the square and visitors must walk around the corner to reach the entrance and see the **bell tower** with the two stone lions carved into its base.

Grand Canal
(CANAL GRANDE)

The Grand Canal, one of Venice's top attractions, is the main waterway that snakes through the center of the city from Stazione Santa Lucia station to Piazza San Marco. The canal is lined with prestigious *palazzi,* churches, and former warehouses. It's very busy, especially on weekday mornings when boats of all kinds move up and down the canal making deliveries, removing trash, and shuttling residents and visitors between *vaporetto* stops. There is no continuous walkway beside the canal except near the train station, just north and south of the Rialto Bridge, and at the entrance to the canal itself in front of Santa Maria della Salute church. You can get inviting glimpses of the canal from the city's bridges, or from the many streets that lead to the water's edge, but the only way to see it all is by boat.

Jewish Ghetto

The word *ghetto* derives from the Venetian *geto,* a part of Cannaregio where iron foundries were located. It became associated with Jews during the 14th century when they were ordered to live in the area. Their lives were closely regulated: Although they could leave during the day, guards stationed along the canals made sure residents remained in the ghetto at night. It wasn't until Napoleon arrived in 1797 that the gates were removed and Jews allowed to live anywhere they liked. A small Jewish community is still based here around several synagogues and a handful of kosher restaurants and businesses.

Campo di Ghetto Nuovo is the center of the neighborhood. It's a large, unevenly shaped *campo* with a handful of trees and marble benches where workers and visitors pause for lunch. There are Holocaust memorials on several walls and a number of restaurants lining the square. (These are closed Saturdays during Sabbath and it's best to visit on weekdays or Sundays if you want to sample Venetian kosher.) The synagogue and **Museo**

Cannaregio

Ebraico (Cannaregio, Campo Ghetto Nuovo, tel. 041/715-359, www.museoebraico.it, Jun.-Sept. Sun.-Fri. 10am-7pm, Oct.-May Sun.-Fri. 10am-5:30pm, €4 or €10 with tour) are in the southwestern corner in front of the old rainwater wells and the tall wooden flagpole. The museum is divided in two parts that illustrate Jewish traditions and recount the story of Venetian Jews through objects, images, and first-hand accounts. **Synagogue tours** depart hourly between 10:30am and 5:30pm and are conducted in Italian and English.

There are several approaches to the Ghetto, but the historic route is along **Calle Ghetto Vecchio.** When approaching from the train station follow Rio Terra Lista all the way to Ponte delle Guglie. Cross the bridge, turn left, and take the second right through the underpass that marks the main entrance to the Ghetto.

Madonna dell'Orto Church
(CHIESA DELLA MADONNA DELL'ORTO)
Chiesa Madonna dell'Orto (Cannaregio, Fondamenta Madonna dell'Orto, Mon.-Sat.

10am-4:45pm, Sun. noon-4:45pm, €3) is one of the largest churches in the *sestiere,* which may explain why German troops used it as a stable during World War II. It was in bad shape for decades until an Englishman (buried in the chapel near the altar) bequeathed funds to restore the church. The elegant façade and modest interior now look as good as they did when the church was built in the 14th century. It's a great example of Venice's take on Gothic architecture and also happened to be Tintoretto's parish church. The artist donated over a dozen large-scale biblical paintings that draw a trickle of tourists. If you're lucky, Chiara (one of the many dedicated volunteers) will be on duty and can answer questions about the building or the artist. **Mass** is held daily at 9am and 11am on Sunday, but the massive organ originally intended for Teatro La Fenice is only played during weddings and funerals.

Tintoretto's former home and workshop are just over the bridge facing the church and to the left on Fondamenta dei Mori. Today, **Bottega del Tintoretto** (tel. 041/722-081, daily 10am-7pm, free) is used by a group of

Castello

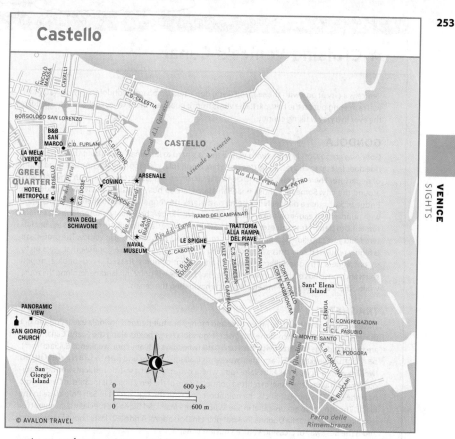

artisans, sculptors, printers, and lithographers. There are occasional tours, and if you're interested in ink and bookbinding it's worth a stop to watch Roberto and other members of the association at work.

Ca' D'Oro

Venice never fully embraced Renaissance architecture, and instead maintained the Gothic status quo long after the movement had gone out of fashion in other cities. This explains the intricate facades lining the Grand Canal. If you're going to enter any of these ornate family residences the **Ca' D'Oro** (Cannaregio, Calle Ca' D'Oro 3932, tel. 041/522-2349, Mon. 8:15am-2pm, Tues.-Sun. 8:15am-7:15pm, €6) is a good place to start. The home dates from the 15th century but it's the later restoration

that is visible today; it was donated to the city in 1916 along with an extensive collection of sculpture, tapestries, paintings, and pottery on display.

The ground floor contains a small courtyard with the original well and early 20th-century mosaic paving that leads to a private dock. Temporary exhibitions of modern artists are staged in the former reception halls upstairs while the smaller rooms are lined with religious paintings, including Mantegna's *St. Sebastian*. The best feature of the building is the terrace that overlooks the water and allows visitors to observe the comings and goings along the Grand Canal below. Ca' D'Oro is rarely crowded and the small museum bookshop can be a lonely place.

★ Cruising Venice's Canals

Venice is a city at one with the sea, and if you don't step on board a gondola, ferry, or water taxi you're missing out on the best part. The views from a boat help make sense of the city and seduce the eyes in a way walking cannot.

GONDOLA

Gondolas are so closely linked with Venice that it's hard to imagine one without the other, and a ride does live up to clichés. If you decide to hire a gondola, it's important to choose a good point of departure. There are eleven **gondola stations** as well as vessels docked in ones or twos around the city. Some, like those near San Marco, are so busy shuttling passengers under the Bridge of Sighs that a ride feels like being on a merry-go-round. You'll also share the experience with hundreds of eager onlookers and end up in who knows how many photographs. It's more romantic to depart from quieter *sestiere*, like Dorsoduro or Castello, where the canals are uncluttered and you can glide past one of the last *squero* (gondola workshops) in Venice. The profession is highly regulated, and prices are fixed at €80 for a 30-minute ride in a gondola that seats up to six passengers. The gondoliers themselves are romantic figures dressed in red- or blue-striped shirts and conscious of the historical role they hold. Some will point out landmarks along the route while others will keep to themselves, silently navigating the canals.

TRAGHETTO

Travelers who do not wish to invest time and money in a full-fledged gondola excursion can get the condensed experience at the *traghetti* (gondola ferry) points along the Grand Canal. There are three landings still in activity: **Santa Sofia** (weekdays 7:30am-7pm, weekends 8:45am-7pm), **San Tomà** (weekdays 7:30am-8pm, weekends 8:30am-7:30pm), and **Santa Maria del Giglio** (weekdays 7am-6pm, weekends 9am-7pm), where two-man teams shuttle residents and adventurous travelers across the canal in refitted gondolas. One of the ferry points is located in Cannaregio near the Ca d'Oro and connects the neighborhood with the fish market in San Polo close to the Rialto. The other two are up-canal in San Marco. Santa Maria del Giglio is especially convenient for reaching the Punta della Dogana lookout point in Dorsoduro. A ride (€2) lasts about five minutes and is the best way of crossing Venice's busiest canal.

VAPORETTO

Vaporetto, the aquatic equivalent of buses, are typical Venetian boats that carry up to 210 passengers and form the backbone of the city's public transportation network. They've been serving the city since the late 19th century. These motorized boats appear frequently at water stops dot-

Scuola Grande di San Marco

With an ornate entrance and a statue of a saint, it's easy to mistake **Scuola Grande di San Marco** (Castello, Rio dei Mendicante 6776, tel. 041/529-4323, Tues.-Sat. 9:30am-1pm and 2pm-5pm, €5) for a church, but the refined *palazzo* facing Campo Giovanni e Paolo isn't a religious building. Scuola Grande is a *scuola*, a Venetian version of the Lion's Club, founded by do-gooders in the 13th century and used as a fancy clubhouse until Napoleon abolished fraternal organizations in the city.

The façade is an eyeful, with interesting use of perspective, elaborate stonework that distinguishes Venetian Renaissance architecture from Florence and Rome—and plenty of lions. The grand entrance on the left leads to a reception hall while the relatively modest doorway on the right provides access to the *albergo*

Grand Canal

ted along the Grand Canal, around the city's circumference, and in outlying islands throughout the lagoon. *Vaporetto* can be crowded and finding a seat is often difficult, but standing along the open railing is the best position from which to observe the city. You can buy a single ticket (€7.50) but the best option is the 24-hour (€20) or 48-hour (€30) passes that allow you to get on and off as much as you like. *Vaporetto* are great any time day or night and make it easy to discover secluded parts of the city like Giudecca, Isola San Giorgio, and the Biennale Gardens, all of which are impossible or difficult to reach on foot.

The number 1 *vaporetto* from Piazzale di Roma is a good place to start. It makes 16 stops along the Grand Canal all the way to Piazza San Marco in 30-40 minutes. If you prefer to avoid commuters and want to learn about the city, board the **Vaporetto dell'Arte** (www.vaporettoarte.com) that stops along the Grand Canal; it is less crowded than standard *vaporetti*. Screens and audio guides recount the city's history and describe the buildings, bridges, and churches you're passing. Tickets are available from the **Hellovenezia office** (Piazzale Roma, tel. 041/272-2249, daily 8:30am-6:30pm), at automated machines, and directly on board. The 24-hour card costs €24 or €10 if you already have another travel card. The service is active from June until October with departures every 30 minutes.

(hotel) and is usually closed. The interior was stripped of artwork after the brotherhood disbanded but the two main rooms upstairs regained their former opulence after a lengthy restoration. *Sala Capitolare* contains a collection of medical artifacts and several paintings by the Tintoretto brothers recounting the life of St. Mark. The walls in *Sala dell'Albergo* next door are also dedicated to the saint. Both rooms have extraordinary engraved ceilings.

The square out front is one of the nicest in Castello and a nice place to linger. Café tables line the southern edge of the square underneath a bronze equestrian statue of a mercenary and gelato is near at hand. The cavernous **Basilica Santi Giovanni e Paolo** (daily 7:30am-6:30pm, €3) is the final resting place of many illustrious Venetians, with enormous stained glass windows from Murano that are best viewed from the inside.

The Smallest Street in Venice

Venice has dozens of streets that are narrow enough that a person could touch both walls at the same time. In these remote, dimly lit passages, silence reigns, and the city seems suddenly distant. Many are difficult to find and some are so narrow they don't appear on maps. Most travelers avoid these secret routes and choose more inviting directions, but the miniature streets of Venice are a remarkable and exciting part of the city's unique urban landscape.

There's debate on which *calle* is the smallest but most locals agree **Calletta Varisco** (Cannaregio, near Campo Widman) holds the title. At its narrowest point the alley measures 21 inches across and turns two-way pedestrian traffic into a game of Twister. Fortunately, there are few people around and once you pass the Doric column time stands still. The *calle* dramatically ends in a canal and one might wonder why it was built in the first place. Dead ends, however, are an essential part of the city's transportation network. Where paving stops, water always begins.

Across the Grand Canal in San Polo **Calle Stretta** (26 inches) connects Campiello Albrizzi with the Furatola underpass. To the north in Santa Croce near the Riva de Biasio water stop is **Calle di Ca' Zusto**, barely 27 inches wide. **Calesela dell'Occhio Grosso** near Campo dell Gorne underneath the walls of the Arsenale is a mere 23 inches wide.

San Giorgio Church
(CHIESA DI SAN GIORGIO)

Greeks have a long history in Venice. They were attracted to the city for its commercial ties to the Orient and tended to settle in Castello, and their numbers grew even larger after the Turks captured Constantinople in 1453. Soon the Orthodox community needed a church of its own. Permission to build the **Chiesa di San Giorgio** (Ponte dei Greci 3412, tel. 041/523-9569, Mon.-Sat. 9am-12:30pm and 2:30pm-4:30pm, Sun. 9am-1pm) was granted in 1498. The single-nave structure was completed a century later in one of the most tranquil parts of the city. The imposing bell tower cannot be visited, but the small museum adjacent contains a collection of Byzantine icons.

Arsenale

Venice wouldn't have been possible without an imposing fleet that controlled much of the Eastern Mediterranean and the islands of Crete and Cyprus. Those ships were built in the **Arsenale** (Castello, Campo del Arsenale, tel. 041/ 241-2020, infrequent openings), the world's first large-scale shipyard. The Arsenale was active for seven centuries, employing more than 2,000 workers at its peak, and takes up 15 percent of the city in the center of Castello.

Today, it's used by the Italian Navy and during the Venice Biennale as an exhibition space. The best view of the complex is from the wooden bridge at the end of Fondamenta dell'Arsenale. Four immense stone lions guard the imposing twin-tower entrance and demonstrate just how important the site was to the city. Although there are plans to transform the Arsenale into a cultural center, most of the area is closed to the public and open only during special exhibitions.

Naval Museum
(MUSEO STORICO NAVALE)

To get an idea of Venice's seafaring past head to **Museo Storico Navale** (Castello, Riva S. Bagio 2148, tel. 041/244-1399, daily 10am-5pm, €5), located near the Arsenale. This museum covers five floors and several centuries of history. The first two are the most relevant and document how Venice created and retained its naval empire. View extensive collections of navigational instruments, uniforms, and models of the vessels used for trade and warfare. Life-size merchant ships, warships, and gondolas can be seen in the adjacent **Padiglione Delle Navi** (Rio della

Tana Castello 2162/C, Mon.-Thurs. 8:45am-1pm, Fri. 8:45am-5pm, Sat.-Sun. 10am-5pm, €5). A single ticket covers entrance to both museums.

Riva degli Schiavone

Venice has a split personality, one that is depressingly crowded and another that's melancholy and panoramic. Sometimes the two can be experienced in a single location, and depending on the hour you may love or hate **Riva degli Schiavone**. In the early morning and evening this wide promenade that stretches from Piazza San Marco to the Biennale gardens is nearly deserted and the dramatic views of the lagoon can be enjoyed in relative peace. In between those times the embankment is lined with pleasure boats, souvenir stands, and itinerant salespeople hawking cheap gadgets to tourists and cruise ship passengers. Choose your time well, and remember that the farther you get from Piazza San Marco the quieter things become until you eventually reach the solitude of Sant' Elena Island at the southeastern tip of Venice.

Sant' Elena Island
(ISOLA SANT' ELENA)

There's little to see in the touristic sense on Sant' Elena Island—and that's what makes it worth visiting. It's out of the way even by Venetian standards and can take ages to reach on foot. It's easier to ride the *vaporetto* and get off at the Sant' Elena water stop. The island is wrapped in a tree-lined park and most of the residential housing in the center was built in the 1920s. There are few businesses and only a couple of simple eateries serving unadulterated classics. On the westernmost point is the modest Chiesa di Sant'Elena, where the remains of Emperor Constantine's mother are preserved. Nearby are two marinas filled with pleasure boats and the rickety stadium that plays host to Venice's lower-league soccer team.

GIUDECCA
Redentore Church
(CHIESA DEL REDENTORE)

Plagues were an everyday reality in 16th-century Venice, and when they hit they decimated the city's population. After nearly 50,000 people died from a plague in the early 1570s, it was only natural to commemorate the event by building a church. Palladio was commissioned and **Chiesa del Redentore** (Campo del SS. Redentore 195, tel. 041/275-0462, daily 10am-4:45pm, €3 or Chorus Pass) was completed in 1580. The exquisitely proportioned façade looks out over the waterfront and is topped with a white dome flanked by twin turreted spires.

Although the interior of the church was decorated by Bassano and Tintoretto, it's the overall harmony of the space that makes the church memorable. This is where the city's most popular festival takes place on the third Sunday in July, during which a pontoon bridge is erected between Giudecca and Dorsoduro that attracts thousands of fervent Venetians.

Food

Venetian culinary traditions have a lot to do with geography and history. Unlike the land-locked cities of Rome and Florence, Venice has easy access to the sea. The fisheries you may have noticed as your train approached the city raise sea bass, sole, and sardines that are available at the central fish market, which also sells shrimp, crab, and other crustaceans that end up on plates around the city.

Venice's status as a seafaring power meant that exotic flavors and spices like pepper, clove, and cinnamon were imported from around the Mediterranean and adapted into local dishes. Large communities of Jews, Greeks, and Turks also contributed a multi-cultural mix of dishes over the centuries.

Each *sestiere* is divided into smaller neighborhoods with their own church and, equally important, a bakery where residents come for bread and local pastries. These are wonderful shops with large gas or electric ovens where holey dough is baked daily for residents.

Dining Tips

Take care when selecting a restaurant in touristy Venice. Many eateries near the train station and along the major routes to the Rialto and San Marco rely entirely on the one-time tourist trade, and no Venetian with an appetite would ever eat there. Unfortunately, some restaurants may also add hidden charges to the bill or forget to inform diners that fish is priced by the gram, which can lead to astronomical bill. Conversely, if something sounds too cheap, it will probably taste cheap, too.

Expect the price of eating out to be higher than in Rome or Florence. (This is due to the added transportation costs, and tourists' willingness to pay high prices). Fish is pricier than meat, and it's hard to find a first course under €10 or a second under €15. Fortunately there are many wonderful places to eat and it's difficult not to be satisfied after a meal in Venice.

A final note: All food establishments are legally obliged to provide customers with a receipt. If they forget, please remind them by stating, *"Il scontrino per favore"* (Ill scon-TREE-no pear fah-VOR-ay). By doing so, you're helping encourage establishments to pay their taxes and therefore doing all Italians a subtle favor.

SAN MARCO
Venetian

With 20 seats, one waiter, and a chef, Ernesto Ballarin's small restaurant, **Vini da Arturo** (Calle Degli Assassini 365, tel. 041/528-6974, Mon.-Sat. noon-2:30pm and 7pm-10:30pm, closed Aug., €15, cash only) is a wonderful place to take a breather just north of Teatro Fenice. While many Venetian restaurants celebrate fish, meat and vegetables are the stars here. There are tender filets of beef, breaded pork chops *(maiale alla Veneziana)*, distinctive salads, and plenty of pasta *(spaghetti alla gorgonzola)*. On the wood-paneled walls are framed photos of satisfied celebrities. If you're curious to see all the famous faces Ernesto has fed, ask to see the photo albums.

La Rosticceria Gislon (Calle della Biscia, tel. 041/522-3569, daily 9am-9:30pm, €10) is the Venetian version of a diner. You can sit at a table or at the counter with locals vying for sandwiches and roast fish and meat dishes laid out in large tins behind the counter. This is where the postman goes for lunch. Most tourists are intimidated by the confusion inside, but it's hard to find a more affordable lunch spot so close to the Rialto. If the downstairs is too crowded there's additional seating upstairs.

Prosciutteria DOK (Ponte del Teatro 3989, tel. 041/296-0764, daily 10am-3:30pm and 5:30pm-1am, €10) has helped reinvigorate the city's culinary scene. DOK is a mini food emporium: The ground floor offers snacks created with local ingredients. Upstairs the open kitchen provides an ample selection of

Best Food and Drink

★ **Beccafico:** Enjoy fresh seafood with a Sicilian twist on an outdoor terrace overlooking one of the most vivacious squares in Venice (page 259).

★ **Caffè Florian:** This historic bar on Piazza San Marco dates back centuries—and has a faded elegance not even tourists can tarnish (page 262).

★ **Al Bottegon:** Enjoy one of the best *enoteche* in Venice from its wonderfully gritty interior or outside along the canal (page 263).

★ **Da Nico:** This century-old shop invented hazelnut and cacao-flavored *giandiotto)*. Its terrace has scenic canal views (page 263).

★ **Antiche Carampane:** The best fish in the city is served in a simple but elegant atmosphere (page 264).

★ **Cantina Do Mori:** Fresh fish, delivered daily, is transformed into delicious creamed cod and fried calamari, accompanied by *prosecco* (page 264).

★ **Vino Vero:** This hole-in-the-wall is packed with grape enthusiasts enjoying tempting *cicchetti* (page 268).

★ **Blue Bar:** This ornate second-story bar at the Aman Venice Resort Hotel overlooks the Grand Canal (page 273).

cured meats and cheeses along with steak tartar, pizza, or burgers that can be enjoyed at the counter or at a table within a bright and modern atmosphere. The rooftop terrace is a good place for sipping cocktails or craft beer. The kitchen closes late and DJs instigate dancing on Saturdays after 10pm.

Seafood

Campo Santo Stefano is one of the most vivacious squares in Venice, and dining on the outdoor terrace of upscale ★ **Beccafico** (Campo Santo Stefano 2801, tel. 041/527-4879, daily noon-3pm and 7pm-11pm, €15) is a treat. The restaurant provides a Sicilian twist on local specialties. The fresh fish and crustaceans are the best reason to come. First courses like pasta with sardines and commendable *zuppa di cozze* (mussel soup) are abundant and flavorful. The delicate seconds include grilled bream with citrus, stuffed swordfish, and large plates of fried fish and

vegetables. Sicilian-style pizza is also served at lunch and the kitchen closes later than most Venetian restaurants.

Antica Carbonera (Calle Bembo 4648, tel. 041/522-5479, daily noon-2:30pm and 6:30pm-10pm, closed Tues. and Wed. lunch, €15) has been maintaining Venetian gastronomic traditions since 1894. Portions are generous and served in copper skillets by an attentive staff. There are several dining rooms and the ground floor is decorated in salvaged nautical furnishings. It's cozy, especially if you sit in one of the booths lining the wall. Upstairs is a modern dining area and small terrace. The menu is all about fish, and *Crudité di Giornata* (raw fish plate) includes fresh salmon, sea bream, bass, tuna, shrimp, and oysters. Pasta and desserts are all handmade daily at this historic *trattoria*.

Cicchetti

Located on a quiet street near the Grand

Venetian Cuisine

Venice offers flavors unlike any others in Italy, and a world away from Rome or Florence. The results will surprise taste buds and make you rethink your definition of Italian food.

APPETIZERS (ANTIPASTI)

- *Sarde in Saor:* Fried sardines served with caramelized onions cooked in a vinegar sauce.

- *Baccalà mantecato:* Boiled and whipped cod spread on thin slices of fresh bread. Often also available as a second.

- *Insalata di mare:* Cuttlefish, shrimp, and celery salad dressed in lemon juice and olive oil.

FIRST COURSES (PRIMI)

- *Risotto:* Risotto plays a major role in the local diet and is usually served with *risi bisi* (peas) or *sparasi* (asparagus) in early spring and summer.

- *Spaghetti con le vongole:* Spaghetti and clams, available year-round.

- *Spaghetti al nero di seppia:* Pasta with cuttlefish ink seasoned with parsley, wine, and garlic.

- Other first courses include *zuppa di pesce* (fish soup), *pasta e fagiole* (pasta and beans), and *bigoli in salsa* (a thicker version of spaghetti) served with a sardine-and-onion sauce.

SECOND COURSES (SECONDI)

Fish is the king of second courses, and restaurants use all available varieties to prepare a vast range of dishes. It comes fried, grilled, baked, creamed, or marinated, and is usually very fresh. To get an idea of what your stomach can expect, take a stroll through the fish market near the Rialto that supplies many of the city's restaurants. *Bisato su l'ara* (eel), cuttlefish, *sardelle* (sardines), lagoon clams, soft-shell crab, sea bass, gray mullet, monkfish, calamari, and octopus are all grilled, fried, and sautéed into original dishes that are difficult to find anywhere else.

- *Fritto misto:* A heaping mixed plate of fried shrimp, calamari, sardines, and squid. Served in restaurants and *bacari*, where it can be ordered to go.

- *Bacalà con polenta:* Cod that's creamed or slowly stewed in tomato sauce and served with polenta.

- *Branzino al forno:* Sea bass baked with onions and tomatoes, topped with a lemon slice.

- *Fegato alla veneziana:* Pork or veal liver with white onions. Best accompanied by polenta.

Canal, **Osteria Enoteca al Volto** (Calle Cavalli 4081, tel. 041/522-8945, daily 10am-3pm and 6pm-10pm, €10) can satisfy any *cicchetti* craving. There isn't much room inside the wood-paneled interior, and most visitors stand at the bar sipping glasses of wine and wondering whether to order the creamed cod or fried calamari on a stick. If you're lucky,

one of the tables outside will be free and you can go back for seconds and thirds of the €2.50 house *prosecco.*

Bacarando (Calle dell'Orso 5495, tel. 041/523-8280, daily 10:30am-11pm) is one of the newer *bacari* bars in the city. It's spread out on two floors and features live music on Wednesday nights. There's seating outside

SIDES (CONTORNI)

Second courses are usually served unaccompanied by vegetables, so if you want to a little variety, you'll need to order a *contorno*.

- *Carciofi impanati:* Breaded artichokes.

- *Patate alla veneziana:* Beans, onions, and potatoes stewed in vegetable broth.

- *Melanzane alla giudea:* Jewish-style fried eggplant dish.

- *Polenta:* Polenta is common in northern Italy, but in Venice it's made from white corn flour and has a smoother consistency than the yellow variety.

WINE (VINO) AND OTHER DRINKS

There are dozens of local appellations to choose from in the Veneto region. White grape varieties tend to do better due to the colder climate, but there are exceptions. The house wine is a safe option.

- **Bardolino:** Dry red wine from the hills around Verona with a hint of bitterness and delicate aftertaste. Goes well with meat.

- **Soave:** Popular white wine produced from garganega or trebbiano grapes. Perfect as an appetizer or with pasta and fish.

- **Prosecco:** Widely produced sparkling white wine that's a valid alternative to champagne. Can be drunk as an aperitif, as a nightcap, or with a meal.

- **Spritz:** A mix of prosecco, Aperol or Campari bitters, and seltzer.

DESSERT (DOLCI)

Venetian desserts have Jewish, Austrian, and Middle Eastern roots and rely on cacao and nuts for sweetness and crunch. During the run-up to *Carnevale* fried *(frittole)* pastries stuffed with cream, raisins, or pine nuts appear in bakery windows, and most holidays are celebrated with a particular dessert. Fortunately, most sweets, like those listed below, are available year-round.

- *Pan di Doge:* Almond-covered biscuits baked in honor of the doge.

- *Moro di Venezia:* A large cookie shortbread, chocolate, and hazelnuts, available in most bakeries.

- *Pinza veneziana:* Rustic cake made with dried raisins and topped with pine nuts.

in a pleasant courtyard where a range of *cicchetti* (€1-2.50) can be enjoyed with inexpensive wine.

Pizza

Not all chain restaurants should necessarily be avoided. If you feel like having a Neapolitan pizza in Venice, **Rossopomodoro** (Calle Larga Rosa 404, tel. 041/243-8949, daily 11:30am-11:30pm, €10) can satisfy a *Margherita* craving. You won't wait long at this large, modern restaurant, which has indoor and outdoor seating and a wood-burning oven in one corner where you can watch pizza being prepared. Toppings are fresh and prices reasonable given the proximity to Piazza San Marco.

Bakeries

The Colussi family has produced six generations of bakers, which means they know what they're doing. Inside their marble-clad shop, **Colussi** (Campo San Lucia 4579, Mon.-Sat. 8am-2pm and 4:30pm-7:30pm), you'll find an array of breads and Venetian cookies including *Zaletti, Pan del Pescatore,* and *Buranelli.* Many are prepacked and make delicious gifts.

Gelato

Suso (Calle della Bissa 5453, tel. 348/564-6545, daily 11am-8pm, €3.50) is a small *gelateria* amid the busy streets around the Rialto and can be difficult to find. Flavors change according to the seasons and they're one of the only shops in the city to offer edible cups and cacao-flavored cones. *Moro di Venezia* and chocolate are the local favorites.

Coffee

The cafes of San Marco are nearly as famous as the square itself and have shared in the history of the city. They're extremely elegant, with chandeliered interiors, plush furnishings, and uniformed waitstaff who have spent a lifetime serving visitors from around the world. Each provides outdoor seating from where you can admire the monuments and listen to classical music played live on small stages facing the square.

This location and history comes with a price tag. Do not expect to pay the same for an espresso or *prosecco* in Piazza San Marco as in Campo Formaso. A cup of coffee that usually sells for €1.20 can cost €7 or more. If you add a couple of drinks, some snacks, and a dessert you could be looking at three-digit bill. Either you don't care and count it as a once-in-a-lifetime experience, or you can go inside and drink at the bar where there's as much atmosphere at a fraction of the cost. Prices vary, especially at institutions like Harry's Bar where Arturo Toscanini, Charlie Chaplin, and Orson Welles hung out. Legends have been replaced by tourists sipping expensive Bellinis and wondering what all the fuss is about.

★ **Caffè Florian** (Piazza San Marco 57, tel. 041/520-5641, daily 9am-midnight, €5 inside) has been in business since getting to the New World meant a long journey on a wooden ship. The cafe attracted Venice's nobles, politicians, and intellectuals. Today, the faded elegance and uniformed waitstaff provide an aura not even tourists can tarnish. The view of Piazza San Marco from the tables is wonderful, while the interior provides more intimacy. Inside there are distinctly themed rooms (Chinese, Oriental, Senate, and Illustrious) decorated in 18th-century style. This is where patriots plotted and artists hatched the idea of a Venice Biennale.

Caffè Quadro (Piazza San Marco 121, tel. 041/522-2105, daily 9am-midnight, €5 inside) doesn't disappoint with its mirrored walls, high ceilings, and gold-leaf moldings. At the counter you'll find a limited selection of high-quality *cicchetti* (€2 each) that can be accompanied by a glass of *prosecco* or spritz (€3.50). The coffee is excellent and quite affordable unless you're sitting down.

Harry's Bar (Calle Vallaresso 1323, tel. 041/528-5777, daily 10:30am-11pm, €15) opened in 1931 and attracted illustrious regulars like Hemingway, Charlie Chaplin, and Alfred Hitchcock. Today the regulars are mostly tourists soaking up the atmosphere at this landmark institution where you can sip expensive Bellini cocktails (€16) from wooden tables or at the counter. Food is available too, but it's equally pricey and nothing to write home about.

DORSODURO

Venetian

One of the places local Venetians can still be found enjoying traditional recipes and tapas is **Osteria da Codroma** (Fondamenta Briati 2540, tel. 041/524-6789, Tues.-Sat. 10am-4pm and 6pm-11:30pm, €14). Under soft lighting and white wooden beams you'll receive a warm welcome and are likely to be the only tourist in sight. Silver-haired septuagenarians and students from the nearby university occupy most of the dark rustic tables, enjoying *sardee in saor* (sardines with onions), marinated fish, spaghetti with cuttlefish ink, and other Venetian delicacies. The kitchen is actually located across the street, but that doesn't seem to bother the waitstaff.

Cozy **Enoteca Ai Artisti** (Fondamenta della Toletta 1169a, tel. 041/523-8944, Mon.-Sat. 12pm-3pm and 7pm-10pm, €14) is a little out of the way but worth finding. It's open from breakfast to dinner and serves creative *cicchetti* throughout the day. Fish is from the Rialto market and transformed into Venetian classics with an edge. The wine cellar is stocked with small Italian producers and the menu changes daily. Tables are limited inside, so if you don't want to be left standing at the bar arrive early or make reservations. Afterwards you can browse the shelves at **La Toletta,** one of the city's oldest bookshops, just down the street.

There is an entire menu of reasons to eat at **Pane Vino e San Daniele** (Campo dell-Angelo Raffaele 1722, tel. 041/523-7456, daily noon-2:30pm and 7pm-10:15pm, €13). Devoted out-of-towners have been known to travel kilometers for the grilled seasonal vegetables. Cured meat and steaks are some the best but vegetarians have nothing to fear. The flowered terrace on a hidden square are icing on the *tiramisu.*

Cicchetti

You can tell from the aging sign above ★ **Al Bottegon** (Fondamenta Nani 992, tel. 041/523-0034, Mon.-Sat. 8am-8pm, €6-10) that this *bacaro* has been around for a while. Inside, three generations of the Gastaldi family keep the institution running on good wine and addictive *cicchetti.* The grape selection is written on a chalkboard and features over 30 labels that can be ordered by the glass or carafe. This is one of the best *enoteche* in the city and the perfect place to enjoy red, white, or *prosecco* in a wonderfully gritty interior or outside along the canal.

Pizza

Order a slice or an entire pie at **Pizza al Volo** (Campo Santa Margherita 2944a, tel. 041/522-5430, daily 11:30am-4pm and 5pm-1:30am), a takeaway *pizzeria* with an oven in view and plenty of toppings from which to choose. It's a favorite with university students and travelers who appreciate the large portions at low prices. You can satisfy an appetite here for under €5 without sacrificing on quality—and you can enjoy the action in the square as you eat.

Gelato

★ **Da Nico** (Fondamenta Zattere al Ponte Lungo 922, tel. 041/522-5293, Fri.-Wed. 6:45pm-11pm, €4) is famous for the hazelnut and cacao-flavored *giandiotto* ice cream (€6) that was invented in Venice and has been served here for over 80 years. Besides the elegant interior there's a scenic terrace facing Canale della Giudecca where gelato connoisseurs gather to enjoy the 25 flavors on offer. The San Basilio water station is nearby, making this a sweet stop before or after a visit to Giudecca on board the number 2 *vaporetto.*

Just off Campo Santa Margherita, **Gelateria il Doge** (Rio Terra Canal 3058a, €2.50-5) quenches sweet cravings. They scoop great ice cream and refreshing Sicilian *granite* ices into cones or cups inside or from a streetfront window. All-star flavors include coffee, hazelnut, *tiramisu,* and the house specialty *Crema del Doge.*

Coffee

Something about Caffè La Calcina, now known as **La Piscina** (Fondamenta Zattera Ai Gesuiti, tel. 041/520-6466, Tues.-Sun. 11am-10:30pm), attracted poets, novelists, playwrights, and their admirers. John Ruskin spent the spring of 1877 at the hotel upstairs working on *The Stones of Venice,* and Rainer Maria Milke would meditate at the bar. Although the name has changed since its 19th-century heyday, the emotion remains. One look at the view and it's easy to be inspired. Beyond the tables set on a pier is the mysterious low skyline of Giudecca. It's hard to resist feeling romantic.

SAN POLO AND SANTA CROCE

Seafood

Being hard to find keeps ★ **Antiche Carampane** (San Polo, Rio Terrà Rampani 1911, tel. 041/524-0165, Tues.-Sat. 12:30pm-2:30pm and 7:30pm-11pm, €20) real. There's no pizza, no tourist menu, and no watered-down traditions here—just some of the best fish in the city served in a simple but elegant atmosphere. If you haven't had a three-course meal yet in Italy this is the place to have it. The raw fish, spider crab (*grancevola*), and turbot fillet (*rombo*) are stalwarts of a menu that changes according to what's available at the fish market. Expect superb desserts you won't want to share and a small, carefully selected wine list. Getting a table here can be difficult especially during the Venice Film Festival when stars like Uma Thurman and Audrey Tautou have been known to make appearances.

Cicchetti

The shelves at ★ **Cantina Do Mori** (San Polo, Ruga due Mori 429, tel. 041/522-5401, daily 8am-7:30pm, €7) are lined with large vats of red and white wine on tap. The long wooden counter fills up fast during *aperitivo* with clients jostling to order triangular *tramezzini* sandwiches stuffed with crab, shrimp, and other lagoon delicacies. Legend has it that Casanova was a regular at this historic *bacaro*, where you can forget about itineraries and just enjoy Venice.

Nearby, **Cantina do Spade** (San Polo, Calle do Spade 859, tel. 041/521-0583, €12-15) has a dark wood interior with a glass case filled with *cicchetti* that include fried calamari, stuffed zucchini flowers, creamed cod, and liver pâté. It's one of the few old-style *bacari*, with inside seating and plenty of red and white wine along with regional beer such as Pedavena lager.

A popular spot with street-side seating and a rustic look is **All'Arco** (San Polo, Calle Arco 436, tel. 041/520-5666, Mon.-Sat. 8am-2:30pm, €8). The friendly staff is always busy making plates of tempting appetizers that often include their famous boiled beef sandwich. Most of the *cicchetti* come from the nearby fish market and the owner will happily explain any mystery ingredients. The only drawbacks are the lines and the early closing time.

There are several *bacari* in the squares adjacent to the Rialto. **Bancogiro** (San Polo, Campo San Giacometto 122, tel. 041/523-2061, Tues.-Sun. 9am-midnight, €8) is under the portico where wealthy Venetians sent their servants to pay and collect outstanding debts. You can sample the miniature surprises chef Jacopo Scarso creates at the small bar, or you can sit down for something more substantial and equally delicious with a view of the Grand Canal. For a great look at the Rialto and fabulous *cicchetti*—all priced at €2 and featuring salmon, cod, and tuna toppings—head to **Naranzaria** (San Polo, Campo Erberia 130, tel. 041/724-1035, daily 10am-midnight, €8). You can stand at the bar or take a seat outside a stone's throw from the bridge. Every Sunday local groups play jazz, rock, and soul. This is also one of the rare *bacaro* that stays open after midnight.

Al Merca (San Polo, Fondamenta Riva Olio 213, 346/834-0660, Mon.-Thurs. 10am-2:30pm and 6pm-8pm, Fri.-Sat. 10am-2:30pm and 6pm-9:30pm, €5) is in the adjacent *campo* and one of the smallest *bacaro* in the city. There's hardly room to enter and consider which of the miniature *panini* sandwiches to sample. Most cost €2.50 and are filled with prosciutto, meatballs, salami, or creamed cod. There's a classic assortment of red and white wines, local beers, and spritz. Diners stand outside holding plates in hand or reclining on the nearby steps.

Street Food

Most of the *frittolini* stands that once dotted the city and served fried fish and *polenta* have disappeared, but **Fritto & Frutta** (Santa Croce, Fondamenta dei Tolentini 220, tel. 041/524-6852, Mon.-Sat. 10:30am-8:30pm, €9) carries on the tradition in an innovative way.

★ Sampling *Cicchetti*

Venetian finger food

A gastronomic highlight of any Venetian vacation is sampling the delicious assortments of finger food known as *cicchetti,* which. Reminiscent of tapas, *cicchetti* consists of sliced bread topped with creamed fish, sautéed vegetables, cheese, and many other enticing ingredients. Chefs take advantage of the abundance of fresh calamari and octopus and serve them raw or dipped in light batter and fried.

You get *cicchetti* at *bacari,* traditional Venetian bars that also serve wine by the glass or pitcher. Most *bacari* are delightfully unglamorous institutions that have been around for generations. They're usually small and darkly lit with rustic interiors where patrons stand around socializing and enjoying an assortment of *cicchetti.* The staff may be brusque, and they open and close early. A crowded sidewalk near a *bacaro* is always a good sign.

To order, get the proprietor's attention and point to the *cicchetti* of your fancy. In a matter of moments, they will be served on a small tray and ready to eat. Individual portions cost €1-2 and are the low-cost way of sampling a variety of local dishes. Be sure to order a glass of prosecco, Venetian sparkling white wine, to savor with your snacks.

Every neighborhood has at least one *bacaro,* though they are particularly common in San Polo, where workers from the nearby markets come for snacks. You'll find many hidden along the narrow street north of the Rialto off the main streets. Once you've tried one, it's hard to resist *bacari* hopping. Start near the fish market that supplies many of the ingredients for this quintessential dish and continue sampling *cicchetti* along the Fondamenta della Misericordia in Cannaregio and in lively squares like Campo Santa Margherita in Dorsoduro.

Here are some good places to get your *cicchetti* fix:

· Al Timon (page 268)

· Vino Vero (page 268)

· Al Bottegon (page 263)

· Cantina Do Mori (page 264)

The owner doesn't use oil for frying; he instead employs an oven technique he will happily explain. Fresh fish, vegetables, and rice dishes are served in paper cones of various sizes that can be eaten at the stools overlooking a canal or on the road. Quantities are generous and prices honest. Andrea also prepares a number of vegetarian options and tasty fruit shakes inside his inviting shop.

Lino Fritto (San Polo, Campo de le Beccarie 319, tel. 041/822-0298, Tues.-Sat. noon-3pm and 7pm-10pm, €10) is opposite the fish market. There's no better location for a *bacaro*. The bright white interior is bereft of seating and it's more of a snack bar serving original fish concoctions and fried calamari. Choose a few of the tempting miniature dishes and enjoy them inside or out.

Vegetarian

Venice has more vegetarian restaurants per capita than Florence or Rome, and going meatless here is easy. **La Zucca** (Santa Croce, Calle dello Specier 1762, tel. 041/524-1570, Mon.-Sat. 12:30pm-2:30pm and 7pm-10:30pm, €14) is a cozy *osteria* with a soothing wood-paneled interior and street-side seating. The kitchen prepares imaginative pasta dishes like *tagliatelle con carciofi e pecorino* and *lasagna con zucchine e mandorle*. Waiters are happy to list ingredients, and there are several fish and duck options for carnivores. Reservations are useful in high season.

Pizza

Venetian pizza is thick and closer to *focaccia* than the thin kind served in Rome. *Pizzerie* and by-the-cut shops are not very common but you can usually find them along the busier streets in the center. **Antico Forno** (San Polo, Ruga Ravano 973, tel. 041/520-4110, daily 11:30am-9:30pm, €4) is a new entry that specializes in reasonably priced takeaway pizza. Toppings aren't overly elaborate and the best sellers are the *marinara* and *margherita*. There's no seating inside but you can enjoy a slice in the tranquility of Campo di San Silvestro a couple minutes away.

Bakeries

You can sample traditional Venetian pastries at **Pasticceria Bucintiro** (San Polo, Calle Fianco della Scuola 2229, tel. 041/721-503, €4). This is where taste matters more than the decoration, which is rigorously old fashioned and hasn't changed since the 1970s-era display cases were installed. Gino Zanin runs the oven and prepares a vast selection of traditional cookies, *brioche*, and *frittelle* that are displayed in the windows beside the small bar. You can order sweets to go or have them inside with tea, hot chocolate, or coffee.

Panificio Albonico (Santa Croce, Calle della Regina 2268b, tel. 041/524-1102, Mon.-Sat. 7:30am-7:30pm, €4) is on a narrow thoroughfare where walking sometimes gets difficult. This homey, wood-paneled bakery provides instant relief from the crowds and during *Carnevale* season prepares all sorts of fried *frittelle* treats. The rest of the year you'll find olive buns, mini pizzas, and *pincia*, a traditional sweet bread that comes in many varieties and that the owners will be happy to explain.

Gelato

Before you proclaim your favorite *gelateria* in Venice visit ★ **Gelato di Natura** (Santa Croce, Campo San Giacomo dall'Orio 1623, tel. 340/286-7178, daily 10:30am-11pm, €3.50), where Pierangelo has been churning out organic ice cream since 1982. All the flavors are made fresh daily using the finest ingredients, including hazelnuts from Piedmont and Sicilian pistachios that are mixed with organic milk, eggs, and mascarpone. There's something for every palate inside this attractive shop with bilingual labels next to every vat. They also create mint, lemon, and pear sorbets on sticks as well as vegan and lactose-free options that don't sacrifice flavor.

Yogurteria White (San Polo, Ruga Vecchia 480, tel. 041/528-5109, €4) is unlike any other *gelateria* in the city. It's a self-service shop with rows of machines where you can fill up cones or cups with gelato and frozen yogurt and decorate them with chocolate, praline, hazelnut, or syrup toppings. The gelato is creamy and fun to prepare but be careful not to get overzealous—price is by weight and quickly adds up.

Coffee

The best thing about Italian coffee bars is that they nearly always serve delicious pastries to accompany a cappuccino or espresso. The selection at **Pasticceria Rizzardini** (San Polo, Campiello Meloni 1415, tel. 041/522-3835, €3) is extensive, and once you've selected a *crostata* or *canolo* pastry you can order a coffee at the metal counter. It's standing room only inside this classic bar with few signs of modernity and plenty of local drama.

Caffetteria Goppion (San Polo, Ruga Rialto 644, tel. 041/523-7031, daily 7am-7pm, €3) combines years of experience with the best-quality coffee. The cheerful staff busily grind beans and serve cups to locals and visitors waiting anxiously at the long counter. There are sweet and salty snacks throughout the day at this pleasant bar with large plate-glass windows through which you can observe the flow of daily Venetian life.

CANNAREGIO AND CASTELLO

Venetian

If you want to find a table at ★ **Al Portego** (Castello, Calle della Malvasia 6014, tel. 041/522-9038, daily 10:30am-2:30pm and 5:30pm-10:30pm, €12) you need to reserve in advance or arrive early. This small *osteria* five minutes from the Rialto is popular and tables fill up fast. Fortunately, you can sample their fish *cicchetti* while you wait. Once you do sit down it can be difficult to get a server's attention, but service is friendly and prices are reasonable. It's a good place to try Venetian classics like *baccalà mantecato* and *bigoli* pasta prepared the old-fashioned way.

Tucked between Chiesa della Madonna dell'Orto and Fondamenta della Misericordia, cozy **Osteria dei Mori** (Cannaregio, Campo dei Mori 3386, tel. 041/524-3677, Wed.-Mon. 12:30pm-3:30pm and 7pm-midnight, €15)

is usually filled with locals. The menu provides a good mix of meat and fish to which the Sicilian chef adds a dash of southern Italian flavor. Notable dishes include the fried fish and vegetable plate along with a memorable *baccalà mantecato* (creamed cod). Rubbing the steel nose of the statue outside is said to bring good luck.

Castello is one of the less-visited parts of the city, which makes it one of the least expensive. **Trattoria alla Rampa del Piave** (Castello, Via Garibaldi 1135, tel. 041/528-5365, Mon.-Sat. 12:30pm-3pm and 7:30pm-10:30pm, €8) is proof of that. The *trattoria* is located at the end of Via Garibaldi in front of a red flagpole and a floating fruit and vegetable market. The decor is nothing special but the simple interior is often packed with locals taking advantage of the fixed-price lunch menu (€13). It's a good place to try *risi e bisi*, *polenta e baccala* (cod), and *spaghetti al nero*. The casual vegan option nearby is **Le Spighe** (Castello, Via Garibaldi 1341, daily 9:30am-2:30pm and 5:30pm-7:30pm, €6), where Doriana sells organic dishes by the kilo and serves them at a convivial communal table.

Put expectations aside and make a reservation at **Covino** (Castello, Calle Pestrin Castello 3829a, tel. 041/241-2705, Thurs.-Mon. noon-3pm and 7pm-1am, Wed. 7pm-1am, €15, cash only). This wonderfully intimate restaurant with a festive host provides a multitude of flavors that blend tradition with creativity. A fixed-price menu (€36) includes a choice of starter, second, and dessert. Depending on the season this could include tartare, sardines, baked cod, veal sausage, tiramisu, and chocolate. Tables are close together and the restaurant gets loud—but that's because everyone is having a good time.

Seafood

Any place decorated with rolling pins, vinyl records, and a vintage hand-cranked cash machine deserves a chance. Fortunately, the food at **Osteria Bentigodi** (Cannaregio, Calle Farnese 1423, daily 7am-12:30pm and 6:30pm-2am, €15) lives up to the rustic and eclectic interior. Cuttlefish with polenta, Venetian sardines, and lightly fried fish come at a price worth paying.

Venetians like their fish fried, and the mother/daughter team at **Frito-Inn** (Cannaregio, Rio Terà Campo San Leonardo, 333/597-819, Tues.-Fri. 9:30am-9:30pm and Sat.-Sun. 9:30am-11:30pm, €8) are happy to oblige this passion. This tiny joint around the corner from a busy street can be smelled before it's seen. They fry a range of fish and vegetables but the house specialty is the calamari and shrimp rolled in flour, fried in sunflower oil, and served in a paper cone perfect for carrying away or eating on the chairs facing the small square.

Cicchetti

★ **Vino Vero** (Cannaregio, Fondamenta della Misericordia 2497, tel. 041/275-0044, Tues.-Sun. 11am-midnight, Mon. 6pm-midnight, €6) is packed with a young crowd of grape enthusiasts. The wine list covers an entire wall and the *cicchetti* are temptingly lined up behind a glass case on the counter where clients jostle to be served. It's a small, modern space, but there are some stools outside and they serve *crostini* on ingenious wooden trays with glass holders that make it easy to eat and drink while standing.

Al Timon (Cannaregio, Fondamenta della Misericordia 2754, tel. 041/524-6066, daily 6pm-1am, €10) is a small *osteria* just north of the Ghetto that caters to snackers and diners. At the counter, the best *cicchetti* in the neighborhood wait to be ordered, while the restaurant prepares Venetian-Tuscan dishes. If you missed out on *bistecca alla fiorentina* in Florence this is the place to go. There's a row of canvas-backed chairs and tables facing the canal but the best seats are on the boat moored out front where musicians occasionally perform and groups of friends gather.

Pizza

Pizza isn't that common in Venice and most *pizzeria* also serve traditional dishes. **Ai Tre Arch** (Cannaregio, Fondamenta San Giobe 552, tel. 041/716-438, Wed.-Mon. noon-3pm and 6pm-11pm, €12) prepares over 50 kinds of pizza, with original toppings that take a while to choose. Staff is friendly and there are shaded tables overlooking Canale di Cannaregio.

Street Food

Fondamenta della Misericordia is a great destination day and night for street food and drink. This canal-side street boasts dozens of restaurants, bars, and *bacari* where locals and visitors huddle outdoors on sidewalks enjoying good food and wine. Don't be intimidated by the chaotic lines—just jump right in and persevere until you're served. Go back and forth between these informal establishments until you find your favorite.

At **Paradiso Perduto** (Cannaregio, Fondamenta della Misericordia 2540, tel. 041/720-581, Thurs.-Mon. 11am-midnight, €10) there's usually a line of people waiting to choose from the counter filled with plates of fried fish dishes. When it's your turn, point to as many delicacies as you can handle. Most of the internal seating fills up early but you can sit along the canal and enjoy a cup or carafe of house wine. There's a regular calendar of musical performances on the small stage inside.

Bakeries and Chocolate

On a busy corner with trisecting streets is ★ **VizioVirtu** (Castello, Calle Forneri 5988, tel. 041/275-0149, daily 10am-7:30pm, €5), a chocolate hideaway. Once you've passed through the well-worn wooden doors of this chocolate boutique, the world disappears. Virtuous Vice is an appropriate name, since this is where cacao gets transformed into tempting pralines waiting to be devoured. There's a fine assortment of sweets, including many exotic flavors, gelatin candies, and homemade gelato. Just point and let Maria Angela place your treats in a small plastic sachet for takeaway.

El Fornareto (Cannaregio, Calle del Forno, tel. 041/522-5426, Mon.-Sat. 6am-1:30pm and 4:30pm-7:30pm, €3) is one of

Venice's oldest bakeries and is equipped with a 19th-century oven in full view. If you're interested, Silvia will open it up and reveal the scorching interior where loaves of bread and pastries are baked. Mornings are the best time to visit—the bread is still warm and the sweets haven't sold out yet.

Gelato

There are fewer *gelateria* in Venice than in Rome or Florence, but the ice cream is just as good and prepared with care and attention to ingredients. The local flavor is *Crema del Doge* (vanilla cream), which is available at **Gelateria Ca' d'Oro** (Cannaregio, Strada Nuova 4273b, daily 10:30am-11pm, €1.80-4.50) alongside some of the shop's own unique creations. Cones and cups come in four sizes and can be enjoyed in the adjacent square off the main street.

La Mela Verde (Castello, Fondamenta de l'Osmarin, tel. 349/195-7924, daily 11am-8pm, €3.50) is located on a pleasant canal near the Greek Orthodox church. The gelato and sorbet are made on site by a friendly staff who take the time to explain the flavors of the day and allow customers to sample them before choosing between pistachio, *torroncino, limone,* and many others. They've recently started serving chocolate filled crepes.

Coffee

It's easy to find a bar in Venice. It's not so easy to find one that serves great coffee and pastries at a decent price. **Pasticceria da Bonifacio** (Castello, Calle degli Albanesi 4237, Fri.-Wed. 7am-8pm, €3) also happens to be around the corner from Piazza San Marco and isn't just a breakfast stop. If you happen in around midafternoon you can enjoy an *aperitivo* along with light snacks before taking a walk along the canal-side promenade at the end of the street.

GIUDECCA
Seafood

Fewer tourists venture to Giudecca than other parts of the city, and as a consequence it has fewer places to eat. Most of these are located along the Giudecca Canal; **La Palanca** (Fondamenta di Ponte Piccolo 448, tel. 041/528-7719, Mon.-Sat. 7am-9pm, €12-15) is near the water station of the same name facing Dorsoduro. There's a good chance you'll be greeted by the jovial Andrea Barina and seated outdoors at one of the tables along the water in the shade of the large umbrellas. The menu has five or six pasta dishes with or without fish and a dozen seconds including grilled calamari, *seppie con polenta,* creamed cod, and a daily fish special.

Nightlife and Entertainment

When the sun goes down, Venice is transformed. An exodus of tourists and workers drains swiftly out of the city, reducing a daytime population of 100,000 to less than half that number. The result is invigorating for anyone who stays behind to explore the abandoned city at night. Take a starlit stroll and enjoy the silence. If you want human contact you can find it, although anyone with images of Casanova-style decadence will be disappointed. You won't find discos or dancing, though there's no shortage of canal-side bars, lively squares, and rustic *enoteche* where wine is decanted. After-dinner diversions include listening to classical music, gambling at the casino, and sipping cocktails inside five-star hotels. The drink of choice is a white sparkling wine called *prosecco* that's produced in the Veneto region and could be mistaken for champagne. It's poured everywhere across the city and accompanied with delicious finger food known as *cicchetti*. Also quintessential to Venice is spritz, a drink consisting of *prosecco,* Aperol or Campari bitters, and seltzer. A spritz or one glass of prosecco may be all the nightlife you need.

One of the most popular nighttime areas with Venetians and visitors is **Campo Santa Margherita** in Dorsoduro. The large rectangular square is dotted with bars that are filled from happy hour to the early hours. **Campo Erberia** overlooking the Ponte di Rialto in San Polo is also reliably animated. Sure signs of nightlife can always be found along Cannaregio's **Fondamenta della Misericordia,** lined with *bacari,* restaurants, and wine bars.

SAN MARCO
Bars

The **Devils Forest Pub** (Calle Stagneri 5185, tel. 041/520-0623, daily 11am-1am) is a favorite with American and English visitors who become remarkably agitated whenever soccer or rugby is playing on the large TVs. It can be fun to partake in the joy and pain of supporters even if you don't know about the offside rule or how to score a *try* (touchdown). Regardless of the results everyone enjoys the beer at this authentic-looking pub with Strongbow, Guinness, and Harp on tap and wooden booths in the back.

    Bar Campanile (Calle Larga 310, tel. 041/522-1491, daily 8am-midnight) is just north of Piazza San Marco and has a different personality depending on the time of day. In the morning it's about coffee, at lunch it's tramezzini sandwiches, and at night the cocktails kick in. Staff are friendly and spritz can be ordered any time, but if the Cuban bartender is on duty you should try his mojito. Prices are cheaper if you stand at the bar, where drinks are served with light snacks, although there's not much room after dark and it remains crowded with Venetians and visitors until closing. There are DJ sets on Saturdays.

    Even if most Hard Rock Cafès make you blush, the **Hard Rock Cafè di Venezia** (Bacino Orseolo 30124, tel. 041/522-9665, daily 11am-11:30pm) is different. You can tell from the red Murano chandelier hanging from the ceiling and the Venetian tiles on the floor. The music is good, the drinks are strong, and the views *do* rock. The café

is located near Piazza San Marco in an historic *palazzo* overlooking a gondolier station. It's the smallest Hard Rock in Europe, which makes it only half a travel sin.

Wine Bars

Wine rarely goes without food in Italy and you can choose either at **Osteria Enoteca Rusteghi** (San Marco, Campielo del Tentor 5513, tel. 041/523-2205, daily 11:30am-3pm and 6:30pm-3am, €12). This wine bar hidden away in a tiny courtyard near the Rialto lies just beyond the tourist masses, and it's where Giovanni D'Este keeps the art of Venetian hospitality alive. He's usually stationed behind the counter pouring difficult-to-find wines to clients who eagerly listen to his gastronomic tales. Most glasses are €6-8 and can be accompanied by *bruschetta,* cheese plates, and other appetizers. It's best after dark when locals take back their city.

Hotel Bars

Inside the expensive **Gritti Palace Hotel** (San Marco, Campo Santa Maria del Giglio, tel. 041/794-611, www.thegrittipalace.com) is the **Longhi Bar** (11am-1am), where you can order the cocktail of the same name and sit back amid the opulence of mirrored walls, 18th-century paintings, and antique settees. Hemingway called this the best hotel in the city and never passed up an opportunity for a drink. Today Cristiano Luciano does the mixing with style, clad in black-tie attire. The bar serves light fare along with champagne and oysters on weekends. The drink of choice is the Longhi, which contains Campari, dry vermouth, China Martini, and orange. If you prefer to drink outdoors try the **Riva Lounge** on the terrace facing the Grand Canal.

Opera and Concerts

There are few large concert halls in Venice. Historically, most nobles had music played to them in their homes, and today associations of musicians perform in churches and historic *palazzi.* These are less formal performances in splendid settings that are accessible to all and a great way to begin or end an evening. Repertoires nearly always feature local favorite and homegrown Venetian Antonio Vivaldi, but baroque and opera classics are frequently performed. *The Four Seasons* is at the top of the hit list and played nearly every evening at different venues. Tickets are reasonably priced given the quality of the music and the surroundings.

Teatro La Fenice (Campo San Fantin 1965, tel. 041/786-672, www.festfenice.com, €38.50-180) is one of the meccas of lyrical music, and if you enjoy opera—or even if you're just curious—this is the place to see it. The season runs from September to mid-July and nearly always includes crowd pleasers like *La Traviata* and *Madame Butterfly*, which are subtitled in Italian and English. Tickets aren't cheap and the most affordable seats in the upper galleries sell out fast. Most performances begin at 7pm and can last up to three hours with several intermissions. Jacket and tie are expected on opening nights, but semi-elegant will do after that; any unnecessary items must be checked into the cloakrooms. The theater also presents a varied symphonic program performed by its own philharmonic (www.filarmonica-fenice.it) and many illustrious guest conductors.

La Fenice may be the most famous theater in Venice but **Teatro Goldini** (S. Marco 4650b, tel. 041/240-2011, www.teatrostabileveneto.it, €8-35) is the oldest still in existence and may have the best acoustics in town. The theater has a capacity of over 1,000 and an intimate four-tiered interior where drama takes center stage. Sundays are reserved for families and shows that anyone can enjoy. The rest of the time many of Italy's finest actors are performing in a variety of plays, and concerts by international musicians are arranged.

The **Interpreti Veneziani** (tel. 041/277-0561, www.interpretiveneziani.com, showtime 9pm, €28) are one of the oldest chamber groups in the city and have recorded dozens of albums and toured widely. The ensemble consists entirely of string players and performs in **Chiesa San Vidal** (Campo San Vidal/Santo Stefano) across from the Ponte dell'Accademia bridge. Concerts are held daily during the summer and there's a pretty good chance of listening to Vivaldi's *The Four Seasons* as well as lesser-known compositions by the Venetian native. Tickets may be purchased directly at the church and performance begin at 9pm.

I Musici Veneziani (Scuola Grande di San Teodoro, tel. 041/521-0294,www.imusiciveneziani.com, 8:30pm, €28/€38) are big fans of Vivaldi, whose works they regularly perform, but they're also passionate about baroque and opera. They play the greatest hits of Verdi, Puccini, Rossini and many others inside an historic *palazzo* with great acoustics. All the musicians and singers dress in 17th-century regalia, which adds instant drama to every performance.

Vivaldi sounds better in Venice and the **Virtuosi di Venezia** (San Marco, tel. 041/528-2825, www.virtuosidivenezia.com, 8:30pm, €28) is one of the reasons why. This small chamber orchestra regularly pays tribute to the composer and performs both *The Four Seasons* along with opera medleys. The arias feature a talented tenor and mezzosoprano who sing in the Ateneo di San Basso overlooking Piazza San Marco.

If you want to experience opera up close, to be within inches of sopranos and listen to the classics in an intimate setting, then **Musica Palazzo** (Palazzo Barbarigo Minotto, Fondamenta Duodo or Barbarigo 2504, 340/971-7272, hwww.musicapalazzo.com, €75) is the ticket. This talented ensemble leads audiences through itinerant performances set in the stunning rooms of a meticulously preserved villa facing the Grand Canal. Doors open at 8pm and shows last two hours. Smart casual dress is encouraged and tickets may be booked online.

DORSODURO
Bars

There are a handful of bars in Campo Santa Margherita, but **Do Draghi** (Calle Renier, Fri.-Wed. 7:30am-11pm) is around the corner on the edge of the square. That doesn't mean it's not crowded—it is, and like many bars in Venice drinkers spill out onto the street. That's what happens in a city without cars, and it's an especially good thing at this colorful bar where it's impossible to go over budget ordering spritz served in large glasses and snacks that keep university students and young travelers merry.

The **Blues Café** (Dorsoduro 3778, tel. 348/240-6444, Tues.-Sat. 11am-2am, Sun. 2:30pm-2am) is a bustling American-style bar that can make you forget you're in Venice. Sometimes that's a good thing, especially when the beer on tap is Belgian and English and you have a craving for a decent hamburger. Live music is scheduled on weekends and soccer games are shown on a couple of screens. If you need an Internet connection just ask the server for the code.

Wine Bars

There are many reasons to love **Estro** (Calle Crosera 3778, tel. 041/476-4914, Wed.-Mon. noon-11pm, kitchen closes at 9:30pm), but best of all are the relaxed atmosphere, delicious food, and two enterprising brothers from Murano that make coming here a pleasure. The wine list includes over a hundred labels the pair have personally selected from small producers they never tire of touting. You can drink at the bar and select from myriad *tramezzino* sandwiches stuffed with boiled meat, creamed fish, and vegetables, or select from the full menu offering fish of the day, vegetarian lasagna, and soups served in a rustic décor around the corner from Campo Santa Margherita.

The fun and friendly staff at **Sora Seca** (San Pantalon 30123, tel. 348/611-8253, Mon.-Sun. 8:30am-3pm and 5pm-12am) don't take wine too seriously but they are serious about hospitality. This is a cozy little bar with a relaxing atmosphere where everyone seems to know each other and regulars can escape from tourists. There is a long list of wines and a surprising selection of whiskeys, as well as a wonderful glass case filled with inexpensive appetizers that are too tempting not to try.

Vivaldi in Venice

Antonio Vivaldi was born in Venice in 1678. His father was a violin player in the orchestra of San Marco and introduced him to the instrument at an early age. He was ordained as a priest at 25 but due to ill health was exempt from celebrating mass. Instead, he spent his time teaching orphans how to play the violin. Vivaldi was quickly promoted to *maestro* of the chorus. He began composing his first sonatas, operas, and longer orchestral works. His legacy was assured in 1725 when he completed Opus 8 that includes *The Four Seasons*. It was an enormous success and spread his name throughout Europe. He was invited to play at royal courts and nominated as the director of the Teatro San Angelo where he continued to compose. Vivaldi was immensely prolific and created over 500 compositions until his death in 1741.

Today, visitors can take a seat in a palace or church and discover how Vivaldi's *The Four Seasons* was meant to sound. Chamber groups keep his melodies alive: the Interpreti Veneziani, Musici Veneziani, and Virtuosi di Venezia are the most notable and regularly perform the composer's masterpiece.

Opera and Concerts

If you're searching for jazz (recorded or live) with a sense of history, turn to the **Venice Jazz Club** (Ponte dei Pugni 3102, tel. 041/523-2056, daily except Thurs. and Sun., 7pm until late, concerts 9pm-11pm). Nights are dedicated to standards, Latin, and Bossa Nova, the cocktails are good, and the wine is priced to uncork. The house quartet performs regularly and entry to live shows (€20) includes a drink. The club is only open weekends in winter.

SAN POLO AND SANTA CROCE
Wine Bars

There are a lot of reasons to stop by **Muro Venezia** (San Polo 2604 B/C, tel. 041/524-5310, www.murovenezia.com, daily

12pm-3pm and 7pm-10:30pm) but probably the best is that it's one of the liveliest places in the city after dark. Inside the intimate bar someone is usually playing guitar on weekends and dozens of people are drinking outside in the little square around the corner from the Rialto. During the day it makes a good happy hour pit stop, and on Saturdays at noon they start serving fried fish and chardonnay outdoors for an unbeatable €8.

Al Amarone (San Polo, Calle Sbianchesini 30125, tel. 041/523-1184, Thurs.-Tues. 10am-11pm) is an excellent place to learn about local Veneto wines. They serve over 30 red, white, and sparkling vintages by the regular and double glass in a spacious, contemporary setting. There are also a number of interesting tastings (five glasses each) with different themes meant to educate palates. Wine can be accompanied with reasonably priced finger food, cheese, and cured meat platters or a selection of reliable pasta dishes.

Any enoteca named **Al Prosecco** (Santa Croce, Campo San Giacomo de l'Orio tel. 041/524-0222, Mon.-Fri. 10am-8pm, Sat. 10am-5pm) should leave no doubt what to order. You can discover different varieties of Venetian bubbly along with organic wines while seated outside in a lively square. Food isn't an afterthought and abundant plates of cheese, grilled vegetables, and gourmet sandwiches are also served.

Hotel Bars

The **Aman Venice Resort Hotel** (San Polo, Calle Tiepolo 1364, tel. 041/270-7333, www.aman.com), around the bend from the Rialto, is the only seven-star hotel in Venice. Its ★ **Blue Bar** (always open) consists of three chandeliered rooms on the *piano nobile* (2nd or noble floor). It's like Versailles with modern furnishings. You can have a seat anywhere but the middle mirrored room with ornate gold fittings, stylish couches, and three low tables overlooking the canal is the perfect backdrop for a proposal of any kind. There's no signature drink but the bartenders can mix anything you like.

Opera and Concerts

Palazetto Bru Zane (San Polo 2368, tel. 041/521-1005, www.bru-zane.com, box office Mon.-Fri. 2:30pm-5:30pm) aims to keep 18th-century classical music alive and presents 30-40 concerts per season (Sept.-June) in a refurbished villa. Concerts are small-scale (the hall seats 100) and feature emerging international ensembles playing chamber, symphonic, and choral works. Tickets are only €15 and free guided tours of the elaborately decorated building are available in English on Thursday afternoons at 3:30pm.

CANNAREGIO AND CASTELLO
Bars

For a pint in a no-nonsense Italian pub, pull up a stool at **Al Santo Bevitore** (Cannaregio, Fondamenta de Ca' Vendramin, tel. 041/717-560, daily 4pm-2am). The attraction isn't the décor but the long row of taps behind the bar. They're all connected to thirst-quenching kegs of stout, bitter, and ale. You can try local brews made from fermenting Japanese and New Zealand hops together (Zona Cesarini), sip Belgian strong ales like La Chouffe (8 percent) and Kwak (8.4 percent), or cross the Channel for a pint of Punks Do It Better (4.3 percent). A small courtyard overlooks a canal and musicians occasionally turn up on Monday nights.

Don't come to Venice expecting bars like the ones back home. In Venice a bar can be more than a place to drink. **Al Parlamento** (Cannaregio, Fondamento Savorgnan 511, 041/244-0214, daily 7:30am-1:30am) is a good example of that: Although you can come to take advantage of their €5 happy hour from 6pm to 9pm you can also order seafood risotto and a couple of other dishes that will help you avoid spritz hangovers. The space has been refurbished with attention to design but hasn't lost the charm, and it still has scenic outdoor tables overlooking the city's second-widest canal.

There's no shame in going to a pub in Venice, especially if you take your drink outside. At the originally named **Irish Pub**

Venezia (Cannaregio, Corte dei Pali 3847, 041/099-0196, daily 10am-2am) you can do just that with a pint of Kilkenny or Bitburger in a little courtyard away from the crowds of Strada Nuova. Inside you're likely to find the television tuned to rugby or *calcio* (soccer).

Wine Bars

If you like your wine bars small and simple, **Cantina Antica Vigna** (Castello, Calle Crosera 3818, tel. 041/523-1318, Mon.-Sat. 8am-8pm and Sun. 9am-1:30pm) is the place you've been looking for. Nothing about this standing-room-only enoteca is fancy and that's what makes it special. That and owner Ferdinando Benettelli, who has a lot of stories to tell and isn't thrifty when it comes to pouring the local wine he's been serving for decades. Try either of the two white wines on tap at the wooden counter with a stuffed tramezzino sandwich—if there are any left.

You can buy wine at a supermarket, bar, or kiosk but Venetians get it at *vinerie*. These shops deal exclusively in the sale of wine. It can't be consumed on the premises; instead it must be taken away in plastic half-liter and liter bottles that are provided. The smaller option is a good investment and an opportunity to sample local wines fresh from the casks lining **Nave de Oro** (Castello, Calle del Mondo Novo 5786b, tel. 041/523-3056, Mon.-Sat. 9am-1pm and 5pm-7:45pm, Wed. 9am-1pm). The husband-and-wife owners have been providing *rosso, bianco,* and *frizzanti* to faithful customers and curious travelers since 1984.

Locals and curious travelers come to fill up their bottles from the half-dozen vats in the shop at **Al Canton del Vin** (Castello, 041/277-0449). They can provide you with a plastic liter bottle if you arrive empty-handed and tempt you with soave or cabernet. It's cheap, it's extremely drinkable, and it's near several pleasant squares where you can drink in peace.

Hotel Bars

Hotel Danieli (Castello, Riva degli Schiavoni 4196, tel. 041/522-6480, www.

Cocktails at Hotel Bars

If you've packed a suit, bow tie, or little black dress, you'll get a chance to wear it in Venice, where lavish hotel bars make wonderful backdrops for a drink. Even if you can't afford a room, you can always soak up the atmosphere at the bar. Don't be intimidated by the number of stars or the luxurious surroundings. Casual elegance and an attitude like you belong are all you need.

There are a dozen five-star hotels and one seven-star resort in Venice; all have bars. Some are classic, a few are modern, and they're all refined. The bartenders at these luxurious haunts are lifelong employees who look like they belong in a Humphrey Bogart film. They're well versed in the art of hospitality and mastered the mixing of cocktails long ago.

Most bars have their own specialty drinks served in Murano glasses and accompanied by light snacks. Seating usually isn't a problem and the sipping goes on until late. Prices range from €10-20 depending on the surroundings and often include light snacks.

danielihotelvenice.com) is located in a 14th-century *palazzo* overlooking the Grand Canal. The narrow front entrance leads to a lavish four-story lobby that has changed little in the last six centuries. **Bar Dandolo** (9:30am-1am), located on the ground floor, is managed by Roberto Naccari, who mixes Vesper martinis and his own creations. Try the After Eight, a drink consisting of Ombra digestif, mint syrup, and double cream. There are comfortable armchairs and velvet loveseats in an intimate room that's perfect for exchanging confidences. The dress code is smart casual and afternoon tea is served at 4pm sharp. The Danieli also has a rooftop bar with wonderful views of the lagoon. It's open from May until September and *aperitivo* is served from 3pm to 6:30pm.

The **Bat Bar Lounge and Terrace** (Castello, Calle Borgolocco 6108, tel.

041/241-1064) inside Hotel Ai Cavalieri may not be the most elegant, but bartenders Giovanni and Claudio know what they're doing and mix their drinks with passion and flair. Signature drinks are €13 and include the easy-to-sip La Dogaressa (vodka, peach liquor, white vermouth, and rose water).

Casinos

Anyone who wants to try their luck in Venice can bet inside the oldest gambling house in the world. **Casino di Venezia** (Cannaregio, tel. 041/529-7111, www.casinovenezia.it, daily 11am-2:45am, tables open at 4pm) opened in 1638 and moved to Ca' Vendramin Calergi along the Grand Canal in the 1950s. If you don't know the rules to *Chemin de Fer, Punto Banco,* or *Midi Trenta* you can stick with roulette, blackjack, or the slot machines. Tables are spread over three floors. When you're ready to spend your earnings (or tire of losing), hit the sophisticated restaurant (Fri.-Sun. 7:30pm-11:30pm, €25-35), modern pizzeria (daily noon-3:30pm and 7pm-11:30pm, €15-20), or metallic lounge bar with nighttime views of the Grand Canal. A jacket is required to enter the upstairs parlors but can be borrowed for free at the door. ID is required and the €10 entry fee includes a chip, cloakroom service, and shuttle from the train station to the casino's private dock. A second Las Vegas-style location is near the airport.

Opera and Concerts

Teatro Malibran (Cannaregio, Calle Maggioni 5873, tel. 041/786-603, €10-100) may not be as grand as La Fenice but it has an equally glorious past. The site of more than a hundred operatic debuts since being inaugurated in 1678, it was restored in 1992 and is now used as the second stage for La Fenice productions and music recitals. These are newer works for the most part and an opportunity for audiences to discover contemporary operas and up-and-coming musicians. Ticket prices are more accessible than La Fenice and start at €10 for seats with partially blocked visibility.

GIUDECCA
Hotel Bars

The **Skyline Rooftop Bar** (Giudecca, Fondamenta S. Biagio 810, tel. 041/272-3311, daily 10am-1pm, Stucky or Palanca water stop) sounds cool because it is cool. This lounge bar in a Hilton hotel occupies a unique location, and the view from the converted factory is one of the best in the city and compensates for the commute. The bar shakes and stirs original drinks at reasonable prices given the surroundings and is perfect for a sunset *aperitivo* or nightcap.

FESTIVALS AND EVENTS
Spring

Su e Zo per i Ponti ("up and down the bridges," www.suezo.it) is a noncompetitive footrace on the second Sunday in April along the streets and squares and over the bridges of the city. The 12km event begins and ends in Piazza San Marco and the route changes every year. There's also a shorter 6km fun run that leaves from the train station. Both start at 10:30am and are open to all. The race attracts over 10,000 runners. You can register online (€6.50) or in person (€7.50) on the day of the race. There are several refreshment areas along the way, and all proceeds go to charity.

Vogalonga (third Sunday in May) is Venice's largest regatta, with over 6,000 participants rowing 1,600 vessels. All types of boats, from gondolas to kayaks, can enter this noncompetitive event. The course is 30km long and follows the major canals around Venice as well as lagoon islands like Murano and Burano before returning to the city and finishing at Punta della Salute.

Festa della Sensa, one of Venice's oldest celebrations, began around AD 1000 as a way of marking the city's maritime rise to dominance and conquest of the Adriatic. The doge's ship would lead boats out of the lagoon into the open sea where prayers were recited to San Nicolo, the patron saint of sailors. The dropping of a precious ring by the doge was later added as a symbolic marriage of the city with the sea. The ritual is reenacted on the last Sunday in May with great pomp. Today, it's the mayor who leads the procession, which is best viewed from the northern shore of the Lido.

Summer

One of the most popular celebrations in Venice is **La Festa del Redentore** (third Sunday in July). It originated in 1576 when locals vowed to build a church if the plague that was devastating the city ended. The disease miraculously relented and Venetians have shown their gratitude ever since. During the day they walk over a pontoon bridge to the Chiesa del Redentore in Giudecca—which was built as promised—and at night thousands watch fireworks that illuminate the sky from 11pm onwards. Riva degli Schiavone in Castello and Fondamenta alle Zattere in Dorsoduro provide the best views but have little elbow room, especially if you arrive late. After the pyrotechnics, younger Venetians continue the celebrations on the beaches of the Lido. The day after a special morning mass is held in the church and the temporary bridge remains in place for several days, offering a rare opportunity to cross the Giudecca Canal on foot.

During late August and early September it's not uncommon to spot international film stars zipping around Venice on motorboats. They're here for the **Venice Film Festival** (tel. 041/521-8711, www.labiennale.org) that's been held on the Lido since 1932 and is one of the oldest festivals of its kind. In Venice the best film is awarded a golden lion and stars walk the red carpet at the art deco Palazzo del Cinema (Lungomare Guglielmo Marconi) facing the Adriatic. The theater has a 1,100-seat screening room where entries are projected day and night. Tickets are available once the program is announced and many showings are open to the general public. It's an opportunity to see great films in an exceptional environment and possibly glimpse a famous face. Exhibitions and collateral events are organized throughout the city during the 10-day festival, including an outdoor cinema in Campo San Polo.

Fall

Gondoliers have been competing with one another for centuries, and the **Regata Storica** (first Sun. in Sept.) fills both sides of the Grand Canal with thousands of spectators. The regatta is divided into four categories according to the type of vessel and number

rowers preparing for the Vogalonga regatta

of oars used. A lucky few watch from *palazzi* balconies while everyone else maneuvers for space on the bridges or along the *fondamente*. The event begins at 4pm with a parade of boats manned by sailors in colorful 15th-century attire and led by someone dressed as the doge. Boats depart from the Giardini Publici (Castello) and row up the Grand Canal to the train station and back to the finish line opposite Palazzo Ca' Foscari. The climax of the event features gondolas oared by teams of two. Each heat has 9 or 10 competitors. The first four to place are awarded cash prizes and a red, white, green, or blue standard depending on how they finished. Winning is a big deal, but the most prestigious honor is the *Re del Remo* (King of the Oar) title that is achieved by winning five consecutive regattas. Only seven gondoliers have won it.

Venice may look old on the outside but it's often brand new on the inside. That's the contrast mayor Riccardo Selvatico wanted to create when he founded the **Venice Biennale** (Castello, Giardini Publici and Arsenale, tel. 041/521-8711, www.labiennale.org, Tues.-Sun. 10am-6pm, May-Nov. in odd years) in 1895. Initially dedicated to sculpture and painting, the event has evolved into the premier showcase for contemporary art. Today the event remains on the cutting edge and introduces leading artists from 89 countries to a global audience of critics, enthusiasts, and collectors. The event has also expanded to include music, dance, theater, and cinema. Each edition has a curator responsible for choosing a theme and selecting participants from hundreds of hopefuls.

The Biennale is centered on a cluster of pavilions in the Giardini Publici and Arsenal warehouses on the eastern tip of the Castello neighborhood. The Giardini Publici at the southeastern corner of the *sestiere* is the original exhibition space where countries built a handful of small pavilions in the gardens over the decades. Arsenal, five minutes north, was added later and provides large industrial spaces where conceptual artists let their imaginations run wild. And the art isn't restricted to Castello—there are installations around the city. If you like art, it's a great time to visit. If you aren't an art fan, Venice goes on as usual, although it is one of the city's peak seasons.

The Biennale offers several ticket options including a single (€25) and two-day pass (€30) valid for both locations and available at either of the ticket offices located at the **Giardini Publici** (Viale dei Giardini Publici) and **Arsenale** (Campo della Tana). If you

a group of *Carnivale* goers

want to have the art explained there are daily **group tours** (€7 for single venue, €10 for both) that don't require advance reservations and are conducted in Italian and English. **Private tours** (tel. 041/5218-828, Mon.-Sat. 10am-5:30pm, €90) can also be arranged. An architectural version of the Biennale was launched in 1980 and is held in even years. It's nearly impossible, therefore, to miss out on the cutting edge and discover a unique contrast of old and new.

Winter

Epiphany usually lands on January 6. It is a holiday throughout Italy but in Venice they celebrate *la Befana* a little differently. A huge stocking is hung from the Rialto and the **Regata delle Befane** boat race is held. Participants are dressed as the legendary witch who provides children with candy or coal depending on how they've behaved. The procession departs from the San Tomà dock at 11am and heads up the Grand Canal towards the bridge. It's a short race that lasts less than 15 minutes. Afterwards there's plenty of steaming *vin brulé* wine and an opportunity to meet *Babbo Natale* (Father Christmas).

Carnevale began in 11th-century Venice as a gluttonous celebration before the arrival of Lent and its period of abstinence. By its 18th-century peak, beautiful, sophisticated, outlandish, and amusing characters all joined the party. Celebrants disguised their identities behind masks and costumes that eliminated social distinctions. Its later decadence brought about a 19th-century decline and eventual disappearance until it was revived in the 1970s. Travelers shouldn't come to Venice during *Carnevale* unless they want to take part. Streets are choked with spectators and orchestrated costume parades while most Venetians are either out of town or at private parties. Piazza San Marco is the center of the action but all the larger squares organize music and dancing. You can watch the gaiety, or better yet, dress up and join the fun. If you haven't packed a costume there are plenty of rental shops, but a simple mask and a little creativity is all you need to join the mayhem.

Carnevale season starts on the ninth Sunday before Easter and climaxes two weeks later on *martedi grasso* (Mardi Gras or Fat Tuesday). The exact dates vary every year according to when Easter falls but it generally takes place in February.

Shopping

Shakespeare never imagined writing a play called the *Merchant of Paris* or *London*. He wrote the *Merchant of Venice* because that's where the shops were. In the 16th century the streets, markets, and docks around the Rialto were jammed with traders. Merchants came from all over Europe to Venice—the most active port in the Mediterranean—to trade with their Ottoman, Indian, and Chinese counterparts. Pigments, leather, textiles, spices, perfumes, precious wood, and foodstuffs were exchanged for gold, silver, and armaments. Local workshops transformed these materials into valuable objects that brought the city wealth and fame.

Many trades have survived, making shopping in Venice an adventure. The most celebrated of these use glass, lace, and papier-mâché. Although the number of craftspeople has declined, they can still be found plying their trades across the city. Historic workshops are common in Dorsoduro, where both and **Calle Bastion** and **Calle della Chiesa** are dotted with one-room galleries where artisans work in the back and display textiles, prints, and jewelry in the front. You can find glass and lace in showroom boutiques and souvenir shops around San Marco, but if you want to go to the source you'll need to board a *vaporetto* and head out to the furnaces of

Made in Venice

Venice is famous for glass, lace, and papier-mâché masks, but that doesn't mean all the glass, lace, and paper masks you'll find in Venice were made in Venice. Local supply simply can't keep up with demand and has led many shop owners to import their wares from other parts of the world. Venetian merchants have been doing that for centuries, but if you've come all this way you may as well get the real deal. That will almost always cost more, but handmade has advantages like craftsmanship and originality that are worth paying extra for.

GLASS

Glass production is centered in Murano but many furnaces supply boutiques in San Marco and offer one-of-a-kind glassware that's difficult to imitate. Genuine glass usually comes with certification (Vetro Artistico Murano, www.muranoglass.com) and large pieces are often signed. There's something for all budgets, from glazed jewelry to colorful vases and immense chandeliers. Many workshops are equipped with ovens where artisans create and sell what they make. That's always a good sign and an opportunity to observe and ask questions about the glassmaking process.

LACE

Lace or *merletti* hasn't resisted globalization as well as glass has; by some estimates over 90 percent of the merchandise in Venice is made outside the city. The school that once taught lacemaking on the island of Burano closed years ago and most practitioners are in their fifties or older—but don't let that discourage you. Authentic Venetian hand-stitched lace can be hard to find, but it's still out there and recognizable by its imperfections and price tag.

MASKS

You'll spot masks being sold as soon as you step out of the train station, but most of these are cheap plastic versions entirely lacking in personality. A papier-mâché mask takes time and, most of all, imagination to shape and hand paint. It's an art that has dwindled down to a small circle of dedicated practitioners. The few remaining shops are crammed floor to ceiling with sensational characters that stop window shoppers in their tracks and can provide a fantastic reminder of your journey to Venice.

VENICE
SHOPPING

Murano or the back streets of Burano where lacemaking refuses to die. Be sure to ask permission before taking pictures of artisans' creations.

Venice has no fashion megastores, but many designer boutiques. Major brands cluster along the most trafficked areas, such as the streets north and west of **Piazza San Marco** or in the **Strada Nuova** in Cannaregio, which stretches from the train station all the way to the Rialto. Both sides of the Rialto Bridge are heavily commercialized, and the arcades and market stalls on the San Polo side are a good place to search for T-shirts, jewelry, and masks. **Rio Terra Lista di Spagna,** the gateway to Cannaregio, is lined with shops, but it's very touristy and best avoided.

Venetian shops are generally open from 9am to 1pm and 3pm to 7pm, though many sacrifice the traditional lunch break, especially during summer. Most shops close on Sundays and many remain closed on Monday mornings.

SAN MARCO

San Marco is one of the most commercial *sestiere* in Venice, but you don't have to scour the entire neighborhood when you can find it all in **Calle Frezzaria.** This narrow street just west of Piazza San Marco provides a mix of new and old boutiques where nothing is off the assembly line and quality, selection, and fun still matter. It's a pleasant walk with stores that are close to each other on a street that isn't overly crowded and is shaded most of the day. Elite fashion brands like Gucci and Prada can be browsed nearby in Calle Larga XXII Marzo, while Merceria II Aprile leading to the Rialto is lined with affordable shops selling clothes, shoes, and accessories.

Glass

The majority of glass shops are located in the busy commercial streets north and west of Piazza San Marco. Lower-end outlets sell fairly anonymous sculptures and jewelry; if you can't make it to Murano they make decent souvenirs. If you want something larger and more impressive, you'll also find dozens of higher-end boutiques in this area.

It's hard to imagine a more inviting location than **FGB** (S. Maria del Giglio, tel. 041/523-6556, daily 10am-6:30pm). This glass workshop is housed within an ancient tower of which only the base has remained. Inside, a couple uses the *lume* technique to create glass jewelry and decorations. They heat colored glass rods up to 500 degrees and shape them into beads of different dimensions that are then used to create earrings, bracelets, and necklaces. You can find a nice gift for under €20 here.

San Marco 801 (Calle Fiubera 801, tel. 334/703-8530, Mon.-Sun. 10am-7pm) is a one-stop souvenir shop just north of Piazza San Marco and especially well stocked in glass. They have a dedicated supplier in Murano and offer a wide selection of jewelry and sculptures as well as larger objects that can be shipped to your door.

To help consumers distinguish between Murano-made and everything else, the glassmakers association created a special Vetro Artistico Murano label that only shops selling authentic local glass can display. You'll find it at **EMI Art Glass** (Calle della Mandola 3803, tel. 041/523-1326, Mon.-Sat. 10:30am-7:30pm), which carries blown vases, marine sculptures, and solid-glass creations that would look good on a mantle or shelf. Pieces are as expensive as they are heavy.

Once you begin shopping for glass it may be hard to stop—but the more time you spend examining the goods, the better you'll become at distinguishing made in China from made in Murano.

Masks and Costumes

The historically accurate costumes, papier-mâché masks, tuxedos, wigs, capes, hats, and shoes at **Atelier Flavia** (Santa Marina, Corte Spechiera 6010, tel. 041/528-7429, www.veniceatelier.com, appointment only) could transform anyone. It's the ideal place to come before *Carnevale* for an *Eyes Wide Shut* (or any other) look. Costumes can be rented or purchased.

Paper Goods

Legatoria Piazzesi (San Marco, Campiello della Feltrina 2511c, tel. 041/520-1978, daily 10:30am-1pm and 4:30pm-7:30pm) is a historic workshop where paper has been produced since 1851, and they continue to do all their bookbinding on site. The small shop with an ancient facade is filled with notebooks, stationery, diaries, and colorful wrapping paper made from antique wood blocks that are also for sale. Prices aren't the cheapest but everything is one-of-a-kind and Venetian-made.

In front of the post office, **La Carta** (San Marco 5547a, tel. 041/520-2325, daily 9:30am-7:30pm) sells handmade paper and specializes in marbleized sheets, calendars, and agendas. If you forgot your diary at home this is the perfect place to buy a new one and start jotting down your impressions of Venice. There's also a decent selection of pens and pencils.

Clothing and Accessories

Anyone with the instinct of a dandy will enjoy a trip to **Al Duca d'Aosta Venezia 1902** (Campo San Zulian 606, tel. 041/523-0145, Mon.-Sat. 10am-7:30pm and Sun. 11am-7pm). This venerated gentleman's brand combines traditional British style with elegant Italian tailoring. It's where princes came for fashion that never fades and modern gentlemen come for wool jackets,

★ Shopping for Masks

Throughout the 18th century, Venetians used masks to enjoy stigma-free decadence. Nobles wore masks to visit brothels, youth to escape from parents, the poor to frequent the rich, the rich to frequent the poor, aristocratic ladies to enter dark alleys, clergy to temporarily break vows, and so on. Famous Venetian Giacomo Casanova wore a mask as he went to meet his lovers at the Cantina Do Mori, where he was a regular.

Masks are still used today and are one of the most common sights at street-side stalls and gift shops around the city, where cheap versions can be had for €5-10. These have little to do with the papier-mâché versions carefully made in a dozen or so ateliers around the city. These versions sell for €30 to €300 and are based on classic molds that have been used for centuries. The most common is the white *Bauta* mask that allows the wearer to eat and drink while remaining hidden from view. It is worn by both men and women and often paired with a black *tabarro* cape. Another popular mask is the *Medico della Peste,* recognizable by the long nose that resembles a bird's beak. It was invented by a doctor in the 17th century who didn't want to be recognized by his patients dying from the plague and was later adopted by *Carnevale* goers. The *Colombina* is a half-mask that covers eyes and cheeks. It continues to be favored by Venetian ladies and often comes painted in silver or gold and adorned with feathers and beads.

These and many other historical masks and newer creations are available at workshops around the city where you can learn more about the origins of your disguise. Castello is a good neighborhood to start shopping for masks. Below are some specific shops to check out:

- **Ca' del Sol** (page 285)

- **Papier Maché** (page 285)

- **Ca' Mancana** (page 282)

---

cashmere sweaters, and cotton shirts that cross seasonal boundaries.

Items at **Giuliana's Longo's** (Calle del Lovo, tel. 041/522-6454, Mon.-Sat. 10am-7pm) hat shop are made right here in Venice. In fact, Giuliana herself makes the hats she stocks. Inside her shop Panama hats, gondolier hats, *Carnevale* hats, felt hats, and straw hats are haphazardly arranged in armoires and antique hat stands. This little corner of hat history is about as far as you can get from mass consumption. Giuliana is usually working away at her little desk on one-of-a-kind pieces that all have their own personality. Try one on and see if it fits.

If you want to dress like a Venetian, visit **Barena Venezia** (Campo San Luca, tel. 041/523-8457, Mon.-Sat. 10am-1pm, 4pm-7:30pm). This men's and women's shop has been creating versatile and functional clothing since 1961. Coats, jackets, and sweaters are made using local textiles and are inspired by 20th-century lagoon style. Clothes are comfortable and easy to wear.

Gentlemen ready for an Italian makeover can head to **Ermenegildo Zegna** (Bocca di Piazza San Marco 1241, tel. 041/522-1204, daily10am-7pm) or **Buosi** (San Bortolomio 5382, tel. 041/520-8567, daily 10am-7:30pm) near the Rialto. The latter has kept Venetian men looking good since 1897. They sew shirts, jackets, trousers, and suits to measure and have a selection of ready-to-wear pieces including ties any man would want to receive.

Men looking to upgrade their wardrobes with Italian fashion can step into **Frezzaria Venezia** (Calle Frezzaria, no phone) for contemporary informal menswear. There is a fine selection of trousers, colored shoes, and Venetian-style hats.

If you need an evening cocktail dress, skirt, or blouse—or even if you don't—**Kiriku** (Calle Frezzaria 1729, 041/296-0619, Mon.-Sat. 10am-7:30pm) boutique is worth a browse.

The wall racks are filled with emerging designers that have a retro-chic style that looks and feels good to wear. A small selection of bags, shoes, and accessories are in the back next to the white revolving armchair where patient partners recline and enthusiastically express approval.

Leather and other materials for both men and women await at **Empresa** (Calle Frezzeria 1586, tel. 041/241-2687, Mon.-Sat. 10am-7:30pm and Sun. 11:30am-7:30pm). You'll find great jackets and accessories in this finely decorated store, which is run by five friendly brothers who aren't in a rush to sell their clothing. Their pieces add personality to any outfit.

Arnold & Battois (Campo San Maurizio 2671, tel. 348/412-3797, daily 10am-1pm, 3:30pm-7:30pm) creates handbags in unique shapes that turn heads and fashionable women adore. Seasonal collections are inspired by and entirely made in Venice. Leather is the material of choice and the original designs are a result of experience and slow production.

Giorgio Armani, Emilio Pucci, Roberto Cavalli, Valentino, Missoni and other renowned designers all also have boutiques in the neighborhood.

Toys
Fanfaluca (Calle Fuseri 4339, tel. 041/847-6891, Mon.-Sat. 10am-7:30pm) is as fun for nostalgic adults as it is for kids. There's clothing, wooden toys, puppets, old-fashioned dolls, and plenty of stuffed animals. They carry difficult-to-find teddy bears, sheep, rabbits, and cows from the legendary Moulin Roty brand. These soft, colorful animals make great presents and become instant friends for toddlers. A majority of the store's items are handmade.

Photography
Arsen Revazov has transformed the **ar33studio** (Calle Frezzaria 1732, tel. 041/296-0129, Mon.-Sat. 10:30am-7:30pm) into a darkroom, laboratory, and gallery. The Russian native uses infrared lighting and multiple exposure times to create black-and-white photos that aren't exactly what they seem.

Markets
Mercatino di Campo San Maurizio (Campo San Maurizio, 333/965-9994, Oct. and Dec. Fri.-Sun. 9am-7pm), a seasonal antique market, is a wonderful place to wander. Dealers from across Italy show a trove of collectibles and curiosities from the 17th to the 20th century and all decades in between. A variety of Murano glass is on display along with silver dinnerware, military regalia from both World Wars, textiles, phonographs, vintage clothing, and more. Browsing the covered wooden stalls is fun whether you're a collector or just interested in history. If you spot something you like, inquire about date and origin before asking the price, which can often be negotiated. The market is generally held the weekend before Easter and the second weekends of September, October, and December but exact dates vary every year.

DORSODURO
Masks and Costumes
Masks are everywhere in Venice but few shops sell their own handmade models. **Ca' Mancana** (Calle de le Botteghe 3172, tel. 041/277-6142, daily 10am-7:30pm) is one of the finest and uses traditional papier-mâché techniques to create both classic *Carnevale* and fantasy characters. Anyone can hide their identity for as little as €30. This is where Stanley Kubrick came when he wanted masks for *Eyes Wide Shut*. If you want to learn how masks are made or are traveling with kids, ask about the maskmaking **workshops** that last a couple of hours and will keep young and old entertained.

Paper Goods
Fabio Pelosin has worked for more than 30 years inside **Stamperia il Pavone** (Calle Venier dei Leoni 721, tel. 041/523-4517) hand-decorating paper that he uses to cover

notebooks, photo albums, bookmarks, frames, and boxes. The process can be observed through the little window that divides the small showroom from the workshop where Fabio can usually be found working on a new creation. He begins by a drawing a motif, which he then carves into a wooden block. The stamp is then covered with paint and applied to paper. The unique results make colorful souvenirs of the city.

Books

Books make good souvenirs, and even if you don't read Italian you can judge by the covers at **La Toletta** (Saca della Toleta 1214, tel. 041/523-2034, Mon.-Sat. 9am-7:30pm, Sun. 3pm-7pm) and choose a novel or nonfiction for the bookcase back home. There are different sections to browse in this shop, which opened in 1933 and has retained a vintage 1970s look. Talks and lectures are regularly scheduled on weekends.

Clothing

Original Laboratory of Design (Fondamenta San Basilio 1643, tel. 041/523-5462, daily 10am-7pm) sounds pretentious, but it's really just vintage women's clothing with a customized twist. Designer Federica and her artistic collaborators transform fashion from the past into original clothes, bags, and accessories that add zest to any wardrobe. The eclectic little shop is a great place to browse and watch Federica at work on her latest creations.

Housewares

Madera (Campo San Barnaba 2762, tel. 041/522-4181, Mon.-Sat. 10am-1pm and 3:30pm-7:30pm) offers a contemporary range of dining and cooking ware. Local designers produce most of the dishes, utensils, and cutting boards and the owner makes many of the wooden items. The style is more Nordic than Venetian, but every piece would be a valuable addition to a kitchen. Nearby is a second store that sells jewelry and accessories with the same artisanal mantra.

Markets

Mercatino di Polvere di Ricordi (Campo Sant'Agnese), whose name translates to "dusty memory market," is just that. But it's the good sort of dust, where patient browsers can find hidden gems among myriad antiques, old books, prints, silverware, and collectibles. The market only takes place three times a year on the second weekend of March, the first weekend of October, and the last day of November. It's spread around the city and stalls are also set up in the Erberia near the Rialto, Campo San Polo, and Campo San Silvestere.

SAN POLO AND SANTA CROCE

Glass

Marco Franzato (Santa Croce, Corte Piossi 2176, tel. 041/524-0770, daily 10am-6pm) is a master glassmaker who has restored the windows of many ancient *palazzi* including Palazzo Ducale. He opened his workshop in 1993. Inside he creates rose glass displays, lampshades, and collectibles. The jewelry is the most accessible in price and ease of transport, although direct shipping can be arranged. Marco uses a number of techniques to create one-of-a-kind earrings, necklaces, and rings that take shape in the lab at the back of the shop.

Masks and Costumes

Period costumes for rent (€160+) or sale (€1,500+) can be had at **Atelier Pietro Longhi** (San Polo, Calle San 2608, tel. 041/714-478, Mon.-Fri. 10am-2pm). They also tailor original costumes to measure from paintings, photos, comic books, or dreams. It usually takes about a week before you can transform reality. Mask are also available to buy or rent.

Clothing

If you've ever wanted to dress differently without shocking anyone you may want to drop into **Altrove** (San Polo, Calle Mori 2659a, tel. 041/476-4473, Tues.-Sat. 11am-6pm). This alternative atelier is off the main shopping drag but easy enough to find and provides a new take on made-to-measure. The clothes are geometrical and difficult to categorize other than being oblivious to trends. Textiles, production, and design are all rigorously Italian-made for originally dressed men and women.

Monica Daniele's (San Polo, Calle dello Scaleter 2235, tel. 041/524-6242, Mon.-Sat. 9am-1pm and 2:30pm-6pm) shop is the kind of place where adults play dress-up. Monica nearly singlehandedly rescued 18th-century Venetian accessories from fashion oblivion. One item in particular she saved from extinction is the *tabarro,* a wool cloak once commonly worn on wintery Venetian *calle.* It comes in blue, black, or gray and goes well with the extensive range of felt hats on display in the window and around the informal shop.

Shoes aren't complicated at **Piedàterre** (San Polo, Ruga degli Orefici 60, tel. 041/528-5513, Mon.-Sat. 10am-12:30pm and 2:30pm-7:30pm). This colorful boutique under the arcades of the Rialto has refashioned traditional footwear for the 21st century. The shoes in question are slipper-like and inspired by those once worn by gondoliers and peasants. Today, velvet has been added but recycled tires are still used for the soles. They come in all colors for children and adults and make a wonderful summertime walking shoe.

The high student population may explain the number of funky and vintage clothing shops in the neighborhood, but these small boutiques are for anyone who values retro style and enjoys hunting for new and slightly used hats, bags, and clothing. One of the oldest is the **Penny Lane Shop** (Santa Croce, Calle Falier 39, tel. 041/524-4134, Mon. and Thurs.-Sat. 9am-noon and 5pm-7pm, Tues. 4pm-7pm, Wed. 1pm-7pm), which stocks colorful northern European brands often made from recycled materials. Try on jewelry accessories in the side room dedicated to haut vintage.

Jewelry

The arcades leading to the Rialto are the traditional domain of goldsmiths, and many jewelers still work along this busy thoroughfare. The brothers who run **Attombri** (San Polo, Sottoportico degli Orefici 65, tel. 041/521-2524, Mon. 3:30pm-7:30pm, Tues.-Sat. 10am-1pm and 3:30pm-7:30pm) combine traditional materials with contemporary design. They create necklaces, bracelets, and earrings made of silver, copper, and glass that are elegant and wearable.

Books

At **Libreria Aqua Alta** (Calle Longa SM Formosa 5177, tel. 041/296-0841, daily 9am-8pm) the books are haphazardly stacked in bathtubs and boats along narrow aisles that would have driven Melvil Dewey mad. Yet it's hard not to like this bookshop and be absorbed by titles that range in subject and language from architecture to Swahili. Outside near the sleeping literary cats are a collection of vintage postcards, prints, and other paper materials that make unusual gifts.

Venice is the perfect location for bookshop dedicated to the sea, and **Libreria Mare di Carta** (Santa Croce, Fondamenta dei Tolentini 222, tel. 041/716-304, Tues.-Sat. 9am-1:30pm and 3:30pm-7:30pm) is lined with nonfiction and fictional accounts where waves are the protagonist. Cristina Giussani is both an accomplished sailor and bookseller who will point you to the right shelf. Most of the literature is in Italian but there's also a great quantity of maps, model boats, prints, and comics.

Woodworking Crafts

It's easy to pass **Dalla Venezia Angelo** (San Polo, Calle Scaleter 2204, tel. 041/721-659, Mon.-Sat. 8am-1pm and 4pm-8pm) without a second thought, but if you're interested in how wood gets transformed into miniature objects step inside and let Angelo show you around. He's been keeping the tradition of woodworking alive since 1959 and will gladly explain the dusty workshop where he carves and sands planks of Swiss pine and Tuscan olive into rings and pyramids using a vintage wood-spinning machine that allows him to shape wood into apples and pears. This isn't mass production and prices aren't cheap, but everything is unique and represents a lifetime of dedication.

Spices

There are rules about what food travelers can bring back to the United States, but fortunately the gastronomic goods on offer at **Mascari** (San Polo, Ruga dei Spezieri 381, tel. 041/522-9762, Mon.-Sat. 8am-1pm and 4pm-7:30pm) will pass customs. This wonderful-smelling shop is full of tempting ingredients like dried porcini mushrooms, sweet paprika, saffron, candied fruits, and mysterious spices. The well-stocked gourmet section also carries truffle-inspired condiments and *mostarda veneta* (Venetian mustard) that elevates meat and cheese.

Rialto Markets

The Rialto is the commercial heart of Venice, and both sides of the Rialto Bridge have been crammed with activity since the 15th century. The area on and around the bridge feels like one continuous market, with arcades and squares filled with all sort of businesses that attract locals and tourists alike. The San Polo side is the busier of the two and where the city's main markets are located. **Ruga dei Oresi**, on the northern side of the bridge, was once the domain of jewelers who worked in the small shops lining the arcades, but most have been replaced with boutiques and stalls selling glass, masks, clothing, and souvenirs of varying quality. You can escape the crush of visitors by exploring the alcoves parallel to the main street or heading north to the nearby **Campo Cesare**. There's a little more breathing room and dozens of kiosks (daily 8:30am-6pm) selling Venetian logoed T-shirts, sweatshirts, and hats in adult and child sizes. **Nicolo** (recognized by his shaved head and good-natured cynicism), like most of the merchants here, offers a discount on multiple purchases. Farther along and facing the Grand Canal are the **fish market** and **produce market**.

Glass

Vetreria (Castello 3868, tel. 349/271-3808) is a fun little shop specializing primarily in jewelry that's made on-site. Prices are reasonable (€5-30) and the style is funky rather than refined. They can also custom make pieces according to your taste and are happy for you to watch while they work.

Masks and Costumes

The walls of **Ca' del Sol** (Castello, Fondamenta dell'Osmarin, tel. 041/528-5549, daily 10am-8pm) are covered in masks. All the classics are here, including *bauta, columbine,* harlequin, plague, and scores of one-off creations that are handmade using papier-mâché, leather, ceramic, and iron. The shop has been around since 1986 and helped revitalize the art of maskmaking in the city. It's run by a collective of artisans who patiently answer questions and aren't uptight about letting customers try on as many masks as they like. They organize maskmaking courses and rent elaborate costumes during *Carnevale.*

It takes a while to distinguish between the different mask types, but the quality of the structure and painted detailing is immediately evident at **Papier Maché** (Castello, Calle Lunga 5174, tel. 041/522-9995, Mon.-Sat. 9am-9pm). Four decades of maskmaking experience is on display in the windows of this boutique, which has a large selection of ornate masks with designs you won't see anywhere else. Prices are a little high, but this is the real deal—and perhaps the finest way to keep your identity hidden.

Paper Goods

Want to follow in the literary footsteps of Bruce Chatwin or Ernest Hemingway? Stop in at the local **Moleskine** (Cannaregio, Stazione Santa Lucia, Fondamenta Santa Lucia 20, tel. 041/740-913, daily 8am-9pm) branch. The modern shop inside the train station sells more than the famed black diary that made the company famous. You'll also find bags, wallets, e-reader cases, and pens and writing implements with the same unmistakable style.

The smell of ink and paper is the sign you've arrived at **Tipografia Basso** (Cannaregio, Calle del Fumo 5306, tel. 041/523-4681, Mon.-Sat. 9am-1pm and 2:30pm-6pm, cash only). Inside the small atelier, Gianni works away on letterpress, lithographic, and offset printers but can always find the time to explain the different printing processes and demonstrate why the old-fashioned way is sometimes the best way. You can buy small prints of Pinocchio and other classic images or order a set of personalized hand-printed business cards.

Bookbinder **G. L. Pitacco** (Castello, Ruga Giuffa 4758, tel. 041/520-8687, Mon.-Sat. 3pm-8pm) specializes in traditional and modern bindings. The little shop stocks diaries, photo albums, and address books of all dimensions. You can also have books bound or repaired. They hand-make sheets of marbleized paper that are different from the Florentine variety; their sheets can also be found at **Domino** (Castello, S. Zaccaria 4685, tel. 041/523-0090).

Antiques

You'll find antique lace, purses, pillows, ceramics, and furniture at **Antichità al Ghetto** (Cannaregio, Calle Ghetto Vecchio 1133/1134, tel. 041/524-4592, Tues.-Sun. 10am-7pm). The shop was opened in 2006 by Elisabetta and Giuliano, who also collect locks. The friendly couple is knowledgeable about the goods they sell and will happily explain the origins of any item.

Clothing and Accessories

Armadio di Coco (Cannaregio, Campo Santa Maria Nova 6029b, tel. 041/523-6093, daily 10:30am-7:30pm) is an elegant vintage shop for women that would make an ideal walk-in closet. Dior, Chanel, Fendi, Valentino, and other designer labels are there, along with bags, belts, shoes, and hats all neatly arranged on secondhand racks and shelves. The clothes may be used but it's nearly impossible

to tell. Many have been given new hems and necklines by the young designer/owner, who wields thread and needles in her backroom workshop.

Prison and fashion may seem incompatible, but over the last decade the woman's penitentiary in Giudecca has collaborated with local dressmakers to help inmates learn a useful trade. The result is affordable and stylish women's clothing stocked in **Banco Lotto no.10** (Castello, Salizzada Sant'Antonin 3478, tel. 041/522-1439, Mon. 3:30pm-7:30pm, Tues.-Sat. 10am-1pm and 3:30pm-7:30pm) in eastern Castello. You can also find original accessories like bags made from discarded coffee sacks that sell for as little as €10.

Markets

Venetian flea markets are never shabby and always offer an opportunity to find unique (often antique) Murano glass, lace, silverware, and mixed oddities with loads of historical charm. If you happen to be in Venice on the right weekend those are the kinds of things you'll find at **Mercatino dei Miracoli** (Cannaregio, Campo Santa Maria Nova, tel. 041/271-0022, Mar.-Dec. Sat.-Sun. all day). Passionate hobbyists and collectors organize this small open-air market in a lovely *campo* where objects of all kinds can be found on the second weekend of month.

Venice's most popular market is held several times a year on the first or last Sunday of the month. **Mercatino delle Robe da Mar** (Castello, Via Garibaldi) translates to *stuff of the sea market*. But that doesn't mean everything here is nautical in nature—you can find everything here from antique stamps to used vinyl LPs. It's also a chance to visit one of the lesser-tread parts of the city and discover the eastern tip of Venice.

GIUDECCA
Textiles

Giudecca is a long way to go for a shopping spree, and there aren't that many shops to begin with. Yet Venice's longest island does have some industrial gems like the **Fortuny textile factory** (Fondamenta S. Biagio, tel. 041/528-7697, www.fortuny.com, May-Nov. Sat. and Sun.). The long brick building overlooking the canal next to the Stucky wheat mill began producing bolts of cloth in 1921 and is still operating today. Though the factory doesn't allow visitors, the showroom does, and it's filled with textiles from the company's past and present. There's also a lovely garden next door that can be visited by appointment.

Activities and Recreation

PARKS AND GARDENS

Grass is rare in Venice and there are few green open spaces. The parks and gardens that do exist are small and simple. They're usually quiet places where tourists have no time to tread and Venetians retreat to push grandchildren around in strollers and read the newspaper.

Giardino Papadopoli (Santa Croce) is located on an island opposite the train station. It's interspersed with gravel paths that circle a surprising variety of trees and bushes. There's a good playground for little climbers, benches, and a small lawn where you can lie down and forget where you are.

On the other side of the canal in Cannaregio **Giardini Savorgnan** (Fondamenta Venier, daily 8am-6:30pm) provides even greater tranquility and a space for street musicians to relax after lunch and toddlers to swing and slide. Like most parks in Venice it doesn't impress in scale or design but it is clean and provides a bucolic break from canals and streets.

The largest park in Venice is **Parco della Rimembranze** (San Elena *vaporetto* station) on San Elena island at the southern tip of Castello. It's as far from the train station as you can get and well off the tourist radar. It's an everyday park that's well kept but not pristine and comes with lagoon views, playgrounds, and shaded walkways. What's also nice is the adjacent neighborhood where residents go about their business seemingly unaware of the rest of the city. There are wide *calle*, occasional greengrocers, and unadorned bars with tables immersed in green.

The **Giardini Publici**, or public gardens

(Giardini *vaporetto* station), are nearby over a bridge. These gardens attract art lovers who come to visit the Biennale held here on odd-numbered years. The playground has seen better days, but the **Paradiso Café** near the dock is a pleasant place to rest a few minutes and contains a small art gallery.

Closer to the center and just around the corner from Piazza San Marco the **Giardini ex Reali** provides a tiny refuge from the tourists wandering along the promenade out front. The beech trees and goldfish-inhabited fountains inside this gated garden were part of Napoleon's royal palace and laid out in the late 1800s. There are plenty of empty benches (red seems to be the favorite color for benches in Venice). The nearby **tourist office** makes it a good place from which to plan your next move or spend a few minutes doing nothing.

ROWING

A number of schools provide lessons on rowing a Venetian boat, and you're better off manning the oars yourself than letting someone else do it for you. A 90-minute lesson with **Row Venice** (Cannaregio, Sacca Misericordia Marina, Fondamenta Gasparo Contarini, 347/725-0637, www.rowvenice.org, 1-2 people €80, 3/€120, 4/€140) costs the same as a 45-minute gondola ride and is twice as fun. Participants learn the basics of navigating a locally made *batellina* boat, which was once ubiquitous along the canals and looks like a gondola without the regalia. Lessons start with a demonstration of basic strokes while the boat is docked. You'll take turns maneuvering the vessel in a wide canal before heading to the open lagoon, gliding through narrow canals, and returning to port. Lessons are conducted in English. Wannabe sailors should wear loose-fitting clothes and comfortable shoes.

BOATING

Why sweat on a rowboat when you can relax in a motorboat? It is a somewhat riskier option and some boating experience is preferable, but Venetian maritime laws are surprisingly lenient when it comes to rentals. No license is required to navigate the small motorboats available from **Brussa Is Boat** (Cannaregio, Fondamenta Labia 331, tel. 041/715-787, www.brussaisboat.it, Mon.-Fri. 7:30am-6pm, Apr.-Oct. Sat.-Sun 8:30am-7pm). All you need is a credit card, valid ID, and a desire for adventure.

Daniele or one of his colleagues will familiarize you with the 23-foot pleasure craft and the essentials of Venetian navigation. The *topetta* (traditional flat-bottomed boat) seat six and the 15hp outboard engine is steered from the tiller. The key is to go slow, stay on the right, and avoid busy or narrow canals. This isn't a free-for-all expedition and you can't go anywhere you like. Instead there are seven preestablished itineraries around the lagoon that cover the islands of the Lido (red), Burano (green and purple), and Venice (yellow). That still leaves plenty of exploring to do for an hour (€35 plus tax) or the entire day (€160 plus tax). Fuel is included and reservations should be made in advance during the summer season. If your nautical skills aren't up to Venetian waterways you can also hire someone to do the sailing for you.

KAYAKING

Vaporetto and gondola aren't the only ways of getting around Venice. Adventurous travelers can do their own paddling and gain full access to the city's waterways. **Venice Kayak** (346/477-1327, www.venicekayak.com, half-day €90, full day €120) offers a variety of guided tours for both novices and experienced kayakers. Daily half-day excursions for 2-6 people depart mornings (9:15am-1pm) or afternoons (2:15pm-6pm) from the island of Certosa and crisscross the *sestiere* of Castello and San Marco, and should be reserved in advance. Expect about 10km of paddling in single or double kayaks at a relaxed pace. Full-day tours of Venice and lagoon islands are also available. Dress with the expectation of getting wet and don't bring a camera unless it's waterproof.

kayaking through the city

Venice by Water (Cannaregio, Corte Morosina 5823, tel. 041/528-0893, www.venicebywater.com) provides shorter tours for a minimum of two participants that last 30 (€35), 60 (€50), or 120 (€90) minutes and explore the lesser-trafficked canals of Cannaregio. All tours are guided and the "sport and snack" option includes a *bacareto* stop.

STAND-UP PADDLING

Stand-up paddling requires a little more expertise than kayaking, and Venice isn't the place to try this sport for the first time. If you are an experienced paddler desiring a board and a guide you'll find both at **SUP Venice** (Cannaregio, Fondamenta Della Sensa 3320, www.supinvenice.com, €50-70 pp). Eliana Argine has been leading tours and navigating the city for over a decade. Routes vary depending on number of participants (max 4), weather, tide, and traffic and take about two hours to complete. Excursions are organized from March to November and comfortable attire is encouraged (no bare chests or swimwear).

TOURS
Walking Tours

There are around 400 licensed guides in Venice and passing the certification exam is not a formality. It takes a combination of historical, artistic, and cultural knowledge as well as excellent language skills. Visitors can choose from group tours organized by the city, private tour companies, and independent guides. While the former costs less the latter are usually smaller and allow for greater personalization. Whatever you choose it's a good idea to have a tour early in your stay so you can become familiar with the urban landscape as soon as possible. Afterwards it will be much easier to recognize details and appreciate local habits. Taking a walking tour around the city is also a wonderful way to put yourself in the hands of someone who doesn't need a map and rarely gets lost.

Private certified guides charge a standard €70-80 hourly fee f[...] two-hour tour. Prices are the [...] two or eight people participat[...] are slightly more imperson[...] clude up to thirty visitors. T[...] cheaper and start from €3([...] 90-minute visit. There are [...] and most generally focus on the [...] area. If you're interested in food or modern art you're better off using a private guide.

PRIVATE GUIDES

Private guides **Sara Grinzato** (tel. 345/850-1309, www.guidedvenice.com) and **Rossana Colombo** (tel. 339/600-8709 www.guide-venice.it) know their city well and love sharing that native knowledge with visitors. After a couple of hours together you'll see Venice differently and things that made no sense will begin to seem normal. They can customize visits according to your interest in art, food, or shopping, but tours often start with an overview of classic destinations like Piazza San Marco and the Rialto. Both will pick you up at your accommodation at the hour of your choosing and can organize fun treasure hunts for restless children and teens.

FREE TOURS

A **Venice Free Walking Tour** (www.venicefreewalkingtour.com) sounds too good to be true—but it isn't. This nonprofit initiative leads 2.5-hour morning and afternoon tours that cover the foundation of the city, traditions, gastronomy, and plenty of facts and figures. Tours start from the old wellhead in Campo Santi Apostoli (Cannaregio) and proceed over a historic two-mile route. Guides are passionate local volunteers who get a kick out of helping curious visitors uncover their city. All tours are conducted in English.

Once you've fallen in love with Venice, you may want to help preserve it, and there are many organizations dedicated to just that cause. **Save Venice Inc.** (Dorsoduro, Palazzo Contarini Polignac 870, tel. 041/528-5247, Mon.-Fri. 9am-5pm) helps repair and restore the city one painting, sculpture, and *palazzo*

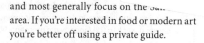

Family-Friendly Venice

Venice is a dream city for kids. It may not have a children's museum or amusement park but it has water, boats, and bridges. Parents can relax knowing there are no cars to look out for and can give kids full reign to run around the squares chasing pigeons and playing ball with local youth. There are no limits to the imagination in Venice, and the city delights and stimulates children in ways they will never forget. Unfortunately, parents with babies and young walkers may suffer, as carrying a stroller up and down the city's many bridges is an arduous task. It's easier to use a hiking carrier or stick to the *fondamente* promenades.

- To generate a little fun, just buy a **mask.** Parents can find cheap plastic versions (€2) in souvenir stands and shops around the city. Let children pick their own and walk masqueraded through the streets. Note: Inexpensive doesn't always mean made in China. Low-priced plastic and rough papier-mâché masks are also fabricated in Italy. They come in many varieties and may be tricky to tie.

- There are several **playgrounds** (Giardino Papadopoli, Parco Savorgnan, Giardini Publici) equipped with traditional swings, slides, and wooden climbing castles. Toddlers to 10-year-olds will love them.

- All ages will love riding the *vaporetto* **boats** that magically eliminate whining—and are free for all passengers under six.

- Hungry kids? That's not a problem in Venice! The mini portions served mornings and afternoons at *bacaro* **bars** make delicious snacks and may convince fussy eaters to try something new.

- Kid-friendly museums include the **Museo Storico Navale** with its collection of ancient sailing vessels and the **secret dungeons** in Palazzo Ducale.

- **Glassblowing** demonstrations on the island of Murano, along with climbable **bell towers** (Piazza San Marco, Isola di San Giorgio Maggiore or Torcello), will captivate even the shortest attention spans.

at a time. You can go to their office and speak with Leslie or Holly about the organization's activities, visit their library, and pick up one of their **self-guided treasure hunt tours** dedicated to art and architecture. Each hunt lasts about 90 minutes and a suggested donation of €20 is appreciated that helps fund future restoration projects.

Boat Tours

Several companies including **City Sightseeing** operate boat tours around Venice. Travelers can compare the options along the **Riva degli Schiavoni** waterfront from where they regularly depart. Journey times and itineraries vary and the biggest advantage is the assurance of getting a seat. The convenience and widespread availability of public *vaporetto*, however, make boat tours nearly superfluous.

Il Burchiello (Padova, Via Porciglia 34, 049/876-0233, www.ilburchiello.it) operates half- and full-day expeditions up the Brenta Canal that connects Venice to Padova. Boats depart at 9am from the Pietà water station (Riva degli Schiavoni) near Piazza San Marco on Tuesdays, Thursdays, and Saturdays. The *bateau mouche*-like vessels have air-conditioned interiors, but the best seats are upstairs on the roof deck. It's a slow ride through pretty countryside, with three or four stops to visit the gardens and interiors of the region's palatial villas. Lunch is extra and the tour is one-way only, but getting back to Venice from Oriago by bus or Padova by train is easy and is an excuse to discover another beautiful city.

kids watching glass being made

- With a little planning you can also organize **papermaking workshops** and classical concerts for artistically minded adolescents.

- Consider booking a hotel room at kid-friendly **Flora** in San Marco, where strollers, high chairs, and cots are all available at no extra cost, or **La Villeggiatura** in San Polo, where children under nine sleep for free.

CLASSES
Cooking

Learn the secrets of Venetian cuisine at the **Gritti Epicurean School** (San Marco, Gritti Palace Hotel, Campo Santa Maria del Giglio 2467, tel. 041/794-611, www.thegrittiepicureanschool.com, 9am-3pm, €290) where a **half-day class** begins by learning about and choosing seasonal ingredients at the Rialto market with chef Daniele Turco. There's time for a *bacaro* break before heading back to the professionally equipped kitchen to prepare a Venetian lunch. It's a practical, slicing-and-dicing introduction to local specialties that nearly always includes fish. The class ends with a well-deserved three-course meal. Participant numbers range from two to eight and courses are held twice a month or

by request. All ingredients and wine are included in the price.

Glassblowing

Once you've seen sand heated to a thousand degrees and transformed into glass you may want to try making some yourself. What looks simple, however, isn't—and most of the glassblowers have been practicing their craft for decades. To understand what's involved in the process you'll need to go to school, and the best place to do that is at the **Abate Zanetti School of Glass** (Calle Briati 8b, Murano, tel. 041/273-7711, www.lascuoladelvetro. it). Students learn how a furnace functions and the basics of shaping raw material through marbling and blowing techniques.

Most courses are for beginners and last 20 hours over several days, but there are also weekend courses in lampworking (€400) and glassworking (€480) for groups of 4-10 people. Single-day private lessons (€120) are also available and participants get to keep their creations. If all you want is theory without practice, the guided tour at the **Glass Museum** (Fondamenta Giustinian 8, Murano, tel. 041/739-586) on Tuesdays and Thursdays at 2:30pm (€18) is followed by the live demonstration at the school, which can answer any questions you ever had about glass.

Accommodations

There's nothing like waking up in Venice, though finding a decent hotel room can be challenging and more expensive than in Florence or Rome. The influx of visitors combined with limited space means low season only lasts from November to January, when rain and falling temperatures dissuade travelers. Italians migrate to beaches and second homes in July and August and hotels often charge midseason rates. Occupancy and prices are high the rest of the year. Advance reservations are essential at peak times like *Carnevale* in February, the Venice Film Festival in September, and major holidays.

Fortunately, hotels aren't the only option. Bed-and-breakfasts and self-catering apartments provide convenient alternatives for travelers who enjoy staying with locals or prefer the independent approach. Many religious institutions also offer accommodation at relatively affordable prices. Rooms are clean and simple, but expect a curfew and less charm. No longer just for youthful backpackers, the city's hostels now often include cool décor and convenient services at significantly lower prices.

Whatever option you choose, it will likely be small. Space comes at a premium in a city where most buildings are more than a hundred years old. There are five-star exceptions, but these are costly and not always stylish. Many rooms around the city suffer from flamboyant furnishings, gilded headboards, and unfashionable floral wallpaper. On the bright side, romantic views of canals, rooftops, and courtyards make up for inconveniences like the absence of elevators (rare except in large establishments) or faulty Wi-Fi. If stairs are a problem, check what floor you're on before booking.

San Marco has the largest concentration of hotels but can be a hassle to reach. It's also the busiest *sestiere*, which means that some may prefer staying in more secluded neighborhoods like **Dorsoduro** or **Cannaregio**. Of course, you can always pay a porter to cart your bags up and down the bridges or hire a water taxi to get wherever you need to go. Just make sure you settle on a price before setting off and ask reception to organize the return journey. If you have difficulty finding accommodation in Venice the nearby towns of Mestre and Marghera or farther-away cities like Padova or Vicenza are easy commutes by bus, tram, or train.

SAN MARCO
Under €100

The flowered façade of **Hotel Locanda Fiorita** (Campiello Novo 3457a, tel. 041/523-4754, www.locandafiorita.com, €80 d) looks out onto a miniature secret square around the corner from the bustle of Campo Santo Stefano. It's a delightful oasis to come home to and hosts Alessandra and Paolo make it even more enjoyable. Rooms have the right amount of baroque along with dark wooden floors, exposed beams, and earth-toned furnishings that soothe the eye. Rooms 1 and 10 each have their own shaded terrace.

Settimo Cielo B&B (Campiello Santo Stefano 3470, 342/636-2581, www.

Rooms with shared baths are heavily discounted. Breakfast isn't served but there are plenty of bars in the area.

None of the 40 rooms at **Flora** (Calle dei Bergamaschi 2283a, tel. 041/520-5844, www. hotelflora.it, €160 d) are the same, though each has custom furniture, tapestries, and Murano glass fittings. The hotel has a worldly atmosphere and has been run by the same family for over half a century. Children are particularly welcome and strollers, high chairs, and cots are all available at no extra cost. The highlight of the hotel is the lovely garden where breakfast is served and guests can relax in bucolic tranquility.

If a friendly face is as important as décor and the size of a bathroom doesn't matter, **Locanda Orseolo** (Corte Zorzi 1083, tel. 041/520-4827, www.locandaorseolo.com, €175 d) is worth considering. The young staff is friendly and readily assists guests before being asked. There are several room types, a lovely breakfast area, and a study with rustic charm.

Prices can range widely depending on your view at **Hotel Violino d'Oro** (Campiello Barbozzi 2091, tel. 041/277-0841, www.violinodoro.com, €200 d). If you come during the low season, ask for a room overlooking the *Campiello* or San Marco Canal. You can sometimes find real bargains at this hotel, which is classically furnished in tones of gold, ivory, and blue.

Over €250

The ★ **Gritti Palace Hotel** (Campo Santa Maria del Giglio 2467, tel. 041/794-611, www. thegrittipalace.com, €415 d) is no ordinary hotel. It's *the* hotel. This is the only 15th-century *palazzo* Churchill, Hemingway, Garbo, Stravinsky, and a long list of 20th-century legends would consider staying while in Venice. Yes, there are five-star rivals, but the Gritti does luxury without trying. The recent €36 million restoration has only made things better and staying here on the edge of the Grand Canal could become the highlight of your entire trip. It's like entering the home of a Venetian aristocrat with plush, old-world

Hotel Locanda Fiorita

settimocielo-venice.com, €100 d) does have flamboyant Venetian style and ornate headboards, but they just seem to work here. This eclectically styled B&B on the edge of Campo Santo Stefano is secluded enough to guarantee a good night's sleep and central enough that guests can reach any *sestiere* in the city in less than 15 minutes. The complimentary breakfast is closer to a banquet than a buffet. The only inconvenience is the stairs, which can be a challenge for anyone on the 3rd floor.

€100-250

If you don't plan on spending much time in your hotel and want to start the day a block from Piazza San Marco, **Hotel Ai Do Mori** (Calle Larga S. Marco 658, tel. 041/520-4817, www.hotelaidomori.com, €150 d) is a good option. Besides location, the advantages are price, a friendly staff, and overall spotlessness. Many of the rooms have views of the *campanile* and basilica. The lower ones are slightly larger and accommodation gets progressively smaller all the way up to the cramped attic.

Best Accommodations

★ **Gritti Palace Hotel:** Churchill and Hemingway once rested their heads at this luxurious 15th-century *palazzo* (page 293).

★ **Hotel Galleria:** This affordable option has helpful hosts, antique furnishings, and views of the Grand Canal (page 294).

★ **Pensione Accademia:** This affordable, hospitable option is in a17th-century *palazzo* that retains all its charm and boasts a peaceful garden (page 294).

★ **Cà del Forno:** Waking up inside a real Venetian home has its advantages, especially if that home is in a 15th-century *palazzo* and belongs to part-time chef Maria Grazie (page 295).

★ **The Metropole:** No two rooms are alike at this stylish hotel, which has a canalside entrance and a Michelin-starred restaurant (page 296).

★ **Generator Venice:** The coolest hostel in Venice is located in a former granary complete with canal views and free walking tours (page 296).

furnishings in every room and a well-mannered staff who know what you want before you do. Staying here will never be a bargain but you get everything you pay for and a lot more.

DORSODURO
Under €100

The **Santa Monica** (Calle delle Pazienze 2885, www.santamargherita-lodgings.com, €95 d) is a small guesthouse with six rooms close to Campo Santa Margherita. Each of the rooms has its own bathroom, safe, and minibar. There's a shared cooking corner in the living area on the ground floor where a self-service breakfast buffet is waiting every morning. The owners also rent out four apartments (€100-235) of different dimensions in the neighborhood. All are clean and convenient with Ikea-like furnishings and a bright, homey feel.

€100-200

Affordable accommodation overlooking the Grand Canal is hard to come by, but views that won't break the bank are still available at ★ **Hotel Galleria** (Rio Terrà Foscarini 878,

tel. 041/523-2489, www.hotelgalleria.it, €150 d). Six of the nine rooms in the hotel face the water and all are decorated with functional antique furnishings. Breakfast in bed can be arranged with Luciano and Stefano, who will happily recommend bars or restaurants and gladly recount the history of their city. The hotel was entirely refurbished in 2016.

★ **Pensione Accademia** (Fondamenta Bollani 1058, tel. 041/521-0188, www.pensioneaccademia.it, €170 d) feels like a five-star hotel at a fraction of the price. It's run by the Salmaso family, who live and breathe hospitality and have been welcoming guests for decades. The 17th-century *palazzo* has retained all its charm and although the rooms are small they are tastefully decorated. The communal hall and garden are great for recovering from a day on the streets and the front desk can assist with dinner reservations, theater tickets, and boots in case the city floods. Romantics can arrange to have *prosecco* and flowers waiting upon arrival.

€200-300

Ca' Pisani Hotel (Rio Terrà Foscarini 979a, tel. 041/240-1411, www.capisanihotel.

it, d €200-480 d) mixes modern with art deco design two minutes from the Ponte dell'Accademia. All 29 rooms are decorated with original 1930s furnishings and come in a number of sizes including family rooms and junior suites. The small restaurant and wine bar offer the perfect end to a long day.

Near Santa Maria della Salute, **Ca' Maria Adele** (Rio Terrà Catecumeno 111, tel. 041/520-3078, www.camariaadele.it, €290 d) offers a variety of styles and prices. These include deluxe rooms with brocades in colors that remind you that gold is neutral in Venice. There are also five themed rooms, including the Doge's Room (for anyone who likes red) and the Marco Polo Oriental Room.

They understand the importance of first impressions at the **Hotel Moresco** (Dorsoduro, Fondamenta del Passamonte 3499, tel. 041/244-0202, www.hotelmorescovenice.com, €190-290 d), where the staff is welcoming and prepared to go the extra kilometer for guests. The hotel is a short distance from the train station and can easily be reached on foot or by water taxi. Each of the 23 elegantly furnished rooms have oak flooring, soundproofed windows, and modern bathrooms. The garden and study are pleasant places to relax after a day exploring the city.

SAN POLO AND SANTA CROCE
Under €100

It's not the number of stars that matters, but the experience, and **Hotel Al Ponte Mocenigo** (Santa Croce, Fondamenta Mocenigo, tel. 041/524-4797, www.alpontemocenigo.com, €90-140 d) delivers in that respect. The décor reflects the fact you're in Venice without going over the top, and the little courtyard where breakfast is served is a great spot to start the day. The Grand Canal is a short walk away and there are dozens of good, reasonably priced restaurants nearby.

€100-200

If you're Italian you might recognize Maria Grazie Calò from her regular appearances on a popular cooking show; if you're not you'll just be happy that breakfast at ★ **Cà del Forno** (San Polo, Calle Forno 1421a, tel. 041/523-7024, d €120) is being prepared by a part-time chef. The B&B she runs on the 2nd floor of a 15th-century *palazzo* near the Rialto is a classic Venetian home with immense ceilings, antique furnishings, and oil paintings on every wall. There are three double rooms, two of which can be converted into triples or quads, with private baths and pleasant views. The price is excellent for Venice and the warm welcome is just what you need after a day meandering through the city.

Pensione Guerrato (San Polo, Calle Drio La Scimia 240a, tel. 041/528-5927, www.pensioneguerrato.it, €145 d) is a one-star hotel with personality. Most of the furniture in this 20-room *pensione* is secondhand, making the 13th-century *palazzo* feel like home. There's a *vaporetto* station five minutes away and plenty of action in the surrounding streets, so it can get loud during the summer when local bars stay open late. Rooms are on the 3rd floor and several overlook the Grand Canal. There's no elevator and Wi-Fi only works in the lobby, but proud owner Roberto Zammattio and his warm and genuine staff make up for any minor drawbacks.

At **La Villeggiatura** (San Polo, Calle dei Botteri 1569, tel. 041/524-4673, www.lavilleggiatura.it, €130-165 d), B&B rooms can be as large as hotel rooms. There may not be a great view and the outside of the *palazzo* could use a wash, but the inside is immaculate and the six rooms on the third floor are spacious (especially Casanova and Doge) and well decorated, and all come with king-size beds. Children under nine stay for free. Rates vary according to the season.

CANNAREGIO AND CASTELLO
Under €100

We Crociferi (Cannaregio, Campo dei Gesuiti 4878, tel. 041/528-6103, www.we-gastameco.com, €80 d) provides student housing inside a former monastery throughout the year and welcomes everyone from July 15 to August 15. It's comfortable, clean, includes breakfast at the adjacent bar and restaurant, and is located on a tranquil square far from any crowds. Rooms and apartments have en suite bathrooms with showers, or you can book a bed in a shared room (€40). There's a major *vaporetto* station less than two minutes away that connects the city with the islands of Murano and Burano.

Istituto San Giuseppe (Castello, Ponte della Guerra 5402, tel. 041/522-5352, sangiuseppe.venezia@virgilio.it, €80 d) is simple, clean, and guarantees a good night's sleep. This comfortable religious house with 14 rooms has an early curfew; if you're not back by 10pm you'll have some explaining to do to the monks.

The best thing about **B&B San Marco** (Castello, Fondamenta San Giorgio degli Schiavoni 3385, tel. 041/522-7589, www.realvenice.it, €90 d) are the hosts, Marco and Alice, who go out of their way to welcome guests. The three rooms of this intimate B&B are large and well decorated and have views of rooftops and canals. Only one has an en suite bath, so book ahead if you don't fancy sharing. Breakfast is served in the kitchen and consists of Nutella, fresh bread, coffee, fruit juice, and homemade surprises.

€100-200

Locanda ai Santi Apostoli (Cannaregio, Strada Nuova 4391a, tel. 041/099-6916, www.locandasantiapostoli.com, €120 d) is a reliable three-star hotel overlooking the Grand Canal. The 11 rooms are located on the 3rd floor of a historic *palazzo* on the main street in Cannaregio that makes finding the hotel and reaching other parts of the city easy. Rooms are large and nicely decorated.

Ponte Chiodo (Cannaregio, Ponte Chiodo 3749, tel. 041/241-3935, www.pontechiodo.it, €125 d) overlooks a canal minutes away from the best *bacari* and nightlife in the neighborhood. The guesthouse provides Wi-Fi, air-conditioning, and breakfast pastries supplied by the local bakery. There's a delightful

garden out back, a railless bridge out front, and an owner inside always willing to talk about Venice.

Foresteria Valdese (Castello, Calle della Madoneta 5170, tel. 041/528-6797, www.foresteriavenezia.it, €140 d, dormitory €35), one of Venice's religious accommodations, is run by Italian Methodists who converted an 18th-century *palazzo* into a 14-room guesthouse. Rooms range from private doubles with en suite bathrooms and canal views to beds in one of two ground-floor dormitories. These are often filled with schoolchildren and youth groups who are quiet at night but vivacious during the day. There's no curfew, complimentary breakfast is served from 8am until 9:15am, and multiple-night stays are discounted.

€200-300

★ **The Metropole** (Castello, Riva degli Schiavone 4149, tel. 041/520-5044, www.hotelmetropole.com, €280 d) is a stylish hotel a short walk from Piazza San Marco. No two rooms are the same at this hotel, which looks out on the lagoon and has an entrance directly on a canal if you want to make a remarkable entry. Doubles, suites, and deluxe rooms are decorated with elegant period furnishings, velvet curtains, rare books, and chandeliers. It's all done tastefully and provides a wonderfully romantic atmosphere. The concierge can handle nearly any request including currency exchange, daily newspaper delivery, babysitting, breakfast in bed, and dry-cleaning. The Michelin-starred restaurant inside the hotel serves a modern mix of fusion dishes that trick the eye and surprise the stomach. Tea is served in the bar every afternoon and live music played every evening.

GIUDECCA
Under €100

★ **Generator Venice** (Fondamenta Zitelle 86, tel. 041/877-8288, www.generatorhostels.com, €16 per bed in shared room, €80 d) is the coolest hostel in the city. The interior of this former granary feels more like a club, and the bar and lounge areas are perfect for recounting Venetian adventures with travelers. There are mixed and female-only dormitory rooms of different dimensions that are modern and comfortable. Rustic double rooms are located in the attic and look out onto the Canale della Giudecca. The property offers complimentary Wi-Fi, 24-hour reception, a restaurant, and free daily walking tours of the neighborhood.

Information and Services

TOURIST INFORMATION
Tourist Information Centers

Hello Venezia (tel. 041/2424, daily 9am-6pm for live operators and 24/7 for recorded info) is the city's call center and provides information about transportation, cultural events, and the Venezia Unica Card. You can purchase tickets to many events by phone or at one of several tourist offices around the city. The **Info Point** (daily 8am-8:50pm) outside Santa Lucia station sells museum and transport passes; if the office is too crowded you can use the automated machines near the canal Venezia Unica Cards. A second **Info Point** (daily 9am-7pm) is located inside Museo Correr in Piazza San Marco. There you can get the latest news on cultural activities, pick up maps, and get any queries answered.

There are additional offices in **Piazzale Roma** (daily 9:30am-3:30pm) and inside the arrivals hall at **Marco Polo Airport** (daily 9am-8pm). During the summer an info point operates on the **Lido** (Gran Viale 6a, daily 9am-noon and 3pm-6pm).

Luggage Storage

There's a **luggage storage facility** (daily 6am-11pm) in the train station on the last platform on the right as you enter the station. The first five hours is €6 and it's €0.90 for each additional hour after that. There's a second storage office in Piazzale Roma (tel. 041/523-1107, daily 6am-9pm) near the Pullman bar that charges a flat €5 per item. There are lines most of the day, so if it isn't absolutely necessary skip it. Most hotels will hold bags before check-in and after check-out.

HEALTH AND SAFETY
Emergency Numbers

For medical emergencies call the **118** hotline or the **Guardia Medica Turistica** (Ca' Savio, tel. 041/530-0874), which is dedicated entirely to diagnosing the ailments of visitors. For emergencies requiring police assistance dial **112.**

Police

Report crimes at the **Police Headquarters** (Ponte della Liberta, tel. 041/271-5511) in Santa Croce near the train station or the smaller **precinct** (Fondamenta San Lorenzo 5053) in Castello opposite Campo San Lorenzo.

Hospitals and Pharmacies

If you need a hospital, try **Ospedale Fatebenefratalli** (Cannaregio 3458, tel. 041/783-111) or **Ospedale Civile** (Dorsoduro 3493, tel. 041/523-0000). There are a dozen pharmacies in the city including **Farmacia Santa Lucia** (Cannaregio, Rio Tera Lista di Spagna 122, tel. 041/716-332) and **Farmacia San Polo** (San Polo, Campo San Polo, tel. 041/522-3527, Mon.-Fri. 9am-1pm and 3:30pm-7:30pm, Sat. 9am-12:45pm). Most pharmacies are located on busy streets and squares, and are recognizable by the green neon cross.

Foreign Consulates

Report lost or stolen passports to the **U.S. Consulate** in Milan (tel. 02/290-351, Mon.-Fri. 9:30am-12:30pm). They can also help with any diplomatic problems you may encounter.

Lost and Found

There's still hope if you've lost something in Venice. Objects forgotten on ferry boats are stored for seven days inside the **lost-and-found office** (San Marco, Ca'Farsetti 4136, tel. 041/272-2723, daily 7:30am-7:30pm) in Piazzale Roma. They are then transferred to the **central office** (tel. 041/274-8225, www.comune.venezia.it, weekdays 9am-1pm). The city issues a monthly online list of objects and the date and location they were found. You can also try the airport lost and found (tel. 041/260-6436) in the arrivals terminal and the **Vigili Urbani** (Piazzale Roma, tel. 041/522-4576). Found items that aren't retrieved are eventually sold at auction.

COMMUNICATIONS

Wi-Fi

Venice (www.cittadinanzadigitale.it) has installed wireless infrastructure around the city, Lido, and smaller islands. Most large squares and major monuments are covered. Usage is limited to 12 hours per day and can be supplemented with the Venezia Unica Card. Many hotels, restaurants, and bars also offer free Wi-Fi access, but if you're feeling nostalgic for a copy shop with Internet access or want some digital photos printed visit **E Copie da Toni** (Castello, S. Lio Calle delle Bande 5645, Mon.-Fri. 9:30am-1pm and 3pm-7pm).

Transportation

GETTING THERE

Air

Aeroporto di Venezia (VCE, Via Galileo Galilei 30, tel. 041/260-6111, www.veniceairport.it) is a medium-sized airport with runways overlooking the lagoon that make for dramatic takeoffs and landings. There are few direct flights to North America but many connecting flights from across Europe. The newly renovated interior is easy to navigate and lines move quickly. The well-organized arrivals hall provides passengers with clear indications for reaching Venice by bus, taxi, or boat. There's also a **tourist office** where travel cards and maps are available. Wi-Fi access is limited and requires registration. There are few scheduled flights from Rome and none from Florence.

The cheapest way to reach Venice from the airport is by **bus**. The **ATVO Shuttle** (tel. 042/159-4672, www.atvo.it) costs €8 one-way (€15 round-trip) and completes the transfer in 20 minutes. Buses operate daily between 5:20am and 12:20am and drop passengers off in Piazzale Roma. If you prefer to be driven in a car you can call **RadioTaxi** (041/5964) 24 hours a day to book a ride, or head to their office in the arrivals hall once you land. Fares

from the airport to Venice are fixed at €40. Taxis do not operate within the city; they drop passengers in Piazzale di Roma near the train station, from where you must walk or board a boat.

The most exciting way of reaching Venice, however, is by water. **Alilaguna** (tel. 041-240-1701, www.alilaguna.it) operates three **ferry** lines (blue, orange, and red) with convenient daily service to stops around the city including San Marco, Rialto, and Guglie. One-way tickets are €15 (€27 round-trip) and allow for one suitcase and one carry-on item with a €3 surcharge for extra bags. Service runs daily from 7:45am to 12:20am and there are several departures per hour. Tickets can be purchased in the arrivals hall or online. The faster and even more dramatic aquatic approach to the city is by **water taxi,** of which there are a number of private companies to choose from. **Consorzio Motoscalfi** (tel. 041/522-2303, www.motoscafivenezia.it) is consortium of water taxis that operate 24 hours a day and can drop you off anywhere you like. A ride for up to six passengers to any point in the city is €100, which can be a small price to pay for getting your journey off to a sensational start.

Train

Getting to Venice from either Rome or Florence is a pleasant journey on board high-speed trains that depart regularly from both cities. Both **Italo** (www.italo.it) and **Trenitalia** (www.trenitalia.it) provide affordable and comfortable service to Venice.

Trains terminate at **Santa Lucia** station, from where the city is accessible on foot. Exiting Santa Lucia train station and seeing the Grand Canal for the first time is one of the most dramatic entrances you can make in a city. Along the canal front are automated machines and ticket offices selling *vaporetto* passes for travelers wishing to make an immediate aquatic getaway. Otherwise there are three choices: You can turn right towards Piazzale Roma and the Dorsoduro, turn left towards Cannaregio, or cross the Ponte degli Scalzi and enter the Santa Croce neighborhood.

From Rome: High-speed trains from Rome Termini and Tiburtina stations to Venice take less than four hours and cost as little as €29 if reserved in advance. There are dozens of daily departures.

From Florence: High-speed trains from Florence Stazione Santa Maria Novella station to Venice take less than two hours and cost as little as €19. All high-speed trains headed to Venice from Rome stop in Florence.

Car

The drive to Venice from Rome or Florence is fairly straightforward and can be undertaken on well-built modern highways. Driving does take longer than the train option and comes with the added expense of tolls, fuel, and occasional frustration. The journey ends once you've crossed the Ponte della Libertà to Venice, where cars must be parked in one of several conveniently accessed garages or lots. Prices range €25-35 per day and parking may be difficult to find during special occasions like *Carnevale* or the Venice Film Festival. A thrifty alternative is to park in the nearby town of **Mestre** on the mainland where rates are about half the price and travelers can reach Venice by bus or train in 15 minutes. If you want to save on rental fees, leave the driving to someone else, and make new acquaintances, try Italian **car sharing** (www.blablacar.it).

From Rome: The route from Rome to Venice is clearly indicated and consists mostly of two-lane highways with a speed limit of 130kph. Follow the signs for Firenze (Florence), which will eventually lead to the A1 highway. The journey to Florence is 377

Santa Lucia railway station

Venetian Vocabulary

Geography combined with foreign linguistic influences have formed a unique language that only exists in Venice and is used to describe the city's unusual urban landscape. The faster you absorb this vocabulary the easier it will be to identify different aspects of the Venetian cityscape and appreciate the beauty of the city.

- *Calle, calleta:* Street, alley, or thoroughfare that can vary substantially in length and width. The former are wider than the latter.

- *Campo, campielo:* Unevenly shaped square of varying proportions. *Campo* means *field*, and these spaces were originally grassy meadows where food was grown and animals grazed. Most have been paved over and today provide visual and physical relief from the narrow *calle*. A *campielo* is a smaller version of a *campo*.

- *Fondamenta:* Any *calle* located next to a canal or *rio*. *Fondazione* means *foundation*, and these streets helped reinforce the islands and allow for urbanization. They can feature stone or iron railings—or none at all—and often have stairs for making getting on and off boats easier. *Fondamente* (plural) are often lined with shops, bars, and restaurants.

- *Ca':* Short for *casa* (house) and used to indicate important residences. The word is usually followed by a family name indicating the original residents.

- *Corte:* A small dead-end courtyard surrounded by residential buildings. They're generally reached from a *sotoportego* or *calleta* and are the center of micro-neighborhoods where Venetians once spent their days washing, sewing, preparing meals, and socializing.

- *Pietra d'Istria:* Dense, impermeable limestone quarried from the Istria peninsula and an essential material in the construction of Venice. Used to build and decorate *calle*, bridges, canals, churches, homes, and palaces.

- *Rio:* Small canal. There are hundreds throughout the city that function both to enhance communication and permit the tides to flow freely through the city and prevent stagnation.

- *Rio Terra:* Any canal that has been filled in and transformed into a street.

- *Riva:* Wide walkway bordering the Grand Canal or San Marco Canal.

- *Sestiere:* Historic neighborhood or district. There are six in Venice and these are symbolically represented by the six metal strips decorating the prow of every gondola.

- *Sotoportego:* Underpass connecting *calle*, *campi*, or *fondamente*. These were usually created by removing the ground floor of houses and often contain small shrines or sacred images of the Virgin Mary and other popular saints.

kilometers and takes a little over 3 hours. Once you reach the city follow the directions below.

From Florence: If you're parked in Florence's historic center, cross the Arno and continue west along the river. You'll eventually see signs for the **A1** highway and should follow indications to Bologna. Once you reach that city take the **A13** all the way to Padua and complete the journey along the **A57** that runs

directly to Venice. The entire journey is 260 kilometers (162 miles), a distance that can be driven in less than three hours.

A section of the journey crosses the Apennine Mountains that run up and down the peninsula and there are many tunnels, turns, and inclines. Be prepared for occasional roadwork and possible traffic jams during the summer. There are several alternative routes in case you prefer a longer and slower drive.

Bus

Passengers arriving by bus are deposited at the **Tronchetto Bus Terminal** on the western edge of the city, the only part of Venice that comes close to being an eyesore. Fortunately, the efficient **People Mover monorail** (daily 7am-11pm, €2) shuttles passengers into and out of the city in a couple minutes and there are continuous departures.

From Rome: The bus journey from Tiburtina station in Rome to Venice lasts an agonizing eight hours, but tickets are cheap (from €9). You can compare fares on Eurolines, Megabus, Baltour, Flixbus, and other operators using the **GoEuro** (www. goeuro.com) travel planner. Buses depart for Venice about a dozen times per day.

From Florence: Flixbus, Eurolines and Megabus operate from Piazzale Montelungo near Santa Maria Novella station. The journey time is close to five hours and one-way tickets start at €7. Buses depart about a dozen times per day.

Boat

You'd think that a city surrounded by water is best approached from the water, but that isn't always practical. It's true that cruise ships arrive every day and disgorge thousands of passengers, but none of these stop in Rome or Florence. The only other alternative would be hiring a vessel, which is costly and time consuming. It's best therefore to save the boats for once you've arrived.

GETTING AROUND

The two most common ways of exploring Venice are by foot or water. Although it's smaller than Rome or Florence you're likely to walk more in Venice than in these other cities. Taking some sort of water transportation is the only way to truly understand the city. The canals are full of different types of boats loading and unloading goods and passengers throughout the day. There are three principle modes of water transportation in Venice: *vaporetto, traghetto,* and water taxi.

Vaporetto

Public transportation is unique, necessary, and rewarding in Venice. It comprises more than 20 **ACTV** (tel. 041/2424, actv.avmspa.it) ferry lines *(vaporetti)*. Each neighborhood has a handful of ferry stations and digital signs indicate how long commuters have to wait for the next boat. Boats on the main routes arrive every twenty minutes, so wait time is minimal. Service is efficient and makes getting around Venice fast and fun. Stations have color-coded maps that can also be downloaded from the ACTV website. Tickets are expensive because boats are harder to maintain than buses and require a captain to steer and a crew member to allow passengers on and off.

Vaporetti are the most common way of getting around Venice. These omnipresent ferries run up and down the Grand Canal, circumnavigate the city, and connect it with outlying islands in the lagoon. There are 24 routes in all that use boats of varying sizes. All have indoor seating and some outdoor seats, which you should try to grab.

Tickets can be purchased at larger stations such as Piazzale di Roma just over the Ponte della Costituzione bridge, or outside the train station. There are many booths, as well as automatic vending machines, so lines are rare. Some newsstands also sell tickets. You can choose from **single tickets** (€7.50) or **24-hour** (€20), **48-hour** (€30), or **72-hour** (€40) passes. These must be validated at the machines outside each station and passengers may be asked to show their passes by controllers. Once validated for the first time you have unlimited travel possibilities.

Vaporetti are even more fun when you ride with no particular destination in mind. If you want to get a good look at Venice, the **4.1, 4.2, 5.1,** and **5.2** lines circumnavigate the city and terminate in **Fondamente Nuove** where you can transfer onto larger ferries heading to Murano, Burano, and Torcello. Lines **1** and **2** go up and down the Grand Canal and you can ride either from Piazzale Roma to San Marco or vice versa in less than 30 minutes.

Vaporetto are usually crowded in summer

and have a capacity of up to 250 depending on the boat. Each line has different hours but service usually starts around 6am and continues until midnight. There's also a night service (N) that runs 11:30pm-5am and runs down the Grand Canal out to the Lido.

Water Taxi

Water taxi is the quicker, more expensive way of getting around Venice. These slick motorboats zip passengers along the canals in style. Pickup can be arranged in advance or simply by going to the nearest taxi station. There are several at Piazzale Roma, Piazza San Marco, and other locations around the city. The fixed price is €120 for a one-hour ride for four people. You can choose any itinerary you like with your driver, and besides going down the Grand Canal you should ask to explore the more intimate inner canals.

The boats are extremely comfortable and resemble miniature floating limousines, with leather seats, wood paneling, and sunroofs that can be slid open or closed depending on the weather. Water taxis are much smaller than *vaporetto* and are susceptible to waves, especially when going down the Grand Canal or out into the open lagoon. Some drivers will point out interesting sights but most are happy to leave passengers alone and periodically check their smartphones.

There are water taxi stations around Venice. Prices depend on distance and time. A ride from Santa Lucia station to Piazza San Marco is €60-70 for 1-4 passengers while a trip to the airport is €100-120. Extra passengers are charged €10 each. Boats can be reserved from **Water Taxi Venice** (342/106-8412, www.consorziovenseziafutura.it) or **Acqua Taxi Venezia** (351 2026881, www.taxiserviceh24.com).

Traghetto

Private gondola rides, which can seat up to six passengers, are expensive (the rate is fixed at €80 for a 30-minute ride), but you can save money by taking advantage of the *traghetti* (gondola ferries, Mon.-Sat. 7:30am-7pm and Sun. 9am-7pm, €2) that operate on the Grand Canal. A ride lasts five minutes and is a fun and practical way to get from one neighborhood to another. Dozens of these ferry points once operated, but today there are only three left—and it's worth riding them all. They can be boarded at the docks near Santa Maria del Giglio opposite the Guggenheim, San Tomà halfway between Ponte dell'Accademia and the Rialto, and next to the covered

vaporetto

fishmarket near the Rialto. Locals usually stand during the crossing, but you can also sit on the side railing and watch as two gondoliers skillfully oar their way from one bank to another.

Bus and Tram

The only place you'll see buses or trams (€1.50 or €3 on board) in Venice is Piazzale Roma, just over the Ponte della Costituzione bridge from the train station. They are primarily used by locals commuting from the mainland town of Mestre and tourists riding the airport shuttle (€15) but are not for getting around Venice itself. **Tickets** are available from automated machines near the modern awning in the center of the *piazza* as well as newsstands and *tabacchi* shops.

Day Trips

There are dozens of islands and countless islets in the Venice Lagoon, but Murano, Burano, and Torcello are the most popular. Each has its own distinct personality and all three can be visited in a day by *vaporetto*. **Murano** is the closest, largest, and most populated. It's famous for glass and could be mistaken for Venice's younger brother. The other two islands are farther away and smaller. **Burano,** known for lace production, is a feast for the eyes and stomach. It's covered with brightly painted houses where fishermen and knitting ladies still reside. **Torcello** is the greenest and least visited, and retains traces of Middle Age glory and American literary greatness.

Murano, Burano, and Torcello are usually visited in that order, but you can reverse the order, or limit yourself to one or two islands. Torcello often gets skipped. If you visit all three, it's hard not to pick a favorite. You can also continue exploring other directions of the lagoon towards the beaches of the **Lido,** where the Venice Film Festival is held and you can get on a bike again.

MURANO

Murano, synonymous with glassmaking, resembles a miniature Venice. It's a quarter of the size and consists of six separate islands interconnected by canals and bridges. The Canal Grande di Murano splits the town in two and can be crossed at the Ponte Vivarini iron bridge. On the northern side you'll find the Glass Museum and Santa Marta e Donato church. Glass boutiques and souvenir shops line most of the *fondamente* and the farther you walk from these the closer you get to the bucolic residential reality of low-rise housing, pretty pedestrian streets, and flourishing vegetable gardens.

The first *vaporetto* stop in Murano is the most popular and where most visitors usually disembark to browse the storefronts and discover how glass is blown. From Colonna station you can walk up Fondamenta dei Vetrai through the center of the town and the lovely little squares where lunch awaits. If you remain on board to the Venier stop you can discover the island from the inside out, get a good look at all the canals, and rub shoulders with locals in Campo San Bernardo.

Sights
GLASS MUSEUM

The **Museo del Vetro** (Fondamenta Giustinian 8, tel. 041/527-4718, www. museovetro.visitmuve.it, daily 10am-6pm, €10 or Museum Pass) glass museum is organized chronologically, starting with ancient Roman glassware. The pieces on display show how 700 years of Murano glassmaking tradition evolved from the 13th century to the present. There are frequent exhibitions of contemporary artists who use glass in creative ways. The collection is located inside one of Murano's oldest *palazzi* and can be visited in less than 30 minutes.

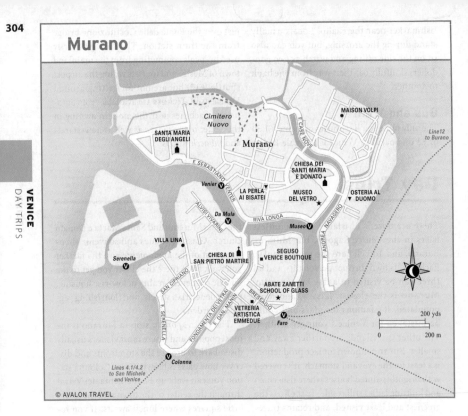

Murano

Unfortunately, there are no demonstrations inside the museum and only the occasional screening of a documentary about technique, which is better experienced at the galleries and workshops nearby.

CHIESA DEI SANTI MARIA E DONATO

Unlike churches in Venice, you can walk nearly all the way around the exterior of **Chiesa dei Santi Maria e Donato** (Campo San Donato 11, tel. 041/739-056, Mon.-Sat. 9am-6pm, Sun. 12:30pm-6pm). It feels like each side is different, and progressive makeovers since 1141 are probably the cause. The Gothic façade is imposing but plain and the only decoration is a relief sculpture of St. Donatus above the entrance. The side is more impressive and lined with windows set within lovely brick arches that could be mistaken for 20th-century design. The back of the church, or apse, provides the biggest eyeful, and the two tiers of arches supported by twin arches and intricate brickwork deserve closer inspection.

Inside is nearly as good. Besides the remains of a saint you'll find a 12th-century mosaic of the Virgin Mary, a Roman sarcophagus, and an incredible floor that feels like it's too nice to walk on. Mass is held on Monday, Wednesday, and Friday at 6pm and Sunday at 11:15am and 6pm.

Food

Most restaurants in Murano are located along the busy canals, and Fondamenta Manin and Venier are good places to start reading menus. **Osteria Al Duomo** (Fondamenta Maschio 21, tel. 041/527-4303, daily 8am-10pm, €12-15), across the bridge from Maria e Donato church, is a pleasant refuge from the heat. The neat white facade hides a large shaded garden where diners can enjoy fish, meat, or pizza prepared in a wood-burning oven.

If you venture down the residential back streets of Murano you'll eventually stumble onto **La Perlai ai Bisatei** (Campo S. Bernardo 1, daily noon-3pm, €6-10). This neighborhood *osteria* on a quiet square is popular with locals who come for *cicchetti* and conversation. The menu isn't extensive but includes essentials like *spaghetti alle vongole* (spaghetti with clams) and grilled fish. It's a jovial, family-friendly place where glassworkers come for lunch and a half-liter of house wine costs €4.

Shopping

Glass is an active export trade and not just for the tourists drawn to Murano. The island once housed thousands of glassmakers and there are still hundreds earning their livelihoods from this ancient craft. The Murano version became renowned for its clarity and color thanks to a unique combination of ingredients and the skills of its artisans.

Murano fuirnaces combine glass selling with glassmaking demonstrations, allowing visitors to witness the magic moment of glass creation. **Vetreria Artistica Emmedue** (Calle Miotti 12A, tel. 041/736-056) puts on demonstrations nearly continuously for groups who arrive by the boatload. Enter the narrow entrance to the shop and head straight to the back, where bleacher seating has been set up around the furnaces and you can get a close-up look as glass takes shape. The expert artisans all over the island tend to make miniature horses for audiences, and things are no different here. There's usually a brief explanation in a number of languages, and once the demonstration is over visitors are encouraged to browse the shop, ask questions, and get a closer look at the tools of the trade. The shop itself isn't that great and is better skipped. But there is a bathroom, which can be useful.

The Seguso family has been blowing glass for 23 generations and keeping their techniques secret since 1397. Inside their **Seguso Venice Boutique** (Fondamenta Manin 77, tel. 041/527-5333, daily 9am-1:30pm and 2:30pm-5:30pm) are vases, glasses, lampshades, and jewels that mix traditions of the past with a desire to innovate and push the boundaries of glassmaking. The showroom (Fondamenta Venier 29) regularly organizes visits to their nearby factory and organizes other glass-related events.

Accommodations

There are a several hotels in Murano but most of these are of the flowery wallpaper-and-gold-plated headboard type and in need of a facelift. The best option if you decide to spend a night or more on the island are the B&Bs and residences, which offer just as much service for double the charm.

Villa Lina (Calle dietro gli Orti 12, tel. 041/527-5358, www.villalinavenezia.com, €130-175 d) is situated five minutes from the Colonna water station directly on a canal. The three comfortable rooms are filled with modern furnishings and equipped with air-conditioning, Wi-Fi, minibar, safe, and TV. It's a B&B that feels like an intimate hotel. Guests have their own keys and can enjoy the enchanting garden after exploring the town. Breakfast is served on the terrace with a distant view of Venice.

Maison Volpi (Calle Volpi 39, 333/456-7561, www.maisonvolpi.it, €120 d) is a good self-catering option. This single-family home is tucked away in the heart of a residential neighborhood where few tourists wander. The spacious house covers two floors and the bright rooms are decorated with an abundance of antiques. The luminous kitchen is a cozy place to come home to and looks out on a little garden. The minimum stay is three nights, although the owner will occasionally make exceptions.

Getting There and Around

Murano can be reached from Venice on the 3, 4.1, 7, 12, 13, or N *vaporetto* lines. The **3** (daily 6:15am-7:15pm) departs from Piazzale

★ Venetian Glass

a glassmaking demonstration

Glassmaking existed in the Venice region since antiquity and was largely influenced by the Middle East, where the craft originated. Murano officially became the center of production when the Venetian Republic prohibited glassmaking in Venice in 1291 to avoid fires and established the island as the center of production. It was a lucrative business and artisans held a prominent role in society. They were obliged to live on the island and not allowed to leave without permission for fear their secrets would be revealed to competitors.

The key to Murano's success was innovation. Glassmakers developed new techniques and designs in the 14th century that found receptive overseas markets. The island produced the highest quality in the world by grinding local quartz with soda ash from the eastern Mediterranean. The

Roma and stops at the train station before heading directly to Murano. The **4.1** and **4.2** (daily 6:10am-11:22pm) are easily accessible; they circumnavigate Venice and terminate in Fondamente Nuove, from where they set off to Burano. All three lines make all seven stops on Murano and take less than 15 minutes to make the crossing.

BURANO

Burano, known for its lace production, is a magical island and pleasant escape from Venice. The photogenic canals and streets are lined with brightly colored houses and shops selling linen, lace, and glass jewelry. Most visitors proceed straight from the ferry dock up

Viale Marcello past a concentration of boutiques. The quieter route is to the left along the lagoon to the first canal that splits the island nearly in half.

There are two other canals to stroll along and many lovely streets to explore, complete with drying laundry and satiated cats. A bell tower leans perilously next to the church on Piazza Baldassarre Galuppo where the Lace Museum is located. Fishing still plays an important role here in both the economy and the gastronomy. There are hundreds of small fishing boats docked along all the canals and three small ports. The entire island can be circumnavigated in under an hour, but Burano is an island that's hard to leave.

formula allowed artisans to create a product that could be tinted by adding ground-up coloring agents that were melted into the glass.

New commercial realities and the influx of tourists have altered the business in recent decades. It's hard not stumble on a demonstration and many have a zoo-like atmosphere in which a *maestro* is on display. Still, it's interesting to see glass heated to 1,000 degrees and scooped out of an oven like molten honey. The heated glass is soft and malleable in the hands of a master, who maneuvers his long metal rod until he's satisfied with the lump of fiery glass he's extracted. He cuts and blows, taking a moment to examine the melting mound until it becomes a recognizable shape (often a vase or a horse) before the amazed eyes of an enthusiastic international audience.

Many of the remaining active furnaces offer demonstrations that are repeated throughout the day. Some of these are free while others involve a small fee. There's usually a brief explanation of the glassmaking process followed by an artisan skillfully creating a small vase or statuette. Demonstrations last 10-15 minutes, after which visitors are encouraged to visit the adjacent galleries. Prices range widely and many pieces are virtually impossible to resist.

There are dozens of workshops around Murano and throughout Venice where you can see glass being made using different techniques. Below are some of the best:

MURANO

- **Vetreria Artistica Emmedue** (page 305)

BURANO

- **Lumeart** (page 308)

VENICE

- **Abate Zanetti School of Glass** (page 291)

- **FGB** (page 280)

Sights

Burano is really about walking and letting the eyes enjoy the scenery, but if you're passionate about lace, visit the **Museo del Merletto** (Piazza Galuppi 187, tel. 041/730-034, daily 10am-6pm, €5 or Museum Pass). The museum explains the tradition, evolution, and commercial importance of lace with a 40-minute documentary and more than 200 intricate patterns. The highlight is watching the little group of skilled ladies working away on new designs and demonstrating an art that is slowly fading.

All the houses on Burano are colorful but **Giuseppe Toselli's house** (Calle Daffan 339) stands out. Giuseppe Toselli, or *Bepi* to the islanders, was a former handyman and candy vendor spent his spare time painting geometric patterns and shapes on his house. The result is something original in an already original town. Although Giuseppe passed away over a decade ago he hasn't been forgotten, and his much-loved facade was recently restored for all to see.

The easternmost canal along **Fondamenta Cao** is another good destination for house spotting. There are few shops or restaurants here but there are wonderful color combos. There are different stories about why the houses were painted in the first place. The most frequent answer is that it had to do with returning fisherman finding their way home

Burano

[Map labels: To Venissa, Line 12 to Torcello, Line 12 to Murano, SAN MAURO, COMARE, MARCELLO, C. S. MAURO, FRITTO MISTO, V, FONDAMENTA CAO, Line 12/14 to Lido, FONDAMENTA DE LA GIUDECCA, I GATTO NERO, Burano, C. PITTONA, LAGUNA BLUE, LUMEART, VIA B. GALUPPI, GIUSEPPE TOSELLI'S HOUSE, FONDAMENTA DEI PIZZO, LIDIA'S, MUSEO DEL MERLETTO, R. T. PIZZO, CHURCH OF SAN MARTINO, VIGNA, F. TERANOVA, 0 150 yds, 0 150 m, © AVALON TRAVEL]

It's always busy and the tables overlooking the canal will be occupied unless you arrive early or reserve. Nearly every dish includes fish or crustaceans and the house appetizer is a wonderful way to start a meal. Firsts are a tempting toss-up between *bigoli in salsa* (thick spaghetti-length pasta in sardine sauce) or the typical *risotto alla Buranella*. Anyone hungry for more can order grilled sole, eel, monkfish, cuttlefish, or sea bream. Otherwise ask for the *griglia mista* (mixed grill) and taste a little of everything.

Fritto Misto (Fondamenta dei Squeri 312, tel. 041/735-198, daily 9:30am-8:30pm, €12) is an informal outdoor eatery opposite the ferry landing. Given its location, you'd be right to avoid it out of principle—but that would be unfortunate for your taste buds. The delicately fried shrimp, calamari, and sardines served over fries on an edible plate made of bread are delicious and go great with a cold beer. The menu option includes a drink and a generous plate of lagoon fish for €16.50. Wait for your order at the counter and then choose a wooden stool in the shade and enjoy the lagoon views.

Shopping

Burano isn't commercial in the way Venice can be, and shopping is a relaxed experienced with little pressure on buyers. Lace is the obvious purchase, but glass and masks are also available. Many products are handmade directly in the little boutiques that dot the island and these are the ones worth seeking out.

Although glassblowing is more famous, the *lime* technique of small-scale jewelry making is how they work glass in Burano. There are a handful of tiny workshops where maestros melt glass rods (at lower temperatures) into earrings, necklaces, charms, and figurines. Massimo Mauro is one of the master artisans on the island and has been perfecting the craft since boyhood. The compact corner studio of **Lumeart** (Via Giudecca 40, tel. 041/527-2278, daily 10am-6pm) is where his wife sells his creations. It is filled with delicate objects

through the morning fog that's frequent in these parts.

Food

It may be impossible to choose a bad restaurant in Burano. They're all more or less good and specialize in fish, which is the most abundant ingredient on the island. Fishermen work hard in Burano and go out five days a week in search of mullet, bream, crustaceans, mollusks, and more. Traditional methods of line and net fishing are still used to supply the island and all of Venice with varieties that you may never have tasted before.

A handful of *trattoria* are concentrated on Via Baldassarre Galuppo that leads to the only *piazza*, but if you ask locals where to eat most will mention **I Gatto Nero** (Via Giudecca 88, tel. 041/730-120, Mon.-Sat. 12:30pm-3pm and 7:30pm-9pm, Sun. 12:30pm-3pm, €12-20).

born from his imagination and one step beyond mass production.

Alice dei Rossi couldn't decide between glass, felt, papier-mâché, or terra-cotta, so she decided to use them all. She transforms the materials into jewelry and clothes inside **Alla Fiera dell'Est** (Via S. Martino Sinistro 166, tel. 041/527-2234, daily 10am-6:30pm), which is painted electric blue on the outside. Nearby, Fabiola creates masks and lace at **La Stramba** (Via San Martino Sinistro 238, daily 9:30am-6pm), which doubles as her home. She will happily explain the three types of traditional Venetian masks and show you how they are made.

Lidia's (Via Galuppi 215, tel. 041/730-052, www.dallalidia.com, daily 9:30am-6:30pm) is the oldest boutique on the island and the largest that only sells locally made lace. Choose from many different patterns on everything from household linen to handkerchiefs, tablecloths, bedcovers, and nightshirts. They even have several racks of women's and children's clothing. Prices are in line with the time and effort employed by the experienced hands who supply the shop.

Fishing Tours

Pescaturismo, or fishing tourism, is an opportunity to go out with fishermen and discover the day-to-day realities of fishing inside and outside the lagoon. Passengers discover the methods for luring different varieties of fish and play an active part in the expedition. Once back on shore you can learn how the fish you've caught are prepared and cooked before tasting the results of your labor.

Igor at the **Cooperativo San Marco** (tel. 041/730-076, www.pescaturismoburano.com) can arrange an excursion. These usually last 2-3 hours and leave daily at 10am. Boats are open and 8-10 meters long during the summer and slightly larger and covered during the winter. This is a relatively new initiative on the part of the cooperative, which is trying to share the fishing traditions of the island with visitors. Although it is primarily aimed at larger groups, Igor will happily give you a quote on smaller groups. A fishing tour for four is around €300. For an extra €25 pp you can also enjoy a lunch of freshly caught fish.

Accommodations

There are no hotels in Burano and few places to stay. The island is out of the way and not the obvious choice for accommodation, but if you're after tranquility and don't mind being 40 minutes from Venice it can make an

colorful Burano

enchanting base for visiting lagoon islands. It's also an opportunity to see Burano after all the tourists have gone and the island can breathe again. **Laguna Blue** (Calle Daffan 379, tel. 041/730-650, €90 d) is a comfortable, recently renovated B&B in the center of town near the main street. Rooms are clean, modern, and above all, silent. Each comes with en suite bathrooms but TVs and telephones are absent.

Venissa (Mazzorbo, Fondamenta Santa Caterina 3, tel. 041/527-2281, www.venissa.it, €100-180 d) is a small estate on the nearby island of Mazzorbo. It's perfect for wine lovers and anyone who isn't in a hurry. The six suites and double rooms combine rustic fittings with contemporary furnishings. They face a small vineyard that was rescued by the owners and now produces a notable white wine. The rural complex is connected to Burano by way of a pedestrian bridge and easily reached from the water station in 10 minutes. Guests can choose between the in-house *osteria* and the Michelin-starred restaurant, both of which use ingredients from the on-site fish farm and vegetable garden.

Getting There and Around

There are daily scheduled *vaporetto* departures from Fondamente Nuove station in Cannaregio to Burano on the **12** line. Ferries operate from 4:20am to 11:20pm and leave every 20-30 minutes. Journey time is 40-50 minutes and there's a single stop in Burano. You can also arrive by **water taxi** from anywhere in Venice. The cost for up to four passengers is €120-130. The entire island is pedestrianized and can be circumnavigated in under an hour.

You can reach other lagoon islands from Burano by foot (Mazzorbo), *vaporetto* (Torcello, Murano), or water taxi to wherever you choose. **Water taxis** can be found at the main dock or near the Carabinieri station behind Piazza Baldassarre Galuppi. They can also be reserved by phone (041/522-2303).

If you want to take a little detour and arrive in Burano on foot without any tourists,

disembark the ferry one stop early on the island of **Mazzorbo**. Turn left from the dock and follow the *fondamenta* along the water until you reach the pedestrian bridge that connects the two islands.

TORCELLO

Torcello was the first inhabited island in the lagoon and was thriving when Venice was still a backwater. The tide has turned: Today, there are only 14 permanent residents, a couple of farms, plenty of flamingoes, and a few stubborn churches and towers that hint at the island's past. The main canal, lined with a smattering of bars and restaurants, is next to the ferry dock and splits the island in half. There's far less frenzy here than in Venice or on most other islands in the lagoon. Torcello is a good place to escape back to nature for a couple of hours, have lunch in a historic restaurant, and reflect on the fragility of civilization.

Sights

Torcello has a single brick lane (Strada della Rosina) that runs along a canal and leads to the island's ancient remains. Along the way there are several possibilities for getting sidetracked into the rural scenery. The first is 180 meters (200 yards) from the dock on the left near the first house. It's a dirt path that leads through grassland to **Casa Museo Andrich** (daily 10:30am-12:30pm and 2:30pm-6:30pm, €12), an informal house museum created by two local artists to display their lagoon-inspired paintings and sculptures.

Continue along the canal (you'll see the *campanile* in the distance) to reach a bridge known as **Ponte Del Diavolo** (Devil's Bridge) because it lacks any protective railing. If you want to give tourists the slip, cross the bridge and follow the gravel path to a second wooden bridge. Cross that one and walk left along another canal. You can take the next bridge back to the main route or continue straight towards the bell tower. You may need to make your own path and cross a wooden plank at some point, but you will eventually arrive at a final bridge leading to the historic monuments of the island. All detours are short and take less than 25 minutes to complete.

The historic center lies at the end of Strada della Rosina where the canal takes a sharp turn and a dirt path commences. Torcello once boasted over a dozen churches but the only ones standing today are the basilicas of Santa Maria Assunta and Santa Fosca. **Santa Maria Assunta** (tel. 041/730-119, Tues.-Sun. 10:30am-5pm, €5 or €9 with *campanile*) is one of the oldest structures in the lagoon and was part of a religious complex that included a baptistery, of which the circular foundations are still visible. The Gothic facade consists of twelve receded arches punctuated by a half-dozen windows. It dates from AD 639 but the present building was more or less completed in the first millennium. The entrance is on the right near the ticket office and reveals a simple interior that shows its age. The back wall is entirely covered in Venetian byzantine mosaics of the *Universal Judgment.*

The *campanile* (Tues.-Sun. 10:30am-5pm, €5 or €9 with basilica) is behind the basilica and worth the climb for a view of the island as well as Burano and Venice in the distance. It's the only tower in the city (open to visitors)

without an elevator and is fun climb. It gets pretty windy at the top and there's not much room along the narrow corridors.

Tickets are available from the basilica office. Adjacent to the basilica is the church of **Santa Fosca** (free), begun in the 12th century. It's vaguely reminiscent of the Basilica di San Marco and is a rare example of a Greek Orthodox plan with Byzantine influences.

Underneath the tree in the grassy yard opposite the churches are several well caps and the marble **throne** on which Attila the Hun is alleged to have sat. The seat more likely served local officials, but it remains a popular photo opportunity nonetheless. Archeologists still conduct digs on the island and their finds are stored in the **Museo Provinciale** (Piazza Torcello, tel. 041/730-761, Tues.-Sun. 10:30am-5:30pm, €3) opposite Santa Fosca. This small museum houses Greek and Roman antiquities, Etruscan and Paleo-Veneto finds from the estuary, ancient documents, and church treasures.

Food and Accommodations

There are a number of *trattoria* along the main canal, but **Locanda Cipriani** (Piazza Santa Fosca 29, tel. 041/730-150, www.locandacipriani.com, Wed.-Thurs. and Sun.-Mon

Ponte Del Diavolo in Torcello

noon-3pm, Fri.-Sat. noon-3pm and 7pm-9pm, €16-24) is the institution. It was opened in the 1930s by the legendary restauranteur who had already turned Harry's Bar and the Cipriani Hotel into international success stories. The Locanda was lower-key but still attracted postwar VIPs including Queen Elizabeth, Charlie Chaplin, and Ernest Hemingway (who became friends with Cipriani and spent a good deal of time on Torcello, where he hunted ducks and wrote *Across the River and Into the Trees*). During the summer you can dine outside on the terrace or garden of this elegant hideaway, whose experienced kitchen turns out carpaccio classics and reinterpretations of Venetian favorites.

Eventually, Cipriani added accommodations, with five rooms (two suites and three singles, closed Jan. and Feb., €140 per person) where Hemingway stayed at various times and guests can enjoy a good night's sleep today. Rooms are spacious and classically furnished with hardwood floors and large beds, and they have pleasant views. The surroundings are romantic and often used for wedding receptions, and you can always make a nostalgic stop at the bar and enjoy drinking in the past.

Taverna Tipica (Fondamenta dei Borgognoni 5, tel. 041/099-6428, www.tavernaveneziana.it, daily 9:30am-7pm, €8-12) is a down-to-earth option and the first eatery along Strada della Rosina. It's a casual *osteria* with outdoor dining on wooden tables and benches next to a large grassy field where children play and parents rest. Rice and fish dishes are the mainstays of the menu that includes *Risotto alla Buranella* and *Bis di Saòr*, both of which can be accompanied with a carafe of great wine.

Getting There and Around

Torcello can be reached on board the **9 shuttle line** from Burano and by the N night service. Journey time from Burano is 7 minutes and ferries depart every 30 minutes. The schedule is posted at the dock and is worth memorizing to avoid a wait. The island is best explored on foot, but if you do decide to get off the main walkway make sure to wear proper footwear—especially if it's been raining.

THE LIDO

The Lido gracefully stretches across the lagoon on its east side and embraces the sea on its west side. The island's original beach bums, who launched its popularity in the 19th century, were Romantic poets like Byron and Shelley. It wasn't long after that the world's largest beach resort went up. The Lido has a stylish, laid-back informality about it. Except for July and August (when the bathing beauties arrive) or during the Venice Film Festival in September, look for hotel bargains here. The Lido could be just the antidote for feet tired from sightseeing. It's possible to swim in the sea, go for a bicycle ride, or play a round of golf at the course near the fort at Alberoni. The Lido's wide promenades also make for good shopping. It's also pleasant to stroll along the Lungomare Marconi and the beach to see the Adriatic Sea, so important to the rise and wealth of Venice.

Nightlife and Entertainment

The first beach platforms went up in 1857, followed in 1888 by the first wooden *capanne* (the family beach spot to change, lunch, and play). Not long after, the luxury hotels followed. Stop in for a cocktail at **Hotel Des Bains** (Lungomare Guglielmo Marconi 17, tel. 041/260-2309) if the renovation has been completed or the **Grand Hotel Excelsior** (Lungomare Guglielmo Marconi 41, tel. 041/526 0201) down the boardwalk to enjoy the posh early-20th-century atmosphere that established the Lido as one of the world's most luxurious beach resorts.

Activities and Recreation
LIDO BEACH

Waves break against the east coast of the Lido. Sunbathers will enjoy the long stretch of yellowish sand that lines the entire eastern side of the island. The strand owes its unique hue to the Piave River, which brings sand from the Dolomite Mountains that contains quartz and magnetic iron. Erosion has become a problem in recent years and the beach narrows considerably the farther away you get from town. In all parts the sea remains shallow for some distance, which makes it a tranquil spot for children and swimmers of all levels. Stroll along the beach to pick your favorite *stabilimento* (beach club), where you can rent a beach umbrella and *lettino* (lounge chair) for €10-15.

CYCLING

Bicycles aren't allowed in Venice, but cycling is popular on the Lido. The island is flat and a nice place to pedal. Lido residents do own cars, but islanders are slow drivers. The Lido's population triples in size during the summer but most Venetian holidaymakers stay on the beaches on the northeastern coast and biking is pleasurable year-round.

There are several rental shops on the main street minutes from the water station. You can get Dutch-style singles, tandems, and fun family bikes that seat four at **Lidoonbike** (Gran Viale Santa Maria Elisabetta 21b, tel. 041/526-8019, Mar.-Sept. daily 9am-7pm). Hourly rates start from €5 and all bikes come with a lock. Deposit and ID are required; make sure to read the rules carefully before setting off. **Venice Bike** (Gran Viale Santa Maria Elisabetta 79a, tel. 041/526-1490, Mar.-Oct. daily 9am-7pm) just down the block offers slightly lower rates for heftier beach bikes that come in all sizes.

There's a **bike path** beside Via Sandro that starts at the Lido *vaporetto* station. It changes names but remains the same road and runs the length of the narrow 12-kilometer-long island. Along the way you can stop in the pleasant seaside hamlet of **Malamocco** and have lunch or resupply. The road skirts the lagoon the rest of the way and becomes surprisingly verdant the closer you get to the ferry dock on the southern tip of the island. On the way back you can ride a different route and skirt the eastern coast facing the Adriatic. To take this path turn right on Via Doge Galla at the Malamocco sign just beyond the water treatment plant and continue until you see water.

GOLF

According to legend, when Henry Ford visited Venice in 1928 he asked his aristocratic host where he could golf. At that time there was no course in the area, but not wanting to disappoint future guests Count Giuseppe Volpi had a nine-hole course built on the Lido. **Circolo**

Lido Beach

Golf Venezia (Lido, Strada Vecchia 1, tel. 041/731-333, circologolfvenezia.it, Tues.-Sun. 8am-7:30pm, €97 weekdays, €116 weekends) was one of the earliest clubs in Italy and later enlarged to an 18-hole par 72 course near a wild beach where Goethe came to watch the waves. It's not particular challenging except on windy days, but it's fun to play and native flora and fauna can be observed along the fairways. Clubs can be rented for €20 from the pro shop and tee times should be reserved in advance.

Getting There and Around

Lido di Venzia lies 10 minutes from Piazza San Marco by *vaporetto* or 50 minutes from the train station. The main Lido water station can be reached on the 1, 2, 4.1, 4.2, 6, and 8 lines. The island extends 12 kilometers from north to south and bus 11 connects the center with the southern tip near the golf course. It's a pleasant place to ride a bike and the summer-only **Info Point** (Gran Viale 6a, daily 9am-noon and 3pm-6pm) can help you find your bearings.

Background

History

ETRUSCANS AND GREEKS
(9TH CENTURY BC-4TH CENTURY BC)

The Etruscans were the first major civilization in what is today called Italy. Recent DNA tests indicate they emigrated from the Near East and possibly originated in Turkey. They began to spread throughout the center of the peninsula in the 9th century BC and established towns in Lazio, Tuscany, and Umbria. Although their language remains a mystery, archeologists have learned a lot from the thousands of tufa rock tombs they left behind. At one point in the 6th century BC, Etruscan kings ruled over Rome, and although the city turned the tables on their occupiers Etruscan culture had a great influence on Roman traditions. The best place to see Etruscan ruins is in the small town of Fiesole overlooking Florence, where their ancient fortifications have remained intact.

Simultaneously, Greek colonists were busy settling the coasts farther south. They were especially active in Puglia, Calabria, and Sicily, where they founded dozens of cities. Syracuse and Akragas dominated central Mediterranean trade routes and became wealthy in the process. Temples at Agrigento and Paestum are nearly as impressive as anything built in Athens and have remained in much better shape. Power struggles between individual cities and the rise of the Romans led to a slow decline, but as with the Etruscans (who were rivals and trading partners) a great deal of Greek culture and philosophy formed the root of Roman philosophy. Romans also preferred to borrow from Greek architectural standards rather than reinvent their own, and temples such as Hercules and Portunus are perfect examples of that.

ANCIENT ROME
(8TH CENTURY BC-5TH CENTURY AD)

No one could have ever predicted Rome would become an eternal city. At its legendary founding in 753 BC, it was little more than a backwater on the banks of the Tiber River. Yet over the centuries that followed the village on Palatine Hill expanded into a city that would dominate the Mediterranean.

There are three distinct periods in Rome's ancient history: Kingdom, Republic, and Empire. The first was the shortest and the only time the city was subjugated. Etruscan kings were overthrown in 509 BC and a republic was established that eventually conquered and consolidated the entire peninsula. Roman customs, language, and law were imposed on native peoples who were integrated into the new society. It wasn't until the turn of the millennium that social tensions allowed Julius Caesar the opportunity to take absolute power and do away with the old checks and balances. Although he was assassinated in the process he changed the course of history and led the way for the emperors to come.

Rise

After the Etruscans were expelled, Rome spent 100 years at war with various cities of Etruria, while gradually subjugating the rest of the Latins and neighboring tribes. Most tribes were allowed to remain independent as long as they accepted Roman hegemony. New colonies were set up in strategic locations so that conquered lands would remain loyal to Rome. Attention was then turned to the only power left in Italy: the Samnites, who were defeated along with their Etruscan and Celtic allies. By 283 BC, nearly the entire peninsula was in Roman hands.

Once Rome had domesticated the peninsula, the leading families of the city began to look overseas. Carthage was another rising power at the time and the Mediterranean wasn't big enough for two ancient superpowers. They faced off in three epic wars. In the First Punic War (264-241 BC) Rome secured Sardinia, Corsica, and parts of Sicily. The defeat did not go down well with the Carthaginians, who broke the peace accords and sent their best general, along with elephants, over the Alps to destroy the Romans once and for all.

Hannibal, one of the greatest military strategists of all time, nearly succeeded in crushing Rome during the Second Punic War (218-201 BC). He inflicted the bloodiest defeat the Roman army had ever experienced at Cannae, and had he received proper reinforcements tourists might be visiting Carthage today rather than Rome. As it turns out, Rome recovered from the losses and the legions made a dramatic comeback at the battle of Zara. Afterwards heavy sanctions crippled Carthage, and the third war (149-BC-146 BC) was just a formality. Rome annihilated its old enemy and became master of the Mediterranean.

Empire

Until Caesar came along, the Republic was governed by two consuls elected to one-year terms by the Senate. Although new territories meant wealth for a few, many Romans were having a tough time surviving. Cheap grain imports from Egypt put farmers out of business, and land was becoming scarce. Famines were frequent, and the ruling class was deaf to calls of reform. Populist statesmen who did advocate change met a violent end.

These were volatile times, and slave revolts like the one Spartacus led in 73-71 BC were common. On the other hand, new conquests gave more power to Roman generals who could count on the support of their troops. Caesar was the most successful of these. After he prevailed over the Gauls (modern-day France), he returned to Rome in 49 BC to outmaneuver the competition. His assassination four years later marked the end of Republic and began an era in which the Senate was reduced to rubber-stamping whatever emperors wanted.

The first of these emperors was Augustus, the adopted son of Caesar, who ushered in a

The Pantheon is the most well-preserved building of ancient Rome.

long period of stability and had the Ara Pacis built to remind Romans of his accomplishments. The empire eventually stretched from the Red Sea to Great Britain. Although some emperors like Nero succumbed to debauchery, the wisdom of Trajan, Hadrian, and Marcus Aurelius in the 2nd century AD led to higher standards of living for all. Slaves performed much of the heavy work, wheat was free, and entertainment was only as far as the amphitheater. Most monuments visible today, such as the Colosseum and Pantheon, were built during the Imperial era, and nearly every large town in Italy was founded during this period; this includes Florence, which Caesar established in 59 BC as a settlement for his veteran soldiers.

Decline and Fall

Over the centuries the Roman legions lost their edge and had to rely on an influx of foreign recruits who were no longer the cream of the crop. Equipment became obsolete and tactics were superseded by those used by the Germanic forces that threatened the empire from the north.

Constantine moved the capital to Constantinople (modern-day Istanbul) in 312 AD, which led to the split of the empire. While the eastern half survived for another thousand years in the guise of the Byzantine Empire, the west could not hold back the hordes of Franks and Alemani pouring over the Alps. The last emperors kept their courts in army headquarters in Medilanum (Milan) and then in Ravenna on the Adriatic. During this time Christianity grew and became an accepted religion; the first Christian temples were built and would later form the foundations on which the Vatican, Duomo, and many other churches were built.

Alaric and his Visigoth army finally sacked Rome in 410 BC. Saint Augustine announced the end of the world and Attila the Hun obliged him with years of chaos when it was no longer possible to distinguish Roman from barbarian. The Dark Ages had begun, and Italy would have to wait a thousand years for

the next golden age. It was around this time that fishermen in northern Italy escaping the violent newcomers formed the earliest island settlements in the Venetian lagoon.

MIDDLE AGES
(6TH CENTURY AD-13TH CENTURY AD)

After the fall of the Western Empire foreign invasion became the rule in Italy. Lombards arrived and founded their capital in Pavia, only to be replaced by the Franks and Charlemagne, who was crowned Holy Roman Emperor. In the south, Saracen pirates landed in Sicily, followed by Normans who went on to build some of their most impressive fortifications in Puglia.

In the fray many cities managed to break free of their feudal lords and win independence. Venice was one of the most successful of these and grew rich importing silk and spice from the Orient and shipping crusaders off to the Holy Land. In 1271, Marco Polo set off with his father on the famous journey to China and returned 25 years later with enough stories from the court of Kublai Khan to fill several diaries. Genoa and Pisa also rose to prominence and were the other great maritime republics of the Tyrrhenian Sea.

Inland Milan and Florence took advantage of conflict between the Papal States and Holy Roman Empire to flex their muscles. Bands of mercenaries were paid by towns to conquer their rivals. Competition was not just about winning on the battlefield: Perugia wanted to outdo Siena in architecture. Florentine rulers demanded grander cathedral doors than Pisa and a dome that would dominate the region. Most squares churches were begun during this time. A sense of civic pride was born, along with a skilled class of tradespeople who paved the way for the Renaissance that was to come.

RENAISSANCE
(14TH CENTURY AD-17TH CENTURY AD)

Although the term "Renaissance" wasn't used until centuries later, people at the time knew they were living something special. Great churches were slowly rising above skylines and overshadowing medieval constructions, and art was taking on new forms. Business was good, and much of it was handled by newly founded Venetian and Florentine banks. Economic expansion required investment, which in turn encouraged greater productivity. The practice of charging interest became standard compensation when lending or investing. A check was used for the first time in Pisa in the 14th century and was commonplace by the middle of the 15th. Modern capitalism spread fast, and once money was available people needed something to spend it on.

The wealthy merchants who vied for control began to take interest in the arts. The Medici in Florence and Sforza in Milan wanted to make a statement with their *palazzi* and interior decoration became important. Art and culture mattered again, as it had under the Romans. Antiquity was rediscovered and an incredible generation of artists was born in the right place at the right time.

Leonardo da Vinci, Michelangelo, Raphael, and Titian all managed to make the transition from craftsman to artist. Painting and sculpture became vital to city life. Competitions were held for important commissions and Brunelleschi's scale model of Florence's cathedral dome is still on display in the Duomo museum. Signs of the Renaissance are still everywhere: Although Florence was the epicenter of the movement, Rome and Venice were also transformed during this incredibly productive period that produced both the Sistine Chapel and Statue of David.

UNIFICATION
(18TH CENTURY AD-
19TH CENTURY AD)

Modern Italy began in the 1750s with the birth of a Republican movement determined to unite a fragmented territory. The *risorgimento* (resurgence) was a difficult endeavor. One of the greatest leaders of the period was Giuseppe Garibaldi. Anywhere you go in Italy

you're likely to find a square or street named after this patriot who surmounted endless hurdles to unite Italy.

The first hurdle was Austria, which after the Treaty of Vienna in 1815 occupied northeastern Italy from Lombardy to Friuli. Garibaldi fought three wars against the Austrians. He lost two, but was on the verge of winning the third when the Austrians surrendered to Prussia, thus avoiding any territorial losses. To this day one of the worst names you can call someone in Northern Italy is a *Croato*, a reference to the Croatian soldiers conscripted to fight for the Austrians.

Garibaldi's other problem was farther south: the Kingdom of Two Sicilies, overseen by Bourbon monarchs who ruled over southern Italy from their capital in Naples. In 1860, Garibaldi set off from Genoa with 1,000 volunteers. Carrying hand-me-down weapons and sporting red shirts for uniforms, what they lacked in training they made up for in spirit. After landing in Marsala, they took Palermo and the rest of Sicily with little bloodshed. The going was tougher in Campania but the Bourbons eventually surrendered Naples and retired to France.

Italy was a little closer to unification, but there was still the matter of the Papal State that controlled Rome and much of central Italy. The real problem was Napoleon III, who supported the Vatican and had sent troops to guard the city. Later that decade, however, the Prussians defeated the French, who were forced to pull out of Rome—thus opening the way for Garibaldi's red shirts. The Aurelian wall was pierced at Porta Pia and a statue later erected on the historic spot. Resistance was light and the Swiss Guard didn't put up much of a fight. An accord was drawn between the new state and the Church that recognized the new Republic.

WORLD WAR I
(1914-1919)

It wasn't until the end of World War I, when Austria ceded Trentino, that Italy reached its current territorial state. Italy entered the

20th century united under a single king but still in search of itself. The country was not threatened, yet politicians and intellectuals alike succumbed to the fervor of war as the events rocking other European capitals spread to Rome. Which side Italy actually joined wasn't settled until the last minute when the Allies made a better offer and promised to expand Italy's borders and regain Trieste from Austrian control.

And so with little preparation and less forethought the Italian war machine mobilized for what everyone predicted would be a short war. The army eagerly set off, badly equipped and ill commanded, towards the Alps. Reality set in after the Battle of Caporetto in 1917. A long, hard-fought campaign ensued that saw very little progress. By 1919 over 650,000 Italians had died and a million had been wounded in fighting of little strategic significance.

FASCISM
(1920-1945)

Postwar Italy was greatly deprived, and it was in this period that many peasants packed their bags and headed for the United States, Argentina, and Australia. Many that remained survived on a meager diet, and a feeling of disappointment filled the air. The promise of war had not been fulfilled and territorial additions seemed small compared to the daily suffering. The economy was weak and the revolution in Russia gave workers something to think about. Extremes began to form and both sides were convinced that the liberal policies of the government were outdated.

One proponent of change was Benito Mussolini. Before the war, Mussolini had been an editor of the Socialist Party newspaper and had displayed a talent for increasing circulation. His idea of Fascism evolved slowly and remained heavy on propaganda and light on philosophy. Economic hardship made recruiting easy, and a private security force known as the Blackshirts was established to protect landowners, fight communists, and beat Slavs. In October 1922 Mussolini announced

he would march on Rome. King Emmanuel III refused to sign a decree of martial law that might have stopped the Fascists, and instead had no choice but to make Mussolini prime minister.

Order was quickly restored, trains started arriving on time, and opponents of the party could still show their faces. Things changed after the elections of 1924 and the assassination of Giacomo Matteotti, who was a rare politician not intimidated by the Blackshirts. Over the following years Fascists used parliamentary means to convert Italy into a virtual dictatorship and inspired other European dictators to do the same. Mussolini started giving his famous speeches from the balcony in Piazza Venezia and a love affair with the Italian people began in earnest. He used large-scale public work projects to keep unemployment down and the new mediums of cinema and radio to glorify his achievements and reinforce his hold on Italy. The neighborhood of EUR was begun at this time and many archeological excavations were conducted in an effort to link the Roman past with the Fascist present.

WORLD WAR II
(1939-1945)

One of Mussolini's favorite slogans was "whoever stops is lost." He could not stop and Italians lacked the democratic means to stop him. He invaded Ethiopia and joined the Spanish Civil War on the side of Franco in 1936. This endeavor forged an alliance with Hitler that would eventually be fatal. Once again Italy was led unprepared into a world conflict, except this time it was on the losing side. The results were even worse than in World War I, and even the magic of cinema could not sugarcoat defeats in North Africa and the Balkans.

Allied troops under Generals Patton and Montgomery reached Sicilian shores in July 1943, by which time it was clear the tide had turned against Mussolini. An armistice was hastily drafted and signed in Brindisi, but it did not end the conflict. German divisions held firm and made the Allies pay a heavy price for every mile they advanced up the peninsula. The battle of Monte Cassino in 1944 was one of the bloodiest and a throwback to the futility of trench warfare. The Allies were aided by an Italian resistance, which organized behind the German lines. Partisans hampered German movement and managed to liberate many parts of northern Italy before Allied tanks rolled into the region towards the end of the war.

Mussolini was caught trying to escape to Switzerland in April 1945. He and his mistress were shot and hanged for all to see in Milan. He remains popular with modern-day extremists and his granddaughter was elected several times into national government.

POST WAR
(1946-TODAY)
In 1946 a referendum was held to choose between monarchy and democracy. Italians opted for the latter. A new constitution was written and passed into law and the Italian Republic was born. There were still many years of rationing and hunger until the country recovered, but by the late 1950s and 1960s Italy began a spectacular period of growth that transformed cities and saw new neighborhoods and highways emerge from the ashes.

Rome was at the forefront of the comeback. Italian style and cinema caught the attention of the world. Rossellini, De Sica, and Fellini portrayed the gritty realism of Italy as the economy slowly rebounded. Factories in the north began to increase production and Fiats rolled off the assembly lines in Turin at unprecedented speed. Roads were built, the Vespa moped became a national success story, and people began smiling again. Inequality still existed but poverty was concentrated in the south, where it remains to this day.

Art and Architecture

If you could put a price tag on all the frescoes, paintings, and sculptures in Italy, you'd approach infinity. The Borghese Gallery alone is stuffed with more beauty than most cities. A stroll in any town is a walk through a patchwork of styles, from classical to baroque to modern.

ARCHITECTURAL STYLES
Classical
The first architects in Italy were Greek, and the temples they erected inspired Romans to lay foundations that remain visible today. The most distinguished feature of these buildings is the column. Often it's the last thing standing. Columns came in three orders: Doric (flat), Ionic (curved), and Corinthian (flowery). All three orders can be spotted on the Colosseum and were recycled by Renaissance designers hundreds of years later. Structures that remain from this period include amphitheaters, triumphal arches, and public baths. Advances in the casting of concrete and the use of the arch allowed Roman builders to think bigger than ever before. The dome was perfected, exteriors adorned with marble, and interiors decorated with elaborate mosaics and frescoes that have survived in Ostia Antica.

Romanesque
Churches are the great architectural legacy of the Middle Ages. The first paleo-Christian places of worship were small and appeared towards the end of the empire. There was a boom in baptisteries around AD 1000 and each region had its own take on the style. Buildings in this era had simple facades and small windows that were later enlarged once glass became widespread. It was common to make alterations throughout the centuries as

fashion and tastes changed, and few buildings from the period escaped without some form of remodeling, especially on the inside. Greater wealth allowed more ambitious building programs. A black-and-white style was developed in Siena and Florence and competition between cities helped spur the movement.

Romanesque ground plans were generally in the form of a crucifix and consisted of single naves. Interiors weren't fancy and nothing was meant to distract worshippers from salvation. Many basilicas were decorated with frescoes recounting the Bible and mosaics were especially popular in Venice. Santa Maria in Trastevere and Santa Cecilia in Rome, along with San Miniato al Monte in Florence and Santi Maria e Donato in Murano, are well-preserved examples of Romanesque style.

Gothic

Architecture eventually exploded beyond the confines of rigid shapes and traditional forms. Gothic emerged in the 12th-16th centuries and seeped down the peninsula from the north. Groups of masons, like the Campionese Masters, built cathedrals and basilicas from Milan to Assisi. In Venice the style was combined with Asian influences, giving the city a look of its own. Ornament

was added to churches and archways pointed the way to heaven. Cathedrals rose higher than ever before, supported by rib vaulting. This meant that walls could be thinner, which allowed for the introduction of stained glass and rose windows imported from France. In Rome, many Gothic buildings were given a baroque makeover, though they reveal their true identity in the mosaics and paintings that were spared. The Basilica di Santa Croce and Duomo exemplify late-Gothic architecture, which also inspired public buildings such as the Doge's Palace in Venice and many private residences.

Renaissance

Renaissance architecture was less spectacular than the art that emerged from the period. There were certainly outstanding achievements—like Brunelleschi's dome in Florence and Michelangelo's cupola for St. Peter's—but it was also a time of confusion and aesthetics that failed to take off the way sculpture and painting did. Antiquity was still admired over creativity, and the imagination of the previous eras was abandoned in favor of austerity. Practitioners like Bramante and Codussi left behind marvelous palaces financed by a growing upper class eager to outdo their neighbors.

Florence's Duomo

Bramante's Tempietto and Michelangelo's Campidoglio square are two of the most famous architectural examples of the period, which left behind thousands of sculptures and paintings now on view inside the Vatican and Uffizi museums.

Baroque

Baroque is easier to identify than Renaissance architecture. A baroque building catches the eye with elaborate lines and unusual flare. It's a love-it-or-leave-it style that grew out of the ideals of the Counter-Reformation in the 17th and 18th centuries. Many church interiors were remodeled during that time, which explains why you can't always judge a cathedral by its facade. It wasn't just churches that were being transformed by the movement—perhaps the best-known example of baroque is the ornate Trevi Fountain in Rome.

The city led the way in the movement, thanks to the genius of Bernini and Borromini. Popes indulged themselves on irreverent designs that were not universally adopted. Florence and Venice mostly passed on the movement and the southern Italian incarnation took the studied excess in a new direction. Italian gardens also sprang up in this era, exemplified by those at Tivoli, and matched the splendor of the palaces they were meant to accentuate.

Neoclassicism

Italy lost her supremacy on the art and architecture front during the 18th century. Neoclassicism dusted off Roman designs and gave them an updated look. Symmetry and the use of architectural standards of the past are its notable characteristics. Grand opera houses sprang up in major towns, along with enclosed shopping galleries. Public buildings became extravagant. Much of the Vatican museums, along with Piazza del Popolo and Villa Borghese park in Rome, were significantly transformed during this period during which the Colosseum was also restored and many ancient monuments began to be recognized and appreciated.

Towards the early 19th century the movement evolved into **Umbertine,** best expressed in the massive Vittorio Emanuele II monument in Rome, which Caesar would have loved but is generally dismissed by modern residents. Harder to find and on a much smaller scale are examples of art nouveau, which spread from France; although short-lived, it marked the beginning of modern architecture. The best examples were usually

The Trevi fountain is a Baroque masterpiece.

related to the burgeoning tourist industry and many luxurious hotels, spas, and casinos on the Italian Riviera and Venice Lido adopted the distinctive style.

Modern

Modern architecture evolved late in Italy, and steel and glass never replaced reinforced concrete as the material of choice. With the rise of Fascism, a stark, monumental style was promoted that's visible in EUR and in many cities in the south, some of which were built from scratch. Train stations also benefited from new ideas in architecture, and old stations in Rome, Florence, and Venice were torn down to make way for sleek marble versions. After World War II, trends mixed and postmodernism slowly snuck into a few skylines. Pier Luigi Nervi was one of the first 20th-century Italian architects to combat dreariness with skyscrapers.

Architecture Today

Getting a building permit in Italy is difficult, and even homegrown architectural stars like Fuksas and Piano have trouble realizing their visions. Today's buildings often look obsolete before the last nail is hammered. There was no shortage of controversy when Richard Rogers completed his Ara Pacis museum in Rome and Calatrava installed a new bridge in Venice. New is often shunned in favor of conventional and downright ugly. Hundreds of buildings could do with a little dynamite and the rationalist mistakes of the 1960s eradicated for good. The best examples of contemporary Italian architecture are in Rome, where structures like the Parco della Musica and MAXXI Museum stand in stark contrast from the buildings around them.

VISUAL ARTS
Medieval

When the Empire fell, creativity wasn't extinguished. It flourished in all three cities and especially in Venice, where contact with the outside world brought new ideas and skills. The mosaics inside St. Mark's Basilica were created during this period, along with many

Giotto's *Ognissanti Madonna* is considered a landmark in Renaissance painting.

of the sculptures and carvings on church facades in Rome and Florence. Craftsmen organized themselves into guilds and specialized in everything from jewelry making to glassware. Most large-scale painting and sculpture was intended for religious purposes and inspired by the Old and New Testaments. Stone remained the preeminent material but metal, glass, leather, wood, and textiles were also used to create highly refined objects.

Renaissance

The Renaissance was a time of artistic leaps and bounds. Tuscany was the cradle of this golden age and Da Vinci, Raphael, and Michelangelo helped lead the movement. Rather than just copy ancient works, they expanded upon medieval traditions and explored new possibilities of expression. Many artists began as apprentices under fine craftsmen before leapfrogging their masters. Florentine style was exported beyond the region by its purveyors, who went on a creative binge throughout Italy and Europe. Painting and sculpture lost its stiffness and began to look lifelike. Space on canvas and walls was redefined and the world was reflected like never before.

Giotto helped redefine perspective and used it in his wooden cross inside Santa Maria Novella and buildings like the *campanile* in Florence. Artists traveled up and down the peninsula painting church interiors, and the greatest were given commissions in Rome. Michelangelo was among these; he spent over a decade at work on the Sistine Chapel, using colors in ways no one had ever seen before. Around the same time Sandro Botticelli was busy painting his *Birth of Venus* (Uffizi) and Raphael was at work on the *School of Athens* in the Vatican. Many lesser-known artists were also busy decorating monasteries, and Florence in particular has an incredible number of frescoes depicting the *Last Supper* and other Biblical scenes.

Mannerism

Mannerism developed in the mid-16th century in response to the High Renaissance and new political realities. Rome was sacked, freedom restrained, and religion was splitting at the seams. Artists became less interested in the observation of nature and more in the style or manner in which they painted. Compositions were unordered and focal points disappeared. Proportions were exaggerated and figures elongated or twisted into graceful or bizarre postures. Colors often clashed and instability was favored over the balance depicted by previous generations of artists. Tiziano was one of the most productive proponents of the style; his paintings can be found inside Basilica di Santa Maria della Salute and hanging throughout the Galleria dell'Accademia. Many Venetian interiors favored the style, and the ceilings of the *Scuole Grande* brotherhoods throughout the city contain many remarkable examples.

Baroque

The Council of Trent (1545-1563) did more than reform Catholic dogma. It started a re-evaluation of art, of which the church was a major sponsor, and began a return to spirituality and tradition. Art was no longer just for the well-to-do but was intended to stir everyone's souls. Inspiration came from the saints, the Virgin Mary, and the Old Testament. Rome was the center of the movement and Caravaggio and the Carracci brothers took turns innovating church interiors, fountains, and living rooms around the city. Drama is the common denominator. Bernini emerged as the greatest exponent of the period. His battling baroque *David* stands in stark contrast to Michelangelo's contemplative version. Viewers could not help being moved and no one could pass the Fontana di Trevi with indifference. Sculpture gained multiple viewing angles and resembled actors on a stage. There was a return to group figures and all sorts of props were used to add to the drama.

Futurism

Futurism was the last great Italian contribution to the art world. It was a response to Cubism and reflected three principal elements: speed, technology, and modernity. The movement was born in the early 20th century with Filippo Marinetti's avant-garde manifesto calling for the burning of libraries. Artists gradually followed in his intellectual footsteps and began portraying sensations and capturing the essence of objects. Canvases and sculpture moved just as fast as the world on the verge of war. Factories and machines were idealized and artists unknowingly paved the way towards Fascism. The movement merged with others around Europe and shared many traits with Russian Constructivism. Good examples of the genre are hanging in Rome's Galleria Nazionale d'Arte Moderna e Contemporanea.

The only other Italian art to attract international attention during the 20th century was the mysterious, metaphysical work of De Chirico and the oddly thin sculptures of Giacometti. The Venice Biennale became a hub for contemporary artists around the world and continues to set artistic trends every two years.

The Landscape

Look out from the plane as you descend towards Italy and you'll see coastline, mountains, and fields. Although the rivers, lakes, and rolling hills may seem miniature from above, they have influenced history and been transformed by centuries of habitation.

The landscape explains a lot. It explains why culture can change within such short distances, why words are pronounced differently from one latitude to the next, how culinary traditions emerge, and why Romans drive the way they do. Nature has played a vital role in the development of urban centers. Look out from a train window speeding up the peninsula and you'll get a glimpse of vineyards, olive groves, hilltop villages, and impervious mountain ranges. It's a land that has fostered genius, and is a hallmark of Italy as memorable as the food, the art, or the people.

GEOGRAPHY

Italy is roughly the size of Colorado but has enough geologic diversity to fill a continent. The long, boot-shaped peninsula was formed millions of years ago in the Cenozoic Era when tectonic plates underneath Europe and Africa slowly collided and transformed the earth's surface. Over the last million years alternating warm and glacial periods shaped the terrain and formed mountain ranges, valleys, lakes, and rivers. A journey down the length of the country reveals Alpine peaks, active volcanoes, hot springs, and desert-like settings.

It's a mountainous and hilly land, and less than a quarter of its total surface is perfectly flat. The Alps lie imposingly to the north and form a natural border with France, Switzerland, Austria, and Slovenia. The Po River starts there and winds its way from west to east forming the country's breadbasket. The Apennine mountain range runs southward down the peninsula. They're rarely out of sight in central Italy, and have both helped and hindered human activity. Today it's still faster to travel north to south than east to west.

The sea is never far away in Italy. Before tunnels were blasted through mountains and highways were built, goods were moved by water. The Mediterranean surrounds most

umbrella pines in Rome

of the country and gives it that characteristic shape. There are 7,600 kilometers of coastline that vary from Dover-like cliffs to long stretches of sandy beaches where Italians spend their summers.

CLIMATE

In Italy, weather follows a fairly predictable pattern, with seasons that are relatively well defined. Temperatures, however, vary considerably from north to south, and it can easily be ten or more degrees warmer in Rome than in Venice. The latter's position in a lagoon makes it susceptible to humidity, fog, and flooding, especially during early spring and late autumn. Snow is not uncommon in Venice but remains a rarity in Florence and Rome, where residents have trouble recalling the last time they saw flurries.

The fact that most Romans hang their clothes out to dry and don't even own clothes dryers says a lot about the city's climate. Summers are hot and dry and skies remain mostly blue throughout the year. Winters are mild except for January and February. The heavy rains arrive in November when torrential storms can disrupt traffic and lead to school and subway closures.

Florence has a similar Mediterranean climate, but its position farther inland makes it slightly cooler and wetter. Over the last hundred years the Arno has flooded dozens of times, most dramatically in 1966 when water reached the Duomo walls. Venice is used to flooding, and Piazza San Marco is regularly covered in water in early spring and late autumn when sirens warn locals to wear their boots and shops start selling disposable rainwear.

From December through February, the average temperature in Rome is around 9°C (48° F). Florence is slightly cooler, and Venice hovers around 4°C (39°F). July is the hottest month, with an average temperature of around 26°C (79°F) in Rome and Florence and 23°C (73°F) in Venice.

ENVIRONMENTAL ISSUES

Italy's environmental concerns range from poor building practices in earthquake-prone areas to pollution. Rome suffers from smog, and the city hall closes the center to cars whenever air quality deteriorates beyond accepted limits. Over the last decade seasons have begun to stray from their clockwork patterns and people have started to recognize the greater variability, which has led to some regional disasters. Summers aren't just hot, they can be excruciating, and local TV broadcasts advise viewers throughout July and August on how to avoid sunstroke and heat exhaustion.

Italy is a breeding ground for environmental criminals who think dumping toxic waste into rivers and fields is the business of the future. Unfortunately, the practice is very profitable and difficult to stop. Many acres of productive agricultural land have been tarnished in southern Italy, and it's not uncommon for Italians living in affected areas to wonder if local food is safe to eat.

Government and Economy

In Italy, not only is the electoral system complex, but there are an infinite number of parties who struggle with each other to reach a majority. There have been over 60 governments formed since the end of World War II and that number seems destined to rise. Elections often end in stalemate, and the 2013 vote resulted in the appointment of a prime minister who wasn't even on the ballot. Often leaders rely more on strength of personality than actual policies—as was the case with Silvio Berlusconi, the most successful politician in the last three decades.

Below politicians are the bureaucrats and government agencies that keep the country running. It's a big organization that has a difficult time slimming down or adapting to new realities. Italians pay more for their government than citizens of other countries, and most wouldn't say they are getting their money's worth. The political system does supply TV talk shows with plenty of content and allows new parties to periodically emerge with promises of reform. Yet change remains elusive, and passing legislation can be an excruciatingly long process.

ORGANIZATION

The Italian parliament consists of a Chamber of Deputies and a Senate. According to the Constitution of 1948, both have the same rights and powers. They are independent of each other and joint sessions are rare. The main business is the enactment of laws. For a text to become law it must receive a majority in both houses. A bill is discussed in one house, and is then amended and approved or rejected. If approved, it is passed to the other house, which can amend, approve, or reject. If everything runs smoothly, the text is proclaimed law by the President of the Republic and enacted.

The president, however, is more of a figurehead than a leader. That job is reserved for the prime minister, who nominates key ministers and is susceptible to losing power if the majority is lost. It's not uncommon for members of parliament to switch parties. A vote of confidence can be called at any time, and should a government fail to pass such a test it must resign and make way for new elections. That means there are no fixed terms and stability can be difficult to attain.

The Italian justice system has its own problems and is regularly in conflict with politicians who seek to reduce its power and openly criticize its judgments. The Constitutional Court is Italy's Supreme Court. It's composed of 15 judges. One-third are appointed by the president, one-third elected by parliament, and the remainder are elected by lesser courts. They have their work cut out for them, and there is a tremendous backlog of cases waiting to be heard.

POLITICAL PARTIES

Italy is as far as you can get from a two-party system. There are dozens of officially organized groups that run the gamut from hardcore communist to right-wing separatist. In between are small and medium-sized groups, none of whom are large enough to govern on their own. The political landscape is divided into right, left, center, and radical. Obtaining a majority can be hard, which explains why the country has experienced so many different governments since the end of World War II. In Italy governments don't last for a designated amount of time; they can be toppled whenever the ruling party loses its majority in parliament. The result has been instability and gridlock that has hampered the country's legislative needs.

The rise of Berlusconi in the early 1990s and opposition to his *Forza Italia* has led to political consolidation. Since the turn of the century there has been a trend towards three or four larger political forces vying for power. The country is currently governed by the *Partito Democratico*, which has managed to unite moderates and has the most adherents among the general public. It's led by Matteo Renzi, the charismatic former mayor of Florence.

The alternatives on the right are the remnants of Berlusconi's fragmented party, now in the faithful hands of political cronies, and the *Nuovo Centro Destra* (New Center Right), whose members would be Republicans if they campaigned in the United States. In between are smaller parties with little influence, as well as the *5 Stelle* (5 Stars) group that capitalized on popular discontent with politicians. Their founder, Beppe Grillo, is a comedian with a sharp tongue and popular blog who has helped nurture a new generation of politicians. They have gained seats in local and national offices and are now the second most important party, with the power to set the agenda and tip majorities one way or the other.

ELECTIONS

The Chamber of Deputies is located in Palazzo Montecitorio in Rome and has 630 members elected by Italian citizens over the age of eighteen. Deputies are elected for five-year terms unless the president dissolves parliament. Reforms in 2005 significantly complicated matters. The electoral system combines proportional representation with priority for the coalition securing the largest number of votes so a ruling government can achieve a majority. That hasn't been the case in recent elections and there's now talk of further electoral reform.

The Senate is located in Palazzo Madama and has 315 members, elected for five-year terms by Italian citizens over the age of twenty-five. Members are elected by proportional representation based on party lists from each of Italy's twenty regions. Six Senators represent Italians living abroad and seven are granted senatorship for life.

Italians don't elect leaders directly. They vote for parties and those parties determine who represents the people. It's like buying a car without specifying the model, and it

guarantees the same old faces. Turnout is generally high and hovers around 80 percent for national elections. Participation has declined of late as electors lose faith in the system, which has led to political mayhem and resulted in compromise leaders. The electoral system is subject to intense debate and regularly modified. Politicians, however, are uniquely unqualified to fix the problem and are more interested in avoiding term limits and guaranteeing perennial power than resolving matters.

ECONOMY

Italy is the eighth-largest economy in the world with a GDP of $2.1 trillion and an average income per capita of over $35,000. The introduction of the euro, however, has taken its toll on disposable income and salaries have not increased as fast as prices. Growth is beneath the European average and has suffered from stagnation since the recession of 2008. In addition, there's a striking economic divide between regions in the north and those in the south. The country's main trading partners are Germany, France, the Netherlands, and the United States. Unemployment hovers around 9 percent and is particularly high among young adults.

Many advanced industries operate in Italy; however, a decline in R&D investment has led thousands of recent graduates and researchers to search for opportunities abroad. Turning this around is one of the political challenges of the future.

Fiscal pressures are high in Italy and tax evasion is common. The Italian tax agency estimates billions of euros goes unpaid every year and their collection would have a significant impact on GDP. For this reason, the government has passed legislation encouraging a transition towards a cashless society.

Industry

Italy has a long history of innovation. Today, agriculture, aerospace, automobiles, light industry, textiles, tourism, and creative services make up the main economic activities. From 1951 to 1963, the economy grew by more than 6 percent per year. Fiat led the economic postwar recovery and its cars still make up the largest slice of the domestic market. Other goods include precision machinery, pharmaceuticals, home appliances, luxury items, textiles, clothing, and ceramics.

The country lacks deposits of iron, coal, or oil. Most raw materials and much of the country's energy sources must be imported. One of Italy's strengths is small and medium-size businesses. Over 90 percent of all companies employ fewer than ten people. These firms take pride in their work and have managed to maintain high levels of craftsmanship.

The Minister of Finance has one of the toughest jobs in Italy. The country must balance a rising trade deficit, high labor costs, and substantial national debt. *Reform* is a dirty word and taxes couldn't be any higher. Italian companies are at a disadvantage compared to their European rivals and competition from Asia has driven many manufacturers out of business. Nevertheless, *Made in Italy* still matters to consumers around the world, and there are plenty of success stories.

Tourism

Tourism represented 10.5 percent of GDP in 2015 and employed over one million people. Still, considering the number of monuments in Italy and the potential for expanding the industry, a lot of investment is needed. Funding from private companies is required to restore many sights, including the Spanish Steps (Bulgari) and Rialto Bridge (Diesel), both of which were reopened in 2016. Newspapers regular report ancient buildings collapsing in Pompeii, along with other archeological disasters. Unfortunately, thousands of architectural and artistic treasures are slowly deteriorating.

In 2014, 48.6 million tourists visited the country. Most are European, but travelers from the United States (4.7 million) and China (2.2 million) represent a steadily growing share. Rome is the most popular destination followed by Milan, Venice, and Florence. Plans to cope with the demands of tourism include expanding airports in Rome and Florence, as well as additional high-speed train links between Italy and France.

People and Culture

DEMOGRAPHY

Italy is one of the most densely populated countries in Europe, with over 58 million inhabitants. Rome is the largest city, with a population of 2.5 million, followed by Naples and Milan. The average life expectancy is 83 years for women and 77 for men. There are also plenty of people pushing 100. Birth rates are low and it's only through immigration that the country has managed to keep the population from declining.

IMMIGRATION

Immigration is a relatively new phenomenon in Italy. Up until 1989 more people left Italy than arrived. Today, the official number of immigrants is around five million, which means 8.2 percent of the population was born outside the country.

The largest immigrant communities are from Romania, Albania, Morocco, and China. Most are male and attracted to Rome and cities in northern Italy where the chances of finding a job are better than in the south. Many work as day laborers, builders, cleaners, and caretakers. The second generation of this immigration wave is starting to make itself felt, and today, it's not uncommon to see Italo Pakistani chefs preparing pasta, Italo Nigerian children on their way to school, and Italo Chinese contestants on TV quiz shows.

Conflict in Syria and sub-Saharan Africa has greatly increased immigration to Europe. The issue has reached crisis proportions, with some nations unable to deal with the influx. Italy is not the primary destination of Middle Eastern refugees, who usually travel

Breaking the Language Barrier

Learning a new language takes time, dedication, and practice. If you want to experience a fundamental aspect of Italian culture you must start before your trip. Set aside 20 minutes per day for undistracted study at least two weeks before arrival. Download an Italian learning app (Duolingo or Babbel), invest in a book, or enroll in a course. Listen to Italian music on your way to work, and browse the headlines of Italian newspapers online. Stimulating your eyes and ears with as many sources of Italian as possible will make it easier to understand and use Italian once you arrive. Find Italian singers you like and add them to your playlist, watch short films or cartoons, and, if you have the benefit of a friend or traveling partner, try out new grammar and vocabulary as often as possible. Imagine situations you're likely to encounter (restaurant, ticket office, bar, etc.) and role-play interactions until you're comfortable ordering a cappuccino and asking for a bottle of house wine. It's impossible to master a new language in a month but you can absorb enough grammar and vocabulary to adapt to the linguistic surroundings and break through the language barrier. The more effort you put in at home, the more gratifying the journey will be.

through Turkey and into Greece on their way to Germany and Nordic countries. Most immigrants to Italy arrive from Africa, and smugglers regularly pack boats with people desperate to start a new life abroad. Many enterprising immigrants wind up selling bags and other trinkets to tourists in the center of Rome or along the seaside and are grateful to be in Italy.

RELIGION

The vast majority of Italians are Catholic, although the number of those who regularly attend church is on the decline. The Lateran Agreement of 1929 officially formalized the relationship between the Italian State and the Vatican, which continues to benefit from substantial tax breaks. Although church and state are divided in the constitution it's not uncommon to see crucifixes in police stations, hospitals, and schools. Every town has a patron saint that is still celebrated with feasts and festivals.

Islam, Buddhism, and Orthodox Christianity are the fastest-growing religions in Italy. Many Muslims face Mecca inside homemade mosques, and some Italian cities have been reluctant to provide building permits for new mosques. Jews have been present in Italy nearly from the beginning, and the remains of the oldest synagogue in Europe can be found in Ostia Antica. Their treatment by the majority varied through the ages, and Rome and Venice both contain ghettos where Jews were once forced to live.

LANGUAGE

Italy's national language derived from Latin and owes a great debt to Dante, who was the first to codify and utilize the dialects spoken on the Renaissance streets of Florence in his tales of heaven and hell. A trained ear can detect the difference between a Roman and a Venetian accent. Besides regional differences, there are minority languages such as Sardo, spoken by over a million people in Sardinia, and Friulano, widely used in Friuli. Ladino and Catalan are confined to enclaves in the Alps and on the northwestern coast of Sardinia, respectively. Both are remnants of foreign occupation, and their gradual mixture with Italian has led to colorful words and expressions that aren't found in dictionaries.

Essentials

Transportation

AIR
Airports

Rome's **Aeroporto di Roma-Fiumicino** (FCO, Via dell' Aeroporto 320, tel. 06/65951, www.adr.it), aka Leonardo Da Vinci Airport, is a hub for intercontinental routes. It has four terminals and scheduled nonstop flights to dozens of North American cities. The airport is 30 kilometers southwest of Rome and there are frequent bus and train connections with Termini station in the center. **Ciampino** (CIA, Via Appia Nuova 1651, tel. 06/65951, www.adr.it), Rome's second airport, is used by charter and low-cost airlines flying to Italian and European destinations.

Venice's **Aeroporto di Venezia** (VCE, Via Galileo Galilei 30, tel. 041/260-6111, www.veniceairport.it) is a medium-sized airport that offers fewer direct flights to North America but many connecting flights from across Europe.

Florence's **Aeroporto di Firenze-Peretola** (FLR, Via del Termine 11, tel. 055/30615, www.aeroporto.firenze.it) is the smallest option, with no direct flights to the United States (although renovations may open the airport to intercontinental routes in the future). Delays and cancellations due to inclement weather are common. Tuscany's busiest airport, **Aeroporto di Pisa-San Giusto** (Piazzale D'Ascanio 1, tel. 050/849-111, www. pisa-airport.com) in Pisa, is less than an hour and a half away from Florence by bus, train, or car. There are direct flights from JFK to Pisa during the summer.

Airlines

There are over 50 daily nonstop flights from the United States to Italy, and most land in Rome. **Alitalia** (www.alitalia.com) operates many of these and flies Boeing B777s and Airbus A330s daily to the capital from Boston, New York, Miami, and Toronto. **Delta** (www.delta.com), **American** (www.aa.com), **United** (www.united.com), and **Air Canada** (www.aircanada.com) also serve Rome from major cities in North America. There are also a handful of direct flights to Venice with Alitalia, American, or Delta; all depart from New York or Philadelphia. There are no direct flights to Florence and only one seasonal flight to Pisa.

Connections within North America or Europe increase options and make it possible to land in all of the destination cities. There are hundreds of connecting flights from London, Paris, and Amsterdam with **Air France** (www.airfrance.it), **BA** (www.britishairways.com), or **KLM** (www.klm.com). Low-cost airlines like **Vueling** (www.vueling.com), **Ryanair** (www.ryanair.com), and **EasyJet** (www.easyjet.com) also fly to Rome, Florence, and Venice from most European capitals. **Aer Lingus** (www.aerlingus.com) runs one-stop flights from Dublin airport, which is equipped with a U.S. immigration office. Passengers are screened in Ireland and bypass customs when returning to the United States.

Alitalia operates most domestic flights, with three daily departures between Rome and Florence and five to Venice. Flight time is around an hour and tickets are inexpensive when purchased in advance. There are no direct flights between Venice and Florence, and a stopover in Rome is required. Other European airlines such as **Swiss** (www.swiss. com), **BA,** and **Air France** cover the routes but require layovers outside of Italy that significantly lengthen travel time.

ESSENTIALS
TRANSPORTATION

TRAIN

Arriving by train from other European destinations often requires a long and tortuous journey. There are daily departures from Paris to Rome on board the **Thello** (www.thello.com) service that leaves in the early evening and arrives at Termini in the morning. If you want to avoid a neckache it's worth purchasing a berth in one of the sleeping cabins *(couchettes)*. There are also many trains from northern European cities to Venice. Single tickets can be purchased through www.trenitalia.it; if you are on a European vacation and will be visiting many countries it can be cheaper to purchase a rail pass from **Eurail** (www.eurail.com) or **Rail Europe** (www.raileurope.com).

Over the last decade successive governments have invested billions in an expanding network of high-speed tracks that have drastically reduced journey times between Italian cities. Today, moving between Rome, Florence, and Venice is fast, easy, and convenient. There are two operators. Both the state-owned **Trenitalia** (www.trenitalia.com) and private **Italo** (www.italo.it) provide frequent daily departures between all three cities. The Trenitalia **Frecciarossa** (red arrow) service is slightly more expensive and operates more trains, making it popular with business travelers; tourists generally prefer Italo. They both use the same track and leave from the same stations. Journey time between Rome and Florence is 90 minutes, Florence to Venice is 2 hours, and Venice to Rome 3.5 hours.

Trains are modern, clean, and equipped with Wi-Fi, electrical outlets, leather upholstery, snack machines, and bar cars. Tickets can be purchased online or at train stations from automated machines or service booths. Both websites are available in English, and the Italo pages are slightly easier to navigate. There are several levels of comfort on board but even standard seating is adequate. High-speed trains depart from central stations in all three cities.

Trenitalia also operates local and intercity trains throughout Italy. These are slower and make more stops. They're also cheaper, and train interiors have a romantic wear and tear about them. The **Regional Veloce** from Rome takes nearly four hours to reach Florence and leaves five times per day. Only high-speed service is available between Florence and Venice.

BUS

Bus service is the cheapest and least comfortable way to reach Italy. **Eurolines** (www.eurolines.com) operates service from 22 European countries.

Within Italy, buses are a cheap alternative to trains or cars. There are a half-dozen companies that operate between Rome, Florence, and Venice. **Eurolines** (www.eurolines.com), **Flixbus** (www.flixbus.com), and **Megabus** (www.megabus.com) provide similar service on buses that seat around 40 passengers. One-way tickets rarely exceed €20 and depots are located near train stations. Most intercity buses leave from **Termini** or **Tiburtina** station in Rome, **Stazione Santa Maria Novella** in Florence, and **Santa Lucia** in Venice. All are equipped with restrooms. There are a few stops along the way, and travel time is two or three times longer than the train.

CAR

The Schengen Agreement removed border controls between members of the European Union and made travel hassle-free. The recent and ongoing immigration crisis, however, has led some governments to reinstate checks. Entering Italy from France, Switzerland, Austria, or Slovenia isn't a problem, but leaving Italy can be trickier.

You will need to take a ticket when entering the country by car and pay a toll when exiting the highway at your destination. As most highways in northern Italy are at fairly high altitudes, snow and fog in winter can lead to some delays. During the summer traffic at borders is common. Smaller roads that cross the Alps are best driven during the day at low speeds.

Italy's *autostrade* (highways) are excellent.

Drivers collect tickets when entering and tolls, based on distance traveled, are paid in cash or credit card upon exiting. Signage should be familiar to North American drivers; however, there's a much greater use of yield and round-abouts are frequent in urban areas. To review the rules of the Italian road, visit the Italian office of tourism (www.italia.com).

You'll need your **passport** and a **driver's license** if you plan on renting a moped or car. An **international driver's permit** is not required but can avoid confusion if you're pulled over. It's available from **AAA** (www.aaa.com) for $15.

CAR RENTALS

Cars can be rented from **Europcar** (www.europcar.com), **Sixt** (www.sixt.com), **Maggiore** (www.maggiore.com), **Hertz** (www.hertz.com), and other companies upon arrival at airports in Rome, Florence, and Venice or from rental offices located near the central train stations in all three cities. The latter option is more practical, as parking can be difficult to find and much of the historic center in Rome and Florence is a **limited traffic zone** (ZTL). The ZTL is only accessible to residents, although drivers renting cars within the zone are exempt.

Skyscanner (www.skyscanner) and **Kayak** (www.kayak.com) can help find the best rental prices. Always get the maximum insurance. Anything can happen on Italian roads, and if you observe cars carefully you'll notice a high percentage of dents. Florence has less traffic and more considerate drivers than Rome. Many streets are partially pedestrianized and it's easy to find a spot on the outskirts and walk or ride a bus to the center. Venice is entirely off-limits to cars except for dedicated lots near the station linked to the center by a light rail system.

You can avoid renting and try Italian car-sharing with **Bla Bla Car** (www.blablacar.it), which connects passengers with drivers traveling throughout Italy. There are several dozen offers per day for rides between Rome, Florence, and Venice. Prices range €15-30 depending on distance. Some Italian is necessary for navigating the website.

GETTING AROUND EACH CITY
Public Transportation

ATAC Rome (www.atac.roma.it) operates subway, tram, bus, and train service to destinations in and around the city. In Florence, **Florence ATAF** (www.ataf.net) operates a smaller network that consists primarily of buses and one tram line (two are currently under construction). Public transit in Venice is made up of over 20 **ACTV** (actv.avmspa.it) ferry lines *(vaporetti)* that circumnavigate the city and connect it with islands around the lagoon.

Tickets and travel passes in all three cities must be validated upon first use in subway stations, on board buses or trams, or at validating machines near ferry landings. Controllers do occasionally check passengers and will fine anyone without a ticket. Daily and multiday travel cards are available in all three cities and can be more convenient and cheaper than repeatedly purchasing single tickets.

Bicycle

Rome has yet to undergo a cycling revolution, and cyclists in the city face innumerable urban obstacles—from cobblestones to distracted tourists to oddly parked cars. Florence is another story, and the rows of bikes locked outside Santa Maria Novella train station and around the historic center demonstrate the city's fondness for two-wheeled transport. Roads are well paved and there is very little traffic. Much of the center is pedestrianized and cyclists are everywhere.

Bicycles and mopeds are banned from Venice and wouldn't be very useful even if they weren't. The city's hundreds of bridges and stairs make these forms of transport impractical.

Car

CAR SHARING

Car2Go (www.car2go.com) and **Enjoy** (www.enjoy.eni.com) are the two largest car-sharing services in Italy. Both are easy to use and provide access to hundreds of vehicles throughout central Rome and Florence. Registration is online and requires a passport, driver's license, and international permit. Once the app is downloaded you can locate and use cars for as little or as long as you like. You're also exempt from parking fees and don't have to pay for gas. It's a practical way of getting around and costs less than a taxi. Car2Go operates a fleet of white two-seat Smart cars while Enjoy uses red FIAT 500s that seat four.

The cost of Enjoy is 25 cents per minute up to a maximum of €50 per day while Car2Go is 29 cents per minute and €59 per day. Cars can leave the zones in each city where they are available but must be returned to those zones once you're finished using them.

PARKING

Parking garages are convenient but expensive, and there's a good chance of being fined if street parking goes unpaid. White lines mean spaces are free of charge, blue is €1.50 per hour, and yellow is off-limits. Meters are located at regular intervals on most streets and can be ignored on Sundays. In Rome (and, to a lesser extent, Florence) unofficial parking attendants appear after sundown to wave drivers into free spots. They expect a euro or two for their effort, but if you want to dissuade them just ignore them or act like you're from a country where such practices don't exist.

Taxi

Cabs are stationed at or near large squares and train stations day and night. Vehicles are privately owned and range from small to reasonably sized. All are white and topped with signage that indicates if cars are free or in service. Spontaneously hailing taxis is possible but rarely done by locals, and it's easier to reserve one by phone. Response time is fast and travelers rarely wait more than ten minutes. All companies operate 24 hours a day and vehicles for passengers with special needs and vans are available. Fares are relatively high and calculated according to time and distance. Weekend and night rates are higher.

Drivers don't expect tips. Fares can be rounded up to the nearest euro, but anything more is unnecessary and un-Italian.

Visas and Officialdom

PASSPORTS AND VISAS

Travelers from the United States and Canada do not need a visa to enter Italy for visits of less than 90 days. All that's required is a passport valid at least three months after your intended departure from the European Union.

EMBASSIES AND CONSULATES

Lost or stolen passports can be replaced at the **United States Embassy** (Via Veneto 119a/121, tel. 06/46741, www.italy.usembassy.gov, Mon.-Fri. 8:30am-noon) in Rome or the **consulate** (Lungarno A. Vespucci 38, 055/266-951, 9am-12:30pm) in Florence. Proof of citizenship and a photo ID are required. Replacements are issued on the spot and cost €135. In addition to assisting with missing passports, the U.S. Embassy in Rome can help travelers deal with medical or legal emergencies. There's also a **consular agency** (Venice Marco Polo Airport, tel. 041/541-5944) in Venice. Citizens with after-hours problems can contact the embassy at any time by calling 055/266-951. The embassy and consulates are closed during Italian and U.S. holidays. For bureaucratic questions before arriving to Italy call the **U.S. Department of State** (tel. 1-888/407-4747 from the United States or 1-202/501-4444 from any other country, Mon.-Fri. 8am-8pm EST).

The **Canadian Embassy** (Via Zara 30, 800/2326-6831, Mon.-Fri. 8:30am-noon) handles all citizen services and is located northwest of the historic center in Rome. The **Australian Embassy** (Via Antonio Bosio 5, tel. 06/852-721) is also located in Rome. Neither country has offices in Florence or Venice.

CUSTOMS

Travelers entering Italy are expected to declare any amount of cash over €6,000 and are prohibited from importing animal-based food products into the country. Duty-free imports for passengers from outside the EU are limited to one liter of alcohol, two liters of wine, 200 cigarettes, 50 cigars, and 50 milliliters of perfume.

Bags are more likely to be heavier upon leaving Italy, and sausage smuggling is common. U.S. citizens are limited to $800 worth of goods deemed for personal use. Anything over that amount must be declared and will be taxed. Fresh fruit and vegetables, cheese, and animal-based products are not allowed into the United States. Further details regarding what can and cannot be imported into the country are available from the **U.S. Department of State** (www.state.gov).

Canadian regulations are fairly lenient and allow cheese, herbs, condiments, dried fruits, baked goods, and candies; for a complete list visit the **Canadian Border Services Agency** (www.cbsa-asfc.gc.ca). Australian regulations are particularly stringent and customs officers go to great lengths to avoid contamination. All fruit, vegetables, ham, salami, and meat products are forbidden. Fake designer goods will also be confiscated and may lead to a fine. If you're in doubt consult the **Australian Department of Immigration and Border Protection** (www.border.gov.au).

Food

There are all sorts of places to eat in Italy, and travelers should attempt to experience as many as possible. When choosing where to eat, avoid restaurants where staff actively encourages you to enter and menus are displayed in more than three languages. Authentic establishments attract Italians and are not located next to major monuments. Generally, however, it's hard to have a bad meal in Italy, and if it looks good it usually tastes good as well.

ITALIAN EATERIES
Restaurants

The most common sit-down eateries are *trattoria, osteria,* and *ristorante.* The first two have humble origins and are cheaper than *ristorante.* The typical *trattoria* serves local dishes within a rustic atmosphere. The best have been in business for generations and have devoted local followings. Service can be ad hoc and waiters are not overly concerned with formality. *Osteria* are similar, but have fewer items on their menus and rarely stray from tradition. *Ristorante* are more expensive and elegant. They may have uniformed waiters, an extensive wine cellar along with a sommelier, and fine table settings. Menus often diverge from tradition and combine flavors in novel ways. *Trattoria, osteria,* and *ristorante* are open lunch and dinner, and continuous service throughout the day is rare. Rome, Florence, and Venice have their share of Michelin-starred restaurants and most offer a tasting menu. Salt is not generally present on tables and if you need additional sodium ask a waiter for *sale* [sah-Lay].

Rome is the best place outside of Naples to order pizza. Although it's available in Florence and Venice, those cities lack pizza pedigree.

Dine Like a Local

Italians have their own way of doing things—especially when it comes to food. Here's how to blend in with locals:

- **Embrace a light breakfast.** Forget about eggs and bacon: Sidle up to locals at the nearest bar and order a cappuccino and a pastry.

- **Know the coffee culture.** Italians drink coffee at specific times. Cappuccinos are rarely ordered after noon or in restaurants, and should never accompany or immediately precede a meal. Espressos are ordered at the end of lunch and/or dinner, and during midday or midafternoon breaks.

- **Skip the salt and olive oil.** Salt, olive oil, and Parmesan aren't meant to be added to food and won't appear tableside.

- **Forget about eating on the go.** Italians eat standing at bars and sitting at restaurants, but you'll rarely see them eating while they walk. The only exception is gelato, which can make a slow stroll through a historic center even better.

- **Accept the slowness.** Service may be slower than you're used to. It might be hard to get the server's attention, or the second bottle of wine may never arrive—just remember the sun is probably shining and you are in Italy. A little patience along with good-natured persistence will ensure a good time. Frustration won't.

Traditional round pies and sit-down service are available at *pizzeria,* which also serve a variety of fried starters such as *suppli* (rice balls stuffed with mozzarella) and *fiore di zucca* (zucchini flowers with anchovies). Pizza is also a staple of many restaurant menus and is easy to find. Quality is generally good and it's hard to pay more than €8 for a pie. The Roman version is thin and toppings tend to be simple.

Rome is an international city with international flavors. Chinese and Japanese restaurants are common but it's also easy to find Middle Eastern, Indian, African, and South American eateries. Kosher restaurants are concentrated around the Roman and Venetian ghettos and closed during Sabbath. New restaurants are opening all the time and recent trends have introduced steak houses, burger joints, vegan-bio, express pasta shops, and sandwich bars to all three cities.

Street Food

The most popular street food in Italy is pizza, which is available on demand at *pizza al taglio* (pizza by the cut) shops from midmorning onward. The pizza inside these small shops with little or no seating is baked in large rectangular tins. There are a dozen varieties waiting to be cut, and customers line up haphazardly to order whatever they like. Slices are then weighed and reheated if necessary, and they can be left open to eat immediately or wrapped up for later consumption. Payment is usually made at a separate cashier.

Markets are another good destination for tasty fast food from morning to early afternoon. Stalls in the Testaccio market in Rome and Mercato Centrale in Florence have been serving the same favorites for generations. This is where to sample beef or tripe sandwiches, drink inexpensive wine out of plastic cups, and sample seasonal fruits.

Bakeries and *Pasticceria*

The day begins in *fornaio* (bakeries), which open before dawn and remain so until midafternoon. There's one in every neighborhood and they supply locals with all types of bread, buns, and sweets. You'll also find cakes, cookies, tarts, pastries, white or red pizza, and unique recipes served during holidays. All items are priced by the kilo and usually purchased for takeaway. *Fornaio* can be crowded in the morning, and some use numbered tickets to avoid confusion. There's a big difference between what's baked in Rome, Florence, and Venice. Each city has its own specialties that vary in form and ingredients.

Pasticceria are entirely dedicated to sweets and keep roughly the same hours as bakeries. They serve cookies, tarts, and cakes along with an array of smaller finger-sized pastries Italians serve as midafternoon snacks (*merenda*) or offer to visiting friends. Some *pasticceria* serve coffee and prepare one or two items for which they are famous. There's a tremendous variety, and pastries in Rome and Florence taste and look different from the ones prepared in Venice.

Coffee Bars

Coffee bars and cafes open nearly as early as bakeries and provide different services throughout the day. In the morning they supply locals with espressos or cappuccinos and *cornetti* (breakfast pastries), which are either plain or filled with cream, jelly, or chocolate. *Cornetti* rarely exceed €1 and are a cheap and tasty way to start the day. Most bars are supplied by bakeries, but some have their own ovens.

By midmorning, coffee bars trade sweets for triangular *tramezzino* and *panini* sandwiches stacked behind glass counters. These cost €2-3.50 and can be eaten at the counter or at a table, or taken away. Larger bars provide *tavola calda* (lunchtime buffets) with a selection of first- and second-course dishes. It's hard to spend more than €15 for a complete meal with water and coffee.

Bars usually operate on a "consume now, pay later" policy with a dedicated cashier off to one side who calculates checks. Counter service is slightly cheaper, always faster, and where most locals do their eating and drinking. There's a big difference between neighborhood bars and those overlooking heavily touristed squares like Piazza Navona or Piazza San Marco. **Cafes** in those squares are far

more elegant and some have been around for centuries. Prices are higher although the food is more or less the same. The biggest advantage is the view, and the tables outside are usually filled with tourists.

Venice is different from other Italian cities in many ways. Although you can find bars similar to those in Rome and Florence, the city has developed its own particular eatery. Venetian *bacari* serve bite-size slices of bread topped with vegetables, meat, or fish called *cicchetti*. These creative and inexpensive appetizers are accompanied by wine or beer from late morning until early evening. *Bacari* interiors are rustic, seating is limited, and service is friendly.

Gelateria

Gelateria are nearly as common as bars in Italy and stay open late during the summer. They specialize in ice cream and sorbet, which come in many flavors. The best are made on the spot with seasonal ingredients, while less passionate owners cut corners by using preservatives and compressed air to give gelato bright colors and gravity-defying forms. Gelato is priced by the scoop and served in a cone or cup. Clerks will ask if you want *panna* (whipped cream) added at no extra cost.

MENUS

Italian menus are divided into courses with an established order. *Antipasti* (starters) are the first thing you'll see and can be as simple as *bruschette* (toasted bread topped with tomatoes) or *fiori di zucchini* (fried zucchini flowers stuffed with anchovies). The point of the *antipasto* is to relieve hunger and prepare stomachs for the meal to come. House starters (*antipasto della casa*) are a safe culinary bet and plates of local cold cuts and cheeses are meant to be shared among friends.

The *primo* (first course) can be pasta, *risotto*, or soup. There are hundreds of traditional pasta shapes, all of which are combined with particular sauces that include vegetables, meat, or fish. This is a chance to get adventurous. Romans tend to serve simple white or red sauces flavored with thick cuts of bacon (*Amatriciana*), pepper and goat cheese (*cacio e pepe*), or clams (*pasta alle vongole*). Soups are popular in Florence and fortified with pasta, beans, and barley. Rice is as common as pasta in Venice and usually served with fish or crustaceans.

Many people surrender after the first course, and that's a shame for stomachs. If you need help getting through a 3-course meal, order a *mezzo porzione* (half portion) and leave room for the *secondo* (second course). It consists of meat or fish and is the gastronomic main event. Let waiters know if you want meat rare (*al sangue*), medium rare (*cotta*), or well done (*ben cotta*). Unless you order a side (*contorno*) your steak will be lonely. These generally consist of grilled vegetables or roasted potatoes and are listed at the end of the menu along with desserts and drinks.

Restaurants often have a separate wine menu and daily specials that waiters will translate when possible. A satisfying 3-course lunch or dinner with dessert and coffee runs around €25-40 per person.

Drinks

Italy has hundreds of natural springs and Italians drink more **mineral water** than anyone. The first question waiters often ask is the type of *acqua* (water) patrons want. You can choose between sparkling (*frizzante*) or still (*naturale*). A liter costs around €3 and sometimes there's a choice of brands. *Acqua di Nepi* is one of the best Roman waters and is said to aid digestion. That's not to say tap water (*acqua del rubinetto*) is bad. It's regularly tested by authorities and is safe to drink.

It's difficult to find a restaurant that doesn't have a decent **wine** list. Many eateries have a separate wine menu that includes local, regional, and international bottles. House wine is also available and generally very drinkable. It can be ordered by the glass or in different-sized carafes. Tuscany is the epicenter of Italian oenology and the place to uncork legendary Chianti and Super Tuscans.

Geography and a cooler climate make Veneto suitable for growing white grapes, and the region is renowned for its sparkling *prosecco*. The Lazio region (Rome) isn't famous for wine production but still turns out respectable vintages and quality has improved in recent years. A glass of house wine costs €3-4, a half-carafe €4-6, and a full carafe €8-10. Prices are nearly always indicated on menus, but if they're not—or if a waiter brings you a bottle—ask the price before indulging.

Most Italians end lunches with an **espresso** and occasionally conclude dinners with a **digestivo** (digestif). The latter are high-grade alcoholic spirits and reputed to help digestion. The most famous of these is *grappa*, which is served in a small glass and meant to be sipped. **Soft drinks** are available but not very common on restaurant tables.

SEASONAL SPECIALTIES

Locals can tell the date by what's on display inside bakeries and *pasticcerie*. Most seasonal specialties revolve around sweets, which are prepared during major holidays.

The weeks preceding Christmas transform grocery and supermarket shelves, with entire aisles devoted to chocolate, nuts, dried fruit, and, especially, **pandoro** cakes made from flour, eggs, butter, and sugar. During *Carnivale*, fried pastries are the gastronomic excess of choice. The most popular are the doughnut-like **castagnole alla romana** and fried dough **frappe** covered with powdered sugar and available in bars and bakeries. Easter wouldn't be the same for Italians without **columba** (dove) cakes topped with almonds and granulated sugar. All are available in bakeries and supermarkets.

New Year's meals nearly always include lentils, which are eaten for good luck, along with **cotechino** (pig's foot). Christmas lunches involve fish while roast lamb tends to be on the menu at Easter. Seasons greatly influence what's on tables the rest of the year. Soups are a mainstay of Florentine menus throughout the winter, while spring is the time to try artichokes prepared *alla romana* or *alla giudea*

Produce Calendar

Italians eat according to the seasons, which means you won't find cherries in winter or kiwis in summer. What you will find is usually fresh and grown both locally and around the country. To get an idea of what's in season visit an open-air market like Campo di Fiori in Rome or Campo della Pescheria in Venice. You can also consult the list below to make sure what you're ordering is fresh:

Spring	Summer	Fall	Winter	Year-Round
artichokes	eggplant	pumpkins	pumpkin	carrots
asparagus	zucchini	white and black truffles	artichoke	endive
green beans	turnips	cabbage	cauliflower	dried beans
fava beans	radishes	mushrooms	broccoli	lettuce
new potatoes	peas	cauliflower	winter melons	leeks
cauliflower	cucumbers	broccoli	Brussels sprouts	celery
broccoli	fava beans	Roman broccoli	radicchio	spinach
cabbage	green beans	chestnuts	oranges	potatoes
zucchini	peppers	grapes	mandarins	chicory
tomatoes	mushrooms	figs	clementines	apples
kiwi	cherries	oranges	grapefruit	pears
strawberries	prunes	mandarins	kiwi	lemons
medlars	peaches	clementines		
peaches	apricots	grapefruit		
	figs			
	melons			
	wild berries			

in Rome. Italian diets are regulated by the harvest and the produce available in outdoor markets has a natural rhythm. Kitchens rely on domestically grown fruit and vegetables that provide variety and delight the palate all year long.

HOURS

Restaurants are typically open 12:30pm-2:30pm for lunch and 8pm-10pm for dinner. Most close one day a week and many take an extended break during August or January. Reservations aren't usually necessary, but to guarantee a seat at popular eateries it's best to arrive early or late. Bakeries open before sunrise and close in the midafternoon, while coffee bars are open all day long and *pizzeria* and *gelateria* stay open late.

TIPPING

Tipping is not required or expected in Italy. This is compensated by a €1-3 surcharge *(coperto)* for bread, utensils, and service per customer. Waiters earn a decent living but no one refuses money, and leaving €3-5 behind after a good meal is one way to show appreciation. Customers at coffee bars often leave a low-denomination coin at the counter.

Shopping

The idea of one store selling everything has yet to take off in Italy. The majority of family-owned shops are dedicated to one thing and one thing only. This can be a single product like shoes, hats, books, clothing, or furniture, or a material like leather, ceramics, paper, or glass.

Most businesses are small and have few employees. Department and megastores exist in the center of Rome and Florence but attract as many tourists as locals, who prefer to shop in malls and outlets on the outskirts of the city. Luxury boutiques are concentrated around major monuments like Piazza di Spagna and Piazza San Marco. Although you're unlikely to find a discarded Giacometti in Roman or Florentine flea markets, collectors with patience will be rewarded. There's a great variety to rummage through and major markets have something for everyone.

SHOPPING ETIQUETTE

People entering a small, uncrowded shop (or bar) nearly always greet assistants with *buongiorno* or *buonasera* (good morning/good afternoon). Most shop owners and employees tend not to be overbearing and welcome browsing. They're happy to leave shoppers alone; however, they are professional and helpful once you demonstrate interest in an item and will happily find your size or explain how something is made. When leaving a store say *grazie* (thank you) or *arrivederci* (goodbye) regardless if you've made a purchase. Eye contact isn't essential but politeness is.

Bargaining

Shopping in Italy is a chance to practice your negotiating skills and discover the thrill of haggling. Price can be theoretical at souvenir stands, flea markets, antique stalls, and even smaller shops, where no one will be offended if you ask for a *sconto* (discount). If a price sounds too high, it probably is—and can likely be lowered.

SHIPPING ITEMS HOME

Don't worry if something that's larger than your suitcase catches your eye. Stores, especially Venetian ones selling glass, are accustomed to tourists and can arrange for shipment directly to your door. Expect to pay up to 10 percent of the purchase price for home delivery.

SALES

January and September are the best times to shop in Italy. All stores begin the sale season in unison during these months and windows are plastered with discounts. Every price tag should contain the original and sale price. Check items carefully before buying and don't hesitate to try clothes on, as Italian sizes generally run smaller and fit differently. The sale season lasts four weeks, but most of the good stuff and sought-after sizes disappear after ten days.

HOURS

Italy has its own unique rhythm, and nowhere is that more evident than in shops. Family-owned stores and smaller businesses nearly always close between 1pm and 3pm. Many also close on Sundays and Monday mornings or another day of the week. Larger stores and those located in heavily trafficked streets have continuous hours. Businesses in the Roman and Venetian Jewish ghettoes observe Sabbath and shut down from sunset Friday until sunset on Saturday.

Accommodations

HOTELS

Italian hotels are graded on a system of stars that ranges from one to five. How many stars an establishment has depends on infrastructure and services. Criteria varies from region to region but most three-star hotels are quite comfortable. Reservations can be made online and most hotels have multilingual websites. A **passport** or ID card is required when checking in and early arrivals can usually leave luggage at the front desk. Many smaller hotels operate a "leave the key" policy in which keys must be left and retrieved whenever entering or leaving the accommodation.

Large international chains like **Hilton** (www3.hilton.com), **Sheraton** (www.starwoodhotels.com), and **Best Western** (www.bestwestern.com) all operate in Italy, along with budget accommodations like **Ibis** (www.ibis.com) and **Mercure** (www.mercure.com). Service may be better and rooms slightly larger in these hotels, but they often lack character and could be located anywhere in the world. Many travelers will find themselves better off staying in smaller boutique or family-operated hotels that have managed to retain their charm.

Valuables are best carried or deposited in a hotel safe if available. In addition to the room rate, expect to be charged a city **hotel tax** of €1-5 per guest/per day depending on the number of stars and accommodation type. It's a small price to pay for waking up in Rome, Florence, and Venice.

HOSTELS AND *PENSIONI*

There's no age limit to staying in the **youth hostels** (*ostelli*) located in all three cities. They provide clean, affordable accommodation and many are less sparse than you might expect. Most include single, double, and quad options in addition to classic dormitory-style rooms. A bed costs around €20 per person and may include breakfast. The best thing about

hostels, however, is the ambience. They're filled with travelers from all over at various stages of round-the-world adventures. All hostels are overseen by **Associazione Italiana Alberghi per la Gioventù** (tel. 06/487-1152, www.aighostels.it). Bathrooms in hostels tend to be shared although many also have private rooms with en suite baths.

Pensioni are small, lower-grade accommodations that are often family-run. Rooms are generally clean and functional, although you may be required to share a bathroom. They're often located near train stations or city centers in large buildings that may or may not have elevators. Some enforce curfews and it's best to check at the front desk (if there is one) before heading out for the night.

AGRITURISMI AND CAMPING

Agriturismi are a wonderful Italian invention that combine bed-and-breakfast-type accommodations with rural living. Most of these are located in converted farmhouses on land used to grow crops and raise animals. Decor is rustic and the number of rooms is limited. Half- and full-board options are often available and meals consist of local ingredients. Owners are happy to show you around and the proximity to countryside provides a relaxing break from the city. Many are located on the hillsides surrounding Rome and Florence and are equipped with swimming pools. **Agriturismo** (www.agriturismo.it) lists thousands of such accommodations throughout Italy.

All three cities also have **campsites** that remain open from April to September. Facilities vary but usually include a bar or restaurant, showers, and telephones. Some locations are better than others and there are several grounds in Florence that are within walking distance of the historic center. Camping in Rome and Venice requires a slightly longer commute. Equipment can be rented if you've forgotten your tent, and bungalows are sometimes also available. For a full list of sites visit the Italian Campsite Federation (tel. 05/588-2391, www.feder-campeggio.it).

B&BS AND APARTMENTS

Italy has experienced a B&B boom over the last decade and the country now offers thousands of options. It allows you stay with local residents and gain an insider's perspective.

To really do as the Romans do, rent an apartment and get an instant native feel. Short-term rental is especially convenient for families. Not only are prices lower than many hotels, but staying in an apartment allows you to call the mealtime shots and relax in a home away from home. Airbnb (www.airbnb.com) and VRBO (www.vrbo.com) are good places to start apartment hunting. Hometogo (www.hometogo.com) searches over 250 international and local rental sites.

Conduct and Customs

LOCAL HABITS

Italians are attached to their habits and especially those related to food. Mealtimes are fairly strict and most eating is done sitting down at precise hours. Locals generally have a light breakfast and save themselves for lunch and dinner, which are served at 1pm and 8pm. You won't see many Italians snacking on the subway or bus or walking while they eat. Meals are usually divided *alla Romana* (Dutch) between friends but no one will take offense if you offer to pay. Rounds of drinks are not offered as they are in the United States; groups of colleagues each buy their own. Drinking in general is done over a meal rather than with any intention of getting drunk, and displays of public drunkenness are rare.

Most of the things considered rude in North America are also considered rude in Italy. One exception is cutting in line, which is a frequent offense. Italian lines are undisciplined and can feel like a fumble recovery. If you don't defend your place by saying *scusi* or coughing loudly you may be waiting all day for a cappuccino or slice of pizza. Fortunately, number dispensers are used in post offices, pharmacies, and at deli counters. Personal space in general is smaller than in Anglo-Saxon countries, and Italians tend to use their hands as well as words to emphasize ideas.

GREETINGS

Italians are exceptionally sociable and have developed highly ritualized forms of interaction. Daily exchanges with friends and acquaintances often involve physical contact, and kisses on both cheeks are common. Bars and squares are the urban settings for unhurried conversation, which is a normal part of everyday Italian life. The proliferation of the cell phone has fueled the passion to communicate, and in some cases has led to an overreliance that can be witnessed on public transportation and the sidewalks of Italian cities.

Kissing is how Italians demonstrate respect, friendship, and love. The practice is as Italian as pizza. The most common form is the double cheek kiss. It can be uncomfortable for the uninitiated but no one will impose it on you, and a handshake is equally acceptable. If you observe carefully you'll see women kissing women, women kissing men, men kissing women, men kissing men, and everyone kissing children.

Kisses are exchanged at the beginning and end of most social encounters. An Italian man introduced to an Italian woman (or vice versa) will exchange kisses. Men will shake hands with each other and women may kiss or shake hands. Non-Italians can greet however they

Italian Survival Phrases

- *Ciao* [ch-OW] This world-famous word is an informal greeting that means both hello and good-bye. It is used between friends or once you have gotten acquainted with someone.

- *Buongiorno* [bwon-JUR-no] / *Buonasera* [bwo-na-SEH-ra] The first means hello (or literally, good day) and the latter good afternoon. These are formal variations of *ciao* and are the first words to say when entering a restaurant or shop.

- *Scusi* [SKU-zee] is an invaluable word that sounds very much like its English counterpart: excuse me. It can be used whenever you want to get someone's attention, ask for something, or need to excuse yourself.

- *Per Favore* [PEAR fa-VOR-eh] / *Grazie* [GRA-zee-eh] are the pillars of Italian politeness. *Per favore* is useful when ordering at a bar or restaurant and can go at the beginning or end of a sentence (*un café per favore* or *per favore un caffè*). Once you've been served something it's always polite to say *grazie*.

- *Dov'è...?* [doe-VAY...?] The Italian phrase for *where* can save you from getting lost. Just add the location to the end and do your best to comprehend the answer. *Scusi, dov'e la Fontana di Trevi?*

- *Parli inglese?* [par-LEE in-GLAY-zay?] should only be used as a last resort, but if you must it's more polite than launching directly into English.

please. While citizens of other countries tend to exchange good-byes quickly, Italians love to linger. The time between verbal indication of departure and actual physical departure can be surprisingly long and is generally spent discussing the next day and making preliminary plans for future meetings.

ALCOHOL AND SMOKING

Legislation regarding alcohol consumption is more relaxed than in North America. Alcohol can be purchased in supermarkets, grocery stores, and specialty shops all week long by anyone over 18 and can be consumed in public. That's a major benefit for North American exchange students who can be spotted staggering down Roman and Florentine streets on weekends. Most locals are not prone to excessive drinking, and public drunkenness is rare.

Smoking has been banned in bars, restaurants, and public spaces since 2005, and if you want to take a puff you'll need to step outside or request an outdoor table. Although there are a high percentage of smokers in Italy that number is falling, and laws regarding nonsmoking areas are respected. Cigarettes are sold at specialized *tabacchi* shops for around €5 a pack. Venice is particularly serious about keeping the city clean, and smokers can be fined for throwing cigarette butts into canals or streets.

DRUGS

Italy's position in the center of the Mediterranean, coupled with the country's 8,000-kilometer coastline, makes drug smuggling difficult to eradicate. There are major markets for heroin, cocaine, hashish, and synthetic drugs that are imported by sea from South America, North Africa, the Balkans, and Afghanistan. That said, it's very rare to be offered drugs in Italy during the day and the hardest drug you're likely to be offered at night is hashish (a substance derived from cannabis and mixed with tobacco). Most dealers aren't threatening and will take no for an answer. Discos and nightclubs are more likely to be the scene of cocaine or amphetamines, which kill their share of Italian teenagers every year. Marijuana and hashish are classified as light drugs and are illegal but have been decriminalized since 1990. Personal use in public will not lead to arrest but may lead to a fine or warning. Enforcement is not strict, as Italian police have more pressing concerns. Still it's not worth the risk, and there's enough perfectly legal wine to go around. Harder drugs such as cocaine, heroin, ecstasy, LSD, and so on are illegal.

DRESS

Italians like to look good. Even if the standards of formality have fallen in recent generations locals of all ages remain careful about appearance. It's not just the clothes, which aren't that different, but the way Italians wear clothes and the overall homogeneity that exists on city streets. Women are elegant, men well fitted, and even retirees look like they're wearing their Sunday best. It's easy to differentiate the locals from the tourists, who are blissfully unaware of the fashion faux pas they are committing. Tourists can usually be spotted a kilometer away: They're the ones wearing the baseball caps, white socks with sandals, and khaki shorts. Fitting in means paying a little more attention to how you look and may require some shopping to acquire that distinctly Italian style.

At Places of Worship

Most churches have a dress code, which is often posted outside. Revealing too much flesh may result in being denied entry. Lower legs, shoulders, and midriffs should be covered. Do not expect to enter St. Peter's or St. Mark's wearing flip-flops, miniskirts, above-the-knee shorts, or cut-off T-shirts. The same rules also apply to some museums and monuments.

Entry may also be restricted during mass and a certain amount of decorum (maintaining silence, refraining from eating and drinking, and acting in a generally respectful manner) should be observed at all times. Photography is usually allowed but rules vary. Flash photography is generally not permitted inside churches and museums where light can damage delicate frescoes.

Health and Safety

EMERGENCY NUMBERS

In case of a **medical emergency,** dial **118.** Operators are multilingual and can provide immediate assistance. You can also contact the **U.S. Embassy** (tel. 06/46741) after hours for matters regarding illness or victimization of any sort. **Carabinieri** (112), **police** (113), and the **fire department** (115) also operate around-the-clock emergency numbers.

CRIME AND THEFT

Italian cities are safe and muggings and violent crime are rare. Still, it's best to travel in pairs late at night and be aware of pickpockets at all times. They're especially common in Rome and operate in fewer numbers in Florence and Venice. Most petty criminals work in teams and can be quite young. Youth often beg for change at traffic intersections or on church steps and supplement that income by playing music on subways, recycling scrap metal, and dumpster diving. They're usually harmless.

Subways and wherever large crowds gather are ideal places for thieves. It's best to keep wallets and other valuables in a front pocket or locked in the hotel safe. Leave jewelry, smartphones, and cameras out of sight and always count your change before leaving a store. Make a photocopy of your passport and other vital documents and call your credit card company immediately if your wallet is stolen. If you're the victim of a pickpocket or have a bag snatched, report it within 24 hours to the nearest police station. You'll need a copy of the police report (*denuncia*) in order to make an insurance claim.

MEDICAL SERVICES

Vaccines are not required for entering Italy, but a flu shot can prevent unnecessary time in bed if you're visiting from November to March.

Italian medical and emergency services are relatively modern and are ranked second in the world by the World Health Organization. First aid can be performed by all public hospitals and urgent treatment is entirely free of charge. A symbolic copayment is often required for non-life-threatening treatment but does not exceed €30. The emergency medical service number is 118. If you can't wait, go directly to the *pronto soccorso* (emergency room) located in most hospitals.

PHARMACIES

Pharmacies are recognizable by their green neon signs and are common in city centers. Many operate nonstop hours and remain open during lunch. If a pharmacy is closed, you can always find a list of the closest open ones posted in the window. If all you need is a condom, many pharmacies have automated prophylactic vending machines out front. Pharmacists can be very helpful in Italy and provide advice and nonprescription medicine for treating minor ailments. You'll also find practical items such as toothbrushes, sunscreen, and baby food.

SECURITY

Security in Italy has tightened considerably since the 2015 Paris attacks and there is a greater police and military presence in airports, train stations, and near major monuments. The new measures are most evident in Rome, where churches, museums, and other popular destinations have adopted new entry procedures involving metal detectors and the depositing of backpacks and oversize bags into cloakrooms. Security around French and United States embassies, schools, and cultural associations has also been bolstered and will remain so for the foreseeable future.

There haven't been any terrorist attacks in Italy since the 1980s, and the country has kept a low profile compared to other allies that have actively intervened in Middle Eastern affairs and become the target of terrorist groups. That could always change, and travelers concerned about security can register with the **Smart Traveler Enrollment Program** (www.step.state.gov) to receive the latest alerts and allow the U.S. embassy to contact them in case of an emergency.

Travel Tips

WHAT TO PACK

What to pack depends on the season and length of stay, but beware of overpacking—traveling to three cities means you'll be unpacking and repacking frequently. It's probably best to leave expensive watches and jewelry at home. Binoculars can be helpful for observing the ceiling of the Sistine Chapel, church facades, and rooftop panoramas. Finally, you can email yourself any important credit card codes or customer service numbers as backup in case you lose your wallet.

Luggage: A wheeled suitcase makes getting around airports and to hotels easier. Backpacks or handbags are good for daily excursions and should have zippers to dissuade pickpockets. A money belt can be useful for storing cash and valuables.

Paperwork: You'll need your passport and a driver's license if you plan on renting a moped or car. An international permit is not required but can prevent confusion if you're pulled over.

Clothing, shoes, and accessories: Select comfortable clothes that can be mixed and matched. Layers are important in spring and fall when mornings are chilly and temperatures vary throughout the day. Formal clothes may be necessary if you plan on any fine dining or clubbing. Remember that knees and shoulders must be covered when entering religious buildings. Flip-flops are fine for the beach but aren't permitted inside the Vatican. Sunglasses are essential during the summer, especially if you'll be doing any driving, and hats are useful. You'll probably do a lot of walking, so bring at least two comfortable pairs of shoes.

Toiletries and medication: A high-SPF sunscreen is vital during summer. If you take medication, make sure to bring enough and have a copy of your prescription in case you need a refill. If you forget something, pharmacies in Italy are useful for replacing lost toiletries or picking up aspirin. Most hotels provide hair dryers, but if you're staying in a bed-and-breakfast or a hostel you may want to pack one. It should be adaptable to Italy's 220 voltage.

Electronics: Voltage is 220 volts in Italy and plugs have two round prongs. Electronic devices that need recharging require an adaptor. Simple U.S.-to-European **travel adapters** are available at Radio Shack for under $10 and double that at airports. They're harder to find in Italy but most starred hotels supply them to guests for free. An extra memory card is useful for digital photographers and a portable battery charger can prevent phones and other devices from going dark.

MONEY
Currency

The euro has been Italy's currency since 2000. Banknotes come in denominations of €5, €10, €20, €50, €200, and €500 (which is being phased out). Denominations are different colors and sizes to facilitate use. Coins come in 1, 2, 5, 10, 20, and 50 cents, €1, and €2; these also vary in color, shape, and size. The euro is used in 19 nations across Europe, and each country decorates and mints its own coins. Take time to familiarize yourself with the different values, and count your change after each purchase for practice.

Currency Exchange

Fluctuation between the dollar and euro can have a major impact on expenditures. Over the last decade exchange rates haven't favored U.S. travelers, but since 2014 the dollar has strengthened considerably, and one dollar is now worth roughly 90 euro cents.

There are several options for obtaining euros. You can exchange at your local bank before departure, use private exchange agencies located in airports and near major monuments, or simply use ATM machines in Italy. Banks generally offer better rates but charge commission, while agencies charge low commission but offer poor rates. The **American Express** (Rome, Piazza di Spagna 38, tel. 06/4211-5561, Mon.-Fri. 9am-5pm and Sat. 9am-12:30pm) office in Rome does well on both counts. Exchange agencies like **Forexchange** (Rome, Termini Station, tel. 800/305-357, daily 8am-7:30pm) in Piazza Barberini are another option, and automated exchange machines operate nonstop at Fiumicino Airport and inside many bank branches. Look for the *cambio* (exchange) sign in bank windows. When changing money request different denominations and count bills at the counter before leaving.

ATMs and Banks

ATM machines are easy to find and are located inside or outside all Italian banks. They accept foreign debit and credit cards, and exchange rates are set daily. Before withdrawing cash in Italy, ask your bank or credit card company what fees they charge. Most have an international processing fee that can be a fixed amount or a percentage of the total withdrawal. Charles Schwab is one of the few financial institutions that does not charge either. Italian banks also charge a small fee for cardholders of other banks using their ATMs.

The maximum daily withdrawal at most banks is €500. ATMs provide instructions in multiple languages. Be aware of your surroundings when withdrawing cash late at night or on deserted streets. If the card doesn't work, try another bank before contacting your bank back home. Italian banks are generally open weekdays 8:30am-1:30pm and 2:30pm-5:30pm. They often have lockers at the entrance for storing keys, coins, and anything else that might activate the metal detectors at the entrance to many institutions.

Debit and Credit Cards

Before your departure, inform your bank and/or credit card company of your travel plans, as many will block cards after unexpected foreign activity.

Debit cards are a ubiquitous form of payment in Italy, and recent legislation meant to encourage cashless transactions has removed monetary limits. You can therefore buy a coffee, museum ticket, or a pair of shoes with Maestro- or Cirrus-equipped cards. Newsstands are about the only place that don't accept plastic, and cash-only restaurants are rare. Most Italian smart cards use a chip-and-PIN system. If your card requires old-fashioned swiping, you may need to alert cashiers.

Credit cards are also widely accepted. **Visa** (tel. 800/877-232) and **MasterCard** (tel. 800/870-866) are the most common. **American Express** (tel. 06/4211-5561) comes in a distant third, and Discover is unknown. Cards provide the most advantageous exchange rates and a low 1-3 percent commission fee is usually charged on every transaction.

Sales Tax

The Italian government imposes a value-added tax (IVA) of 22 percent on most goods. Visitors who reside outside the EU are entitled to **tax refunds** (www.taxrefund.it) on all purchases over €155 within stores that participate in the tax-back program. Just look for the **Euro Tax Free** or **Tax Free Italy** logo, have your passport ready, and fill out the yellow refund form. You'll still have to pay tax at the time of purchase but are entitled to reimbursement at airports and refund offices. Forms must be stamped by customs officials before check-in and brought to the refund desk, where you can choose to receive cash or have funds wired to your credit card. Lines move slowly and it's usually faster to be refunded at private **currency exchange agencies** such as **Forexchange** (www.forexchange.it), **American Express** (www.americanexpress.com), **Interchange** (www.interchange.eu), or **Travelex** (www.travelex.com) located in Rome, Florence, and Venice. They facilitate the refund process for a small percentage of your refund. All claims must be made within three months of purchase.

COMMUNICATIONS
Telephones

To call Italy from outside the country, dial the **exit code** (011 for the US and Canada) followed by **39** (Italy country code) and then the number. Most large cities have a specific 2-4-digit **area code** (06 Rome, 055 Florence, and 041 Venice) and numbers vary in length.

To call the United States or Canada from Italy, dial the 001 **country code** followed by **area code** and **number.** For collect calls to the U.S. dial 172-1011 (AT&T), 172-1022 (MCI), or 172-1877 (Sprint).

Numbers that start with 800 in Italy are toll-free, 170 gets you an English-speaking operator, and 176 is **international directory assistance.** Local calls cost €0.10 per minute and most phone booths have disappeared. Numbers starting with a 3 are cellular, for which fees are higher.

CELL PHONES

Your smartphone will work in Italy if it uses the GSM system, which is the mobile standard in Europe. All iPhones, Samsung Galaxy, and Google Nexus devices function, although rates vary widely between operators. Voice calls to the United States can vary from as much as $1.79 (Verizon) to 20 cents (T-Mobile) per minute depending on your plan. Most companies offer international bundles that include a certain amount of text messaging, data transfer, and voice traffic. If you don't want any unexpected bills, compare offers and choose one that meets your expected needs.

You can also purchase a SIM card in Italy at any mobile shop and use it in your phone. **Wind** (www.wind.it), **Tim** (www.tim.it), and **Vodafone** (www.vodafone.it) are the most common operators, with stores in all three cities and at airports. This option will require a passport or photo ID and may take a little longer, but it is the cheapest option if you plan to make a lot of domestic and international calls.

If your phone doesn't use GSM you can rent or buy one in Italy. Rentals are available at the airport but are expensive. New phones are a cheaper option and available from the European telecom operators mentioned above. A basic flip phone can cost as little as €29 and be purchased with prepaid minutes. ID is required and some operators have special deals for foreign travelers.

You can save on telephone charges altogether if you have access to Wi-Fi. Many hotels and bars have hot spots, and using Skype or other VOIP operators is free.

PAY PHONES

The advent of cell phones has led to a steady decline of public pay phones. Those that remain operate with coins or phone cards that can be purchased at *tabacchi* or newsstands. Ask for a *scheda telefonica* (phone card), which can be inserted into a slot in the telephone.

Wi-Fi

Getting online in Italy is easy. Rome, Venice, and Florence all have Wi-Fi networks that make it easy to stay connected throughout a journey. Access is free; however, registration is usually required and there are time and traffic limits. Both Trenitalia and Italo train operators provide onboard Wi-Fi, as do most Italian airports.

Postal Services

Francobolli (stamps) for standard-size postcards and letters can be purchased at *tabacchi* shops. Larger parcels will require a trip to the post office. **Poste Italiane** (tel. 800/160-000,

www.poste.it) offices are yellow, and larger branches are usually open weekdays 8:30am-7:30pm and Saturdays 8:15am-12:30pm. Grab a numbered ticket at the entrance and prepare for a short wait. A postcard to the U.S. costs 85 euro cents as long as it doesn't exceed 20 grams and remains within standard dimensions. The cost of sending letters and other goods varies according to weight; such items can be sent *posta prioritaria* (express) for a couple of euros extra. Mailboxes are red and have slots for international and local mail.

Stamp collectors may be disappointed, as most post office clerks slap computerized stickers onto correspondence. However, there are special philatelic branches in Rome (Piazza San Silvestro 20, tel. 06/6973-7273, Mon.-Fri. 8:20am-1:35pm and Sat. 8:20am-12:35pm) and Venice (Fondamenta del Gaffaro 3510, tel. 041/522-1614, Mon.-Fri. 8:20am-1:35pm and Sat. 8:20am-12:35pm) dedicated to collectors.

WEIGHTS AND MEASURES

Italy uses the **metric system.** A few helpful conversions: 5 centimeters is about 3 inches, 1 kilogram is a little over 2 pounds, and 5 kilometers is around 3 miles. **Celsius** is used to measure temperature, and 20 degrees (68 F) is a good air-conditioning setting inside hotels and cars. Summers often break the 35-degree (95 F) barrier, and it's best to stay indoors during the early afternoon when this is the case.

Italy is on **Central European Time,** six hours ahead of the U.S. East Coast and nine of the West Coast. Military/24-hour time is frequently used, so 1500 is 3pm, and 2015 is 8:15pm.

Italians use commas where Americans use decimal points, and vice versa. That means €10,50 is 10 euros and 50 euro cents, while €1.000 is a thousand Euros. Italians order dates by day, month, and year—which is something to remember when booking hotels and tours.

ACCESS FOR TRAVELERS WITH DISABILITIES

Special-needs travelers may find life in Rome, Venice, and Florence challenging. Italy is not especially accessible to the blind or wheelchair bound, and sidewalks can be narrow and uneven. One positive is that many museums and monuments are free for special-needs travelers and their companions.

The situation in Rome is gradually improving. All museums are now accessible, and most of the city can be reached with relative ease. The Vatican museums in particular are simple to navigate and provide **tactile tours** (tel. 06/6988-3145, www.mv.vatican.va, free) for the visually impaired. Most subway stations are equipped with elevators, braille maps, and raised floor trails for safely getting from entrance to platform. Stations on the Metro B line all have lifts, which isn't always the case with Metro A. However, bus 590 follows the same route above ground and is wheelchair accessible, as are many buses in the capital. These are entered from the doors in the center with the assistance of drivers.

Florence is the most accessible of the three cities. The center is flat, pavements are in good condition, and traffic is limited. Many museums are easily navigated and free for the otherly abled and their companions. There's also no need to wait in line to enter the Uffizi or Accademia as long as you have proof of any medical conditions. You can rent wheelchairs from the tourist office near the train station. There are 14 fully accessible public bathrooms in the Historic Center, and many museums have created special **tactile tours** (tel. 055/268224) for the visually impaired. A group of specialized guides provide tours and the list is available online or from the **tourist office** (Piazza Stazione 4, tel. 055/212-245, Mon.-Sat. 9am-7pm and Sun. 9am-1pm).

Venice may seem impenetrable to special-needs travelers, but 70 percent of the city is actually accessible to all. The city has created a bridge-free itinerary with descriptions in French and English along with a useful accessibility map that highlights options for avoiding urban barriers. Both can be downloaded online (www.comune.venezia.it) or picked up from the *citta per tutti/ city for all office* (San Marco, Ca' Farsetti 4136, tel. 041/274-8144, Thurs. 9am-1pm) or other tourist offices around the city. Raised **tactile pavements** for the visually impaired have recently been installed along many canals and several flat footbridges and nonslip ramps set up along key routes. Wheelchairs can be rented from **health care stores** (*Sanitaria ai Miracoli,* Cannaregio 6049, tel. 041/520-3513 or Farmacia Morelli, San Marco 5310, tel. 041/522-4196), and up to four can board *vaporetto* lines 1 and 2 at a time. Users and companions benefit from reduced fares (€1.50) on all public transportation. There are seven fully accessible public toilets within the city and one in each of the major outlying islands. Museums in the city are free for otherly abled travelers.

Traveling between cities by train is convenient for anyone with reduced mobility. **Italo** (tel. 892929, www.italo.it) goes to great lengths to accommodate passengers. Seat numbers and other signage are written in braille, and two seats in car 8 are reserved for wheelchairs. These are located next to restrooms and snack machines designed for maximum accessibility. In-station assistance can be arranged up to one hour before departure at Florence SMN and Venezia Santa Lucia stations daily from 8am to 10pm and with 12 hours advance notice in Rome Termini and Tiburtina. **Trenitalia** (tel. 800/906-060) provides similar services and assistance.

TRAVELING WITH CHILDREN

Italians go crazy for kids, and if you're traveling with a baby or toddler expect people to sneak peaks inside the stroller or ask for the name, age, and vital statistics of your child. Restaurants and hotels generally welcome young travelers, and some high-end accommodations offer babysitting services for parents who want to sightsee on their own. Many restaurants have children's menus, and most have high chairs. Half-size portions (*mezza porzione*) can also be requested for young appetites.

Tickets to museums, amusement parks, and public transportation are discounted for children under 12, and kids under 6 can go anywhere for free. **Trenitalia** has several offers geared towards families, who can save up to 20 percent on high-speed rail tickets. **Italo** has similar deals and toddlers sit on laps unless an extra seat is reserved. Trains are roomy and give kids plenty of space to roam or be entertained by the landscape outside. There are diaper-changing facilities, and Italo has a cinema car with eight high-definition screens showing family movies in Italian.

Italian tots are used to taking naps, and a midafternoon break back at the hotel can prevent evening tantrums. Parents may want to intersperse fun and high-octane activities, like horseback riding on the Via Appia or cycling through Villa Borghese in Rome, with visits to monuments and museums. Most parks are equipped with playgrounds and Roman and Venetian beaches provide a refreshing break from city streets. Involving kids as much as possible in the journey will help leave an impression they will never forget.

FEMALE AND SOLO TRAVELERS

Women attract the curiosity of Italian men whether traveling alone or in groups. For the most part advances are good-natured and can simply be ignored. If you do feel threatened, enter a shop, bar, or public space. Should harassment persist, call the **police** (113) and remain in a crowded area. At night, it's best to avoid unlit streets and train stations. If you must pass through these areas walk quickly and keep your guard up. Having a cell phone is a wise precaution, and keeping in touch with family back home never hurts. Hotels often go out of their way to assist single travelers and will be happy to order a cab or make reservations whenever necessary.

SENIOR TRAVELERS

Italy has one of the highest life expectancies in the world (83), which makes gray a common sight and visiting seniors feel young again. There's also a general respect for older people, who are an integral part of economic and social life.

Seniority also has financial benefits. Anyone over age 65 is entitled to discounts at museums, theaters, and sporting events as well as on public transportation and for many other services. A passport or valid ID is enough to prove your age, even if they are rarely checked. **Carta Argento** (Silver Card) is available from **Trenitalia** for over-60s traveling by train and provides a 15 percent discount on first- and second-class seating. The card costs €30 but is free for those over 75. It's valid for one year and can be purchased at any train station. **Italo** offers those over 60 a 40 percent discount on all first-class train tickets.

If you are on medication, bring as much as you need because prescriptions can be hard to fill.

LGBT TRAVELERS

As of 2016, homosexual couples can benefit from the same civil union status as heterosexuals. Italy was one of the last European countries to enact such legislation, doing so more than 20 years later than Denmark. This was a big step, and a sign that Italian society (or Italian politics) is ready for change.

Italians in general are accepting and take a live-and-let-live approach. It's not uncommon to see same-sex couples holding hands. Violence against LGBTs is rare, although cases of physical and verbal harassment do occasionally make headlines. The Roman community is the most active of the three cities; there's an annual summer gay village and a pride march, and many businesses display rainbow stickers in their storefronts (rainbows also represent peace in Italy). There are plenty of LGBT-friendly bars and clubs in the capital; Florence and Venice have fewer such options.

Tourist Information

TOURIST OFFICES

Each of the destination cities have a tourist office where city cards, maps, and event information can be obtained. Hours vary but most are open nonstop from 9:30am until 6pm. Staff are multilingual and can help reserve local guides, order tickets, or get directions. Offices are located in airports, train stations, and near major sights such as the Colosseum in Rome, Duomo in Florence, and Piazza San Marco in Venice.

SIGHTSEEING PASSES

City cards provide entry to monuments and museums as well as unlimited access to public transportation for one or more days. They also offer line-skipping privileges at popular sights. Options include the **RomaPass** (www.romapass.it) or **Omniacard** (www.omniakit.org) in Rome, the **Firenzecard** (www.firenzecard.it) in Florence, and **Venezia Unica** (www.veneziaunica.it) in Venice.

Cards are expensive and do not always guarantee savings. They will save you time entering the Colosseum or Uffizi and are useful for travelers who plan on doing a lot of sightseeing. All cards are available online or directly from tourist offices. They are active upon first entry and meant for individual use only, although there's no real way to prevent cards from being shared.

LOST AND FOUND

Hopefully you'll never need an *oggetti smarriti* (lost and found), but if you do they exist in Italy. All three airports have dedicated offices at baggage claim. If you forget something on board a Trenitalia train, contact the passenger assistance office located inside Termini (Rome, 6:35am-midnight), Santa Maria Novella (Florence, 7am-10:30am), or Santa Lucia (Venice, 6am-9pm). Italo has fewer staff inside stations but you can call **Italo Assistance** (tel. 892/020, daily 6am-11pm) for help finding things. Fortunately, objects lost on high-speed trains have a high recovery rate. Objects lost in the historic centers may wind up at central lost-and-found offices.

MAPS

Maps are available at tourist offices, for a small fee in Rome and Venice and free in Florence. They are also sold at newsstands and bookstores. Examine the offering carefully and select a map that's easy to read, easy to fold, and small enough to store conveniently. Paper quality varies, and some maps are laminated and come with sight descriptions on the back. Once you have a map, try to orient yourself and memorize major landmarks and rivers. You should try to study maps and memorize the layout of each city before arriving.

Finding the name of a street you're standing on is simple, but finding that same street on a map can be tricky. Often, it's quicker to locate a *piazza* or a nearby cathedral, museum, or monument. Also, asking for directions is the best way to start a conversation with a stranger.

Resources

Glossary

A
aeroporto: airport
albergo: hotel
alcolici: alcohol
alimentari: grocery store
ambasciata: embassy
analcolico: nonalcoholic
aperitivo: appetizer
aperto: open
arrivo: arrival
autista: driver
autobus: bus
autostrada: highway

B
bagaglio: suitcase
bagno: bathroom
banca: bank
bibita: soft drink
biglietteria: ticket office
biglietto: ticket
buono: good

C
calcio:: soccer
caldo: hot
calle: street (in Venice)
cambio: exchange
camera: room
cameriere: waiter
carta di credito: credit card
cartolina: postcard
cassa: cashier
cattedrale: cathedral

centro storico: historic center
chiesa: church
chiuso: closed
città: city
climatizzato: air-conditioned
coincidenza: connection (transport)
consolate: consulate
contante: cash
conto: bill

D E
destinazione: destination
discoteca: disco
dogana: customs
duomo: cathedral
edicola: newsstand
enoteca: wine bar
entrata: entrance
escursione: excursion

F G
farmacia: pharmacy
fermata: bus/subway stop
ferrovia: railway
fontana: fountain
forno: bakery
francobollo: stamp
gratuito: free
grazie: thanks

L
letto: bed
libreria: bookshop
lontano: far

M N O

macchina: car
mare: sea
mercato: market
metropolitana: subway
moneta: coin
monumento: monument
mostra: exhibition
museo: museum
negozio: shop
orario: timetable
ospedale: hospital
ostello: hostel

P Q R

palazzo: building
panino: sandwich
parcheggio: parking lot
parco: park
partenza: departure
passeggiata: walk
pasticceria: pastry shop
pasto: meal
periferia: outskirts
piazza: square
polizia: police

ponte: bridge
prenotazione: reservation
prezzo: price
quartiere: neighborhood
ristorante: restaurant

S T

sconto: discount
soccorso: assistance
spiaggia: beach
spuntino: snack
stabilimento: seaside resort
stazione: station
strada: road
tabaccherie: tobacco shop
teatro: theater
traghetto: ferry
trattoria: restaurant (casual)
torre: tower
treno: train

U V

uscita: exit
vaporetto: ferry
via: street
viale: avenue

Italian Phrasebook

Most Italians have some understanding of English, and whatever vocabulary they lack is compensated for with gesticulation. It can, however, be more rewarding to attempt expression in the melodic vocals of Dante rather than succumb to the ease and familiarity of monolingualism.

Pronunciation is straightforward once you understand the sounds of the letters. There are 7 Italian vowel sounds (one for *a, i,* and *u* and two each for *e* and *o*) compared to the 15 in English, but the most audible difference is the consistent pronunciation of Italian letters—as opposed to English, which has multiple, seemingly arbitrary sounds that change without warning. Consonants, by and large, are used the same in both languages and Italian has

fewer letters in its alphabet. If you have any experience with French, Spanish, Portuguese, or Latin you have an advantage, but even if you don't, learning a few phrases is simple and will prepare you to take a linguistic dive into Italian culture. Inquiring how much something costs or asking for directions in Italian is thrilling and much more fun than using English.

PRONUNCIATION
Vowels

a like a in father
e short like e in set
é long like a in way
I like ee in feet
o short like o in often or long like o in rope
u like oo in foot or w in well

Consonants

b	like *b* in *boy*, but softer
c	before e or i like *ch* in *chin*
ch	like *c* in *cat*
d	like *d* in *dog*
f	like *f* in *fish*
g	before e or i like *g* in *gymnastics* or like *g* in *go*
gh	like *g* in *go*
gl	like *ll* in *million*
gn	like *ni* in *onion*
gu	like *gu* in *anguish*
h	always silent
l	like *l* in *lime*
m	like *m* in *me*
n	like *n* in *nice*
p	like *p* in *pit*
qu	like *qu* in *quick*
r	rolled/trilled similar to *r* in Spanish or Scottish
s	between vowels like *s* in *nose* or *s* in *sit*
sc	before e or i like *sh* in *shut* or *sk* in *skip*
t	like *t* in *tape*
v	like *v* in *vase*
z	either like *ts* in *spits* or *ds* in *pads*

Accents

Accents are sometimes used to indicate which vowel should be stressed in a word and to differentiate those that have the same spelling.

ESSENTIAL PHRASES

Hello *Ciao*
Good morning *Buongiorno*
Good evening *Buonasera*
Good night *Buonanotte*
Good-bye *Arrivederci*
Nice to meet you *Piacere*
Thank you *Grazie*
You're welcome *Prego*
Please *Per favore*
Do you speak English? *Parla inglese?*
I don't understand *Non capisco*
Have a nice day *Buona giornata*
Yes *Si*
No *No*

TRANSPORTATION

Where is...? *Dov'è...?*
How far is...? *Quanto è distante...?*
Is there a bus to...? *C'è un autobus per...?*
Does this bus go to...? *Quest'autobus va a...?*
Where do I get off? *Dove devo scendere?*
What time does the bus/train leave/arrive? *A che ora parte/arriva l'autobus/treno?*
Where is the nearest subway station? *Dov'è la stazione metro più vicina?*
Where can I buy a ticket? *Dove posso comprare un biglietto?*
A round-trip ticket/a single ticket to... *Un biglietto di andata e ritorno/andata per...*

FOOD

A table for two/three/four... *Un tavolo per due/tre/quattro...*
Do you have a menu in English? *Avete un menu in inglese?*
What is the dish of the day? *Qual è il piatto del giorno?*
We're ready to order. *Siamo pronti per ordinare.*
I'm a vegetarian. *Sono vegetariano*
May I have... *Posso avere...*
The check please? *Il conto per favore?*
beer *birra*
bread *pane*
breakfast *colazione*
cash *contante*
check *conto*
coffee *caffè*
dinner *cena*
glass *bicchiere*
hors d'oeuvre *antipasto*
ice *ghiaccio*
ice cream *gelato*
lunch *pranzo*
restaurant *ristorante*
sandwich(es) *panino(i)*
snack *spuntino*
waiter *cameriere*
water *acqua*
wine *vino*

SHOPPING

money *soldi*
shop *negozio*
What time do the shops close? *A che ora chiudono i negozi?*
How much is it? *Quanto costa?*
I'm just looking. *Sto guardando solamente.*
What is the local specialty? *Quali sono le specialità locali?*

HEALTH

drugstore *farmacia*
pain *dolore*
fever *febbre*
headache *mal di testa*
stomachache *mal di stomaco*
toothache *mal di denti*
burn *bruciatura*
cramp *crampo*
nausea *nausea*
vomiting *vomitare*
medicine *medicina*
antibiotic *antibiotico*
pill/tablet *pillola/pasticca*
aspirin *aspirina*
I need to see a doctor. *Ho bisogno di un medico.*
I need to go to the hospital. *Devo andare in ospedale.*
I have a pain here... *Ho un dolore qui...*
She/he has been stung/bitten. *È stata punta/morsa.*
I am diabetic/pregnant. *Sono diabetico/incinta.*
I am allergic to penicillin/cortisone. *Sono allergico alla penicillina/cortisone.*
My blood group is...positive/negative. *Il mio gruppo sanguigno è... positivo/negative.*

NUMBERS

0 *zero*
1 *uno*
2 *due*
3 *tre*
4 *quattro*
5 *cinque*
6 *sei*
7 *sette*
8 *otto*
9 *nove*
10 *dieci*
11 *undici*
12 *dodici*
13 *tredici*
14 *quattordici*
15 *quindici*
16 *sedici*
17 *diciassette*
18 *diciotto*
19 *diciannove*
20 *venti*
21 *ventuno*
30 *trenta*
40 *quaranta*
50 *cinquanta*
60 *sessanta*
70 *settanta*
80 *ottanta*
90 *novanta*
100 *cento*
101 *centouno*
200 *duecento*
500 *cinquecento*
1,000 *mille*
10,000 *diecimila*
100,000 *centomila*
1,000,000 *un milione*

TIME

What time is it? *Che ora è?*
It's one/three o'clock. *E l'una/sono le tre.*
midday *mezzogiorno*
midnight *mezzanotte*
morning *mattino*
afternoon *pomeriggio*
evening *sera*
night *notte*
yesterday *ieri*
today *oggi*
tomorrow *domani*

DAYS AND MONTHS

week *settimana*
month *mese*

Monday *lunedi*
Tuesday *martedi*
Wednesday *mercoledi*
Thursday *giovedi*
Friday *venerdi*
Saturday *sabato*
Sunday *domenica*
January *gennaio*
February *febbraio*
March *marzo*
April *aprile*
May *maggio*
June *giugno*
July *luglio*
August *agosto*
September *settembre*
October *ottobre*
November *novembre*
December *dicembre*

VERBS

to have *avere*
to be *essere*
to go *andare*
to come *venire*
to want *volere*
to eat *mangiare*
to drink *bere*
to buy *comprare*
to need *necessitare*
to read *leggere*
to write *scrivere*
to stop *fermare*
to get off *scendere*
to arrive *arrivare*
to return *ritornare*
to stay *restare*
to leave *partire*
to look at *guardare*
to look for *cercare*
to give *dare*
to take *prendere*

Suggested Reading

CULTURE

Barzini, Luigi. *The Italians: A Full Length Portrait Featuring Their Manners and Morals*. This classic semi-sociological work may be over 50 years old, but many of Barzini's observations still hold true. He provides detailed portraits of Italians that are often quite hilarious and examines the origins of everyday rituals that have left travelers baffled for generations.

Hofmann, Paul. *That Fine Italian Hand*. With an outsider's perspective and an abundance of curiosity, Hofmann reveals the paradoxes of his adopted country.

Severgnini, Beppe. *La Bella Figura: A Field Guide to the Italian Mind*. Severgnini has made a living out of explaining Italians to the rest of the world. He does it with humor and manages to dissect and explore many of the habits that are uniquely Italian without condescension or oversimplification.

Stille, Alexander. *The Sack of Rome*. Few individuals have influenced modern Italy as much as Silvio Berlusconi. Stille takes an objective look of the consequences of life under a media tycoon and tracks how Italians have changed under his reign.

TRAVELOGUES

James, Henry. *Italian Hours*. A collection of essays about Rome and Venice that balance romantic vision and the realities Henry James wasn't afraid to write about.

Morton, H. V. *A Traveller in Rome*. Morton was a pioneer traveler at a time when tourism was still in its infancy. This diary-like account is filled with impressions of the

Eternal City told in an erudite yet easy-to-read manner.

HISTORY

Crowley, Roger. *City of Fortune: How Venice Ruled the Seas*. A historical page-turner recounting Venice's rise as a naval power and the lasting repercussions trade had on the city.

D'Epiro, Peter, and Mary Desmond Pinkowish. *Sprezzatura: 50 Ways Italian Genius Shaped the World*. The authors detail how advances in politics, banking, and music—and many other innovations taken for granted today—originated in Italy. After a few pages it becomes evident how different the world would be without Italian ingenuity.

King, Ross. *Brunelleschi's Dome*. The Duomo in Florence may appear like a forgone conclusion today, but in 1418 building the dome was anything but certain. The story of its completion is a tale of how a Renaissance genius solved the greatest engineering challenge of his day and reinvented architecture while he was at it.

McGregor, James H. S. *Rome From the Ground Up*. A concise study of Rome's evolution through the millennia. Each chapter describes a different epoch and the city's gradual transformation. The book's clear prose, color photos, engravings, historical maps, architectural plans, and drawings help make sense of Rome.

Scirocco, Alfonso. *Garibaldi: Citizen of the World*: A Biography. Garibaldi was the George Washington of Italy and one of the most extraordinary figures of the 19th century. A soldier, politician, farmer, and one of the founding fathers of modern Italy, he played a vital role in the country's unification. His story reads like the best drama—except it's all true.

Kemp, Martin. *Leonardo da Vinci: The Marvelous Works of Nature and Man*. Kemp takes readers on a revealing journey across Leonardo's long and improbable life, describing the artistic, scientific, and technological achievements at various stages of his monumental career.

King, Ross. *Michelangelo and the Pope's Ceiling*. The behind-the-scenes story of the Sistine Chapel and how an egotistical artist and manipulative pontiff created the most famous fresco in history. King's prose reads like fiction but is well documented. It paints a colorful picture of the political drama of the time and how the ceiling came to be.

Murray, Peter. *The Architecture of the Italian Renaissance*. A comprehensive illustrated guide to the art and architecture of the Renaissance. Leonardo, Raphael, Michelangelo, Palladio, and Brunelleschi are the protagonists of this ambitious work that segues between Rome, Florence, and Venice.

Vasari, Giorgio. *Lives of the Artists*. Vasari (1511-1574) was a well-known painter and architect but this book is his lasting legacy. It contains short biographies of Italy's greatest Renaissance artists and traces the development of art and architecture across three centuries.

FICTION

Forster, E. M. *A Room with a View*. Although the novel is set in Florence, this love story of a young Englishwoman caught between two suitors provides few descriptions of the city. It does offer a jolt of romanticism, which is an essential part of any visit to Italy.

Preston, Douglas. *The Monster of Florence*. For something contemporary and more plausible than Dan Brown, try this thriller about an author's quest to solve a Florentine mystery. The plot traces Preston's semiautobiographical investigation into the city's most infamous double homicide and has kept readers up at night since it was published.

KIDS

Collodi, Carlo. *The Adventures of Pinocchio.* Kids have adored the puppet who came to life for over a century and Pinocchio souvenirs abound in Florence, where the author was born. For ages 3 and up.

Macaulay, David. *Rome Antics.* The story of Rome as told by a vagabond pigeon who takes readers on a journey through time. Illustrations will fascinate young minds and prepare their eyes for the cobblestone streets and surprises the city has to offer. For ages 8-11.

Sasek, Miroslav. *This is Rome.* A wonderfully illustrated book that explains the past and present of Rome. Landmarks and everyday life are unveiled in a playful narrative that will keep kids tuned in and build their expectations for the real thing. *This is Venice* also available by the same author. For ages 7-10.

Suggested Films

ROME

Open City (1945) Roberto Rossellini. One of the first films released in Italy after World War II recounts the chaotic days between German occupation and Allied liberation. The film launched the neorealism movement and won the Grand Prize at Cannes.

Bicycle Thieves (1948) Vittorio De Sica. All-time classic that depicts the mood of a country still recovering from war. Different strata of Roman society are depicted along with an epic relationship between a desperate father and a faithful son.

La Dolce Vita (1959) Federico Fellini. This film marks a turning point in Italian cinema away from the past and towards a rapidly brightening future. The good life, however, is tainted for the protagonist played by Marcello Mastroianni. He spends his days following fading aristocrats, second-rate movie stars, and aging playboys and remains trapped in an empty life of lonely dawns. The film coined the word *paparazzi* and earned Fellini the second of four Oscars. Every scene is iconic and the midnight dip in the Trevi Fountain is ingrained in popular culture.

Ben Hur (1959) William Wyler. American film made at Rome's Cinecetta studios that set the standard for sword-and-sandal epics. It may not have held up as well as Fellini, but the chariot scene was shot on a monumental scale and reproduces racing at the Circus Maximus.

Caro Diaro (1993) Nanni Moretti. Moretti is as close as any Italian actor/director gets to Woody Allen. *Caro Diaro* is a cinematic triptych that begins with a meandering moped ride through the deserted streets of Rome, accompanied by a Keith Jarrett soundtrack and an itinerant monologue pondering cinema, sociology, and urban planning.

To Rome with Love (2012) Woody Allen. After New York, Paris, and Barcelona, Woody Allen couldn't resist making a film in Rome. Although the plot may be forgettable the setting isn't.

La Grande Bellezza (2013) Paolo Sorrentino. In this Oscar winner for Best Foreign Film, Rome appears highly stylized and there are plenty of day and night scenes revealing its majestic beauty. The hedonistic storyline may divide opinion but the cinematography is beyond repute.

FLORENCE

A Room with a View (1985) James Ivory. Florence never attracted the film crews of Rome or had a chance to make the cinematic impact of Venice. The most famous film shot in the city was James Ivory's *A Room with a View*.

VENICE

The Talented Mr. Ripley (1999) Anthony Minghella. This book-based film is set in the late 1950s and was shot in southern Italy and Rome but climaxes in Venice. There are scenes of the Grand Canal and a final confrontation inside Café Florian in Piazza San Marco.

Merchant of Venice (2004) Michael Radford. The *Merchant of Venice* may have flopped at the box office but it wasn't because of the Venetian cityscapes, which feature heavily in the period drama based on Shakespeare's play.

007. James Bond is a frequent visitor to Italy, and there are scenes of Venice in *From Russia with Love* and *Moonraker*. The city gets more extensive screen time during *Casino Royale* when Bond sails down the Grand Canal past the Rialto Bridge. He returns to Rome in *Spectre* for a long car chase and a short-lived romance.

Internet and Digital Resources

TRAVEL AND TOURIST TIPS

www.italia.it
The official Italian tourism website is a good place to start browsing. Find information about upcoming events along with links to regional and local sites.

www.travelforkids.com
Find hundreds of activities for kids in Italy.

www.viator.com
Global guide platform that satisfies a wide range of interests and facilitates the purchasing of tickets to museums and monuments.

izi.Travel
Free audio platform with hundreds of narrated explanations and extended tours through Rome, Florence, and Venice. An accompanying app includes maps that function offline.

TRANSPORTATION

www.skyscanner.net, www.kayak.com, www.hipmunk.com
These flight aggregators help you find the cheapest fares. Hipmunk is one of the latest and has paid a little more attention to design and practical features like timelines and maps that simplify planning. All three have expanded into hotel and car-rental bookings.

www.rome2rio.com
Door-to-door transportation details with distances, departures times, and prices of the planes, trains, buses, and ferries. There's also a carbon emissions estimate for the ecologically inclined.

www.seatguru.com
Learn your legroom options and read unbiased advice on where to sit on a flight. The database includes all major airlines along with

diagrams, photos, and descriptions of Airbus and Boeing interiors.

www.jetlagrooster.com
Avoid jet lag by creating a personalized sleep plan for a smooth transition between time zones. Just log on 3-4 days before departure and follow their recommended bedtimes.

www.italo.com, www.trenitalia.com
Open both of these rail operators' sites to compare prices for travel between cities. Purchase tickets that can be printed out at home or saved on mobile devices. If your trip is months away, sign up for the Italo newsletter and receive monthly discount offers.

www.autostrade.it
Drivers can calculate mileage (in kilometers) and toll costs for planned routes. Rest areas are listed, as are the cheapest gas stations along any itinerary. Useful for learning about possible roadwork and brushing up on the rules of the Italian road.

ACCOMMODATIONS

www.airbnb.com, www.slh.com, www.tablethotels.com
Search for B&Bs, apartments, or boutique hotels. Sites include reliable visuals and advice from those who have traveled before you.

www.tripadvisor.com
Read feedback and user ratings on hotels. Comments are detailed and often highlight inconveniences like a bad view or small bathroom.

www.xe.com
Calculate what a buck is worth and know exactly how much you're spending. The site's sister app is ideal for the financially conscious and allows travelers to track expenditures as they happen.

APPS

There are plenty of well-designed apps for locating restaurants and mastering public transportation in each of the cities. They're available for all operating systems and a search in any app store will turn up a plethora. The following have English versions and are free, although some may incur data roaming charges and it's wise to check with your carrier before using them. Many of the larger museums and monuments such as the Vatican, Duomo, and Uffizi have official and unofficial apps that include maps and detailed descriptions of their collections. Some are free; others charge a small fee.

ADR Roma
Real-time flight, boarding, and baggage claim info for both of Rome's airports.

Alitalia
Airline carrier app. Provides flight, boarding, and baggage claim info.

Trenitalia, Italo
Purchase tickets for high-speed trains. Italo also provides departure times, track numbers, and updated info.

Enjoy, Car2Go
These car-sharing companies' apps allow vehicles to be located and used in Rome and Florence.

AppTaxi
Order taxis throughout Italy.

Autovelox
Avoid speed traps on Italian highways.

Muoversi a Roma
Official public transportation app for Rome. Provides real-time planning, suggested routes, and expected arrival times.

AVM Venezia
Official public transportation app for Venice. Currently only allows users to purchase tickets.

Moovit

Public transportation tips for Rome, Florence, and Venice.

Maps.me

Good source for offline maps.

Duolingo

Good for learning basic Italian before your trip.

Word Reference

Decipher (and learn to pronounce) Italian on the go.

Index

UV

WXYZ

List of Maps

Photo Credits

All photos © Alexei J. Cohen except page 5 © Dreamstime.com; page 6 (top left) © Dreamstime.com, (top right) © Dreamstime.com, (bottom) © Dreamstime.com; page 7 (top) © Dreamstime.com, (bottom left) © Dreamstime.com, (bottom right) © Dreamstime.com; page 8 © Dreamstime.com; page 9 (top) © Dreamstime.com, (bottom) © Emicristea | Dreamstime.com; page 10 © Dreamstime.com; page 12 (top) © Dreamstime.com, (bottom) © Dreamstime.com; page 14 (top) © Dreamstime.com, (middle) © Dreamstime.com, (bottom) © Wieslaw Jarek | Dreamstime.com; page 15 © Dreamstime.com; page 16 © Dreamstime.com; page 17 (top) © Dreamstime.com, (bottom) © Andreirybachuk | Dreamstime.com; page 19 (top) © Mildax | Dreamstime.com, (bottom) © Dreamstime.com; page 20 (top) © Dreamstime.com, (bottom) © Patricia Hofmeester | Dreamstime.com; page 21 (top) © Dreamstime.com, (middle) © Juan Moyano | Dreamstime.com, (bottom) © Timurk | Dreamstime.com; page 22 © Dreamstime.com; page 24 © Dreamstime.com; page 26 © Dreamstime.com; page 28 © Dreamstime.com; page 29 © Paha_l | Dreamstime.com; page 31 © Dreamstime.com; page 32 © Dreamstime.com; page 33 © Dreamstime.com; page 35 © Dreamstime.com; page 37 (top) © Scaliger | Dreamstime.com, (bottom) © Dreamstime.com; page 39 © Dreamstime.com; page 45 © Dreamstime.com; page 50 © Dreamstime.com; page 51 © Rostislav Glinsky | Dreamstime.com; page 53 © Erica Schroeder | Dreamstime.com; page 55 © Dreamstime.com; page 60 © Dreamstime.com; page 61 © Dreamstime.com; page 62 © Photoanto | Dreamstime.com; page 65 © Dreamstime.com; page 66 © Valeriya Potapova | Dreamstime.com; page 69 © Dreamstime.com; page 70 © Nicknickko | Dreamstime.com; page 71 © Dreamstime.com; page 75 © Dreamstime.com; page 82 © Salmassara | Dreamstime.com; page 102 © Michel Dreher | Dreamstime.com; page 131 © Dreamstime.com; page 135 © Dreamstime.com; page 136 © Dreamstime.com; page 141 (top) © Dreamstime.com, (bottom) © Dreamstime.com; page 143 © Mix7777 | Dreamstime.com; page 150 © Dreamstime.com; page 151 © Dreamstime.com; page 155 © Dreamstime.com; page 159 © TasFoto | Dreamstime.com; page 164 © Raluca Tudor | Dreamstime.com; page 165 © Anibaltrejo | Dreamstime.com; page 171 © Liv Friis-larsen | Dreamstime.com; page 175 © Dreamstime.com; page 195 © Dreamstime.com; page 214 © Dreamstime.com; page 216 © Dreamstime.com; page 221 © Dreamstime.com; page 223 © Dreamstime.com; page 224 © Dreamstime.com; page 228 (top) © Dreamstime.com, (bottom) © Dreamstime.com; page 229 © Dreamstime.com; page 238 © Dreamstime.com; page 239 © Dreamstime.com; page 240 © Dreamstime.com; page 242 © Ioana Grecu | Dreamstime.com; page 243 © Infomods | Dreamstime.com; page 245 © Richard Van Der Woude | Dreamstime.com; page 246 © Dreamstime.com; page 247 © Dreamstime.com; page 249 © Dreamstime.com; page 250 © Milosk50 | Dreamstime.com; page 255 © Dreamstime.com; page 277 © Claudio D'Armini; page 299 © Cristi111 | Dreamstime.com; page 309 © Dreamstime.com; page 313 © Dreamstime.com; page 315 (top) © Dreamstime.com, (bottom) © Dreamstime.com; page 317 © Dreamstime.com; page 322 © Dreamstime.com; page 323 © Dreamstime.com; page 324 © Public domain via Wikimedia Commons; page 332 © Dreamstime.com

Acknowledgments

This book is a collective effort and would not have been possible without the dedicated team at Avalon. No one was more instrumental than my editor Nikki Ioakimedes, who never lost sight of the big picture. Although Berkeley is a long way from Rome, it felt very close for all the months we worked together. Thanks also to Grace Fujimoto, who got the ball rolling; Kat Bennett, who designed the maps; Darren Alessi, who oversaw photographs and design; Kevin McLain who guided the project over the finish line; Katie Mock who got the word out; and all of the fact checkers and copy editors who made this book a reality.

Italy is an inexhaustible subject. Understanding it requires asking lots of questions. Fortunately, Italians like to talk. No one was more patient or provided more answers than Roberta Romoli at the Florence Office of Tourism. Other Florentines deserving of thanks are Caterina for her hospitality, Elisa Acciai for her insight, and Professor Artusi, whose knowledge of the Renaissance has few limits. I'm also grateful to Sara Grinzato and Rossana Columbo in Venice for taking the time to show me parts of the city I would have never discovered on my own; and Mariagrazia Calo, who both housed me and fed me local delicacies during my stay. Back in Rome, Rosa Romano was my chief source of inspiration. We had many conversations about all three cities and she encouraged me to visit the Last Suppers of Florence and look beyond the usual thoroughfares of Venice. She was right. Scores of artisans took the time to explain their craft, waiters patiently listed local ingredients, and countless strangers who pointed me in the right direction.

Finally, I must thank Alessia who assumed many of the parenting duties while I was away from home and kept my spirits high whenever I became overwhelmed with the history, art, and culture of Italy. This book is dedicated to her, to Sacha and Emma, and of course to Carl and Cecile, who took me on my first journeys and introduced me to the joys of travel.

Alexei Cohen
Rome, Italy

Also Available

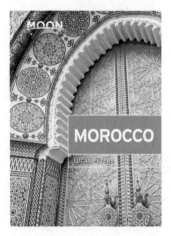

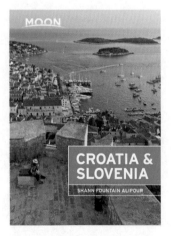

MAP SYMBOLS

═══ Expressway	○ City/Town	✖ Airport	♣ Golf Course
─── Primary Road	◉ State Capital	✗ Airfield	🅿 Parking Area
─── Secondary Road	⊛ National Capital	▲ Mountain	⛰ Archaeological Site
┄┄ Unpaved Road	★ Point of Interest	✚ Unique Natural Feature	⛪ Church
─── Feature Trail	• Accommodation		⛽ Gas Station
┄┄ Other Trail	▾ Restaurant/Bar	⚶ Waterfall	⬭ Glacier
⋯⋯ Ferry	■ Other Location	⚑ Park	▨ Mangrove
═══ Pedestrian Walkway	▲ Campground	⬛ Trailhead	▦ Reef
▭▭▭ Stairs		⛷ Skiing Area	▨ Swamp

CONVERSION TABLES

°C = (°F − 32) / 1.8
°F = (°C x 1.8) + 32
1 inch = 2.54 centimeters (cm)
1 foot = 0.304 meters (m)
1 yard = 0.914 meters
1 mile = 1.6093 kilometers (km)
1 km = 0.6214 miles
1 fathom = 1.8288 m
1 chain = 20.1168 m
1 furlong = 201.168 m
1 acre = 0.4047 hectares
1 sq km = 100 hectares
1 sq mile = 2.59 square km
1 ounce = 28.35 grams
1 pound = 0.4536 kilograms
1 short ton = 0.90718 metric ton
1 short ton = 2,000 pounds
1 long ton = 1.016 metric tons
1 long ton = 2,240 pounds
1 metric ton = 1,000 kilograms
1 quart = 0.94635 liters
1 US gallon = 3.7854 liters
1 Imperial gallon = 4.5459 liters
1 nautical mile = 1.852 km

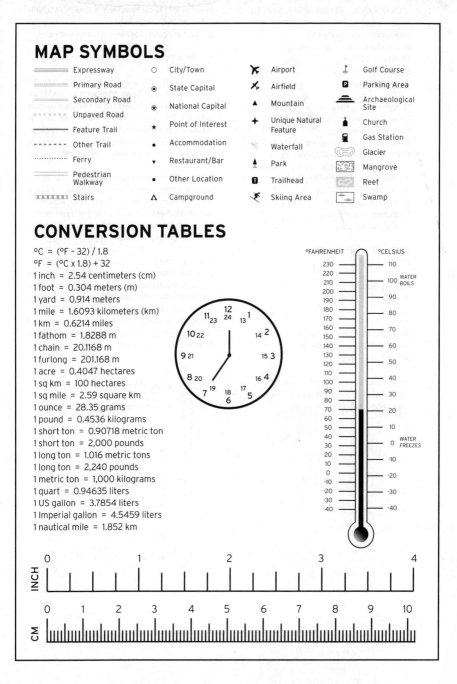

MOON ROME, FLORENCE & VENICE
Avalon Travel
An imprint of Perseus Books
A Hachette Book Group company
1700 Fourth Street
Berkeley, CA 94710, USA
www.moon.com

Editors: Nikki Ioakimedes, Kevin McLain
Series Manager: Kathryn Ettinger
Copy Editor: Brett Keener
Production Coordinator: Darren Alessi
Graphics Coordinator: Kathryn Osgood
Cover Design: Faceout Studios, Charles Brock
Interior Design: Domini Dragoone
Moon Logo: Tim McGrath
Map Editor: Kat Bennett
Cartographer: Kat Bennett
Indexer: Rachel Kuhn

ISBN-13: 978-1-63121-331-1
ISSN: 2474-8803

Printing History
1st Edition — April 2017
5 4 3 2 1

Text © 2017 by Alexei J. Cohen.
Maps © 2017 by Avalon Travel.
All rights reserved.

Some photos and illustrations are used by
  permission and are the property of the original
  copyright owners.

Front cover photo: Pantheon in Rome © Michelle
  Zassenhaus/Getty Images
Back cover photo: © Stevanzz | Dreamstime.com

Printed in China by RR Donnelley, Shenzhen

31901060466770